Praise for Howard Bryant's

THE LAST HERO

"Brawny. . . . *The Last Hero* had the forceful sweep of a well-struck essay as much as that of a first-rate biography."
—*The New York Times*

"Perfect for the sports fan and the history buff."
—*Good Morning America*

"No one was more important to the game of baseball in the last half of the twentieth century than Henry Aaron, and no one writes about that supremely talented man, that tumultuous time, and this treasure of a game better than Howard Bryant. Together, they are an extraordinary combination, and the book Bryant has written gets to the heart of the complicated and dignified, patient, and consistent genuine hero that is Henry Aaron."   —Ken Burns

"Marvelous. . . . Wrists, legs, heart, brain—here is the full picture of a great man and ballplayer who finally gets his due."
—David Maraniss, author of *Clemente*

"There will surely be other books on Hank; there may never be a better book on Henry Aaron than Bryant's *The Last Hero*."
—*Mobile Press-Register*

"A fascinating and at times a troubling book, which revivified the lovely old game for me."   —Tracy Kidder

"A must read for baseball fans of every generation."   —*Booklist*

"We already know Henry Aaron as one of the greatest players in the history of baseball. Now, in Howard Bryant's impeccably researched and nuanced biography, we know Henry Aaron not just as a great ballplayer, but as a remarkable man. In *The Last Hero* Bryant asks the hard questions and cuts through the myths to create a timeless and unflinching portrait of an American icon and his times. And as in any great biography, in learning about Aaron's life we also learn something about our own."
—Glenn Stout, series editor, *The Best American Sports Writing*

Howard Bryant

THE LAST HERO

Howard Bryant is the author of *Shut Out: A Story of Race and Base-ball in Boston,* which won the Casey Award for best baseball book of the year and was a finalist for the Society for American Baseball Research's Seymour Medal; and *Juicing the Game: Drugs, Power, and the Fight for the Soul of Major League Baseball.* He is a senior writer for ESPN.com and *ESPN the Magazine*; appears regularly on ESPN's *The Sports Reporters, ESPN First Take,* and *Outside the Lines*; and serves as sports correspondent for NPR's *Weekend Edition Saturday. The Last Hero* won the 2010 Casey Award. Bryant lives in western Massachusetts.

www.howardbryant.net

THE LAST HERO

THE Last Hero

A LIFE OF HENRY AARON

Howard Bryant

Anchor Books
A Division of Random House, Inc.
New York

FIRST ANCHOR BOOKS EDITION, MAY 2011

The Library of Congress has cataloged the Pantheon edition as follows:
Bryant, Howard.
The last hero : a life of Henry Aaron / Howard Bryant.
p. cm.
Includes bibliographical references and index.
1. Aaron, Hank, 1934–   2. African American baseball players—Biography.
3. Baseball players—United States—Biography.   4. Baseball—United States—
History—20th century.   I. Title.
GV865.A25b79 2010
796.357092—dc22 [b]   2009040573

Anchor ISBN: 978–0–307–27992–7

Author photograph © Erinn Hartman
Book design by Robert C. Olsson

www.anchorbooks.com

Printed in the United States of America
10 9 8 7 6 5 4 3 2

In memory of Nona Bryant,
and for Donald Bryant,
my parents

CONTENTS

PART FOUR: **FREE**

INTRODUCTION

Nearing the crest of Manhattan's Upper East Side, all Henry Aaron wanted was a milk shake. It was June, and the weather was humid— an uncomfortable day gathering momentum toward oppressive.

Initially, the line out front wasn't much, just a couple of kids in baseball caps and shorts, holding baseballs and cellophane-protected glossies. Then it grew longer, sloping eagerly down Ninety-third street toward Second Avenue. New York had never been one of Henry's favorite cities, yet he had awakened on this particular Saturday at 4:00 a.m. so he could catch a 6:15 a.m. flight from Atlanta to La Guardia.

This autograph signing was the latest example of concept marketing: an event held in an upscale ice-cream parlor that doubled as a high-end memorabilia store. The idea that the upper-middle-class gentry from Westchester and North Jersey would spend their disposable income on mint chocolate chip cones and autographed three-hundred-dollar baseball jerseys was the brainchild of Brandon Steiner, the head of New York collectibles juggernaut Steiner Sports.

Inside the brightly colored, baseball-themed storefront sat Henry Aaron, seventy-four years old, in an air-conditioned back room across from clear plastic containers of Gummi Bears, Swedish Fish, and bobblehead dolls. Behind a folding table, Henry was flanked by candy and enough photographic evidence of his life to suggest a forensic exhibit.

There were black-and-whites from his high-flying days in Milwaukee, when he was all muscle and torque and potential; there were plastic blue-and-white batting helmets with the cursive letter *A*, for the Atlanta Braves, and pictures of when Hank hit a home run in the

1972 All-Star Game, played in Atlanta, the first major-league All-Star Game played in the Deep South. And there were snapshots of his jaunty, jowly American League finale, the career National Leaguer sporting the powder blue double knits of the Milwaukee Brewers.

Overwhelming it all were images from the night of April 8, 1974, at Atlanta–Fulton County Stadium. The images recorded that evening showed the follow-through from the batter's box, when his eyes lit up, and the moment he'd made impact. They showed the two kids catching up with him as he crossed the plate. They showed Joe Ferguson, the dumpy Los Angeles catcher, looking as though he were standing on the wrong subway platform. And they showed Hank Aaron holding up the historic ball returned to him by the teammate who had caught it, relief pitcher Tom House.

The line gathered outside and Henry girded. He knew it was time to reach into himself and get into character and become, once again, Hank Aaron. Each of the hundreds of photographs of the moment that had made him an international hero filled Henry with a special sense of dread.

This had been true for the last fifty-five years, this uneasy relationship. Inside, Aaron would do an in-store interview with ESPN Radio, trying to sound as though he actually cared about baseball in 2008, about which of today's players reminded him of himself (none!), and whether Yankee third baseman Alex Rodriguez could hit eight hundred home runs. ("I don't get to see him much," Hank said, "except in the play-offs and World Series.")

During a commercial break, a perky staffer filling a waffle cone promised Henry she would make him a milk shake. ("Coming right up!") Henry stood up and stretched a bit while the eyes on him— from the few dozen fans inside the store to the throng still waiting on the sidewalk, tapping on the glass—bulged at the sight of him. They didn't yell, just stared at him, soaking in the deep creases of his face, the protruding belly, the white tennis shoes, and the limp, a souvenir from knee surgery that had left him on crutches for virtually the entire winter.

The ones who didn't speak tried to attract his attention with hand gestures and provocative clothing (a middle-aged woman sporting a

Mets cap and cottage-cheese thighs, backpack slung over both shoulders, wore a T-shirt that read 755: THE REAL HOME RUN RECORD). He smiled politely, wading easily through the crowd, unpretentiously close physically yet at a complicated emotional remove.

The words from the crowd solidified for him the idea that Hank was a necessary creation, a public conduit for his considerable fame, his tremendous ability, which had been sculpted into legend, and it was this distance, impossible to navigate, between what he represented to them and who he was, that Henry Aaron truly detested the most. The most obvious clue could be found in the name itself, for nobody who really knew him ever called him Hank. Well, almost nobody. Only one member of the inner circle, a kid Henry had met back in 1966, ever got away with calling him Hank. Henry had promised Johnnie and Christine Baker that he would take care of their son Dusty when he arrived in his first spring camp, and maybe that was why the rules were a little different for Dusty Baker.

To everybody else who mattered, he was Henry. Neither his first wife, Barbara, nor his second, Billye, ever called him Hank. As a boy, his name was Henry. That was what his mother and father and all seven siblings knew him by. His best friend from grade school, Cornelius Giles? To him, he was Henry. When he'd first entered the big leagues a lifetime earlier, the name was how he differentiated the familiar, the friendly, from the rest. "When he first came up, if you called him 'Hank,' he wouldn't even hear you," recalled Billy Williams, who grew up close to Henry in Whistler, Alabama, a fingertip's reach from Mobile. "I remember we were in Chicago one day and everybody was yelling for him. They were screaming, 'Hank! Hank!' and he just kept walking. Then, when everything died down, I said, 'Henry!' and he immediately turned around. That meant you were a familiar face. That meant you knew him, and that was the only way he'd ever turn around."

The adorning of him as the people's champion ("You're still the home run king, Hank!") did not evoke a response. He did not respond to the dozen offhanded variations of the same theme—the Barry Bonds question. It was the public's way to broach the unspeakable, and by his total lack of reaction, you would have thought the numbers that used to define him—714, 715, and 755—as well as the names of Mays, Ruth, and Bonds, were by now just street noise to him.

The names and iconic statistics are, of course, much more than that and the oceanic space between the public Hank, who avoids confrontation, and the private Henry, who is clear and passionate and committed, explain why he can never do enough or say enough to satisfy supporters thirsty not only for his statesmanship but his fire. Bonds was where the collision between Hank and Henry was often the fiercest, where the facade came closest to dissolution. It was Hank, the public man, the legend, who wished Barry well in his quest to break the all-time home run record, who avoided controversy. It was Hank Aaron who publicly drove down the avenue of gracious cliché. Records were made to be broken, he would say. He had enjoyed his time as the record holder, and now it was time for someone else to take over.

Aaron would be called bitter, an assessment that hurt him deeply. Henry would often say he wanted the people to know him, yet he was convinced that all the public wanted to know about was Hank. "People don't care about me. They don't care about the things that made me into the person I am," he said one wintry day in January 2008. "They don't care that I raised five children and try to help people do whatever they can to get the most out of their lives, to allow them to chase their dreams. All they care to talk about is that I hit seven hundred and fifty-five home runs or what I hit on a three–two pitch. There is so much more to me than that." The space between Hank and Henry wasn't supposed to be such difficult terrain. He was supposed to be like Reggie or Ruth, Ted Williams and John Wayne, where the person and the legend meshed so seamlessly that the individual *became* the myth. And whatever gulfs did exist, Henry believed most people felt it just wasn't their problem. The fans didn't care that what drove him was not the unremarkable desire simply to be left alone (many superstars before and after him were uncomfortable with the demands of fame), but the wish to use the enormous advantage of his talent, first to avenge the devastating limitations racism placed on previous generations of Aaron men, and, second, like Robinson, to be complete, to develop an important voice on important subjects beyond the dugout.

Henry believed the fans had no interest in these concepts, in his moral indignation; they just wanted Hank. He was on their baseball card. He was supposed to make them happy, and for all his gifts on the baseball field, Henry Aaron lacked the oratory skills and unrestrained charisma (he loathed public speaking) to bridge the gap between Henry's smoldering drive and Hank's reticent celebrity. Roxanne Spillett, a friend and philanthropic partner of Henry, said, "When I think of Henry Aaron, I see an introvert in an extrovert's role. Anyone who has ever been put in that position knows just how difficult it truly is."

To memorabilia collectors, Henry was nothing but a commodity. They were the ones who pushed the bats in the man's large hands, their eyes cold marbles, devoid of nostalgia or awe. They were the ones who demanded specifics. ("This one *has* to say *seven hundred and fifteenth home run,* not seven hundred and fifteen home runs.")

The ones in line who weren't, however, who waited in the heat to trudge an inch closer to him, they were the ones who told him stories (or at least tried; the line had to keep moving) about what Hank Aaron meant to them, then and now. He was their happiness before and, in a baseball universe ethically complicated and corrupted by drugs and money, the person they looked to for their conscience today. ("I just want you to know you're the *real* home run champion.") It was Hank whom the public came to see, and each and every one of them, in their shorts and tank tops and Yankees and Mets caps, stared into the lines of the old man's face, hoping—in fact, begging—to make eye contact, so that when their turn to have their picture signed of Hank breaking the record or a souvenir baseball or their tattered copy of his face on the cover of the *New York Daily News,* April 9, 1974 ("Mr. Aaron, I just wanted you to know that I've been saving this newspaper for thirty-four years. . . . Just to meet you . . . this is my pleasure. . . .") finally came, they would find just the right words with just the right pitch that would separate them from the rest, and their words alone would bridge their distance, personalizing for him the impersonal chore of signing merchandise for money.

And they all so desperately wanted different slices of the same pie: for him to soak in his moment back in 1974 and carry it with him with ease and joviality and reverence, as they did. They approached the line and pleaded with their eyes for him to regale them with a story and a laugh about 715, an anecdote, one gold nugget from the man himself about that night, which would make his glory a little bit more theirs.

Henry would not accommodate this request; a photo and a hand-shake and a signature would have to be enough. When he did pause with a glint of energy in his eye, it was not for a fan who had triggered a warm baseball memory; it was at the moment he looked to his left up at the television, put down the vanilla milk shake he had finally been handed, and saw the tennis player Venus Williams finish off her match in the Wimbledon quarterfinals.

"It's going to be Venus and Serena," Henry said. "And Venus is going to win the whole thing again."

Henry always enjoyed the interaction with people that came with being Hank, but rarely the duty itself. Brandon Steiner would hand over a check for more than ten thousand dollars to Henry (Hammerin' Hank Enterprises, to be exact), who would, in turn, donate the money to the Friendship Baptist Church in Atlanta, the church he'd been attending for forty years. He was ruefully cognizant that Hank was the one who provided the fuel, generated the interest, and provided the platform for Henry to exist as a person whom universities would line up to offer honorary degrees to, whom corporate CEOs would pay tens of thousands of dollars to play a round of golf with, and whom governors and presidents would listen to.

Hank made all that possible, and Henry knew it. With Hank's popular muscle, Henry could continue to grow even more iconic, even bigger in his nearly invisible, powerful way, like that horrible day in 2007 when the Bluffton College team bus skidded off Interstate 75 in Atlanta, killing five members of the baseball team. Henry sat by the bedside of one of the survivors, a boy in a coma, whom Henry had never met in his life, never telling a soul about the visit. That was Henry, elevated above the creation of Hank and his nemesis, Willie Mays, who would never acknowledge that Hank had been every bit his equal in spikes and had soared far past him when the final outs of their careers were recorded. "Willie," a Henry confidant told me bitterly, "Willie ceased being a person the day he retired. Who did Willie ever help except Willie?"

Without Hank, there were no platforms that would, he believed, give Henry a greater and more lasting significance, one that would rival whatever Hank had done in the outfield. There was only Henry Aaron of Mobile, Alabama, making deathly sure he did not look whites in the eye, a man with much to say but with no platform from which to say it.

And all of them, especially the round-bellied sports fan high rollers, would make the same mistake: They believed the way to get to Hank was to mention 715 more lovingly than they spoke of their own children, unaware of, or just tone-deaf to, the nuances (warning signs, all) that so much of that night had suffocated him like a boa. He would grow silent and distant, and they would call him bitter. Perhaps they should have listened to Henry a little bit more during those few times when he let his considerable guard down.

"It still hurts a little bit inside, because I think it has chipped away at a part of my life that I will never have again. I didn't enjoy myself. It was hard for me to enjoy something that I think I worked very hard for," he had said a decade earlier. "God had given me the ability to play baseball, and people in this country kind of chipped away at me. So, it was tough. And all of those things happened simply because I was a black person."

He had been living with the conflict for over half a century, was convinced nobody cared about the price of the moment that gave them so much joy, and so Henry retrenched and let Hank play pretend, dutifully and professionally signing everything—lithographs, batting helmets, bats, baseball cards—with the remove and distance of an insurance agent. Like an insurance agent, being Hank was, after all, a job.

Yet he did not blame them for loving Hank without understanding Henry—or, more accurately, for not making the distinction between the two men who lived in one body, each providing the foundation for the other—by being surly and churlish. Hundreds of fans arrived at an ice-cream shop for their wide-angle view of 715, and he obliged.

When the afternoon of make-believe had ended, both parties

were satisfied. The public was ecstatic: Fathers and sons and mothers and daughters got to see Hank, got to breathe his air. He especially softened for the impatient, uncomprehending children born three decades after he'd swung his last bat, all of them unsure why their wistful and dutiful fathers were pushing them in front of this grayed, unfamiliar man, and even more bewildered why they spoke with reverence in their creaking voices instead of displaying unbending fatherly authority. ("Son, take a good look at this man. . . . You're going to tell your grandkids about this.")

Henry won, too, for he was one step closer to sending Hank away permanently, secure in the knowledge that at this stage, the days of make-believe would become even fewer. Henry left the room, shaking hands with the staff, signing one last round of stuff while thanking them for a "pretty good milk shake." "I wasn't sure I was gonna get it," he said cheerfully, "but I'm glad I did." He seemed more convinced than ever before that it was time to head to West Palm Beach, to the secluded home he had built, where he could say good-bye to Hank Aaron and his glossies, his Sharpies, his enormous shadow and public obligations, in favor of Henry.

"You know what the hardest thing is? What nobody wants to understand—is me. People want their memories of me to be my memories of me," Henry Aaron said. "But you know what? They're not."

PART ONE

ESCAPE

CHAPTER ONE

HERBERT

DURING THE QUIET times, always in a small group, or more prefer-
ably, a one-on-one setting—in the back of a cab on the way to the airport, over dinner after an exhausting afternoon of smiles, greetings,
and waving to the aggressive gaggle of fanatics that always made him
nervous—he would try and let people in, try to help them understand
him. Henry Aaron would drift back, far past his life and his own individual achievements. You had to go back to the first decade of the last
century, and then flip the calendar back further still into the bitter
contradictions his people lived, to the land of the ghosts that forever
remained inside of him. He would try to explain rural Alabama,
across the southern Black Belt into the corner of America that
created him.

Even the name, "Black Belt," meant different things to different
people, spoke of conflicting layers. Some people said its origin derived from the dark hue of the southern soil, moist as a chocolate
cake. Others said the name referred to the immense financial potential of the land, which offered such lucrative possibilities that its owners would always be, at least according to financial ledger, in the
black.

And yet for others still, the etymology of the Black Belt simply
described those black people, Henry's people, whose dark hands dug
deep into the land every day for centuries, from sunrise to dusk,
whose feet trudged thanklessly across acres of unrelenting realities:
the richest land in the country would always be worked by the poor-
est people—once for free, and then for pennies.

It was into this life that the original Henry Aaron was born, on
December 20, 1884. In the spring of 1910, a part-time federal em-

ployee named Louis J. Bryant combed an important southern set-piece—the wide swath of cotton fields and dirt roads—collecting data for the United States government. In late May of that year, he arrived at Camden, the venerable county seat of Wilcox County. Rich in harvestable soil and advantageous geography, Wilcox County had been one of the richest cotton-producing counties in Alabama during most of the eighteenth and nineteenth centuries. From Camden, the Alabama River twisted southward, then turned into the Mobile River before emptying free into the Gulf of Mexico.

Slavery had long been the lifeblood of Wilcox County. Paddle-boats carrying cotton and tobacco crowded the Alabama, but it was the transportation of slaves from down the river that gave Wilcox County its special economic power. So important were slaves to the financial fortunes of the region that whenever a prominent slave ship docked in Canton Bend—the county seat during slave times—town business effectively stopped. Auctions for newly arrived blacks commenced promptly at noon each Thursday, and the ships that served Wilcox County were so well known for producing quality slave man-power that Canton Bend bankers would close early on Thursdays in order to attend auctions in the town's center. The custom was so deeply ingrained into the fabric of Wilcox County that even a century later, after slavery had become only a haunting memory, many south-ern banks in the old Black Belt areas still closed at noon midweek. Just before the Civil War, the county seat was moved from Canton Bend to Camden, and its preemancipation customs moved along with it.

The black population of Wilcox underscored the county's eco-nomic reliance on slavery. According to the 1860 census, twenty-six blacks were listed in the county rolls as "free colored," but each lived uneasily, in constant danger of being captured and resold into slavery. Government records show 905 whites owning 17,797 African slaves. Even with a relatively low white population (slightly under seven thousand), Wilcox County nevertheless held the ninth-highest total of slaves in Alabama and the nineteenth-highest in the entire country.

The county was run by influential families with deep Confederate pedigrees. The two leading family names in Wilcox were Tait and Gee. The Gees were the first white inhabitants of the county, and the northernmost arch of the river was named Gee's Bend, after the ten-thousand-acre cotton plantation settled on the banks by Joseph Gee. The Gees facilitated slave trades between the family estates in North Carolina and Wilcox County, while the Taits routinely enjoyed the privilege of having among the highest number of slaves in the county, and generations of Tait men, led first by the patriarch, Charles Tait, would hold prominent positions both in southern politics and social circles. Powerful Confederate organizations, such as the Daughters of the Confederacy, were, in part, founded in Wilcox County. Slavery and cotton combined dominated the economy, and the Tait name was an affluent one, the family exploiting one of the most profitable of slave-trading corridors in the state. A few years after Bryant's visit, on April 1, 1913, another former slave owner recorded his recollections for the state archives in a typed letter:

My Dear Sir,

Your favor of recent date received. I take pleasure in furnishing the following information regarding slavery.

CABINS AND QUARTERS

The cabins were generally one-and two-roomed. They were constructed of pine poles, had plank windows and floors and were ceiled.

The slaves were required to make their own furniture. This was plain, nude, and consisted mainly of a table, benches and a few chairs.

The cabins had one and two rooms. A slave family was housed in a two room cabin. The rooms were all ceiled up well, and were very comfortable in the winter.

CLOTHING, SHOES, ETC . . .

The slaves were furnished with good warm clothing which was made of kerseys and osnaburg. They were allowed four suits a year. These were made by the white women and the negro seam-stresses on the place. The "Lady of the White House" superin-tended the making.

FOOD

Their food mainly consisted of bacon, bread, potatoes and peas. 3¼ to 4 pounds of meat was the allowance per week. They had little "extra patches" which they worked at odd times and made money to purchase extras.

They did their cooking at night for the following day. They generally ate their breakfast at home and carried their dinner to the fields in a little bucket.

WORK AT THE HOUSE, IN THE FIELD, IN TOWN, ETC . . .

Their work was mainly ploughing, hoeing, and splitting rails, and any work that would naturally be performed at a plantation. The work hours was from sun-up to sun-down. They were allowed holidays on Christmas and 4th July.

The region, like the nation, collectively could not envision a world without slavery. In Wilcox County, slaves were not merely purchased but also bred by slaveholders, with the intention of creating a workforce in perpetuity. In *The Reins of Power,* his memoir of growing up in Wilcox County, Clinton McCarty wrote that when James Asbury Tait, son of Charles Tait, the first federal judge from Alabama and later a U.S. senator, inherited the family business following his father's death, he perfected the practice of maximizing the financial value of slaves.

Charles Tait rejected the convention of paying more for slave boys, McCarty wrote, and instead would pay an average of $625 for girls. Because any baby born to a slave became by law the property of the plantation owner, Tait set out upon breeding his future workforce, routinely paying as much as fifty dollars more for slave girls just reaching puberty than for teenage boys. The Tait plantation, for example, owned 180 slaves in 1835, but between 1819 and 1834, Tait estimated that fifty-eight slaves were born on his property.

In the surviving family business journals, James A. Tait left a portrait of his slaves' living conditions and their necessity in providing labor for the Tait plantation. In memorandums titled "The Sickly Season" and "Negro Housing," he wrote:

More care must be always be taken about health during the sickly season than at other times. . . . There is more danger to Negroes picking cotton than any other, the hot sun shining on their backs whilst stooping. . . . 30,000 lbs of cotton total Negroes equal to 18 bales . . . crop of 1837. . . . Negroes housing ought to be moved regularly once in two or three years . . . this is essential to health. The filth accumulates under the floors so much in two years to cause disease. This is cheaper and easier than to pay doctors and nurse sick wages. The putrid threat that prevailed so fataly [*sic*] in the winter of 1837, 38 was caused by the filth under the houses, and I have no doubt 4 little Negroes died of it.

During the Reconstruction years, when the plantation system gave way to sharecropping, blacks in Wilcox County fared no better than they had prior to emancipation. By 1890, well after the war, blacks outnumbered whites by four to one, the slavery system was dead, and the depression in cotton harvesting had dramatically reversed the affluent position of many whites, but the culture in Wilcox County of whites living in complete dominion over blacks endured. The ensuing result was a region that housed thousands of blacks working the unforgiving land, generation following hopeless generation, prospects as bleak as the granite sky. The topography of the county had virtually guaranteed that change, if at all, would take place at a lethargic pace. The river opened into a teardrop called Millers Ferry, which isolated the portions of the county—such as Gee's Bend—that had yet to be bridged, leaving the great plantations essentially walled off from the rest of the area. As one visiting writer observed, "Gee's Bend represents not merely a geographic configuration drawn by the yellow pencil of the river. Gee's Bend represents another civilization. Gee's Bend is an Alabama Africa. There is no more concentrated and racially exclusive Negro population in any rural community in the South than in Gee's Bend."

Over the days Louis Bryant visited Camden, he discovered just how little life had changed for the black people of Wilcox County. The homes that bordered the pockmarked dirt roads were virtually identical to those that had been written about in the old letter: dilapidated wood-planked cabins that had once been slave quarters balanced unevenly on wooden blocks to protect the rough pine floors against worms and flooding, the rot the moist Alabama soil so easily accelerated. The raised floor also provided marginal relief against the intense heat of the summer months—just enough so little kids could play and cool off underneath the houses. The roofs were comprised of a patchwork of rectangular shingles varying in length. The cabins were spartan, having only one or two rooms, a woodstove with cooktop, and a small four-paned window on each side, patched with newspaper to insulate its borders. Some cabins were constructed with pine logs, insulated by a crude combination of mud and grass. Bryant's recordings would be included in the vast database that would become the thirteenth Census of the United States.

Bryant recorded on May 23, 1910, that Henry Aaron lived with his family in a rented cabin on 325 Clifton Road in Camden. The 1910 census listed Henry as twenty-five years old, the head of the household, living with his twenty-three-year-old wife, Mariah, born 1887, and their eighteen-month-old son, Herbert, born October 24, 1908. Family members would describe Henry as a man who did not speak unless spoken to and who was slow to come to his opinions of people, but once he had reached a conclusion, his assessments were firm and accurate. Once he had become a famous baseball player, Henry would often say not only that he had been named after his grandfather, whom he referred to as "Papa Henry," but also that he owed his methodical approach to work and his deliberate style of communication not to Herbert, his father, but to Papa Henry.

Papa Henry told the census taker that both he and Mariah had been born in Alabama, as had their parents. His occupation was listed as a "laborer" who worked as a "general farmer." According to the census, Papa Henry could neither read nor write and had never attended formal school. Mariah, according to the same data, was recorded as able to read and write and was listed as being school-educated, making her one of the very few blacks on Clifton Road who had attended school. Mariah was among a small percentage of blacks in Wilcox reported to be literate.

Official documents paint a skeletal picture of Papa Henry's roots. A basement fire at the Commerce Department in 1921 destroyed most of the data from the 1890 census, leaving little, if any, paper trail to Henry's father, who was likely either one of the last children born into slavery or part of the first generation of southern blacks born free in the United States. Poor record keeping, gaps in memory, and, most disastrously, the disinterest in the black community expressed by local and federal record keepers—the official term to describe this phenomenon was *undercounted*—would leave mysterious but not uncommon holes in the family story. The irony was that it was easier to keep track of blacks in captivity—slaves were, after all, property no different from a horse or a wagon or a house—than the freedmen who comprised the first generation of post–Civil War American blacks.

When the census was done again in Camden ten years later, on January 24, 1920, the census taker, a man named Joseph H. Cook, recorded the family name as "Aron." Cook reported that that the Aarons now had six children: Herbert, eleven; Cottie, nine; Mandy, seven; Olive, seven; William, five; and James, three. Herbert would say in later interviews there would be six more children. "I am the oldest of twelve children and father of six," Herbert told an interviewer in 1985. Age would always pose a riddle throughout the family. On the 1920 form, Mariah, whom Henry and his siblings called "Mama Sis," was listed as being born in 1894, making her seven years younger than she was listed as being on the 1910 report, which would have made her fourteen years old when Herbert was born.

Like most people connected to Wilcox County, the Aarons were touched by the enormous shadow of the Tait dynasty. Charles Tait's grandson, Robert, was a Confederate captain, and in 1860, he owned 148 slaves. During the ruthless white reclamation of power that dissolved Reconstruction, the foundation of the sharecropper system was born and blacks who had once worked the land as slaves now tended to the same land as free blacks, and for many—because of the illegitimate bookkeeping and other shady practices that left blacks in a perpetual state of debt—there was no escape from the system. According to the 1920 census, Papa Henry and his family lived next door to Frank S. Tait, Charles Tait's great-grandson. The Taits were the only white family on the street, suggesting that the black families on that street rented their housing from the Taits and worked the family land accordingly as sharecroppers. This was almost certainly true in the case of Papa Henry, whose World War I civilian registration card listed F. S. Tait as his employer.

As a boy, Herbert worked the fields in Camden, picking cotton into his teens. Though public records are unclear, it is likely at some point or another he worked the enormous Tait property, as had his father.

Herbert was restless and dreaded a life of dreary, hopeless agrarianism. The routine in Camden had not changed for a century: work the land for nonexistent wages, with little chance for self-improvement or respect from the white community, which for the better part of two centuries had held absolute power. In later interviews, he would say the members of his family lived in the fields and the church. As he grew older, he was aware of an important, curious phenomenon: Many blacks he knew were leaving Wilcox—for Mobile, and even Chicago and California—and he decided he would be one of them. From the time of Herbert's birth, in 1908, up until his twentieth birthday, the black population in Wilcox County dropped nearly 30 percent.

And yet, despite the obvious contradictions, whites still clung to the old paternalisms. In *The Reins of Power*, Clinton McCarty recalled the prevailing attitude regarding blacks in Wilcox County during the time Herbert Aaron was coming of age in Camden:

> Blacks as a race were commented on in routine white conversation mostly in terms of the care they needed, the trouble they caused, or the anecdotes and jokes they lent themselves to. Except for those long loyal to and productive for one's family, they were said to be lazy, shiftless, promiscuous, addicted to petty theft, quick to ingratiate for a purpose, childlike in their intellectual capacity; on more than one occasion, I heard adult white males address adult black males in the sort of sing-song cadence usually heard when adults talk to small children. Blacks were described as incapable of good taste, humorous in their speech, often amusingly animated in their actions. But with it all they were credited with being the occasional sources of heart-of-the-matter descriptions and homely wisdom. Always there was the suggestion that whites were still the blacks' truest friends . . . and would come to their aid in time of trouble.

Herbert had been secretly dating a young girl, also from Wilcox County, named Stella, whose family names were Pritchett and

Underwood. In the records, Estella's birth year ranged from 1909 to 1912, and the exact dates of her family origins would also remain unclear, even to the family.

Herbert had plans to leave Camden, with its grim prospects. He was heading for Mobile. Herbert and Stella waited until she was old enough to leave town, but in 1927, Stella became pregnant and the two moved south down the river, four hours from Mobile. Later that year, Stella gave birth to their first child, Sarah, most likely out of wedlock. As much as movie theaters and water fountains, city records were segregated during those days, and the records of blacks were not nearly as accurate as those of whites. According to Book 36 of the Mobile Colored Marriage License Book, page 503, Herbert and Stella Aaron were married in Mobile on August 22, 1929, by justice of the peace and notary public Thomas B. Allmann. On his marriage certificate, Herbert spelled the family name "Aron," and he was listed as twenty-two years of age, five eight, and weighing 142 pounds. Stella was listed as nineteen years of age, five seven, and weighing 115 pounds. The license book stated both were Protestant and were marrying for the first time.

The original surname, the first one the clan would claim as a free American family, had been Aaron. As the country moved through the wrenching antebellum period, the hope and disappointment of Reconstruction, and then the subsequent establishment of Jim Crow as the southern rule of law, the Aaron name would move along with it. For a man who would carry his name with an eaglelike pride, Henry recalled his name weathering numerous variations, from Aron to Arron and occasionally Aarron, a stinging byproduct of the lack of educational opportunities afforded blacks at the turn of the twentieth century. By 1930, the family name had returned to its biblical origins, and would not change.

"Our name changed often," Henry would explain. "My mother and father, they could not read or write, and so it was spelled differently many times over the years."

Herbert Aaron had come to Mobile as a slender nineteen-year-old without prospects beyond labor, and although he was unable to read or write, he was determined nevertheless that life would be better for him than it had been for his father. He considered himself religious—

he attended Episcopal Sunday services in Mobile—but, unlike his predecessors, did not envision a life rooted in the church.

In Mobile, work was plentiful but unpredictable in its reliability. Mobile was Alabama's main port city, and in the years following World War I, it boasted a growing economy and a diversity of jobs. This optimism stood in strong contrast to the city's sagging economic fortunes in the decades following the Civil War. In later years, when his son grew famous, Herbert would tell interviewers that, in terms of manual labor, he had done it all. In Camden, he had picked cotton, as well as operated heavy machinery and motorized farm equipment. According to city records, Herbert and Stella moved to 1170 Elmira Street in Down the Bay, one of the two major residential areas for blacks inside of Mobile's city limits. Rent was six dollars per month. In the Mobile city directory, Herbert listed his first job as a laborer, and later he drove a truck for the Southall Coal Company.

Down the Bay was situated in the southern part of the city, blocks away from the idyllic magnolia-lined beauty of Government Street, bordered by the Magnolia Cemetery to the south, Government Street to the north, and Cedar and Ann streets to the east and west, respectively. Demographically, Down the Bay was poor, unemployment high. The neighborhood was primarily black, but, unlike Davis Avenue—the main thoroughfare, which served as the center of the other predominately black section of Mobile—not without diversity. The 1930 census listed fifteen dwellings on Elmira Street, seven white households, eight black. Whites lived on each end of Elmira, the blacks in the middle. To the north, by contrast, was Davis Avenue, once known as Stone Street and then renamed before the Civil War for Jefferson Davis. It was called "Darkey Town" by blacks and whites alike before adopting the more modern and proud nickname "the Avenue."

To northerners, Mobile seemed both formidable and chilling. The city was situated in the deepest part of the Deep South, just miles from the Mississippi border, a frightening pocket of intolerance, where good people who said or did the wrong things might just disappear. To white and black southerners alike, however, Mobile was one of the more livable cities for blacks. Bienville Square, with its rushing alabaster water fountain and softly blossomed magnolias and oaks, represented the best of Mobile for its whites, the middle- and upper-class gentry, and on special days—birthdays, holidays—the white poor. The park represented southern beauty, especially on those perfect spring days before the heat soared, and for a time in the late nineteenth century, both blacks and whites had come to see Bienville Square as a place representative of all of the city's residents.

Both races, naturally, came to resent the northern view of Mobile as another intractable southern monolith. It was not uncommon for blacks to rise to the defense of Mobile as an example of southern tolerance. One of the reasons Mobilians tended to take a more benign view of race relations was due to its population. Unlike Wilcox County, where a small number of whites controlled four times as many blacks, the white population in Mobile hovered around 50 percent.

By the time Herbert and Stella arrived, legal and social segregation had been firmly entrenched for nearly two decades, and in that regard Mobile was no different from the rest of the South. Locals believed that despite the law, daily accommodations had allowed both blacks and whites to live in relative dignity. It was an idea, of course, that rested on the notion that moderation resided in the eye of the beholder. If you were the ones on top, daily life might have been fine, acceptable, without the coarse and brutal edge of, say, Birmingham.

If you were black and did not upset the social order, it was not necessary to live in fear. Moderation also depended on one's standard of measurement, and in the South, the measure had always been Birmingham, two hundred miles to the north, centered in the heart of the Black Belt, both in the agricultural and racial sense. The locals would always use the backbreaking rigidity of Birmingham as the standard, and the contrast always worked in Mobile's favor. Compared to Birmingham, Mobile appeared almost sleepy.

Part of the reason for this was its quirky history. Where most regions in the South were demarcated by the oppressive and linear weight of slavery, Mobile's racial lines were somewhat less obvious. The city had been inhabited by the French and the Spanish. Where in much of the South there were just blacks and whites, Mobile was populated with another racial group, Creoles of Color. Though the event would first be co-opted and later defined by New Orleans,

Mobile was the first city in the United States to celebrate Mardi Gras. The historical demographics of the city—with its high number of French and Spanish and a high number of citizens of mixed racial origin—made it difficult to strictly enforce the emerging racial codes that had effectively destroyed the promises of Reconstruction.

The truth was, however, that during the final decade of the nineteenth century and the first decade of the twentieth, whites across the South organized a massive resistance to whatever gains blacks had made during Reconstruction. If fond memories existed of Bienville Square as a gathering place for all Mobilians, it was also true that long after the nation had abolished the slave trade, illegal slave ships docked on the Mobile River, next to the L&N Railroad and the Mobile and Ohio docks, and chained-together captured Africans were sold at auction in Bienville Square during the week. Another old slave market stood blocks away, on Royal Street, between St. Anthony and Congress.

During the first two and a half decades of the twentieth century, southern whites methodically restored the old social order through a punishing combination of legal and extralegal means. Mobile, despite an exterior gentility and a favorable comparison to some of the harsher southern cities, did not escape this organized assault on black freedoms.

In 1900, Montgomery adopted a series of segregation ordinances. Mobile was under similar pressure to enact stricter segregation laws, though the city had been relatively free of major incident. The following year, numerous states, including Alabama, rewrote their state constitutions, legally imposing segregation orders, disenfranchising blacks from voting and other social freedoms they had enjoyed during Reconstruction. Between 1895 and 1909, the first year of Herbert's life, a massive campaign of disenfranchisement had begun.

South Carolina enacted laws severely limiting people of color from voting and prohibiting contact between the races in terms of education, marriage, adoption, public facilities, transportation, and prisons. During the same period, similar laws were enacted in Texas, Oklahoma, Missouri, Arkansas, Louisiana, Mississippi, Kentucky, Tennessee, Georgia, Florida, North Carolina, Virginia, West Virginia ("White persons who marry a colored person shall be jailed up to one

year, and fined up to $100. Those who perform such a marriage cere-
mony will be guilty of a misdemeanor and fined up to $200"), Mary-
land, Washington, Idaho, California ("Persons of Japanese descent in
1909 were added to the list of undesirable marriage partners of white
Californians as noted in the earlier 1880 statute"), Colorado, Arizona,
New Mexico, North Dakota (literacy tests) and South Dakota (inter-
marriage or illicit cohabitation forbidden between blacks and whites,
punishable by a fine up to one thousand dollars, or by imprisonment
up to ten years, or both), Kansas, and Nebraska.

In justifying separation of the races, the press served as an effec-
tive tool to incite fear among whites. It purported that blacks did not
possess the social capacity to be treated with the same courtesies as
whites, and that blacks were dangerous, uncivilized, a grave threat to
the safety of the white women of Mobile. (In 1915, Alabama passed a
statewide law prohibiting "White female nurses from caring for black
male patients.")

The social order had been upset by the large influx of blacks who
inhabited the city during the final decade of the 1800s. The *Mobile
Daily Item* was the most actively hostile newspaper in the city toward
blacks—its coverage only spurred growing insistence among whites
for the return of segregation. During a ten-day period in October
1902, its coverage proved even more relentless:

FURY OF A TEXAS MOB

Finds satisfaction in lynching of negroes

HEMPSTEAD, TEX., OCTOBER 21 — After being tried with legal
form and procedure for criminal assault and murder and given the
death penalty in each case, Jim Wesley and Reddick Barton, negroes,
were, late this afternoon taken from the authorities and lynched in
the public square by an infuriated mob

NEGRO PEEPER

*Is discovered on the gallery of a
citizen residing on Espejo Street*

Mr. Charles Helmer, while on his way home Tuesday night last with
his wife and a party of ladies saw a negro on the gallery of Mr. George
McCary, on Espejo Street, near Government. The Negro was on the

gallery peeping through the blinds and when one of the ladies discovered him, he jumped to the ground. Mr. Helmer chased the man across a pasture but was unable to capture him.

The black response derived from the old paternalistic relationships with whites. The famous educator Booker T. Washington appealed to the white city elders across the South to confront the "criminal colored elements" but not to "punish the entire Negro race" with segregation ordinances. Washington's disciples began echoing a similar theme in Mobile. Washington was already a national figure, and his presence in Mobile increased the influence of two black businessmen, Charles Allen and A. N. Johnson. Washington would vacation with Allen, often fishing at his home. Johnson owned a funeral home prominent in the black community and published his own newspaper, where he often broke with Washington's doctrines of appeasement with whites. Washington appealed to whites to recall the positive relationships between the two races, a relationship that in large part favored whites. Johnson seemed to have a clearer notion of white intentions. Through his writing, he sought to challenge the existing structure. He understood that a single increase in restrictions would only lead to more.

Johnson was right in his belief that a movement to undo current relationships between the races was afoot. Erwin Craighead, the editor of the ostensibly moderate *Register*, endorsed in an editorial the necessity of segregation on streetcars. These sensational headlines and editorials only heightened racial tensions in the city, and any idea that Mobile would be different from the rest of the South crumbled. The newspapers increased their character assault on Mobile's blacks, including a decision by the newspaper editors to publish on the front page reports of crimes committed by blacks hundreds of miles away.

BOUND FACE TO FACE

*They had murdered a young farmer
while on his way home
One of the negroes escaped into Arkansas*

NEWBORN, TENN., OCTOBER 8—Garfield Burley, and Curtis Brown, negroes, were lynched here at 9 o'clock tonight by a mob of

500 persons. . . . The mob would not listen to the judge and forcibly took possession of the two men. . . . Ropes were presented and the two men were taken to a telephone pole where they were securely tied face to face. At a given word, they were strung up and in a few minutes both were pronounced dead. The lynching programme was carried out in an orderly manner, not a shot being fired.

BAD NEGRO

Sam Harris Riddled with Bullets at Salem Ala.

USED AXE ON WOMEN

The negro was placed in custody and held until Miss Meadows had sufficiently recovered to identify him. This she did at 4 o'clock this afternoon, and the negro was taken in charge by about 125 armed men and his body riddled with bullets on the spot. He denied his guilt until the first shot was fired, when he acknowledged the crime.

By October 16, 1902, Mobile reacted with a sweeping ordinance that had been adopted in New Orleans, as well as in Montgomery and Memphis.

TEN MORE POLICEMEN PROVIDED FOR CITY: SEPARATION OF THE RACES ON STREET CARS

Petitions, circulated by the Item and Signed by More Than 500 People, Read and Favorably Acted Upon— full text for the Ordinance Requiring the Separation of the Races on All of the Street Cars.

Be it ordained by the mayor and general counsel of the city of Mobile as follows: That all street railcars operated in the city of Mobile and its police jurisdiction shall provide seats for the white people and negroes, when there are white people and negroes on the same car, by requiring the conductor or any other employee in charge of said car or cars to assign passengers to seats on the cars, or when the car is divided in two compartments in such manner as to separate the white people from the negroes by seating the white people in the front seats and the negroes in the rear seats as they enter said cars; but in the event such order of seating might cause inconvenience to those who are already properly seated, the conductor . . . may use his discretion in seating passengers, but in such manner that no white person and negro must be placed or seated in the same section or compartment arranged for two persons; provided that negro nurses having in charge white children or sick or infirm white persons may be assigned seats among the white people.

Be it further ordained, that all conductors and other employees while in charge of cars are hereby invoked with the police power of a police officer of the city of Mobile, to carry out rail provisions, and any person failing or refusing to take a seat among those assigned to the race to which he or she belongs, if there is any such seat vacant, at the behest of a conductor . . . shall, upon conviction, be fined a sum not less than five dollars and not more than fifty dollars.

And so it was done. Jim Crow laws were now established in Mobile, if not as violently enforced as in other southern cities, although equally rigid. Two weeks later, on November 1, the black leaders A. F. Owens, A. N. Johnson, and A. N. McEwen staged a boycott, which lasted barely two months. During the time of the boycott, some white business owners, unconvinced the city would benefit from the segregation ordinance, openly defied it. James Wilson, the owner of the Mobile Light and Railroad Company, told his conductors not to enforce the law. Whites sat anywhere they chose on Wilson's cars, and blacks were, for a time, seen seated in the front. The courts intervened and the segregation laws were not only upheld but strengthened. On streetcars, conductors could use their own discretion in upholding the ordinances. After December 1902, whites faced jail time and a fifty-dollar fine for not upholding segregation statutes.

Streetcars were the first step. Total segregation came next, followed by the vigilante violence Mobile thought it had avoided. The outspoken black leaders, who once believed they had a voice, fled the city. A. N. Johnson escaped to Nashville in 1907.

"With the disintegration of the boycott and the court's decision, segregated public conveyances legally became an established element of life in Mobile—a condition that persisted unchanged until the 1950s," historian and Mobile native David Alsobrook wrote in his comprehensive 1983 dissertation. "By 1904, Mobile's blacks, as in other southern cities, were separated from whites by municipal and state laws and by customs. Mobile had segregated public conveyances, schools, parks, restaurants, hotels, theaters, hospitals, cemeteries, saloons and brothels. With the single exception of public transportation, segregation was maintained without the passage of municipal ordinances."

By the time Herbert and Stella arrived, whites and blacks alike now lived under a new, terrifying system, naturally worse for blacks but also not easy for whites who didn't believe in segregation. David Alsobrook recalled walking down the street in Mobile one day as a boy and seeing the charred remains of a cross. In addition to the legal segregation codes was the daily etiquette whites demanded, unwritten codes that, if not followed, could be deadly. Herbert knew them all by heart:

1. No offering handshakes with whites, for it assumed equality.
2. No looking at or speaking to white women.
3. No offering to light a white woman's cigarette.
4. All whites were to be addressed as "sir," "mister" or "ma'am," but whites were free to address blacks by their first names or "boy."

This was Herbert Aaron's America. He knew where he stood.

CHILDREN WERE BORN frequently to the Aarons. The combination of children and Herbert's constant (and not always successful) search for work forced the family to look for housing as often as Stella bore children. A son, Herbert junior, was born in 1930, and the family moved again, this time to 10 O'Guinn. Then the family moved to 1112 Elmira, before renting another apartment in Down the Bay, at 666 Wilkinson, for nine dollars per month.

Four years later, on February 5, 1934, at 8:25 p.m., Stella gave birth again, this time to a twelve-and-a-quarter-pound boy named Henry Louis. The baby was so large that Stella nicknamed him "the Man."

A year before Henry was born, Herbert took a job as a part-time riveter at the Alabama Dry Dock and Shipbuilding Company, on Pinto Island, on the Mobile River. The company had been in business since World War I. Herbert worked as a boilermaker assistant and riveter on coal barges, minesweepers for the U.S. Navy, and tank barges for oil companies. The work was hard and often irregular, but a few years later, as the war in Europe escalated and tensions with Japan increased, a job at ADDSCO became one of the plum ones to have in Mobile, especially for blacks. At the company's peak, a third of ADDSCO's workers were black, though that did not mean the workforce was treated with complete equity. The riveting and manufacturing and labor crews were largely segregated. Blacks and whites entered together through the large main gate, but both proceeded through designated separate entrances. When he first accepted the job, Herbert was paid sixteen cents an hour.

With the family now numbering five, the apartment on 666 Wilkinson was no longer sufficient. In 1936, Gloria Aaron was born. Two more children followed, Alfred, who did not survive pneumonia, and Tommie, in 1939. At this point, Herbert began forming a bold vision for a semiemployed black person: owning his own house. In Down the Bay, both Elmira and O'Guinn streets were fairly integrated, but, according to census data, only the whites on the streets where Herbert lived owned their homes.

For Herbert, ownership meant protecting his family from outside forces that could, at any time, take away what he had. Herbert had lived in Mobile for thirteen years and had already moved four times. "When you own something," Herbert would tell his children, "nobody can take it away from you." Herbert chose Toulminville, once an all-white enclave within the city limits, roughly seven miles northwest from Down the Bay. To black Mobilians, Toulminville was considered a step down from Down the Bay socially, and Henry would later recall that when he was a child, Toulminville kids absorbed insults from the blacks who lived closer to the city.

Local blacks called Toulminville "Struggleville," because people who had moved out to Toulminville, or so went the local folklore, did so anticipating a rise in social status but routinely found it difficult to pay the rent. Unlike Down the Bay, Toulminville was considered lower-middle-class by black standards, as the city housed numerous teachers within its borders. Herbert purchased two adjacent lots for fifty-three dollars apiece on Edwards Street and began culling wood. Herbert collected ship timber from Pinto Island. Young Henry, all of six years old, collected wood from abandoned buildings. Some of the wood came from houses that had partially burned down, and some of the original walls of the house still contained deeply discolored streaks, charred from fire. Herbert constructed a six-to-twelve-foot triangular gabled roof above the front door. He used the smaller, miscellaneous pieces of wood for the inside walls. The floor was made of yellow pine. Like most of the houses in the South, the structure itself stood on concrete blocks, both to cool the house and to protect the flooring from the damp southern soil.

In 1942, when the house was completed, Herbert moved the family into 2010 Edwards Street, a narrow dirt road on the southwest side of Toulminville. Edwards Street bordered a wide playground and baseball field, Carver Park, to the west. By this time, Stella had given birth to six children. The house consisted of two rooms and a small kitchen area, the backyard big enough for a small garden, a livestock pen, and an outhouse. For lighting, Stella kept a kerosene lamp nearby. There were no windows, no electricity, no indoor plumbing, but the house did not belong to the bank, or a landlord, white or black. Herbert had built a piece of the world for himself, and it would become the cornerstone of the family for the next four generations.

"The only people who owned their houses," Henry would often say, "were rich people, and the Aarons."

Ownership was not a concept easily entertained by blacks in the South, but Herbert Aaron keenly understood its value. As much as southern whites would become stereotyped in their collective racial attitudes, so, too, did blacks in the Deep South suffer from the opposite labels of docility, too easily accepting of the withering effects of Jim Crow.

As an adult, regardless of his actual position, Henry Aaron would always be perceived as too accommodating when it came to social conditions. The same was true with Herbert in Mobile. Such clichés were misleading at best. The truth was that Herbert Aaron developed a wide and serious strategy for dealing with the limitations placed on him by society; the first was ownership. He was sophisticated in his knowledge of the social code of Mobile, and fortified by a core toughness that was easily underestimated. Herbert fought for his space, but he used nontraditional weapons.

Residents and historians routinely agreed that daily life in Mobile was not as hostile as in other southern cities. What was less easy to agree upon, however, was why. David Alsobrook believed the crackdown beginning with the streetcar ordinance at the turn of the century—and the violence that followed—served as a powerful-enough deterrent to any new generation of prospective black protesters. Other Mobilians, black and white, took a more benign view, saying that Mobile was simply an easier, less volatile place to live.

Nevertheless, along Davis Avenue during the first years after Herbert arrived from Wilcox, the black community still kept fresh in its mind the handful of events designed to maintain order. There was the 1906 dual lynching of seventeen-year old Jim Robinson and twenty-year-old Will Thompson. Both had been jailed on the vague charge of "improper conduct" toward white women. A mob of forty-five men wearing masks captured the two and hanged them together from a tree just outside city limits. According to Mobile legend, whites heard about the lynching and boarded the streetcar to visit the hanging tree and collect souvenirs, cutting off pieces of clothing from the two victims as well as shaving off bark from the tree.

Herbert possessed a keen sense of self-determination and self-sufficiency, and he knew what it took to survive in Mobile on his own terms. He had suffered humiliations too familiar to southern black males. During the days living in Down the Bay, Herbert was frequently laid off from jobs, although whites were retained in similar positions. Herbert would keep his family close, reminding the two oldest boys, Herbert junior and Henry, that whites wanted to "cut the head off of the snake," which meant emasculating a black male in order to break his family. That was why Herbert may have responded to whites in a way that appeared subservient. But Herbert Aaron would not be one of the black men in town easily goaded into making an emotional mistake around whites, giving them a reason to break him.

"My grandfather believed in the work," said Tommie Aaron, Jr. "It got passed down to this day. He used to say it all the time, 'Nobody is going to give you anything.' "

As a young boy, Henry would watch as his father was forced to surrender his place in line at the general store to any whites who entered. There were boys who were never the same after they saw their own fathers back down, the leader of the family reduced. And there were men, unable to live after having been diminished, who lashed out at their own families. Herbert told his children that the psychological destruction of the black man, and by extension his family, was the white man's true game. Living in the South was a daily contest of restraint, for one weak moment could finish a family. The newspapers were full of stories of black men who wound up dead for a minor offense. Herbert knew that, too, and told his boys. White overreaction was a dangerous weapon. If it were possible to be jailed simply for addressing a white person improperly, blacks in general would hardly dare broaching a more serious offense.

Psychological intimidation was always reinforced by the physical. Periodically, in Toulminville, Stella would hear the ominous sound of a Klansman's drum, first off in the distance and then closer. She would wake the children and force them under the bed. Peering out from the door, she would see the rows of Klansmen marching down her muddy street, armed, dressed in white robes and hoods, their torches terrorizing the night sky. The children remained quiet, lying on the hardwood floor, waiting for the danger to pass.

"That was the way it was," Tommie Aaron, Jr., recalled. "We used to hear stories like that all the time. But my grandfather also used to say, 'Don't let anybody break your will.' "

By the time the family moved to the house in Toulminville, when Henry was eight, Herbert had been promoted to a full-time riveter at ADDSCO. The country was at war, fighting with bombs and bullets but also with its own contradictions of equality and fairness. In 1941, President Roosevelt had signed Executive Order 8802, which prohibited discrimination in the federal workplace, an edict that confronted southern segregation and discrimination patterns directly. One practical application of the order occurred at ADDSCO, where a number of black assistants were promoted to welders, with the same title, same responsibilities, and same salary as their white counterparts. On Tuesday, May 25, 1943, at approximately 9:00 a.m., a fight broke out between whites and blacks, which escalated into a full-scale riot. Black workers, fearing for their safety, were sent home for two days. Roughly 350 state and federal troops arrived to maintain order.

For the press, it was 1902 all over again. The *Mobile Register* used the disturbance as justification for universal segregation.

ABSOLUTE SEGREGATION OF RACE
THE ANSWER TO ADDSCO PROBLEM

The bomb on Mobile's doorstep has not been extinguished. It still smoulders and will continue to do so unless and until officials of the Alabama Dry Dock and Shipbuilding Company adopt a clear-cut policy of absolute racial segregation in the preparation of this great war enterprise.

The son who would one day become the great Henry Aaron, from his earliest days on, would always be called a mama's boy, but it was the desire of the father to escape the debilitating roots of Wilcox County and, in turn, to give the Aaron name meaning beyond its past, thereby setting the course the son would one day navigate.

"Obviously," Herbert said in an interview forty years later, "the black color of my skin presented many unnecessary problems in my life."

HENRY HAD BEEN taken with baseball ever since the family lived in the cramped spaces of Down the Bay. Herbert junior would toss bottle caps at him at top speed. Henry would watch the caps, flat and convex and erratic, whiz toward him and, unflinchingly, eyes steady and even, he would batter them with a stick. In Toulminville, his brothers and friends like Cornelius Giles would play baseball until the sun disappeared and it got so dark—streetlights were years away—that the kids couldn't see their hands in front of them. So instead of going into the house, the boys would light rags on fire, toss them up into the dark sky, and hit the descending fireballs. These stories were true, and they would serve the legend.

If there was a dominant memory of Henry during his boyhood days, it was that of a kid who perhaps more than anything else wanted to be left alone. When he was on the baseball field, he was dynamic, but the hard part often was getting him there. Henry was a loner. He would leave his house and venture alone through the tall brush to reach Three Mile Creek. There he would escape from the world and fish and think. He caught catfish and trout and would not be seen for hours at a time. Stella would always call him a loner and mentioned in interviews later in life that when he played baseball, it was not a social event, but his personal avocation. Unlike most kids, for whom sports was as much for camaraderie as for score keeping, Henry played for the game and not to make friends, she said. Many times, the kids with whom he played remained there on the diamond, cardboard cutouts for his ambition. Sports, in other words, did not transform him into a social creature. A female former classmate recalls Henry as certainly having been "interested in girls . . . but not as interested as he was in playing baseball."

When he wasn't wandering along the riverbanks, Henry was playing baseball. His desire for solitude explained in part why he was so comfortable in the batter's box, playing the game of baseball, the most individual of team sports. There, standing at the plate, he was alone, relying on his own ability to sustain him. No one could hit the ball for him, and no one else could take credit for what he did in the batter's box. Hitting, it could be argued, represented the first meritocracy in Henry's life. In a world where virtually everything could be qualified, hitting was the most unambiguous of activities.

Part of Henry's emphasis on baseball in future retellings would obscure a more revealing element of his upbringing—that he was an unexceptional student. This was not due to unintelligence as much as to disinterest. Aside from his enormous baseball ability, his enjoyment of the game was, for an American boy growing up in the 1930s and 1940s, fairly unremarkable. School never held his attention, and he would admit, though only partially, that as a child the limitations placed on a black person weakened his young spirit. He would talk to

Herbert about his dreams, and the old man could be withering in not sparing his children the bitter realities of his life, and, for the moment, theirs.

At 2010 Edwards, Henry, Herbert junior, and Tommie slept in the same bed. Above the bed hung a sign—most likely hand-painted by Sarah—which read RELY ON GOD AND ACT ON THE THINGS YOU CAN CHANGE. Henry wanted to be a pilot and a baseball player, and the sign just above his head said that such things were possible. But Herbert disagreed. He said, "There ain't no colored pilots. And there ain't no colored baseball players, either."

It is safe to say Jackie Robinson's signing was a transcendent day for America, and for Henry, it signaled the first time in his life that neither Papa Henry's nor Herbert's America would necessarily be his. The path of the son did not have to follow that of the father. Henry was eleven. Before Robinson signed with Montreal, Henry had played baseball, basketball, and football nearly equally. After, baseball was transformed into an obsession that did not diminish. Indeed, Henry's connection to the sport only intensified as Robinson ascended. Conversely, his interest in school waned even more.

In March 1948, Henry was fourteen, starting his high school career at Central High in Mobile. Robinson and the Dodgers arrived in Mobile for an exhibition game as the club made its way north to begin the season. The details of the day would always be sketchy— Henry recalled listening to Robinson in front of a drugstore on Davis Avenue; others recalled Robinson speaking at an auditorium. Henry had skipped school to see Robinson (though in those days, Henry did not need a reason to avoid classes), and for the next six decades of his life Henry would say that outside those with the members of his own family, no moment ever affected his outlook on what was possible in the world more than that day. "I knew I was going to be a ballplayer," Henry wrote in *I Had a Hammer*. "There was no doubt in my mind, and so school didn't matter to me. School wasn't going to teach me how to play second base like Jackie Robinson. I could learn that better by listening to the Dodgers on the radio. And that's what I did."

Robinson would have been disappointed by what the young Henry Aaron took from his message that day on Davis Avenue. Robinson told the throng of kids to stay focused on school, to gain an education, to work hard. Robinson's words were not the preachy adult bluster that the kids ignored, but a blueprint for an America that had not yet met its enlightenment on civil rights. When Henry met Robinson in Mobile, Robinson was a college man, from UCLA, a prestigious, integrated school. He not only had a college degree but was a veteran, and yet he still was subject to the limitations of what blacks would be allowed to accomplish. The only way to combat such obstacles was through education, Robinson said, a path in which Henry had little interest.

Instead, Henry would be mesmerized by Robinson. He would listen to him but not hear him. From that day forward, Henry started down a road Robinson himself never dared travel. Henry would bet his life on his talent, his ability to connect a piece of wood with a ball covered in horsehide. He would attend school sparingly, spending his time on the Avenue, in the pool halls, dodging Herbert, who knew his son was drifting away from his studies. Henry missed so many days of school—forty by the end—that he was expelled from Central High. He was enrolled at the Josephine Allen Institute, a small private school in Toulminville, on the corner of Sengstak and Walnut streets, run by a local educator, Josephine Blackledge Allen. The school, a long two-story rectangle, did not emphasize sports, but "basic grammar, mathematics and cultural refinement."

As the Aaron legend was being spun, an interesting caveat would find its way into each subsequent profile: Henry had promised Stella that if he didn't make it in baseball, he would go to college. Stella would repeat the tale that Henry was headed to Florida A&M, a black college.

For his part, Henry would debunk certain portions of the myth, denying that had he chosen not to play baseball, A&M would have been interested in offering him a football scholarship. This was almost certainly not true, as Henry did not play football as a junior or senior in high school. Henry would go so far as to say that he *purposely* stopped playing football because it would guarantee no school would have an interest in him. In later years, he would laugh at the suggestion that he'd ever had any intention of playing college football or that a college existed that wanted him on its team.

The truth was that Henry Aaron bet his entire life on baseball.

The college promise was, given his high school academic career, empty and illogical, but the words sounded good. They created the fiction that Henry Aaron, who spent more time in a pool hall than in the classroom at a time when a young Negro with little education wound up working in the fields, a factory, or on a chain gang, had a backup plan. What Henry never told anyone was that he was so confident in his ability to hit a baseball that he never thought he needed one.

"It was never one, two, three with me," Henry would reflect. "It was never 'this or that.' I knew it had to work. I knew I had to do it. It was that or, well, I didn't think I was going to the cotton fields, but it was going to work somewhere for one-fifty a week. It had to work. There wasn't anything to fall back on."

CHAPTER TWO

HENRY

HENRY AARON SET out to be a professional baseball player, having hardly been an amateur one. At Central High, he had dabbled in football, and once, either in 1947 or 1948, he played a regular-season game against Westfield High and its sensational running back, Willie Mays. Central, however, had no baseball team, and Henry would not play football with great enthusiasm, for fear an injury would ruin his baseball prospects. He was expelled from Central, and was uninterested in anything but baseball while at Josephine Allen, which only fielded a softball team anyway. Henry's résumé consisted of hitting bottle caps with a broom handle.

As he grew older and more prominent, journalists would seek to know more about his early years, about his upbringing and his family, about how he could have been so sure he possessed the special ability it took to play baseball at the highest level. A lot of kids were the best in their neighborhoods, but it wasn't exactly a given that Henry was even *that*. Henry would depend on a few of the old chestnuts that would be repeated for the next half century. The stories were odd and colorful, but none was particularly true or carried the kind of insight that would fill in the important pieces of his personal puzzle. At differing times, he told various tales about the origin of his legendary wrists. He told one writer that despite his wiry frame, his bulging forearms came from a job hauling ice in Mobile; he told another he benefited from mowing lawns; and he told people that for all of his right-handed greatness, he would have been an even *better* switch-hitter. That was because he batted cross-handed, which for a right-handed hitter was to say with his left hand on top, as a left-handed hitter would.

In 1959, the writer Roger Kahn would attempt to profile Henry for *Sport* magazine. He encountered the same frustration that sports editors of the Mobile newspapers had: Depending on the day, Henry would tell a different story about his origins, and, when placed side by side, no two stories ever exactly meshed.

Kahn was never quite sure if he found himself more frustrated by Henry's early story or by Henry's unwillingness to tell it. "I did not find him to be forthcoming," Kahn recalled. "He wasn't polished and really did not have the educational background at that time to deal with all of the things he was encountering in so short a time. If there was a word I would use to describe him then, it would be *unsophisticated.*"

Even as a teenager, Henry was expressing his lack of comfort with public life. On subjects both complex and innocuous, he would not easily divulge information, and he developed an early suspicion of anyone who took an interest in him. The reason, he would later say, was not the result of any personal trauma, but, rather, that of growing up in Mobile, where the black credo of survival was to focus on the work and let it speak for itself. It was a trait that was equal parts Herbert and Stella. Not only did Stella remind him never to be ostentatious but Herbert and all black males in Mobile knew what could happen to a black man who drew too much attention to himself. "My grandfather used to say all the time, 'They don't want you to get too high. Know your place,' " recalled Henry's nephew, Tommie Aaron, Jr. "I think a lot of that rubbed off on all of us."

In fact, Henry would employ the recipe for star power best articulated in the old Western *The Man Who Shot Liberty Valance*: "When the legend becomes fact, print the legend." That, too, was fitting, because as a movie fan, Henry fell in love with Westerns. He did not volunteer much truth, so the scribes printed the legend. There was more than one drawback to Henry's approach, however: As difficult as it was to piece together his early years, writers—virtually all of them white, carrying the prejudices against blacks that were common at the time—filled in the blanks for him, defined him, creating a caricature, from which he would not easily escape.

There was no magic moment to his childhood, no secret formula or bolt of lightning that transformed the broomstick-swinging boy into a baseball-playing man. He was not a particularly charismatic teenager, but he was single-minded. When he was not playing baseball, he spent his time on Three Mile Creek or in the pool halls of the Avenue, smoking with the adults.

Henry would occasionally cut the postage stamp of grass in front of the house. He would gather wood as Herbert demanded and he did his chores dutifully. Sometimes the two would clash, as fathers and sons do, over the future. Herbert, who earned sixteen cents an hour on Pinto Island, would have three quarters in his pocket and give his son two. There was, Herbert would say, an opportunity for Henry to have more than three coins in his pocket, to have, perhaps, an easier go of life if he would care more about school.

Like the rest of the Aaron children, Henry attended Morning Star Baptist Church, a mandatory requirement in Stella Aaron's house. For his part, Herbert didn't care much for the fire-and-brimstone carrying-on that was part of the tradition of the southern black Baptist Church. He preferred the more sober Episcopal Church, and attended somewhat regularly. After church, Henry would rush over to Carver Park, and that was where part of the legend was actually true.

In another place, just being a good ballplayer, better than the rest, would have been enough to attract the attention of someone who mattered—an influential college coach or one of the big-league scouts who seemed to know someone in every corner of the baseball-playing world. But Henry Aaron came of age in Mobile at a time when baseball was the lifeblood of the city, and being a good ballplayer in Mobile had all the distinction of a sunny day in California. It had been that way—for the odd, unquantifiable reasons that certain regions seem to breed highly skilled professionals of any stripe—since the 1920s. On the black side of town, before Henry's time, there was Satchel Paige, who had come from Down the Bay— he'd lived on Alba Street—and became the most celebrated pitcher in the history of the Negro Leagues. There was the great Negro Leaguer Ted Radcliffe, who caught at one end of a doubleheader and pitched at the other so many times, they nicknamed him "Double Duty." Radcliffe played for thirty-six years in the Negro Leagues. He and Paige were the big names of black baseball, but the culture of the sport was not rooted in the success of a couple of players. Across the tracks, on the white side of town, there were the Bolling brothers, Milt and Frank. Both would play in the big leagues, as would Henry and Billy Williams, but state law and local custom forbade interracial competition, and a generation of talented players lived in parallel universes.

Neighborhood kids would collide on the sandlots. On the black side of Mobile, the boys from Toulminville would play a group of kids from the other black areas, like Whistler or Plateau (which happened to be pronounced "Platt-toe"). Plateau was a depressed, historically rich, and significant part of Mobile. The town was nicknamed by the resident blacks "Africa Town," because Plateau was the docking point for the *Clothilda,* the final slave ship to land in Alabama. During Henry's childhood, Africa Town was also the part of Mobile where many former slaves had relocated following Emancipation. In Plateau, when the Mobile establishment grew more determined to enact Jim Crow statutes, blacks founded the Hickory Club in 1906, a local organization formed to police black neighborhoods from within (black policemen were not hired in Mobile until the mid-1950s) but also, if necessary, to protect them from the Ku Klux Klan.

There was a boy from Plateau who happened to be best in that neighborhood. He was just a little kid at the time Henry was on the field in Toulminville, so Tommy Agee just watched the big kids play.

The boys from Whistler would ride their bikes (the ones who had bikes) over to Toulminville for weekend epics that would last on the Carver Park dirt for hours and in memory forever. Another kid, five years younger than Henry, used to sit and watch unless the teams weren't even and they needed another body. When he got the call to play, Billy Williams would follow his big brother and do whatever he was told. The boys used their imaginations, the way kids do. Billy Williams recalled calling the dusty little park Carver *Stadium* instead of Carver Park, to give the place its proper regality, lending dreams their proper setting.

Billy's brother Clyde, a left-handed pitcher, often used to pitch to Henry. There was another younger kid in a different part of Mobile, Magazine Point, named McCovey, and people were already talking about keeping an eye on him, as well as another kid, Charley Pride, who wasn't sure if he wanted to be a baseball player or a musician.

Mobile's obsession with baseball was like something out of an old movie. Many of the factories in the city sponsored company teams, as did other industries. The men who played were grown and grizzled; they were welders and riveters and boilermakers in their mid-twenties and early thirties who ran down fly balls and threw in on the hands. Interspersed on these teams were some teenagers. Some of the kids could play, while others were bodies who filled out the rosters on days when numbers were short.

For a time, Henry played with the Pritchett Athletics, earning two dollars per game, and then he joined the Black Bears for three bucks a game. The traveling Negro League teams would come into town and play the industrial teams, and as a fifteen-year-old, Henry would play against Negro League competition. He played infield mostly, third base and shortstop, and as much as how he wielded the bat, players remembered the odd, slingshot style he used to throw the baseball, wide and to the side—"three o'clock," Billy Williams said. Williams himself played against the adults, first on the Mobile Black Shippers as a teenager, and also on the Mobile Black Bears, the Negro equivalent of the minor-league Mobile Bears. Saturdays and Sundays would showcase doubleheaders. There was also another team, in a different part of the city, the Mobile Mohawks. The games were scheduled for 3:00 p.m., just after church. Willie McCovey played for the Mobile Buckeyes.

Periodically, Henry would have a chance to play in a game and dream a little bit bigger. Other times, he would have his ambitions temporarily broken, like the time he showed up at an open tryout held by the mighty Brooklyn Dodgers but couldn't generate the nerve to stand up for himself and get in the batter's box. The older kids intimidated him and he skulked off the field without ever holding the bat in his hands.

The story might have ended right there except for two important but underplayed factors: the confidence Henry possessed in himself to hit any pitch from any pitcher, and the sureness of a man named Ed Scott, who had been watching Henry since 1950, when Henry was sixteen. Henry was not a prodigy and had played in only a handful of organized games. Billy Williams remembered his demeanor as unchanged even then. "A lot of guys were playing a helluva baseball game. Every day, he didn't stand out. He was just *good*."

There were bigger kids and more confident ones who might have been further along in their development at the time, but there was something about the way the ball sounded when Henry hit it, a sound the untrained ear might have missed. Ed Scott was convinced that the raw talent Henry displayed on the dusty sandlots of Toulminville might just be sufficient to allow him to play baseball at the next level.

Ed Scott worked in one of Mobile's factories, but on the side he provided the eyes and ears for a Negro League team, the Indianapolis Clowns. Their time was essentially over, and everybody knew it. Robinson had integrated the big leagues, and the unintended—or, depending on whom you talked to and how much money was being taken from their pockets, the *intended*—consequence of integration was the end of the black leagues. But in 1951, the Clowns could still attract young black ballplayers, and the major leagues still turned to the Negro Leagues as a source of talent. It was a relationship that would end before it began, for it would only be a matter of time before big-league clubs hired their own scouts to find black players.

Scott estimated he spent "every other day" with Henry. They would meet at Carver Park and Scott would shag flies for him. He believed Henry had a special ability, not simply because of Henry's swing but also because he was able to make such consistent contact with crude equipment. "He could hit the ball with a broken piece of wood. That was hard to do," Scott recalled. "Especially the black kids. You'd see them out there hitting and running and catching, with a tennis ball or broken pool stick. A broken pool stick was a Louisville Slugger to us."

The more Scott talked to Henry about his ability, the more he understood that Henry was afraid of Stella. More to the point, he was afraid of telling his mother he wanted to find out if what Ed Scott was saying about him was true, that he truly did possess the ability to be a big-time baseball player. Scott recalled needing to summon all his courage to approach the Aaron household and confront the formidable Stella with his thoughts about her son's future. On a few occasions, Scott would hide behind the side of the house. Stella Aaron sat on her porch. It was her favorite place at the house, her grandchildren thought.

In the fall of 1951, Scott made his case. Henry Aaron had the talent to go as far as he wanted as a baseball player. The Indianapolis Clowns were willing to give him a look. The Clowns were a legendary Negro League team, known for being the Harlem Globetrotters of baseball. The team featured good ballplayers but also high circus-style entertainment. Toni Stone, a woman, played second base. King Tut, an enormous man with a round belly, served as a mascot, wearing nothing but a grass skirt. If Henry made the club, the Clowns would pay him two hundred dollars per month, which was twenty-five dollars a week less than what Herbert brought in at ADDSCO. At first, Stella said no. After more discussion, the reality that college was not going to be an option settled in. Henry's gaining a college education had been, understandably, a mother's fantasy. The harder truth was that Henry had no interest in school and no track record as a student.

In those days, children in Mobile were not obligated to attend school for their senior year. Students could enter the workforce after eleventh grade. That rule created an opening: If he did not make it, Henry promised his mother, he would return to the Josephine Allen Institute for his final year. Stella agreed. Henry Aaron would then report to Winston-Salem to meet the Clowns. Bunny Downs, the Indianapolis business manager, would be at the depot to meet him. Unlike Stella, Herbert tended to lean toward Henry's way of thinking. Perhaps Henry's leaving Wilcox as a teenager to discover his own destiny influenced Herbert's viewpoint.

Ed Scott recalled the difficulty in convincing Stella to let her son go. As much as she wanted Henry to attend college, she was also largely unaware of just how talented her son was.

"I told her, if this kid was Satchel Paige, I wouldn't be bothering you," Scott said. "But you really don't know what you have."

ED SCOTT WAS born near Dade City, Florida, in 1917 but was raised in Hobe Sound, ten miles from Jupiter, a few miles west of Jupiter Island, on the eastern coastline. The town was split into two distinct sections. There was White Town and Colored Town. "Hobe Sound proper was what we called White Town," Scott recalled. "There wasn't nothing in Colored Town back then. Now, there's a golf course owned by Greg Norman."

Though he was born years before integration, baseball was the center of Scott's life. Unlike Henry, who was always something of a homebody, Scott was convinced at an early age that he would be a creature of the road.

A product of the Depression, he had a harsh childhood. According to the 1945 Florida state census, Scott's formal education ended in the sixth grade, just before his twelfth birthday. Baseball provided an escape from a life of few possessions, and even less freedom. As a boy, one childhood memory stood out from the rest: the patch of field right outside of Colored Town, where a large slanted oak tree sat. To both races, it was known as "the Hanging Tree." The Hanging Tree was where, Scott recalled, "you went when they wanted to teach the colored a lesson." This was no product of a child's imagination. During the first quarter of the twentieth century, more blacks were lynched per capita in Florida than in Alabama, Mississippi, or Georgia, the states with the most notorious reputations.

Baseball provided the diversion from such terrifying realities. It also provided Scott with an escape from his chores, especially the ones at which he was not particularly adept. Killing a chicken for supper was one such task. It was a chore that made him especially queasy, and he would never be particularly good at it. His mother, Anna May O'Neil, was unsympathetic.

"Back then, you didn't tell your parents what you could and couldn't do. She always used to tell me to take the chicken before the killing and put him in the pen. You're supposed to hold and twist, in one motion. My mother came out and watched me. Instead of holding tight and twisting his neck, I was just twirling him. She'd just go out there and wring his neck like it was nothing. I never did kill one."

When food supplies were low, the family subsisted on whatever was available. "We had a garden in the back. We ate gophers and sun turtle during the Depression. That, and biscuits and corn bread. No sliced bread," he recalled. "That's what you survived on."

He set out for the road as a teenager, determined, not unlike

Henry, to make baseball a part of his life. Unlike Henry, however, Ed Scott could not entertain the dream of playing in the major leagues. He caught on for a time with a Negro League team, the Norfolk Stars, where he considered himself an average player. He batted and threw right-handed, and had better than average speed and some power, but not enough to make a living playing baseball in the black leagues.

It was in reflecting on his own development as a player that Scott found the most kinship with Henry. In Henry, he saw a kid with raw ability who had not been taught the game of baseball. That made it easy for teams not to recognize his talent. It also made it easy for baseball scouts to make rash, inaccurate judgments about black kids who may have possessed the proper tools to play baseball but had never been taught *how* to play the game or told *why* certain elements of the game required specific skills.

"In those days, especially with blacks, you taught yourself how to play. You weren't judged on how you caught the ball. You were judged if you *didn't* catch the ball," Scott recalled. "Fundamentals? Hitting was the fundamentals. If you could hit, you could play. You didn't have a guy show you how to go after a ball and how to catch. The only thing they would tell you was to put two hands on it. Two hands on the ball, but I didn't like that, because you can't reach as high with two hands and you can't run as fast. You had to learn it all yourself."

Scott lived along the Florida Panhandle and arrived in Mobile in 1940. For him, Mobile was a haven. In many ways, Scott best represented the example of Mobile as a destination for blacks, in that it was, by degree, a more tolerant place than other southern cities. "It was a seaport town, so everything was a little easier. People came and went about their business."

Herbert Aaron dealt with segregation by focusing on becoming self-sufficient. Herbert owned his own house. Most of his food came from his own garden. He restricted his interaction with whites whenever possible and did not assume equality.

Ed Scott was different. He was, in his own way, openly political, and his tongue could be sharp. He did not seek to confront whites, but nor did he shy away from contact with them, either. Segregation in Florida was far more debilitating, he thought. Scott believed Mobile's whites seemed less convinced of the necessity for segregation. If he was wrong, he said, he felt at the very least that in Mobile he had encountered more whites who seemed willing to treat black people with dignity, if not total equality. Scott referred to them as "the good ones," whites who would treat him with a measure of humanity, people who may have been frustrated as much by the racial environment as he. Mobile, he said, was full of "the good ones," and they made his life in the city far easier. "That was why I fell in love with the city," Scott recalled. "I found out that Mobile was one of the better places as far as the South. Later on, we had problems.

"Once, I was working at a country club, and I said something like 'Okay' to a white lady," Scott recalled. "She turned away and later came back at me and said if I couldn't address her as miss or missus or ma'am, then I should not say anything. When she was finished, I looked at her and said, 'Okay.'

"See, that's what you needed to survive. You needed the good ones, the ones who understood you were a person just like them. They had to go along with it all, because that's the way things were, but they didn't put their knee in your back, either."

He always remained attuned to black life around the country, even though in those days blacks who simply read the Negro papers—the *Chicago Defender* and the *Pittsburgh Courier*, especially—were often branded as "agitators" and threats to the social order. "I would always buy the *Defender* and the *Courier* at the newsstand because all the Negro baseball—Paige, Luke Easter, Mule Suttles, Buck Leonard— was in there. I could keep up with them.

"Then one day, a white man said to me that the *Pittsburgh Courier* just caused a lot of problems. I told him that I bought the paper to read about the hangings and all the other things going on, because the *Courier* was the only way I could get my news."

When he met Henry, Scott worked as a porter at the Scott Paper Company. He played with the Mobile Black Shippers and began to settle into a good life in Mobile, working during the week, playing baseball one day a week and doubleheaders on the weekends. On the side, as a way to maintain a toehold in black professional baseball, he became a part-time scout for the Indianapolis Clowns. Word got around that Scott was a conduit to professional ball. The kids began calling him "Scotty," and he quickly became the most connected black baseball insider in Mobile.

One day in 1940, when he was using the Black Shippers team bus to transport WPA workers back from Brookley Field, a woman, Rebecca Deal, came out of the gate. "It was funny. I just happened to go out that way and she was standing at the gate. Before you know it, we ended up married."

He used his old contacts in the Negro Leagues for a special purpose. Though the idea of playing in the big leagues would be unavailable to him, Scott never found himself embittered that post-Robinson blacks would enjoy opportunities denied him. He had always been close to the generations of black ballplayers who arrived too early to play in the major leagues and took seriously their brotherhood as men who would pave the road for the next generation. Scott was particularly close to Buck O'Neil, who, when he signed with the Chicago Cubs, became the first black scout in the major leagues, and the two maintained a friendly scouting rivalry over the years. Scott had taught O'Neil how to play golf, and then he became known as the man who had discovered the great Henry Aaron. Scott had the inside track on Henry, but a few years later, O'Neil and Scott were jousting over Clyde Williams's little brother Billy, who had scouts buzzing from Florida to Texas. Buck O'Neil told everyone that Scotty had no chance at signing Williams. Scott, for his part, figured he had Williams to himself, as they shared the same outfield with the Black Shippers. But there was another scout for the Chicago Cubs, Ivy Griffin, who had been watching Billy Williams all along. And it was Griffin, working for the Chicago National League Ball Club, not O'Neil, who delivered Billy Williams to the Cubs.

There would be no place for men like O'Neil and Scott as players in the big leagues, but both would end up working for major-league clubs, and their satisfaction would have to come through developing the next generation of black players. For both men, that would have to do.

On the platform of the L&N Railroad, the train station on the southeast side of Mobile, Ed Scott said good-bye to Henry. It was March 1952. Stella and Herbert were there, as was Henry's eldest sister, Sarah. He wore a dark work shirt with large pockets on each breast. His pants were neatly creased and pleated, and he wore a dusty pair of wing-tip shoes. To his right was not a cardboard suitcase, as was part of the lore, but a duffel bag. The bag contained two sandwiches, a baseball, and a baseball glove. Henry stood on the tracks, a frown on his face, his eyes closed against the sun, while Ed Scott took his picture. He then headed for Winston-Salem to meet the Indianapolis Clowns.

The story was that Henry promised his mother that he would return to finish high school, but the Josephine Allen Institute closed in 1953, and there would be no surviving document of a high school diploma. Henry would never answer the question directly as to whether he finished high school with a diploma or finished high school simply by not going back.

There was one thing about Henry that never made sense to Ed Scott, and throughout the decades he would be the only person to confront this piece of bedrock that was central to the legend of Henry Aaron.

"I never once saw him hit cross-handed," Scott said. "I know, because I've seen guys who hit cross-handed and he didn't. But that was something I missed, something I know for a fact I would have noticed. I'm telling you, I never saw it, but that became part of the legend. No point arguing about it now."

HENRY AARON WOULD have the distinction of being the last Negro League player to be promoted to the major leagues who was talented enough to reach the Hall of Fame. After him, the best of the black talent would be cultivated directly by big-league clubs. Jackie Robinson represented the beginning of the end of separate baseball leagues and separate societies in general. Henry represented the end itself. When Henry met Bunny Downs in North Carolina to begin his career with the Clowns, it marked the final time the Negro Leagues would factor into the story of a black player ascending into the integrated world of big-league baseball.

The Negro American League in 1952 consisted of only six teams—the Indianapolis Clowns, the Kansas City Monarchs, the

Philadelphia Stars, the Chicago American Giants, the Memphis Red Sox, and the Birmingham Black Barons—and the biggest name in the league, the legendary Oscar Charleston, was the Birmingham manager. The Clowns, and by extension the rest of the league, were ghosts-in-waiting. The team took Indianapolis as its name, but the Clowns were on the road every day of the year. They did not play in Indianapolis, nor did they have a home stadium there. Henry Aaron never played a game in Indianapolis.

The eighteen-year-old Henry would not enjoy the same experience as, say, Jackie Robinson on his way to the majors. When Robinson joined the Kansas City Monarchs in 1945, he was twenty-six years old. His teammates were Josh Gibson and Satchel Paige. Buck O'Neil was the manager. The Monarchs were the kings of black baseball and therefore on a par with the great black entertainers. The Negro Leagues were always financially challenged and record keeping was, at best, temperamental, but during Robinson's time, the Negro Leagues were still a vital part of black entertainment life.

In 1952, the dominant baseball team in black America was not even a Negro League team, but the Brooklyn Dodgers. The Negro League had lost its place. Henry knew if he showed any ability at all, it would only be a matter of time before a major-league team discovered him. Before he left Mobile, he had already seen the pathway to the big leagues. Willie Mays, for example, had played just a few months with the Birmingham Black Barons in 1950, and by the time Henry joined the Clowns, Mays had already played in a World Series.

It was only a matter of time. Within a week of the Clowns season opener, May 11, 1952, in Nashville, against the Philadelphia Stars at a ballpark called Sulphur Dell, the wheels were already turning. From his home on 472 East Ridge Road in Mobile, Ed Scott had begun a letter-writing campaign, keeping big-league teams informed of Henry's talent. Scott had written to Billy Southworth of the Braves, and Branch Rickey in Pittsburgh. By 1952, Branch Rickey had left Brooklyn and was now running the Pirates. Nearly as much as Jackie Robinson himself, Branch Rickey had a name that was of great currency to black players. To be associated with the man who had desegregated the major leagues was no small thing. It was the reason why so many black kids wanted to play for the Dodgers, and why so many black adults from all over the country had adopted Brooklyn as their team.

On May 23, Scott received a letter from George Sisler—"Gorgeous" George Sisler, who hit .400 twice in his fifteen years in the big leagues—confirming Rickey had received Scott's letter, dated May 21, 1952, "regarding Henry Aaron, 17 years old, 170 lbs, 5'11". We will send the contents of your letter to our scout in the area who will endeavor to see him play. Mr. Rickey wishes to thank you for having thought of him." Scott had already contacted the Boston Braves, and Dewey Griggs, the club's top scout, was watching Henry. Griggs, in fact, had been following Henry since he first joined the Clowns. The New York Giants were watching Henry, too, the luscious prospect of Mays and Henry in the same outfield tantalizingly close.

Henry joined the Clowns in Winston-Salem, but his Negro League career lasted all of fourteen games. He was skinny and poker-faced, quiet around older, calloused men who had grinded on the black baseball circuit for years. Teammates barely knew what to make of him—until he stepped into the batter's box. There was the double header against the Memphis Red Sox, June 1, 1952, in Buffalo. Jim Cohen went the distance, winning 6–4. Henry went four for five with a home run. In the finale, an 11–0 washout, Henry went three for four, and Dewey Griggs was on the phone to Boston faster than Henry's first home run left the park. John Mullen, the Boston Braves general manager, authorized Griggs to "do whatever it took" to wrest Henry from the grip of Clowns owner Syd Pollock. The secret was out.

MAJOR LEAGUE SCOUTS TAKE GANDER AT CLOWNS' SHORTSTOP, HENRY AARON

KANSAS CITY, MO—... Rookie Henry Aaron, Clowns' sensational shortstop, continued his blazing slugging, getting four of five in the opener including a long home run over the right field wall.

Major league scouts are swarming into parks where the Clowns are playing. ... All seem to agree he stands at the plate like a young Ted Williams.

By June 7, four teams had scouts tracking Henry. Fay Young, the venerable *Defender* sports columnist, had already signaled to any fans interested in seeing Henry to head to the nearest ballpark to catch their "last glimpse of Henry Aaron, the league-leading Clowns short-stop." With the first half of the Negro League season complete, Henry had run away with the league.

CLOWNS' AARON LOCKS UP
NAL SLUGGING HONORS

Rookie Henry Aaron will win slugging honors in the Negro American League, according to the latest figures of the How News bureau.

Aaron leads the league in batting with .483, in runs with 15, hits, 28, total bases, 51, doubles, 6, home runs, 5, and runs batted in, 24.

Henry was destined for greatness, but there was a certain melancholy to it all. A decade earlier, Henry would have been a major attraction for the league, a drawing card in the vein of Josh Gibson or a Satchel Paige or Oscar Charleston, or any of the old-time greats of the black leagues. But Henry was heading beyond the segregated life. He represented progress, and for as many avenues as the future opens, it closes just as many. Henry Aaron's month in the Negro Leagues was nothing less than the final period on the obituary of the great black leagues.

Bunny Downs had promised Henry that the Clowns would pay him two hundred dollars per month. Henry lasted with the Clowns exactly one month. On June 11, 1952, the Boston Braves and the Clowns completed a deal for Henry Aaron. Henry's last act as a Negro Leaguer, according to the *Defender,* was to rap two singles in the opener and play a "whale of a game" in splitting a doubleheader at Comiskey Park against the Chicago American Giants. The Braves sent Henry to its farm club in Eau Claire, Wisconsin, and sent Syd Pollock and the Clowns a check for ten thousand dollars.

Six weeks earlier, Henry had never been outside of the Mobile city limits without his parents. The farthest from Mobile he had been was to visit Papa Henry and Mama Sis in Camden—on horseback. But now, during the second week of June 1952, Henry was boarding a North Central Airlines plane for the first time in his life, choking on his own panic from Charlotte to Eau Claire, close to retching on each turbulent bounce across the Appalachians to the broad expanse north. He was eighteen years old and had never had anything close to an extended conversation with a white person. He would now engage in activities that Alabama had drafted laws to prevent: He would live among whites, play ball with and against them on the same field, and talk to them—at least under the strict definitions of the law—as equals.

Henry had never played against white players—interracial competition had been prohibited by custom in Alabama since the late 1880s and would soon be enacted into law during the 1950s. Unlike Robinson, he did not have the advantage of social refinement afforded by education and experience. One would have had to look hard to find a kid less prepared to navigate this sudden new world. He was completely on his own.

Clell Buzzell, the sports editor of the local Eau Claire paper, picked Henry up from the airport and took him home so his wife, Joyce, could meet the newest member of the Eau Claire Bears. As author and Eau Claire native Jerry Poling wrote in his book *A Summer Up North,* "The introduction might have been a pleasure for Joyce but not for Aaron. Seeing the scared, skinny young man in her living room, she thought he was fourteen or fifteen years old and feeling out of place. She felt sorry for him."

"He was shaking," Poling quoted Joyce Buzzell as saying. "He had never been in a white person's home before."

The Eau Claire Bears had been integrated three seasons earlier by Sam Jethroe. Jethroe himself had played a small role in the early story of integration in April 1945, when he and Marvin Williams accompanied Jackie Robinson to Fenway Park for a notorious, humiliating tryout with the Boston Red Sox. Jethroe would never be contacted by the Red Sox, but in 1950 he became the first black player with the Boston Braves, and won Rookie of the Year. Another top black prospect, Bill Bruton, had played for Eau Claire in 1950.

The population of Eau Claire in 1952 was virtually 100 percent white—35,000 residents, seven blacks, twenty more nonwhites.

Henry kept his distance, adopting the proper code of conduct for southern blacks: Do not approach whites unless directly addressed. He would walk the streets of Eau Claire and the young children would stare at him as though he were a foreign species. Sometimes their mothers would apologize with polite nods to him; the children had never seen a black person.

The adults weren't much better. At least the children had the excuse of being young. It was as though he had entered an alternate universe in that Henry walked around town among whites but did not sense the inherent hostility that was an ingrained element of the Mobile social atmosphere.

Henry rented a room at the Eau Claire YMCA at 101 Farwell Street, which was located downtown, a mile and change from Carson Park, where the Bears played their home games. The two other blacks in the club—outfielder John Wesley Covington and the catcher, Julius "Julie" Bowers—also lived there, while the white players roomed with families.

Henry did not often socialize with Covington or Bowers, though the three men lived in the same YMCA building. In later years, Covington recalled the young Henry as distant, hard to read. Even in private settings, even around his black teammates, Henry wasn't exactly the guy cracking jokes at the card table. He was guarded, mostly trying not to betray all that he did not know. "He just would not open up to you. Hank was as far away from me at times as he was from anybody else on the ball club," Covington recalled in 1993. "I don't think at that time we were trying to be close."

For the prospects, Class C ball was just a stepping-stone to bigger things, a place to start an expected ascension. For the others, baseball might never be as good as it was in the Northern League, which made it the perfect place to travel and party and bond.

In June 1952, Henry was neither the can't-miss phenom nor the teenager happy to stretch a baseball dream as far as his middling talent would take him. He knew he had the ability to play, but he also knew that he could be right back with the Clowns should anything go wrong in Eau Claire. He had, the contract said, thirty days to prove that he was worth the investment.

And so he kept his distance, adopting an immersion technique his family would have immediately recognized as belonging to Papa Henry: he kept to himself, studying others and forming opinions without volunteering much. While it was a protecive device, designed not to expose his limits in education and sophistication, it was within this total immersion into the white world where a damaging Aaron caricature first took root. Marion "Bill" Adair, the Eau Claire manager and a southerner from Alabama, began what would become a career-long commentary on the Aaron demeanor, and by extension, his intellect. "No one can guess his IQ because he gives you nothing to go on. He sleeps too much and looks lazy, but he isn't. Not a major-league shortstop yet, but as a hitter he has everything in this world."

Eau Claire was a lonely and distant place. From the hallway phone at the YMCA, Henry would call Stella not only to hear a familiar voice but to tell her he was coming home, he was quitting. Each day the conversation was similar: he wasn't afraid he would fail. He just didn't care for being so far away from home. Homesickness was especially acute for the first generation of black players integrating the game. Virtually all of them, before reaching greatness, told a story about wanting to quit. Some of them, like Billy Williams, actually jumped their clubs and went back home. More than half a century later, Williams remembered leaving his farm club in Amarillo, Texas, and returning to Mobile, not picking up the phone even when the big club, the Cubs, called personally to bring him back. And the stories always ended the same, too: Once a player arrived home, it was his family who sent him back out into the world, making sure a special opportunity to escape was not wasted.

The difference was that these kids weren't just learning how to adjust to curveballs far from home, nor were they integrating the game. They were integrating society. Henry would answer for the next half century the question of what those days in Eau Claire were like, being the only black person sitting at the drugstore counter, but the inverse was also true: The overwhelming majority of his white teammates had never engaged in a meaningful conversation with a black person, either.

And the worst thing of all for an eighteen-year-old ballplayer was the lack of girls. Naturally, there were girls all over the place. Black girls, however . . . well, that was a different story. The Northern

League consisted of teams in Eau Claire, Duluth, Fargo-Moorhead, Grand Forks, Aberdeen, Sioux Falls, and St. Cloud—not exactly the best advertisement to meet eligible black women.

Herbert junior would often be the one to tell him to forget about the idea of coming back to Mobile, that there was nothing in Mobile for him. He would do himself no good being just another southern black boy without prospects. Herbert had persuaded him, boosted him, revived him. Then came the moment that transformed two lives: June 20, Carson Park, Eau Claire versus the Superior Blues, the White Sox farm club. Henry is playing shortstop. In the top of the eighth, Gordie Roach hits Superior's Gideon Applegate and then walks the next batter, Chuck Wiles, the Superior's catcher. The next ball, a chopper to second, would play in slow motion to anyone who was at the park that day.

Bob McConnell fields the ball and flips to Henry for the first out, and Henry steps on the bag and winds to throw back to first for the double play.

Wiles is racing for second but has not yet gone into his slide. Henry fires sidearm to first. These were the days before batting helmets. Wiles took the full force of Henry's throw in the flesh of his right ear. He stood for a moment before crumpling to the ground, unconscious, while Applegate rounded third for the tying run. Wiles was taken off the field on a stretcher and rushed by ambulance to Luther Hospital.

That might have been the end of the story, one of those fluky baseball accidents. Except that upon arriving at Luther Hospital, Wiles slipped into a coma, in which he remained for three days. His career was over. The doctors consoled the young catcher by telling him had his outer ear not borne the brunt of the impact, Henry's throw would have killed him.

Wiles spent two more weeks in the hospital, his inner ear crushed. He lost his equilibrium. Periodically, he would entertain the thought of returning. The next year, Wiles and his family moved to Albemarle, North Carolina, where he signed on with a semipro club, the Cotton Mill Boys, but the experiment ended in a heartbreaking finale, Wiles losing his orientation while on the base paths, to the amusement of fans, who thought he was joking. "One time I got to second base. I was determined I was going to get home," Wiles told Jerry Poling. "I don't think I even knew where I was. I missed home plate by a lot. The fans thought I was clowning." Chuck Wiles never played baseball again.

The Wiles incident rattled Henry, as would the vitriolic response from the Superior fans when Eau Claire next arrived. During moments of despair, he called home and told Stella he was returning to Mobile. Each time Henry called, Stella would hand the phone to his brother Herbert, who took the receiver and told him the same thing each time: "The future is ahead of you, not back here in Mobile."

For years, Henry would recall how close he came to quitting the game, fearful that he could kill someone on the baseball diamond. Not an interview regarding his Eau Claire years would pass without a reference to Chuck Wiles. Henry would be betrayed by his lack of world experience, for while Wiles lay in a coma, Henry hit his first home run for the Bears, June 22, against Reuben Stohs. Wiles would never hold a grudge against Henry and he would say he believed Henry was remorseful about the accident. But he also would never forget that Henry did not apologize or console him in person.

Henry tore apart the Northern League. He played shortstop, wearing the number 6. He batted seventh in the order, consistent with the old-time custom of infielders batting low in the order. It was almost as if the isolation helped him. He had no distractions after the Wiles incident. On the field, he focused on his talent, developing an uncanny ability to compartmentalize, an attribute that would become a trademark. He played eighty-seven games for Eau Claire, hit .336, made the all-star team, and was named Most Valuable Player in the league. He was competing against players his own age, but they were just kids. In the Mobile industrial games and in the Negro Leagues, Henry had played against older competition for years.

His homesickness subsided, his batting average soared, and Henry began to shed his introverted personality. The moment that best illustrates Henry's evolution from a shy and uncomfortable young man, hamstrung by his southern upbringing, to a more confident one was his relationship with Susan Hauck, a white teenager who frequented Bears games with her girlfriends and hung out with the players away from the ballpark.

The girls did not seem to care about how interracial friendships—or romances—were viewed by their friends or the community at large, but their nonchalance put Covington and Henry in a potentially dangerous situation. For example, there was the time Henry, Covington, and a group of Susan's friends, all female, went to Elk Mound, Eau Claire's stunning vista point—and designated make-out spot. As Hauck recalled for Jerry Poling, a group of white teens followed the group to the peak of the hill, only to find Susan and her friends—unaware that Henry and Covington were hiding in the bushes, petrified that they might be forced to duke it out with a gang of white boys.

"It was never a romance. It was a friendship. I suppose people thought we were dating. I liked him," Poling quoted Hauck as saying in *A Summer Up North.* "I guess you could say I was infatuated with him. Back then, if you would talk with a black person you were awful. I used to think that was wrong. I was never raised that way."

While Susan and Henry clearly shared a heightened level of intimacy, their relationship was not something Henry would ever again mention. Over the next fifty years, he would coauthor two books and write an autobiography, and never mention Susan Hauck and his relationship with her family. He ate dinner regularly with them, the guest of her parents, Arnold and Blanche Hauck. The two held hands often at her house. Two years earlier, in 1950, the Haucks had welcomed Billy Bruton into their home as warmly as they did Henry. The relationship between Susan and Henry, however, was more intense.

"When you think about who Henry Aaron is and where he came from, it was all pretty remarkable," Jerry Poling recalled. "Never mind what may or may not have gone on between them. Here was a guy who came from the worst segregation in the country and here he is holding hands with a white girl. I thought that was pretty amazing."

For the 1953 season, Henry was promoted a level, to the Braves Jacksonville club, but for a .336 hitter, it was not a major ascension. The club didn't want to rush Henry, and thus it classified him at the A-ball level. Jacksonville was part of the notorious South Atlantic

League, otherwise known as the "Sally League." Jackie Robinson had just completed his sixth year in the majors, but the Sally League had not yet been integrated. Henry Aaron and a handful of others would be the first black players in what was widely considered to be the most hostile league for blacks in the minor-league system. Perhaps more than any minor league, the Sally represented the major challenge to integration. *The Sporting News* marked the moment:

JACKSONVILLE AND SAVANNAH
SHATTER COLOR LINE IN SALLY

COLUMBUS, GA. — After Savannah broke the color line for the first time since the circuit was organized in 1904 . . . Jacksonville . . . followed suit by taking on three colored performers. . . .

The . . . Tars picked up three from Toledo . . . Shortstop Felix Mantilla, outfielder Horace Garner and Second Baseman Henry Aaron.

HENRY WOULD HAVE a more difficult time even than Robinson. Where Robinson would have the benefit of going to his home ballpark in Brooklyn half of the time, the Sally League would play all of its games in the Deep South. Even the home park, Jacksonville, would not always be a friendly place. Henry knew he might be able to win over the home fans with spirited play, but off the field, he found that Jacksonville was another southern town that was not ready to treat him with any degree of humanity.

Robinson played under the glare of the national press, which provided a certain degree of protection against the most virulent opposition. In the minor leagues, Henry would be isolated, and press coverage would be minimal. When Henry arrived in Jacksonville, another minor league, the Cotton States League, attempted to ban the Hot Springs franchise from competition for signing two black players—Henry's old teammate with the Clowns, Jim Turgeson, and his brother Leander.

His nerves were on edge. "We were in spring training and it was way across Georgia, and it was an old army camp field and they still had the bunk houses and that's where we stayed," one teammate remembered. "They had a couple of fields there. And Hank was playing left field one day, and now keep in mind he was young just like I was. All of the sudden he takes off from left field right during the ball game and heads towards the barracks where we were staying and nobody knew what the hell was going on. We talked to Hank later and he said there was a big snake out there in left field."

The small towns that comprised the league were notorious—societies with little sophistication that enforced Jim Crow laws ruthlessly. Jim Frey was a teammate of Henry in Jacksonville. Frey would be another one of those baseball men who was an average minor-league player, not quite good enough to reach the majors, but someone who possessed such an eye and enthusiasm for baseball that he would draw a paycheck from the game for his entire working life—as a manager, a general manager, a scout, and in numerous other capacities, as well.

Jim Frey had been raised in the southern part of Ohio, a northern state that often possessed a southern mentality. He grew up in Bridgetown, west of Cincinnati, which was known during that time as a "sundown town," which meant no blacks after dark. When Frey was a kid, his father, John, worked with a black handyman who did carpentry and stonework for the family. Frey recalled how his father had had to rush to escort the man out of town before the sun went down. Violating such local customs could be fatal for blacks, but it also posed danger for any sympathetic whites.

"It was toward the country, just a little itty-bitty town. There weren't many people there. In this particular town, at that time, and this was in the forties and fifties, the blacks had to get out of town, had to get to the next town in, which was Cheviot, Ohio. My dad had to get them to the car line by six o'clock. That was the rule."

Jim Frey held Henry in high esteem. He loved his talent, but he also felt acute personal pain because of the abuse Henry endured in Jacksonville during that 1953 season. "It was just terrible what he was subjected to," Frey said. "And he just took it all and hit. Baseball is a hard-enough game when everyone is rooting for you. You cannot believe what it must have been like to be Henry Aaron in 1953. It was a heartbreaking thing to watch."

If Frey was aware of the treatment the black players faced, a certain reciprocity was also taking place. Henry and, to a lesser extent, Felix Mantilla were watching the white players, taking in how they responded to their teammates' humiliations, who they were as men. If Frey was learning about the American South, Henry was learning about his white teammates and whether they would be friend or foe.

Frey recalled the segregated grandstands at Luther Williams Field, where the Macon Peaches played. Every park in the Sally League separated its black fans from its white ones. Frey remembered being taken by the different elements of America colliding on the field one day in Jacksonville as he stood in the outfield, surrounded by the black faces in the crowd while simultaneously watching Henry fielding his position at second base as the home crowd, the whites, screamed at Henry to "go back to the cotton fields."

This was, both Mantilla and Frey agreed, how the 1953 season progressed, either in Jacksonville or on the road. "Which city was the worst?" Henry said. "You couldn't say, because they were all bad." Frey, who became great friends with Horace Garner, remembered being handed gifts by the black fans at the end of the season, thanking him for engaging with them all season. Previous white outfielders, Frey thought, must never have acknowledged the paying black fans, who sat in the corner sections.

"My exposure to blacks mostly came [from baseball], because in the minor leagues, starting in Evansville, Indiana, in '51 and then '52 and then later in Jacksonville in '53 and '54, they were some of the first blacks that were allowed to play in professional baseball at that time," Jim Frey recalled. "We went to a high school, Western Hills High School, which had about two thousand students at that time, and we only had a handful of blacks in the school. I doubt if there was more than one [black] family or two. I don't think there were more than three or four black students in our school, which was a pretty big school. We had to go into Cincinnati to go to high school. We didn't have one out in the country. We never had a lot of exposure to the blacks at that time.

"It was first the Three-I League in the Midwest and the Sally League in the Southeast. I played with, I don't know, several on each of those teams, and those players were the first or among the first who were allowed to play in the minor leagues at that time. A couple of them were Latins and the others were Americans and blacks, but they weren't allowed to eat with us. In many areas, they weren't even allowed to get off the bus at night, and they had to stay in different quarters. It was a different world then. It was tough on 'em. It was really tough on 'em."

In Jacksonville, three important events took place in Henry's life. The first was his friendship with Felix Mantilla. Mantilla was brought to Jacksonville from the Toledo club specifically to room with Henry. Clubs in those days always fielded an even number of black players to keep white players from having to room with a black teammate. Mantilla's presence soothed Henry, even though Mantilla, a dark-skinned Puerto Rican, did not speak much English. He relied on Henry while adjusting to the Deep South.

Mantilla recalled his time in the minor leagues as horribly oppressive, where race was consistently the determining factor in virtually every encounter, on or off the ball field. He remembered his difficulties in learning English and understanding the culture.

"When you're seventeen or eighteen years old, you see things very differently. I was lost. I used to go to the movies to learn, but the movies didn't have subtitles. I didn't always pay attention to the segregation laws, and I found out when it was too late.

"When I joined the team in Evansville, I didn't know the city was segregated, either," Mantilla recalled. "One day, the team got tickets to go to the movies, and when I walked in, they said, 'What the hell are you doing here?' They looked at me like I had the plague.

"There was another theater that didn't allow blacks, and Henry and I walked in. You had to know all the rules, all of the things you could do and couldn't do. Believe it or not, Jacksonville was one of the better towns for us. It was Hank who always kept me away from the things that could have gotten me in trouble. Hank and I relied on each other. We tried not to let the other out of our sight."

There were humilating moments, Mantilla recalled. "The whites used to yell from the stands and call us 'alligator bait.' Jacksonville wasn't so bad. But places like Columbus and Macon, those places were wicked."

There was the time Mantilla and Aaron combined to propel Jacksonville closer to the Sally League pennant. Jacksonville hadn't finished first in the league since 1912. Mantilla and Henry had both been all-stars. By midseason, the crowds had warmed to their presence. They wore the right uniform. They were helping the club win. Once, after a particularly satisfying victory, a fan caught up to Henry and Felix Mantilla as they left the park. Mantilla remembered the game as being a considerably hard-fought contest and, having won, both he and Henry were smiling, their guards down after nine innings of concentration. The fan approached the two players easily.

"I just wanted to say," the man said, "that you niggers played a hell of a game."

Mantilla remembered the good white teammates who made his and Henry's time a bit easier. Pete Whisenant, an outfielder with Jacksonville, often made sure the black players were not isolated. Whisenant, Mantilla remembered, would often go out to dinner with Henry and Mantilla after games, looking for an integrated place where the teammates could hang out together. Often, Mantilla recalled, such a small gesture could put them all at risk.

And then there was the time Mantilla put everyone at risk. Henry had always told him about southern culture, about how to interact gingerly with whites. At the start of the 1953 season, Sally League umpires warned Aaron, Mantilla, and Garner not to engage with hostile white fans or opponents. They were also warned not to argue calls with umpires, in order not to incite white fans. Montgomery had even held off integrating its club, because it wanted to see how Jacksonville and Savannah—the two integrated teams in the league—were received both at the ticket gate and inside the clubhouse.

One result of the umpire edict was open season on black players. Pitchers threw at Henry, constantly sending him into the dirt. Mantilla thought when he went to the plate that his ears were being used for target practice.

Then came the game in July when a career minor-leaguer named John Waselchuk threw at Mantilla's head one time too many.

Waselchuk was a pip-squeak from Peabody, Massachusetts—five eight, 150 pounds—but a hard-throwing one, with the best curveball in the Sally. Waselchuk was a tough kid, a veteran; he'd joined the navy directly after graduating from high school, then sailed the Mediterranean for three years before signing with the Cubs organization in 1949.

Mantilla had been hit before—they'd been throwing at him all year—but this time, instead of heading for first base, he stalked to the pitcher's mound. The game was already tense. Henry recalled that not only were the fans on the black players that day but insults were being hurled between the segregated sections, and he was convinced he was about to be part of a race riot.

The benches had already cleared. The police, having been alerted, formed a circle around the field, sidearms at the ready. Additional officers kept the blacks and whites in the crowd from tearing one another apart. And then it was Horace Garner who intercepted Mantilla and dragged him to the ground, averting catastrophe.

"I never saw a black player who did anything but put his head down, play well, weather the storm. They had to," Jim Frey said.

Perseverance remained a prerequisite for the black players. Mantilla possessed a temper quicker than either Henry's or Garner's but the possibility of humiliation remained a constant. Henry proceeded gingerly, not assuming that even his own teammates were sympathetic to his situation. The reverse was often true: on more than one occasion white players who reached out to their black teammates could find themselves outcasts as well.

"One of the first bus trips we took, we had Hank and Felix Mantilla, the shortstop, and Horace Garner, an outfielder," said one member of the Jacksonville team. "Three colored guys, and we were going to Columbia, South Carolina, and Charleston. In those leagues back then you played at home for six games and then you went away for six games in two places. So we would stop and get a pop or a bag of chips or a chocolate bar or something.

"Hank and Felix and Horace didn't get off the bus so I said, 'Aren't you guys going in?' And they said, 'Oh, we'll never get in that place.' So anyways, I said, 'Well, do you want me to get you something?' And they said, 'Yeah, that'd be nice if you did.' They paid for it and everything, but I got them stuff, and so the rest of the guys, the white guys on the club, the southern guys especially, they hated me just as much as they did Hank and Felix and them because I would do that.

"He was real quiet in the clubhouse. Those guys, they knew they weren't accepted by everybody, so they didn't say and do a lot of things that we would do. It was just a lot of bullshit. It was the worst part. I was down there nine years and that was the worst thing in the nine years."

Henry's relationship with Jacksonville manager Ben Geraghty eased the tension. Geraghty was known for being strict but fair. He chided Henry constantly. The aspects of Henry's game outside of his hitting were in need of improvement. Like most baseball men, Geraghty accepted physical errors—making a fielding or throwing error—far more quickly than he did mental ones. Some of Henry's mental mistakes bordered on the apocryphal, like the time he stole four bases and—either due to oversliding or failing to ask for time— was picked off each base. Another time, Henry blew a sign and Geraghty asked him why. Henry responded, "I can't remember all that."

The difference was that Geraghty also seemed to understand Henry's sense of humor, that his responses were not always referendums of his intelligence. He knew that Henry often answered questions with a dry wit to diffuse the embarrassment of missing a sign or not executing his responsibilities. Even in criticism, he talked to Henry like an adult.

But most important, Ben Geraghty recognized Henry's potential almost immediately. He knew that even as a nineteen-year-old, Henry Aaron possessed the ability to be not just a major-league player but a great, possibly transcendent one. "If Henry has a strike zone, it is from the top of his head to his ankles," Geraghty said. "In a year or so, he'll make the fans forget Jackie Robinson, and I'm not exaggerating. He never pays attention to who's pitching. He hits them all."

The third event, and the most important, occurred just as the season started. Henry had met Barbara Lucas, a young student at the local business school. Barbara was from Jacksonville, and Henry was immediately taken. She was tall and thin, with sparkling green eyes. Her younger brother, Bill, was also a baseball player. Bill Lucas attended Florida A&M—ironically, the school Stella wanted Henry to attend—and was a strong infield prospect. Within two years, Ed Scott would sign Bill to the Braves farm system. In the meantime, Henry and Barbara dated throughout the summer, although, according to family legend, Barbara's parents did not want her to become serious with a baseball player.

Yet on the field, Henry destroyed the opposition, such as on April 1, 1953, in Jacksonville, against a big-league club, the Boston Red Sox. The Braves were demolished, 14–1. Mel Parnell, the veteran Red Sox left-hander, gave up just five hits, but two were to Henry. Another pro, Ike Delock, gave up a long home run to Henry in the eighth inning.

The competition did not seem to matter all summer long: two doubles against Columbia. Later that season, in back-to-back double-headers against Columbia, Henry went twelve for thirteen. Jacksonville won the pennant and Henry was named the Most Valuable Player of the Sally League. The numbers, again, were staggering: .362 average, 22 home runs, 36 doubles, 14 triples, 115 runs scored, 125 runs batted in, and 208 total bases.

He was assigned to winter ball in Caguas, Puerto Rico, and before going, he asked Barbara to marry him and join him on the island.

In the span of eighteen months, Henry had gone from standing on the platform at the L&N Railroad station to playing in the Negro Leagues to being a married man. He spent the winter of 1953 preparing for his first major-league spring training. He was told from the start that no matter how he hit, he would spend the entire 1954 season in Toledo.

AND SO THE comet soared. Bill Slack, the longtime baseball man known as the pitching guru of North Carolina, worked with Henry in the 1980s. Slack never played in the big leagues, but he was one of those legendary baseball men who had given his life to the game, one dusty back road at a time. He and his brother, Stan, had played with Henry in Jacksonville, and one day in Richmond, Henry and Bill knocked back a beer after a day of meetings.

"I remember one day I asked Henry when he was his most afraid," Slack recalled. "I was thinking he was going to tell me the stories about being chased by the Klan or something like that. But he didn't. He told me the most scared he'd ever been was getting on the train for the first time, heading to Winston-Salem."

Ed Scott never left Mobile. In 1961, he became a scout for the Boston Red Sox, a job he would hold for the next thirty-three years. Scott led a rich baseball life, one that was both raucous and sober. He had become the first black scout for the Red Sox, a team with a notorious history in terms of race relations. He was the man who first discovered Henry Aaron, but he recalled losing out on the kid from Whistler, Billy Williams, to Ivy Griffin. Scott later signed big leaguers Dennis "Oil Can" Boyd and George Scott for the Red Sox. The picture he took of Henry at the train station is the oldest surviving photograph of his journey as a professional baseball player.

"I'll never forget that day at the depot," Scott said. "I remember his mother putting him on the train. I still have a picture of that day. He wound up signing it for me. It really was something, an amazing day. I can tell you one thing: As that train was leaving the station, he sure didn't look like he was headed to the Hall of Fame."

CHAPTER THREE

STEPIN FETCHIT

ANTICIPATION of Henry's arrival in the spring of 1954 was heightened by the fact that no one, apart from the Milwaukee scouts, minor-league personnel, and occasionally the owner, Lou Perini, or the general manager, John Quinn, had actually ever seen him play. He was famous, mostly, in the Braves anticipation of him, but his fame stemmed from the exotic, sumptuous ingredients that were critical to the baseball publicity machine: dewdrop reports from the bird-dog scouts, who, in turn, whetted the appetite of fans and management alike. "Any amount you ask for that kid Henry Aaron in right field wouldn't be too much," exuded Red Sox scout Ted McGrew. Word of mouth traveling from exuberant minor-league coaches and managers (HANK AARON IS FABULOUS FELLOW, SAYS FORMER PILOT BEN GERAGHTY read a March 1954 *Milwaukee Journal* headline) and sports writers ("If Aaron is 75 percent as good as the glowing reports about him, he will be worth keeping around for pinch hitting, if nothing else," R. G. Lynch wrote in the *Journal* a full month before spring camp opened) only increased the anticipation. But so much of it was more talk about the latest next big thing, just word of mouth, just so many words on paper.

There was only one element, however, that provided the real fuel to the churning engine: the staggering offensive numbers Henry had produced over the past two seasons. His statistics leaped out of the morning box scores (best found in the weekly agate of *The Sporting News*), from Eau Claire to Jacksonville to Caguas. After Henry and Barbara were married, in October 1953, Henry kept his promise and the two went to Puerto Rico. Henry played for Caguas, and the manager was Mickey Owen, the old Brooklyn catcher and owner of the worst moment any ballplayer could ever endure: 1941 World Series, game four, Ebbets Field, the Yankees leading the series two games to one but down 4–3, with two out and two strikes in the top of the ninth. Tommy Henrich was the batter when Owen dropped a called third strike that would have ended the game and tied the series. Henrich reached first; the Yankees scored four runs on the melting Dodgers and won the game, 7–4, and the Series the next day. That was how it was in baseball. Mickey Owen played thirteen years in the big leagues, but he might as well have played one inning of one game one afternoon in October.

Henry would always say Ben Geraghty was the best and most influential manager he had ever had, but Mickey Owen qualified as a close second, for it was Owen who in Puerto Rico took a raw Henry Aaron, a kid who had taught himself everything he knew, and over a tropical winter molded him—made him a ready, big-league package. It wasn't that Henry didn't already have Olympian tools, but no one at the professional level ever did anything more than gawk at him and snicker about how unorthodox he was. Owen was different. It was Owen who taught him weight distribution and how to hold his hands steady. Owen received credit from Henry for all the things he did, and for one thing he did not do: change Henry's peculiar front-footed approach to hitting the ball.

It all started somewhere between Central and Josephine Allen, when during a game Henry injured his right ankle, his plant foot. Rather than rest, he compensated for the pain in his right leg when he swung by shifting his weight to his front foot. Any hitting coach would have been tempted to tinker with Henry's mechanical footwork, but instead of giving him instructions, Owen gave Henry confidence. During the first week of December, Henry was hitting .295. A week later, he was at .343. A week after Christmas, Henry had scored the batting title at .357.

Still, to the most hard-boiled of baseball men, even those numbers could be tempered. Swinging a bat in the thick breezes and among the uneven talent of the Caribbean was one thing, especially as the rum flowed. Hitting in Ebbets Field with the bags full was quite another.

Dugout chatter was the only advanced billing most of the world ever received about a player—even one considered as special as

Henry—and that was one of the beautiful, enduring characteristics of baseball. Anticipation provided that magical component—the verbal mythmaking—that built the American game and set up the inherent challenge (whether or not the kid could make the big time) that resonated with millions of fans . . . that's what brought them in. Until a player succeeded with the big club, in the big leagues, even great prospects like Willie Mays, Mickey Mantle, Ted Williams, or Henry Aaron amounted to nothing more than a string of press clippings. Buzz was the special sauce that heightened anticipation about a prospect, a trait that neither time nor technology would ever change.

BOSTON GLOBE writer Harold Kaese was in town to take his first look at the Red Sox, but he somehow found himself talking about this kid Henry. Well, not exactly *somehow.* In Red Sox camp, trying to squeeze out another year behind the dish for the Red Sox was none other than Mickey Owen, still raving about Henry. A few days later, the Braves were in Tampa to play the White Sox, and Paul Richards— the Chicago manager who one day would become the Braves general manager—yelled out to a couple of Braves coaches, "Where's Aaron? I've heard a lot of reports on him." In baseball, words were a carelessly tossed match to dry grass, and Kaese—who two decades later would be awarded with the J. G. Taylor Spink Award, induction into the writers' wing of the Baseball Hall of Fame—had been around long enough to know a prairie fire had been sparked. Kaese, who was standing at the batting cage, sidled up to Richards and parroted what he'd heard from Mickey Owen. "Over in Sarasota," Kaese told Richards, "Mickey Owen told me the other day that Aaron is good enough to run Bruton off the ball club."

Baseball was so different, because with the other sports, all you had to do was follow the paper trail. A college basketball star left a roughly one-hundred-game outline, a skeleton for anticipating the body of work that would soon follow. A college football player left at least thirty games. Nobody who hadn't been sleeping under a boulder wondered if Lew Alcindor or O. J. Simpson could play; no one was unsure of their physical characteristics as players. Certainly there was anticipation to watch a college player make the transition to the pro game, but it was eagerness based on information, eyewitnesses, and reams of newspaper exposure from actual game coverage. In later years, during the video age, film highlights on a player could be wound, rewound, dissected, and analyzed long before a player scored his first touchdown at Lambeau Field.

But no matter how talented, minor-league baseball players were nothing. They were not to be counted upon, except maybe to sweeten the allure of a trade. In those days, they were not treated charitably as young stars ready to lead. That's why the entire universe of minor-league towns, from Louisville to Atlanta, Wichita to Jacksonville, Kenosha to Visalia, was called "the bushes." Charlie Grimm, the Braves manager, had never laid eyes on Henry. No one knew what he looked like, how he moved, how he talked, how he swung, or what the ball sounded like off of his bat. It was the constancy of the numbers and the volume of the talk that had made him a prospect.

The words had been plentiful enough, the praise from baseball men who had spent their lives sharpening their antennae to pick up the slightest deficiencies certainly convincing, but no one quite knew for sure if the hundreds of column inches devoted to him should be framed for posterity or used as kindling, thereby designating him as another overhyped kid who couldn't play. In later years, the arrival of a highly rated prospect would provide a certain degree of protection from management, but during Henry's time, when salaries were low and security virtually nonexistent, veterans waited to see hotshot prospects, and not particularly enthusiastically, for if Henry was as good as advertised, someone, perhaps a friend or a roommate, was going to lose his job. The first person waiting to see Henry was third baseman Eddie Mathews, the young heart of the Braves lineup, who was just two and a half years older than Henry and was expected to be the face of the Milwaukee baseball club for years to come.

Over the first few days of March, the picture came into full focus. The match caught, and the impressions scorched each side of the Florida coast. They talked about how he looked—the vitals first: six feet even, about 175 pounds, slim in the shoulders, tapered at the waist. He was a skinny kid, especially when he stood with the burly, rugged Mathews and Joe Adcock, the hulking first baseman. Baseball was a physical business, and baseball men talked about players crudely, as if they were horses. Henry's bottom half was bigger than his upper body, and his legs and ass, the scouts all said, formed a sturdy base of power.

Charlie Grimm watched Henry's mechanics, and the old baseball men, from Duffy Lewis, the Red Sox outfielder who was teammates with Babe Ruth and who, along with Tris Speaker and Harry Hooper, was part of Boston's "Million-Dollar Outfield" back in the teens, to Hall of Fame right fielder Paul "Big Poison" Waner, the Pirate great, in Bradenton as a special instructor, were writing the legend with their eyes.

There was plenty about his game that made them all wince, especially when they watched him around second base, allowing base runners dangerously close before firing off a relay throw with that sidewinding whip that had finished Chuck Wiles's career. "As a second baseman," Charlie Grimm said, cringing, "Aaron is a very good hitter. But we'll find a place for that bat."

AARON GIVEN DIVIDED VOTE BY PROPHETS

. . . whether he will make the big team . . . has nearly everybody out on a limb. His hitting is of slight worry—practically all insist he can club big-league curving right now—but there are many pros and cons as to whether he can cut the buck at second base.

In the cage, too, there were funky elements to his approach: that stomp on the front foot as he met the ball, which brought forth murmurs among the men that with his hitting style, Henry would never have substantial power (And why didn't his coaches at the minor leagues break that habit? they asked). They noticed how Henry swung almost as quickly as the ball left the pitcher's hand, leaving him to commit to pitches at eyebrow level or near his shoelaces.

And yet . . . *and yet* . . . when the baseball men took a snapshot of the moment the ball met the bat—the moment that mattered most—twenty-year-old Henry Aaron was pure gold. He would stand in the box, legs tight in a closed stance, leaning and crouched. And he would strike, catlike, hands back, then bring them forward with a thrusting motion, and at the last millisecond—everything about hitting in the big leagues was measured in milliseconds—the wrists that looked too skinny to produce power would snap through the zone, the hips would twist and uncoil, and the ball would just leap . . . to left . . . to center . . . and especially to right field. And the men behind the cage, the ones who would have killed to be able to cut at a baseball like that just once in their lives, to watch it sizzle upon impact, well, they just salivated. These were men who had spent their entire lives in the game, were collectively older than God, and all had seen Olympus in the form of Ruth, Gehrig, Greenberg, Cobb, all the very best. And it was Cobb, of all people, the old racist but inscrutable baseball mind, who seemed to like Henry the best. "Incidentally, Ty Cobb rates Henry Aaron, Braves' Negro newcomer, one of the best young players he has seen in years," reported Al Wolf in the *Los Angeles Times*. "Calls him a hitting natural."

Henry was not on the Braves major-league roster, but Charlie Grimm wouldn't let the kid out of his sight. One Saturday morning in early March, Henry was told to remain in Bradenton with the rest of the minor leaguers while the big club played four games on the east side of the state. Grimm would have none of it. Grimm told Henry—who had not yet even been issued a Braves uniform—that while he did not know what position Henry would be playing, he was to take orders only from him. "Pack a bag," Grimm told Henry, "and stick with me." That meant games against the Dodgers in Miami and the Philadelphia A's in West Palm Beach and Pittsburgh in Fort Pierce.

Each day, Grimm would watch Henry hit, and the baseball men would look at each other slyly—grim-faced on the outside, because no matter how good a player might be, you couldn't ever give away too much praise too early. That could ruin a kid. But inside, where it counted, Henry's talent reduced them all to giddy schoolboys bubbling with a secret. And smile they would at their good fortune, because Henry belonged to them, and the general manager, John Quinn, always made it a point to remind the newsmen first of his shrewdness: He'd got Henry for the bargain price of ten thousand dollars, and he would reaffirm his belief that the Braves could fetch ten times that sum from other teams. "I understand now," Paul Richards said, "why everyone raves about that kid. He's got powerful wrists, the kind all great hitters have."

The only man in the Braves organization who wasn't smiling was

George "Twinkletoes" Selkirk, the former Yankee outfielder, who through the thirties and forties had teamed with Ruth, Gehrig, and DiMaggio during an all-star career and won five World Series championships. He was now the manager of the Toledo Sox, Milwaukee's Class AA affiliate, and in January, Quinn told Selkirk he would have Henry for the entire 1954 season. Yet here it was, not even St. Patrick's Day, and Selkirk was already groaning to Red Thisted of the *Milwaukee Sentinel.* "I don't think," Selkirk said, "that we'll ever have him in a Toledo uniform." And he hated himself even more because he knew he was right.

FOR ALL THE commotion, young Henry Aaron was not a particularly comfortable or secure baseball player. He received the most attention of any rookie in any spring camp in baseball, but he was still not a member of the Milwaukee Braves, still not a major leaguer. He did not have a position. He knew he wasn't a major-league-caliber second baseman, and yet he didn't feel comfortable in the outfield. Second base would not be an option anyway. The day after Christmas, 1953, the Braves had given $200,000 and traded seven players to Pittsburgh for the rugged Irishman, second baseman Danny O'Connell. A month later, Milwaukee traded the promising left-hander Johnny Antonelli to the New York Giants for Bobby Thomson, the man who never had to buy another drink in his life in New York City after winning the pennant for the Giants over the Dodgers in the famed 1951 play-off game, the man a seventeen-year-old Henry had dreamed about at Josephine Allen.

Henry figured there was no place on the big-club roster for him with Thomson in left field, Billy Bruton in center, and Andy Pafko in right. Pafko was the man who had played left field for Brooklyn when Thomson's two-out, ninth-inning, pennant-winning three-run home run sailed over his head. Even the Milwaukee bench was crowded. Grimm was counting on Jim Pendleton, the former Negro League utility man who surprised the Braves in 1953 as a twenty-nine-year-old reserve with a .299 average and seven home runs. Moreover, Henry knew he was too talented to sit on the bench with the big club. Prized prospects needed to play every day, and that wouldn't happen on a veteran team that believed, even without him, it would be contending for the pennant.

However realistic or pessimistic Henry was about making the big club in 1954, he still handled his daily chores by crushing the baseball every day in the spring. Henry's hitting wove a tale that blended fact with the spurious. It was true that the best baseball minds wanted a piece of him, if for no other reason than to solidify their reputations as acute talent evaluators. Branch Rickey had been on the Grapefruit League scene less than a week before he declared Henry the "top prospect in the country." Rickey said he'd offered the Braves $150,000 for Henry, a figure confirmed with no shortage of glee (even the great "Mahatma" wanted in on Henry, although it wasn't as if Ed Scott hadn't warned him) by John Quinn.

When Henry took his cuts in the batting cage in Sarasota, and later in that game mashed a 450-foot home run against the Red Sox, a story was born that grew sweeter with each retelling. As Henry whipped blistering line drives through the strike zone, the contact of ball and bat was so pure that one man could recognize its significance by pitch alone. That man was none other than Theodore Samuel Williams.

"In his first spring training, during a game against the Red Sox," George F. Will wrote of Henry in 2007, "Ted Williams came running from the clubhouse to see whose bat was making that distinctive sound." In the book *Hammering Hank: How the Media Made Henry Aaron,* the authors Mark Stewart and Mike Kennedy offered a slightly different version:

> Aaron laid claim to a permanent roster spot with the Braves after slamming a long home run against the Red Sox. The blast even got the attention of Ted Williams. "Who the hell is that," Williams demanded of some nearby sportswriters after hearing the crack of the ball off Aaron's bat. When told it was a newcomer named Aaron, he responded, "Write it down and remember it. You'll be hearing that name often."

And still another version existed, the one that had Williams sitting in a lounge chair, his eyes closed, his back to the field, but aroused by the perfection of Henry's swing cutting the Florida air. Even Williams himself, in a 1999 book about Henry by the writer Dick Schaap, recalled the moment with trademark Williams aplomb:

> I was playing in Sarasota, and because I was an older, more experienced player I got to play the first three innings and then—Boom!—they take me out. I went in and showered because I wanted to watch the rest of the game. In Sarasota there was a nice little field and you had to go through a little dugout door and then sit on the bench. So I went out, and just as I dove through the door, I hear 'WHACK!' and then the roar of the crowd—it was a small crowd but it was a helluva roar anyhow—and one of my teammates said, "Did you see the guy hit that ball?"

It was a great story, with plenty of local detail—especially regarding the intimacy of Payne Park, the old Sarasota ballpark—except for one key point: It never happened, at least not the way the legend had it. Williams did not play against the Braves in March 1954. In fact, he did not play against anyone, because he wasn't even in Red Sox camp that year. He was on the operating table twelve hundred miles away in Cambridge, Massachusetts, having a four-inch metal spike inserted into his left collarbone. On March 1, while Henry was making the old-timers drool, Williams broke his collarbone shagging fly balls and was then admitted to Sancta Maria Hospital in Cambridge, where he remained from March 9 until his discharge from surgery a week later. He stayed in Boston following his discharge and didn't play his first game until May 15.

For the record, only the Williams portion of the story was fiction. The rest was true: Henry had them talking.

RED SOX SHADE BRAVES, 3–2; AARON'S HOMER STEALS SHOW

SARASOTA, FLA. — . . . However, even the final result . . . could not detract from the stir created in the third inning by a tremendous home run by Hank Aaron, the 20-year-old Negro rookie outfielder. Veteran observers called the blow the longest ever hit at Payne Field here.

True or not, the hype machine had accomplished the desired effect, and Williams and Aaron were both well served by repeating the tale: Williams because it reinforced his considerable reputation, proof that the Greatest Hitter Who Ever Lived not only had the keenest eye but also the sharpest ear (it wouldn't have done the Splinter any good if he'd told future generations of hungry listeners that the sweet sound that day was produced by the hitless bat of Jim Pendleton); and Henry because no greater authority than Williams had instantly elevated him into the honors class of power hitters— before he had ever played in a single big-league game that counted. He had been anointed, first by Cobb, and now by Williams. It was true that Williams had seen Henry swing a bat, for the Red Sox and Braves played numerous times that spring and, later, in All-Star Games (they appeared in seven All-Star Games together). He also might have seen Henry during subsequent spring-training seasons, as the Red Sox trained just a dozen or so miles away. It just didn't happen in 1954, when everyone believed it had.

The Williams story was emblematic of how legend could feed upon itself and how, as the tale was repeated, the names grew bigger, everyone just a bit closer to the simple and titillating beginnings of the Henry Aaron story, making it easier for him to be adopted by the baseball people, who, because of their reputations, couldn't allow anyone to think Henry had taken them by surprise.

The next day, March 2, Henry helped destroy the Yankees 11–3 by turning the baseball into a white blur that hit the base of the wall of the 433-foot marker in center field, over the head of outfielder Irv Noren. "It was not hit as hard as the tremendous home run at Sarasota Wednesday but went almost as far," the *Journal* reported. "The young Negro now has a .417 batting mark (5 for 12) and looks more like a fixture every day."

And it was at that precise moment when fate took over at the keyboard and tapped out a new narrative. When he arrived at Braves camp, Henry was not incorrect about his prospects. The club was set and he was headed to Toledo. He wouldn't be part of the Braves until 1955. The Braves paid handsomely for Thomson, an established power player and veteran outfielder acquired to provide protection for Mathews and first baseman Joe Adcock. And it was true that at the end of the 1953 season, Charlie Grimm so liked what he saw from Pendleton that he began to rely on him as a reserve.

But what Henry did not anticipate was that at the end of 1953, Jim Pendleton was feeling so good about himself and his sudden contribution that by January, he had decided to hold out for a better contract. A week away from the opening of camp, Pendleton still wasn't signed. When camp opened on February 28, and Henry was slashing line drives while the old-timers drooled over his potential, Pendleton was nowhere to be seen. Two days later, on March 2, Pendleton arrived in camp, a big, mushy tire around his waist. He and Henry would room together, but the challenge for a roster spot, for all intents and purposes, ceased the day Pendleton arrived, twenty pounds overweight, at 205.

Pendleton chomping away at the buffet table while Henry tore the cover off of the ball was fate just warming up. In the eighth inning of a spring game between the Braves and Yankees eleven days later, on March 13 at Al Lang Field in St. Petersburg, Pafko bounced a one-hopper to the mound. The Yankee pitcher, Bob Wiesler, caught and fired to second baseman Woody Held, who threw to first for a routine double play. But when the play was over, Held looked down, to find the first out of the double play, Bobby Thomson, crumpled in a heap over second base, yowling in pain. Held yelled over to the Braves bench, fear in his eyes at the sight of Thomson's twisted frame, and the world changed in an instant. Thomson had slid to avoid Held's relay and suffered a triple fracture of the right ankle. He was taken off the field on a stretcher and was put in a temporary splint by the Yankees physician, Dr. Sidney Gaynor. When Thomson arrived at St. Anthony's Hospital, he received the news that he would be out at least six to twelve weeks.

The next day, March 14, 1954, at a game against Cincinnati, Charlie Grimm wrote Henry's name into the lineup. He would be starting in right field, batting fourth. Henry rapped out two hits.

WITH THOMSON GONE for three months, Pendleton wearing a rubber suit to, in the words of the *Sentinel,* "work off the extra blubber," and Henry's incessant pasting of the baseball ("Aaron Shows

Power Again But Phils Down Braves, 12–10," announced the *Journal* after Henry homered and tripled over the head of the center fielder Richie Ashburn), a job on the big-league club seemed all but certain. His new teammates, however, were not exactly sure what to make of him. Despite his wrists, his surprising power, and his obvious ability, there was still something about the kid that just didn't quite compute. The scouting reports said Henry could run, and since he never was thrown out on close plays, it was clear that the scouts were not exaggerating his speed. But instead of blazing down the line in a thrust and flash, Henry would beat throws easily but somehow unconvincingly. Mickey Owen raved about Henry's arm, and at second base, Henry made all the necessary plays. He would snap off a throw that would beat the runner, but the ball didn't *pop* into the first baseman's glove, the way a throw from a legitimate major-league arm should. He would release his throws sidearm, at a three o'clock angle, his arm never higher than his shoulder. In the outfield, the sidearm delivery was the same languid motion, producing the impression that he was not concentrating enough on improving his mechanics. In the outfield, Henry would catch the baseball the old-fashioned way, two hands directly in front of the chest, allowing the ball to travel as close to his body as possible, to cushion the sting of the ball. That was the way poor kids caught the ball, the ones who played baseball every day without gloves or with gloves whose pockets had been worn painfully thin.

He was reticent to engage. Henry did not often speak to many players on the team, preferring, in the eyes of some teammates and writers, to position himself at a distance, yet no one accused him of possessing a rude demeanor. When he did speak, it was largely to the other Negro players on the team, Bill Bruton, Jim Pendleton, and Charlie White. At no point was he considered by the coaching staff to be lazy, but nor did he move with the frothy enthusiasm and frightened eagerness of most rookies.

So what was the reason for the disconnection? Was it simply that Henry was a green twenty-year-old of blossoming expectation, unsure exactly how to navigate his vast and rapidly expanding universe? Upon his arrival in Bradenton, he knew only three members of the Braves: catcher Bill Casey and pitcher Ray Crone, both of whom were white teammates of Henry in Jacksonville, and Bob Buhl, the promising young right-hander with the serious face and distinctively dark brows, who had earned a slot in the starting rotation by winning thirteen games in 1953 and was quickly being viewed as a potential third starter behind the snarling Burdette and the great Spahn. Buhl hailed from Saginaw, Michigan, and as a teenager had been a paratrooper in World War II. Henry and Buhl were teammates under Mickey Owen in the winter of 1953 in Caguas, and, like Owen, Buhl had made it his personal crusade during the spring to talk up Henry as the next great player.

The opposite was more likely true. In Henry, the Braves had the kind of player who could reverse the fortunes of an entire franchise, but no one in the organization—or in the game, really—knew quite how to deal with what Henry truly represented: the first signature black player in Braves history. Henry's invitation to the Braves training camp was a telegram with the address in Bradenton of Mrs. Lulu Mae Gibson.

Although Henry did not expect an invitation to stay at the Dixie Grande, the posh hotel in Bradenton where the white players lived during the spring, he was not comfortable with the accommodations provided him. The Gibson house was located in the colored section of Bradenton, and it had been the spring-training home for the Braves black players since 1950, when Sam Jethroe arrived as the first black member of the franchise.

In the spring of 1954, Barbara remained home in Alabama, pregnant for the first time. Henry and Barbara had already agreed that the spring-training conditions would not be conducive to living together as a family, as it was unlikely that apartment rentals would be available for colored players, and he was certain that the ball club would not pay for him and his pregnant new wife to be together. Henry would simply follow the other black players—Bruton, Charlie White, Jim Pendleton, and George Crowe—from Mrs. Gibson's house to the ballpark.

The Gibson house was a brick five-bedroom duplex. The main house was connected to a smaller addition, "a little house on stilts," as Henry recalled. During that first spring, he lived in the addition. "Mrs. Gibson was a schoolteacher, and I remember the house was right next to the J. D. Rogers funeral home. She would cook and clean for us and was happy to have us in her home. I remember living in the small house when I first came up."

Henry and the black players were treated better in the private homes of black professionals than in the mainstream, but housing represented the first stage in confronting what it meant for a black prospect to be a full member of the organization. A common attitude regarding racial questions in baseball was that with the arrival of Jackie Robinson in 1947, long inequitable scales had now been balanced. Blacks had been allowed to play at the big-league level for seven years, and thus it was believed that nothing much was left to be discussed. It was a perspective that didn't take into consideration the racial distinctions that existed despite the initial breakthrough. When Henry arrived at the clubhouse at Braves Field that first day, Joe Taylor, the Braves clubhouse man, showed him his locker, a wooden stall with a couple of diagonal nails inside for his jerseys, which would be clumped in with those of the other black players. The lockers of the white players were set apart. During the early weeks that spring, Henry noticed an unspoken practice that was common in baseball: The white players would shower first, then the black players.

And there were many discrepancies with regard to race: what could be said and what could not, who could speak and how, what types of people carried themselves in a given way and why, and what it all meant.

Most importantly, the presumption about who would be forced to sit and take it until the times were different remained. As Henry found during that first spring in 1954, Robinson was only the beginning. The real matters, the ones that made life *normal,* had not yet been addressed to any real degree, evidenced by his living in a rooming house while the white players (and their wives and kids) sat by the pool at the Dixie Grande. Henry tore into the baseball as the black leadership anxiously awaited a verdict in an important Supreme Court case that had been argued for the previous year and a half, *Oliver L. Brown et al. v. Board of Education of Topeka et al.* The case centered on equal facilities in public schools, but it spoke directly to the contradictions that defined Henry's life: Was it possible for two parallel societies to exist? In Henry's case, to play in the same outfield as white players, to use the same showers (*perhaps one day at the same time, even*), to hit in the same lineup, and yet be prohibited to sleep under the same roof? Henry received a six-dollar per diem for meals, the same as the white players, but in vivid ways he was being shown he was not on an equal basis with his teammates. Across the country, in Arizona, the New York Giants faced similar contradictions. Bill White played for the Giants minor-league system in 1954. He would play thirteen years in the major leagues, hit 202 home runs, and become the first black president of the National League, and to him, the absurdity of the situation was obvious. "I remembered thinking, If the accommodations were equal, why did they have to be separate in the first place?" he recalled. "Equal had nothing to do with it once you stepped off the field. They never thought we were equal. That's why we couldn't live where they were living."

MOTHER GIBSON SERVES VERY TASTY TABLE TO THE NEGRO MEMBERS OF BRAVES SQUAD

Bradenton, Fla. — "Come and get it, boys."

Three of the Braves' Negro players answered the breakfast call at Mrs. Gibson's home where they live.

"This is really like home," said outfielder Billy Bruton as he sat down to his platter of bacon, fried eggs and hot biscuits.

"It sure tastes like home cooking," agreed outfielder Henry Aaron. . . .

"Wonderful boys, all of them," said Mrs. Gibson, a broad smile lighting her face.

There were no complaints about the food. ("Mrs. Gibson must be the original home of southern fried chicken," Braves assistant trainer and clubhouse man Joe Taylor said. "Hers is the best I've ever eaten." But in a low and steady murmur, plenty of dissent was expressed regarding the system that forced Henry Aaron and Sam Jethroe to sit at Mrs. Gibson's dinner table in the first place. When the time was right, it was Bruton (always beware of the quiet ones) who led the fight to eliminate segregated housing during spring training in the major leagues, thereby bringing to an end a valuable source of income and a sense of belonging for Mrs. Gibson and the other middle-class black families that took on the traveling famous—baseball players, jazz and bluesmen, all the blacks who were good enough to provide entertainment to whites but not good enough to occupy a hotel room. That spring, when integration existed in theory only, Lulu Gibson took pride in caring for her Braves, and she soon felt betrayed by the fact that Henry and "her boys" were angling to leave.

"Mrs. Gibson's was the best choice at that time," Henry recalled. "When integration came, she thought we were turning her down, and she was not happy about that. To her, it was a choice. To us, we wanted to have the same opportunity everyone else on the ball club had."

During a meeting of player representatives during the 1961 All-Star Game in Boston, Bruton and Bill White canvassed support from the nascent players association and the white players, of whom Bill White said, "[They] only see us at the ballpark." White by then was playing with St. Louis, Bruton with Detroit. It was White, focusing in the 1961 meeting on the new franchise awarded to Houston, who suggested that black players refuse to participate in cities that did not offer integrated housing. It was Bruton who said it was time for white players to support their black and Latino teammates off of the field.

"Behind the scenes, we made things happen. We integrated before the military, before the schools. We were the first ones," Bill White recalled. "In a lot of places, we integrated hotels and housing in Florida before the civil rights movement. It started with Jackie, but Henry and Billy Bruton and Frank Robinson and me, too. When Atlanta came in the league, Willie Stargell said in a meeting that unless everyone could buy a ticket and sit wherever they wanted to, we shouldn't play there. We all had to deal with it. People always talked about how we handled living while America was changing. Hell, *we* were the ones who changed America."

In the spring, in between the long home runs that created myth and the nervousness of being a twenty-year-old trying to make a big-league roster, Henry represented the upsetting of another social layer. He was, along with Willie Mays, baseball's first black super-prospect, touted as a teenager, groomed by a big-league organization through the traditional, integrated minor-league system. Henry played in the Negro Leagues, but as a teenager who hadn't finished high school, and his future would be radically different from that of his Indianapolis Clowns teammates, the men for whom the times wouldn't change fast enough. The Negro Leagues were never a destination for Henry, and that made him different from the rest. Even Robinson at first believed Branch Rickey had selected him to be part of a potential Negro League rival.

Evaluation of baseball talent was one thing—everybody in the Milwaukee system during spring training knew Henry had a special talent. Judging him as a man, however, was a completely different story. Two years earlier, in Buffalo, Henry had been questioned about how he conducted himself. Milwaukee scout Dewey Griggs, who signed Henry, asked him if he had another gear, which meant could he throw harder, put more snap on the ball, run harder, look like he was putting a full sweat into it. Griggs thought that Henry's pace—languid to his coaches—might be problematic in a baseball environment where players were constantly and openly testing one another's commitment level, and he asked Henry if he could run faster, if he could play more quickly than he was showing at that particular moment, and Henry said that he could. And Griggs asked him why he didn't show maximum effort, each time, all the time, and Henry told him he was following old advice from Herbert Aaron: "Never move faster than you have to."

If you came from Wilcox County, where the work was merciless and the future nonexistent, the maxim might have made more sense. *Never move faster than you have to.* In Herbert Aaron's America, these were genius words, essential passages in his personal survival guide, the strategy employed by poor blacks to conserve the energy they would need for the backbreaking tasks they would face every day for rest of their lives, tasks that would weigh on Herbert Aaron, with no relief and no justice in sight. And the words represented something else: a subtle articulation of the black man's revenge, the poor man's only fighting weapon. For whether you moved quickly or leisurely, the day's worth of work still awaited; the load never lightened. There was no reward of promotion or of prosperity, hope just a dream on a kind horizon. Working faster would not lead to more respect or more rest, a larger share of the profits, or a better life. It would not change your prospects in the eyes of the boss or create a reexamination of the system that profited from your sweat and crushed you in the process. If you asked for more, the southern system would rather kill you than make you an equal partner in the American dream. Working faster would not better your position in the company. The only thing fast work produced was more work. In Herbert Aaron's America, appealing to the boss was the *worst* thing you could do. It was just a waste of energy, because the status of the black laborer in the South always remained the same.

On the ball field, Henry had not yet learned this key piece of survival, and on the sun-and-dust ball fields in Bradenton, Dewey Griggs attempted to clue Henry in on how baseball's version of office politics really worked. In baseball, perceived effort was often as important as actually working hard, and the appearance of working hard carried a great deal of value. Players with less physical talent knew it the best, for they were the guys whose very survival in the game depended on a manager or a coach believing that his lack of talent gave him a greater desire than the more gifted players, thus making him more valuable. Baseball managers often connected best with these players, the ones whose arms pumped and teeth clenched when they chugged helplessly to first, out by a mile. Since the great majority of baseball managers at one time themselves had had marginal ability and had to compensate with toughness and maximum effort, the player who used tenacity to compensate for a lack of foot speed often reminded the skipper of himself when he was young. It was the guy who couldn't run who had to run the hardest, to prove that he was willing to overcome his physical limitations with extra effort. And in the dugout, there was no shame in that—unless, that is, you were trying to score unearned points with the manager. Baseball linguistics provided terminology for the culprits who embodied each end of the scale. The term was *jaking it* for the player who did not hustle and lacked work ethic, and *goldbricking* was the special designation for the players who mastered the fine art of false hustle. And it was always surprising just how many people in the big-league hierarchy—

players, managers, executives, coaches, and members of the press—
fell for the act.

There was a difference between the player who played hard but
could make it look easy and the guy who *gave it his all,* buttons popping, tumbling in the outfield, all to make a routine catch. The latter
was a guy the shrewdest players in the dugout could sniff out faster
than a bloodhound.

In the beginning, Henry paid a severe price for not exploiting
these subtle, variable distinctions, which took on greater significance
with black players. In later years, once his talent had secured his legend, he would be applauded for running and fielding so effortlessly.
As a twenty-year-old in his first spring camp, the unscientific art of
reading body language never seemed to work in his favor, even as he
revealed the depth of his awesome potential to his teammates. The
initial impressions of his teammates were often harsh, exposing less
about who Henry Aaron was as a man and more about the racial attitudes that supported an order that was supposed to be crumbling.

"SLOW MOTION" AARON BECOMES
COLORFUL FIGURE IN BRAVES' CAMP

BRADENTON, FLA. — Henry Aaron is gradually becoming accustomed to major league surroundings. When he joined the Braves
here three weeks ago, the 20-year-old Mobile (Ala.) Negro acted
scared. . . . The bewildered rookie now acts like he is one of the gang.
He smiles when Joe Adcock calls him "Slow Motion Henry" because
he shuffles on and off the field.

OFTEN, the white boys would slip beyond the light joshing, and the
true face behind the mask would reveal itself. Joshing with Henry was
never easy anyway, because while he liked to laugh, he did not like to
be teased. Sometimes his teammates would watch him in the field,
walking easily, and it would reinforce not only stereotypes about how
a black man moved but the widely held paternalist belief that blacks
did not take work, whether baseball or otherwise, as seriously as

whites. Sometimes the slights could feel like pinpricks, nagging and annoying, reminders to the black players that they were different. Whenever a black power hitter reached the majors, the adjective du jour was *husky*. "[Grimm's] first sacker was George Crowe, husky Negro, a graduate of the Eastern League," the *Journal* wrote in 1951.

Where matters became sticky was in the eye of the person doing the evaluating and whether he recognized his own prejudices, for the belief systems about what people were, in the case of black players in particular, of how hard they were willing to work, were capable of playing tricks on even the sharpest eyes. And that was why, if you were a white player watching Henry in those days, you had to ask yourself a question: Was he actually acting any differently from the thousands of inexperienced rookie ballplayers who had come before him?

Joe Adcock was the first player about whom Henry was wary. Adcock was a son of the South, the South Henry Aaron had escaped either by daydreaming as a boy or by leaving as a teenager. Adcock was born two years before the onset of the Depression in the unsparing poverty and rigid segregation of Coushatta, Louisiana. He would grow to six four and 220 pounds. He was a star athlete in football and basketball. He played college football at Louisiana State University in the mid-1940s and chose baseball over the National Football League because Cincinnati signed him first.

When southern resistance to Reconstruction reached its violent apex, Coushatta was the town best known for the Coushatta Massacre, when in August 1874 a mob of whites calling themselves the White League accosted members of the town's political leadership, whites and their black followers, and threatened to murder each if they did not leave town. As the group of sixty blacks and six whites left the town limits, heading to Texas unarmed, they were followed and murdered by a gang of forty Coushatta whites, who chased them down and shot each one of them to death.

Once in the spring, Adcock noticed Henry's running style, nearly motionless from the waist up. Because Henry compensated for an ankle injury suffered when he was young, his stride was not always fluid. Adcock decided that Henry ran stiff-legged, and he coined another new nickname for the rookie, one that the press occasionally repeated. "Slow Motion Henry" wasn't enough. Adcock now called him "Snowshoes." In these instances, Henry might smile or pretend he did not hear. Spahn, he of the extensive vocabulary and cutting wit, might call you out, yelling something clever across the diamond or the clubhouse, shredding his tormentor into verbal ribbons. Mathews, on a dark day, might just break your jaw if you pushed him the wrong way. Henry was not an emotionally confrontational man. He would not say anything, and that made him in those years easy to underestimate. If Jackie Robinson would spark and combust, Henry would collect information about the people around him, quietly sharpening his judgments while smoldering privately at the same time, like the day he sat in a bathroom stall and overheard Adcock talking about "niggers." "He was talking about something," Henry said. "I don't remember the whole conversation, but he said to somebody, 'You couldn't see a nigger if they put you in the middle of Harlem.' " There was no confrontation with Adcock that day, or any other during the decade they would play as teammates, but Henry knew he would never let Joe Adcock take him by surprise. He knew where Adcock stood, and to Henry, that gave him an advantage.

To Chuck Tanner, Henry was a threat both to the order and to his new teammates. Like Henry, Tanner had been invited to the big-league camp and, like Henry, was not on the Milwaukee roster in the spring of 1954. Tanner was an outfielder who had first been signed by the Boston Braves in 1946 but had advanced slowly through the ranks. Tanner was born on Independence Day, 1929, in the tough mining town of New Castle, Pennsylvania, three and a half months before the stock market crash. Tanner immediately understood racial and ethnic divisions, divisions that were often muted because of the grinding poverty of the region. "We had so many different people from where we came from—Germans, Poles, Ukrainians, and a few blacks—you couldn't pronounce the last names of most of the people on my block," Tanner recalled. "And believe me, when you had that many different people in one area, things could get heated. But none of us *had* anything, so it was hard for anyone to feel superior. When I was a kid, we all traded fruits and vegetables with one another instead of money, just so we could eat."

By 1954, Tanner had been in the Braves minor-league system for seven years and was not exactly certain he would ever make the major leagues. Tanner's experiences gave him special insight into how established players could view a player so extremely gifted as Henry. While it was not a surprise to him that those from the Deep South, like Adcock, would be difficult, Tanner believed that racism, or even simple insensitivity, was secondary to a certain kind of professional jealousy and a certain amount of fear both on the part of some of Henry's peers as well as the writers.

"The bottom line is that they were jealous of him," Tanner recalled. "In those days, nobody wanted to go back to the farm, and Henry Aaron was so good, they knew that. They knew *he* wasn't going to be the one going back to the farm. He made everything look so easy that even the writers hated him for it at first. Henry didn't run; he *glided.* He just had so much ability. He could make everything look so easy, and I think people resented him for that."

The hazing was more a by-product of the players' insecurities reaching the surface, Chuck Tanner believed. What increased the intensity was another layer of change white players were being forced to confront: There now would not only be black players in the game but the greater number of black players on a roster, the more white players who would be losing their jobs to blacks. It was bad enough to get sent out to the minors because a better player took your job, but it was even worse for a white player to lose out to a black. The thing the white players feared most, Tanner thought, was having to explain to all the guys back home that they weren't as good as the black guys coming into the league.

And Henry left Bradenton leading his team in home runs, extra base hits, and runs batted in. On the final day of spring training, the Braves purchased his minor-league contract from Toledo. George Selkirk's premonition had come true. Henry would never play a game in Toledo. His big-league contract paid the major-league minimum salary of six thousand dollars per year. Charlie Grimm told him he was the starting left fielder, with Bruton in center and Pafko in right. As the team headed north to begin the season, Joe Taylor, the Braves equipment manager, told Henry to keep the number he wore during the spring. He would wear number 5.

CHAPTER FOUR

MILWAUKEE

IT WAS A strange way to start a renaissance, by leaving a big town full of history and power and influence for a medium-sized midwestern town with an inferiority complex, virtually anonymous, both in terms of national prominence and importance on the baseball map.

Since the end of the Spanish-American War, the Braves had been looking for love, and they never quite found it in Boston. The team was formed in 1871, thirty years before the Red Sox, first as the Boston Red Stockings of the National Association and then, in 1876, as the Boston Red Caps, one of the inaugural eight franchises of the newly formed National League of Professional Baseball Clubs. The Red Caps finished fourth that year, but they were fortified by an admirable stamina—they didn't finish in the money, but they remained in business. Neither the New York Mutuals nor the Philadelphia Athletics (both of which were expelled after one season) could say that. The Hartford Dark Blues, the St. Louis Brown Stockings, and the Louisville Grays all folded after the league's second season. The Cincinnati Red Stockings were expelled by the league following the 1880 season, in part for the high offense of selling beer to fans. Of the original eight franchises that comprised the National Association, only the Chicago White Stockings (later to become the Cubs) and the Red Caps would survive the years.

For a time, life in Boston was beautiful. The franchise played in Roxbury, at the South End Grounds and later at Braves Field, both parks within throwing distance of Fenway Park, later the home of the newly formed Red Sox in the upstart American League. The Braves were an immediate dynasty, winning four pennants in the five-year existence of the National Association, and in their first twenty-two years after joining the National League, they won eight more. The team was managed by accomplished baseball men Harry Wright and Frank Selee, men who would wind up in Cooperstown, and it would forever live in memory for the magical year of 1914, the year the Braves were in last place, sporting a record of 33–43, eleven and a half games back of John McGraw's New York Giants on July 15, and yet the Braves were popping corks by October, finishing the season winning sixty-one of their final seventy-seven games, to end up with the pennant, ten and a half games in first. The "Miracle Braves," as they would be known forever more, completed the conquest a week later, sweeping Connie Mack's legendary Philadelphia A's in four straight in the 1914 World Series.

Over the years, the name changed, from the Red Caps to the Beaneaters to the Doves to the Rustlers to the Braves to the Bees and, finally and permanently, in 1941, back to the Braves. Yet three truths remained constant: The first was that despite the changing nickname, the team always remained a bedrock constant in Boston. The second was that once the twentieth century began, the Braves were patently awful. It didn't matter if the manager was Rogers Hornsby (50–103 in 1928) or Casey Stengel (373–491, for a .432 winning percentage over six seasons), or the players were Walter "Rabbit" Maranville or a forty-year-old fat and finished Babe Ruth (.181 batting average in twenty-three games for a team that would finish 38–115 in 1935). In the seasons between the Miracle Braves and the 1948 club that surprised everyone by winning the pennant (and were one agonizing one-game play-off away from playing the Red Sox in what would have been the only all-Boston World Series), the Braves finished in the second division. That was the kind way of saying fifth place, or worse—twenty-six times in the thirty-two seasons between pennants.

The third truth was that almost from the start, the American League Red Sox possessed an uncanny ability to attract attention in a way their august, stiffer National League counterparts certainly could not. The Red Sox arrived in 1901, and they were champions by 1903 after winning the first-ever World Series between the rival leagues, dousing Pittsburgh in a raucous affair. While the Braves puttered around in the muddy old confines of the South End Grounds in Roxbury, the Red Sox built their grand ballpark, Fenway Park, in the Fenway section of town in 1912. The Red Sox were interesting in victory and defeat during the teen years, building a following with championship teams in 1912, 1915, 1916, and 1918. The Braves were established, but the Red Sox were exciting, with big names and bigger personalities—among them Cy Young, "Smokey Joe" Wood, Tris Speaker, and, of course, one George Herman Ruth—names so big that, despite the unquestioned dominance of the Braves before the Red Sox ever existed, future generations would accept as fact that Boston always had been an American League town.

It was a momentum that never slowed. Thomas A. Yawkey purchased the Red Sox in 1933, and the Braves had no one to compete with the headline-generating bombast of Ted Williams or Yawkey's fruitless opulence. Winning the pennant in 1948 did not change the Braves second-place status, and Frank Lane, the general manager of the Chicago White Sox, began to articulate a prediction about the future that seemed too scary, too foreign to accept as anything but radical.

"Two-club cities, with the exception of New York and Chicago," Lane said, "are doomed."

MILWAUKEE WAS ONCE a big-league town. The year was 1901, the first year of the American League, and the team, the Milwaukee Brewers, was ironically an early incarnation of the St. Louis Browns/Baltimore Orioles. The Brewers that year won forty-eight games (out of 137, a winning percentage of .350, good for last place) in their only season in Milwaukee before moving to St. Louis. It wasn't that the good people of Milwaukee ("Good Burghers," the press called them) didn't love their baseball, but more that the barons, who ran the game, didn't exactly love them back. Another edition of the Milwaukee Brewers arrived in 1902 and played in the minor-league American Association for the next fifty years, and that's what Milwaukee would be, *minor-league,* through two world wars and the Depression. For a time, being called "minor-league" did not sting, for the city took pride in its baseball team and Borchert Field, its rickety old home, adopting the position that it, like much of the

rest of the custom and personality of Milwaukee, may not have translated easily to the outside world but, inside, was representative of
how the community viewed itself.

Milwaukee was a city founded by French fur traders and speculators. Nestled on the western edge of Lake Michigan, it united originally by conflict. Two independent, rival communities—Juneautown
on the east banks of the Milwaukee River, founded by Solomon
Juneau, and Kilbourntown, on the west, founded by Byron
Kilbourn—lived in relative hostility during the early 1840s. When the
Kilbourntown supporters dumped a whole section of a proposed
drawbridge into the river, ostensibly to hamper and isolate the economic prospects of Juneautown, the famous Milwaukee Bridge War
ensued. The weeks of fighting resulted in the unification of the two
factions into one city in 1845.

The French arrived first, but the enduring fabric of the city was
shaped by the heavy influx of German immigrants in the mid-1800s
and the social and political customs they brought to their new world.
There would be lasting examples of the city's uniqueness. Milwaukee
would be the only major American city to elect three Socialist may-
ors, and even as late as World War I, no city outside of New York City
would house as many different immigrant groups as would Milwaukee. And in line with its German-Austrian immigrant roots, there
would be agriculture and education and social progressiveness and
beer, not always in that order.

The population surged, and the powerful German heritage mixed
with that of the fast-rising pockets of Poles, Jews, Hungarians and
Austrians, and some Western European immigrants (the first Milwaukee City Hall, built in 1891, was designed in the Flemish Renaissance style). During the first fifty years of incorporation, Milwaukee
grew from roughly 20,000 residents to nearly 300,000. Between 1880
and 1890 alone, the population grew by 76 percent. World War I
threatened the social fabric of the city as the allegiance of German
immigrants was tested, prompting the *Milwaukee Journal* to inflame
tensions by accusing the *Germania-Herold,* the German newspaper,
of disloyalty. The sensibilities of Milwaukee Germans were so frayed
that by the end of the war, many believed Prohibition became a reality in part as a reaction to a disturbing backlash of anti-German senti-

ment. Still, the city grew. By the late 1940s, the population exceeded 600,000 (times were so good that even the *Milwaukee Journal,* on the flag of the paper, right next to the weather and the date, listed its circulation, proof of its muscle, its upward mobility). In the years following World War II, with the population booming, Milwaukee wanted more. It wanted baseball, big-league baseball, and there was no longer anything quaint or endearing about the term *minor-league.*

The layers of change that enveloped baseball in the early 1950s were not limited to white players growing accustomed to having black teammates. The changes also presented a challenge to the barons of the game to see more clearly beyond the confining borders of the past and determine which of them possessed the vision to navigate a fluid future.

No team had relocated since 1903, when the Baltimore Orioles moved to become the New York Highlanders, or its better-known *nom de voyage,* the Yankees, but the larger forces of postwar expansion and advances in technology and travel could not be suppressed. Frank Lane had predicted that the two-team city structure that had been a fixture since the turn of the century was dead, and only the most stubborn owners could disagree with him. There was a new baseball phrase for the growing number of cities in an expanding America that hungered for baseball. The term—*big-league ready*—was one that only a few members of the old guard were ready to adopt, but Braves owner Lou Perini and Cubs owner Phillip K. Wrigley were baseball's two biggest evangelists for expansion. "The entire map of Organized Baseball should be reorganized so that baseball can keep pace with the growth of the nation," Wrigley said in 1951. It was a sentiment that spoke directly to Lou Perini.

Louis Perini was a New Englander, born and raised in the rural town of Ashland, Massachusetts, about twenty miles west of Boston. Yet Perini was never limited in his worldview. As a boy, he worked for his father's construction company, and according to the family legend, six-year-old Louis would fetch pails of water for his father's crew of hungry workers. In 1924, when Louis was twenty-one, his father died and left the family construction business to his sons. Louis became president of the new company, and even through the Depression years, he was able to amass and maintain a hefty fortune.

Nearing the end of World War II, in January 1944, Lou Perini partnered with Joseph Maney and Guido Rugo, along with a consortium of minority partners, to purchase a controlling interest in the Braves from Bob Quinn. The three construction men turned baseball owners were known as "the Three Little Steam Shovels," and their first order of business was to bounce Stengel as manager and revive the moribund franchise. Within three years, the Braves were contenders. In the fourth, in 1948, the Braves drew 1.3 million fans and won the pennant, although they lost to Cleveland in the World Series.

Lou Perini saw himself as a visionary, and compared to the owners whose idea of progress was to view the coming of television as the death of baseball, he was. Perini believed in expansion. In the 1940s, he wanted baseball scouts to begin searching in Europe—both to in his words, "spread the gospel of the game" and to develop new talent markets outside of the United States. Perini believed Los Angeles deserved a baseball team, and he saw California as the great growth area of the country. "And let's interpolate this opinion: in 25 years California will have more people than any state in the U.S.A.," he said in 1951. "Can the major leagues afford to stand still?" He thought Milwaukee and Houston were "big-league ready," which was where one of his key visions entered the picture in 1951: a twelve-team league with franchises in California, Montreal, Mexico City, and even Havana, Cuba.

For a time, Perini did not believe his own club a candidate for relocation, and he had his reasons. One was his commitment to Boston. In the years 1947 through 1949, both the Braves and Red Sox drew over one million fans, suggesting that if both clubs fielded competitive teams, the city possessed the resources and will to support both. But the Braves never outdrew the Red Sox during those years, and at least some of the attendance figures on both sides were boosted by American euphoria over the end of the war years. Cleveland, for example, drew 2.6 million fans when it won the World Series in 1948, but the next season, when pennant-winning clubs usually enjoyed a significant spike in attendance, the team drew 400,000 fewer fans.

Another of Perini's convictions in 1951 was that within five years the Braves would be the powerhouse in baseball, on a par with—if not better than—the Dodgers and the Yankees. One key piece—the pitcher Warren Spahn—was already in place, and in 1950, the Braves had traded for another, moving an aging Johnny Sain to the Yankees for a young right-hander named Selva Lewis Burdette. There were third baseman Eddie Mathews, the young shortstop Johnny Logan, and two black prospects, the lightning-fast outfielder Bill Bruton and George Crowe, a hard-hitting first baseman. Even more promising for Perini was that at each level the Braves farm system had been tearing up the minor leagues.

In 1950, Perini invited two friends to attend the All-Star Game at Comiskey Park in Chicago, the legendary Notre Dame football coach Frank Leahy and Fred C. Miller, the president of the Miller Brewing Company. During the game, Miller asked Perini if he was interested in selling the Braves to him and expressed his intention of moving them to Milwaukee. Perini declined, but he agreed to Miller's request that Perini not move or sell the Braves without first speaking with him. The following year, on July 1, 1951, the *Boston Traveler* published an item about a group of Milwaukee businessmen interested in purchasing equity in the Braves, with the intention of relocating the team to Milwaukee. Perini, not willing to accept the old Hollywood adage that the rumors are always true, laughed the story off as ridiculous. "The whole thing is utterly fantastic. The Braves will remain in Boston, which is where they belong," Perini said. "I believe that some day Milwaukee will have a major-league franchise, but that will not come to pass until the entire structure of baseball is changed. I can assure everyone that the franchise that Milwaukee may obtain eventually will not be the Braves franchise."

Less funny was the massive financial hit the Three Little Steam Shovels were taking with the Braves in Boston. In 1950, Perini lost a quarter of a million dollars. The following year, the attendance at Braves Field dropped by nearly half, to 6,250 fans per game.

Future retellings of the Braves demise would always contain a delicious element of the unknown—of what might have been had the Braves remained in Boston another few years and the flowering of the club had taken place there instead of in Milwaukee. Perini had alienated fans, in part by selling off key members of the 1948 pennant team, such as Alvin Dark, Johnny Sain, and Eddie Stanky, but a powerful young nucleus was forming on the club, just at the time when the Red Sox were about to begin a deep and precipitous slide into irrelevancy.

Bill Veeck, the iconoclastic owner of the St. Louis Browns, had realized that St. Louis was not big enough for two teams, and Veeck began searching for relocation possibilities. Suddenly, the gold rush was on, and the teams that never had a prime market to call their own were racing to find the promised land. Milwaukee was first, or a booming equivalent. Veeck wanted to move to Milwaukee, to return the Browns to their original home of fifty years earlier. A group of businessmen from Houston took an interest in purchasing the Cardinals when the owner, Fred Saigh, under federal investigation for tax irregularities, put the team up for sale. Veeck disclosed that a year before Fred Miller's discussion with Perini at the All-Star Game in 1950, Fred Miller had contacted him and spoken of the possibility of moving the Browns to Milwaukee, and the two would speak again for the next two years, even though Veeck's real dream was to move the Browns to Los Angeles. He'd tried in 1944, but wartime travel restrictions made it impossible for one team to be located two thousand miles from the next closest club. Plus, Veeck was never popular enough with his fellow owners to be allowed so audacious and potentially lucrative a move.

Perini held the advantage in Milwaukee. His relationship with Miller was strong and he also owned the minor-league club, the Brewers, and held an existing lease on Milwaukee County Stadium. He promised five million dollars in stadium renovations, ostensibly for the Brewers, who had outgrown Borchert Field. The true motive for County Stadium, naturally, was to attract a big-league team. When Perini denied he would ever sell the Braves to any consortium of Milwaukee businessmen, he was being accurate, albeit in a convoluted way. Parse the words, peel off the layers of the onion, and in many ways Perini had shown his hand back in 1951. Milwaukee wouldn't land a team "until the entire structure of baseball is changed." It was true: He was not going to sell, but he was going to change the entire structure in one stroke. He was going to move the Braves to Milwaukee himself.

In January 1952, Perini wagered his greatest and last gamble in

Boston, spending thirty thousand dollars to charter a Pan American Airways jet to publicize the star players of the Braves farm system. Perini invited five Boston writers, plus a radio commentator and his publicity man, to fly to the hometowns of eighteen of the club's top prospects, as well as five more who were playing in Puerto Rico and Cuba. The final stop of the 10,361-mile journey was Santa Barbara, California, home of Eddie Mathews, the twenty-year-old slugging third baseman. The jet was dubbed the "Rookie Rocket," and had it departed six months later, an eighteen-year-old Henry Aaron, playing shortstop in Eau Claire, likely would have merited a stop on the tour.

In the end, the 1952 season broke Lou Perini. On April 15, Spahn lost to the Dodgers 3–2 in front of an opening-day crowd of 4,694. On May 14, 1,105 showed up for the Braves-Pirates game. In the final home game of the season against the Dodgers, 8,822 watched Joe Black beat the home team. The final attendance for the season at Braves Field was 281,278, or an average of 3,563 fans per game, an 80 percent drop in attendance from the 1948 World Series team just four seasons earlier.

The Braves arrived in Bradenton as vagabonds. Perini knew the club would not likely return to Boston for the 1953 season, and he began planning his escape. The cover of the 1953 spring press guide had been redone, removing the name Boston. The new guide did not specify a city, reading simply "The Braves." During the winter of 1952, Perini engaged in a little behind-the-scenes horse trading. He cajoled his fellow owners to relax the tight restrictions on franchise moves by allowing a major-league team to move into the same territory of a minor-league team without permission from the team or its league. The rule allowed Perini to move into Milwaukee, since he already owned the Brewers. Perini then consolidated his power base, buying out all of his minority partners—including two of the original Steam Shovels, Guido Rugo and Joseph Maney—and replacing them with his two brothers, thus eliminating any potential objection within ownership to a move to Wisconsin. Of the owners, Perini was particularly focused on canvassing Phil Wrigley of the Cubs, Ruly Carpenter of the Phillies, and Connie Mack of the Athletics for support, the owners who shared their cities with another club. He was also keeping a watchful eye on St. Louis, where the Cardinals were for sale, knowing a group of Texas businessmen were hot to move the venerable Redbirds to Houston. Perini told his old friend Wrigley that he needed to support the proposal to make it easier to one day have the city of Chicago to himself. When the sale of the Cardinals to beer magnate August Busch was approved, Perini knew he could count on the support of Bill Veeck, who realized the Cardinals were not going to Houston and now had the resources to become a St. Louis institution once again. That confirmed what Veeck long knew: His St. Louis Browns would again be on the move and would need support.

On March 19, 1953, at a meeting in St. Petersburg, Florida, the league owners approved Perini's request to transfer the Boston National League franchise to Milwaukee, while rejecting Veeck, who had accepted the second-place prize of Baltimore. At the time of the approval, the Braves were in the fifth inning, playing in a spring-training game. On the scoreboard in Bradenton, the name for the home team read BOS. By the end, the home team was MIL.

The Braves now belonged to Milwaukee.

The sale was complete, but not without a touch of irony. Five years after Perini had successfully lobbied the owners to ease the relocation process, Walter O'Malley, the owner of the Brooklyn Dodgers, engineered the most famous and polarizing relocation in the history of American professional sports. He had voted for the rules and the relocation, while lamenting that the changes would create a "shifting carnival."

Still, it galled Perini that he, a native son of Boston, was being forced to move, while that Michigan–South Carolina carpetbagger Yawkey, who would never even purchase a permanent residence in the forty-three years he owned the Red Sox, positioned himself as the guardian of Boston baseball. Yawkey and Boston never warmed to each other until 1967, the single most important year in the baseball history of the city (the Red Sox went to the World Series, losing to St. Louis), when more than a decade of losing was wiped clean by the "Impossible Dream" Red Sox. Before then, Yawkey had been disillusioned with baseball and, more to the point, the city politicians who refused to build him a new stadium with public money. To Johnny Logan, it was just another reason why he felt the gods rained on the Boston Braves. If Mathews, Bruton, and Aaron could have reached the majors together as a unit, it might have been the Red Sox who left town. "With the team we had, we would have turned Boston upside down," Logan said. "If we had stayed, we would have owned that city. I was hoping we could stick just a little longer. But we left."

Even Perini's successes were somehow either obscured by or co-opted by the Red Sox. In a city always unable to escape its racial contradictions and confrontations, Perini was never part of Boston's racially unattractive narrative. The Braves were one of the first teams in baseball to integrate, with center fielder Sam Jethroe winning the National League Rookie of the Year award in 1950, and had the Braves remained, the Boston sports scene would have showcased Henry Aaron and Bill Russell (not to mention a fading but always compelling Ted Williams), both at the height of their powers. It was Perini and his ownership group and not Tom Yawkey or the Red Sox that founded the Jimmy Fund, and yet over the decades the famous charity would become synonymous with the Boston Red Sox.

And it galled him equally that he truly was a man of vision, a person who embraced the future as a place of wide opportunity—indeed, the leagues would expand to California, expand internationally, and embrace television, ideas that Perini supported years before his contemporaries. By comparison, Yawkey would be one of the least dynamic owners in the history of the sport, one who viewed change as something to be suppressed. Following the first transcontinental broadcast of a baseball game in 1951, the common attitude toward television was that televising home games would not be a great advertising tool to attract fans or build a greater following for teams whose fans could not attend a game. Instead, it would negatively affect the home gate. Yawkey refused to broadcast even a third of Boston's home games at Fenway Park. Perini, meanwhile, broadcast sixty-three of the seventy-seven Braves home games. Yawkey would be the name synonymous with baseball ownership in Boston, while Perini was left ashen and melancholy. "Ever since I got into baseball I have given considerable thought to making it more attractive to the fans and the idea of attracting new fans," Perini said. "Perhaps several of my ideas were too extreme for some, but they were always motivated in the best interests of the game." Yet, Perini's hometown simply would not respond to his baseball team, and it was that curious and fatal apathy that created the momentum toward Milwaukee. Perini saw himself as a man of vision, and men of vision did not fight momentum.

THE BRAVES WERE welcomed to Milwaukee as saviors. In most towns, the bars and restaurants jockeyed to curry favor with the local ball club, everyone wanting to be *the official* establishment of the home team. Milwaukee was no different.

After home games, Duffy Lewis, the Braves traveling secretary, would call Ray Jackson's Barbecue and tell the bartender to put some bottles on ice—the players were coming over. Wisconsin Avenue was full of hot spots willing to cater to the team. There was Ray Jackson's, but there were also Fazio's and Frenchy's and the authentic German restaurants Mader's and Karl Ratzsch's. There was Mick Lewin's, and for the best steak in town, there was the Hotel Schroeder.

In most towns, the gratuity stopped there—a steak and a beer and a handshake. In Milwaukee, grateful to finally be big league, the red carpet extended to gasoline (Wisco 99 filled the players' tanks for free), dry cleaning, and furnishings for the wet bar, courtesy of Fred Miller.

"We got automobiles to drive. We got dairy products. We got free gasoline. We got free dry cleaning," Frank Torre recalled. "A case of beer a week, and a case of whiskey a month, I remember. They just fell in love with the team. I was one of the luckiest players in the world. What a unique era it was."

The ballpark, County Stadium, was supposed to be a minor-league park, and except for the two-tiered grandstand that made a half-moon behind home plate, this was obvious. Down the lines, the grandstands stopped, replaced by odd single-level bleachers that would have looked more at home at a high-school football field. The light stanchions stood 115 feet in the air beyond the outfield fences, tall and alone, except for a row of fir and spruce trees in left center field planted in 1954, called, oddly enough, "Perini pines."

The best feature of County Stadium was outside of the park's grounds. On Mockingbird Hill, beyond the right-field fence, sat the

National Soldiers VA Hospital. On game days, the vets could sit outside their rooms and watch the games for free.

The park offered glimpses of the future. It was big and roomy, unencumbered by the funky city blocks and angles that defined the old crackerjacks in Boston and Brooklyn. Hugging the outfield in a crescent beginning at third base and stretching to first was enough parking to satisfy an airport.

The 1953 team responded with immediate success—and magic. On opening day at County Stadium, Billy Bruton beat the Cardinals 3–2, with a tenth-inning home run. Mathews, all of twenty-one years old, hit 47 home runs, scored 110 runs, and drove in 135 to go with a .302 average and a second-place finish for the MVP, behind Roy Campanella. Spahn won twenty-three games, losing only seven. Primarily out of the bull pen, Burdette won fifteen games and saved eight more, while the new acquisition from Cincinnati, twenty-five-year-old Joe Adcock, drove in eighty runs. The club finished a distant second, thirteen games behind the 105-win Dodgers, but a 92-win team was something to embrace. At the gate, Perini led the league in attendance at 1.8 million fans, and the $600,000 loss he took in Boston was turned into a profit of nearly three-quarters of a million. The Boston experience did, however, erode some of Perini's vision. Once in Milwaukee, Perini retreated from his position that television promoted the game and retrenched, refusing to broadcast a significant number of games to his new and excited fan base.

He had been the first owner to move a franchise in half a century, and it worked. Every sad-sack owner in baseball, either saddled behind a more profitable club in the same city or pessimistic about the lump of mud they called home, suddenly wanted to be just like Lou Perini. That was what men of action did with momentum. They found a way to make it work for them, to cultivate it, to give the world the impression that the happenstance of the day was exactly the lucky break for which they had been searching all along.

THE MILWAUKEE IN which Henry Aaron arrived in 1954 was still growing, though not at the rapid pace it had at the turn of the century.

It was adjusting to another transition, one that occurred in the years immediately approaching and following World War II: the arrival of thousands of southern blacks during the great migration north. The postwar increase in the black population would produce for Milwaukee one of its great contradictions, for despite its reputation for tolerance, high-quality-of-life Milwaukee earned a reputation as one of the most severely segregated cities in the country.

Blacks were marginalized in a tight quarter of the city, nicknamed "Bronzeville," which was roughly the rectangle bordered by State Street to the south, North Avenue to the north, and Third and Twelfth streets to the east and west, respectively. The name Bronzeville was most likely a descendant of the black section of Chicago, the destination city for so many southern blacks during the great migration. Bronzeville was managed so tightly by the restrictive housing patterns and lending practices of area banks that a study undertaken by the Milwaukee Commission on Human Rights—titled *The Housing of Negroes in Milwaukee, 1955*—concluded:

> The free choice of residence in the open housing market which ecologically stratifies most of our population in terms of income, education and occupation is not operative in the case of Negroes. All those restricted within the arbitrary confines of the racial ghetto must find shelter as best they can within its circumscribed bounds. The Negro middle and upper classes, regardless of their education, skills, professional accomplishments—if their skin is dark—must reside in the slum. The fact that they dislike the disorganizing and predatory features as greatly as do their white social status counterparts avails them naught.

Henry and Barbara, who was now pregnant, rented an apartment on Twenty-ninth Street, close to Bill Bruton and Jim Pendleton. Henry was eager to breathe the air of the big leagues—to measure his ability against the top competition in the sport, to absorb the fullness of the dream of being a major-league ballplayer—but navigating his new city outside of the ballpark was a far less attractive challenge. He had always been the boy who wanted to escape, the one most comfortable in his own private space or on the baseball diamond, not easily gregarious by nature. Thus, it wasn't with great enthusiasm that Henry went about the inevitable but important chore of wading through the idiosyncrasies of his new city, even though he was immediately taken by the nightlife there. Milwaukee was not Chicago, but when it came to hoisting a glass, it was on par with any city. "The first thing I noticed about Milwaukee," Henry would say, "was the number of bars. Milwaukee was definitely a drinking town."

More than any other player on the Braves, it was Billy Bruton who eased Henry's transition. "If it weren't for Bill Bruton," Henry would say, "I don't know if I would have made it those early years. He was like a big brother and a father to me, all at the same time. He showed me the way."

Eight years older than Henry, William Haron Bruton was born November 9, 1925, in Panola, Alabama, on the outskirts of Birmingham. Unlike most of his teammates, including Henry, for whom baseball was the only destination, Bruton saw baseball as a vehicle that could provide greater opportunities and acceptance for him off of the field, opportunities not yet existing for blacks. As an adolescent, he moved to Wilmington, Delaware, with the childhood dream of becoming a chemist, but he would later say that he chose baseball because he believed that chemistry was not yet a field in which a person of color could succeed. He had not even begun to think of baseball as a career, because during his youth, the game had still been closed to black players. By the time he had been discovered playing center field for the San Francisco Cubs, a barnstorming club that toured the Midwest, Bruton was twenty-four years old, talented enough to play in the major leagues but too old to be taken seriously as a prospect by a major-league club. After the legendary scout Bill Yancey instructed Bruton to shave four years off of his age to make him more attractive to big-league clubs, the Boston Braves signed Bruton to a minor-league contract to play at Eau Claire. He was a tall and lean left-handed hitter, six feet tall but weighing barely 170 pounds, possessor of blazing speed and sharp defensive instinct. When Bruton was promoted to Denver before joining the Braves, he had been nicknamed "the Ebony Comet" by the local fans.

It was Jackie Robinson who received the attention, but Billy Bruton was one of the many unsung black players who had a special role in the integration of the game. Along with Roy White, he had integrated the Northern League two years before Henry arrived, and, like Henry, he had been welcomed into the home of Susan Hauck. Few players were as committed to challenging the conditions for black players in the game as Bill Bruton. He was as frustrated and impatient for equal opportunity as Robinson, yet he possessed interpersonal skills that made him popular with the overwhelmingly white Milwaukee fans—but not at the price of his dignity—without having to play the caricature of the disarming Negro. He did not raise his voice, or often show flashes of temper, but almost immediately after reaching the big leagues, Billy Bruton had become the de facto ambassador to Braves management for the black players of the team. He would be the first black player on the Braves to live year-round in Milwaukee, and being an older player—he was a twenty-seven-year-old rookie when he made his big-league debut in 1953—he was more mature than the younger players.

Bruton was serious and religious, and he immediately commanded the respect of his peers, even during a humiliating time. His wife, Loretta, did not attend spring-training games, because she refused to sit in segregated seating, apart from the wives of the white players. "There were beaches everywhere in Florida, but none where she could go with the other wives," Bruton once said. "I had to eat in the kitchens of roadside restaurants . . . or wait for a Negro cab driver to come along and tell me where I could get a meal. All I could ask myself was, 'How long would I have to suffer such humiliation?' "

Bruton was the black elder of the Braves, and he had immediately taken Henry under his wing. He taught Henry important aspects of the big-league life: how to tip, which cities were particularly difficult for black players, which parts of Milwaukee were friendly and which were not. Duffy Lewis had, in effect, made Bruton his deputy when it came to dealing with the logistics of the separate life black players were required to live. Lewis made Bruton his proxy. It was Bruton who handed out meal money and, most important in spring training, learned the transportation schedules of black cabdrivers and buses, as well as restaurants, barbershops, all of the details black players needed to know, being apart from the rest of the team.

. . .

INSIDE THE CLUBHOUSE, the youth of the team served as a major benefit. It meant there would be less sifting through an established, rigid culture. Unlike most clubs that contended for a championship, the 1954 Milwaukee Braves possessed an optimism that stemmed more from talent than experience. The Braves were in gestation, a talented club high on potential but low on actual checks on their big-league résumés. The Rookie Rocket may not have been able to keep the club in Boston, but Perini was correct in his belief that his club was on the verge of becoming a force. Henry was now another addition to the Braves stockpile.

The lone exception was Warren Spahn, who represented the dominant personality of the clubhouse. In 1954, Spahn was thirty-three, eleven years older than Mathews, thirteen years older than Henry. He had been with the organization since before Pearl Harbor, having signed as an amateur free agent with the Boston Bees in 1940. When the Braves were poised to rise to prominence in their new home, Spahn was already the most gifted and prolific left-hander in the game.

He came from Buffalo and was from the outset a star athlete. His father, Edward, pitched in the semipro leagues and city teams in Buffalo and played on and managed traveling teams in Canada. The city teams had no age limits, and Edward Spahn and young Warren played on the same team.

He was, like most superior athletes, always competitive, on and off the field, but perhaps not exactly by choice.

"My grandfather was a shortstop, played third base on occasion when the team needed him to," Warren Spahn's son, Greg, recalled of his grandfather Edward Spahn. "He was a little, wiry guy. He absolutely loved baseball. He drove my father so much, he always told me he wasn't going to do to me what his father had done to him. My father was given no other option but to play baseball. Looking back on it, I wish he would have driven me more. It was just an over-reaction to what his father had done to him."

There were qualities in his personality and background that set

Warren Spahn apart from his contemporaries. The writers consistently made note of his extensive vocabulary, erudition, and wide interests, taking great effort to paint him as the pitcher as intellectual. His arrival in the big leagues in 1942 as a twenty-one-year-old was nearly his downfall. Casey Stengel, salty and unsentimental, was the Braves manager. Stengel banished Spahn to the minor leagues one day after he refused to throw at Brooklyn shortstop Pee Wee Reese during a spring-training game. "He told my father he did not have enough guts to be a major-league pitcher, and that became a big point of contention for my family over the next couple of years," Greg Spahn said.

Spahn was drafted in 1942 and served three full years with the U.S. Army Combat Engineers. Unlike that of many higher-profile players, his military service was not a country club existence, putting on baseball exhibitions stateside for starry-eyed superiors. He saw combat in Europe, was wounded in Germany, and fought in the Battle of the Bulge, the monthlong battle along the Rhine, where 19,000 Americans were killed and another 47,000 wounded. He received a battlefield commendation in France. During the European campaign, Spahn suffered a shrapnel wound to the leg. For his wartime service, he would be awarded two Bronze Stars and two Purple Hearts.

"At the Bridge at Remagen his foot was hit by shrapnel from the bridge being bombed. At the Battle of the Bulge he suffered a laceration across the back of his neck," Greg Spahn recalled. "He had a six-inch scar across the back of his neck. After he came back from the war, he would always say, 'Pressure? This isn't pressure. No one's going to shoot at me if I don't pitch well.' "

During the war, Warren met his wife, LoRene, a native Oklahoman, and the family settled in Broken Arrow, near her hometown. When he returned to the major leagues in 1946, Stengel was gone and Spahn, at twenty-five, won his first big-league game. He posted an 8–5 record in 1946 and then began one of the great pitching streaks in baseball history. In 1947, Spahn won twenty-one games and lost ten. The next year, the Braves won the pennant for the first time since 1914, with Spahn immortalized in baseball history by *Boston Post* sports editor Gerald V. Hern.

First we'll use Spahn
then we'll use Sain
Then an off day
followed by rain

Back will come Spahn
followed by Sain
And followed
we hope
by two days of rain

The poem survived the years as a two-verse rhyme, "Spahn and Sain and Pray for Rain." For his part, Spahn went just 15–12 in 1948, producing the second-lowest win total of his career between 1948 and 1963. Johnny Sain, who won twenty-four that year, was the legitimate ace of the staff, but legend never worries about such details.

Like Johnny Logan, the shortstop, Spahn was hesitant about the move to Milwaukee. Months before Perini petitioned the National League to relocate, Spahn opened a restaurant in Boston, Warren Spahn's Tavern on Commonwealth Avenue, just across from Braves Field.

Spahn was simply different, distant in age and experiences from the younger players. He was a practical joker but could possess a cruel sense of humor, one that could make other players uncomfortable. Over the years, the relationship between Warren Spahn and Henry Aaron would fluctuate. Henry thought Spahn took pleasure in being a merry antagonist, the kind of person who would locate someone's most sensitive spot and use it as fertile ground for humor. Spahn's personality was exactly the kind Henry disliked the most— the guy who needled others for fun. "Spahn and I," Henry would say fifty years later, "we had our problems."

While always respectful of each other's considerable ability, the two were not always friendly. "Hank didn't always get Dad, but they definitely had great respect for one another," Greg Spahn recalled.

If Spahn was the established veteran on the young team, Eddie Mathews was symbolic of its youth and vitality. If Spahn was the old pro, Logan the gritty street fighter, Lew Burdette the wily and guileless old pro, and Henry the prodigy, Eddie Mathews was the instant star, the matinee idol who immediately gave a face to the Braves. From the start, though he played his first season in Boston, Mathews captured the imagination of the Milwaukee baseball fan in a way no other member of the Braves would.

Edwin Lee Mathews, Jr., was born October 13, 1931, in Texarkana, Texas, but was raised in Santa Barbara. His father, Edwin senior, moved the family in 1935, in search of work during the Depression. He eventually landed a job as a wire chief, transmitting, among other news, baseball games for Western Union. As a boy, young Edwin was not close to his father. While the elder Mathews made a great effort to play catch with his son, Eddie's earliest memories of his father were the odd hours Edwin senior worked, which prevented him from being home during the hours most fathers were, and the small bottles of alcohol Eddie would find hidden around the house.

Eddie was a two-sport athlete while growing up, excelling both in football and basketball. It was clear even in middle school that he had a special talent. In other, less forgiving cities, a player would have to be homegrown to truly reach the soul of the hometown. When the New York Giants relocated to San Francisco in 1958, Willie Mays was clearly the signature player of the franchise, but the city would not warm to the team until it produced Willie McCovey, its first star without ties to New York. Mathews was different. He was a hero almost from the beginning and would grow as a baseball player as the city became one of the new capitals of the sport. It was a glossy photograph of Mathews swinging away one night in 1954 at County Stadium that served as the initial cover for a new, sports-only magazine, *Sports Illustrated*.

He played baseball with a rugged intensity, wore his emotions nakedly, and was, on the surface, an uncomplicated competitor. What drew Milwaukee to Mathews was his grinding drive, often bordering on a rage, which, because of his passion, seemed glamorous. His youth and power made him something of a heartthrob to female fans. He connected to Milwaukee, Chuck Tanner thought, because of his almost pathological drive to succeed. That, plus Mathews's rages, gave Milwaukee a player who reflected the city's idealized vision of itself as a blue-collar, hardworking city.

He did not back down, ever. Mathews once engaged in a fistfight at third base with Frank Robinson after a hard slide, and brawled with six-foot-six-inch Don Drysdale for making a habit of throwing at Johnny Logan. Mathews, it was said, intimidated even fellow players with a look.

He was so gifted an offensive player, blessed with a smooth, slashing left-handed swing, that players and coaches alike underestimated his defense. In turn, Mathews played with a persistent self-consciousness regarding his abilities as a defensive player. Spahn was considered a sophisticate around the press, while Mathews was prone to fits of silence. He was wary of the writers in general and especially of the ones who did not cover the team on a daily basis. Mathews, even as a young player, was combative with the press. It was Mathews who fit the role of the prototypically tough third baseman, short on words, long on home runs, quick in temperament. He was not a vocal leader, the kind of player the press referred to in those days as a "holler guy." Mathews could be dark and moody, prone to fits of anger and, some of his teammates thought, depression. He was to be feared when he drank, which was often. Mathews was the enforcer in the clubhouse and in the lineup. Almost immediately, Eddie Mathews earned a reputation as a player not to be crossed.

He would be anointed as a superstar not long after he was legally able to drink. Mathews possessed an uncanny level of star power, which attracted immediate attention. Within months of his arrival in the big leagues, he had been forecast to become among the greatest of players. In 1954, it was Mathews whom Charlie Grimm predicted had the best chance to break Babe Ruth's single-season record of sixty home runs, even though County Stadium, with its symmetrical dimensions, did not favor left-handed hitters. The connection to Ruth had begun a year earlier, when before the all-star break, Mathews was ahead of Ruth's 1927 pace, the year he hit sixty home runs. Mathews did not sustain his level of home-run hitting, but he had given everyone a taste.

The Milwaukee hierarchy was so taken with Mathews that one day during the spring, as Henry put on another batting exhibition, Red Thisted of the *Sentinel* asked Mickey Owen if he thought Henry would ever hit for power on a par with Mathews.

"No way," Owen said.

Mathews, dark and distrusting, took time to warm up, but once he did, he could be the fiercest, most loyal of friends. It would be Mathews who would attempt to lessen the pressure on Henry by shielding him from the press when he played well and especially when he did not. "He knew Henry was going to have it rough," Chuck Tanner recalled. "Not that the writers meant anything by it, but Henry was so quiet, so soft-spoken at first that he wasn't going to defend himself when some of the writers got out of line. Eddie used to tell them, 'Get out of here. Leave that kid alone.' And here he was, just a kid himself."

Spahn, Mathews, Burdette, and Bob Buhl formed the core of the most influential clique on the Braves. Burdette and Spahn were roommates in spring training and on the road, as were Buhl and Mathews. They were the best players and the closest friends. Henry was not part of that group, partly because as a black player there were simply too many uncomfortable moments to navigate socially. The other part, however, was because Henry did not drink much, if at all. Growing up as a clubhouse kid in Milwaukee, Henry, Greg Spahn would recall, occasionally sipped a beer after a game, but most times, Greg Spahn would take a bottle of Coca-Cola over to Henry.

The rest of the Braves lived in orbit around the Spahn clique. The pitchers Gene Conley and Carl Sawatski roomed together. Conley was a six-foot-eight-inch right-hander, and after the Antonelli trade for Bobby Thomson, he was expected to be the fourth starter in the rotation behind Spahn, Burdette, and Bob Buhl. Conley, like Spahn, grew up in Oklahoma and was a natural athlete. He played football, baseball, and basketball. He accepted a scholarship to Washington State and found himself in the fortunate position of being in the middle of a bidding war between John Quinn and Red Auerbach, the coach of the Boston Celtics.

Gene Conley was the athlete as individual. He cut his own figure in an industry where a certain unchallenged conformity was expected. He was not apolitical, nor, despite coming of age during a time of political and social upheaval, did he share strong views on race. He often spoke of himself as somewhat naïve about the pressures of racial separation. Once as a ten-year-old living in Muskogee, Oklahoma, Conley took a black friend to the municipal pool. The two swam and enjoyed themselves without incident. When young Gene walked home, the director of the pool stopped him and told him never to bring his friend to the public pool again or both would face serious consequences.

In later years, when playing for the Boston Celtics, Gene Conley was drawn to the complexities and talents of Bill Russell, but at the time he was not attuned to the different, harsher road for black baseball players. Conley remembers the early black ballplayers on the Braves—George Crowe, Bill Bruton, Jim Pendleton, and Henry Aaron—dressing in the same corner of the clubhouse. The clubhouse man, Joe Taylor, gave the black players lockers in the same corner, away from the whites. Henry and his black teammates were unofficially segregated from the rest of the team, often showering together and dressing together when the white players had finished, unsure about crossing in the clubhouse the racial divide that had not yet been erased in society at large. Conley recalled the dynamic being appalling, but he also did not remember knowing quite how to confront an obvious wrong.

Henry's inaugural season in the major leagues would be more a challenge of maddening perseverance than Broadway triumph. The pennant forecast for 1954 never materialized. He was quite good, proving that the spring hype surrounding him was no mirage, but the dream of duplicating the grand entrance to the big leagues of his two childhood idols—both Joe DiMaggio and Stan Musial won the World Series in their first full seasons—was a fantasy best left to the silver screen.

The Braves jerked around in the standings, wobbly at sea all season long, at times fearsome, only to then nose-dive into the mud. No team in baseball—not the perennials, the mighty Yankees and Dodgers, nor the two teams that actually won the pennant, the Giants and 111-win Cleveland—would beat other teams as manically as Milwaukee, only to follow such wins with fatal stretches of mediocrity. Three times over the course of the campaign, the Braves would catch fire, winning at least ten games. On a fourth occasion, they were nearly as good, winning nine in a row. But while those torrid streaks represented nearly half of the Braves eighty-nine wins, the rest of the season wasn't nearly so glamorous. Spahn won his requisite twenty-one games, but Burdette was a languid 15–14. One of the Rookie Rockets, Buhl, lost his first seven starts and lost his spot in the rotation, while another, Conley, won fourteen and kept an uneven team interesting.

HENRY WOULD EXPERIENCE much of the same, his rookie season resembling a volatile stock. There was opening day, April 13, at Crosley Field in Cincinnati, facing Joe Nuxhall, and Henry Louis Aaron, twenty years old, starting left fielder, batting fifth between Andy Pafko and Joe Adcock, bounced into an inning-ending double play in his first big-league at bat, debuting with the goose egg, zero for five. Two days later, at home against the Cardinals in the bottom of the first, he doubled in the right-center gap off Vic Raschi for his first big-league hit. Eight days later, in St. Louis, it was Raschi again, the ill-tempered ex-Yankee, who served up home run number one. It came in the sixth inning of a fourteen-inning, 7–5 win. And two days after that came the first breakout game, when Henry went five for six.

And then there would be games like the epic one on the afternoon of June 10, against Willie Mays and the first-place Giants. The Braves were home, playing the twelfth game of what would be a disastrous seventeen-game home stand, in which they had already lost nine games and were falling out of the pennant race before the solstice. Henry endured a day to remember. He went two for four that day, and while in the box score that was all that mattered, Henry just might have played the worst game of his life. Twice he came to bat with runners on. First, he bounced into a double play, only to follow up by hitting into a force play while each pitcher tossed zeroes at the other.

NONE OF THIS would have mattered much under normal circumstances, but on this day, Gene Conley and Rubén Gómez weren't pitching; they were fighting for the last scrap of beef on the table. Plus, Willie was in center, and the rookie Henry would always feel a special twinge when playing against Mays. Neither pitcher had given up a run, nor had either one of them any intention of giving in. Henry singled in his other two at bats, but once he got on base, that was when the trouble started. Standing on third, with one out, Bruton lofted a fly to center. Mays camped under the ball, squaring himself to throw. Henry tagged and broke for the plate, the *rookie challenging the great Mays in a 0–0 game.* Mays uncorked a good one, a hard one-hopper that skidded off the dirt cutout at home plate and into the mitt of the Giants catcher, Wes Westrum. The throw was true, and the home plate umpire, Jocko Conlan, waded into the choking cloud of dust, looked at Westrum and Aaron tangled on top of home plate, threw up the right hand, and signaled Henry out. It didn't matter that Johnny Logan dressed Conlan down for blowing the call (Logan got tossed, and so did Burdette, who seconded Logan's argument); Mays had won the battle, and Henry skulked to the dugout.

It was still scoreless in the ninth, and Henry singled again to start the winning rally. Danny O'Connell sacrificed him to second, and the managerial wheels started turning. Leo Durocher, the Giants manager, walked Catfish Metkovich to get to Conley, who even in the ninth inning was hitting for himself against Gómez. Conley looped a short fly to right. Don Mueller, the right fielder, snared the ball and, to his surprise, saw Henry off the bag between second and third. Mueller fired to second, and for the third time in one game, Henry ended an inning with a double play.

Only the finale made it worse. Conley started the tenth by striking out Mays and then gave up a pinch home run to Bill Taylor, losing the game, 1–0.

THROUGH IT ALL, Charlie Grimm, the skipper, took on the persona of a double agent. On the good days, he would talk about Aaron as they all did in the spring, the can't-miss, a member of the millionth percentile club, the guy with talent to spare.

But during the bad times, when Henry struggled through a slump in May and Grimm benched him, replacing him with a trimmer, slimmer Pendleton (it lasted one day; Pendleton went zero for three), it was "Jolly Cholly" (as the papers called him), who so very much enjoyed being one of the guys, who would join in with the razzing of Henry. Grimm told the writers that Henry had seemed tired from playing baseball year-round, and that he was probably a little stressed that the draft board had contacted him and it wasn't quite clear if he would be wearing a different type of uniform in 1955. But Grimm still borrowed Adcock's line and referred to Henry as "Snowshoes," yukking it up with the boys at the rookie's expense. It was Charlie Grimm who would remark to the writers that Henry looked as though he were sleepwalking, except when he was hitting. Occasionally, even Grimm, the manager, would call Henry "Stepin Fetchit," a nickname the press—since it came with the imprimatur of the skipper—was all too willing to pick up and print.

AARON GOOD NOW, MAY TURN GREAT

Young Braves Fielder Has Won Respect of Pitchers over League as Dangerous Hitter

NEW YORK, N.Y. — He throws sidearm from the outfield and runs the bases like Stepin Fetchit with a hopped up motor. But . . . Henry Aaron is one of the most promising hitters in the major leagues. . . .

. . . the 20-year-old Negro is deceptively fast, and at least an ordinary hand at getting his outfield chores done, even if he has his own way of going about them.

On the Braves, the prevailing view of Charlie Grimm was one of benevolence. Johnny Logan loved Grimm, as did Conley and Mathews. Mathews believed Grimm to be one of the better baseball men he'd encountered, but he knew Charlie was too close to his players. Henry, however, did not care much for Grimm. Aaron believed it was Grimm who was responsible for much of the hazing he took from his teammates and the press during the season.

If nothing else, Henry believed that Grimm should not have encouraged the creation of a minstrel character. It was Grimm's responsibility, Henry believed, to shield him from some of the harsher layers as fans adjusted to seeing blacks on the same field as whites. Robinson had such protectors, Branch Rickey and Charlie

Dressen, as did Mays with Durocher. Henry had a guy calling him "Snowshoes" to the press.

The Sporting News would devote an item on April 15, 1954, a full seven years after Robinson reached the majors, to the moment in the Braves-Cardinals game when, in the eighth inning, Milwaukee became the first team to field an all-black outfield during a regular-season game.

But he kept hitting, not to the .300 mark, which was the gold standard for good hitters, but not under .270, either. In late May, Grimm moved Henry to the cleanup position and Henry struggled with the responsibility of hitting fourth, at one point posting a dreadful mark of just five hits in forty-one at bats. He was fourth in the all-star balloting, but making the all-star team as a rookie was, in those days, a long shot (though it wasn't lost on Henry that DiMaggio was the first to ever accomplish the feat). At one point during the season, Henry admitted that there were a couple of pitchers who were intent on giving him the business. One was Larry Jackson, the hard-throwing lefty with the Cardinals, and the second was a journeyman with the Philadelphia Phillies named Herm Wehmeier. "I don't know what I did to those fellows," Henry said. "But they both worked me over pretty good."

At the all-star break, the Braves were fifteen and a half out. By August 1, the Braves had shaved six games off the lead. Being a mile away from first place wasn't part of the plan, but the Braves were especially galling, considering they were in fourth place, with the best pitching staff in the league. But they won twenty of twenty-two games in August to make it interesting. By the fifteenth, the lead was three and a half.

In the second game of a doubleheader at Crosley Field, where Henry had made his big-league debut, fate reappeared. The Braves won the first game 11–8, their sixth in a row. The lead was still six and a half games, with twenty-three to play, but they were alive and still had three games left with the league-leading Giants.

In the nightcap, the Reds had leaped all over them. First it was Jim Wilson, then Joey Jay, the bonus baby, and, finally, Spahn in relief. Down 7–1 in the top of the seventh, Pendleton singled for Spahn and the dam burst. The Braves batted around. Henry singled and scored a run and a poor sucker named Corky Valentine walked off the mound at the end of the inning, down 8–7.

The next inning, Henry faced a big left-hander named Harry Perkowski and boomed a cannon shot into the deepest part of the old park. Adcock raced around with an insurance run and Henry dashed to third, sliding hard. His body carried past the bag. His left ankle did not. The bone snapped cleanly. The stretcher came next. Bobby Thomson, the man whose broken ankle in spring training had put Henry in the big leagues in the first place, ironically ran for him at third.

Once Henry went down, the end came quickly. On September 10, down four games to the Giants and two ahead of the Dodgers, with seventeen to play and riding another ten-game win streak, the Braves arrived in Brooklyn for a two-game showdown and lost both. Adcock, who made a habit of wearing out the Dodgers (Clem Labine had already beaned him earlier in the season), followed Henry to the hospital, after Newcombe fired a fastball headed for Adcock's cheek in the opener. Big Joe threw up his right hand in defense and the ball cracked the bone. Then they lost another in Philly, and all three at the Polo Grounds to the Giants. They finished in third place, eight games behind the Giants and four behind the Dodgers. Henry underwent surgery, had pins set into his ankle, and thought about 1955.

After the World Series, Henry found the price of losing wasn't just the pennant. He'd lost the final month of the season and, with that, a chance at the Rookie of the Year award. He finished fourth, behind his teammate Conley, a young shortstop with the Chicago Cubs named Ernie Banks, and the winner, Wally Moon of the Cardinals.

IN LATER YEARS, Henry would reveal modest disappointment at not having won the award, and even a bit more at having finished fourth. By the time the season was over, however, Henry Aaron had learned something far more valuable than a trophy. He had seen them all up close—Willie Mays, the rookie Ernie Banks, the great Stan Musial, and, as a player, even the great Jackie Robinson—and none had intimidated him. He would later say he had learned how deeply his pride ran, and how that pride, comparing his abilities with those of his contemporaries, was the ingredient that truly fueled his motivation.

In the off-season, after the pins were taken out of his ankle and he could walk without crutches, Henry did not think about the 1955 season or about fitting in with his new team. He thought of the big picture, about his legacy. He had been in the big leagues for all of five months, and he had resolved to pursue one goal: He wanted three thousand hits. It was a goal that seemed far outside what he had accomplished in just one injury-shortened season, the place of immortals. At the end of the 1954 season, only seven players in the history of the sport had crossed the three thousand mark, but after only one season in the big leagues, Henry had reached a seminal conclusion: There was nothing on a baseball diamond that he could not do.

PART TWO

MAGIC

CHAPTER FIVE

WEHMEIER

ON THE FRIGID, festive evening of January 22, 1956, in the middle of Milwaukee's most prestigious banquet room, the Grand Ballroom of the Wisconsin Club, Charlie Grimm took out his banjo and strummed "Has Anybody Seen My Gal?" When Charlie followed up with "When You Wore a Tulip"—a capella, *in German,* no less—the place went wild.

That was the night the Milwaukee chapter of the Baseball Writers Association of America descended upon the Wisconsin Club and honored Charlie as the inaugural recipient of the Sam Levy Memorial Plaque, for meritorious service to baseball. Not a whiff of negativity interrupted the bonhomie. Jolly Cholly was in his element, awash in the moment, whooping it up with the scribes, sharing the dais with two of his best kids, Chuck Tanner, the outfielder whom the writers had chosen as the 1955 team's top rookie, and Henry Aaron, who in his second year had been chosen—over the forty-one-homer Mathews—as the team's Most Valuable Player.

Pretty heady stuff, all of it was—a harbinger. The season itself had been anticlimactic: the Braves had spent all of 1955 looking up at the Dodgers—who not only dusted the rest of the National League but finally beat the Yankees in the World Series after five losses—but individually, Henry had turned in a star performance: .314 average, 27 home runs, 106 runs driven in. In keeping with their unflattering portraits of Henry the person, the writers would have been remiss had they not reminded the world that Henry that night was about as animated as a three-toed sloth: "Aaron, who rarely shows emotion of any kind, admitted he was 'thrilled' by the honor," *The Sporting News* reported. The truth was that Henry was quite proud of his 1955 season. He was upset that the year before, in 1954, Wally Moon had hit .300, while he had not, and it likely had cost him the Rookie of the Year award. In later years, he would remark that he was "disappointed at not winning. Not because Moon didn't deserve it . . . he did. I just thought I could have done better. I figured if he could hit .300, I could, too." He had better than doubled his home run total and by crossing the 100-RBI mark had initiated an enduring history as a devastating run producer.

The banquet was held ten days before his twenty-second birthday, and Henry was already enjoying a healthy sampling of the big-league caviar: single-breasted tuxedo with notched lapels, white carnation and winged collar, rubbing elbows with Frank Zeidler, the Socialist mayor of Milwaukee, National League president Warren Giles, and the commissioner himself, Ford Frick. The Grand Ballroom packed in over six hundred that night. But the club, as a general rule since opening its doors in 1891 with a goal of "promoting and providing a venue for German-American understanding and fellowship," did not yet routinely admit blacks. For Henry, the rules were waived for one evening.

The night belonged to Grimm. No less an authority than *The Sporting News* reported that even sharing the stage with an obvious comer like Aaron and the kid Tanner, shining brightly as a future star of the Braves, it still was Grimm who "stole the show," strumming "Shanty Town" on his left-handed banjo. While Grimm gushed about his excitement over the coming year, Henry reached the podium with characteristic deference. "We'll be striving," he said, "to bring all you fine Milwaukee people a pennant in 1956." Tanner, green as the outfield grass, did not veer off of the reservation: "I'm sure we have the men who can do it."

In only three years, Grimm had placed twice and showed, finishing third in 1954. In public, the Braves tipped their cap to the Dodgers, who rushed out of the blocks so quickly that nobody was going to catch them. There was no shame in losing the pennant to a team that had started the season 18–2 and went wire-to-wire. It was a boat race, Charlie said, just one of those fluky years when everything went right for a club; it just happened not to be his. The Dodgers were hungry—starving, in fact—for that first World Series and nobody, not even the

Yankees this time, was going to stand in the way. Brooklyn had been schlepping for that first title since 1884, and with that group—Robinson and Reese, Duke Snider, the hard-hat Furillo, all soon to be Roger Kahn's famed "Boys of Summer"—well, you had to figure they were going to make a last stand.

That was one way to look at it. Another way was to say that something was terribly wrong with a franchise that had Spahn, Burdette, Mathews, Adcock, and a rising Aaron and yet could only look at the Dodgers backside for six months. Tipping the cap was for the public. Internally Perini and his brain trust believed that, the Dodgers aside, maybe the problem existed from within. The Braves lost the 1955 pennant by thirteen and a half games and the closest they got to the Dodgers for the whole year was a distant ten and a half. It was indeed a boat race, and the Braves, supposedly a powerhouse, were left drifting harmlessly in the East River wake.

Showdowns between the two clubs further convinced Perini. Twenty-two times Milwaukee took the field with Brooklyn in 1955, and fifteen times the Brooks came out on top. And it didn't matter if the games were held in narrow, boxy Ebbets Field or in the wide-open spaces of County Stadium, because while the Braves dropped eight of eleven games in Flatbush, they did only one better at home, losing seven of eleven at County Stadium. If Milwaukee couldn't beat Brooklyn straight up, there would be no pennant. As the winter progressed, Perini began asking himself the question with a bit more frequency. Maybe the problem wasn't Don Newcombe and Jackie and Pee Wee, as the conventional wisdom suggested. Maybe the problem was Charlie Grimm.

AT THE END of 1955, Grimm realized that the question of his survival was a fire he had to contain. While the Dodgers were about to taste the champagne, the word was that Grimm was out in Milwaukee, heading back to his beloved Cubs for a front-office position. No matter how much sand he applied, it was a rumor he could not extinguish. "I shouldn't dignify either question with an answer," he told the Associated Press. "I can't deny anything which has no basis to it. I have not been contacted by the Cubs. I have another year on my contract here, and as far as I know, I will be back. And I am definitely not throwing in the towel here." The Cubs rumor wasn't exactly hearsay; Grimm was at his baseball best on the North Side, both as a player and a manager, and he didn't hide just how much he loved that franchise.°

Perini was no coffee shop owner, oblivious to the day-to-day operation while Quinn made him money. He read the papers, kept his radar tuned, listened to what was being said around town. In 1956, Perini toured England to explore an expansion of a different type: He wanted baseball owners to consider buying financial stakes in English cricket and soccer teams, a foreign exchange of sorts, a cross-marketing endeavor that would be consummated in full nearly a half century later, when George Steinbrenner entered his New York Yankees into a partnership with the English soccer dynasty Manchester United.

Perini was aware of the knocks about his club: Milwaukee wasn't tough enough in the clutch. They liked chasing the girls as much as chasing the pennant, and maybe a whole lot more. Even Adcock, their man-mountain first baseman, might have been a little more Jane than Tarzan. Adcock was a beast. He could rip a phone book in half with his bare hands. But Joe would never charge the mound. Pitchers could throw at him. Newcombe had put him in the hospital not once, but twice. Mathews used to try to fire him up—"Kick his ass, Joe. We're right behind you"—but it did no good.

They had good players, and the boys weren't afraid to mix it up, either. Henry used to say that Johnny Logan was the best at starting a fight, and Mathews the best at finishing it. But leadership, the kind that won pennants and not split decisions during a rhubarb, was another matter.

Perini knew his team's weakness because everybody else did, too. Put all the clichés in a hat and pick one—"Baseball is a funny game"; "Sometimes a team just has your number"; "Those guys in the other uniforms are getting paid, too"—but none of the old saws could beat

°If anyone ever needed proof where Charlie left his heart, it was provided by the choice of his final resting place. Following his death in 1983, his widow received permission from the Cubs to spread his ashes over the Wrigley Field outfield. The Cubs heartily agreed and the widow Grimm did just that.

the trump-card edict of all winning ball clubs: "Beat the teams you're supposed to beat."

The two bottom-feeders of the National League—eighty-four-loss St. Louis and ninety-four-loss Pittsburgh—beat Milwaukee a combined twenty-two times in 1955. Getting beaten by the patsies of the league, more than anything that was happening at Ebbets Field, was what cost the Braves the pennant. Within the organization, the Braves knew too many games were being lost to the previous night's hangover. Perini knew it, Quinn knew it, and the Braves coaches knew it. And if that wasn't bad enough, the Brooklyn Dodgers knew it, too. And it was, of all people, the furious Robinson, who would always tell his mates, and sometimes the press, too, that when the Braves were good enough to get to the table, Milwaukee just didn't have the fire to close the deal.

To make it official, *The Sporting News* put the Braves business in the street for all to see, summarizing with a simple, deadly sentence: "What the Braves need, more than anything else," read a paragraph on September 28, 1955, "is that intangible thing called spark."

Grimm *was* in the final year of his contract, but instead of providing security, not having a guaranteed future in Milwaukee beyond 1956 only made him look like a lame duck should the Braves struggle early. Add to that a little extra kindling: the persistent rumor that Perini and Quinn didn't just want to ax Cholly; they wanted to replace him with the ferocious, canny Leo Durocher, who had just been bounced by the Giants. Everybody knew "the Lip" could wear out his welcome in places faster than he could drop an *F* bomb on the home plate umpire, but the man could manage. Charlie never got to the Series as a player, and as a manager, he saw his Cubs lose to the Yankees in 1932 and to the Tigers in 1935 and 1945. Durocher, meanwhile, won it all as a player with Ruth and won it all again with Dizzy Dean, and he would go down as the guy who inspired the nickname "the Gashouse Gang" for the 1934 Cardinals. He was hated, especially by the umps and the commissioner's office, and maybe by some of his players, but in those days, Leo's teams didn't get worse when the leaves started to change. They didn't miss when they sniffed a pennant, like they did in 1941 with the Dodgers—also in 1947, though Durocher had been suspended for a year for associating with gamblers—and in the miraculous 1951 season and the title year of 1954 with the Giants. No Durocher team would get shut out by the Pirates three times in a season when there was money to be had.°

Durocher didn't just know how to manage; he lived the game, turned it inside out, studied the seams, felt baseball the way a pianist fingered his keys. "Baseball is a lot like church," Durocher used to say. "Many attend, but few understand."

Putting Durocher in charge of the Braves held special portent for a young Henry Aaron. It was Durocher who was Jackie Robinson's manager when Robinson reached the majors in 1947. It was Durocher who took Willie Mays under his wing when Mays was called up in 1951 and the Giants won the pennant. The day after Aaron was honored in Milwaukee, Mays was in Minneapolis, attending a banquet in honor of Bill Rigney, the Giants new manager for 1956. That "the Franchise" flew to Minneapolis in January to welcome his new manager was significant, especially because Mays *still* walked on water for hitting .477 for the Minneapolis Millers before being called up to the big club for good in 1951. But instead of concentrating on Rigney, Willie talked nearly as much about how much he would miss Durocher.

"He was more than just a manager to me. I can't explain it, but I know what Leo did for me," Mays said, adding, "but certainly I'll give Rigney 100 percent."

Mays would be professional for Rigney, but he was no Durocher. Durocher knew how to talk to Willie, how to motivate him, coax the best performances out of him. Durocher was caustic, but knew how to chastise Willie without breaking his confidence. While Willie would have run through a brick wall for Durocher, Henry had Charlie Grimm calling him "Stepin Fetchit." It was Grimm who repeated the old stories about how Henry didn't know who Ford Frick was, even though the commissioner was seated next to him while Cholly sang like it was Saturday night at the *hofbrau.* And while it was

---

°And then Durocher signed on to manage the Cubs. In 1969, the Cubs appeared headed to their first World Series since 1945, holders of a nine-game lead over St. Louis and a nine-and-a-half-game lead over New York on August 15, only to lose the division to the Mets by eight games. Durocher would manage five more seasons and would never again come so close to a pennant.

Durocher who clashed with Robinson in the way that intense, driven men do, each stoking their similar, smoldering fires, Robinson would always respect Durocher for extracting from him the competitive elements that would make him great. But Durocher, who came from the bare-knuckle town of West Springfield, Massachusetts, didn't care about skin color, not if you had the goods to be a ballplayer.

"I don't care if the guy is yellow or black or has stripes like a fuckin' zebra," Durocher said in early 1947 when white Dodgers resisted the idea of being Robinson's teammate. "I'm the manager and I say he plays."

Durocher, Perini also knew, provided instant credibility, the big New York name that would trumpet to the baseball universe that Milwaukee wasn't the bushes. By drawing two million fans twice, Perini was already the financial envy of the baron class, especially the owners who chafed at being second in those two-team cities—the Philadelphia A's and St. Louis Browns had skipped town to Kansas City and Baltimore, respectively, within a year after Perini left Boston—and he knew he was close to fielding a dominant team, as well.

All of which added up to one nagging, significant thing: *expectations*, the kind that defined hungry baseball cities like New York and Boston, the kind that were just descending on Milwaukee and threatening to upset the idyllic equilibrium, free eggs and free cheese and free gas for a smile and an honest effort. Big-league baseball may have existed in Milwaukee for less than five years, but the attitude shift from just "happy to have a team" to "We deserve a pennant" was happening faster than Henry's wrists whipped through the strike zone.

And there was the pressure of time. Financially, Perini recognized a window of opportunity when he saw one. There was already talk of more franchise moves. Philadelphia had left for Kansas City and St. Louis left for Baltimore in 1954, and it was only a matter of time before baseball expanded to the West Coast and the South. The night at the Wisconsin Club was good hot stove fun, but the truth of the matter was that in little unassuming Milwaukee, Perini was outdrawing the big boys of New York. On the field, with Spahn and Burdette on the hill, plus Mathews, Adcock, and Aaron, the Braves owned a front line that was better than that of the Giants, and rivaled that of the Yankees and the Dodgers. Yet all three had titles, while Milwaukee had a manager who proved he could play the banjo and come in in second place. In the weeks leading up to spring training, before the Braves reported to Bradenton, Perini hit the Milwaukee dinner circuit, where he often said publicly, "We should win the pennant." The simmering message in Milwaukee for 1956 was an obvious one, and it was being sent to Charlie Grimm, by his own bosses, special delivery: Win it now. Win the pennant . . . *now* . . . or else.

HENRY DID NOT live in Milwaukee during the winter. He, Barbara, and their daughter, Gaile, now almost two years old, went back to Toulminville, living in the house on Edwards Street. Unlike the year before, when he'd hopped around on crutches and wondered how his ankle would respond, Henry had been healthy when preparing for 1956. At the end of the 1955 season, he had accepted an invitation to join an all-black barnstorming team assembled by Willie Mays and Don Newcombe. The touring team, originally formed by Jackie Robinson following the 1947 season, was inherited by Mays from Roy Campanella, and it might have been the best barnstorming team ever assembled, even rivaling the Satchel Paige teams in the 1930s. For Henry, the invitation served as another indication that if he was not yet being discussed as one of the game's elite players, his potential was obvious. He belonged.

The most telling element of the team wasn't who played—in addition to Mays, the club featured Henry and the whiz shortstop Ernie Banks, who banged forty-four homers in 1955—but who didn't play. Most specifically, it was how little of the American League was represented. Aside from the Cleveland Indians, American League team owners would fight being on the wrong side of history for decades, but the proof lay in their rosters: Integration was virtually nonexistent in the American League. Of the powerful men who ran the league—Boston's Yawkey and Cronin, George Weiss of the Yankees, Calvin Griffith of the Washington Senators, Campbell and Briggs of the Tigers—none could boast an even discussable record in regard to racial progressiveness. The great migration of black players to the major leagues was almost entirely a National League phenomenon.

Crowe and Charlie White joined Aaron from the Braves. Newcombe, fresh from beating out the Braves in the regular season, joined the team after the Dodgers finished the Yankees in the World Series. Banks and Gene Baker of the Cubs made up the double-play combination, while the great Negro League and White Sox pitcher Connie Johnson teamed with Joe Black and Brooks Lawrence of the Cardinals on the mound.

The first downside of the tour for Henry was that Sam Jones was also on the squad. Jones, he of the big curveball and famous temper and love of the bottle, was the rare black player who publicly fought with other blacks. Aaron would recall that Jones would even fight with Mays, who had invited him to join the squad in the first place. There really were two Sams: the one who was drunk and the one who had been drinking. Neither was pleasant to Aaron, who saw no advantage in an extended quarrel with Sam Jones. Since Robinson, the unwritten rule among black players was ironclad: Whatever grievances that existed, blacks did not fight other blacks on the field or throw at them. The reasoning was simple: When it came to integration, the real game being played was not taking place on the field. Everyone knew the stereotypes about blacks—how they were short-tempered, quick to fight. Each black knew what he had left before being promoted to the majors, and no one wanted to go back. The first wave of integration was too important to have progress halted by petty gripes between players.

Sam Jones would be his greatest antagonist. Each of Henry's first few seasons would contain at least one new chapter of his twelve-round battle with Jones. For one month in 1955, they were teammates.

The team played thirty-two games. It played against white teams and against Negro League all-star teams. And it was on that barnstorming trip that Henry witnessed the sheer incandescence of Mays. The dates were full, sellouts all. The big stars all had their homecomings: Banks in Dallas, Aaron in Mobile, Mays in Birmingham. The players earned, for the month, between three thousand and four thousand dollars, a big number, considering that in his rookie year of 1954, Henry earned just six thousand dollars for the whole season. Willie played at a thousand watts. In Longview, Texas, the game was delayed twenty-five minutes because even at game time, the line of fans still waiting to enter the ballpark snaked around the block. Mays treated the crowd to a single, a triple, and a home run, and, of course, a signature defensive play that would leave the crowd buzzing. The *Defender* was there, and the main subhead of the story put Mays in lights: "Willie Puts on Power Show."

"The Giants' outfielder also made a tremendous throw from the four-hundred-foot wall in deep center to third base to nail a runner attempting to stretch a double," the paper reported.

They would win every game, laughers mostly—13–3 in Longview, led by Willie; 9–2 in Austin; 12–2 in Waco, with Willie homering and doubling; 10–1 in Corpus Christi, when Willie homered twice; and a 20–1 rout in Hazelhurst, Mississippi, when Willie cleared the fences against an overmatched ragtag band of Negro American League All-Stars.

When the tour concluded with three games at Wrigley Field in Los Angeles, Willie was a supernova; all eyes were trained on him that noted day Americans tuned in to baseball, *November 6*. The barnstormers had won all thirty-one games, but in the finale against the Southern California All-Stars, the music was all but stopped when Willie stepped up to the plate to offer a proper demonstration of how to do the hero thing. Down 4–3, with two on and two out, Mays sliced a three-run job that curved the left-field foul pole, winning it, 6–4.

WILLIE'S WALLOP WINS WINDUP
ON BARNSTORMING TRIP

Los Angeles, Calif. — The Willie Mays–Don Newcombe All Stars concluded their 32-game tour in practically the same way they started the junket. . . .

The team won every game. . . . In the finale at Wrigley Field, 12,012 turned out to see Mays apply a spine-tingling finish to the contest.

. . .

HENRY WASN'T EXACTLY invisible, and in another time, under a different sun, maybe he would have been the headliner. As it was, he was difficult to miss. The *Defender* ran his photo with the story of the Longview game, and when it had finally finished tripping over itself in praise of Mays, the story did eventually note that, yes, Henry had gone four for four with two home runs. Henry homered in the 20–1 destruction at Hazelhurst, again in El Paso, and in the opener in Los Angeles. If Henry had already been convinced of his abilities, the barnstorming trip proved that he could hit with anyone, Willie Mays included. But in building a legend that would live in the mind as well as on the stat sheet, Mays emitted his own unique pheromones—the sweet aroma of stardom—which could not be duplicated.

In small ways, Mays could even transcend Jim Crow. Henry recalled that once, in Birmingham, he and Mays walked into a department store. Mays, eyeing a few suits, pulled out a healthy roll of hundred-dollar bills, more money than a black man was supposed to carry in the Deep South. The store clerk began dialing the telephone, when Mays told him he wasn't just any Negro, but *the* Willie Mays. That changed everything.

"It was okay to be black in the South," Henry would say years later, "but only if you happened to be Willie Mays."

After the trip, Henry returned to Mobile. He worked at Carver Park, the old playground a few blocks from his house, as a recreation supervisor for the city, busy working, with a goal in mind: the batting title. During the early years of his time, before the home run became the definitive measure of a hitter, batting for average was a far more important barometer of a hitter's true ability than hitting for power. It was a combination of hits and power in the tradition of Musial and DiMaggio that was the mark of a true hitter. Anybody could run into one and yank it over the fence, but it took an accomplished batsman to back it all up with a consistently high level of hitting. That's why Musial was so great. Musial would win the batting title seven times, and six times would lead the National League in hits. And he was no Punch-and-Judy hitter. Musial led the league in doubles eight times, triples five times, and though he would never hit 40 home runs in a single season, he would wind up with 475 home runs.

For the bulk of his career, more than Mays, more than Williams, Clemente, or even Ruth, Musial would be Henry's standard of success. When he dreamed about records during the first half of his career, it was not with Ruth in mind, but Musial's National League record for hits.

In early January, Quinn sent Henry his contract for 1956, which called for a salary of twelve thousand dollars. Aaron sent the contract back in the mail, he said, with a note to Quinn that read, "You must have sent me O'Connell's contract by mistake." He would sign for seventeen thousand dollars that season. At home, he enjoyed something of the celebrity life, but the humiliating reminders of Mobile were always close. Six days after sporting the tux at the Wisconsin Club, he was named "Negro mayor" of Mobile for Mardi Gras, the signature event of New Orleans, but whose American roots dated back to 1702, when Mobile was the first capital of the Louisiana Territory. Henry was the guest of honor for dinner at the Elks Club. But Mobile's withering segregation rules immediately reduced Henry, and an incident ensued that he would carry with him for the next half century.

The Elks Club invitation came with a condition: He would be a welcome guest of the club for *one night only* and could bring no guests. When he arrived with Herbert, his father was not allowed entry to see his son's big night. When the evening was complete, Henry would not be allowed to leave the building through the front door with the white guests. Herbert was not just turned away at the door; he was instructed to meet Henry at the back entrance. Henry never forgot this slight. It was America at its most contradictory— saluting excellence while demeaning the individual.

The hype for 1956 started in January at the Wisconsin Club and continued when the trucks rolled out of County Stadium for Bradenton. Lou Perini may have been unsure about Charlie Grimm, and the rest of the league had its doubts that the Braves were capable of staring down the Dodgers, but apart from complaints about his charisma level, no one in baseball took a dissenting view of Henry.

Barbara did not join Henry in Bradenton. She was aware of the local customs, and the routine of having to walk around the outside of the park to the colored entrance (which was hardly an entrance as much as it was a wooden fence slat that had been removed to allow blacks to enter—at full price, of course) would have been too humiliating. She did not want to listen to the jeers and the jibes from the adjacent white sections of Ninth Street Park. She remained in Mobile until the regular season started and the team headed up north.

FOR MOST OF his postcareer life, Henry—and even more passionately his supporters and teammates—would bristle at the lack of star power that accompanied his accomplishments. They would call him the most underrated superstar of all time, a man who never received proper respect for everything he had done in the game. Johnny Logan would tell anyone who would listen that Aaron, day in and out, was a better player than Mays.

"All Mays had over Henry was *flash*," Logan would say, as if star power was valueless.

Yet, in later years, Henry would reflect on those years and conclude that he *was* something of a hotshot, after all, the rising star in the same class as Mantle and Mays. He really was the can't-miss. The personal awards were piling up—MVP in Jacksonville in 1953, team Rookie of the Year in 1954 (Henry's first invitation to the Wisconsin Club), all-star and team MVP in 1955, before he was twenty-two— and he may not have known the details, but he knew he had value. Had he been unaware that he was being projected as an all-time great, he likely would never have sent Quinn's contracts back with sarcastic notes attached.

Branch Rickey, the bushy-eyed Mahatma who was running the Pirates, had tried during the 1955 season to buy Henry from the Braves, offering Perini $150,000. Had he accepted, the Pirate outfield would have featured Aaron and the newest Rickey prospect, a gifted Puerto Rican outfielder who went by the name of Clemente. The careers of Clemente and Aaron would always circle each other. When Clemente was a teenager and Aaron was tearing up the Sally League, it was the Braves that offered Clemente three times what the

Dodgers put forth. But Clemente desired to play in New York more than he wanted money.

The problem of perception had nothing to do with Henry's skills, which were universally admired. The problem was that there was always a new boy on the street—someone with a prettier swing or a better press agent, somebody with more panache, a stronger arm, or that special intangible you built magic around.

This time, in the spring of 1956, when Henry came to Bradenton, lashing line drives and fully healthy, it was another Robinson from California he encountered, this one in the Cincinnati system. His name was Frank and he was from Oakland, where, like Mobile, ballplayers seemed to grow out of the ground. Robinson had been a two-sport star at McClymonds High, on Oakland's west side, the alma mater of Bill Russell, the star basketball player. Oakland would always be fertile baseball territory, and Cincinnati had hit the trifecta. In addition to Robinson, the Reds had just signed a young black center fielder from Oakland Technical High named Curtis Flood, and they had the inside track on another McClymonds kid everyone was talking about: Vada Pinson.

Frank Robinson was listed as being six one and weighing 190 pounds, just an inch and ten pounds bigger than Aaron, but he was built like a football player and possessed an intimidating presence. Where Henry was slender in the arms and calves and thicker in the waist, Frank Robinson carried his muscle in his chest and shoulders. Virtually overnight, Henry's stage grew crowded even before the curtain went up. Mays was omnipresent, Banks hit for more power than any National League shortstop, and now the word was this kid Robinson might be so good that the down-and-out Reds could even make a little noise. The hype machine was always looking for fresh material, especially during spring training, when for every legend born, thirty never produced a thing.

ERNIE WHITE, the old pitcher who won seventeen games for the Cardinals in 1941 and was a teammate of Warren Spahn in Boston, was the first to feed the machine enthusiastically, this time in an INS news wire item on March 17, 1956. After watching big Frank tattoo a couple of balls, White gushed, and in the process, he started a trend that would hound Henry Aaron for his entire career.

ROBBY HAS REDS BUZZING

Ernie White, former hurler for the St. Louis Cardinals and the Boston Bees who managed Robinson last year at Columbia, added:

"I was managing Columbia when Hank Aaron tore the Sally League apart for Jacksonville. Robinson can outdo Aaron in everything. He'll outrun him and he'll outhit him. He has great power to all fields."

During spring training, Henry seemed especially focused on the Dodgers, perhaps just to show that at least one member of the Braves wasn't intimidated by Newcombe or Drysdale, Robinson or the moment. Henry dominated the champs all spring, hitting .552 against them, including four home runs. Walt Alston, the Dodger manager and Aaron admirer, said, "What's more, he's likely to hit .552 all season."

Even Robinson, ferocious competitor that he was, understood Henry possessed the ability to be feared, and he was forced to give a tip of the cap. Roger Kahn recalled a story about Henry stealing second base during spring training that year. When he swiped second a second time, Robinson landed on Henry, pinned him hard to the dirt, and began filling Henry's spikes with handfuls of dirt.

"Jackie, what are you doing?" Henry cried.

"I'm making sure you don't steal on me again."

CERTAINLY, there were chances for populism, magical opportunities for the words and deeds to meld, chances to be beautiful. *Look* magazine loved Aaron, naming him "a lock" to win the batting title. "Hank is a '3-L hitter': lean, loose and lethal," the magazine said. "His batting secret is his supple, powerful wrists." *The Chicago Defender*, the influential black newspaper, ran an AP story, following *Look*'s lead, predicting Henry would win the batting crown.

AARON PICKED TO WIN
NATIONAL BATTING TITLE

Some of the keenest baseball observers are convinced that the leading hitter . . . will be a 22-year-old . . . outfielder for the Milwaukee
Braves. This unobtrusive athlete is Hank Aaron.

Aaron does not have the dramatic flair of Willie Mays or the oversized press buildup of Mickey Mantle.

The AP continued the drumbeat, comparing him to white stars
like Hall of Famers Paul Waner and Joe Medwick (so what if the
comparison to Ducky was a tad backhanded, ripping Henry for his
Medwick-like ability to stretch the strike zone from his ankles to his
forehead and points north). Best of all, there was the bus ride back
north to Milwaukee and the start of the campaign, when Bob Wolf,
the *Journal* beat man who was moonlighting for *The Sporting News,*
sat with Grimm for what must have been hours. Grimm believed the
Braves were going to win the pennant, and he told Wolf just how
they were going to do it, how despite Conley's fragile arm, the pitching would be better than ever and that pitching was how championships were won. Grimm chewed Wolf's ear about how the Braves
young guns were going to be a threat for years, well into the 1960s,
sizzling past the Dodgers, the Reds, the Cardinals, all of them. But
his most melodic tones were saved for his twenty-two-year-old right
fielder.

"Aaron," Charlie Grimm said. "Aaron, of course, is the prize."

GRIMM BELIEVED and the Braves believed, but when opening day
neared, the scribes weren't sold. Maybe they didn't want to get
burned again (the year before, the writers had said the Braves had
arrived, only to eat crow after the first week of the season). The New
York hold on the World Series, at least in the minds of the writers,
wasn't going to be broken in 1956, with the fierce-swinging Henry or
without him.

DODGERS, YANKS PICKED TO WIN FLAGS BY FOUR OF EVERY FIVE WRITERS IN POLL

The vote of 109 writers who "experted" the pennant races for The Associated Press was so lopsided it was almost no contest. . . . The Yanks had eighty-eight firsts and Brooklyn had eighty-six. A similar poll of 110 writers a year ago predicted pennants for the Cleveland Indians and Milwaukee Braves.

THE 1956 CURTAIN went up on a drizzly afternoon, April 17, and Henry immediately set about his business. The first victim was Bob Rush of the Chicago Cubs. Aaron drove in the game's first run in the fourth and then broke Rush in the sixth. Rush had appeared to be breezing toward the seventh: two quick outs and a 1–0 lead. Aaron took a strike and then roped a long homer to make it 2–0. Shaken, Rush fell apart. Thomson singled. Adcock hit another homer to make it 3–0, and Bruton tripled. Rush headed to the showers and the Braves cruised to a 6–0 win.

The Braves swept the Cubs three straight, and it seemed that maybe Charlie had a better handle on his team than Perini thought. Grimm's charges won nine out of twelve, but everything seemed just a bit off. Rain wiped out a week of games, and every hot start was followed by a sputter. The Braves were 13–7 after twenty games, in first place, during which time the Dodgers couldn't get out of their own way. But instead of building on the lead, the Braves fell back, getting demolished in a doubleheader by the Pirates (Pittsburgh *again*) 5–0 and 13–8.

In the opener of a Memorial Day weekend doubleheader at Wrigley, the Braves tied a big-league record by hitting three consecutive home runs in the first inning. Mathews hit a two-out homer off the short-fused former Dodger Russ Meyer. Henry followed with another and Bobby Thomson yanked yet another over the left-field fence. Meyer, now breathing fire, guaranteed his next pitch would stay in the park by throwing a strike off Bruton's right cheekbone.

Bruton crumpled. After a moment, he steadied himself with his bat, took a few wobbly steps toward first base, then raced toward Meyer. Bruton dropped the bat and caught Meyer with a left to the body. Grimm raced from the third-base coaching box and corralled Meyer by the neck. As the benches cleared, Meyer and Bruton kicked each other at the bottom of the pile. The *Chicago Defender* would call the brawl a "near riot." Aaron, years later, would call it the worst fight he'd ever seen. *The Sporting News* said Meyer and Bruton fought to a "split decision" but that the big loser was battered and bruised Charlie Grimm, who paid the price for trying to make the peace.

Nothing could awaken the Braves like a good fight. They hit five homers that night but lost the game 10–9. The next night, Thomson hit two more and Henry exploded with a homer, a double, three RBIs, and three runs scored in an 11–9 demolition of the Cubs.

In the finale, a 15–8 win the next afternoon, the Braves led 14–0 after four innings and, in a ten-inning span over the two-game onslaught, hit *seven* homers off one guy, sad-sack Cubs hurler Warren Hacker. In the three games, the Braves hit fourteen home runs, incited the Cubs to fisticuffs, and had their best record of the season at 19–10. They were in first place, with six fewer losses than the Dodgers. A power display, plus wins, and punching out the other team added up to the sort of weekend that provided the best kind of energy boost for a club. Plus, the Braves were coming home for fifteen games against lowly Pittsburgh, the Dodgers (a chance for an early knockout, perhaps?), Mays and the Giants, and the hard-luck Phillies.

But in the opener, Spahn took a 1–0 lead into the eighth against the Pirates and gave up four runs in a 4–1 loss. Something was wrong with the meal ticket. He had started the season 3–0 and was now 3–4. "You didn't even worry about Spahn," recalled Gene Conley. "Even before spring training began, you penciled him in for his twenty wins, because he was doing the same thing. To see him not win, you had to wonder a little bit." Pittsburgh beat Conley the following day and then split a doubleheader the next to take three of four.

Then came the Dodgers, who were 20–19, the defending champs standing in place. These were the games where great teams both revealed themselves and could use the emotional currency of winning to deflate their opponents in future meetings. In the opener, in front of a buzzing, nervous 27,788 souls, Sal Maglie led Burdette 1–0 in the eighth before Lew gave up homers to Pee Wee Reese and Gil Hodges, while Maglie walked away with a complete-game, three-hit shutout. Perini stood and smoldered as the home folks who were good for complimentary dry cleaning booed his team. The catcalls increased the next day, when Roger Craig beat Spahn 6–1 on a two-hitter. Spahn had collected just one out in the second inning and was gone. He was now 3–5, but the guy whom fans wanted to see with an apple in his mouth was Grimm. When Newcombe beat Conley 5–2, the Braves were 1–6 on the home stand and suddenly in fourth place.

Expectations had swallowed them whole, and under the weight of having to perform, the Braves were disintegrating. Spahn told writers that the team was under "terrible tension." Charlie Root, the Braves pitching coach, who had played for Grimm's pennant winners with the Cubs in 1932 and 1935, the man who went back decades with Grimm, said the skipper was "jittery" and that he had been able to feel the tension on the club since joining the team before spring training. Following a 7–2 loss against the Giants—when Adcock and Logan made errors in a four-run third—John Quinn told Grimm he wanted to talk to the team. Like a dad scolding his little kid, Quinn made Grimm sit in the clubhouse and listen while he let the Braves have it. They weren't hustling, Quinn said. Quinn looked around the room—at Aaron and Mathews, Burdette and Spahn and the rest—frothing that they were "letting down the fans" and "letting down the club as well."

When Quinn finished setting fire to their tail feathers, a somber Grimm closed the door and told his boys, "I may not be here much longer, but as long as I am, nobody is going to tell you fellas anything like that. You are hustling. You're hustling so much that you're pressing. I know darn well that you want to win as much as anybody."

Against the Giants, Spahn lost again, 3–1 to Johnny Antonelli, the man traded for the plummeting Thomson. Playing left, Henry committed an error and, representing the tying run, flied out to left to end the game. Before the final game of the home stand, Grimm composed himself, confronted Quinn, and told him he'd had no right to dress down his team. That was Charlie's way. Quinn and Perini had never played the game at the big-league level and, as far as he was concerned, they didn't know how hard it was. He was the manager, but the player in Charlie Grimm always ruled. In the meeting, Grimm was fired up, and he decided he wanted answers. He wanted to know where he stood as the manager, not just on that day but in the future. He wanted an assurance that Quinn would leave his team alone and let him manage. What he got instead was a phone call from Perini, who said coldly, "We're going to discuss your case when you get to New York."

Spahn finished the home stand by striking out ten in a 5–2 win over the Giants to snap the losing streak and save face. Willie went three for three with a homer, but the Braves had finally won a game. Even so, the Milwaukee fans didn't bring milk and cheese to the yard, but more boos. In losing ten of the fifteen games of the home stand, Milwaukee scored forty-one runs. In those three games against the Cubs alone, the Braves had scored thirty-five. They may have been only two games out after the carnage, but the Braves had come home in first place and now left for the longest road trip of the year in fifth, officially in the second division behind Cincinnati, St. Louis, Pittsburgh, and the Dodgers. The Braves hit the road with a record of 24–20. The first stop—and the last for Charlie Grimm—was Brooklyn.

Once in Brooklyn, the end came quickly. In the opener, Friday night, June 15, Perini watched from the Ebbets Field press box during the game and was pelted with questions by the blood-smelling reporters.

"Are you prepared to say that Grimm is your manager for the rest of the year?"

"I am prepared to say nothing."

"Are you thinking about making a change?"

"I'm not prepared to say anything about that, either."

BURDETTE STONED THE Dodgers for seven innings, up 4–2 in the eighth. But with one out, Rocky Nelson (batting average, .208) homered and Hodges walked. Grimm sent for Dave Jolly, who walked Campanella and gave up the game-tying single to Furillo. In the bottom of the ninth, Lou Sleater got Pee Wee Reese, but Duke Snider doubled. Randy Jackson was walked intentionally and Nelson grounded out.

If Perini was still unsure what to do with his manager, what happened next sealed the fate of Charlie Grimm. With Snider on third and Jackson on second and two out in a tie game, Grimm ordered Charlie Root out to the mound to replace Sleater with Ernie Johnson. With forty-one years in the game, Grimm's logic was sound: Campanella followed Hodges, and the left-handed Sleater would not face the right-handed Campanella.

Except that Rube Walker, the lefty, had already replaced Campanella in the top of the inning. Now, with the losing run on third, Grimm had put himself in the disadvantageous position, his right-handed pitcher facing the lefty Walker. Root was halfway to the pitching mound and Johnson had left the bull pen when Grimm pulled the fire alarm, yelling frantically for Root to get back to the dugout. But the switch had already been signaled to home plate umpire Artie Gore. Grimm caught a lucky break when Gore allowed him to rescind the switch, leaving the lefty Sleater to face the lefty Walker. The Dodger manager, Walter Alston, went ballistic, telling Gore he was playing the game under protest. But it didn't matter. Lefty or righty, protest or not, brain cramp forgiven, fate still had other plans for Charlie Grimm. Sleater threw a first-pitch fastball, which Walker ripped for the game-winning base hit. The Braves lost anyway, 5–4.

After the game, Perini left the press box, muttering, "We're not getting as much out of this club as we should."

The denouement came the next afternoon, with Roger Craig shutting Milwaukee down again, 2–0 in the eighth. Adcock banged a pinch homer to make it 2–1 and Mathews singled to tie it. The Dodgers did it again in the bottom of the inning when Snider homered off Ernie Johnson. The Braves put two on in the top of the ninth, but Bruton grounded out to second to end it. In the span of two weeks, the Braves had lost twelve out of seventeen, and against their rivals, the Dodgers, the team they knew they had to beat in order to be considered big-league, championship-level, Milwaukee was 1–5.

When the game ended, Perini invited the Milwaukee writers to his suite at the Commodore Hotel for a drink. Shortly after they arrived, Grimm walked in and told the group he was finished. "I've decided to give someone else a crack at this job."

He was out. It wasn't Durocher, however, who walked through the clubhouse door the next night, but one of his old disciples, white-haired, five-foot-five-inch Fred Haney. Haney had joined the Braves as a coach to start the season, after having managed the Pirates the previous three years, the same Pirate team whose success against the Braves in 1955 had cost them the pennant. Haney was now the boss.

As for Perini, he lamented how his little mom-and-pop baseball operation had succumbed to the sudden hunger of the fans and a flash flood of expectations.

"I can't understand the people," he said. "We get two or three games behind and they want Charlie to be fired or they want him to resign. I think it's a terrible thing."

The truth, as always, was quite different. The fans wanted Grimm's scalp, in no small part because it was Perini who had whipped up the expectations in the first place. It was Perini who had told anyone who would listen that these Braves were nothing less than pennant winners.

Bob Wolf pecked out his column for *The Sporting News,* and concluded that Grimm had never been able to overcome his banjo-playing, roll 'em out and let's drink image. He was too close to his players. They wanted to laugh with Charlie and drink with him, feel safe with him, win or lose. But camaraderie was one thing. Not being able to beat the Dodgers had proven something else: With a pot of gold in the middle of the table, the Braves didn't know how to collect. The Dodgers had been dizzy, reeling, and instead of a kayo, six games against the Braves were what had gotten them straight. The Braves had Burdette and Spahn and Mathews and Adcock and Aaron, Wolf wrote, and still didn't know how to reach across the table and bring the money home.

> Why did Grimm fail to produce the pennant winner Perini and the fans of Milwaukee thought they should have had? The consensus is that his easy-going manner got the best of him, just as it apparently had in his two terms with the Cubs. The club appeared to lack the competitive spark.

For the papers, Charlie gave Milwaukee one last smile. Sporting a polka-dot shirt and cream-colored blazer, a cigarette in his left hand,

Charlie mugged for the cameras, shaking Fred Haney's hand with his right.

ALTHOUGH FRED HANEY knew a Cadillac when he saw one, he knew he wouldn't have it for long if he didn't learn how to drive, and fast. Haney had been around the Braves enough to know his wasn't a 24–22 team. His first act as commandant was to crush the element on the Braves that preferred barmaids to first place. Over the first weeks of his tenure, Haney would manage quite differently from the way Grimm had. Haney called frequent meetings, if for no reason other than to give the drinkers on the club something to think about. He promised to deal with the "two or three playboys" on the club. One, of course, was Mathews, but he wasn't going anywhere. Mathews had trouble even when he wasn't exactly involved. Take the night of May 12, when he hit his fourth homer of the year in a 10–6 loss at Cincinnati. Mathews showed up at the ballpark for a doubleheader the next day sporting cuts on each side of his face. It turned out that a woman had thrown a glass in his direction and shards of glass were now deeply lodged into his face. No matter, Mathews went four for eight in sweeping two from the Redlegs, but too many times the edge the Braves needed was being left in the bar.

Jim Pendleton, the versatile utility man who was also Henry's roommate, was another story. Pendleton, who possessed a big appetite for long legs and drink but couldn't hit his weight, was sent out to Wichita the day Haney was hired. Felix Mantilla, the infielder from Puerto Rico who had been Henry's teammate in Jacksonville, was called up. The two would room together.

There was something else about Haney that differed dramatically from Grimm. Haney had no problem pointing out a player's mistakes in front of the whole team. He was, after all, a Durocher man, and he knew the value of peer pressure, of being embarrassed in front of the club. Mental mistakes would not be tolerated. A ball getting by or a throw coming in low was one thing, but not knowing how many outs there were or not taking the extra base was quite another. Under Fred Haney these types of errors would definitely cost players money. The difference was that Durocher was a better psychologist than Haney. Durocher knew that he needed Willie Mays to win and never embarrassed Willie. To do so would have sent Mays retreating into his shell. On the Braves, Henry was the rising star. Even at this juncture in his career it was clear he possessed the most all-around talent.

Yet Haney had no problem criticizing Henry. Or anybody.

In the Braves first test under Haney, a doubleheader at Ebbets, Adcock won it in the ninth with a home run that went over the roof. The *New York Times* photo caption said it was the first time anyone had hit a ball out of Ebbets. In the nightcap, Adcock hit another, this time off Don Newcombe, and the Braves had not only swept the day, 3–1, but done something they hadn't done all season. They'd beaten the Dodgers in consecutive games.

And so it went for Fred Haney, two months of rolling sevens. As they headed into Forbes Field for four games, it wasn't lost on any of the Braves that no team gave them more trouble than the Pirates, but Haney handled his former club. Spahn and Burdette won the first two games, and the Braves broke the Pirates for a five-run fifth in winning the third, and Henry's first-inning triple started a rout in the finale for a four-game sweep. The Braves went back to New York for four with the Giants in Harlem, and it was more of the same. Mathews bombed a home run to win the opener. The Braves rallied for two in the ninth to win the second and swept a doubleheader for their tenth win in a row. In Philadelphia the next night, Pakfo started a three-run eighth with a bunt single and the Braves won 8–5.

The streak ended the next day in Philadelphia, but after Grimm was fired, the Braves had catapulted four teams in the standings, suddenly playing .600 ball and leading the league over an upstart Cincinnati club as well as the Dodgers.

ON MAY 8, the Milwaukee cleanup hitter, Henry Aaron, went zero for four, struck out twice, and made an error in a 5–0 win against Pittsburgh. His average dropped to .167. He'd started the season with three hits in his first seven at bats, including demoralizing the Cubs with a home run on opening day, but over the next nine games,

Henry could do next to nothing. The average wasn't there, and neither was the power. He went thirteen games before hitting his first double of the season. He had three home runs up to that point. The consolation was that Milwaukee was in first place without its cleanup hitter doing anything at all.

The trouble with Henry was that there were few signals his teammates could point to that suggested his problems were over. Some slumping hitters got themselves out of the dumps by taking more pitches, by walking more and cutting down on their strike-outs. Not Henry. A low number of strike-outs would always be a central source of pride for him, and even when he was cranking, he didn't walk. On May 15, he went one for four in Philadelphia, raising his average to .208, but he had struck out five times and walked five times all season. Others would try to take the ball the other way, to shoot the ball into the right-center gap. That meant the hitter wasn't overanxious to pull the ball, which meant he wasn't trying to meet the ball too quickly and thus was missing good pitches.

The hitting coaches would all tell Henry the same thing: to stay back, wait on the ball, and then stride toward it. Henry hit differently. Since the ankle injury in high school, his hitting approach was to balance and drive off of his *front* foot, to use the combination of his quickness and power to drive the ball. Despite the results, few of his coaches knew exactly what to do with him, because they'd never seen anyone hit like that and be successful over the long term. Committing to the front foot should have left him vulnerable to late-moving pitches, made him susceptible to strike-outs, but he was just different.

Henry's gifts at the plate were unpredictable except in their roots. He thought along with the pitcher and tried to beat him to the spot. It had been that way in Mobile, when Ed Scott first saw him. Henry had always banked on his ability to make contact with any pitch, in any location.

When he did catch—a three-hit game with a triple in a 2–1 loss in Philly—it was without warning, an innocent spark turned wildfire. The next day, in the Polo Grounds against the Giants, Henry rapped two more hits, a double and a two-run triple, to put on a show with Mays, who would also double and triple, just to keep the universe in balance. Then it was time to break out the adding machine: three straight multihit games against Pittsburgh and Brooklyn. By the end of the month, Aaron was suddenly hitting .352.

If Charlie Grimm knew Aaron had the potential to be a transcendent talent, it was Haney who worked unsentimentally to refine him. When Grimm resigned, Aaron was hitting .313. Indeed, in Haney's first game, Henry went three for four, and Haney presented him with a reward: early batting practice when the team arrived in Pittsburgh. Henry responded that night with two more hits.

Meanwhile, the hype machine had found its man, and it was true: twenty-year-old Frank Robinson was indeed the real deal. At the all-star break, he was running away with the Rookie of the Year award, and for all of his blustery spring-training oratory, maybe Robinson's old minor-league manager Ernie White had *underestimated* his former protégé. Robinson wasn't just killing the ball; he was second in the league in hitting. He wasn't just hitting the ball over the fence; he led the league in runs scored, even though he was not a base stealer. Like Aaron and Mays and Banks, he was a complete hitter, and that other rumor about Robinson was also true: You couldn't intimidate the kid. It wasn't yet August, but Robinson had already been hit twelve times. He stood there snarling, right on top of the plate. He ignored the customary batter-pitcher compact of giving up one half of the plate, and for it, Robinson would be hit twenty times in 1956 alone. It would be a hallmark of his long career. By the time he retired, in 1975, he would be hit a total of 198 times. By contrast, Henry was hit by pitches thirty-times over twenty-three seasons.

Robinson was not a beneficiary of the kingmakers in the East Coast media machine. He played in dowdy Cincinnati, which by all accounts was a city hostile toward blacks. Cincinnati was so fearful of offending the conservative middle-American attitude that in 1956, in the age of McCarthyism, the Reds changed their name to the Redlegs, lest anyone think the baseball team had sided with the Communists. It was only a matter of time before Robinson chafed in Cincinnati, but in the summer of 1956, Frank Robinson was the most exciting player in the National League.

Then, for Henry Aaron, came the unkindest cut: Robinson was named to start in right field in the All-Star Game. Robinson, in fact, would be the only black starter in the game, with Mays, Aaron, and Ernie Banks on the bench.

FOLLOWING THE ALL-STAR Game, the Dodgers traveled to Milwaukee for four games. The standings showed Cincinnati in first place, up on Milwaukee by a game and a half and by two on Brooklyn, but no one really believed the Redlegs would be around for the whole 154 games. The Braves knew beating Brooklyn would be the only measure by which they were judged. For the doubleheader opener on July 12, 41,000 burghers packed County Stadium, Bob Buhl versus Roger Craig. Adcock boomed a long homer in the fifth to make it 1–0, and Buhl led 2–0 into the ninth. Jackie Robinson grounded to third for the first out. Hodges fouled out to third. Buhl, too close to victory, grew nervous, pitching as though he were defusing a bomb. Nelson rapped a single to center; Furillo followed with one to left. The groans in the crowd grew more unsettled. Against the Dodgers, this was the kind of game Charlie Grimm always found a way to lose. Haney didn't move. Roy Campanella stepped to the plate, salty on about a hundred different levels. The first was that he was having the worst hitting year of his career. Campy, who'd won three MVP awards, couldn't crack .240. The second was that on this day, he was already zero for three with a strike-out. Buhl threw two quick fastballs by him, and then pitched to him carefully, so carefully, in fact, that Campanella walked to load the bases. That brought up Rube Walker, the same Rube Walker who had singled in the ninth inning in Grimm's penultimate game as manager, the game in which Grimm had forgotten who was on deck. Walker stepped in on Buhl and broke the Braves hearts again, lashing an apparent game-winning drive down the first-base line.

Except that Frank Torre, who had just entered the game as a defensive replacement for Adcock, leaped and stabbed the ball out of the air, saving the game for Buhl. He was now 10–4 on the season and had beaten the Dodgers five times.

The rest of the weekend was pure magic. The second game was rained out and in the rescheduled doubleheader—Friday night, July 13—the Braves gave Milwaukee something to remember and the

Dodgers something to fear. In the first game, in front of 40,169, New-combe lasted but one inning, blasted out of existence by Adcock's two-run homer, which led a six-run first.

The Dodgers pieced together two runs in the second as wheels within wheels turned. It was only mid-July, but a referendum on the Braves toughness was taking place. The score was 6–2 and it should have been more. Don Drysdale, all six feet, six inches of him, with his nasty slider and nastier disposition, didn't really have it. They should have punched him out in the second, his first inning of work, but Henry bounced into the rally-killing double play with two on and one out. Milwaukee had Drysdale again in the third and the Dodgers looked rattled. Covington singled and Campy dropped a foul pop. Two more on and one out again, but Drysdale walked into the dugout, untouched, when Rice grounded into another double play. The Braves held a four-run lead, but they were leaving ducks on the bases every inning.

In the fourth, Drysdale gave up a double to Danny O'Connell and Campy let the next pitch roll through his legs. With O'Connell dancing off third, needing just a grounder or fly ball to bring him home, Logan bounced a chopper to Robinson at third, forcing O'Connell to scamper back. Drysdale, the magician, escaped again when Mathews, ever dangerous, ended the inning by lining to Robinson.

More than any other member of the Dodgers, it was Robinson, thirty-seven years old and rancorous, who was convinced that Mil-waukee couldn't play in the thin air of a pennant chase. And here, again, when the details of the game seemed to be showing that the Braves were the more talented team, it was being proved. Drysdale should have been toast, putting men on in every inning, and yet he hadn't broken, hadn't even given up another run. The score may have looked like a blowout at 6–2, but that was the thing about baseball—one swing of the bat could tie it. The Braves hadn't shown Robinson anything. The Dodgers should have been dead and yet they were one rally away from recovery.

Drysdale received his cosmic reward in the top of the fifth, bouncing a liner off Ray Crone that caromed from the pitcher to Logan for an infield single. Then the flood came: a single by Gilliam, a double by Reese, which made it 6–3. Bat held high above his head, Robinson stepped up on Crone, with runners on second and third and with one out, and ripped a two-run single to center, and it was 6–5. It was Durocher who famously said Robinson "didn't come to beat ya. He come to stick the bat up your ass."

And so here was Jackie, having snared the final two outs the previous inning, driving in two runs in the middle of this rally, taking the game into his hands. The next exchange would detail why no single statistic could properly summarize his impact as a winning ballplayer. With Crone shaking, the Milwaukeeans sitting on their hands as they watched their big lead melt like a July snow cone, Robinson went for the jugular, faking twice before finally stealing second. Crone was so rattled, he walked Hodges, and Haney came out with the hook.

Dave Jolly entered and chucked a wild pitch that sent Robinson to third. Without the benefit of a hit, Robinson tied the game at 6–6 on a fielder's choice.

In later years, these games would be deliciously remembered for differing reasons. Johnny Logan believed what transpired over those next days as the moment the Braves transformed themselves into a championship personality, finally discarding a reputation as carousers who spit the bit when the pressure rose. The writer Roger Kahn would remember the Robinson performance as another example of the Einstein adage "Everything that can be counted does not necessarily count; everything that counts cannot necessarily be counted."

Robinson was largely finished as an everyday player, as his diminished skills could no longer support his furious activism. But in short bursts, during big games, he could still be a devastating impact player. From the vantage point of the score book, Robinson had done nothing remarkable that Friday—a couple of putouts, an RBI base hit, and a stolen base—but placed in the context of the game and the season and the intensifying relationship between the two teams, he had once again made the difference.

For spending the afternoon in the pressure cooker, Henry had not done much. He'd struck out. He started a Brooklyn rally with his tenth error of the season and killed a rally by hitting into a double play.

But when he doubled off Clem Labine to lead off the seventh in a tie game, it was the seasoned Dodgers who crumbled. Labine's error allowed Aaron to advance to third and score the go-ahead run on a Bruton sacrifice fly. In the eighth, it was Labine again, giving up a leadoff double to O'Connell and committing another error on the very next batter. With O'Connell on third, Mathews walked to keep the double play intact.

That brought up Henry, with a duck sitting on third and Mathews at first. Labine wanted to pitch Aaron inside, hard at first, and then soft enough to force a double-play grounder. Henry took a pitch. On the next, O'Connell broke for home, and Henry, the power hitter, pulled a Robinson, dropping a perfect bunt in front of Labine as O'Connell raced home with an insurance run in a sweaty 8–6 Milwaukee victory.

Burdette took the mound in the second game and immediately gave up four in the first. Naturally, Robinson was at the center of the fray. Winning the game was important, but beating Burdette came with an even bigger payoff, for it meant there was no one the Braves could run out to the mound with a psychological advantage. Three batters into the game, Burdette was already down 2–0, with Snider on first. Robinson followed with a single. Nelson reached on a bunt single to third, loading the bases. That's when Robinson sensed a chance to break Burdette's will.

Furillo bounced a double-play ball to O'Connell at second. No harm there, because with Snider on third, Haney was conceding Snider's run to get two outs. Being down 3–0 in the first inning wasn't ideal, but he had twenty-seven outs to make up the difference.

But Robinson raced to third, as he was supposed to do, and *then kept on running*. Surprised, Adcock took Logan's relay and spun toward the plate, a flying Robinson careening for the plate, Burdette screaming, "Home! Home!" Adcock hit Del Rice in the glove with the throw, but Robinson was already dusting himself off, trotting gingerly toward the Dodgers dugout, and it was 4–0.

It was the kind of play few players would ever dare to attempt, the kind of play even fewer had the skills to consider, and the kind an even smaller percentage thought could work. Even though he was now on one knee in the dugout, gingerly holding his crotch, while Burdette spewed venom at him, he had scored from second on a dou-

The great educator Booker T. Washington (fourth from right) vacationed in Mobile and spent much political capital fighting unsuccessfully to prevent the implementation of Jim Crow policies there. It was into a strict culture of segregation that three generations of Aaron men were born.

Almost as if preordained, the specter of Babe Ruth would never be far from Henry Aaron. Ruth was born February 6, Henry a day earlier. Ruth finished his career with the Braves, the team that would one day draft Henry. In the same year Herbert and Stella Aaron moved to Mobile, Ruth poses before an exhibition at Hartwell Field.

The pool halls of Davis Avenue appealed to a young Henry Aaron far more than education, leading to his expulsion from high school. He attended the Josephine Allen Institute, but Henry bet his entire future on baseball.

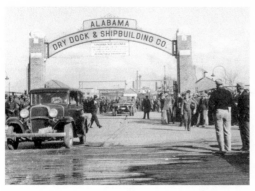

When Herbert Aaron finally found steady work, it was as a riveter with the Alabama Dry Dock & Shipbuilding Company on Pinto Island. Until a 1942 riot, white and black employees worked alongside one another, though they would still suffer the humiliation of segregated entrances at the main plant.

Henry joined Jacksonville, part of the notorious South Atlantic League, as a second baseman in 1953. Along with Felix Mantilla and Horace Garner, he would integrate the league while winning MVP honors.

A staple of the segregated era: black players living in a boarding house in the Negro section of town. White players on the Braves resided at a resort hotel in Bradenton, Florida, during spring training, while Henry, Charlie White (center), and Bill Bruton (right) lived at the home of Lulu Mae Gibson.

During his early years, no player would have as much of an impact on Henry as Bill Bruton (second from right). Bruton taught a young Henry Aaron how to dress, how to tip, places to avoid on the road, and, most important, how to begin pressing Braves management to end the segregationist practices during spring training. From left: Jim Pendleton, Charlie White, Bruton, and Henry Aaron.

Few teams in history ever boasted as powerful a trio in the middle of the batting order as did the Milwaukee Braves, with Henry hitting fourth, between Eddie Mathews (center) and Joe Adcock. Henry loved Mathews, but he and Joe Adcock were never close. Henry believed Adcock to be the most racist member of the Braves. It was Adcock who was responsible for the saddling Henry with the unflattering nicknames "Stepin Fetchit," "Snowshoes," and "Slow Motion Henry."

While baseball focused on his rivalry with Willie Mays, it was Jackie Robinson after whom Henry patterned his career, and Robinson who inspired Aaron to be a person of import following his retirement. Aaron always remembered that Robinson was never offered a job by Dodgers owner Walter O'Malley (right) when he left the game, and he resolved to cultivate relationships with the game's power brokers.

Fresh off of winning his first batting title, Henry arrived in Bradenton for spring training in 1957. By season's end, he would hit a pennant-winning home run, win the World Series, and secure the Most Valuable Player award for the only time in his career.

On Henry's first trip to Boston, in May 1957, he and Ted Williams posed before a charity exhibition game at Fenway Park between the Braves and the Red Sox. It was Williams, the curmudgeonly perfectionist, who was both taken by Henry's accomplishments and perplexed by his unorthodox hitting style. "You can't hit for power off your front foot," Williams often said. "You just can't do it."

The Wrist Hitter: Perhaps no player in the history of the game would be as celebrated for his lightning-quick wrists as Henry Aaron. "You might get him out once," Don Drysdale once said, "but don't think for a minute you're going make a living throwing the ball past by Henry Aaron."

Warren Spahn won 363 games and was the unquestioned leader of the Braves pitching staff. Spahn was a decorated World War II veteran, awarded the Purple Heart and Bronze Star. Along with Henry and Eddie Mathews, Spahn would be elected to the Hall of Fame, but while Henry and Spahn shared mutual respect, Spahn's irreverence and unprogressive racial attitudes made for a professional but sometimes uneasy relationship.

Henry at home with Barbara, a young Gaile, and infant Lary. The Aarons lived on North 29th Street, in the segregated Bronzeville section of Milwaukee. As Henry's celebrity increased, the family became the first and only black family allowed to move to the suburb of Mequon, a source of pride and tension on both sides of the roiling civil rights movement in the city.

No set of teammates hit more home runs than Eddie Mathews (left) and Henry Aaron, or better symbolized the glory days of baseball in Milwaukee. After the 1965 home finale, the two walk up the runway at County Stadium for the final time before the club moved to Atlanta.

Henry voiced his reluctance to return to the South, the scene of so many humiliations. Ironically, it was living in Atlanta, the center of the modern civil rights movement, that shaped his views and deepened his conviction to become more than a baseball player.

Perhaps the three most historically significant players of their era: Henry's consistency was often overshadowed by the charisma of Willie Mays (center), while Roberto Clemente (left) displaced Henry as the premier defensive right fielder in the National League. It was Clemente, however, who would be the most notoriously underpaid.

After Henry hit his 500th home run, on July 14, 1968, the baseball world realized it was Henry Aaron—and not Willie Mays—who represented the best chance to reach Babe Ruth's all-time record of 714. For the next seven seasons, as he became the focal point of a national obsession, the smiles would be scarce.

ble play. If he had to do it alone, Jackie Robinson would make the Braves crack.

Except that Milwaukee did not fold. Erskine led 4–1 in the sixth when Henry followed a Mathews single with another, and Bruton, too, reached on a one-out error. Then Adcock blasted a grand slam and gave the Braves a 5–4 lead. Four outs away from being swept in the doubleheader, Robinson again came up, sore groin and all, and tied the game with a two-out homer in the eighth, only to see Bruton win it 6–5, scoring on a sacrifice fly.

Afterward, it was Smokey Alston who blew his stack. They were the champs, and yet in each game it was the Dodgers who had folded in a critical moment. In three games, they'd committed six errors. Campanella was zero for eight with four whiffs. Adcock had homered in every game. Gutless is what they were, Alston said. And in the next day's paper, in the genteel *New York Times*, no less, that was exactly the word attributed to Alston in describing his defending world champs: *gutless.*

In the Saturday finale, the Dodgers on the brink of being swept four straight, Robinson left after the first inning, his sore groin finishing him for the afternoon. Maglie put the Braves down, except for Henry Aaron and Adcock. Still, up 2–0, with two out in the seventh, "the Barber" gave up a dribbler to Bruton and a game-tying homer to Adcock. When Alston walked to the mound to relieve Maglie, the Barber didn't want to give him the ball. The game stayed that way until the tenth, when Henry stepped to the plate. He already had three hits, and now Logan was on second with the winning run. That wasn't all. Alston walked Mathews intentionally to get to Aaron. Don Bessent threw a one-strike fastball and Aaron crushed it four hundred feet against the base of the wall in left center, sending the 39,105 at County Stadium into a frenzy. The beer was on ice at Ray Jackson's.

The Dodgers were now four and a half back. Robinson was brilliant, but Milwaukee had its sweep. Since Grimm had been bounced, the Braves had beaten Brooklyn six straight. Adcock now had sixteen homers, half of them coming against Brooklyn. With Charlie, Brooklyn had won eight of thirteen. The lead, though, was only two ahead of second-place Cincinnati, but those mashers weren't supposed to have the pitching to stay in it, lending a certain degree of inevitability to a Dodgers-Braves showdown.

For all the commotion—letting the Dodgers up off of the mat earlier in the summer, the home fans booing relentlessly, being embarrassed like a bunch of Little Leaguers by a raving Quinn, and having to witness the public sacrifice of Charlie Grimm—the Braves were the best team in the league by the end of July, and had they hit like they were supposed to, they might have been even better than the Yankees.

As Grimm had predicted, Milwaukee had the best pitching in baseball. On July 26, the top four pitchers in ERA (earned run average) were the Braves starting rotation, Buhl and Spahn, followed by Burdette and Conley. The Braves had stretched out a five-game lead over Cincinnati and six games over the third-place Dodgers.

Henry was the catalyst. Mathews could still get behind one, but he couldn't get his average higher than .250, and Adcock was devastating in stretches, but it was Henry who was there, delivering every day. Two days after the Brooklyn sweep, on July 15, Henry singled in a 4–1 win over Pittsburgh, and then the hits rushed downriver, with multiple-hit nights over the next seven games. By the end of the month, he was leading the league in hitting, just as he had set out to do while working on his swing in Carver Park. The hitting streak had reached sixteen games when the press started to take notice.

On August 8, at County Stadium, a doubleheader against the Cardinals, Henry singled in a 10–1 laugher to stretch the streak to twenty-five. In the second game, he stepped in against Herman Wehmeier. Henry was leading the league in hitting, and he remembered Wehmeier from his rookie season. Wehmeier was then with Philadelphia, but he was one of the few pitchers who had consistently tested Henry with knockdown pitches. In his first three at bats, Henry twice flied out to Bobby Del Greco, the center fielder, and once grounded to Ken Boyer. Meanwhile, Burdette and Wehmeier traded runs and outs. Tied 2–2, with one out in the eighth and O'Connell on second, Henry lashed a meaty fastball from Wehmeier, which Del Greco ran down.

In the tenth, Del Greco doubled, and with two out, Wehmeier

rapped a single off Burdette's glove. By the time Burdette could locate the ball, Del Greco had scored from second with the go-ahead run. The Cardinals won 3–2, and the streak was over, personally extinguished by Wehmeier and Del Greco, two names Henry Aaron would never forget.

THE DODGERS and Braves met for the final time for a two-game set September 11 and 12 at Ebbets Field. The Braves led the Dodgers by a single game and a stout Redlegs team by three. The Braves had held on to first place since taking that July doubleheader from Brooklyn, but as Henry's streak sent him toward the batting title, the Braves lost half their lead. There was payback in Ebbets Field. After Henry destroyed the Dodgers in the opener (three for five, a double, a homer, and four RBIs) to run Haney's win streak against Brooklyn to seven straight, Brooklyn won the next three. In the first, a 3–2 victory, Robinson accounted for all three runs with a two-run homer and an opposite-field game winner in the bottom of the ninth, which a streaking Aaron snagged for an instant before the ball dropped out of his glove, ending the game. In the second, a 2–1 Brooklyn win, Robinson led off the eighth inning of a 1–1 game by singling to left, taking second on Bobby Thomson's error, and scoring what would be the winning run on an infield chop. In the finale, Newcombe needed only a run (a home run by Furillo) in a 3–0 win. The Dodgers would go 40–19, shaving five games off the lead.

Over the decades that followed, the Dodgers would be judged harshly for their inability to defeat the Yankees. But they also would be romanticized for that moment in time during the mid-1950s when Brooklyn and the Dodgers seemed to exemplify innocence and simplicity, virtues fast slipping away in modern society, virtues that disappeared with the Dodgers as they moved to the West Coast. Much of it was a myth, certainly, as were most notions of simpler times. The Dodgers leaving Brooklyn would serve for the next half century as a metaphor for virtues lost to progress. Brooklyn's failure at the hands of the Yankees would burnish the dynastic traits of the Yankees while obscuring another immutable truth: The Dodgers, as the Braves discovered during 1956, were one of the more resolute and determined baseball teams in history. For the length of the baseball season, the Dodgers and Braves believed in the symbols they ostensibly represented.

The Dodgers were the old guard, representatives of a standard in sharp decay. The daily dramas on the baseball field were rivaled only by the confrontations in the boardroom and at Borough Hall, when Walter O'Malley danced with politicians around the construction of a new ballpark for the Dodgers. One plan in 1956 called for a retractable dome, another for a park in Staten Island. The Dodgers were already playing games in Jersey City, the explanation for this being that O'Malley was exhausting all options to stay in New York. The truth was that the old days were dead, and, far ahead of his time, O'Malley knew it, even as the heart of the city still seemed to be beating strong.

The Dodgers, these Brooklyn Dodgers at least, represented the last vestige of a disappearing time, a fact complicated by their unwillingness to go away on the field. Change was what the Braves and Dodgers September showdown truly represented. Change was why Perini, the old Steam Shovel, took his team to the open spaces of the Midwest—where parking was plentiful—rather than remain in the tight corners of Boston, fighting for space with another team, feeling unwanted virtually the whole time. For years, Logan would lament Perini's decision to leave Boston. "We would have been the powerhouse," he said. "Look at the guys we had coming up. But they made the decision to go."

Maglie, one of the many signature faces of New York baseball, would say the same. Like Robinson, Maglie was not quite ready to give way to the Braves or O'Malley's grand vision, which did not include him. During the furious Dodger run in August, Maglie posted a 1.99 ERA. In September, a 1.77 ERA and a no-hitter September 25 served as proof that the Dodgers were breathing down the Braves neck. Winning the pennant now was, they all knew, their last best chance to win, to say good-bye to the old days in style. Furillo, Erskine, Labine, Hodges, Newcombe, and especially Jackie . . . they were nowhere men, all of them, with no choice but for the uncertainties of the future to sweep them up, with each leaving the best of himself behind in Brooklyn.

O'Malley was playing games in Jersey City not because he wanted a retractable dome in Brooklyn, but because he knew Perini had it right: If the future was a place no one could yet imagine, it could only be realized by a man of vision who wanted to be remembered for something grand. Such a destiny could not be attained by staying in Boston, or, for that matter, in Brooklyn. Being remembered didn't mean acquiescing to a politician's compromise. It meant starting over.

The future was inevitable. Less certain was whether the Milwaukee Braves, set up to be the Next Big Thing, could take the pennant, the prize all season long Henry and Perini and Spahn all thought belonged to them. The old saying that water finds its own level was never truer than in baseball, because of the grueling length of the season. For much of the season, Mathews couldn't get himself straight, and yet with two weeks to go in the season, the slugger had pounded thirty-two home runs. Adcock would finish with thirty-eight. Spahn was near twenty wins. There was the attrition of the season, as well. Chuck Tanner, the team rookie of 1955, would play only sixty games, bat .238, and spend time in the minors, looking more like a traveling salesman than a ballplayer.

Yet here they were, battered and alive, cradling a wafer-thin one-game lead for the pennant, with sixteen left to play.

PERINI AND THE brain trust flew to Brooklyn for the series. Before the game, John Quinn called Haney for a meeting and announced the manager would be returning in 1957. He had taken a 24–22 team and gone 59–31. Maglie and Buhl warmed in the dugout, and by happenstance, Robinson and Burdette met under the bleachers. Instead of payback for their July rhubarb, what resulted was an unexpected peace accord. Burdette, the West Virginian with a reputation for not only throwing at black players but *enjoying* it, told Robinson there was no place in the game for racial taunting and—in perhaps the most backhanded compliment of the century—said he hadn't called Robinson "watermelon" during their bitter confrontations following the all-star break out of racial animosity, but because he was commenting on Robinson's weight, his "watermelon stomach."

"Burdette told me that there is no place in baseball for racial references," Robinson told the *Times*. "He said that he merely had been making a point that I am getting a bit thick in the middle. Lew's statement about how he felt is one of the most gratifying things that has ever happened to me."

Still, these were difficult words to accept, coming from Burdette, a man with a reputation for little love toward black players. Henry respected Burdette's professionalism, his toughness on the mound, and his commitment to protect his hitters from headhunters like Maglie and Larry Jackson of the Cardinals, but he would never speak of Burdette warmly as a man. In 1955, Burdette knocked Campanella down twice during an at bat in a game at County Stadium, calling him a "black motherfucker" in between dustings. With Campanella in the dirt, Burdette called out, "Nigger, get up there and hit." After Campanella struck out, he rushed the mound, clearing the benches.

Brooklyn hadn't held sole possession of first place since April 28, and yet here they were, poised to steal the golden goose at the end. In the opener, a Tuesday night sellout at Ebbets, Maglie gave up a homer to Mathews in the second and another to Adcock and stifled the Milwaukee lineup in between for nine innings. Buhl didn't even make it into the fifth, chucking the ball around the ballpark. Seven walks in three and two-thirds got him the quick hook from Haney, and the two teams were tied at 83–55 apiece.

In terms of failure, Burdette topped Buhl in a quick turnaround the next afternoon, getting yanked after recording just two outs. But this game, with the fall air and cigar smoke intermingling around the old ballpark and Fred Haney chomping on his fingernails, turned into a September classic. The Braves trailed 3–0 after the first, with Don Newcombe, leading both leagues in wins, on the mound for Brooklyn. But big-pressure games and Newcombe did not often mix well, and Newcombe lasted but an inning himself, and the score was tied 4–4 after two. Milwaukee led 6–4 when Mathews doubled and Adcock (*again*) bombed a two-run homer in the sixth. Del Crandall wafted one into the seats in the seventh to make it 7–4.

But the Dodgers chased Conley and Taylor Phillips in the seventh, the old hands not quite ready to relinquish their pennant. It started with two singles and a run-scoring twelve-hopper by Pee Wee Reese, and a walk to Duke Snider. In came Buhl, once the Dodger killer, who hit Robinson in the elbow to load the bases. On the next pitch, Sandy Amoros tied it on a two-out, two-run error by Danny O'Connell.

Now tied at 7–7 and with Haney reaching a fever point, Bruton's single scored Adcock in the eighth. A redeemed Buhl would get the win in relief, but not before Crone sweated out the ninth, with Robinson singling, with two out, before Amoros ended the game on a grounder.

The Braves led Brooklyn by a game. Henry had gone three for five. All season long, the personality of the Braves had been defined by Spahn, Mathews, Adcock, and Logan. The frustrations of reaching the pennant had been illustrated by Perini. Henry was only twenty-two, and while he had been the team's most consistent player, he had not yet affected the pennant race with a defining moment. The Braves left Brooklyn and took the train to Philadelphia, checking into the Warwick Hotel on Seventeenth Street between Walnut and Locust, a block from Rittenhouse Square. Henry and Felix Mantilla grabbed a cab to the ballpark, where Henry took over an epic doubleheader against the Phillies.

Jack Meyer, the twenty-four-year-old Phillies pitcher (who would die of a surprise heart attack in 1967), was throwing the game of his life, shutting out the Braves through six innings. With the Braves trailing 2–0 in the seventh, Henry doubled in O'Connell to cut the lead in half and then scored to tie it. In the twelfth, Thomson from left field erased a streaking Puddin' Head Jones at the plate to preserve the tie.

In the thirteenth, Meyer—still in the game—retired the first two batters before making the critical mistake of hitting O'Connell (career average: .260). Henry stepped to the plate. Up until that point, Meyer had pitched twelve and two-thirds innings, had given up only six hits (Henry had one) and two runs (Henry scored one and drove in the other). The Phillies manager, Mayo Smith, did not blink, nor did he offer even a token look to the bull pen, not during these tough-guy days, when starting pitchers (even in the thirteenth inning) finished the game they started. The bull pen was empty. Meyer worked Aaron gingerly, outside and low, until Henry laced a rocket down the right-field line. O'Connell raced home from first and Aaron stood on third with a lead-taking triple. All Bob Trowbridge—who himself had pitched eight innings of scoreless relief—had to do was finish off the bottom of the thirteenth, which he did easily.

The nightcap at Connie Mack Stadium went twelve innings, with Spahn pitching the whole dozen. The game stayed 2–2 until the eleventh inning, Spahn and Robin Roberts, two future Hall of Famers, trading ground balls for pop flies, when Aaron led off the inning with a home run. Spahn couldn't close the deal, giving up a two-out, two-strike home run to Ted Kazanski (batting average at the time: .211; career average: .217). In the twelfth, Spahn reached third—he had been on base all five times—and Aaron rocked a game-winning sacrifice fly off of another old pro, old Aaron antagonist Curt Simmons.

Now the lead was two, with thirteen games remaining, but only Spahn could win a game. The Dodgers took a one-game lead after Burdette (three and two-thirds), Buhl (three), and Conley (one and one-third) all failed to get out of the fourth inning and the Braves lost all three, two to the Phillies and one to the Giants. On September 25, Spahn won his twentieth, eliminating the Redlegs with a complete-game six-hitter, 7–1. Still, the Braves led by a game—91–60 to the Dodgers 90–61—with two left to play.

The venue was St. Louis. The wobbling Buhl and Spahn were scheduled to pitch, with Burdette slated for the finale.

BRAVES OPEN WITH CARDINALS
TONIGHT WITH CHIPS DOWN
IN TIGHT PENNANT RACE

Three is magic number in closing series;
Buhl to start against Tom Poholsky
By Bob Wolf of the *Journal Staff*

ST. LOUIS—Operation Pennant is at hand. Tonight, against the fourth-place Cardinals, the Braves will enter the final phase of their campaign. . . . Three is the magic number.

The Braves lead the second-place Dodgers by one game with three to play. Any combination of Milwaukee victories and Brooklyn defeats adding up to three will now decide the race.

Perini and Quinn flew in for, as the *New York Times* put it, "the kill." Buhl, in complete free fall, didn't retire a single batter. After two hits and two walks, Haney wasn't taking any chances. The only batter who did make an out, Don Blasingame, did so by getting thrown out while trying to steal second. By the end of the first inning, St. Louis led 3–0.

The Braves clawed back—home run number thirty-eight by Adcock in the second, two doubles, a single, and a sacrifice in the fifth to tie it at 3–3—but Milwaukee was undone by a case of the shakes. In the first inning, Musial pushed a roller to no-man's-land between Adcock at first and Dittmar at second. But when Jack Dittmar fielded the ball, he looked to first, to find it unoccupied. Buhl was late to the bag. Dittmar made a desperation flip—high and late—that went for an error.

In the sixth, Bobby Del Greco singled home a run to break the tie. With the bases loaded and one out in a one-run game, Blasingame bounced an inning ender to Adcock, who threw home for the first out. But Crandall rushed his throw, wide of the bag and low past Adcock. Del Greco scored to make it 5–3.

The Crandall error cut even deeper, when Bruton led off the eighth with a double and Aaron drove him in. The Braves went quietly in the ninth; the final score was 5–4, Cardinals.

Only Spahn remained. He took the mound at Sportsman's Park, determined to carry his team to the World Series. On the mound was Herm Wehmeier, 11–11 on the season and going nowhere, but no insignificant figure in the drama. Six weeks earlier, it was Wehmeier who had beaten Burdette in ten innings, on the same day ending Henry's twenty-five-game hit streak.

A special train, dubbed the "Pennant Express," darted from Milwaukee to Union Station, carrying four hundred eager Braves fans.

Perini liked his chances after Bruton stepped in, with one out in the first, and homered to left, but the remaining two hours and forty minutes were nothing less than torture by baseball. Everything Wehmeier threw came in clear and flat. No suspense, no blinding fastball. The game went twelve innings. In nine of them, the Braves put a man on base, but only one, Henry, passed second base. Aaron stood on third, with two out in the eleventh, but was left to watch the season disintegrate before him. He had singled in the sixth and was exterminated with another double play by Mathews.

Robert George Del Greco, born April 7, 1933, in Pittsburgh, grew up in the Hill District of the city. He was a playground star when he hit his one-in-a-million shot: a tryout with the Pirates. By 1952, he would be the youngest player in the major leagues, playing as a nineteen-year-old for his hometown team. He would play nine seasons for seven teams, including two stints with the Phillies. In no season would he come to bat more than one hundred times and hit better than .259. But Bobby Del Greco could catch the baseball.

He would hit .215 for his career, and that weekend in St. Louis, along with Herm Wehmeier, he became one of the most infamous characters in Milwaukee baseball history. His two hits in winning the opener broke the 3–3 tie and gave the Cardinals insurance. Playing behind Wehmeier, he made eight putouts in center, dousing every rally with his glove. He chased down a vicious drive by Aaron in the eighth. In the ninth, Mathews led off with a bomb to deep center. Del Greco turned to the wall, racing straight back 422 feet to center, the longest part of the old yard. At the very worst, even a plodder like Mathews would have wound up on third, giving the Braves two chances to play for the pennant without even needing a hit . . . and yet Del Greco snared the ball. The pain multiplied when Adcock followed with the single that—had it not been for Del Greco—would have sealed at least a play-off with the Dodgers. Next up was Dittmar, who screamed a liner into the right-center alley that might have scored a run . . . but Del Greco ran it down.

With one out in the twelfth, Musial doubled. Rip Repulski hit a smash to Mathews, who was not sure he had a play anywhere but thought he could at least keep the ball in front of him. But, at the last instant, the ball caromed over his right shoulder and rolled fatally down the left-field line. Mathews gave a helpless half chase, feverishly at first and then with heartbroken steps as Musial careened around third to score the winning run, and wipe out the season.

The next day, the Dodgers swept the Pirates. For the next half century, the final weekend of the 1956 baseball season would haunt members of the Milwaukee Braves. Johnny Logan, the little tinder-box of a shortstop, would remember each sequence where they stared the pennant in the eye, cradled and caressed it, only to see the unlikely Del Greco snatch it away. Spahn, with his eaglelike confidence, would live for forty-seven more years, and would pitch nine more years, win 160 more games, pitch in the World Series twice, face fellow Hall of Famers Gibson, Koufax, Drysdale, Ford, and Marichal. And yet Herm Wehmeier, who would finish a thirteen-year career in 1958 with a career record of 92–108, was the one name he would never forget. On the eve of the World Series, when the Yankees would defeat the Dodgers yet again in seven memorable games, the *Journal* ran a story under Bob Wolf's byline, with a headline that pleaded for an explanation.

WHAT HAPPENED TO BRAVES?
MANY ANSWERS POSSIBLE

Fade Out of Burdette, Buhl Placed
Heavy Burden on Warren Spahn

Why didn't the Braves win? Wherever you go these days, the same questions are asked.

And the answers? . . . One explains the loss of the pennant.

Failure to play even .500 ball after Labor Day is the first thing that meets the eye. . . .

Had the Braves gone just one game over .500 during that time, they would have tied for the flag.

The story went on to say, "With Adcock and Mathews not hitting, Henry Aaron, the new batting champion, was the only member of the one-two-three-punch that hit consistently." For the first time in his career, Henry played a full season of pennant-tight baseball, and he did not disappoint. He did not flinch against the Dodgers, and proved the difference in two extra-inning games in Philadelphia, games without margin. There was not a moment during the pennant chase where Henry succumbed to the pressure. When the Braves soared to the lead in July, Aaron hit .424. When they were gasping in September, Henry hit .357. Against the top two teams in the league, Aaron hit the best: .350 against Cincinnati, .409 against Brooklyn, .450 at Ebbets Field. He had three hits in the epic between Spahn and Wehmeier.

The papers would devote many column inches and thousands of words to the bitter end of the season, to Burdette's fade and Buhl's September fizzle, but the totality of what was lost that season was best summarized by the man often ridiculed the most for saying the least.

"In 1956," Henry Aaron said years later, "we choked."

CHAPTER SIX

JACKIE

JACKIE ROBINSON did not go away easily. The spindly fingers of time caressing his shoulders, Robinson willed a last immortal charge, leading the Dodgers past the Braves for the 1956 pennant. Periodically, the old fire could sustain him, tricking him into believing his competitiveness meshed with O'Malley's and Alston's view of the future. And it was a fact: Even though he'd hit only .275 (his career average would be .311), played in the second-fewest games of his career, and wouldn't even finish the season with one hundred hits, Jackie Robinson was brilliant in 1956, especially in those big games against Milwaukee, when it was clear that the difference between success and defeat would not be commodities as easily definable as simple talent or statistics.

Against the Braves, Robinson hit .347. In June, when the Brooks were struggling to stay afloat in a five-team race, he hit .321. In July, when most players and teams couldn't keep their tongues from dragging the infield, the old man of the Dodgers led the club by hitting .368. Finally, in September, when it was time to win the pennant, Robinson hit .290 but scored seventeen runs and drove in twelve, his highest and second-highest totals of any month of the season.

He was stubborn and driven and dangerous, an asset to a team that lacked that furious thirst to compete, the critical difference to one that seemed oddly luckless, tougher than the Braves but insufficiently resilient against the Yankees. In a final World Series showdown with the Yankees, the last Subway Series for nearly half a century, Robinson was fierce and smoldering: a home run off Whitey Ford in the triumphant opener, two hits the next day as the Dodgers went up 2–0. As was the case during the season, he had a talent for discovering those lush patches of brilliance, as in the tenth inning of the sixth game, after the Dodgers had lost three straight and were facing the end, when Robinson singled home the only run of the game and pushed the Series to its winner-take-all conclusion. The finale, a 9–0 Yankee rubout at Ebbets Field, was explosive only in its confirmation of the Yankee mandate—over a ten-year period, the Yankees met the Dodgers in the World Series six times and lost but once, in 1955—and for being the final humiliation of Don Newcombe. Game seven ended Newcombe's run as one of the signature pitchers of his time and sealed his reputation as a pitcher who came up the smallest when there was so much to be gained. Naturally, it was never that simple. Newcombe won 27 games in 1956 (the rare daily double of the MVP and Cy Young, too) and 123 as a Dodger, but in his career he never won a single postseason game.

In the end, Newcombe finally broke under the weight, and he would never be the same. Over the course of the Series, he punched out a fan after being tagged by the Yankees for six runs over the first two innings in game two, finished the Series with a 21.21 earned-run average in two starts, and, after being demolished again in game seven, left not only the field but the ballpark before the game was complete, disappearing for days before reappearing just before the team plane took off for an exhibition series in Japan. He would never win fourteen games again in a season and would never again pitch in the postseason.

Robinson, in the short term, did not fare much better. The two-out liner in game six (made all the sweeter because the Yankee pitcher, Bob Turley, intentionally walked Snider to get to Robinson) would be the last hurrah in a big-league contest. He went one for ten over the final three games, ending the Series when Johnny Kucks struck him out. On the Japan trip, a goodwill exhibition designed to spread the gospel of baseball, Robinson's temper ignited in Hiroshima and made the lead of the United Press dispatch, "An out-burst by Jackie Robinson highlighted the Dodgers' 10–6 victory over the All-Kansai Stars today in the city that suffered the first atom bomb attack." The story continued to state that Robinson's "run-in with the umpire occurred in the third inning. He protested a decision so long and so loud that he became the first Brooklyn player to be ejected since the start of the Japanese tour."

Robinson made two more pieces of news in Japan. The first was that he was not planning to retire to become manager of the Montreal Royals, the Dodger minor-league affiliate with which he began his career (Robinson was never offered the job). The second was that he said he expected to return to the Dodgers for an eleventh season in 1957. Walter Alston also said he expected Robinson back.

And then, eleven days before Christmas, the Dodgers traded him to the New York Giants. "Dear Jackie and Rachel, I do know how you and the youngsters must have felt," Walter O'Malley wrote Robinson on December 14, 1956. "It was a sad day for us as well. You were courageous and fair and philosophical on radio and television and in the press. It was better that way. The roads of life have a habit of recrossing. There could well be a future intersection. Until then, my best to you both, with a decade of memories. Au revoir, Walter O'Malley."

If he had been caught unawares by the trade—the word he often used for the press was *shocked*—it was only because he forgot that first great rule of baseball, and maybe of life in the competitive world: There are going to be a lot of folks waiting for you on the way down. Baseball always had a way of reminding players that at the end of the day, they were just ballplayers, a reminder that the players always seemed to forget when they were at their weakest. Players had the shortest shelf life; they were, on balance, the easiest to replace, and would live on, if they were lucky and good, in the memory of the people who watched them and enjoyed their play. The real game took place far from the pitching mound, away from the batter's box. That game was invitation-only, and most players, especially the superstars, were not invited. Ruth had left the game a whimper of his bombastic self, a panhandler for a coaching job, who would come up empty until the day he died. DiMaggio, too, would cut an awkward figure when it was time for him to leave the game, and so it would be for Jackie Robinson.

LOOKING BACK, it required an impossible leap of imagination to think of the retirement of Jackie Robinson as anything other than a moment of statesmanship, but the truth was just the opposite. In the winter of 1956, while Henry was basking in the afterglow of his first batting title, Robinson was at best remarkable, dynamic, polarizing. He was, for the first time, vulnerable: Age and sharply declining skills were unable to protect him from his controversies. On team letterhead that contained a photo of the 1955 title team—the team that won Brooklyn's only World Series, with Robinson injured and on the bench in game seven—Alston wrote to Robinson on December 18, 1956.

Dear Jackie,

I appreciate your letter very much and I'm glad to know how you feel. As far as I'm concerned there was never any serious trouble between us, and what little we did have was greatly exaggerated by the press.

I have always admired your fine competitive spirit and team play. The Dodgers will miss you, but that is baseball.

Good luck to you and your family in the future.

Sincerely,
Walt Alston

FEW TEARS INSIDE baseball were shed when Robinson made his retirement official in January 1957, but Robinson's walking away from the game had a tremendous effect on Henry. The two did not share many conversations and were not great friends, but Robinson was a nearly mythic figure for Henry, and his retirement seemed, in an indirect way, to close the first chapter of Henry's baseball life. It was Robinson who had hatched the dream of playing major-league baseball, against white competition, succeeding in what had once been the foreign, prohibited land of white baseball. And here Henry was, twenty-two years old, winner of the batting title, fast being considered in a league with Mays, Musial, and Mantle at a time when Robinson was closing the book on his career—one ending and the other just getting started.

O'Malley may have admired Robinson, but he never exactly enjoyed him. There was no money in it for Walter. Robinson was part of the old regime, a Rickey hand, and O'Malley had never received any residual benefit from Robinson's pioneering. History never credited O'Malley with any portion of the Noble Experiment. Alston and Robinson were never exactly warm. Robinson was a Charlie Dressen man, and Alston kept trying to replace him by trotting out new candidates for his position, as he did when the Dodgers acquired third baseman Ransom Jackson from the Cubs in 1956. Robinson muscled and flexed and reduced Jackson from an all-star in 1955 to a part-time player. Randy Jackson would be out of the league after 1959. "And when Jackie wants to try extra hard," wrote Arthur Daley in the *Times,* "he's a matchless performer, the best money player in the business."

Certainly the skill to defeat an opponent physically and psychologically could have helped a club. Henry W. Miller of 29 Lincrest Street in Hicksville, New York, thought so. After the Dodgers won the title in 1955, Mr. Miller wrote a letter to Joe Brown, the Pirates general manager—the same Joe Brown to whom Ed Scott had written four years earlier about a younger Henry—suggesting the remedy for the sagging Pirates was Jackie Robinson . . . as *manager.*

"Thank you for your letter of October 25 in which you recommend Jackie Robinson for consideration as manager of the Pittsburgh club," Brown wrote in response three days later. "You were most kind to offer your advice, and I can assure you that I have the same high regard for Jack Robinson as you do." In other words, Mr. Miller, leave the front office work to the professionals.

The *Defender* promulgated the Montreal rumor, advocating that Robinson be given the opportunity to make history once again, this time by becoming the first black manager in professional sports. At the same time, Robinson was rumored to be in the running for the Vancouver managerial position in the Pacific Coast League. In this case, the rumors were off by nearly twenty years, for baseball would not hire a black manager until 1974.

If anything, the first month of his retirement was far from tranquil. Warren Giles, the National League president, had no comment upon receiving Robinson's retirement filing, not even the slightest recognition that the game Robinson left was not the game he had entered. Robinson gave an interview later in the month, saying the Dodgers were justified in their concern about the hand injury that reduced Campanella to a .219 hitter in 1956. Jackie and Campanella, two men who saw race in starkly contrasting terms, were never particularly close. Campanella's nonconfrontational style appealed to writers in general and to one in particular, Dick Young. Young found Campanella and told him Robinson had said he was washed up. When Campanella struck back ("A lot of people are happy to see Jackie gone," the catcher said), Robinson found himself at the airport in Chicago, preparing a statement in between connections from New York to San Francisco.

"Campy is quoted as saying that our relationship had 'cooled off' over the past few years," the statement read. "Absolutely no good would be served by my saying why it 'cooled.' I have no argument with Campy and I don't want one. In addition, I'm too busy as chairman of the NAACP Fight for Freedom campaign to concern myself with arguments of this type."

Robinson had taken a swat at his vanquished foes, the Braves, telling one captive audience that the Braves lost the pennant because "one or two of the key Braves players were out 'nightclubbing' with the pennant on the line." It was bad enough that the Braves had lost the pennant on the second-to-last day of the season, and now on his way out, Jackie was pouring a fifth of bourbon into the open wound. That sent Johnny Logan into a lather. Logan chafed at Jackie Robinson for publicly flogging the Braves. If Robinson was going to suggest the Braves partied their way out of the money, Robinson, Logan believed, should at least name the players he knew to be carousing. Otherwise, Logan thought, Robinson was being a coward for covering the entire team under one blanket accusation, for there were players like the catcher Del Crandall—whom Grimm used to call without admiration "the milk shake drinker"—who almost certainly were not burning the midnight oil.

Spahn said Robinson had developed a real hate for Milwaukee, ever since a couple from that city sued him for forty thousand dollars when he accidentally flipped his bat into the stands. Still, Robinson's greatest crime was his candor. Days after being traded to the Giants, he received a letter from his favorite manager, Charlie Dressen, who by that time had begun what would be a short managing stay in Washington. Dressen wrote the letter in his squat, loopy longhand on Washington Senators stationery ("Office of the Manager") and thanked Robinson sweetly for never failing to mention Dressen's considerable influence on him ("Players rarely give their managers any credit," he wrote). The letter was written with a sense of warmth, which underscored the fact that the relationship between the two men went beyond the professional, proof that during the tumultuous period of integration, a legitimate friendship had formed. Dressen had always believed that Robinson was the best baseball player he'd ever managed, and it was clear that Robinson was never more comfortable than when he played under Charlie Dressen. Dressen invited Robinson to Yankee Stadium when the Senators traveled to New York, and said he understood if it was too early yet for Robinson to step into a big-league ballpark, having quit the game so recently. Dressen then asked Robinson to remember, even in retirement, a key portion of the ballplayer code:

> Had something in mind, of course it would not help you now. Just want to give you a tip but I think you are well aware of the same. Anyhow, Jack, don't let anyone trick you into nameing [*sic*] players in regards to night life. You will have to be careful because you will be asked many times about the Milwaukee club. Off the record, or on, don't name anyone.

Then, there was the small matter of Jackie Robinson versus Florence and Peter Wolinsky, the Milwaukee couple who had sued Robinson for forty thousand dollars two and a half years earlier on the grounds of "severe nervous shock" when Robinson conked the couple on the head with a bat he inadvertently tossed into the stands after being ejected by home plate umpire Lee Ballanfant. On February 5, Henry Aaron's twenty-third birthday, Robinson paid each of them three hundred dollars.

On January 31, Robinson's thirty-eighth birthday, Maglie came out swinging. "Jackie Robinson is a pop-off who hurts people and 'then writes them a letter of apology,' Brooklyn's clutch pitcher Sal Maglie said today," a United Press wire story reported. Robinson may have been retired, and it may have been January, but the Barber was still trying to dust Robinson. Robinson was out of shape, Maglie said. He played when he wanted to. His reflexes were shot.

"I admire his playing, but it's a shame that a great ballplayer like he was does that," Maglie was quoted as saying.

Maybe Robinson was cracking under the burden of responsibilities and symbolisms that had weighed him down for too long. His physical appearance would always be the best giveaway—gray hair at thirty-eight would turn porcelain white by forty-five. Only sitting presidents would age on the job as severely as Robinson. His physical appearance was proof of the anecdotal rhetoric: His journey was killing him.

The thing of it was that Robinson understood his special place, his burden, his *mission* more clearly than anyone else. Though Robinson was always described, quite clumsily, in fact, as "breaking the color barrier," the mission itself was by no means the removal of a singular obstacle. First there was the goal of getting onto the field, of making being the first a reality. Then it was necessary to make sure that when he finally did play, he did not do so only as a novelty, but as someone who would be remembered as one of the very few transformative figures equal to the moment. That was the only way integration could gain its proper weight, provide the appropriate momentum for the larger movement that was to follow. Robinson's 1947 roommate, Dan Bankhead, for example, was the first black pitcher in the major leagues, but no one remembered him, because he couldn't play. Baseball's first dominant black pitcher would come a few years later, when Don Newcombe arrived, but it would be nearly twenty years after Robinson before a black pitcher—in this case, Bob Gibson of St. Louis—began a Hall of Fame path and in fact wound up in Cooperstown.

The third stage was full membership in the club, at a level of every white person born in the United States of America—not only for Robinson but for the twelve million Negroes in the country at the time. Well, that one would be a bit more complicated. That was why his contemporaries understood and applauded the early Robinson, the one who took the spikes to exposed shins, the mitts to the face, and the knockdowns, and yet would be so offended and threatened by the assertive, bolder Robinson of later years, the one who realized full equality did not mean staying in your place, but not *having* a place at all. The early Robinson accepted his road by facing down his adversaries with that dangerously double-sided word—*dignity*—which could be at once reverential and patronizing (as Henry would one day discover), and that fit the narrative the kingmakers with the typewriters wanted to tell.

The Robinson who turned the other cheek fit the rules, the perception of how blacks were expected to deal with white aggression, as well as the perception of what the noble experiment was supposed to be all about, the nonviolent protest of being above aggression and thus better than his oppressors. The writers could bask in his forbearance, as long as they had control over and approved the narrative. In truth, Robinson waited for the day to drop a knuckle sandwich on some clown who put him in the dirt one time too many, and when he did—just ask Davey Williams, the Giant second baseman Robinson buried back in the old days, when Maglie (the real target) ducked the responsibility of covering first base after throwing at Robinson—the results were messy and merciless. He once told Roger Kahn that he had no intention of being turned into "some pacifist black freak."

The hard truth was that even as the mid-1950s were producing an unprecedented generation of Hall of Fame black ballplayers who surpassed him in statistics, if not overall raw baseball talent—Willie Mays, Roberto Clemente, Elston Howard, Roy Campanella, Ernie Banks, Frank Robinson, Larry Doby, and Henry Aaron all made their debuts between 1951 and 1955—Robinson was still alone in front.

The 1950s were not a time when Negro ballplayers voiced confrontation in the press, except for Robinson. *Happy to be there* wasn't full membership; neither was *stay in your place.* It was also true that it did not matter what was being said to the umpire or to the press, but, rather, that it was Robinson doing the talking. During Robinson's first five seasons in the big leagues, from 1947 to 1951, he was ejected a total of sixteen times. A loudmouth like Eddie Stanky, the hard-charging adopted southerner, got tossed seventeen times, but it was Robinson who earned the nickname "Pop-off." On August 3, in a death grip for the pennant with Milwaukee, Robinson would go four for six with three RBIs in a twelve-inning loss at St. Louis. That same morning, an item appeared in the *Los Angeles Times:*

SOUTHERN SCRIBE BLAMES
JACKIE FOR RACE LAW

NEW ORLEANS, AUG. 2 (AP)—Bill Keefe, sports editor of the Times-Picayune, said the new law received a push from the "insolence" of Robinson. . . .

"He has been the most harmful influence the Negro race has suffered . . . and the surprising part of it is that he wasn't muzzled long ago."

Unbowed, Robinson responded, "You call me 'insolent.' I'll admit I haven't been subservient, but would you use the same adjective to describe a white ballplayer—say Ted Williams, who is, more often than I, involved in controversial matters?"

It would take another generation of players, the Jim Brown, Bill Russell, Muhammad Ali generation, to embrace Robinson's role of the political figure as athlete, confident in his standing, willing to take a sledgehammer to the old order. And perhaps more importantly, the writers who most passionately championed Robinson's right to exist as a player in 1947 did not appear to appreciate this final leg of the Robinson quest.

Men like Arthur Daley of the *New York Times* and Shirley Povich of the *Washington Post* were not of the appropriate generation to recognize this next challenge as a first assault on a paternalistic order. Instead, they saw Robinson as oversensitive, hot-tempered, irrational, and in many ways betraying the nobility of the experiment. In a sense, their attitudes were no different from the attitude expressed one day in Bradenton, when Spahn would shake his head after reading the latest headline about the Montgomery Bus boycott and ask Henry uncomprehendingly, "Henry, just what is it you people want?"

The writers did not understand their own inherent paternalism. When Robinson formally petitioned for his retirement, Daley recalled in print an early exchange with Robinson.

"If you'll forgive a personal experience, it will be offered as an illustration of Robinson's shrewdness," Daley wrote. "Midway in Jackie's second season . . . this reporter suddenly realized that Robbie had never once addressed him by name. . . . He did not want to set himself apart . . . by using the clumsy 'mister' and he wasn't certain . . . whether the first-name approach would be too familiar.

". . . in his second season, I asked him an inconsequential question. 'You know the answer as well as I do, Arthur.' . . . He'd smuggled in the first name. . . . He was never troubled thereafter."

Daley was so sure of his position, convinced of his birthright to be addressed in a certain formal fashion by a black person, for the reinforcement of his class superiority to Robinson's surely occurred daily. Yet Daley seemed so secure within that order that in his report he did not offer to break the caste system himself by simply inviting Robinson to call him by his first name.

And it made sense that so many began to hate Robinson, because the shift toward a new society did not just come suddenly and without warning; Robinson did not ask for permission to change these unspoken rules. He did not ask to speak in turn. He did not issue a press release announcing he was upgrading his membership, appointing himself one of the first leaders of the movement, years before it was given a proper name.

And the ones who remembered the noble Robinson turned on him because he saw faster than they that his audacity in showing he was unsatisfied was part of that movement. What the Art Daleys and Shirley Poviches of the world did not understand was the difference between perceived and actual equality. Robinson knew the critical difference lay in who sat at the controls. Through Robinson, a meteoric shift was taking place right in front of their eyes, and men like Dick Young and Daley and Povich were of the wrong generation to see it.

He would not play for the Giants, and inside the game he did not have many friends in that insular, exclusive club called baseball. DiMaggio eventually went back to the game, to coach in Oakland after a long disillusionment. Robinson never would. There would be no offers to coach, work in the front office, or manage, few reconciliations, and plenty of calamity, but that was the thing about Jackie: No matter how unsure he looked in his endeavors off the field (sparring with Malcolm X and JFK, supporting Nixon before recognizing the enormity of his error), compared to his grace and fire on it, baseball in a sense would always seem too limiting for him.

That was always the tricky thing about history: You never quite knew in which direction it would turn. Induction into the Hall of Fame required approval on 75 percent of the ballots. When Robinson was elected in 1962, the first year he was eligible, he was safe, by a hair, receiving a mere 77.5 percent of the vote. His Hall of Fame plaque served as proof that baseball at the time did not comprehend its own larger significance: Nowhere did his inscription note that he was the first black player in the major leagues.°

THEY CAME AND went in baseball, but face it, how many actually changed the rules of the game, how it was played, who was allowed to play, and how they were allowed to act? There were really just five— Ruth, Landis, Rickey, Robinson, and Marvin Miller—while the rest served at the pleasure of the ruling class, some doing their part but most maintaining the status quo. And of that five, only one could say he was just as influential on the political front, in protests and events outside of the ballpark, as he was dancing off third base. Following the second game of the 1956 World Series, Robinson received letters on White House stationery from both Vice President Nixon and Frederic Morrow, the first black White House aide, congratulating him and the Dodgers. Nobody else in baseball was getting letters from the Oval Office, and they hated him for that, too. "What? Is he running for president, too?" snorted a bitter Allie Reynolds when Robinson criticized the recalcitrant Yankees for not signing black players. It went back to what the writer Leonard Koppett used to say about Robinson, that before him, black people did not really exist in the eyes of white America. Certainly they were there, in the streets, on the sidewalks, in the kitchen, as the objects of jokes but invisible to the touch, never anything more than stage props.

Robinson was the first black American to play his piano in the

---

°In 2008, the Baseball Hall of Fame and Museum in Cooperstown, New York, took the unprecedented step of replacing Robinson's original plaque with an updated version, one that notes his batting average and awards, but also his place as the first African-American to play in the Major Leagues in the twentieth century.

foreground, with no intention of ever being anything else but the leader. Joe Louis came first, but boxers didn't fight every day, and while the fights were big, the racket itself lacked the social legitimacy of baseball. While Maglie was throwing heat his way, Robinson soared beyond, his legacy secured by progress, redrawing the canvas of society, giving the discussion an entirely different starting point. His enemies chafed at the unfairness of it all, but virtually all would stand on the wrong side of history. It was history that would vindicate him, and the men who sparred with Jackie, the ones who were sick of him, who could least see those transformative qualities, stood alone, sounding little more than bitter. As Robinson's influence as the single most important political figure in baseball history grew all the more obvious as the lifetimes piled up, his enemies began looking horribly small, insignificant signposts disappearing in the rearview mirror.

AT THE TIME, there would be no publicity marking the moment, and it would take years before he articulated his position publicly, but Henry Aaron had carefully watched Robinson, and he did not admire him as much as revere him. Where others saw audacity, Henry saw a road map. For years, Henry would be paired with many players. For if no other reasons than their outsized production and contrasting playing personalities, Henry would always be connected to Willie Mays. For their annual rivalry for the Gold Glove and the starting spot in the All-Star Game, Henry would face comparisons to Roberto Clemente. Naturally, as he reached the pinnacle of his baseball achievements, Henry would always live with Babe Ruth.

For the rest of his playing career, Henry Aaron would be paired with Willie Mays instead of the one player who truly mattered, the one who provided the template not for him as a player but for the man he sought to become. When Robinson retired, to the business world and the somewhat foreign but important arenas of politics and philanthropy, Henry saw the value, the necessity of not being limited by baseball. Only in following in the footsteps of Robinson could Henry realize his true path: to use whatever influences his baseball life afforded him to have some effect on society at large.

CHAPTER SEVEN

SCRIPTURE

It would take one of those years when it all came together—
when he could not only hear the notes in his head but play each and
every one of them beautifully—before the legend could officially
commence. It needed to be the kind of season where all you had to
do was say the year and the heart of every fan would spontaneously
flutter, carrying that person easily back into the warm currents of
memory, and when, even decades later, the faces of his peers would
firm with professional respect. Sometimes, the faces would betray
envy, other times admiration, but in all of them would be the recognition that he was one of the very special ones, that millionth percentile, someone who may have stood on the same field with them
but, because of his enormous talent, was playing a game completely
different from all the rest.

Henry rang in the year 1957 with the same ritual he would begin
every year of his first decade in the big leagues—by sending his contract back to the Braves unsigned. He'd earned $17,500 in 1956 and
had no illusions about his value to the team. First for Charlie Grimm
and then for Fred Haney, Henry had chopped the wood. Adcock had
his best year in home runs, drove in more than a hundred runs, and
most importantly, it seemed as if all of those home runs were against
the Dodgers late in games. But as the season reached its devastating
conclusion, with every at bat critical, Adcock's batting average
dropped nearly twenty points in September, highlighted by a disastrous zero for seventeen in four games against bottom-feeders
Philadelphia, New York, and Pittsburgh. Mathews was second in the

league in home runs, but he was stuck in low gear for the whole season, hitting .229 at the all-star break before grinding his way to a .272
average.

Henry hit thirty-seven points higher than Adcock, fifty-six points
higher than Mathews, and was more consistent than both. Adcock
was certainly the signature clutch player on the team in 1956, but
Henry had shown, as he did in the Philadelphia doubleheader, that
he was not frightened of the moment. Mickey Mantle won the American League Triple Crown in 1956, but Henry was the only player in
the majors with two hundred hits, a twenty-five-game hit streak, and
340 total bases.

Thus, he sent the contract back to Milwaukee blank. Two hundred
hits had to count for something, and on January 26th, a two-
paragraph Associated Press brief hit the wire, filling a corner of the
next day's *Chicago Tribune.* Henry was home in Mobile and spoke by
telephone to John Quinn, who by the end of the conversation understood Henry's idea of his own market value. He didn't just ask Quinn
for a pay raise; he wanted his salary *doubled.*

BRAVES' AARON ASKS PAY
BOOST OF 100 PER CENT

MILWAUKEE, JAN. 26 (AP)—A report tonight said that Henry
Aaron of the Milwaukee Braves, the National League batting champion for 1956, is asking for a 100 per cent salary boost—or $35,000.

"I think I deserve it, after the year I had last season," Aaron said
in a telephone interview from his home in Mobile, Ala.

The Braves had the reigning batting champion, but little sentimentality existed in dealing with John Quinn during contract time.
The salary figures offered to players were hard, for lesser players usually final, and for the more gifted, a higher number was merely far
below what a player was actually worth. In those days, there were no
agents and no lawyers negotiating deals, no salary arbitration, and no
ability to attract interest from another team. And what if you didn't
like the numbers that were being offered? Well, there was always bar-
tending. The big leagues—or O.B., which stood for Organized Base-

ball, as the clubs liked to be called collectively—even negotiated a lockout deal with the independent leagues in Mexico and the Pacific Coast League, blocking a player who did not sign his contract from playing ball anywhere else.

The Players Association was still two decades away from power. Players walked into the front office, virtually always undereducated and, lacking the leverage to play for another team, always overmatched. Quinn understood management's inherent advantages and did not hesitate to flaunt his power. The front office turned making players sweat for a few extra pennies into a sadistic little sport.

"I was making ten grand one year and Mathews was holding out. Logan was, too. Quinn was a good baseball man but tough with the negotiations," Gene Conley recalled. "One day, he calls me over to his office right as my kids are having a birthday party," Conley said. "He's got a couple of cups on the table and a bottle of whiskey. He says to me, 'I'm not giving you what you want.' I tell him I'm not signing, that if this is the offer, then I have no choice but to go back and play basketball. He pours a couple more cups, and says, 'You're going to get it, but you're not worth it.' And then he starts asking me about the family again. He knew the highest number I was asking for was low, but he wanted to make me fight for that. The next day, I saw him and he was all smiles, and asked me about my family and the birthday party, like nothing ever happened. Still, he knew baseball."

Three days after his twenty-third birthday, on February 8, Henry signed his contract for 1957. The papers said he would be making between $25,000 and $30,000, and that Henry's tough stance with Quinn had gotten him close to the seventeen-thousand-dollar raise he sought. Throughout the season, the papers would refer to Henry as earning $28,000. The actual figure was $22,500. Henry had won the batting title, and a measly raise of five thousand dollars was his reward.

"I think back then we all realized just how powerless we were," Henry said. "I didn't have any great strategy. Nobody taught me anything about how to negotiate a salary. A lot of times, you had to take what they gave you. But I figured I would ask. They never gave any of us what we were worth."

. . .

THE ROBINSON sentiment that the Braves were underachieving echoed in a Milwaukee press corps that began to reflect the subtle changes in coverage that would be a harbinger for the contentious years ahead. Traditionally, the writers allowed the explanations for winning and losing to remain within the field of play, but the evidence that the Braves were simply not focused enough, not driven enough, simply not tough enough to be champions was an angle too obvious to ignore.

The Braves were leaving the pennant in the bar, and Milwaukee fans began sending anonymous letters to the local papers in Milwaukee and Chicago, listing the favorite haunts of the players.

The attitudes of the players were one part of the discontentment, and the national writers followed. "The National League pennant has been a mirage for the Milwaukee Braves the last three seasons following their second-place finish in 1953, the year they left Boston," Edward Prell wrote in the *Chicago Tribune.* "Haney realized he had a discipline problem when he succeeded Charlie Grimm as manager last June." What was jarring to the players was the speed with which the Milwaukee writers—and, to a lesser extent, the fans—had become so jaded.

Chuck Tanner recalled the difference in the coverage of the *Journal* and the *Sentinel.* "Bob Wolf always kept it to the game, whether we won or lost," Tanner said. "But that Lou Chapman at the *Sentinel,* he wanted the *story.* He wanted to know who was getting along with whom. He wanted a spark. I remember when they traded me to Chicago, Lou used the old trick to get me to say something bad when I walked out the door. He came over to me and said, 'Chuck, got a pretty raw deal, didn't you?' The fact was, I was grateful to the Braves because they gave me the chance. But you could see the change starting then. Talking about the game on the field wasn't enough. Now look at it."

The transformation had begun the previous year, when the Braves had been embarrassed by the Dodgers during a June home stand, but in 1957, the press had begun intensified scrutiny of the franchise.

Since Perini's arrival in Milwaukee, his leadership had not been in question. With attendance soaring and competitive teams close to a pennant, the Braves were the model for franchise relocation, but now the scrutiny was as much about whether Quinn and Perini had chosen the right players as it was about when the players were going to perform.

O'Connell and Logan were to form the top double-play combination and more: Together they would give the Braves the toughness and fire the team had always lacked. "Danny was to be the holler guy who would make the club seem less placid on the field," wrote the *Tribune*. "The Braves have no quarrel with Danny's vocal enthusiasm, but the chunky Irishman has fallen short of their expectations as a player."

Bobby Thomson suffered similar wrath. He had been acquired from the Giants for Johnny Antonelli and hit but .235 as an everyday left fielder. The Thomson injury had expedited Henry's path to the big leagues, but now another key and expensive deal was starting to look like a failure.

In turn, the manager tightened the screws. This was a championship team, he said. The team didn't make any moves in the offseason, Haney said, because the Braves were already good enough to win. What they needed was more discipline. Wanting to win wasn't enough. Relying on fundamentals to buttress talent was what Haney believed separated a championship team like the Dodgers from his own team.

There could be no greater difference between Haney and Charlie Grimm than in spring training. A half century later, Gene Conley recalled Grimm with a reminiscent lilt in his voice. "Jolly Cholly," he said. "Charlie ran us out there and let us play." Grimm drank with his players, and gave them plenty of free time in the spring, relying on their professionalism instead of using a hammer. Players brought their golf clubs to Bradenton. Charlie brought the banjo. Chuck Tanner recalled a spring training when Grimm cut workouts short because he had a special surprise for his team. "We were working out and Charlie Grimm called us over because he had invited one of the most famous banjo players in the country over. Here it was, spring training, and we were sitting there listening to this guy play the banjo."

Haney was different.

Haney instituted two practices per day, plus meetings, and the golf clubs disappeared. Spring training was not to limber up the muscles and get ready for the season, but more a clinic, with repetition of the most mundane baseball drills. Haney used spring training to redraw the rules. Under Grimm, Bruton had been free to steal bases. Grimm had told him to follow his instincts and ignite the ball club, as a leadoff hitter should. Haney announced that no player would steal without his command, or any who did could expect a heavy fine.

Grimm had given Charlie Root, the pitching coach, the authority to make pitching changes. Haney stripped Root of that responsibility. Haney, however, followed the growing trend of the 1950s by managing from the dugout, allowing his third-base coach to wave or hold runners on the base paths. Grimm had managed in the Durocher style, from third base. By 1957, a manager positioned on the coaching lines neared extinction. Only Bobby Bragan, the Pittsburgh manager, managed away from the dugout.

If Grimm had enjoyed being one of the boys, Haney forged a clear line of authority: The Braves were his team. While Charlie Grimm had not criticized his players in public or exposed them to management, Haney, it seemed, used every spring-training interview to expose a player he believed had not performed for him in 1956.

When Arthur Daley of the *New York Times* came to see him in Bradenton, Haney offered the *Times* columnist strike one: "We came close to winning the pennant without anyone having an outstanding year. I'm discounting Henry Aaron, who won the batting title, because he's a kid just starting to develop as a great hitter." Then came strike two: "Joe Adcock, Bill Bruton and Johnny Logan all had average years. And you can't tell me Eddie Mathews isn't better than a .272 hitter." And finally, in talking to the Associated Press about Thomson, came strike three: "I can't play a .235 hitter in left field."

When the *Chicago Defender* showed up, Haney took a few more hacks at his club, this time taking aim at Danny O'Connell: "He hurt us a lot." There was one player, though, who made the craggy, five-foot-five-inch Haney's lips curl into a smile.

"No one on our team had a really big year. Not even Hank Aaron, though he led the league in hitting," Haney told the *Defender.*

"Aaron's the best hitter in our league. Yes, better than Willie Mays. He's easily capable of bettering his 1956 figures."

IN LATER YEARS, when the power of the player (and in the 1990s the general manager) would eclipse that of the manager, what Fred Haney had done with Henry Aaron on the first day of spring workouts would be the kind of move that got managers fired. Aaron had won the batting title hitting cleanup. Henry had been the cleanup hitter since midway through his rookie season, but Haney told him he would be the subject of a radical experiment: Henry would be batting second.

His reasoning was simple: The top of the order was not producing, and no one in baseball hit more than Henry. O'Connell couldn't be trusted in the second spot in the order, yet Haney decided to bat him first. Bruton, normally the leadoff hitter, had been demoted by Haney during the previous year. That left Henry as the most versatile hitter on the team. Haney believed that having Henry hit second would give O'Connell better pitches to hit. The move would also give him more at bats, as he was guaranteed to hit in the first inning of every game. Mathews would remain in the third spot and Adcock would move up to cleanup.

The second spot was usually reserved for crafty batsmen, the ones who weren't expected to hit the ball over the fence. Henry may not have been in Mathews's category as a slugger, but he was a run producer. Hitting second would limit his opportunities: In the first inning, he could hit only a two-run homer at best, and later in the game, he would be hitting behind a leadoff hitter, the pitcher and eighth hitter.

But the real reason Henry did not want to hit second was because he knew that being in the two-hole, where you hit behind the runner, wasn't where the money was.

"Hell, I'll never drive in one hundred runs hitting second," he said one day.

Henry set the Braves camp afire. March 11, against the Dodgers in Miami, Aaron yanked a fastball over the left-field fence off Sal Maglie. The next day, against the Cardinals, he hit another. Two days later in Bradenton, against Cincinnati, he hit his third home run of the spring. Against the Dodgers again the next day, Aaron took a fastball from Don Elston and blasted it over the four-hundred-foot sign in dead center, over the center-field fence, with seventy-five feet to spare. The *Times* called it the "king-sized wallop of the day." March 16, against the Phillies in Clearwater, Aaron pounded another home run.

It was, thought Gene Conley, as if Henry had decided to focus on another element of his game—power hitting—just for fun.

And that was just the thing about being in the one-millionth-percentile club: It wasn't hyperbole, for the great ones *could* do just that. In baseball, you could separate the good ones from the great with your eyes closed—literally, to the veteran baseball ear, it was often that easy. Contact with the ball just *sounded* different—clearer, cleaner, sharper. When a hitter like Musial or Williams stepped into the cage, there was simply the sound of perfection. The bat didn't graze the pitch, but caught it flush, not just once every four or five swings, but a dozen times in a row if they found their groove. Teammates would tell stories about Henry *choosing* which field—left, center, right—he would drive the ball into. Against the fastball, Henry could fire his hands and wrists and hips through the strike zone without hesitation, level and deadly, unleashing the perfect power swing against the sport's ultimate power pitch.

On breaking balls, the best ones did not shift their bodies too quickly, anticipating a fastball, only to be struggling woefully out of hitting position. They were different. Henry was one of them. He could defy physics and not be caught unbalanced. They could rattle off that mental checklist before the ball reached the plate. They could do what sounded so easy—*see his release point . . . look fastball, adjust to the curve . . . don't pull your head off of the ball . . . stay tight . . . shoulder in . . . wait on the ball . . . be quick!*—and make it look like cake. Everybody else in baseball told themselves the same thing before the pitch, and yet they were the ones walking back to the dugout.

And when all else failed, when the pitcher made a great pitch in a great location—and with a different pitch than expected—a fooled, beaten hitter like Henry could simply summon the gods, weight heavy on the wrong foot, looking for the wrong pitch, and *still* tag it. With Henry, the wrists were already becoming legendary, but unlike the great power hitters, Henry had still not taken to pulling the ball. His power still remained in the right-center-field alley, which meant he could still swing a fraction of a second late and generate tremendous power.

It was true that at times he could look funny, for, unlike Musial or Williams, he did not possess classic mechanics. His teammates and coaches wondered how he could generate such power when finishing on his front foot, instead of his back leg or at his waist, yet they immediately found themselves in awe of just how technically sound he truly was at the actual moment of impact. One day, he tried to explain it to *The Sporting News*. "Whether I'm hitting good or not depends on my timing," he said. "I never have any trouble seeing the ball. I can't even say I see it better when I'm hitting good than when I'm not. When my timing is off, I have trouble, and when it ain't, I don't." To veteran hitting experts, it was something of a remarkable admission. Normally, slumping hitters would decide they were picking up the ball leaving the pitcher's hand just a fraction too late.

Upon contact, everything was in perfect place, as if Henry were a model: His head was down, his eyes focused on the ball. His hands were back, clearing through the strike zone at the same time his hips whipped through, steady and then lethal. On contact, the ball jumped, spring-loaded.

When Henry stepped into the cage for batting practice, players marveled at his bat control, how he could lash line drives to any part of the ballpark. "I remember it probably better than anybody," recalled Frank Torre. "I am left-handed, and many times I had to throw batting practice to Henry. He damned near killed me. He was the scariest guy." During the six weeks of spring, Henry seemed intent on tearing through the league, retribution for stalling in 1956, payback for Herm Wehmeier. He slid into second base against Washington, sprained his ankle, and missed a week, but by the end of March, he was still leading the Braves in runs driven in. When he returned, and the Braves began making their way back north, the rampage continued. He hit a home run in Tampa against Cincinnati, and again April 5 against the Dodgers in San Antonio. When he was finished, and the Braves completed the exhibition season against Cleveland at County Stadium, the Braves were playing with the kind of furious purpose that Haney had long craved.

HANEY, BRAVES SURE 1957 WILL
BE THEIR PENNANT YEAR

The headlines followed along similarly, all dwarfed by one that appeared in *The Saturday Evening Post,* quoting Mr. Warren Spahn, who declared three days before the season started that the Braves would not only win the pennant but would play the Yankees in the World Series, and beat them.

At no point during the 1957 season did Henry's average drop below .308. He homered in every park, against every team, home and away. If he hit when the Braves were ahead, he gave them insurance. He hit when the game was close. He did not steal bases in large numbers, but he stretched singles into doubles, doubles into triples. While Haney had credited him for being a consistent player in 1956, from the beginning of the season in 1957, Henry exuded a special star power that at once elevated him into the elite class of the league.

Take the second game of the season, the home opener in front of 41,506 at County Stadium April 18 against Cincinnati: Burdette and the left-hander Hal Jeffcoat pitched briskly, as if they had a plane to catch, trading fastballs and sliders and double-play balls for five innings. In the bottom of the sixth, Aaron caught a Jeffcoat fastball and golfed it into the Perini pines, the high row of trees that stood between the outfield fences and the miles of parking lot, for the only score of the game. Burdette closed his own deal, forcing the mighty Ted Kluszewski to ground into a double play in the eighth, sealing the 1–0 win. The Braves mashed the Redlegs three straight, and won their first five games.

On April 24, at home against St. Louis, the Braves faced their old nemesis Herm Wehmeier, the man who in 1956 first snatched away Henry's twenty-five-game hitting streak (after dropping him with cheek-high fastballs during his rookie season), then beat Spahn and ripped the pennant away that fateful final Saturday. Wehmeier lasted just four innings, giving up home runs to Adcock, Aaron, and Mathews before departing. Yet Wehmeier escaped with a no-decision. Crandall bombed the winning home run in the bottom of the ninth.

The Braves played three straight extra-inning games to start May, once at the Polo Grounds over the Giants and twice in Pittsburgh, and won them all. Tied at 1–1 in the tenth against the Giants, Henry drove in the game winner that gave Spahn a ten-inning, complete-game win. The next night, Henry went five for six against Pittsburgh. Burdette was up 5–2 in the bottom of the ninth, only to give up a pinch-hit, three-run homer to John Powers (.195 average, six homers for his career). The Braves scored three unearned runs in the tenth, the second coming when the Pittsburgh right fielder, Roberto Clemente, allowed Henry's single to skip past him to win, 8–5. The next night, Henry doubled in the fourth to score Gene Conley, smoked a two-out, three-run homer off Bob Friend in a six-run sixth, and scored the winning run after tripling to lead off the eleventh. Henry was muscling his way onto the big stage, armed with a sudden and complete command of his game. His teammates thought of him as a gifted hitter, if not a bit aloof, but during the first weeks of 1957, he took on the look of a superstar. The surge of confidence went back to the first days of spring training, when Henry arrived in Bradenton convinced not only of his own ability but that 1957 would be the year when his talent and self-confidence would intersect. Moreover, he had begun to force the writers and his teammates to view him as a leader.

DURING HIS FIRST three seasons, Henry had escaped the criticism leveled at the rest of the Braves. He was portrayed mostly as a comet, a player too talented to miss as a prospect but too green to be part of the Braves cultural problem. He was just reaching his potential as a player and was asked only to let his play provide his leadership. The press had not yet collectively come to a conclusive opinion of Henry. He was twenty-three, entering his fourth season, and while the Braves did not appear to have the experience of the Dodgers, they were a veteran team, whose leaders were all in their thirties. Spahn was thirty-six, Logan and Burdette were thirty, and Bobby Thomson was thirty-three.

Henry was not quoted often, and when the paper previewed the Braves, it talked about the psyches of Spahn, Mathews, and Burdette as keys to the Milwaukee season. In later years, Henry would see these characterizations as subtle forms of the racism he had dealt with his entire life. He would take the writers' underestimation of his influence as proof of their cultural reluctance to position a black player ahead of established white stars—even in the late 1950s, when Robinson had already retired and proved that a black player could lead a club without the visible on-field fissures baseball people had long feared.

More than simple racism, the uncertainty of the press with regard to Aaron seemed to prove another vexing phenomenon: the inability of the writers close to Henry to read him properly. Had one, whether it was Bob Wolf of the *Journal* or Lou Chapman of the *Sentinel,* been able to connect with him, he would have seen Henry's confidence upon his arrival in Bradenton as obvious. Henry told the *Defender* he saw the National League Triple Crown as a goal, and that Willie Mays was one player who could keep him from leading the league in average, home runs, and RBIs. If he could stay ahead of Stan Musial for the batting title, he figured, he would have a chance. The story may have been one of many light spring-training features, that time of pastel optimism. Henry's comments could have even been considered reckless for a young player, and quickly dismissed. Expecting to have a good year was one thing; talking about surpassing Mays and Musial was quite another, even for a defending batting champion. But in Henry's case, it was indicative of his emergence as a star player, emblematic of his circuitous method of revealing just how sure he was of his ability. Just a year earlier, it was Henry who had barnstormed with Mays, outperformed other star players, only to be enveloped, swallowed whole, by Willie's aura.

In just a year, he no longer considered his abilities with deference toward other players, even Mays or Musial, who had won his first batting title when Henry was nine years old and had won six batting titles before Henry turned eighteen. They were great players. Musial had been his idol, true enough . . . but now they were his *peers.*

.   .   .

SUNDAY, MAY 5, with the Braves playing the Dodgers at Ebbets Field up a game in the standings, Haney gave the ball to Bob Buhl, the same Buhl who had beaten Brooklyn eight times in 1956. This night, a heavy bag would have taken less punishment than the shots leveled at Buhl. He recorded just two outs, gave up five runs in the first, and was gone. Before he left the shower, Brooklyn led 7–3.

But it didn't matter, not with Henry flying. With one on in the top of the first, Henry singled up the middle off Sal Maglie, but the ball got past Duke Snider and rolled 410 feet to the wall. O'Connell scored easily and Henry raced around the bases and scored all the way from first. In the third, Henry doubled to right and scored again. In the fourth, he lashed a two-out, three-run homer over the fence in right to cut the lead down to a manageable 7–6. By the end of the fifth, the Braves led 9–7.

Henry capped the evening by singling off Sandy Koufax in the eighth. He had rattled Snider in the first and then strolled home from third when Koufax chucked a wild pitch. The Braves had won, 10–7, and when the smoke finally cleared, Aaron had gone four for five, with a home run, a double, two singles, four runs scored and three batted in. His average was now .417.

Then there was the frigid forty-degree afternoon of May 18 at County Stadium, when Henry pounded two homers against Pittsburgh, first off Vern Law in the third and then, in the next inning, a two-out, three-run backbreaker that did in Bob Smith, fueling a three-for-four, four-RBI day and a 6–5 win. Henry was now leading the league in home runs and RBIs, and close to the top in everything else. During the first week of June, Haney realized that a hitter of Henry's gifts couldn't be a two guy, a power hitter in a Punch-and-Judy role. On June 7, Haney finally came to his senses. He made the switch and restored Henry to cleanup.

The machine was coming together. A year earlier, Eddie Mathews had been dying at the plate, hitting .250 on a good day, under .230 when things went sour. But now he battled Henry for the home-run lead and was hitting over .300. Spahn, Burdette, and Buhl were all winning, and then there was the Kid, twenty-year-old Juan Ramón

Cordova Pizarro, the lefty phenom from Puerto Rico, who made the team out of spring training and already was being called the next War-ren Spahn.

The Braves played like a team still smarting at having given away a golden opportunity the previous year. There was, thought Johnny Logan, no joy in the chase, as there had been in the years before, that spark of titillation when the writers would put the Braves in the same class as the Dodgers, the Giants, and the Yankees. Instead, Logan recalled, there could be only one outcome that would satisfy the play-ers. "You have to remember. We had been close for probably five years. We felt it was our time. We had earned the right to think that way."

The beauty of winning is that it always provides a soft landing dur-ing the rough spots. The problem with losing is that no one lets you forget it, ever. When the Braves surged, *The Sporting News* reminded them of their old nemesis, running a forty-eight-point headline above the fold that read JACKIE'S RAP NO SPUR TO BRAVES' SPURT, in reference to Robinson's contention that the Braves drank themselves into second place in 1956. "Did Jackie Robinson's blast at the Milwaukee Braves last winter fire them up and send them away flying in the National League Pennant race?" read the lead paragraph of the story. It was a charge that more than fifty years later still bur-rowed into Johnny Logan.

"Ah, that was complete bullshit. When we went to the bar, it was to talk baseball. When we won, it was to enjoy getting the job done. When we lost, it was getting the guys together to see how we could win the next day. Total BULL-*shit!*"

If they had been criticized in the past for not playing their best against the league's best, the Braves now sent the message to their National League rivals that they weren't gorging themselves only on the cupcakes. Against Cincinnati, they mashed the Reds the first six times they met and seven of eight, and even started a row with Reds manager Birdie Tebbetts, who railed against Burdette and his spit-balls. Haney responded that he was "tired of this spitball wrangle," and said that maybe the Braves routine coldcocking of the Reds was the real reason Birdie had a beef with the Braves. But there was something special about Cincinnati. The two second basemen,

Johnny Logan and Johnny Temple, waged their own little private war, jawing and spiking. Adcock had no love for the Reds, the team that gave up on him. Milwaukee beat St. Louis and the Dodgers both five of eight. The Braves played with the kind of angry drive that vindicated the common belief that Milwaukee was the best team in the National League. These ingredients were supposed to fuel the engine for the whole 154 games.

And yet—and *yet*—Milwaukee was just as close to the pennant as they were to fifth place. During the first week of June, five teams were separated by only a game and a half. The Dodgers were supposed to be fossils. Newcombe was down, but Koufax, Drysdale, and Johnny Podres entered June a combined 14–6. The writers said the Cardinals would compete, maybe the toughest out in the league, but in the end didn't have the horses, or so went the conventional wisdom. But the Cardinals were trading afternoons in first place with the Braves. The same was true for the big-hit, no-pitch Reds. Even the Phillies, who could pitch with Brooklyn and Milwaukee but couldn't hit off a tee, were in the race.

The Braves were hungry and angry and focused, playing each day with a singular intensity, but it just wasn't possible for a club to get mad and thrive off that rage for the entire season. Baseball is a game of stoic concentration, requiring a maestro's sense of timing for knowing when to get mad, when to clown, when to floor the accelerator or to forget an especially tough loss and just let the tide pass.

Beyond the star players were real problems. Covington (.143), Pafko (.143), and Thomson (.156) weren't hitting. Chuck Tanner was swinging—and missing—at .192. Haney had already benched Thomson in May after starting the season three for his first thirty-four. Conley was 0–4. On May 15, Haney shipped Covington back to the bushes, to Wichita, of Class AA ball. Haney had already been victimized by the left-field situation in 1956, vowed it wouldn't happen again, and yet his left fielders combined to hit .163.

The writers knew Haney wanted to make a deal, and they sniffed around to find out what the Braves next move would be. Haney did his best to play coy, but the little general wasn't so good at this. Despite the fact that Milwaukee had paid a quarter million for

O'Connell, who was still hitting .230, it was rumored that the old hand Red Schoendienst would be traded to Milwaukee to stabilize a position that, in truth, had been an expensive disaster.

"Now there's a funny one," Haney told *The Sporting News* the day Covington was sent out. "I have been asked about Schoendienst for months." Haney added, "In short, there has been a lot of player trading—in the newspapers. I am not beefing. It doubtless makes interesting reading, and it's no hair off my thinning noggin. I think we have a fine ballclub, and if you get the impression that I think it's good enough to win as it stands, you have caught my sentiments."

Haney focused on two targets for his anger since the spring: they were Bobby ("I can't play a guy hitting .235") Thomson and Danny ("He hurt us a lot") O'Connell. Haney had told just about anyone with a press card that second base and left field would either cost the Braves the pennant or win it. Exactly one month after Haney laughed off the Schoendienst deal, O'Connell and Thomson were shipped to the Giants for Schoendienst, the hard-driving nine-time all-star who at twenty-three had won a World Series title with Musial in St. Louis.

The baseball life would be a bittersweet one for O'Connell. After placing third for Rookie of the Year with Pittsburgh in 1952, O'Connell would never hit better than .266 after being traded from Milwaukee. He hated playing for San Francisco manager Bill Rigney, who, he said, destroyed his confidence. After the Giants moved west to San Francisco, O'Connell played two more years, ceasing to be an everyday player. He played two uninspired years in the cellar with Washington and was finished in baseball after the 1962 season. He caught on as a coach with the Senators. On the night of October 2, 1969, O'Connell's car skidded off a rain-slicked street near Clifton, New Jersey, and hit a telephone pole, the crash killing him. He was forty-two years old.

For Bobby Thomson, the trade from Milwaukee would be an especially bitter one. For the next fifty years, he would be an American hero, but words like *hero* and *icon* could be savored only when the playing stopped. Thomson would have one good season with the Giants, but the broken ankle he suffered his first year with Milwaukee effectively ended his career as an impact player.

. . .

AT THE NATIONAL LEAGUE All-Star Game played in St. Louis July 9, 1957, three future immortals were unanimously voted to start the game: Stan Musial, Willie Mays—and Henry Aaron. Normally, the fans did the voting for the eight starting lineup spots, while the manager voted for the reserves and the pitching staff. The All-Star Game was, after all, the fans' game. But Commissioner Ford Frick stepped in and took over the voting after an exuberant ballot-stuffing campaign in Cincinnati threatened to hijack the integrity of the Midsummer Classic. Ten days before the game, the *Cincinnati Times-Star* added 550,000 new ballots. Had the coup succeeded, Cincinnati would have started all eight positions. In later years, both the league and the individual teams would *encourage* the kind of ballot stuffing Frick believed it was his duty to stop. And if the commissioner had had much of a sense of humor regarding the matter, he would have concluded that the Cincinnatians deserved credit for their moxie, if nothing else.

Without Frick, Wally Post, who trailed Aaron by fifty thousand votes before the flood, would have started. Henry's old teammate George Crowe would have beaten Musial, and Gus Bell would have toppled Mays. The new starting outfield for the game was a bit more representative, especially for posterity: Frank Robinson in left, Willie Mays in center, and Henry Aaron in right.

Henry had gained more fan votes for the game than Mays. Henry batted second behind Johnny Temple and in front of Musial and Mays. Frank Robinson hit sixth. Henry didn't do much in the game, going one for four against Jim Bunning, Billy Loes, Early Wynn, and Billy Pierce.

If Henry's arrival as a player was undeniable, the greater problem was in understanding him as a man. That would be infinitely more difficult, because it required considerably more introspection on the part of the writers and Henry's teammates than watching his mechanics or marveling at his bat speed.

The local Milwaukee reporters didn't quite know what to make of him, because they didn't quite know anything about him, and often they restricted their commentaries to Henry's latest game-winning hit. His leading characteristic off the field was to be the first person dressed in the clubhouse, often gone from the room before reporters arrived.

From the time Henry arrived in Milwaukee, the more complicated task of confronting the social customs of the day, all of their uncomfortable layers and Henry's level of acceptance, required skill. In the eyes of the traveling Milwaukee writers, considering the Braves as anything other than belonging in mind and spirit to Spahn and Mathews meant veering from the expected script, one that had been anticipated since the Braves arrived in Milwaukee from Boston.

Henry forced a change of thinking. Outside of the Dodgers and Giants, no team had yet possessed a black player who was not only the most talented player on the team but also its emotional core. The Braves were a raucous and rowdy team. The leaders of the team were Burdette, Spahn, Mathews, and Logan. All were big drinkers, and few took the time to consider Henry as anything but shy. *Shy* was the operative word.

"You *had* to drink to hang out with that crowd. That wasn't Henry's way," Johnny Logan recalled. "He never did stay around much. He kept to himself in what was the colored part of town." Logan reflected a common attitude among white ballplayers, which suggested that Henry and other black players did not socialize with their white teammates merely by choice. So much of it was a question of knowing where you stood. The reality was that in American society, there were too many layers of negotiation. There were no clear rules, no road maps to follow in 1957. "I kept to myself because I didn't want to be humiliated," Henry recalled. Inviting a black player and his wife over for a barbeque might have offended half the club, causing everyone discomfort. An invisible line cut through America that no one was quite sure how to cross. Henry wasn't a big drinker, it was true, but he wasn't often invited to join the crowd, either.

Frank Torre, the Milwaukee reserve first baseman, was one of the few white teammates to spend time with Henry, and what he saw was a man who was sensitive to slight but who also kept his emotions regarding segregation buried. Henry did not want to be a burden to his teammates, Torre thought, so he often remained solo, preferring to spend time alone. "He went through terrible times. We used to go to the Milwaukee Athletic Club, used to go there all the time, and people would make a big stink because he was a Negro," Torre recalled. "And that was here, where the Braves were heroes."

Alcohol provided a subtle yet vitally important subtext of race relations. Black players were often wary of drinking around whites because of its potential dangers. The clubhouse, a relatively controlled environment, was one thing. Being away from the park, in bars that may not have been friendly to blacks, when players unwound and released their inhibitions, was quite another. It was when the alcohol flowed that the real danger lurked, and all it took was one drink, one shot too many, for a potentially explosive situation to develop. The writer Roger Kahn recalled that when Jackie Robinson was playing cards with his Dodger teammates, Hugh Casey, a big right-hander from Georgia, said he fought losing streaks—both on the field and at the card table—by "rubbing the teat of the biggest, blackest nigger woman I could find." Scenes could be bad enough among teammates when a player got drunk, but add to it the simmering tensions and resentments that existed just under the surface during the first decade of integration and the decision on the part of many black players not to mix socially seemed a wise one.

Gene Conley saw Henry socially on similar terms as Johnny Logan. "He really was all business. He had a job to do and he did it. Then he was out of there." Conley had competed with and against blacks for years. The racial codes, both real and clumsily ignored by the Braves players, made him uncomfortable even decades later. Conley would be especially aware not because he was a social activist but because he was a basketball player.

"I just didn't go for that stuff. I didn't make a big deal of it then or now," Conley recalled. Logan, too, who came from upstate New York, was not uncomfortable or distant with his black teammates, but he wasn't unaware of the difficulties.

There were days when Conley seemed intrigued by Henry, but he also knew the strict codes about mingling socially with his black teammates. Conley recalled knowing specifically that during spring training, when teams developed their collective personality, hanging out with blacks in town after games was prohibited. More than his other white teammates, Gene Conley found he was uncomfortable to the point of anger when discussing the racial questions of the day. Conley recalled that later, when he joined the Boston Celtics, he often spent more social time with Russell than with Henry. It all seemed so stupid, he thought. "The 1950s," Conley said ruefully one day a half century later, "were hard."

The other power brokers on the team were less predictable, which made the concept of drinking with them less palatable. Spahn wasn't from the South, but nevertheless he held racial attitudes not always considered progressive. Spahn and Aaron had something of an odd relationship. Throughout the league, Spahn had developed a reputation for being, if not a strident racist, a man who was less sympathetic toward the black situation and, despite his education and combat service in World War II, less willing to change. Both Spahn and Aaron would profess respect for each other's Hall of Fame talent, but Spahn was glib and aloof, while Henry was known for his deliberate and shrewd assessment of people. Henry, like Bob Gibson, was constantly, if not openly, measuring what kind of men the white people around him were. Spahn could make a joke and if you didn't get it, well, that was *your* problem. If it offended you, then maybe you were just being too sensitive, like the time he offered and answered a riddle in the clubhouse. This was during the season the Braves were receiving national attention for being the first big-league club to field an all-black outfield. There was Bruton in center, Wes Covington in left, and Henry in right.

"What's black and catches flies?" Spahn asked one day in the clubhouse.

"The Braves outfield."

In the baseball culture, that was Spahn's right. He had been a star pitcher for so long that he did not have to adjust to his teammates as much as they needed to learn about him, a dynamic especially true in the case of Spahn's black teammates.

Burdette was from West Virginia, and his hostile attitude toward blacks had been well established, while Adcock and Henry already knew where they stood. Some players engaged in a spirited talk about "niggers" without realizing Henry was within earshot. The Braves may have been teammates, determined to win the World Series together, but Henry did not assume he was necessarily welcome in every situation.

"You had to remember that integration was a new thing," Henry said. "We had players coming from places where that wasn't accepted. Everybody had to learn to live differently."

With the Braves grinding through another tight National League race with four other teams, the national press descended on Henry for a closer look at the man who was, even in July, the leading candidate for Most Valuable Player and the Triple Crown, goals he had set for himself back in spring training. And that wasn't all. Two days after he joined the All-Star Game, the Associated Press announced that Henry had invaded the thinnest airspace possible for a baseball player.

HANK AARON TIES RUTH HOMER
MARK AFTER 77 GAMES

With the 1957 major league season at the halfway mark, young Hank Aaron is even with Babe Ruth's record home run pace. Mickey Mantle of the New York Yankees is four behind.

Aaron, who also leads the National League in batting (.347) and runs batted in (73) has hit 27 home runs in 78 games, the same number Ruth totaled in the same number of games en route to his record 60 in 1927 with the Yankees.

On Monday, July 29, the Braves enjoyed one of their most rousing wins of the season, a 9–8, tenth-inning affair over the Giants at County Stadium. Spahn, taking a terrible pounding, couldn't get out of the fifth, while Willie and Henry played tit for tat. Mays was thrown out while trying to steal home in the third; then Aaron beat him deep with a triple over his head, and scored when Covington drove him in, to tie the game at 4–4. Willie broke the tie with a long homer off Pizarro in the seventh, and the Giants broke it open in the eighth with three more.

Down 8–4, with one out, in the bottom of the ninth, Crandall homered and started a four-run rally that tied it at 8–8. With two out and the bases loaded in the bottom of the tenth, Al Worthington walked Mantilla home for the victory.

That morning, the latest issue of *Time* magazine hit the news-stands, a sultry illustration of the actress Kim Novak on the cover. Inside were 589 words under the headline THE WRIST HITTER.

> In the wildly unpredictable street fight for the National League lead, the Milwaukee Braves were last week's team to beat. . . . But the man mainly responsible for the Braves' surge into first place was a lithe Negro outfielder named Hank Aaron, who is hitting the baseball better and more often than any man in the National League.

The story recounted the old Aaron chestnuts—his days with the Clowns, Dewey Griggs scouting him in Buffalo, the Mobile beginnings—but in the final section of the piece, the subheadline referred to Aaron as "The Talented Shuffler."

> Aaron claims to enjoy playing right field . . . because ". . . I don't have as much to do, especially not as much thinking." Thinking, Aaron likes to imply, is dangerous. But by now everyone knows that Aaron is not as dumb as he looks when he shuffles around the field ("I'm pacing myself"), and some . . . think he will . . . rank among the game's great hitters.

In later years, when the country's attitudes shifted and talk that had been common for centuries became socially unacceptable, Henry would gain an annoying reputation among writers for being bland, the same writers who would later attempt to deify him. More likely, Henry had erected a wall around himself, a protective barrier designed to prevent, or at least minimize, the lasting damage of the words written about him.

"I wouldn't have taken that shit," Bill White recalled. "I would have had to have a talk with a lot of people had they said those kinds of things about me. But you also have to remember that a lot of those first black players were from the South, and this is what they knew. It had been reinforced in them and their families for so long and they had been taught not to fight back. That's why it used to anger me when people accused Willie of not saying enough. The reason why Henry is a man of respect is because of things like this. He did not respond with words, but with his bat. But Henry Aaron took a lot of crap."

The press had traveled to Milwaukee to see Henry before. It was in 1956, when Charlie Grimm was still managing the club and the Braves were the fashionable choice to end the Dodger reign. A month before Haney took over, *The Saturday Evening Post* ventured to Milwaukee to profile Henry. Like every top prospect or signature player on a club, he had been featured in the local papers, but *The Saturday Evening Post,* with its Norman Rockwell covers and decades-long residence on American coffee tables, was another matter altogether.

Even in the mid 1950s, as *The Saturday Evening Post's* influence had begun to wane and television accelerated its final demise, few magazines reached the heart of America like it did. Its interest in Henry represented his arrival in just his third season, but it also seemed to validate the Perini claim that Milwaukee would one day become the country's baseball capital. *Sports Illustrated* and *Sport,* the two national sports magazines that would carry the industry for nearly a half century, were still in their infancy. *The Sporting News* had not been surprised by Aaron, but the Baseball bible in those days was more a trade magazine for the industry. A feature in *The Saturday Evening Post* meant Henry would be introduced to the mainstream. This form of recognition was reserved for only the most gifted players, the ones who either had transcended their own sport or achieved a degree of cultural significance beyond the limits of the batter's box.

Ted Williams and Joe DiMaggio had been on the cover of *Time* and *Life,* as had Jackie Robinson. Willie Mays made the cover of *Time* in 1954 and would win the cover of *Life* for the first, but not the last, time in 1958, as the Giants arrived in San Francisco. With the interest in him expressed by *The Saturday Evening Post,* Henry would have two important breakthroughs: He would begin his ascent into the ruling class of baseball players, and for the first time in his career, he would be introduced to a larger American audience interested in reading about important people.

The writer of this profile was Furman Bisher, a thirty-seven-year-old reporter, whose full-time job was covering sports for the *Atlanta Journal.* Bisher had been raised in Denton, North Carolina. A speck of a town in the central portion of the state, it claimed just six hundred people. As a boy, when he was not milking cows and completing his farming chores, Bisher had longed to be a third baseman, a dream only enhanced when one of his high school friends, Max Lanier, went on to pitch in the major leagues, primarily for the St. Louis Cardinals. Through good luck and good connections, Bisher landed a freelance writing contract with *The Saturday Evening Post* to write periodic sports pieces. He had gained the trust of a top editor at the magazine after a pair of profiles of college football coaches were well received by the New York office.

Bisher knew Henry from years before, having covered the Sally League in Atlanta when Aaron played for Jacksonville. Bisher liked to tell the story that he supplied the great New York columnist Red Smith with a variation on one of the more memorable lines regarding Henry Aaron. Smith wrote that in Jacksonville, Henry "led the league in everything except hotel accommodations."

For the better part of a week, Bisher absorbed the life of Henry Aaron. He dined at the apartment on Twenty-ninth Street and watched television with Barbara and little Gaile. Bisher would recall particularly enjoying the company of Barbara, whom he would refer to as "shy," "trim and pretty," with a "great personality." "We got along quite well," he recalled. Early during the visit, he decided that Henry wasn't equipped for the fame that his talent would ultimately create, but Barbara seemed more readily inviting and eagerly curious about the life of a sports star, a life that was beginning to define their environment.

Bisher talked to Grimm, who told him that Henry was "one in a thousand. You can't make a Willie Mays out of him. He's not that spectacular. He does things in his own way. But he'll probably be around a long time after Willie's gone." He retold the few chestnuts about Henry's early life that became boilerplate for every writer attempting to shape Henry Aaron for the next half century: his brief time with the Indianapolis Clowns, Dewey Griggs's signing him with the Braves, his brief and wondrous play at each level in the minor leagues. Bisher recalled being taken by the Aaron family and considering Henry a friend.

When the Bisher profile appeared in the August 25, 1956, issue, Henry's introduction to America in *The Saturday Evening Post* would not be the triumphant moment that trumpeted his arrival onto the national scene. Instead, it was the most influential and devastating piece of journalism ever written about Henry Aaron.

BORN TO PLAY BALL

*Milwaukee's prodigious Hank Aaron
doesn't go in for "scientific" hitting.
He just grabs a bat and blasts away.*

In Jacksonville, Florida, where he carried off almost everything except the franchise during the South Atlantic League baseball season of 1953, there is still a considerable degree of puzzlement about Henry Louis (Hank) Aaron, now one of the mightiest warriors in the tribe of the Milwaukee Braves. There was, for instance, the time in Jacksonville that summer when Aaron was in the grip of a rare batting slump, and one of his teammates asked in conversation how he was going to cure it.

"Oh, I called Mr. Stan Musial about it," was Aaron's dead-pan reply, "and I coming out of it."

"What did Musial tell you to do?" asked the teammate, an infielder named Joe Andrews.

"He say, 'Keep swinging,' " Aaron said.

Shortly the slump passed and Henry thundered on to a .362 finish. Meanwhile, the Musial story was repeated often in dugouts around the league. On the day when Aaron got the league's most valuable player award, manager Ben Geraghty decided it might be well to have Henry repeat his Musial tale to the sports writers who were inquiring into the reasons for his success.

"Man, I never called Stan Musial," Aaron said, shaking his head vigorously.

"But you told Joe Andrews you did," Geraghty said.

"I liable to tell Joe Andrews anything."

Spec Richardson, general manager of the Jacksonville Braves, is representative of the perplexed local opinion that Aaron left behind.

"Tell you the truth," he says, "we couldn't make up our minds if he was the most naïve player we ever had or dumb like a fox."

For decades, journalists would speak of Henry with a mixture of respect for his baseball achievements and deep frustration bordering on anger for what they considered to be Aaron's unnecessary suspicion of them. Henry would not dispute the writers' descriptions of him. Often, he would confirm what the writers believed, for his wariness of the press was real. He did not believe that how he thought about himself as a person had ever been accurately conveyed in print, that the gap between his recollections of a given interview and the finished product was always far too wide. Furthermore, it was a gap that never seemed to tilt in his favor. Yet Henry also would not explain that the roots of his remove could be found in the pages of *The Saturday Evening Post:*

> Even in Aaron's earlier days with the Braves, there were occasions when he surprised everybody with his mental nimbleness. . . .
>
> Off the field, the Aarons stay pretty well tied to the little apartment when the Braves are at home. For all his natural rhythm, Henry doesn't dance a step. . . .
>
> One of the biggest moments in Henry's career so far was the 1955 All-Star Game, which was played in Milwaukee. Henry scored a run, walked and singled twice. His second single, combined with Al Rosen's error tied up the game and sent it into extra innings. Stan Musial finally won it with a twelfth-inning home run.
>
> "I enjoy that," Aaron said. "but my first year in the league I play in Jim Wilson's no-hit game. That's the most kick I get out of baseball."

Over the three-page spread, Bisher exposed, though perhaps unintentionally, an important subtext of the baseball culture at the time. Integration by 1956 was clearly a success—only the Tigers, the Phillies, and the Red Sox had not yet integrated. But in the eight full seasons since Jackie Robinson had debuted, black players had dominated the sport, yet having star black players on major-league rosters did not amount to actual equality. He noted that Henry's Braves teammates had nicknamed him "Snowshoes" for his stiff-legged running style. At no point did Bisher mention that Henry did not engage with his teammates easily because he, along with Joe Andrews and Felix Mantilla, were the first black players ever to play in the Sally League. Integrating a southern league was no insignificant task; in 1953, most southern states still carried laws on the books prohibiting competition between whites and blacks. Certainly entering such an environment could have explained much of Henry's hesitation, but Bisher, a southerner comforted by his own sense of normalcy, saw Henry merely as an unsophisticated black character. Even Jackie Robinson, insulated in the minor leagues by playing in Montreal, had not had to endure the indignities that came with playing in the South on a daily basis.

The Sally League had long been considered perhaps the most notorious of the minor-league systems, and baseball people believed the league seemed the most unlikely to transition smoothly to integration. The Sally League's reputation (combined with the cities and states that comprised it) was so formidable that big-league teams (the Red Sox and Cardinals primarily) used the fear of conflict in their minor-league affiliations in the South as reasons the big-league teams did not integrate. Bisher, and by extension Henry's teammates and the men in the Jacksonville front office, captured Henry's reticence, but they interpreted his hesitancy as an inability to navigate or a lack of intelligence, instead of recognizing the social forces at work. In the South, blacks were forced by habit, custom, and the law to be careful about how or if to approach whites. Henry had been taught from birth not to assume, and thus he would not have believed that he was entitled to the perk—which likely seemed extravagant at the time— of choosing a personal collection of bats.

In the fifteen hundred words he used, Bisher painted a disturbing portrait of Henry as nothing more than a country simpleton. Bisher wrote of him in the most condescending of terms, portraying a kind of hitting savant unaware of the larger, sophisticated world around him and without a passable IQ. The device Bisher used most effectively was language. Sharp and yet subtle, language could convey intelligence, stupidity, or *nothing*. It could be deftly used to feed into racial stereotyping.

> "I guess the thing I'd most rather do of all," he said, cocking his head and biting his lower lip, "I'd rather hit four hundred. A lot of guys are hitting forty homers nowadays, but nobody is hit four hundred since Ted Williams a long time ago."

In 1955, Henry and two other Braves players arrived in Bradenton to begin early work before spring training. Today, players are allowed to work out at a club's minor-league facilities during spring training but are prohibited from arriving at the major-league grounds until the league-scheduled reporting date.

But in 1955, players were not allowed to use the club facilities at all until the mandatory reporting date. Commissioner Ford Frick wired the Braves and fined the players fifty dollars. Charlie Grimm alerted Henry with a note, telling him he'd been fined by Frick, and Aaron's reply was, "Who's that?"

The Frick story had been told many times and would become an apocryphal anecdote that would follow Henry. FRICK—"WHO'S THAT?" HENRY ASKED WHEN TOLD OF FINE, read one headline in *The Sporting News*.

> Aaron, so the story goes, crumbled a telegraphic notice of his fine without reading it. Manager Charlie Grimm asked if Aaron knew who sent him the wire. Aaron said he didn't.
>
> "Ford Frick," Grimm told him.
>
> "Who's that?" asked Aaron without batting an eyelash, tossing the wire into the wastebasket.

Bisher retold the Frick story in his profile.

> When Manager Charley [*sic*] Grimm handed Aaron his copy of the telegram, Henry shoved it into his pocket unopened.
>
> "Better read that thing, Henry," Charley said. "It's from Ford Frick."

The picture of innocence, Henry looked at Grimm and said, "Who's dat?"

As even the best hitters must, Aaron has his batting slumps. He got into one at the end of spring training, going nine straight times without a hit. "I saving up for opening day," he said.

If Bisher was taken by Barbara, he did not spare her in his writing.

In Milwaukee, the Aarons live in a little upstairs flat at the rear of a faded brown house on North 29th Street, just off busy West Center. Two pieces of furniture eat up most of the limited space in the living room—a big leather easy chair and a large screen television set. "He just sit there and watch those shooting westerns and smoke cigarettes," his wife says, chuckling at the chance to poke fun at her mate.

Later, Bisher asked Henry if he had been motivated to play baseball because Satchel Paige, one of the great pitchers of the day, had grown up in Mobile. "I never heard of him till I was grown," Bisher quoted Henry as saying. "I didn't know he come from Mobile, and I never seen him till yet."

With language, that was all it took—a little manipulation in pronunciation here, a phonetic license there—and the desired effect could be achieved. Though both were southerners at a time when social issues were reaching the confrontation point, Bisher did not ask for Henry's opinion of the emerging fight for civil rights. Bisher did not believe Henry to be particularly bright, and the clear picture he painted of Henry is unmistakable for any reader.

The most devastating effect of the profile would be its influence on future profiles about Aaron. A profile on him would always be some form of referendum on his intelligence. It would, however, be misleading to suggest that Furman Bisher alone created the composite that would become Henry Aaron's public personality. He did not. It would be more accurate to say that the Bisher story legitimized that point of view, for ever since Henry's rookie season, a certain type of scrutiny had always been reserved especially for him.

Three weeks before the Bisher's story was published, *The Sporting News* took note of Henry's batting surge and ran a two-page feature. If Bisher focused on Henry's diction, *The Sporting News* article, written by Lou Chapman of the *Milwaukee Sentinel,* portrayed Henry as graced with natural hitting talent but insufficiently intelligent to grasp such a complicated game.

BRAVES' BLAZING AARON BIDS
FOR BATTING TITLE

Amazing Wrist-Action Gives Outfielder Whiplash Power

The accompanying cartoon—a montage of illustrated anecdotes that underscored the widely held perception of Aaron's disdain for hard work or hard thinking—was more demeaning than the story itself, but one section remained with him.

> Aaron was guilty of particularly atrocious base-running in one game. . . .
> . . . one of the veterans took Henry aside to give him some pointers. . . .
> "Henry," he said, "you've got to watch the ball when you're running the bases and you've got to decide whether and when you should tag up and go to another base."
> "I can't do all that," Aaron said, thus ending the discussion.

For years, Henry would speak about Herbert's determined pride, and the admiration he held for his father, who had been able to carve out an existence despite his harsh circumstances. The early portrayals of Henry were painful. He had endured the taunts and assumptions of the Sally League ("Just wanted to let you niggers know you played a hell of a game") and now was in the major leagues, beyond the reach of his expected place in Mobile, beyond the reach of the old limitations. Race was never America's dirty little secret, for it was never a secret at all. The real secret was class, and all of its insidious tentacles. If Henry had thought he had finally escaped and was ready to be introduced to the American public as the new force on base-ball's emerging team, Bisher, with a pen stroke, brought Aaron, if not physically then at least mentally, back into the condescending caste system of the South.

A FEW WEEKS before the all-star break, Fred Haney was in the dugout, grousing about his bench. The reserves, usually the strength of a balanced team, were melting over the summer months. Pafko wasn't hitting. Frank Torre was an excellent defensive first baseman, but he didn't scare anyone at the plate, and Haney had already sent Covington out. The front liners—Aaron, Mathews, Bruton, Logan, and Adcock—were holding up their end and more. The starters who weren't—Thomson and O'Connell—well, they'd been shipped out, responding to being traded from the Braves by going on hitting tears for the Giants. During one pregame bull session, a reporter asked Haney, "What would happen to your club if Adcock were to break his leg?"

It was one of those apocryphal baseball stories, surreal, ridiculous, and, of course, 100 percent true. On the afternoon of June 23, in the second game of a bitter doubleheader with the brash, contending Phillies at County Stadium, Joe Adcock broke his right leg. He would be gone until mid-September.

On July 11 in Pittsburgh, two days after the All-Star Game, Bill Virdon led off the bottom of the first with a dying quail to short cen-ter. Bruton raced in from center, Mantilla out from short, and neither slowed down. When the play was over, Virdon was on second with a double. Mantilla and Bruton were both knocked cold. When Bruton came to, he was on a stretcher, out for the year with a knee injury that would affect him for the rest of his career. Even Haney spent a week in the hospital, missing six games due to ulcers.

With Bruton gone, Haney chose Henry to fill the space in center field. To Fred Haney, acknowledging Aaron's versatility was a compli-ment. Henry filled in at second base a few times. He had batted sec-ond, and now, in the middle of a five-team race, he would be the new center fielder.

But for Henry, the constant shifting hampered his development as a player. He wanted to learn how to be a great right fielder, and play-ing center would not help. Haney had placed him out of position in the batting order and now in the outfield.

IF THE PENNANT had been lost at happy hour in 1956, the 1957 flag was being left in the emergency room. Already Bob Wolf in the *Jour-nal* crafted a preemptive epitaph, referring to the Braves as "fading."

John Quinn made two moves. He acquired first baseman Vernal "Nippy" Jones to back up Frank Torre at first. Second, he purchased from Wichita the contract of light-hitting outfielder Bob Hazle, who then put on the greatest five-week show in the history of baseball.

And that was the other beauty about the American game of base-ball: There isn't just one way to become an immortal. The gods could go to Mobile and touch Henry Aaron, giving him so wondrous a gift that he could hit a baseball four hundred feet with his hands in the wrong position, or you could be twenty-seven-year-old Bob Hazle, a guy held in such low esteem that the Braves tried to give him away for free in the draft and nobody wanted him.

That included Quinn, who told his farm director, John Mullen, that Ray Shearer, hitting .330 at the time, was the guy he wanted. Mullen convinced Quinn that Hazle was the better choice, because with Frank Torre in the starting lineup, the Braves did not have a left-handed batter on the bench.

On August 1, Conley shut out the Dodgers, 1–0. It was the kind of day Conley craved. He had started the season 0–4 but had evened his record and was beginning to see the results reflect how good he felt about his arm. The Braves were 61–41 after the win, in second place by half a game to St. Louis and two and a half games ahead of the Dodgers. Three days later, Hazle rapped two hits in another win over Brooklyn.

Then came the showdown for first place at Sportsman's Park against the Cardinals. In the opener, Henry doubled home a run in the first. Hazle led off the second with a long homer off Lindy McDaniel. Henry hit a two-run homer in the third, and it didn't mat-ter that Buhl was in the middle of another heinous masterpiece (com-plete game, nine hits, eight walks, but only two runs), because Hazle went four for five with two runs scored, two RBIs, and a home run in a 13–2 demolition. The next day, Hazle ripped three more hits and drove in three more in a 9–0 win. In two games, Hazle was seven for nine with five RBIs and a home run, and the Braves swept. In Cincinnati, Hazle led a sweep of the Reds by scores of 12–4, 13–3, and 8–1, going seven for ten with a home run and five RBIs.

Robert Sidney Hazle was born December 9, 1930, in Laurens, South Carolina. He grew to cut an imposing figure at six one, 190 pounds, but baseball had never come easily at the professional level. After two years in the army, Hazle played two games for Cincinnati before being traded to the Braves as a throw-in as part of the deal for George Crowe. He remained in the minor leagues, with their punishing schedule and meager pay. He had often thought about quitting. At the time Quinn called him to the Braves, Hazle was hitting .289, but even the Braves front office hadn't thought his streak was anything more than that of a mediocre player enjoying a rare hot month; thirty days earlier, Hazle had been hitting .230.

The Braves had won ten straight, and Hazle's average was .556. In forty-one games, Hazle hit .403, and now the press was making up nicknames for Hazle. Within a year, his career would be over, a rash of swings and misses, harmless outs and feeble explanations, either for his miraculous 1957 season or his inexplicable inability ever to hit the ball safely again. For the next thirty-five years, until his death in 1992, Bob Hazle would forever be known as "Hurricane" Hazle, named by teammates and writers after Hazel, the deadly 1954 hurricane that killed close to two hundred people from North Carolina to Toronto. He would be the greatest of comets, and when Milwaukeeans would speak of the Braves years in Wisconsin in elegiac tones, he was as important and beloved a figure as Henry, Spahn, and Mathews, his more accomplished Hall of Fame–bound teammates.

For the month of August, Hazle hit .493. By the end of the month, the Braves finally had separation. Twisted in the wreckage were the Dodgers (seven back), the Cardinals (seven and a half out), Philadelphia (Good night and good luck at fourteen and a half out), and the Reds (fifteen and a half back: See you next year and drive safely!). The Hurricane rampaged, and all that was left in his wake was the inevitable clincher.

The great irony was that as the Hurricane was unleashing his greatest damage and the Braves had engineered that championship run that distanced themselves from the pack, Henry Aaron, the Triple Crown threat and MVP leader, endured his worst month of the year, hitting .255 during August.

WHEN THE HISTORY of the great ones is written, the words are never merely a mundane compendium of numbers. Somewhere, there must be a singular feat that stands as a calling card. Just being good every day by itself does not merit a ticket to Olympus. It is the reason why there is a difference between stars and *superstars*.

Ted Williams took his team to only one World Series, and in it he hit poorly, but people *still* talk about the Williams starbursts: the home run in the World Series in 1941, going six for eight over the season-ending doubleheader to hit .406, instead of sitting out to qualify for .400 at .3995, the home run in the final at bat of his career.

Ruth? Too many to count, but leave it at the 1932 World Series. Mays wasn't just electric. He was a one-man power grid. Every great Yankee pennant run contained some DiMaggio stretch where he was the difference maker. In Clemente's lionish pride, you could practically *hear* the Puerto Rican national anthem with each and every one of his raging steps. Then, lonely on the other side of the trail, was Ernie Banks, who carried that heavy and unfortunate asterisk of being the greatest player never to take his team to the World Series, of never having the *moment* that separated winning from losing, and him from the rest.

That's why they were different, these millionth-percentile players. Just having one on the team meant somewhere, at some point, even if it occurred just once, there would be champagne at the end of the summer journey. They would do something that made the words sparkle when they hit the page, leaping magically, like a child's eyes on Christmas morning.

THE OLD BRAVES modus operandi of squeezing the bat just a little tighter as the September leaves changed did not disappear without resistance—old habits die hard—and the result was a tension that could have been felt from County Stadium up and down Wisconsin Avenue. The "Slop Thrower," Herm Wehmeier, journeyman to the rest of the world but a Walter Johnson against Milwaukee, pitched a twelve-inning complete game, striking out eight, and St. Louis beat the Braves 5–4. The losing streak hit three; it swelled to eight out of twelve when the Phillies beat Spahn 3–2 in ten innings September 15. The lead was shrinking, and that wasn't the only part of the trouble. Two of Henry's greatest pitching enemies were the ones threatening to steal 1957 the way one of them had taken 1956. While Spahn was losing, Wehmeier beat the Pirates in the first game of a doubleheader, and Sam Jones finished the sweep in the nightcap, cruising 11–3. The lead was two and a half games.

During the next seven days, Henry Aaron took hold of the National League pennant, wrestled it to the ground, and stomped the life out of it: two hits and an RBI against the Phillies, three hits and home run number forty-one in the eighth inning to finish the Giants, two runs scored and an RBI the next day as Burdette beat the Giants again.

And on it went: back-to-back two-hit games in routs of Chicago, the first a 9–3 win for Spahn's twentieth, home run number forty-two in the 9–7 finale September 22, when Hazle won it with a homer in the top of the tenth. They had won six straight and the lead was now five, with six games left to play.

The Cardinals arrived at County Stadium, with the Braves needing a win for the pennant. As is so often the case in baseball, the parallels were delicious, poetic. The Braves had been here before at the end, looking at the World Series, only St. Louis blocking their view of the promised land, when the Slop Thrower snatched the title away and Fred Haney promised them a summer of hell.

The night was September 23, Burdette versus that old cur, Wilmer "Vinegar Bend" Mizell. They would play three hours and thirty-three minutes, the second-longest game of the year, topped only when Gino Cimoli had homered off Red Murff in the bottom of the fourteenth at Ebbets way back in May. Burdette had been on the mound that day, too, a twelve-inning, eleven-hit, six-walk no-decision. Koufax was the winner.

Forty thousand came to County to witness the completion of the mission. One, a twenty-three-year-old history major at the University of Wisconsin named Allan Selig, was faced with a difficult choice: go to a night class or go to the game, with the hope that the Braves could clinch it that night. In later years, Selig would recall that the choice was not such a difficult one after all. He bought a bleacher ticket. In the first, Burdette escaped the first two batters before giving up an opposite-field double to Stan Musial, who would be stranded at second. Schoendienst singled in the bottom of the inning, only to have Logan kill the momentum with a double play.

Henry pulled a single to lead off the second. Adcock, back from his broken leg, and Pafko followed as the crowd fidgeted, eager for a reason to explode. Covington drove Henry home with a sacrifice fly that sent Fred Hutchinson out of the dugout. After one inning, Mizell was finished.

Into the game came another Aaron nemesis, head-hunting Larry Jackson, the same Jackson whom Henry had accused of throwing at him back in his rookie year, the same Jackson whom Chuck Tanner would refer to only as "that right-handed son of a bitch."

But Jackson was good this night, quelling the insurrection. He would pitch the next seven innings on a wire, dancing into trouble as Milwaukee waited to erupt. In nine of ten innings, the Braves would put a runner on, and yet there would be no celebration. In fact, the place was at times monastery-quiet.

With one out in the sixth, Wally Moon singled and Musial doubled again. This time, Alvin Dark bounced a two-run single to center and Burdette would not escape.

In the seventh, Schoendienst singled. Logan sacrificed him to second and Mathews doubled him home to tie the score. Fred Hutchinson's next move made clear Henry's influence. With none on and one out in a tie game, the Cardinal manager *intentionally* walked Aaron— the go-ahead run—with another right-hander, Adcock, on deck to face the lefty Jackson. Adcock bounced into a rally-killing double play.

The Cardinals increased the pressure. Moon singled in the eighth and Musial knocked him to third with his third hit of the game. Irv Noren grounded to short and Logan threw out Moon at the plate.

For the Braves, dying to exhale, the game was excruciating. Milwaukee loaded the bases, with one out in the tenth, off Billy Muffett. Haney called Burdette back for Frank Torre, who hit into a double play to end the inning.

Fifty years later, Chuck Tanner sat behind the dugout at the Pittsburgh Pirates minor-league facility in Bradenton, not far from the Pink Motel, where he and Gene Conley had been roommates, and where he and Henry had become friends those dusty years past. He had been traded to Chicago earlier in the summer and hadn't been part of the final pennant race, but Milwaukee was never far from him. He had struggled badly before he was traded and understood that being a bench player, sitting around for days, cold without being in the action and being asked to produce without the benefit of rhythm, was the hardest of jobs. Tanner was fond of Fred Haney, and it was Haney who'd given him his first job managing in 1963. The Braves were long gone from Bradenton, but Tanner thought about Henry.

"I don't know if there was a way to figure it, but I felt it then and I feel it now. There wasn't a player I'd ever seen get more hits with two outs than Henry Aaron. A two-out hit, one that scores a run, is just *devastating* to a pitcher. It's like a tease. You think you're gonna get out of it, but you're not. Before you know it, you're dead meat, mister."

Muffett retired Henry in the ninth, but the two had met in extra innings before, on August 17, when the Cardinals were taking three of four from the Braves. With a chance to sweep the series and make a tight race even closer, Henry hit a game-winning, one-out double off Muffett in the tenth for a 5–4 win.

Now, here they were in the eleventh. Logan singled between outs by Schoendienst and Mathews. Henry stood at the plate, with two outs. With none on back in the seventh, Hutchinson had walked him intentionally. Now, Adcock wasn't even in the game, having been lifted for a pinch runner, and the pitcher, Conley, was on deck. Yet Fred Hutchinson made the fateful decision to pitch to Henry.

Bud Selig would not forget the sequence. It was the first pitch, and Henry leaned forward, hands back, and sliced the ball into the right-center gap. He quickly rose to his feet, more hopeful than certain that the ball would drop, that Logan could score from first. The right fielder, Irv Noren, took a hard angle racing toward the fence.

Chuck Tanner had seen that kind of swing from Henry many times before. "You wanna know how quick his hands were? There was a game when Henry had two strikes on him. The umpire was an old, tough bastard, Al Barlick. The ball was on the outside corner and Barlick had raised his right hand to call strike three. *Henry was out!* The ball was by him. The signal was up. And he swung and hit the ball out of the ballpark. Never saw anyone do it as many times as he could. Hit it right out of the park."

Logan ran furiously, head down, and only the crowd told him the ball had cleared the fence. Henry had won the pennant. During the weeklong stretch that turned a close race into a title, Henry had come to bat twenty-eight times, nailed fourteen hits, scored eight runs, and hit three home runs.

The next day, after a night of beer showers and champagne and thinking about the Yankees in the World Series, "Toothpick Sam" Jones took the mound for the Cardinals. It was a meaningless game, but no confrontation between Henry and Sam Jones could ever be entirely meaningless. Jones loaded the bases in the first inning, and Henry, looking for an appropriate exclamation point to the regular season, blasted home run number forty-four—a grand slam—into the left-field seats.

When the pennant-winning home-run ball cleared the fence, Henry's teammates carried him off the field. *Time,* which two months earlier had referred to him as "The Talented Shuffler," now used words out of Scripture, Exodus 8:17, to paint the deed: "For Aaron stretched out his hand with his rod, and smote the dust of the earth."

When Henry was a boy, tossing stones in the air, driving them into the right-center-field gap of his imagination, he wanted to be Bobby Thomson, carried off the field by his teammates. The front page of the *Journal* the day after the Braves-Cardinals game served as a bittersweet reminder of the conflicts and contradictions that would define the rest of his life.

On the left side of the newspaper was a photo that even the notoriously conservative *Sporting News* would say reflected the true ideal

of America: Henry's dark body hoisted in the air above a sea of jubi-
lant, mostly white teammates.

Above the fold, adjacent to the photograph of Henry, was a news
story, dateline Little Rock, Arkansas, detailing a white mob beating
several black students attempting to enter Central High School.

CHAPTER EIGHT

BUSHVILLE

THE STORY HELD that the Pittsburgh Pirates lost the 1927 World Series to the Yankees before a single pitch was thrown. Overmatched by the greatest team ever assembled, the 110-win New York Yankees of Ruth, Gehrig, and Lazzeri, the Pirate players watched the mighty Yankees take batting practice and crumbled, piece by piece, player by player, immediately deciding that they could not win.

The lore of the 1949 pennant race captured a similar tone. The Red Sox players believed they were equal to the Yankees that year, but their manager, the ex–Yankee skipper Joe McCarthy, feared the great DiMaggio and the innate toughness of the Yankees to such a degree that his players sensed his lack of confidence in them. Needing to win just one of the final two games of the season at Yankee Stadium for the pennant, the Red Sox folded just when they needed their championship wits the most. Boston lost both, and the Yankees won another pennant and World Series.

Even against those tough-as-hell Brooklyn teams, the ones that could run away with the National League or beat you at the end—take your pick—the Yankees always found a way to get in their heads—a play here, a stolen win there. Take 1953, when Brooklyn was armed to the teeth—105 wins, 955 runs scored, Robinson, Reese, Snider, the MVP in Campanella, the best club in the world—and the Yankees still handled them in six games.

That was how the Yankees cut teams down, first mentally and then by bleeding them, game by game, inning by inning. Each generation of New Yorkers told a story of some pennant race that reinforced Yankee October dominance, and in each, there was always a worthy team good enough or even better than their Yankees, only in the end to be forced to kneel before the lordly pinstripes, and the shadow of the big town itself. All of which reinforced the Yankees—and the city's—sense of superiority. There was a lesson in the mythology: All things being equal, New York itself would be the critical difference.

Charlie Root, the Milwaukee pitching coach, knew firsthand a consequence of losing to the Yankees was a hagiographic blend of truth and myth, and how, once written, the legend could be impossible to overcome. For Root was on the mound during the fifth inning of the third game of the 1932 World Series, October 1, 1932, at Wrigley Field. Babe Ruth had already homered in the first, been pelted with tomatoes and fruit from the Wrigley fans, and verbally abused from the Chicago dugout. In the fifth, he took a strike, two balls, and another strike from Root before jawing with the pitcher. At that precise moment, he pointed his bat toward the center-field fence, toward the great beyond—Ruth *called his shot.* And then the Babe parked Root's next pitch, a sloppy curveball, over the center-field ivy and into the land of fable. Whether Ruth had actually called his shot, or was simply adjusting himself to hit, or was pointing out a local species of pigeon did not matter, nor did Root's salty protestations for the rest of his life that he would have "knocked Ruth on his ass" had the audacious Bambino tried to show him up like that, in the World Series, in his home park no less.

All that mattered was that the story would have been different had Root not served the Babe such a juicy morsel in the first place. And it was like that for every unfortunate soul who suffered through the monotony of spring, fought through summer, and clutched the pennant, only to be caught in the sticky web of the Yankee mythology. Had they put up a better fight, even won just a couple of games, the 1927 Pirates might have been able to escape the idea that they cringed under the immense shadow of the Yankees, the story that would haunt each one of them till the end of their days. *Maybe . . . might have . . . if only*—loser's words, every last one of them. Like Charlie Root and the Cubs, they didn't. Pittsburgh was swept into the Yankee mist in four easy games, and the legend became fact.

The Yankees were intimidating because they didn't lose. After winning the first of their seventeen titles in 1923, the Yankees lost the World Series just three times in thirty years. The Cardinals beat them in 1926, when in the seventh game, trailing 3–2, Ruth ended the Series in a spectacularly boneheaded fashion, getting thrown out by a mile while trying to steal second with big Bob Meusel at the plate and Lou Gehrig on deck. It was again the Cardinals—and their prized rookie Stan Musial, fresh from the hills of Donora, Pennsylvania—who beat the Yankees in 1942, back when Henry was eight, hitting bottle caps with a broom handle. And the Dodgers, after failing five times, beat the Yanks in 1955, only to lose to them the following year.

The city grew to expect the exclusivity of the fall. Since 1949, no team outside of New York had even won a single Series *game*. Both teams outside of the boroughs in the World Series had lost badly. The 1950 Whiz Kid Phillies were swept out of the Series by the Yankees, which would be the last Series between two all-white teams in base-ball history. The 1954 Indians of Feller, Wynn, and Garcia steam-rolled to 111 wins, only to be swept four straight under the brilliant spell of Mays and the New York Giants.

In the days leading up to the 1957 World Series, the New York writers naturally suggested a similar psychological phenomenon would overtake the Braves as they landed in New York. Only two reg-ulars, Warren Spahn and Red Schoendienst, had ever played in a Series. When Johnny Logan and Del Rice entered cavernous Yankee Stadium for the first time, the word that reached the newspapers was that two seasoned pros, tough, grinding competitors, both spent that first walk-through slack-jawed, looking up at the familiar moldings and trellises of the majestic ballpark, overcome by small-town won-der, no different from a family of four visiting the Empire State Building for the first time. When Fred Haney disembarked from the Braves charter bus, a reporter approached and asked if the Braves expected to be another good-intentioned victim of the famed dynasty.

"Fred, do you think your team will choke up against the Yankees?"

"What the hell is the matter with you?" Haney barked. "What kind of question is that?"

That the midwestern Braves, whose naïve and grateful fans deliv-ered milk and eggs to their heroes, contrasted so sharply with the cold and impersonal victory machine that was the Yankees made for an irresistible—and to the Braves, wholly irritating—story line. Still, Logan was convinced that his team held an edge over the Yankees because of the rugged terrain of the National League. The Braves had won a five-team race, had finally beaten the Dodgers, and relished the opportunity to stand with the Yankees.

The Yankees took over sole possession of first place June 30, two full weeks before the all-star break, and polished off Chicago by eight games. The third-place team, Boston, finished sixteen games out, and the writers and fans (and to no small extent the Yankee organization) spent the final days of the regular season positioning the Braves as fodder, just another fill-in-the-blank October opponent.

The facts were, as always, just a bit different.

Johnny Logan *was* wide-eyed that first day at the Stadium, but not because he had adopted the role of awestruck newcomer. He had spent the final week of the season leading up to the Series working *himself* into a competitive lather to beat the Yankees. The only way for the Braves to avoid being folded into another Yankee yarn, he decided, was not to make it close, not just to give a better showing than the Dodgers, but for the Braves to win, plain and simple. Logan had grown up in Endicott, New York, but quickly had identified with Milwaukee. He settled on the south side of Milwaukee, a working-class neighborhood, and like a few of the Braves—Felix Mantilla was another—Johnny Logan would never leave Milwaukee. "Before the thing even began, we were hearing it from Casey Stengel and the smart guys from New York, who started calling the town 'Bushville.' Believe me, we sincerely wanted to stick it to them. We wanted to show them that there were some ballplayers in Bushville."

Logan heard the old saws regarding the Yankee mystique and how even great teams buckled under its power. How else, he would often recall having been asked, could he explain how a bunch of tough bastards like the Dodgers, who grew tougher in the roughest clinches of a fight in the National League, lose to the Yankees so many times, in 1947, 1949, 1952, 1953, and 1956, winning only once, in 1955? Logan believed the questions were designed only to produce doubt, and that those critical dips of self-confidence, invisible to the eye, were precisely what gave the Yankees that intangible edge.

Spahn, who would start the first game against Whitey Ford at the Stadium, was blunter. Spahn had been vindicated, for when the season began, he had told Furman Bisher in *The Saturday Evening Post* that the Braves would win the pennant and face the Yankees in the World Series. He said in that April article that the Braves would beat the Yankees in seven games, and days before facing Ford, he told the writers that the Yankees did not, during the long season, have to face the same level of competition as the Braves. "They had to beat the White Sox," Greg Spahn said. "They had to beat the Dodgers, Philadelphia, Cincinnati, and St. Louis. They faced tougher teams."

There was something else, a score to be settled from many yesterdays. Spahn hadn't forgotten that the Yankee manager, Casey Stengel, had sent him to the minors years earlier for not decking Pee Wee Reese when Stengel managed Spahn in Boston. More importantly, Spahn's father, Edward Spahn, hadn't forgotten, either.

"Before the start of the 1957 World Series between the Braves and the Yankees, Stengel was walking through the lobby of the Commodore Hotel in New York. I'm not sure why he was there, probably for some promotional thing," Greg Spahn recalled. "My grandpa saw him and threw him up against the wall. He said, 'Now what do you think of my son? You think he has enough guts to play in the major leagues?' They were about the same size, not very big people. My dad and a few other guys had to pull my grandfather off of him."°

Logan had another concern. When his eyes scanned the three-tiered stadium, he wasn't buckling at the thought of the Yankees, but doing a certain amount of math in his head: Yankee Stadium held nearly seventy thousand people, County Stadium more than forty thousand. World Series earnings were based in part on stadium capacity. That meant the winner's share of the Series was going to be a considerable amount of money. In that regard, Logan couldn't have been happier to be playing the Yankees.

Playing the Yankees meant money, and winning the World Series meant even more. Gene Conley recalled a similar sentiment. "We weren't scared of the Yankees," he said. "We knew we were finally going to get some postseason money. For some of the guys, that check was a pretty good chunk of what they were making in the regular season."

°Greg Spahn also noted that short memories also exist in baseball. "My father and Casey became good friends later on." (Spahn finished his career with the Mets, where, in 1965, Stengel was his manager.)

Fifty years later, Logan, still pugnacious, tar-throated at eighty years of age, said it even better: "When we went in 1957, we wanted to win, yes sir. We wanted to show Casey Stengel we weren't Bushville.

"And you know what? I'll tell you something else. We wanted the money, too."

HENRY DID NOT say much during the buildup to the World Series. Both the *Journal* and the *Sentinel* ran daily front-page stories, with the Braves (IKE CONSIDERS ATTENDING GAME HERE OCT. 5) competing for space above the fold with local news (TAVERN PATRON SLAIN BY NERVOUS ROBBER) and national (LITTLE ROCK SCHOOL IS QUIET AS NEGROES ENTER AGAIN). The local angle from the Yankees centered on the success of the sensational rookie from Milwaukee, Tony Kubek. Henry was the fulcrum of the Braves offense, the front-runner for Most Valuable Player honors, but he stood far from the front of the club publicly.

From a motorcade that spanned two and a half miles, from Wisconsin Avenue to Lake Michigan, Spahn and Burdette kissed babies during a pre-Series rally that caught 150,000 Milwaukeeans in a state of pride. Henry and Wes Covington shared a convertible, with Barbara sitting regally in the back. Fred Haney received a gold statue nearly equal to his five-foot-five-inch frame. On two occasions, Henry found his name prominently mentioned in ink: The first was a front-page story in the *Journal* detailing a three-way scrum for the pennant-clinching home-run ball, the participants being Henry, who hit it off Billy Muffett, Hubert Davis of 1307 McKinley Avenue, who caught it, and Donald Davidson, the Braves public-relations man, who wanted to showcase the famous heirloom for the public and offered Davis World Series tickets in exchange for the ball.

THE PENNANT VICTORY BALL
FLIES INTO SERIES SQUABBLE

Henry stated his claim to the home-run ball modestly: "Sure, I'd like to have it"; while Davis assumed the position of insulted practitioner of English common law, which held that possession was nine-tenths of the law: "I wasn't gonna settle for no bleacher seats," he said. "If he offers me grandstand, I'd consider it." Davidson was on the defensive: "I didn't offer him any tickets. I just asked him if he wanted to see the World Series. I didn't mention bleacher tickets."

The second instance was the revelation that the ankle injury Henry had suffered in Philadelphia had not only cost him five games but likely the Triple Crown, as well. At the time of the injury on July 17, Henry was hitting .351, and he wound up losing thirty points off his average. In later years, when age would transform Henry from phenom to elder statesman, he would stress to younger players the importance of playing through pain, coining a slogan that one of his future protégés, Ralph Garr, never forgot. "You can't help your club from the tub," Garr recalled. "Henry used to say it all the time."

AARON'S SWAP: CROWN FOR PENNANT

"Few fans understand how seriously Aaron was handicapped," Manager Fred Haney said. "His ankle was not completely mended for weeks. He favored it somewhat for all the rest of the season.

"Of course it hurt his chances for the batting championship. He made the sacrifice for the good of the team."

Henry produced magnificent results in 1957—his forty-four home runs led both leagues, as did his 132 RBI; Musial beat him out for the batting title, .351 to .322. There was that famous publicity shot with Henry and Mantle posing in their batting positions, but Henry was not instantly propelled into a leading role at the dawn of the World Series. That said more about the times than it did about Henry Aaron. The common response to his relative lack of public notoriety in contrast to his offensive achievements was attributed to his demeanor and his desire for fame. Henry was ill-equipped for the hero's role. He was not quick with a verbal jab or glib with the writers. He chose to avoid the spotlight. He did not want publicity. These were simple elements of a more complicated equation. While each description of Henry was true to varying degrees—as was the very real fact that Henry often contributed to his own misrepresentation with sarcasm or evasion during interviews—the image of the Milwaukee Braves was a loud one. The public image of the club reflected more the personalities of Burdette, Spahn, Mathews, Logan, and Charlie Grimm, even though the latter had been gone for over a year. To a large extent, that image steered the press and the public away from Henry Aaron.

Most importantly, 1957 was still years away from the time when a black player would represent the public face of a franchise with all of its unspoken facets. That meant being the player who would speak for the club during winning and losing streaks, the player who held enough clout in the clubhouse to criticize elements of the team's or an individual player's performance. It meant being the highest-paid player on the team, the player upon whom management would rely, not only by offering kind words but by fortifying rhetoric with financial investment. Black players led on the field, by the examples of their play, but in 1957 did not do the talking.

In 1957, Henry Aaron held none of these titles. He was arguably the best player on the team, and even at twenty-three years of age, it was clear to the Braves that he was the most versatile player and possessed tremendous long-term potential. As the Series approached, Henry was not an underestimated talent by the press. Frank Finch, the longtime *Los Angeles Times* baseball writer, called Henry "already one of the game's great hitters." The *New York Times* referred to Henry as "Milwaukee's answer to Mickey Mantle."

For all of Henry's potential, the personality of the Braves belonged to Eddie Mathews. By 1957, Mathews was nearly two hundred home runs ahead of Babe Ruth at a comparable age, and it was Mathews, not Aaron, who was considered the best candidate (if there ever was such a thing) to break Ruth's career home-run record.

Henry did not have particular influence in the clubhouse, a domain belonging to the rugged, moody Mathews, the diffident Spahn, and the other veterans on the team. As a black player, his locker was not centrally located, but in the far corner of the home clubhouse, geographically sealed away, along with those of the other black players, from the mainstream areas of the clubhouse. During spring training, the most important bonding time for a team, Henry and the black players did not even stay with the team at the Dixie Grande Hotel. In later years, when the rigid line between the sports world and the real world would be effectively erased, it would have been impossible for a player of Henry's status to escape discussing the current events of the day, especially during the World Series, when baseball lived on the front page in every American city.

But as the World Series commenced and the violence during the dramatic integration of Central High School in Little Rock intensified, dominating the front pages of newspapers across the country, at no point did an interview with Henry on the subject appear in either the Milwaukee or the New York papers.

In regard to political issues facing black players, such as lodging and dining concerns during spring training and the regular season, it was Billy Bruton, not Henry, who held sway in the home clubhouse and the front office. Outside of macro predictions ("I think we'll win the pennant this year"), Henry did not often discuss in print the direction or mood of the club.

Henry earned $22,500 in 1957, nearly three times less than Spahn and slightly more than half of what Mathews was earning. Burdette, Schoendienst, and Logan ($25,000) also earned more than Henry. Moreover, the sport was far from reaching the point (which would be common in the future) when one of the youngest players on the team, regardless of ability level, could command the kind of salary that gave him instant credibility in the clubhouse. Young players were still expected to play and not be heard.

Given that perspective, it seems wholly appropriate that Henry played a secondary role on the Braves outside of the batter's box. The day before the Series began, he did his part in turning the crank on the hype machine by posing for the newsreels with Mantle, but in general, he left the publicity to the more established stars. In a sense, it was a position that reinforced his own sense of isolation, a belief that he could spend 180 days a year with people and still not have them know or understand him. He was not invisible, but his persona was shaped in the papers and, to a lesser extent, in terms of his teammates solely in the field of play, beginning with his stride at the plate, ending when he made contact. In later years, as Henry grew more comfortable with himself and his heightened stature, he would admit he had not helped very much when it came to letting people know him.

Periodically, a precious nugget of information would appear—for example, that one of Henry's sisters, eleven-year-old Alfredia, was living with Henry and Barbara and attended the Phipps School in Milwaukee. His contemporaries seemed fuller, more three-dimensional: Mathews brooded with hunger for drink and women, quick-tempered and protective of his turf, desperate to be known as a truly great player. Spahn was the single-minded, often distant intellectual on the mound. But both were quicker to reveal their emotions. Henry was not without opinions, but they remained in him, grounded. "Henry didn't volunteer what he thought about you," Felix Mantilla recalled. "But that didn't mean he didn't have thoughts about who you were."

IN THE YANKEE scouting meetings, however, Henry was far from anonymous. He was central to every discussion about pitching to the Braves. The scouting reports were sparse, and at times they reflected the traditional condescending Yankee attitudes toward their opponents, but they were of questionable benefit anyway, because Henry was an unpredictable hitter. As pitchers would say in later years, a scouting report on Henry Aaron was of lesser value than the paper on which it was printed.

In the first game, in front of an overflow, sun-splashed crowd of 69,476, Ford was masterful, beating Spahn 3–1. While Spahn labored early and was finished in a sixth-inning flurry, Ford pitched a five-hit complete game. Henry knew at once that the Yankees did not regard him lightly. Though only twenty-eight, Whitey Ford was an October veteran of four World Series. Throughout the first game, Ford gathered information on Henry, testing his patience in his early at bats. Young players, especially run producers, liked to hit when they knew they were being challenged, so Ford took a different approach, waiting out Henry. Henry's first three at bats were emblematic of the great duel taking place between two future Hall of Fame players. Henry led off the second by seeing the first of an afternoon's worth of curveballs. Ford, the left-handed master of pace, stayed on the outside corner without challenging in the at bat. Henry waited for Ford to challenge him inside, a challenge that never came. Frustrated, he bounced weakly to second base.

In the fourth, after a one-out walk to Mathews, Ford started Henry with another curve on the outside corner, which Henry pasted to right for a single, and the scouting report went into the garbage. For the rest of the series, Ford would pitch to Henry according to the feel of his pitches. With runners on the corners and one out, Ford then jammed Adcock, forcing a double play.

In the sixth, Henry faced his first controversy of the series. Trailing 1–0, with two on and none out, Haney chose not to have Henry bunt, opting instead to give Henry a chance to break the game open. "No way," Haney said fiercely to the writers afterward, "am I going to bunt with my best hitter up."

Henry looked for the same slop on the outside corner, and Ford obliged, but Henry fouled the pitch. Ford's next pitch was a beauty, a shoulder-high curve that sloped down and in over the middle of the plate, belt-high for strike two. The third pitch was a throwaway. Ford hadn't challenged Henry inside all day and threw a nothing curve inside and down around Henry's ankles.

Henry, who flailed and checked, was fooled that Ford had finally come in with a soft, hittable curve. Home plate umpire Jocko Conlan said Henry did not hold up, and called him out, a call that left Henry fuming in the clubhouse to Conley and anyone else who would listen afterward. "It isn't often that Aaron squawks," Ollie Kuechle wrote with local pride in the *Journal*. "But he squawked here, and he had a right."

The Yankees had struck first. The skipper, Haney, was unbowed. "No complaints. We just didn't get the hitting we needed and they whipped us in a good ball game," Haney said afterward. In the opener, the Yankees won all the key points, plays that went their way by a sliver, plays that *always* seemed to go their way by a sliver in October. Hank Bauer hit a two-out, run-scoring double to center, which Henry could not reach and which the writers believed he should have been able to catch ("No way," Haney said). In the sixth, with Spahn gone and Ernie Johnson pitching, with one out in a 2–0 game, Jerry Coleman dropped a squeeze bunt. The crowd gave a resigned roar, thinking that Coleman had tapped it too hard to the pitcher, leaving Berra doomed at the plate. But Johnson opted to retire Coleman at first, and another run scored, leaving Haney to defend not just Henry's defense but Johnson's decision not to throw home. And there was Henry's check-swing strikeout. Ford had won the first round. "I've never seen so many curveballs in my life," Henry said.

Game two, another perfect day in New York, the luster of the bunting having worn off. The Braves and Yankees traded runs early in the second game, which featured less pomp and more fight. Bobby Shantz, the five-foot-six lefthander who in 1952 had beaten out Mickey Mantle for AL MVP, was going against Burdette, the pitcher the Yankees did not trust because of his reputation for decking hitters and wetting the ball, not always in that order. For his part, Burdette still seethed at the Yankees for trading him from the organization in 1951. From the start, it was clear the second game would be more intense than the opener, when Ford had cast a spell on the Milwaukee hitters. Henry led off the second with a triple over Mantle's head in center and scored on Adcock's single. The Yankees tied in the bottom of the inning on consecutive two-out singles by Kubek and Coleman and nearly broke the game open when the Braves made their first decisive play of the series, with Shantz nailing a two-out fastball from Burdette into the left-field corner. Kubek and Coleman dashed for the plate. Wes Covington sprinted toward the left-field corner, where the low wall narrowed sharply. With his back to the infield, Covington stretched his glove in the direction of the fence and caught the ball, saving two runs.

Pushed back to even in the second, Shantz immediately gave the lead back, with Logan tagging him for a long, quick home run down the skinny left-field line. Bauer counterpunched, taking Burdette out of the park in the bottom of the inning. In the top of the fourth, Adcock and Pafko led off with singles. Covington followed with another hit, a run-scoring single that Kubek mangled in left for an error and another run, and it was 4–2, with nobody out.

Then, suddenly, the fireworks stopped, and game two turned tough and nasty. Stengel, bowlegged and annoyed, removed Shantz after just three innings. Art Ditmar entered the game and first decked Crandall with a fastball, then Aaron in the fifth, forcing a warning from home-plate umpire Jocko Conlan.

Burdette held on to his two-run lead. The Yankees got close in the sixth, putting runners on second and third, with one out, but Burdette, growing irascible and working faster as he neared victory, retired Kubek on a grounder. The Yankees put two more on in the ninth but did not score. After Ditmar dusted Henry, Burdette waited patiently for his chance, then sent Coleman into the dirt.

The Braves won 4–2 and headed home for three games. Afterward, Burdette and Haney were terse. Henry, who had been decked by Ditmar, said, "We don't worry about such things." If the Braves had seemed unable to match the Yankee toughness in the opener, Burdette had evened the scales, and the all-slug, no-field Covington— who spent the postgame interviews apologizing for the irony of a power hitter changing the day's momentum with his glove—had provided the unexpected magic.

FRANK ZEIDLER munched on a sandwich from a box lunch as he waited for the team charter plane to arrive at General Mitchell Field. The mayor was not, by any account, a rabid baseball fan, but as a politician he understood how to connect with his constituency. When Zeidler arrived at the airstrip to greet the Braves, a policeman notified him that the team flight would be late. He used the extra time to eat, crushing a box lunch.

Zeidler noticed something of an oddity: The crowd of a few hundred diehards waiting to welcome the Braves home had swelled to more than a thousand. As the gathering increased, Zeidler told Emil Quandt, the Milwaukee police chief, to add additional officers. Instead of buses, Dan Fegert, a local auto representative, arranged for thirty convertibles to meet the team plane and carry the players and their wives from the airport. The team had not won the World Series. They did not even have a lead in the Series. They had played only two games, but the welcome for the Braves had turned into a full-on motorcade. When the American Airlines DC-7 touched down, airstrip officials rolled out a red carpet leading to the waiting fleet of convertibles. The Milwaukee police estimated the crowd had grown to as many as 7,500.

For eleven miles, out of the airstrip grounds and along the streets of the city's south side to the Eighteenth Street viaduct, the sound of cowbells collided with that of banging pots and pans and yells and screams. The next day, city officials estimated the gathering at 200,000. Zeidler called the greeting "the biggest spontaneous celebration in the city's history."

BRAVES WELCOMED AT AIRPORT BY THOUSANDS OF WELL-WISHERS

The turnout, it should be remembered, was not for an elaborate parade, with bare-kneed majorettes and marching bands. It was for a bunch of tired baseball players who are still on the short end of the odds in an unfinished competition for the baseball championship of the world.

Over the years, after the Braves had long since left town, Henry would be known in Milwaukee for three major things: the home run off Billy Muffett, the way he carried himself, and his unwavering position that Milwaukee owned a greater piece of his heart than any place he'd ever visited.

At 11:25 a.m., the Yankees seventeen-car sleeper pulled into Milwaukee to a great and unwelcome surprise. A delegation of Milwaukee civic and political leaders greeted the Yankee officials with booklets titled *Milwaukee USA* and welcomed the Yankees and the World Series to the city. The players walked with no small degree of annoyance past the congregation and silently boarded a Greyhound bus, which would take them to County Stadium. Stengel had slipped onto the bus and refused to come out, despite the pleadings of Judge Robert Cannon and the civic group, who wanted Stengel to say a few words. The Yankees were here for a World Series, not a banquet. Cannon, the Milwaukee circuit court judge who would precede Marvin Miller as head of a fledgling players union, remained on the bus as it peeled off, and the welcoming gesture fell about as flat as Mantle's crew cut. According to the *Journal*, "the Yankees hurried off. The fans and welcoming committee moved forward, smiling. A cheer was heard. The Yankees ignored the reception. Heads down, faces grim they walked rapidly to the three chartered Greyhound buses east of the station."

"This," a Yankees official was quoted as saying as he boarded the team bus, "is strictly bush league."

FOR THE THREE games to be played at County Stadium, six thousand standing-room tickets were made available. Art ("Happy") Felsch slept in a tent for ten days to guarantee he would be first in line. The ballpark, draped in bunting even along the outfield fences in front of the Perini pines, was sold out, with 45,804 there for the first World Series game ever played in Wisconsin. On a fifty-three-degree afternoon, Saturday, October 5, the Yankees responded to the pageantry by beating the tar out of Bob Buhl in the third game. For the first time in the Series, the Yankees showed off their vaunted power. Mantle, leveled by a bad back and ineffective for the first two games, ripped two hits, including a home run, and drove in a pair. Kubek, coming home, hit two homers, including one in the first inning as a nervous hum flitted through the stands. The Yankee first four in the order went seven for seventeen with three homers, eight runs scored, and eight more driven in. For a brief moment, it appeared that the Braves would have an easy time, as Bob Turley, the New York starter, gave up three hits and four walks and couldn't get out of the second inning. The only problem was that Buhl couldn't get out of the first. Don Larsen was staked to a 5–0 lead after two innings, on the way to a 12–3 final. Down 7–1 in the fifth, Henry laced a Larsen fastball for his first home run of the Series.

In the fourth game, when the blustery lake winds laced a chilly fifty-degree day, the Braves came face-to-face with the Yankee mythology. Spahn was brilliant, avenging the opener when he couldn't escape the sixth. He gave up a run to start the game, then settled, retiring eleven straight Yankees at one point. His counterpart, the knuckle-baller Tom Sturdivant, held a 1–0 lead until Logan led off the fourth with a walk and Mathews followed up with a double. Stengel walked to the mound. Not particularly interested in facing Aaron with two on, nobody out, and first base open, Sturdivant suggested walking Henry. Loading the bases wasn't great baseball strategy, but perhaps putting

Aaron on would solve two problems. The first was that Sturdivant wouldn't have to face Henry; the second was that the on-deck hitter, Covington, might hit into a double play and minimize the damage.

Stengel listened, felt the wind whip past his ears, and rejected the suggestion.

"No, pitch to him," Stengel told Sturdivant. "With this wind, Babe Ruth couldn't get one out of here."

Stengel retreated to the Yankee dugout. Sturdivant tried to drop a knuckler in on Henry, one that danced belt-high. Henry destroyed it for a three-run homer. The next batter, Covington, hit a one-hop grounder to second—a sure double-play ball, in other words—and Frank Torre homered later in the inning to make it 4–1.

When Sturdivant reached the top step of the dugout at the end of the inning, he said to Stengel, "I thought you said Babe Ruth couldn't get one out of here."

Shortly before his death in 1995, Mickey Mantle appeared in the documentary *Hank Aaron: Chasing the Dream,* and recalled Stengel's reply.

"Well," the Perfesser told his pitcher, "that wasn't Babe Ruth you were facing."

By the ninth, Spahn had been masterful, holding a 4–1 lead and needing only three outs to tie the Series. Bauer lofted a soft fly to Henry in center. Mantle chopped to Logan at short. But McDougald and Berra singled to right. One strike away, Elston Howard hit a game-tying three-run homer. The Yankees took the lead in the tenth when Spahn retired the first two men of the inning, only to see Kubek single and Bauer triple him home.

And this is why these were the Yankees, why the mythology spread like honey to New Yorkers, like cholera to the rest.

Deflated, the Braves came to bat in the tenth. Tommy Byrne hit Nippy Jones on the foot with a pitch, the home-plate umpire awarding Jones first because of a faint mark of shoe polish on the ball. Mantilla ran for Jones, and took second when Schoendienst sacrificed off Bob Grim. With Mantilla on second, Stengel did about a year's worth of managing. He called Mantle off the field, and moved Kubek to center. Mantle jogged off the field, replaced by the old pro Enos

Slaughter, whose arm was better in left. After Casey's shuffling, Logan sent a double into the gap in left to tie the game. The next batter was Mathews, who ended it with a two-run homer. The series was tied again.

THE SERIES WAS going back to New York after Burdette defeated Ford in a taut 1–0 masterpiece. The Yankees, masters of creating luck through intimidation, had put runners on in each of the first four innings but could not score, while consecutive singles by Mathews, Henry, and Adcock accounted for the only run of the game. The Braves would return to New York one win from taking the Series.

Bob Buhl started game six, a title on the line. He had won seventeen games during the season. For more than two seasons, he had been the Braves best pitcher in those blood wars with the Dodgers, and yet he collapsed in the World Series, folding at home in game three. Given a second chance, Buhl gave up four hits and four walks, which amounted to two important runs. Down 2–1, Henry tied the game at the top of the seventh with a home run to deep center, past the 402-foot sign and into the Braves bull pen, where reliever Taylor Phillips caught it. The Yankees retook the lead off Ernie Johnson in the bottom of the inning. In the ninth, Mathews walked to lead off the inning, but Henry struck out and Covington bounded into a double play to end the game. And so it came down to a seventh game, Burdette versus Larsen.

In two hours and thirty-four minutes, Milwaukee had its answer to Lou Perini's boast that the city would be the baseball capital of the country.

It was over early—four runs in the third, and the pinstripes never recovered. The final score was 5–0. For the final out, Skowron bounced a short hop to Mathews, who raced to third and stepped on the bag, and the Braves were champions. Burdette was the hero, winning three games. In the crowd, frenzied Milwaukee fans unfurled signs that read BUSHVILLE WINS.

Henry hit .393, with three home runs in the World Series, eleven hits in the seven games, including a twelve-hop, RBI single up the middle during the winning third-inning rally. Three weeks later, in a close vote, he was named National League Most Valuable Player, beating out Ernie Banks, Stan Musial, and Willie Mays. It had been ten years since Herbert had taken him to see Jackie Robinson, ten years since he'd told Estella he would be a major-league baseball player. He was twenty-three years old, and though his journey was just beginning, in many ways it was already complete.

A MONTH LATER, on December 15, 1957, Barbara went into labor at St. Anthony's Hospital in Milwaukee. She delivered premature twin boys, Gary and Lary, and the immediate hours after their birth were perilous. Neither child weighed four pounds. Lary would spend three weeks in the intensive care unit at St. Anthony's, kept alive only by the protection of an incubator. Gary, who weighed three pounds, three ounces at birth, arrived ten minutes before Lary, but he would not survive a week, dying two days after he was born.

Suddenly, the afterglow of a world championship as well as the personal awards and baseball achievements were tempered by events beyond the reach of Henry's baseball abilities. He began the year celebrating the birth of one son, spent an incandescent summer furiously chasing dual pursuits, both seeking vindication for 1956 and establishing himself as one of the truly great young players in his sport, neither quarry eluding him. And now, eight days before Christmas, he faced the coming year emotionally halved by his professional success and profound personal loss. He had seen death before, years earlier in Mobile, when his brother Alfred did not survive childhood, but the death of a son presented a different dynamic altogether. When he was a child, it was Stella and Herbert who provided the family support and stability in dealing with family tragedy. Now, though only twenty-three, Henry was the head of his own household, and the responsibility to maintain and support his family fell to him. This did not mean explaining death to little Gaile, who was three, or to Henry junior, nicknamed "Hankie," who was nearly ten months old, but it did mean that he would have to confront the various and unpredictable emotional repercussions that always accompany death. Over the years, throughout six decades of public life, in thousands of interviews, numerous books, and even in his own autobiography, Henry would never discuss Gary's death beyond acknowledging that the little boy did not survive long past birth, choosing instead to leave the wound buried deep under accumulated layers of scar tissue. During the months that followed, as 1957 moved into 1958, Henry moved forward stoically and privately, focusing publicly on the upcoming challenge of defending his World Series title and striving to be the first player in National League history to win consecutive Most Valuable Player trophies. And his was the appropriate course of action, for 1957 was not a time culturally when the press probed into the personal lives of professional athletes, or when the athletes themselves felt compelled for public-relations and image reasons to permit revealing and candid interviews about personal topics not directly related to their craft. *The Sporting News* and the *Los Angeles Times* ran only wire-story briefs about Gary's death, and the local Milwaukee newspapers did not challenge the Aarons' privacy.

But, as is so often the case, it was during this period of grief that important and lasting threads in Henry's life would be formed, where the public life of Henry Aaron, the man who would seek not only acceptance as a potentially great baseball player but respect as a person of substance, would begin to take shape. Both professionally and personally, things would change after 1957—between Henry and Barbara, in the way Henry was viewed as a baseball player and the way the people of Milwaukee would view their baseball team, and, most importantly, in the way Henry would see the larger world around him, and his place within its uncertain, bittersweet confines.

CHAPTER NINE

ALMOST

By FOUR O'CLOCK on the afternoon of October 5, 1958, Warren Spahn knew exactly how a dynasty was supposed to feel. For seven innings he had sparred with Whitey Ford, just as the two had a year earlier in the opener of the 1957 World Series, again pitching in Yankee Stadium. Yet where Spahn had pitched bravely but labored and lost a year earlier, here he basked in the wonderfulness of being in total command, in complete control of every pitch, both in velocity and location, regardless of hitter or situation.

For any pitcher, especially one as fiercely competitive and driven as Spahn, walking off the mound that way represented a supreme moment. The fourth game of the 1958 World Series was over and Spahn soared, lifted by the importance of the victory and his part in it. In a World Series rematch with the Yankees, the Braves were not simply unafraid of the vaunted New Yorkers but were in the process of embarrassing them as no team had since before the end of the war, when in 1942 St. Louis smothered DiMaggio and Berra and the dynasty in five easy games to win it all.

The final score was 3–0, and the details of the game were to be savored and replayed. Spahn went the distance, besting Ford, who was gone after seven. He had given up but two hits and struck out seven. Only one batter, Mickey Mantle, even advanced past first base the entire game. Mantle hit a booming triple over Covington's head in the fourth but was left stranded, unable to score. While the game had been close, with the valiant Ford equaling Spahn frame after frame early on, the delicious part was that it was the Yankees, those ice-cold, steel-nerved veterans of the fall who always relied on their opponent to commit that crucial psychological lapse, who were faltering. Norm Siebern lost a ball in the sun in the sixth inning. Tony Kubek muffed a ground ball, which led to the first Milwaukee run. After years of making the opposition wilt, it was the Yankees who were now falling victim to the pressure.

The Braves were now winning in games three to one, with one more to go to defend their championship and become the first National League team to repeat as champions since the days before players had numbers on their jerseys, back when the New York Giants beat the Yankees in 1921 and 1922. That was before Yankee Stadium had been built, before the Yankees had won their first title, before the Yankee name really meant much of anything. The Braves monument was being erected, and Spahn stood at its center, for consecutive titles, both over the Yankees, no less, would cement their place in history, simultaneously erasing the bitter disappointments of 1956.

Lew Burdette, that Yankee killer, was scheduled to be on the mound for two of the final three games, if the Series even went that far. For the team, a win away from a championship, the victory represented something far larger than a win in a seven-game play-off series; it was as if the Braves had finally reached their collective apex, their formidable individual and team abilities coalescing at once in a shimmering display.

SPAHN AND COMPANY had done nothing that dusky afternoon at Yankee Stadium that they hadn't done for virtually the entire 1958 season. For the first time, it was Milwaukee, and not Brooklyn or the Giants or the Yankees, that entered the baseball season not needing to explain away what had gone wrong—not only why they hadn't won, but how they'd continued to lose. They entered 1958 as champions, and could soak in that perfectly decadent feeling of reaching the peak of their powers. That was the greatest spoil that came with winning. Nobody stood around second-guessing.

After defeating the Yankees three times, Burdette returned to his hometown of Nitro, West Virginia, the conquering hero, the MVP of the World Series, the recipient of beers on the house, literally, for the rest of his life. Instead of being haunted by the needling presence of

Herman Wehmeier, Warren Spahn basked in a championship over the winter, the king of Broken Arrow, Oklahoma, even though it was his wife who was actually the Oklahoma native. Instead of wanting to punch every wiseass fan in the chops after a bittersweet season, Eddie Mathews stood awash in the winner's sunshine during the 1957 off-season. These days, there was no reason to want to rip a guy's lungs out for asking the wrong question, at the wrong time, as he had after the bitter defeat of 1956. With Mathews, the bitterness of losing revealed itself most forcefully whenever he tried his best *not* to be bitter.

"When you come close to winning a championship and don't win it, everybody wants to know why you didn't win, or how it feels to come so close and lose. Nobody wants to hear about the 92 games you won or the great things you did; they only want to know about the one terrible game you lost," Mathews wrote in his 1994 autobiography, *Eddie Mathews and the National Pastime.* "It gets old, though, talking over and over about the same moment of disappointment in your life. You want to say, 'Hey, a month before that I beat the Cardinals with a three-run homer.' But nobody cares about that."

Those concerns were part of the old days, the old Braves. Even one of the most important pieces of the scary old days—the annual showdowns at Ebbets Field—would never return, for the Dodgers didn't live in New York anymore. Having tormented and tortured the Braves for years, the Dodgers were gone from Brooklyn. Nobody was happier that the Dodgers had left than Spahn, who literally couldn't win a game in Brooklyn. The Giants were gone, too, to San Francisco, and now train rides were replaced by DC-7 jets and five-game series on the West Coast. The National League would not host a regular-season game in New York for five years.

When the 1958 season commenced, the Braves danced around the quicksand that sinks most title teams, but only barely. In his own way, each player found himself let down by the painfully temporary nature of winning. Whether it was Spahn or Adcock or Aaron, each discovered that winning was not so unlike a good massage: It felt otherworldly, but too briefly. The feeling never lasted long enough.

As spring camp opened, the stars did not report there fat and they did not squabble among themselves over money or credit for their part in finally winning the title. Many of the players arrived in Bradenton as if they still had something to prove. For a time, they even continued to listen to Fred Haney.

That wasn't to say that money was irrelevant. In baseball, money was still the best way to measure value, especially when it flowed at a trickle from the penurious wallet of John Quinn. And when it came time for the reward of finally being the best, the money spring was drier than Fred Haney's scalp. During the first week of January, the week before the deadline when teams were required to mail out offers to the players, the Associated Press and the *New York Times* ran dueling stories about the two pennant winners, the *Times* placing the Yankee payroll unofficially at $500,000, led by Mantle at $65,000 per year and Berra at $58,000. "So far as is known, only the Braves and possibly the Dodgers can be regarded as being anywhere near the Bombers' salary bracket," the *Times* wrote on January 5, 1958. "The world champion Milwaukeeans have a few high-salaried performers such as Warren Spahn, Red Schoendienst and Eddie Mathews. Hank Aaron is moving up rapidly, but they haven't quite the array of high financiers the Yankees have to satisfy." The AP did not place a payroll figure on what the Braves would spend on player salaries in 1958, but it was assumed that after a world championship, the players would expect more.

In fact, everybody wanted more.

If winning the championship was a team effort and the greatest moment in Milwaukee baseball history, the city was more appreciative of the victory than management. Nineteen of the players, including Aaron, Burdette and Mathews, did not sign their original contracts. Billy Bruton, who missed the Series after the violent collision with Mantilla during the pennant run, made $14,500 in 1957 and exactly that the following year. When camp broke in Bradenton the first week of March, Burdette stayed home. Haney said the holdout had nothing to do with the money (Burdette was really earning $25,000 instead of $28,000, but in an age when player salaries were as well guarded a secret as any at the Pentagon, the press could hardly be faulted for guessing). Instead, it was because Burdette didn't like Haney's strict camp style, which required the pitchers to run for miles. In later years, the smothering degree of control ownership exerted over the players made them sympathetic figures; it paved the way for massive change. How management treated its champions in 1958 served as an undisputed example. Spahn, the twenty-game winner and defending Cy Young recipient, received a raise of three thousand dollars, bringing his salary to sixty thousand dollars. Mathews, who had hit the big home run in game four that saved Spahn and left the city delirious, received a five-thousand-dollar raise, for a salary of $55,000, and Burdette eventually received more money, if not fewer calisthenics. After the second spring-training exhibition, Quinn gave Burdette a $10,000 raise, for a total of $35,000.

Burdette got his money, but only one other player came close to receiving his salary demand, and that was Henry. He indeed had asked for forty thousand dollars, the second straight year he'd asked that Quinn virtually double his salary. In 1957, he'd asked for a $17,500 raise and received just a $5,000 increase, bringing his salary to $22,500. In 1958, he'd asked for another $17,500 and received $12,500, for a total of $35,000.

The Braves began the defense of their title on April 15, a breezy day at County Stadium, Spahn versus Pittsburgh's Bob Friend. Vernon Thomson, the Wisconsin governor, threw out the first pitch, but not before Perini beamed his gap-toothed smile as the Braves fifteen-by-thirty-seven-foot pennant was raised before the game. Mathews hit a home run in the first, a towering drive into the center-field bull pen, and then another in the third. Spahn labored but persevered—except in facing a hungry Pirate outfielder named Roberto Clemente, who in four appearances against Spahn rapped three hits, including a double. Friend was better than Spahn on this day—Henry could attest, going hitless against him and one for six on the day—but the pennant magic still held a flicker. Trailing 3–2 in the bottom of the ninth, the Braves tied the score before Conley lost it with two out in the fourteenth. At three hours and forty minutes, the game was the longest opener in the National League in twenty-three years and was the first time Spahn or the Braves had lost a home opener since moving to Milwaukee.

There was first the money and then the business of defending the pennant, and the tough, militaristic Haney knew only one way: keeping his foot on the necks of his players. One result was inevitable clashes—both with the club's free spirits, who always needed a short leash, and the sturdy veterans, who believed their performance the previous year had earned them the right not to have Haney turning another training camp into boot camp.

Another result was a certain loss of the innocence that surrounded the entire Milwaukee affair, and each player lamented the sober reality that chasing a goal is far more romantic than achieving it, and while the 1958 season would be a highly successful and efficient one, it felt to Henry, and especially to Mathews, a little less sparkly, a little less fun.

Take the case of Bob Hazle and the cool afternoon of May 7, 1958, a Wednesday afternoon, in St. Louis, when Herman Wehmeier took the mound against the Braves. This time, Burdette was on the mound and Wehmeier, for once against the Braves, looked exactly like the ham-and-egg pitcher he was to the rest of the league.

Schoendienst led off the game, Logan to follow. Both singled. Mathews flied to right. Henry doubled in both runs, and Frank Torre doubled him in. Then Covington stepped up and took a Wehmeier offering and sent it clear into Kansas. Wehmeier faced six batters, five of whom got hits, three of whom nailed extra base hits, all five of whom scored. Fred Hutchinson, the Cardinals manager, called for Larry Jackson out of the bull pen. Hazle stepped up, and Jackson chucked a fastball, hard and straight and deadly, slightly behind Hazle, who instinctively backed into the ball. Hazle was knocked unconscious.

Exactly seventeen days later, Quinn had two things to say to Hazle. The first was to ask him how he was doing. The second was to tell him he'd been sold to Detroit.

This was the way management always made sure to remind players that yesterday's news was today's liability, and the reminders could be as icy as the wind off Lake Michigan. As much as Spahn or Burdette or Henry Aaron, Hurricane Hazle had won the 1957 pennant. Sure, he had stopped hitting (he had actually stopped against the Yankees during the Series), but no matter how many years a player played in the big leagues, few could ever get used to the callousness of management. Mathews recalled the moment in *Eddie Mathews and the National Pastime:*

The other ballplayers were completely stunned and upset about it. We thought it sucked. Here was a guy who came out of nowhere and led us, not single-handedly, but led us to our first World Series. He was in a slump the first month of 1958, but he'd had some ankle trouble in the spring. We figured the ballclub owed him more than that. He was 27 years old and a super-nice kid. After he came up in 1957, he was just a part of us. Whenever we'd go out, he'd come with us, just a nice guy, what I would call a good old Southern boy, fun laughs, the whole bit. Of course, I never understood a lot of the stuff that went on in baseball, but we were pretty disappointed when Hazle was dumped. We all said, "What the hell did he do wrong, have an affair with the general manager's wife?"

Gene Conley was next. Never a Haney favorite, Conley found himself banished to the bull pen. Then his arm started to hurt, and he spiraled; he would never be as promising as he once was. Conley would not look back on 1958 fondly, for it represented one of those curious phenomena in sport when the team did well, while the individual player struggled. For years, the two stalwarts of the pitching staff, Spahn and Burdette, would tease Conley about his mechanics. Neither had to deal with Conley's height, but both men knew potentially dangerous mechanics when they saw them, and Conley's motion tended to place a great deal of strain on his elbow and shoulder.

And in those days, there was no pitch count, no video, and no wet nurse catering to every need of the pitcher, as would be the case in the future, when teams poured so much money into pitchers that they actually took an interest in their investment. With the exception of the great former Brave Johnny Sain, the pitching coaches in 1958 were not much more than cronies.

"Those guys, all they did was carry the balls to BP," Gene Conley recalled. "That was it. Whitlow Wyatt and all, come on. Their job was to drink with the manager, keep him company. I took the ball and threw. No one helped me with mechanics. I threw the ball until it hurt, and then I threw some more."

Yet, the Braves were a better team than in 1957. Spahn won his first six decisions. Bob Rush, picked up from the Cubs in the off-season, won six of his first nine. The Braves didn't mash the ball as they had in earlier years, but they pitched as never before. Nevertheless, the season hadn't been a wire-to-wire finish, and in the early months there were small surprises, such as the sudden ascension of the Giants—the *San Francisco* Giants—as well as that of the emerging Pittsburgh Pirates and the resilient Cardinals. An equal surprise was that the *Los Angeles* Dodgers were nowhere to be seen. They would finish twenty-one games out of first and, for the first time since 1945, cease to be a threat during the season. (But finishing even more than twenty games out of the money didn't stop the Dodgers from being hell on the Braves: Los Angeles beat the Braves fourteen out of twenty-two times.)

On June 5, the wind cutting hard and nasty across Seals Stadium in San Francisco, Willie Mays singled off Conley in the bottom of the twelfth inning of a 4–4 game. The next batter, Jim Finigan, drilled a double into the right-center gap. Mays took off, a determined low-flying missile on the base paths. In later years, even Henry, who rarely ceded advantage to another player, would marvel at how Willie ran, surgically slicing the bases, his arms pumping furiously through the air. As Mays hit third base, Bob Stevens, the veteran baseball writer for the *San Francisco Chronicle,* yelled "No!" from the press box. Mays had blown through the sign and rushed home to win the game. Henry dug the ball out from the wall, turned, and fired a low-flying missile of his own toward the plate. The ball skidded once in the dirt cutout and bounced directly into the glove of the catcher, Del Crandall. In one motion, Crandall caught Henry's relay, wheeled to his left, and waited to tag Mays. When the home-plate umpire, Frank Secory, raised his right hand to call Mays out at home, Stevens let out a loud yell for all the scribes to hear. "Stupid!"

The next batter, Orlando Cepeda, singled home Finigan with the winning run. The loss left Conley at 0–4, and the Giants and Braves were tied for first place, with Cincinnati, St. Louis, Pittsburgh, and even the Cubs within six games. They would lose the next four, fall out of first, while leaving all eight teams of the National League separated by only seven and a half games.

The Braves had finally reached the top levels of the sport and spent much of the year learning how to stay there, but their cleanup hitter, Henry Aaron, had already begun charting an entirely different course for himself.

It was in 1958 when the dual tracks of his personal life and his athletic life would begin to intersect.

IN THE WEEKS that Lary Aaron held on to life at St. Anthony's, Henry grew friendly with Michael Sablica, a Catholic priest who introduced himself to Henry following little Gary's death. Barbara's nurse was a member of Sablica's parish in Milwaukee, and when told of the Aarons' ordeal, the young priest sought out Henry to express his condolences. Sablica was just thirty-three, ten years older than Henry, and was newly ordained. He, too, had been an athlete, a linebacker on the football team at Marquette during the war years.

In the months that followed, Father Sablica and Henry strengthened their bond, playing handball at Marquette University and occasional rounds of golf. With his considerable hand-eye coordination, Henry was drawn to handball and was a formidable player, but Sablica had been an accomplished player himself, and the two engaged in spirited matches. They talked about family and baseball and Milwaukee, for Henry had now been in the city for nearly four years and had begun to feel a fondness for Milwaukee he hadn't anticipated. Henry's affection for the city grew quickly, despite some uncomfortable moments, most obviously his sister Alfredia's difficult school experience in 1957 and the foreseeable unease that would come with his next ambition: to buy a house in what were the virtually all-white suburbs.

Even though Henry was now a member of the beloved Milwaukee Braves, he understood that such a decision would test the limits of Milwaukee's tolerance and would determine how he assessed the people of Milwaukee as a group. He also understood, however, that regardless of the result, his would not be a typical experience. Henry would often say that how he was treated in Milwaukee would always be enhanced by his own special status as a famous athlete, that he knew the daily life of the average black person in the city was not nearly as welcoming.

Henry and Father Mike, as he had come to be known, talked

about many issues, but mostly, they talked about faith. More accurately, they talked about the intersection between faith and the growing question of civil rights. Henry told Sablica that while he had been raised in the traditions of the southern black church, he had been intrigued about other religions and denominations. Whether this interest was a direct by-product of Gary's death or Lary's struggle to survive—or merely because he saw an opportunity to increase his own religious knowledge—Henry seemed open to the teachings of Catholicism, certainly willing to expand his worldview beyond baseball and the safety and comforts of his own situation. One day, after a round of golf, Father Mike noticed a small book Henry kept in his glove compartment; it was titled *The Life of Christ.*

That the booklet surprised Father Mike said as much about his own presuppositions as it did about Henry's religious curiosity. Sablica was, like most Milwaukeeans, a Braves fan, and he didn't want to run afoul of management by approaching Henry without first going through the proper channels. At the time they met at St. Anthony's, Father Mike didn't know much more about Henry than what he'd read in the newspapers and sports periodicals. He later admitted he had been influenced by the depictions of Henry as something of a simpleton, the characterization of Furman Bisher in *The Saturday Evening Post,* uninterested in the larger questions of the world, lacking the articulateness to express whatever feelings he did have. It was an attitude confirmed by John Quinn, who told Sablica he believed Henry would have little interest in speaking to him. Quinn told Sablica that Henry was "uncomplicated" but that there was no harm in the priest approaching him.

More accurately, Quinn likely preferred that Henry be uncomplicated, for Sablica hadn't approached Henry that day at St. Anthony's only for friendship. For years, even before he had entered the seminary, Michael James Sablica had possessed a passion for activism. He would be one of the early members of that small and often courageous group of Catholic priests who would take a passionate interest in the fight for equal rights.

What particularly aroused Father Mike was the condition of Milwaukee's black poor. The Sablicas had grown up in Milwaukee, and from an early age, Michael Sablica maintained an integrated lifestyle, one that revealed the disparities, both clear and subtle, existing between blacks and whites. There would be other American cities with more notorious reputations for segregation and the racial unrest that ensued—Birmingham, Boston, and later Detroit and Los Angeles, for example. But Milwaukee residents—despite the lack of national attention their city received—knew just how pronounced the lines of segregation truly were. They knew how staunchly the city's banks and real estate agents protected those boundaries with sinister selling and mortgage practices that not only served to keep the races separate but made it increasingly difficult for blacks to purchase property even within their own circumscribed boundaries.

The south side of Milwaukee, where Johnny Logan lived, was overwhelmingly white. The neighborhood was made up of predominately Italian and Irish working-class families. Clergymen of the Catholic Church who felt passionate about civil rights understood that change could come only with an assault on the northern preference for de facto segregation, meaning no laws barring blacks from equal opportunity existed on the books, but because of the social conditions and business practices in Milwaukee, the end result was the same.

In a short time, the more activist members of the clergy would find themselves in the center of the civil rights movement. Sablica was a forerunner of James Groppi, the most famous of Milwaukee's civil rights leaders. Groppi, born the eleventh of twelve children to Italian immigrants who settled on the south side of town, would be ordained in 1959, the year after Sablica. Like Sablica, Groppi was appalled by the living conditions in the black section of Milwaukee, and in the late 1950s he began a slow and relentless campaign against the city's segregationist practices.

As Henry rose to prominence as a player, one of Groppi's prime targets was Judge Robert Cannon, the same Judge Cannon who rode the team bus with Casey Stengel before game three of the 1957 World Series, the same Judge Cannon who preceded Marvin Miller as head of a toothless organization called the Major League Baseball Players Association. Cannon was a Milwaukee insider and was a prominent member of the Fraternal Order of Eagles, a Milwaukee club that did not admit blacks. Cannon denounced the membership practices of the Eagles but did not resign his membership. In turn, Groppi organized demonstrations in front of the good judge's house.

For the priests committed to improving the conditions in the black slums, finding an appropriate place of entry into the social struggle represented a perilous journey, for convincing their blue-collar parishioners of the worthiness of the cause was often a difficult task. Sablica and Groppi faced resistance from clergy peers and elders, and clearly they did not advance as swiftly or as highly within the Church's ranks as they might have had they not been so contro-versial. But the clergymen also understood that times were changing, and social forces were moving at a speed that required action from the Church.

Whites who had become more affluent in the postwar years sought the appeal of the suburbs, which, in turn, reduced the num-bers of children who attended Catholic schools within the city. With enrollments potentially affected and the racial composition of the city changing, the Church began looking for potential converts. Sablica held to a singular conviction: The Catholic Church could be a power-ful instrument in the advancement of the black cause. It was only through Catholicism, he told Henry, that blacks could achieve the dignity and rights that had long been outside of their collective reach. It was a point he stressed to Henry during the spring of 1958.

Henry was not unaware of the racial transitions taking place in Milwaukee. He and Barbara lived in Bronzeville, as did Felix Man-tilla and Wes Covington. They represented the very demographic the Milwaukee Commission feared; affluent people who could afford the neighborhood of their choice but, because they were black, were forced to live in subpar conditions. Nor were the racial contradictions that came with being a famous baseball player lost on Henry. By being Hank Aaron, the rules could be bent and exceptions could always be made. Life could be easier, and it would be. Being awarded dispensation not afforded other blacks was an element of being famous that made Henry uncomfortable, especially given the dynam-ics of professional sports.

Given the perspective of time, Sablica's approach with regard to Henry now appears paternalistic, and more than a bit naïve. In fact, Sablica would later refer to this early view as naïve, a reversal of opinion that stemmed from the deep resistance toward social activism he experienced from his parishioners and fellow clergymen. Sablica also learned the complexities of the race and religion nexus from Henry. Once, before Henry headed for Bradenton and spring training, Sablica wished him good luck and reminded him to "attend mass every Sunday." According to the 1972 book *Bad Henry*, Henry "looked his friend in the eye and answered softly, 'Down there, they won't let me go to mass.' "

In the book, Sablica recalled the exchange. "I wouldn't blame him personally if he never went to mass again for the rest of his life," Sablica was quoted as saying.

JOHN QUINN believed drawing Henry into the nascent civil rights movement of Milwaukee would only be a distraction, and within a short time, he attempted to discourage Henry's contact with Sablica. What Quinn underestimated was Henry's attitude toward racial and social inequalities, which was shaped long before he had ever met Father Mike. Mobile had often provided the bitterest reminders of his place in the social order, and the fearlessness of Jackie Robinson had inspired him. The attitude Sablica projected reflected Henry's own belief system, and perhaps for the first time in Aaron's life, it was being amplified and articulated by a white man. Father Mike had been voicing a message in Milwaukee that was slowly being formulated across the country, led not by the Catholic Church but the black Baptist churches in the South: It would be the clergy who would fuse the dual purposes of religion and social justice. It was a message that immediately appealed to Henry. He had long been awaiting its arrival.

BILLY BRUTON's knee did not heal as quickly or as well as the doctors had forecast in the off-season, turning those optimistic pieces that ran in *The Sporting News* ("Bruton to Report on Time: Knee Healing Satisfactorily") into more kindling for the winter fire. That meant the team's best defensive outfielder would not be available when spring 1958 began and could not be counted on for the regular season. The truth was that Bruton would never again be the same player he was before the injury. When Danny O'Connell suffered at second base, Haney asked John Quinn to make a trade. When Bobby Thomson struggled in left, Haney and Quinn used a platoon of players—Pafko and Covington, mostly—for production.

But when Haney was told that Bruton would not be back until mid-May at the earliest, and even then it was unclear what kind of player he would be, Haney's solution was simple, and it wasn't to look to the trade market for help: Put Henry Aaron in center, permanently.

At the major-league level, there would not be a manager who Henry Aaron ever believed helped him become a better player. He would credit only two men in the minor leagues with improving him as a player and as a hitter. The first was Ben Geraghty in Jacksonville and the second was Mickey Owen, his manager with the Caguas team in Puerto Rico. Geraghty was quite likely the first white man who took an interest in his success, an invaluable dynamic for a young player, especially given the task of integrating the notorious South Atlantic League that faced Henry, Felix Mantilla, and Horace Garner. Watching him play with Caguas, Owen saw that Henry possessed an uncommon ability as a hitter, and he took it upon himself to help refine that ability.

In the major leagues, Charlie Grimm was more a drinking buddy than a skipper, and Henry hardly drank. Henry didn't wish any man to lose his job, but he wasn't exactly distraught when Grimm got the guillotine in June 1956. Gregory Spahn recalled that as an adolescent roaming the Braves clubhouse, he never saw Henry drink anything heavier than a soda. "If he ever had one beer, I don't ever remember him having two," Spahn said. But at least Grimm left him alone. Once Henry became a fixture in the lineup, Charlie let him play, batting fourth, playing right field.

But Fred Haney just couldn't leave Henry alone. He had put him in center in 1957, after Bruton was hurt. Henry could understand that at least. The team had been in a pennant race and was faced with an emergency situation. In the heat of July, Henry had been his only option.

But now, in the dead of winter, with a full six weeks of spring training before the season began, this was no emergency. The team had known for months that Bruton would not be available, and yet playing Henry out of position was the choice Haney decided was appropriate.

Henry was insulted by Fred Haney. In addition to being convinced that Haney was uninspiring as a leader, Henry believed that his manager was stunting his development as a player both at the plate and, quite obviously, in the field. It was Haney, after all, who had come up with the grand idea of batting Henry second. Haney had even stuck Henry at second base a few times.

Henry saw something else, and when he thought about it, the smoke would billow from his ears: Why was he always the lucky one who got screwed? He may have been quiet, but no player ever possessed a greater sense of his own ability than Henry Aaron. And it wasn't just that Henry had an overly inflated opinion of himself. Willie Mays was the biggest attraction in the game and had won an MVP and a world title. Mantle had four titles, an MVP, and a triple crown to boot. But Henry was now an MVP, a world champion, a batting champion. He'd had one two-hundred-hit season, and on August 15, 1957, in the seventh inning of an 8–1 rout over the Reds at Crosley Field, Henry had bombed a two-run homer off Don Gross. The home run was the one hundredth of Henry's career. Before his twenty-first birthday, Henry was averaging 180 hits a season.

Back in those days, before guaranteed contracts and performance incentives and a union that made the players more than hired hands, it was more common for managers to tinker with players and their positions, but in general, the great ones didn't get messed with—at least not as easily as Haney seemed to be doing with Henry. Mays played center field and batted third. You could write his name in the lineup in *pen*. Duke Snider? Center field. Mantle? Ditto. Ted Williams? Left field. DiMaggio? Exactly. (Though, it was also true that Haney told Eddie Mathews, who would one day be elected to the Hall of Fame and be considered perhaps the greatest third baseman of all time, that he was thinking of playing him in left if Covington didn't get it together.)

Haney was mucking with another subsection of the ballplayer code: Don't send me out there to look foolish. Playing defense was hard. It required repetition, and time, and study. Henry didn't want to stand in center field in the Polo Grounds, with its 485-feet straightaway to center, only to be embarrassed by balls coming at him from angles from which he'd never grown accustomed. By putting him in different positions each year, there was no way he would be recognized for his defensive ability.

In his previous four seasons, Henry might have voiced his displeasure with Haney's moves, but only to intimates, a Mantilla or a Bruton, for example. In the spring of 1958, Haney would not tell Henry what position he would play, waiting to find out if a couple of kids, the former Duke star Al Spangler or Harry Hanebrink, would work out. Henry believed it should have been the other way around. Haney should have told Aaron what position he'd play, then filled in the gaps around him.

"That position in center is like no other in the outfield." Henry told the *New York Times* before a spring game with the Dodgers. "You're in on all the plays, either backing up the guys on your right and left or running in to back up throws to second, keeping your eyes out for the pickoff throw to second that might go wild and having to run all over the outfield, covering more than I'm used to."

And there was something else: "I'll be cut short in some things like the All-Star game if I play center. With guys like Willie Mays playing there what chance have I of making the team?"

Maybe it was a question of accumulation, of too much of everything: the tragedy of losing one child and praying for the survival of the second, combined with the whirlwind of publicity and demand for public time that came with being in the spotlight. During the offseason, Henry had appeared on *The Steve Allen Show.* He traveled to New York to be honored for "high principle and achievement" from the Sports Lodge of B'nai B'rith. Fred Miller gave him a job in the Miller publicity department, traveling the country to say nice things about beer, Milwaukee, and baseball. He went from Boston to Manchester, New Hampshire, to New York, Denver, and Salt Lake City. Before the tour, Henry joined Logan, Conley, Mathews, Torre, Covington, and a few other teammates in Chicago to play a benefit basketball game against the Harlem Globetrotters. In that game, the Trotters featured a new showman named Meadowlark Lemon.

When the 1958 season began, Henry couldn't hit. There were a couple of flashes—a two-homer game April 24 in Cincinnati that capped a three-for-three day—but after going one for five in the first game of a doubleheader May 30 in Pittsburgh, Henry was hitting .232. Between the two-homer game against the Reds and a two-run shot off Ron Kline in Pittsburgh, Henry homered just once—a two-out shot off Robin Roberts in a 5–2 loss—for his only home run in a span of 121 at bats.

Henry slogged through the first half of the season. For the first time in his career, he would spend the entire first half of the baseball season unable to enjoy consecutive days with his batting average over .300.

THE BRAVES TOOK over first place two weeks before the all-star break and held on to it for a month. During that time, Henry began to experience that phenomenon special to baseball: of water somehow reaching its natural level. He had not hit for power for the first month and a half of the season, could not find the rhythm that made him the most dangerous man of the summer, and, like every ballplayer, did not offer much insight as to why he was not hitting. Nor did he explain how and why he came out of it so forcefully—thirteen hits in twenty-one at bats in one five-day stretch against the Dodgers and Reds, and all of them rockets. In a week, his average shot up thirty points.

Then the thunder came. July 21–22, against the Cardinals at County Stadium: Henry came to bat ten times, raked seven hits— three for six the first day, followed up with a four-for-four afternoon— but the Braves gained little daylight in the standings. The day before, at Forbes Field, Bob Friend recorded but one out, and the Giants bombed the Pirates, 7–3. San Francisco had caught and passed the Braves in the standings, taking a half-game lead. Nine days later, the two met for a critical four-game series at County Stadium, a game in Milwaukee's favor separating the two.

Raw numbers never tell the complete story. Maybe the sense of ambivalence that seemed to wash over Milwaukee was nothing more than a natural leveling of things, what the economists call a "market correction." The civic enthusiasm that welcomed the Braves when they arrived from Boston was so overwhelming, the passion so complete, that it was impossible to sustain. Perhaps, even, the growing attitude among the players, fans, and ownership that baseball had lost some of its magic was not quite accurate in the first place. The Braves were still leading the league in attendance. They had been in first place or near the top for the previous three years. What passed for concern in Milwaukee would have been welcome in cities that couldn't pay their fans to come watch a ball game. And yet there was concern: concern that the magic of Milwaukee baseball was fading away, that perhaps the arrival of baseball after decades of being strictly minor-league had amounted to nothing more than temporary euphoria. Maybe Perini hadn't discovered oil in the form of baseball prosperity and Milwaukee was not, after all, a lasting model of sport and community. Maybe the town was nothing but a boomtown in disguise.

What made them all nervous—Lou Perini especially—was the sudden *feel* of the place, especially in comparison to the time before the championship. If you weren't careful, the numbers could be very deceiving, even the sellouts, for there was a big difference between a crowd of forty thousand, with twenty thousand more fans unable to get into the ballpark, and a sellout of forty thousand, with some fans at the park because they were unable to get rid of their tickets. The concern was real, and too many people—from Henry to Eddie Mathews to Perini—sensed an ominous, intangible difference for all of them to be wrong.

Still, on a warm Friday night, August 1, with Willie Mays in town, having designs on taking the pennant from the home team, more than 39,000 packed County Stadium for the first-place showdown between the Braves and Giants, Burdette versus McCormick. The game was thrilling, tense, the Giants playing desperately and inefficiently, a wheezing team clawing to save itself. Burdette was hit hard, eleven hits in eight and two-thirds innings, but he managed to escape each problem, striking out eight, forcing double plays, giving up harmless two-out hits. The game was 1–1 until both teams tallied in the late innings. In the top of the ninth, Burdette labored to hold a 4–2 lead. With one on and two out, Willie Kirkland ripped a double to put the tying runs at the corners and the go-ahead run—Mr. Mays himself—at the plate. Burdette wouldn't get the chance to face him. Haney called on Don McMahon.

McMahon threw a fastball, and then another. And then he threw another. And then he threw four more fastballs. Mays wouldn't budge, fouling off one, taking another close for a ball, pushing the count full. Del Crandall was behind the dish, playing sign language with McMahon. Now, this was war. Willie took McMahon's best, one heater after another. And that was the way to pitch to Mays, because you didn't throw him breaking balls.

But then Crandall called for a curve and McMahon agreed reluctantly. He wound and tossed a little spinner at Mays, who lunged and chipped it foul.

Now Crandall was calling for *another* curve . . . and that was like trying to pet an alligator. You could double up fastballs on Mays, but not curveballs, not if you were fond of living. But that's what Crandall called, and that's what McMahon threw, a little teardrop of a pitch that kissed the sky and spun easily into Crandall's glove, just perfect enough for home-plate umpire Dusty Boggess to raise his right hand and call strike three and the game over, leaving Mays frozen as the Braves celebrated.

That night, in his suite at the Knickerbocker, Fred Haney poured himself a drink and chatted with one of his California chums, *Los Angeles Times* columnist Braven Dyer. "I have an idea," the skipper said, "that that was the big one tonight."

The next afternoon, Henry enjoyed the kind of day power hitters craved—four for four, with a home run, two doubles, and three driven in. The sun-drenched crowd of 34,770 watched the rout, prompting John Drebinger of the *Times* to remark, "Anyone of the opinion that baseball is waning in this sector had better recheck his figures. When a town produces a capacity crowd on a Saturday afternoon it can scarcely be said to be disinterested."

The end of the Giants as pennant contenders came the next day, when Spahn completed the doubleheader sweep, 6–0. San Francisco had come in having lost three in a row and now had been bounced four straight by the division leaders. The Braves lead was now six. By the time the losing stopped, the Giants skid had reached ten out of eleven. They would not contend again, finishing twelve games out. Chiefly responsible for the San Francisco demise were the Braves—who beat them sixteen out of twenty-two times during the season—especially Henry, whose fire glowed with the sight of Mays in the other dugout. Henry hit .333 against the Giants, with nineteen runs driven in, his most against any team.

That left the Pirates, and the rising Roberto Clemente, who were now a half game out of second place, five games back.

If the Giants pennant hopes had been undone by their head-to-head meetings with the Braves, the Pirates knew the Braves couldn't keep them from winning the pennant, for Pittsburgh gave Milwaukee trouble, on the mound and at the plate. That the Dodgers, Giants, and Pirates would come to County Stadium in succession was a gift from the schedulers to the fans, who enjoyed watching the most driven players play with added passion.

For years, Henry would downplay his rivalry with Mays. There was no advantage in it for him, he would say. Henry wanted to be a great player, regardless of the competition. Mays was cool and confident, the older brother to the young lions who were dominating the game. He was the first transcendent black superstar. Jackie was the first black player, admired, respected, but Willie was beloved, a player whose talents were undeniable and whose disposition, unlike Jackie's, didn't threaten whites. Mays would never betray any rivalry with Henry, or any player, for that matter. Willie even used his confidence to influence the debate. Whenever he was asked who was the greatest player he ever saw, Willie would reply, "I thought I was." Still, despite each man's protestations, there was never a great deal of warmth between the two. Henry wanted to be the best. Willie played as if he was always in the lead—and he was.

And then there was this new kid Clemente, who saved his fury for the Dodgers. Games with Los Angeles would always mean more to Clemente, for the Dodgers were his first team, and they had traded him. That was not to say that the Braves didn't hold special value to Clemente. Henry was the all-star in right field—Clemente's position—and the two staged a quiet but furious rivalry each year for the title of best right fielder in the National League. Only one could be the leading man, especially when it came time to start the All-Star Game.

In the opener, Juan Pizarro pitched brilliantly. Perhaps more than any other pitcher on the staff, Pizarro was weighted by expectations. All of twenty-one years old, he couldn't go to the watercooler without hearing how he would one day be the next Spahn.

Through six innings, the score was tied at three—the big kids playing tit for tat. Clemente singled and scored in the first. Aaron drove in the Braves first run on an RBI grounder. For a moment, it appeared Pizarro would escape the ninth, after pinch hitter Roman Mejias led off the inning with a single to center and was called out for not touching first base. But after Bill Virdon flied to left, there was Clemente (three for four, three runs scored), who lofted a two-out, game-winning home run to center field.

Burdette beat the Pirates the next night, and Henry's two-out home run in the first stood up in the third game. Spahn finished the Pirates in the finale, and the lead over Pittsburgh was eight. A week later, the Pirates went on a final tear, winning seven in a row, cutting the lead to four and a half on August 20 after thumping Milwaukee twice at Forbes Field, 6–4 and 10–zip. They would beat the Braves four more times down the stretch but couldn't get closer than five games for that most quintessential of baseball reasons: They couldn't beat last-place teams. The Phillies and Dodgers beat the Pirates seven times in the final thirty games of the season.

Meanwhile, an inch away from defending their pennant, it was Henry who made short work of Cincinnati Sunday afternoon, September 21, at Crosley Field.

Fifth inning, scoreless game: Henry hits a three-run double. Later, he hit a two-run homer, his thirtieth, to take away the suspense. The score was 6–0. Then in the seventh, Frank Robinson boomed a homer off Spahn, who later admitted he let up because he was "feeling cocky." Then the lead shrank to 6–5 in that same inning. Only when McMahon got Ed Bailey to fly out to Bruton did the sweat ease. The final score was 6–5. Fourteen thousand fans awaited the team at the airport. The race was over, the pennant secured, and, once more, the Yankees were waiting.

.   .   .

AND NOW, game four over, Spahn had beaten Ford. The Braves were a game from repeating as champions. Burdette took the ball for game five of the World Series. Outside the Milwaukee clubhouse, two cases of champagne stacked on top of each other sat on a hand-cart in anticipation of the fact that by the end of the afternoon, the baseball season would end as it had a year before, with Burdette beating the Yankees at Yankee Stadium.

As metaphors went, this catastrophe was no hurricane. With a hurricane, you can see it coming a hundred miles away, days before it hits, swirling in its menacing formation. You can anticipate its angry acceleration. Nor was it an earthquake, for though earthquakes strike without warning, their damage is quick and immediate. The fall of the Milwaukee Braves was more like buying the newest, nicest house on the block, the envy of all the neighbors, only to discover upon closer, belated inspection, the basement is damp with moisture, the pretty wood frame has rotted from underneath, the trusses bow, and the roof probably won't survive the winter. Yet on the outside, everything looked fine.

October 6, 1958. Bob Turley was on the mound for the Yanks. Turley was no pushover. He was, in fact, a hard-throwing right-hander, a strikeout pitcher who had pitched well against the Braves in the previous World Series. But in game two, in the same pitching matchup at County Stadium, the Braves had clubbed Turley for seven runs in the first inning, when he retired exactly one batter. Bruton had led off the game with a home run and Burdette had poured bourbon in the open wound, ending the scoring that inning by ripping a three-run homer that not only made the score 7–1 but knocked Elston Howard—who careened into the chain-link fence in left while trying to keep the ball in the park—right out of the game.

Even before the legendary shadows could descend on the Yankee Stadium grass, Lou Perini, sitting in the box seats with his wife and Joe Cairnes, knew to send the champagne back to the icebox.

The final score was 7–0. Turley had struck out ten, fanning Henry twice. There would be no celebration, only a long flight to Milwaukee and two chances to win one game at County Stadium.

But you wouldn't have known the Braves had blown a chance to win the World Series by the scene in the Milwaukee clubhouse. Haney was gray, Burdette embittered, but the rest of the Braves were as light as a Fourth of July barbecue.

BRAVES FROLIC IN CLUBHOUSE AFTER LOSS
BUT HANEY AND BURDETTE ARE GLOOMY

Aaron imitates Covington lapse

Fred Haney . . .wasn't happy after yesterday's loss to the Yankees. . . .

But there was no evidence of unhappiness among the other Braves. . . .

Wes Covington, smiling as always, said "no comment" when asked whether he had lost McDougald's long drive in the sun in the sixth inning.

At that moment, his team-mate, Henry Aaron, who had just emerged from his shower, put on a clowning act that he intended as an imitation of Covington staggering aimlessly as the ball dropped. Covington only grinned some more.

Haney decided to start Spahn on two days' rest, and if need be for a deciding game seven, Burdette on two days' rest.

Overconfidence comes in many forms. With the Braves, it revealed itself in a total lack of concentration, which undermined Spahn. Bauer hit a two-out homer in the first to make it 1–0 before the Braves chased the great Whitey Ford in just an inning and a third, taking a 2–1 lead. Spahn held the lead until the sixth, when Mantle and Howard singled to lead off the inning. Berra hit a game-tying sacrifice fly that scored Mantle, who had advanced on an error by Bruton in center. It was the second error of the afternoon and it cost Spahn the lead.

Haney, of whose managerial abilities Henry would always be critical, allowed Spahn to pitch into the tenth in a 2–2 game. McDougald led off the inning with a home run. Spahn responded by retiring Bauer and Mantle. One strike away from going into the bottom of the tenth down a run, Howard and Berra singled. Then Haney got the message and brought in Don McMahon, who gave up a run-scoring single to big Moose Skowron.

And so it was 4–2 in the bottom of the tenth, the Braves facing Ryne Duren, who had breezed fastball after fastball by them. Duren had entered the game in the sixth inning, had struck out the side twice, in the sixth and ninth innings. With two out and Logan on second, Henry rifled a run-scoring single to center to make it 4–3. Then Adcock singled to put the tying run on third, and the Series-winning run on first. Stengel replaced Duren with "Bullet Bob" Turley, who threw three pitches to Frank Torre. The third was a soft liner to second that floated over McDougald's head. Henry raced toward home and the game-tying run, only to see McDougald's legs churning, his arms outstretched, before he leaped and snared the ball into his glove to end the game.

New York won the World Series in Milwaukee, 6–2. And it was there Henry's doubts about Fred Haney exposed themselves.

Nearly four months earlier, the Yankees and Braves had met for an exhibition game at Yankee Stadium to support the Jimmy Fund, the Boston charity created by Perini to fund cancer research. Before the game, Stengel and Haney shared a jocular moment, with Haney relishing the license to crow, since he had beaten Stengel in the World Series. Both had spent their lives in baseball. Stengel was seven years older than Haney, and at their ages, in other occupations, both would have been retired instead of standing at the center of the sports world.

But that was where similarities ended. Stengel's ability to butcher the English language beyond recognition made him colorful to the newsmen. But like most theater, it was an act, and the true face behind the Stengel mask was that of a shark. The kindly old clown who picked up his knowledge not from books but the streets was nothing more than a routine. Stengel did not spare feelings for victory. There was no sentimentality for the moment. Take the Yankee starter for game seven, Don Larsen, who held a 2–1 lead. Billy Bruton led off the inning with a single. Frank Torre popped up, and Henry singled to put two on and one out. And what happened next? The old man tramped up the dugout steps, grim and crotchety. He wasn't coming out for a pep talk. He took the ball from Larsen, *in the third inning.*

The game was 2–2 in the eighth. Burdette retired Bauer and struck out Mantle. Judging a pitcher by his pitch count, especially on two days' rest, was still four decades away, but back in 1958, common sense was still available. Burdette had pitched forty-eight hours earlier, had given up just two runs. The entire Braves bull pen would not pitch again in a game that mattered for another six months. Blame it on the times, when men were men and pitchers were not removed from games, or blame it on Fred Haney, his five-foot-four-inch frame a motionless little package as Berra doubled to right.

Haney didn't move. Then Howard singled Berra in to break the tie. Andy Carey hit a smash to third, which Mathews kept in the infield but couldn't make a play on to put out runners at the corners, while Henry fumed in the outfield and the bull pen waited for the skipper to lead them into action and save the season. Haney let Burdette face the next batter, Skowron, who had already driven in the go-ahead run off Burdette way back in the second that put the Yankees ahead, 2–1. Skowron, naturally, homered, a big majestic drive that sent an entire city into grieving. Four runs with two out and the manager reduced to being a spectator: The score was now 6–2.

Just as he had been on the mound in game five, when the Braves were cavalier about losing, Turley was on the mound at the end, when Schoendienst lined to Mantle, thereby giving the Yankees the World Series. "Going into the eighth, when Burdette still had his tie game, the scent of victory was still strong among Milwaukee's burghers," wrote Shirley Povich in the *Washington Post*. "Coming out of the eighth, after those four Yankee runs, a sickly quiet reigned in the stands, and wooden men went to bat against Turley in the last two innings."

Over the final three games, Turley had beaten Burdette twice and saved the game in between. The Braves committed six errors over the final two games and struck out twenty-five times over the final three. Henry was brilliant, with nine hits and a .333 average, while Eddie Mathews set a World Series record with eleven strikeouts and a .160 average for the Series.

There was bitterness to spare, and the Braves knew they had cost themselves greatly. They had become the one thing they detested the most. They had become a chapter in the Yankee legend, and Henry would lament often that instead of being a team that won consecutive championships and dominated an era, they had been reduced to, in his words, "just another team that won the World Series."

Of course, they'd become more than that. They had also become one of the rare teams that gave away a championship with a 3–1 lead in games. You had to go back thirty-three years, to 1925, when the Pirates beat Washington and Walter Johnson lost game seven, to find another team that had a 3–1 lead in games and came away with nothing but dust. There were no pantomimes in the clubhouse after this one. The 1958 season was over, and nobody was laughing.

PERHAPS MORE THAN any other sport, baseball is a game of self-sufficiency, a team game that lives in the individual's domain. Nobody can hit for you. By virtue of the strikeout, a pitcher can barely include his fielders in the flow of the game. Even defensively, where a team must work together on cutoffs and relays and backups, only one person can catch the ball. On certain days, an outfielder can play the entire game and not even have an opportunity to touch the ball. Sink or swim. If the shortstop is the best player on the field but a ball is hit to deep center, there is no defensive scheme that can be concocted to shield his team from the center fielder's defensive weaknesses, no way to showcase the better players and hide the mediocre as in football and basketball. In basketball, the player who can't shoot can always pass the ball to a more gifted offensive player. In baseball, you can't give an at bat to a teammate. You catch the ball and hit it, or you fail.

Conversely, because of baseball's individualist nature, it is also virtually impossible for a position player to dominate every moment of every game. A few basketball players can account for the majority of their team's shot totals. In extreme cases, one player can score nearly half of his team's points. In baseball, both halves of the batting order—the first five and the bottom four—each receive approximately the same number of at bats over a single game, regardless of a player's abilities.

And that was the reason why the National League season of 1959 was so special. It combined the individual and the collective. It featured a supernova eclipsing the established star. And it spotlighted a three-team pennant chase deep into September—the Dodgers, the Giants, and the Braves vying for the prize—a chase that would have lasting consequences for each franchise, and the players involved.

The supernova was Henry Aaron, and for the first month of the season he began to chart his course toward a place more rarefied, more exclusive. He began the season with fury—extra base hits in each of the first seven games of the season, including three in an opening-day destruction of Bob Friend and Pittsburgh at Forbes Field, then three more for the home opener, including singling and scoring the winning run in beating Philly in front of 42,081 at County Stadium. At the end of April, Henry was hitting .508.

Henry did not necessarily need a reason to tear into the league at a more vigorous pace, but two spring-training incidents clearly would have motivated him. The sting of the World Series loss would never go away, and during the spring, Haney did not intend to let any of the players forget, especially the ones who didn't produce. One day in Bradenton, Mathews, who had died at the plate during the Series, wanted to stay in the batting cage for a few extra swings. "You didn't want to swing it last October," Haney bellowed for all to hear. Throughout the length of spring training, Haney's jabs contained just a bit more acid.

Of course, Haney did not seem to blame himself for nodding off at the wheel in game seven, but he gave the players the works. "We could use some more speed," Haney told Shirley Povich of the *Washington Post*. "Pitching and hitting sound pretty good, but you can't overlook other ways to win ball games. In a close game, the big play can beat you. Willie Mays can beat you four ways. He can beat you with a hit or a throw or a steal or a big catch in the outfield. We don't have one like that on our club."

For three years, Henry had listened to Fred Haney take his whacks at various players on the team, and now he had taken a shot at him, too. *We don't have one like that on our club.* It was true that Henry did not have big stolen-base totals. It was bad enough that Haney had sat in the dugout while the World Series turned to ashes, and now the players had to wake up to the morning paper, with him cutting them off at the knees. And now there was this, Haney waxing nostalgic for Mays.

So Henry swung with purpose, setting the Phillies, the Pirates, the Cardinals, and the Reds aflame. When the Giants came to Milwaukee for three games to start May, Henry had to swallow Sam Jones walking away with a victory in the opener and Willie going four for five in the second game, a Saturday win for San Francisco.

In the finale, Burdette against Johnny Antonelli, the two stars put on a show in a sideways Milwaukee rain. With one on in the first, Mays took a sidearm fastball from Burdette and sent it four hundred feet to dead center, the ball landing softly in the Perini pines in right-center field. In the bottom of the inning, with two out, Henry pounded a home run of his own to make it 2–1. The next time up, Mays lashed a drive into the left-center gap and raced for second, only to be erased by a laser from Pafko. Leading off the fourth, Henry faced Antonelli and wafted another home run, this one close to where Mays's ball had landed. An inning later, the Braves finished Antonelli with five runs and took the game, 9–4. When Mays and Aaron were finished sparring, Willie had gone two for four, with a home run and two runs driven in. Henry was three for four, with two home runs, three driven in, and two runs scored.

The Dodgers came to County Stadium the next night and Drysdale posted a classic line—eleven innings, ten hits, nine strikeouts—which meant nothing, because he was long gone by the time the matter was decided, at the end of the sixteenth inning, which happened to be three minutes before the National League curfew of 1:00 a.m.

BRAVES SHADE DODGERS, 3–2

Aaron's long double breaks up
thriller just before curfew
By Frank Finch/*Times Staff Representative*

MILWAUKEE — With first place at stake, the Dodgers and Braves battled for 4 hrs, 47 minutes . . . before Hank Aaron doubled Eddie Mathews home . . . to give Milwaukee a 3–2 victory. . . .

. . . Aaron, the greatest hitter in the game today, drove in the tying tally with an accidental bloop single . . . and then demonstrated his greatness with the clutch clout that ended hostilities at 12:47 a.m.

Even if Fred Haney didn't believe he had a game breaker the caliber of Mays, Henry played with a certain type of ferocity. Most players played with purpose, but few could make their bodies do what the mind wanted. On May 10, Henry singled in the ninth inning off Joe Nuxhall to cap a doubleheader sweep of Cincinnati.

The Braves took over first place three days later. In the meantime, Henry maintained a scorching pace. In a particularly painful loss in Philadelphia on April 23, he doubled for his first hit of the game in the seventh inning and then homered in the ninth to give the Braves a 3–1 lead, only to see Pizarro give up two homers in the bottom of the ninth and lose 4–3. He would hit in every game for nearly the next month, a twenty-two-game hit streak. In the final game of the streak, a crisp afternoon at Seals Stadium, with the Giants and Braves slugging it out for first place, Sam Jones held on, trailing 2–1 in the fifth. Mays had already homered, and even though he was down in the game, Jones was pleased by his shackling of Henry, who bounced out weakly in his first at bat and struck out in his second.

Jones quickly retired the first two batters of the inning and, with the pitcher, Spahn, standing at the plate, was about to cruise into the dugout. But Spahn singled. So did Bruton. Then Mathews flipped a single to the opposite field in left to make it 3–1. Jones was breathing fire when Henry stepped to the plate. Henry took a Jones delivery and blasted it into the gap in center, over Mays's head. Bruton scored from second and Bill Rigney made his quick trot across the infield with the hook. Jones left the mound, turning as he headed to the showers to stare down Henry, who was staring right back at second base.

SAM JONES GUNS FOR HANK AARON

MILWAUKEE (AP)—Sam Jones of the San Francisco Giants was quoted . . . as saying, "The next time Henry Aaron sees me on the mound, he is going flat. He's going to get a face full of dirt." . . .

"Don't let 'em print what you said," Willie Mays pleaded with . . . Jones. . . .

"Aw, go ahead and print it. I said it."

And with a little self-satisfied twinkle in his eye, Henry responded, "Sam must have been a little upset at getting beat," but he knew Jones was a little upset at getting beaten by him. Sam Jones would die of cancer in 1971, at forty-five years of age, and there would not be a moment of reconciliation. Sam Jones took his fight with Henry to the grave.

On June 16, at the cavernous L.A. Coliseum, the trio of Johnny Podres, Clem Labine, and Art Fowler held Henry to a hit in five at bats, dropping his pregame average from .402 to .398. He would not threaten .400 again, but he assaulted pitchers, especially in late innings. Once, it was easily Mays in the National League, Elston Howard and Berra in the American as holders of the clutch-hitting title, but now Henry had elbowed in on the discussion.

But the Braves could not escape their own drift. They had lost first place at the all-star break and would trade places in the standings with the Dodgers throughout the remainder of the summer. In the second week of September, the Giants still held the lead, but the Dodgers and Braves played two bitter games at the Coliseum. In the first, Bob Buhl beat Drysdale, 4–1. The next night was a game the Braves would not forget. Henry struck hard again, going four for six, singling and scoring in the tenth to break a 6–6 game. Up 7–6, with one out in the bottom of the tenth, Maury Wills singled off McMahon, then raced to third on another single by Chuck Essegian. Junior Gilliam wafted a sacrifice fly to tie the score at 7–7 and rejoiced when McMahon walked in the winning run. The Dodgers and Braves were now tied for second, both 79–65.

ON SEPTEMBER 15, the Giants led by two games. The next five games would likely decide the pennant, home games with Milwaukee and the Dodgers. San Francisco had held on to first place since July 10. Bad things always seem worse when they happen to you, and that was why the San Francisco Giants generally lacked sympathy for the Braves. The Giants proceeded to split the series with the Braves, lose all three to the Dodgers—which put Los Angeles in first place for the first time in consecutive days in May—and then lose two more to the Cubs and the Cardinals. The Giants lost eight of their final ten games, and by the final weekend, they were finished.

The Braves, meanwhile, entered the final two games of the season trailing by a game, thanks to Jack Meyer (now pitching for Philadelphia) beating Burdette 6–3 at County Stadium. Losing was one thing, but there were still two games left. But on that night when Mathews hit his forty-fifth home run, staring the Braves in the face should they find a way to take the pennant was not the perennial New York Yankees, but the Chicago White Sox, who had won the pennant for the first time in forty years, not having done so since the infamous year 1919. These Sox, the "Go-Go Sox," as they were called, couldn't break a pane of glass with their bats, but they ran all the way to the pennant, beating out Cleveland. The dreaded Yankees were thirteen back.

It wasn't the losing that night that galled Perini and Burdette and the rest, but the sparse and uninspired crowd of 24,912 that showed up at County Stadium. Had winning become so old so quickly? Was the circus in town? Then came the chilling extrapolations of thought: If the fans weren't showing up for a team that played for the pennant, the whole franchise would fall through the floorboards if they'd ever had a losing season.

On September 26, at Wrigley Field, the Cubs jumped all over Podres. It was 9–0 in the third, heading to a 12–2 Cub pounding of the Dodgers. Meanwhile, up Route I-94 in Milwaukee, Spahn and Robin Roberts wrestled to a 2–2 standstill against Philadelphia until the bottom of the eighth, when Mathews and Aaron started the inning with singles. Needing a run to tie for the pennant on the final day, putting their destiny in their own hands, Fred Haney decided to do some managing. Adcock put down a sacrifice, advancing Mathews, who scored on Bobby Avila's force play. Spahn struck out the first two batters of the ninth and finished the job for his twenty-first win of the season in a tidy one hour and fifty-nine minutes. Both teams would win the next day, setting up a best-of-three play-off, the Dodgers versus the Braves again, to begin Monday, September 28, at County Stadium, the winner to take on the awaiting White Sox in the World Series.

Henry figured his team would go to the World Series a third straight time. This Dodger team simply didn't scare anyone with its lineup. Snider was old, and so was Hodges. Pee Wee was at the end; Robinson was long gone. They played in the sun and not the tough corners of Brooklyn. They certainly could pitch, but the Braves had

Burdette and Spahn, who had both won twenty-one games. Besides, both teams would have to hit to win the series, Henry believed, because the big pitchers on each side had already pitched just to make the play-off possible. The opener would be two middle-rotation guys, Danny McDevitt for L.A. and Carl Willey for Milwaukee.

But when he walked out to the field to take a quick look at the conditions, Henry could not believe his eyes. There was hardly a soul at the ballpark—County Stadium empty . . . for a play-off game, no less. It was bad enough that the Saturday-afternoon game, with a pennant on the line, had been witnessed by exactly 23,768 paying spectators. The weather had been gloomy that weekend, a slashing rain pelting the field, but that couldn't stand as the reason for why the hungriest city for baseball in the league suddenly had better things to do.

"A disgracefully small crowd of 18,297 watched in apathy," wrote Arthur Daley of the *New York Times.* "No one seemed to care much and the players responded with the routine job the uninspired surrounding seemed to demand." Henry's worst fears were realized.

The Braves knocked out McDevitt with one out in the second. They led 2–1, but like Bob Turley's relief appearances in the World Series, the Braves couldn't touch the new man, Larry Sherry. Sherry pitched the rest of the way, not giving up a run. In the sixth, the game tied 2–2, Willey gave up a long home run to Dodger catcher Johnny Roseboro that wound up being the game winner.

He blasted a pitch over Henry Aaron's head and into the right field bleachers. . . .

Once upon a time Milwaukee was rated as the most rabid town west of Flatbush. . . . Nothing deterred them. They braved rain, snow, discomfort and second-place finishes. . . .

. . . The support Milwaukeeans gave their Braves must have been moral. It certainly wasn't physical. The bleachers were virtually empty. . . .

. . . Maybe the Braves shouldn't have given their followers the bonus of two pennants and one world championship. They have nothing left for an encore.

—Arthur Daley, *The New York Times,* Sept. 29, 1959

Once in Los Angeles, the finale was emblematic. Aaron and Mathews, invisible in the opener, jumped on Drysdale in the first for two runs. The Braves led 2–0, and 3–1, and, in the bottom of the ninth, 5–2. Burdette was tough and ornery, ready to force a winner-take-all gambit in Milwaukee. Then Wally Moon led off the ninth with a single, and it was the old Dodgers, the ones who had roamed Brooklyn, made the name famous, trolled the archives for one last reminiscing. Snider, thirty-three and gray, singled. Two on, nobody out, and the tying run at the plate, and Fred Haney about as motionless as a cigar store Indian.

Only after Gil Hodges singled to load the bases did Haney finally call for McMahon, but putting a pitcher in a bases-loaded, nobody-out situation in the other team's stadium is not a blueprint for success. Norm Larker hit a two-run single to make it 5–4, and still nobody out. Another Brooklyn legend, Furillo, tied it at 5–5 with a sacrifice and the game went into extra innings.

In the eleventh, Henry stood on third, with the bases loaded and two out, but Stan Williams stymied Adcock. Bob Rush entered the game in the bottom of the eleventh and did the same, escaping with the bases loaded. With two out and nobody on in the bottom of the twelfth, Hodges walked, and then took second when Joe Pignatano singled off Bob Rush.

That brought up Furillo, thirty-seven years old, leg-heavy, and out of place in Los Angeles, another member of the Brooklyn old guard soon to be phased out by progress. Furillo took a fastball from Rush and drilled it past short, or so it looked. Mantilla dived and stabbed the ball, keeping it in the infield, seemingly saving the season . . . but then he scrambled to his feet and fired wide to first. The ball screamed past Frank Torre, heading toward the dugout. Hodges, big number 14, skipped home deliriously, holding his head with both hands in disbelief before spreading them wide, anticipating the embrace.

Mantilla could not speak afterward, unashamed that he cried on his stool, unable to compose himself, unable to give interviews. The Braves had led in both games and yet lost each of them and the season.

Fifty years later, Frank Torre could still see the final play of the season, clear and in slow motion. "The Coliseum was a football field. Mantilla was in for Logan. Gil Hodges was a slow runner. Mantilla got the ball and he threw it in front of me, and what I was trying to do was put my body in front to block it. The infield was football sand, and football sand was a beachlike sand. It went into the sand and bounced over my head. It was impossible to block it—and the winning run scored. I'm six-foot-three, and you had to listen to the crap, 'Gil Hodges woulda blocked that ball.' . . . It was pathetic."

THE NEXT DAY, in Los Angeles, Joe Reichler of the Associated Press ran a story saying that Fred Haney would be leaving the club as manager, the victim of another bitter defeat and the change of management. Birdie Tebbetts, the needling former catcher and manager of the Reds, was now in the Braves front office. Haney blew a small gasket when denying the rumors. "Absolutely untrue," he said. "Anyone can write a story and ascribe it to a 'trusted source.' "

Two days later, he quietly and solemnly resigned as manager of the Braves, and the Braves did not try to stop him.

AND SO FRED HANEY left, and with him the magic and allure of Milwaukee baseball during the 1950s. Haney was merely the symbol of the change, not the catalyst. He was sixty-one years old, and despite having won six of every ten games he managed with the Braves, he would never again manage at the big-league level. Haney had arrived in Milwaukee having never finished higher than sixth in the previous six years he'd managed, but he left with a World Series title, two pennants, and the bittersweet memories of a moment in baseball history that would not last long after he and his wife headed for California.

For all the disappointment about the way the season had ended, Henry saw the future as something to look forward to. He'd played hard, had played to win, and looked at his teammates with respect. Nevertheless, there would be the lasting pain of failure, of coming up so short. That part, Henry could handle. Losing when his teams should have won more, well, that would gnaw at him for fifty years.

In his autobiography *I Had a Hammer*, Henry commented on his disappointment:

Every team has its "ifs" and "buts," but that doesn't make it any easier. It still bothers me that we were only able to win two pennants and one World Series with the team we had. We should have won at least four pennants in a row. The fact is, we had them and we blew them. If we had done what was there for us to do, we would have been remembered as one of the best teams since World War II—right there with the Big Red Machine and the A's of the seventies and the Dodgers and the Yankees of the fifties. But we didn't do it, and in the record book we're just another team that won a World Series. Damn it, we were better than that.

Though deep in his heart he felt the atmosphere of Milwaukee had changed, he was the most brilliant young star in the game, who, at least statistically, may have competed with more dynamic rivals, while looking up at no one, the great Mantle and Mays included. He had played in pennant races virtually every year since he'd entered the league. He had been disappointed before the first game of the play-off that so few Milwaukee fans had showed up, but he did not place the appropriate significance of the moment until years later.

Henry had fallen into the lethal baseball trap of believing in the endless summer. The pain of losing again to the Dodgers was considerable, but to Henry's mind, a great team losing was nothing more than the awful price of competition. The year 1960 awaited, the players coming back would be the same, and as a group they had always played at or very near the top.

To Henry, they would simply win it all next year. He had no way of knowing that the day Spahn walked off the mound at Yankee Stadium after game four would be as close to winning the World Series as he would ever come again.

PART THREE

LEGEND

CHAPTER TEN

RESPECT

You ache with the need to convince yourself that you do exist in the real world, that you're a part of all of the sound and anguish, and you strike out with your fists, you curse and you swear to make them recognize you. And, alas, it's seldom successful.

—Ralph Ellison

IN FEBRUARY 1964, Henry celebrated his thirtieth birthday, and the various rivers of his life, both competing and complementing, reached a critical convergence. Gaile was ten, Hankie six, Lary six, and Dorinda two (she was born on Henry's birthday, February 5, 1962). Months earlier, he and Barbara had celebrated a decade of marriage. So much of what he had envisioned had coalesced: Months before, he had completed his tenth season in the major leagues, his position not only as a premier player in the game but as quite possibly one of the greatest to have ever played the game cemented. All of his benchmarks, active or retired—Robinson, Musial, DiMaggio, and Mays—were now peers.

For a place that had once been foreign and unsettling, Milwaukee was now home. The family had lived in the suburb of Mequon for five years, Henry's connection to the city and its people growing only stronger. He at once understood the contradictions that came with his stature: He was often subject to the humiliations and limitations that came with being black, and yet his fame insulated him from some of the very conditions suffered by the average black family. Indeed, Henry was aware that the Aarons were *allowed* to move into Mequon in the first place only because he was *the* Hank Aaron, a fact

Father Groppi and his supporters often noted with increasing volume during the turbulent rallies for housing desegregation that came to define 1960s Milwaukee.

There was a reason, the Groppi followers always said, that the Aarons were the only black family living in Mequon, and the reason was certainly not the city's heightened level of tolerance. Groppi and Aaron did not have any formal relationship. Henry was not active in the desegregation battles in Milwaukee, but Groppi nevertheless used Henry and his fame as an example of the racial inequities in the city's housing practices.

If Henry remembered the difference between how he and his fellow black teammates were regarded and the treatment afforded Willie Mays back during his barnstorming tour of the South following his second year in the league, he also now understood that in Milwaukee, being Hank Aaron represented no small advantage, either. In certain situations, the disparity between the famous Henry Aaron and the common black person in Milwaukee was so great that it made him uncomfortable, for Henry's internal compass had never been turned toward superiority over others—especially other blacks—regardless of the perks gained because of his talent. While he would for fifty years hold a special place in his heart for Milwaukee, he would acknowledge the painful merits of the Groppi argument: It was definitely his fame, he later decided, that had made his time there so special.

This was a position common to famous blacks in the 1950s and 1960s, the movie stars, singers, and athletes whose talent provided opportunities that otherwise did not yet exist for the general black population, and being able to taste, even briefly, a world where color was not the defining aspect of life created a bittersweet worldview. There were some players, such as the St. Louis Cardinals pitcher Bob Gibson, who were cognizant of being treated with more humanity and dispensation by whites simply because of their athletic gifts. Gibson understood the uneasy balance of his position, and the worst part of it all was how immediately transparent the change in disposition of those same whites could be once they discovered he was not Pack Robert Gibson, taxi driver from Omaha, Nebraska, but *Bob Gibson,* the great Cardinals pitcher, who provided so much success and glory to the home team and enjoyment to the paying customers, the majority of whom were white. "It's nice to get attention and favors, but I can never forget the fact that if I were an ordinary black person I'd be in the shithouse, like millions of others," Gibson once told the writer Roger Angell. "I'm happy I'm *not* ordinary, though."

Similarly, such discomfort did not fail to have an effect on Henry. As he grew more prominent, he resolved that he must do more with his special status than buy a house in a nice neighborhood or receive a better table at the exclusive restaurants that did not admit blacks but made exceptions for him. His abilities, he believed, needed to translate into his having greater significance than those vapid, individual perks. As he rose, Henry believed his responsibility included helping the less fortunate.

For his years in public life, Henry would become known for his consistency on the baseball diamond, far past the point of weary cliché. Yet, to the people closest to him, it was his sense of duty, combined with a certain steely, uncompromising compassion, that struck them the most. One example was his friendship with Donald Davidson, the Braves publicity man, who went back with the franchise to its days in Boston. Davidson happened to be a dwarf, all of four feet tall, and if the news stories always contained a mention of a black player's race, Davidson could not escape mention of his diminutiveness. There were some members of the Braves who played tricks on him— Spahn and Burdette, naturally—but Henry was very protective of Davidson.

"You always knew he was a serious man," said Joe Torre, Frank Torre's kid brother, who joined the Braves in 1961. "You always knew he had strong commitment to people. And it's not something that he bragged about. And I think that was one of the most admirable things about Henry. He was quiet. He didn't advertise it, but you just knew."

HUNTING SATISFIED Henry's need for adrenaline. It also served as an extension of his desire for open space and solitude, in a sense no different from his days as a boy in Toulminville, when he would escape to an isolated fishing spot on Three Mile Creek, being at a peaceful distance, seeking a retreat from the world. Early in his career, he and Barbara would return to Mobile almost as soon as the season ended, but after Henry had purchased the Mequon house, he would spend at least part of the off-season in Milwaukee, even though Lary and, periodically, Gaile still lived in Mobile with Estella and Herbert. In 1960, an old friend of Henry, Lefty Muehl, who played in the long-since-vanished Illinois-Iowa-Indiana league and was a part-time scout in the Braves organization, invited Henry to Doland, South Dakota, to shoot pheasant, and fall hunting became something of an annual pastime for him.

Soon, a routine formed: Henry would leave Milwaukee and head west, through Minnesota and into South Dakota, at some points along Route 90 and Route 94, stretches of the nascent Eisenhower Interstate System, the new superhighways that were connecting towns and cities across America. Henry and Lefty would scour little Spink County, the cluster of a half dozen cities nestled in the northeast corner of the state, hunting game. There were Doland (population 267, boyhood home of Hubert H. Humphrey), Frankfort (where Lefty Muehl grew up), Ashton, Conde, Mellette, and especially Redfield (known locally to South Dakotans as the "Pheasant Capital of the World"). Henry and Lefty would snare the legal limit (and maybe then some). Muehl told Henry he would introduce him to a hunting paradise. He was not exaggerating, for the region was famous for its pheasant, attracting hunters, as well as celebrities from the sports world and from Hollywood, the enclave rich who fancied shooting. There was just one problem: When the rich and famous arrived in Spink County, everyone knew who they were. Privacy and discretion were essential, and that was where Audrey Slaughter came in. She and her husband, Rich Wilson, were the proprietors of the Wilson Motel. According to local legend, Audrey ran the tightest switchboard in America. The kids in the neighborhood may have heard the rumors that a big name was in town—the great stunt cyclist Evel Knievel would be a frequent visitor in the 1970s—but the phone at the Wilson Motel leaked no secrets. Once, word swept through Redfield like a dust storm that Ted Williams, the Splendid Splinter himself, was in town. "My mother was so mad," recalled lifelong Redfield resident Ted Williams, who as a teen heard that his namesake and hero was staying at the Wilson. "She knew the woman who ran the hotel. They were friends and she *still* wouldn't tell us what room Ted Williams was in."

It was while hunting in Doland that Henry met State Senator Lawrence E. Kayl, whose daughter attended the school. When the hunting ended, Henry would not return to Milwaukee immediately, but would leave Doland and drive twenty miles to Redfield, continuing along State Road 212 until he reached a cold eleven-building complex that stood ominously above the reddish clay flatlands. Each time when he arrived, the children were waiting for him.

THE MISSION STATEMENT for the Northern Hospital for the Insane, written near the turn of the twentieth century, stated the complex was not designed for the mentally ill, but for people suffering from a "developmental disability." In 1913, the institution was renamed the State School and Home for the Feeble Minded, and it would be officially known as such for nearly the next four decades. Between 1951 and 1989, the name changed once more, to the Redfield State Hospital and School, and today, the buildings still stand, though in a time when attitudes regarding mental illness are more tolerant. Officially, it is now known as the South Dakota Developmental Center, a kinder, more clinical name, for certain. But for generations of South Dakotans, the old name stuck, and locally and colloquially the hospital would always be known as the "Feeble Minded School." Ted Williams, the Redfield boy once rebuffed by Audrey Slaughter at the Wilson Motel in his attempts to meet his namesake, would years later become superintendent and resident historian of the school. He would accept the former names of the school as at once embarrassing, painful reminders of the society's lack of sensitivity toward mental disabilities, but he also understood the terminology reflected the orthodoxy of the day. In that, Redfield was not alone. In 1881, years before the school first opened, Minnesota dedicated the Minnesota Institute for the Deaf, Dumb and Blind, adding a wing to that institution in 1887, officially known as the School for Idiots and Imbeciles, the critical difference between the two—according to medical definitions that would in later years be recanted—being that an idiot maintained an IQ under twenty, an imbecile slightly above. In 1890, Indiana opened the Indiana School for Feeble-Minded Youth, and the famed American eugenicist Henry Goddard, generally credited with inventing the term *moron* as a clinical definition, was the director of the Training School for Backward and Feeble-Minded Children, in Vineland, New Jersey.

When Henry arrived in Redfield, he would be surrounded by hordes of eager small children. Some inmates, institutionalized for life, were nearly adults, and some were within five or six years of Henry's age. Henry would stay for hours, spread out with the residents on one of the two large baseball diamonds on the property, patiently instructing the young ones how to run and throw and swing a baseball bat, encouraging strong throws and vigorous swings, the actual lessons far less valuable than the time spent. "I remember it well. I was working with one of the youngsters and he was about three feet away from me. He took the ball, wound up, and threw as hard as he could. He hit me right in the chest," Henry recalled with laughter. "I was happy to go up there and spend time with the children, but it was *dangerous*." Howard Chinn, superintendent of the school from 1961 to 1973, recalled that Henry was eager to organize a game with the kids, except for one major problem, which scotched the idea: gopher holes. Chinn remembered gophers burrowing into the grass, creating dangerous divots in the field, and Henry had no intention of having to explain to Lou Perini that he was out for the season because he'd snapped one of his brittle ankles by catching his foot in a gopher hole in South Dakota.

The practice of an athlete visiting sick children dated way back, like so much in American sporting culture, to the legend of Babe Ruth, and over the years, in the face of image burnishing, it would be met with great and often deserved cynicism, considered hardly much more than an exercise in manipulation: the fail-safe photo op. Against the current backdrop, such visits are often viewed as the ultimate cliché, athletes paying social penance for enormous salaries that in years to come would engulf and distort the sports culture. And, worse, they are often viewed as a self-serving opportunity for athletes to cleanse their reputations, thereby increasing their own marketability. In today's world, even a nonpublicized visit can hold great currency in the image-making business, transparent acts of self-aware selflessness. But 1963 was different. With Henry, there were no television crews in tow, no photographer, and no publicist. There were no friendly local columnists trading access for some good publicity (who knew the real Henry Aaron sneaked away on goodwill missions to South Dakota, and snagged a bagful of birds, too?), and there were no well-timed, perfectly managed news leaks designed to get the word out that a big-time ballplayer hadn't forgotten the little people. On the dusty plains hundreds of miles from his own cultural sphere, there was no advantage for Henry to gain except in whatever he offered of himself to the children of the Redfield school, and whatever emotional currency they could return to him. Henry told virtually no one about his visits. He never even told anyone on his own *team.* In later recollections, his closest teammates—Mantilla, Mathews, Covington—had never heard of the school, and they certainly didn't know Henry knew anything about South Dakota. Howard Chinn did not remember Henry as a celebrity making an electric appearance that kept the town buzzing for weeks. Nearly fifty years later, living in Enid, Oklahoma, hard of hearing but sharp of mind, he recalled "a lone black fellow who played baseball" coming by for several years.

Even when he was finally exposed as a Samaritan, Henry still refused the opportunity to engage. Once in 1964, Al Stump, biographer of Ty Cobb and prominent freelance writer, profiled Henry for *Sport* magazine. The two met in Los Angeles before a series with the Dodgers. In Henry's hotel room, Stump asked him about Koufax and Drysdale and then about his trips to South Dakota. About everything except the hunting, Henry was frustratingly vague. When the article was published, Henry, if not enshrouded in mystery, remained distant—not hostile, but certainly private. The story did not mention Redfield as the location of the school, stating only that it was "near Frankfort." Stump did not mention the name of the school or explain why Henry seemed drawn to it. Though the piece promised an opportunity for Henry to present himself in fuller dimension to a national audience, he did not seem interested. Stump came away with a story for *Sport,* a lengthy profile ("Hank Aaron: Public Image vs. Private Reality"), where the hook was the contradiction between the Henry Aaron who slept except in the batter's box and this other

Henry Aaron, who took an interest in the mentally disabled, grew anxious about civil rights, and breathed a simmering political fire. Thirty years later, in his own autobiography, Henry never mentioned the quiet but important visits to the little school in South Dakota, though the people of the town never forgot.

WHAT HENRY AARON desired most during the first half of the 1960s was to be complete, to be more than just a guy who could rip a line drive to center. He wanted to be considered great in his profession, certainly, but given the framework of the 1960s, when at last the time had come to redraw the lines of society, he also sought to be a person of substance. For his decade in baseball, Henry's place on the diamond was undeniable, but being known as an athlete of social impact seemed far less certain, even inadequate within the confines of the sport upon whose record books he began a massive and methodical assault. Henry was in conflict not only with society but with his caricature—uninterested in things apart from hitting—both by a press corps that continually seemed to misread him and by many of his peers, who took his silence to mean he was uncomplicated.

The reality was that Henry craved to be part of the larger world, contributing to important subjects and issues beyond athletics. Even some of the people closest to him did not understand his own yearnings, and they would find themselves off balance in those instances when they saw Henry on the political offensive. He sought to cultivate an important voice about the significant issues that were shifting the ground underneath his feet, and it was a desire that that had always been present, even if invisible to his closest contemporaries.

In baseball, he never worried about his voice or his impact or his abilities; on the diamond, Henry Aaron always knew he could play, and his sheer talent gave him instant credibility. Yet credibility was not the same as respect, and one lost its full value without the other. During the spring of 1960, Henry, along with Covington, had spoken to Tebbetts and Lou Perini about the spring-training conditions for the black Braves players. Henry and the other black players had begun to take Billy Bruton's lead. Henry, now one of the veterans on the club, second in seniority to Bruton among the Braves black players and clearly its most important, began to speak more actively about the daily inequities of spring-training life.

The black players had lived in Mrs. Gibson's Bradenton house each year Henry had been in the big leagues. Like their peers in most ball clubs, Tebbetts and the Braves management had not used their leverage in the cities where spring training took place, and they told the players there was little they could do to improve conditions for black players. The team members were merely six-week tenants in a town, and they could not interfere with local customs. Years earlier, Henry had lobbied Perini and John Quinn (who left Milwaukee for Philadelphia after the 1958 season) to abolish the policy of maintaining separate facilities at the ballpark, for it stung each time he walked around the Bradenton park, where the Braves played their games, and saw white and colored seating sections, water fountains, and rest rooms. The worst parts for blacks weren't just the rusted fountain pipes and filthy toilet bowls, but the signs reinforcing every inferior accommodation, as if blacks weren't sure *which* water fountain—the one a person would want to drink from or the one that awaited them—was meant for them to use without being given a humiliating reminder.

Quinn, following the missteps of baseball men before him in completely misreading the social landscape, told the press (via Bob Wolf of the *Journal*) that not a single black player had complained about the accommodations of the boardinghouses in the Negro section of town. It was an old saw. When that explanation failed to mollify the players, Quinn would say the club lacked the political influence to affect local custom.

Segregation issues consumed the Braves black players and had been gaining momentum with all the clubs that trained in Florida and Arizona, and the fight for equality was led by Bruton and Bill White and journalists in the black press like Wendell Smith. Even Judge Cannon, the figurehead of the largely ineffective Major League Baseball Players Association and target of Father Groppi's protests in Milwaukee—Groppi periodically sent hundreds of protesters to Cannon's house when it was revealed that Cannon had maintained his membership in the Hawkeye Club, a restrictive organization prohibiting blacks and Jews—began to press teams to adopt an aggressive position with regard to integrating the team accommodations in Florida. Across the American landscape were signs that the old customs were finally vulnerable, and this was a fight in which Henry wanted to play a part.

Even as he expressed an opinion on racial matters—a voice that, to him, was clear about the injustices and humiliations of segregation—Henry was nevertheless wary about being labeled a troublemaker. In many ways, the appearance of caution he presented to the public undermined his true passion for civil rights. One example could be found in his words. He was convinced that the time had arrived to press for equality, and yet he referred to the louder voices in the movement, the ones who clearly stood on the right side of the issue, as "agitators." He would refer to himself as a person interested in the cause of change but not one who would instigate. "I don't consider myself an agitator," he would often say, thus indirectly creating a certain degree of distance between himself and the public figures whose positions he admired and encouraged.

Why Henry did not hurl himself into the burgeoning civil rights movement in the driven, public manner of the handful of his contemporaries had much to do with his natural reticence, and the reticence of professional athletes in general. Certainly a more aggressive approach would have left no question as to his feelings about the necessity for change—and the imperative of speed to effect that change—but Henry did not see appealing to the public as anything but a last resort. His political strategy would always begin behind closed doors. Part of his reasoning was practical: Using the public for leverage could be embarrassing to the people he most wanted to cultivate, and while he might have scored points with the public by being audacious, making people look bad would tend to harden their stance and thus make achieving the ultimate goal that more difficult.

More important, Henry dreaded public speaking. He was, thought Felix Mantilla, self-conscious about his southern accent, an insecurity Mantilla (whose English was layered with a strong Puerto Rican accent) could appreciate. Henry was particularly self-conscious in northern or East Coast settings—in interviews with New York newspapermen, for example. He did not trust how his words would be interpreted.

Indirectly, his pragmatism led to another enduring label from which he could not escape: that Hank Aaron was accommodating on civil rights. In his heart, no conflict existed: Civil rights was precisely the onrushing movement he had craved since he was a boy. It was, in fact, not a topic at all, but the story of his life. Henry was as passionate about equal rights as any of the more outspoken voices around him. In later years, he would express a certain regret that he had not been more firm in his conviction. "I know I did not make it easy for people to understand me, but there was nothing to me more important than civil rights and what Jackie Robinson and Dr. King started."

In many ways, he was more passionate than most of his contemporaries, for Henry *was* a child of the South, and the distance between his rights and equal rights was as wide a gap as existed in the country. Henry knew how much change was needed, for his examples were so distinct and so personal. He would never forget how Herbert had labored each day with such nervous uncertainty, unsure from week to week if work would be plentiful or sparse, and yet each day, no matter how hard he had worked or how dutiful and disciplined he had been, Herbert would always have to relinquish his place in line at the store whenever a white man entered. Better than most, Henry understood the debilitating effect of segregation, not only on society but on the individual family, and too often he could summon a litany of offenses, which now suddenly seemed right to address.

Henry would always be reluctant to speak out, both because of his lack of formal schooling and his desperate fear of addressing people in public, but in the first half decade of the 1960s, he began to sharpen his own attitudes on racial equality. He found himself taken with the writings of James Baldwin, whose position that blacks had persevered despite their overall condition and could no longer wait on the goodwill of whites resonated deeply with him. There was a particular passage in Baldwin's *The Fire Next Time* that seemed to illustrate Henry's attitude precisely at this moment in time: "Things are as bad as the Muslims say they are—in fact, they are worse, and the Muslims do not help matters—but there is no reason that black men should be expected to be more patient, more forbearing, more farseeing than whites."

For a time, Henry had been interested in Baldwin, but he had never actually read his books. He had learned of Baldwin from seeing the writer on television. Like most baseball players, Henry was a night creature; he would flip channels, hoping for a Western on the late show. He first saw Baldwin by accident, on a late-night talk show, and the writer's words clicked with him in an important, personal way. Baldwin initiated the type of dialogue Henry had sought, and he was impressed by Baldwin's considerable ability to articulate the frustrations of his fellow black citizens, the imperative of taking advantage of this special moment in time. In later years, Henry would say he felt the urgency of the times not because of his own experiences but because of his childhood recollections of Herbert. Herbert was powerless to challenge the impenetrable white structure that had been in place for his entire life and that of his father, Papa Henry. These two people had been the most important male figures in Henry's life and he remembered the immense power whites had held over both.

And here Henry was, up late, watching the black-and-white television, hoping for a Western but finding something else instead, unsure of exactly what he was watching. It might as well have been science fiction, but all the while Henry was completely riveted as he watched the small-shouldered, large-eyed Baldwin broadcasting the singular, clear, and ferocious message across the entire nation that the time had come to challenge openly the smothering social conventions that had suffocated three generations of men like Herbert Aaron and Papa Henry. The particular Baldwin theme of rejecting the idea of waiting for change resonated powerfully with Henry. "We've been waiting all this time. My parents are waiting right now in Alabama," Henry said in a profile piece. "The whites told my parents, 'Wait and things will get better.' They told me, 'Wait and things will get better.' They're telling these school kids, 'Wait and things will get better.' Well, we're not going to wait any longer. We're doing something about it. That's what Baldwin says, and he's right."

It was a revelatory moment, for Baldwin had articulated the very sentiments that Henry had long believed but had never thought the time would be right to voice outwardly. Henry may not have considered himself an agitator, but certainly in private he adopted a position to the left of the black mainstream.

As a teenager, Henry had bet on his athletic ability, forgoing higher education and sailing through high school with only minimal interest, but as a parent he was bitterly strict when his children spoke of skirting the educational system and relying only on their own talent (as he once had). More upsetting to him was when his children believed in their elevated position, when Gaile or Henry Junior anticipated an easy and bountiful road ahead because of their father's celebrity. When he believed that the children grew a bit too spoiled, he would recoil, Gaile recalled, reminding them, "I'm Hank Aaron, and you're not."

"I was sensitive to what they would face out there in the world, but I also did not want to do anything or say anything to my children that would break their spirit," Henry said. "I didn't want them to think my experiences had to be their experiences, but I also didn't want them to just think it would be easy, just sticks and stones. It's not just sticks and stones out there."

Henry's public positions during the mid-1960s shook those who thought they knew him. In 1964, he was approached by a representative from J. B. Lippincott, the Philadelphia book publishers, on behalf of Jackie Robinson. Robinson was writing a book of profiles of players, white and black, about their roots and experiences in the game during the first generation of integrated baseball, and he wanted Henry to be a part of the project. Henry agreed, and his first-person transcript appeared in the book as a thirteen-page chapter, which was entitled "Baseball Has Done It." Henry's contribution would be remarkable both for its content and because it represented the first moments Henry would begin to strike back at the press.

> I've read some newspapermen saying I was just a dumb kid from the South with no education and all I knew was to go out there and hit. They didn't know how to talk to me and then wrote that I didn't know how to talk to them . . . you know how newspapermen build up a lot of stories, and they built 'em about me, me saying this and me saying that. I got wise to 'em, but what could I do? In spring training I hit a triple off Curt Simmons. Well, you know how it is in spring exhibitions, when they keep bringing in pitch-

ers after pitchers. So, when one newspaperman asked me if I knew who I hit that triple off of, I said, "No." He said, "That was Curt Simmons." And then they wrote that I didn't know who the pitcher was . . . that's how the story started.

I've saved my money. I have four kids. We live, my wife and me, in a little country town 18 miles from Milwaukee called Mequon. Living's been very good there. The kids go to school and don't have any trouble; they play with other kids in the town. Of course, Milwaukee is a pretty good city as far as Negroes are concerned, but all places could stand improvement regardless of where you go. There's no other Negroes in Mequon but us. My wife has one friend across the street; we have other neighbors who talk to us. Baseball has done a lot for me, given me an education in meeting other kinds of people. It has taught me that regardless of who you are and how much money you make, you are still a Negro.

Periodically, Henry would question whether he was doing enough. His public position was never as outwardly firm as his inner convictions and the result was a public position that did not always represent his passion for civil rights issues. Everyone in America was watching, watching to see who would step up and speak out, who was standing on the sidelines, and who was standing in the way. Jackie Robinson himself was watching, and though Henry did not know it at the time, Robinson had been as quietly impressed by Henry as he was vocally disappointed by Mays. It wasn't that Robinson doubted Mays' enormous power as the premier player in baseball, but that he wanted Mays to use his influence in a way that Mays would not. Robinson was deeply disappointed that Mays refused to be part of *Baseball Has Done It,* and criticized Mays heavily for it. Over time, Robinson deepened his conviction—and would say as much in interviews—that if his mission of integrating all levels of baseball were to go forward, Henry was the active player most capable of carrying the responsibility. "I never knew Jackie said that about me," Henry recalled. "I knew that I couldn't go forward with my life saying things were all right because they were all right for me."

I COULD DO THE JOB

By Hank Aaron With Jerome Holtzman

The Braves' star names the Negroes—and includes himself—who could manage in the major leagues. He also discusses the problems they might have.

—SPORT, October 1965

The writers listened to Henry and did not believe he had simply evolved politically, as had so many Americans during that period. Instead of approaching him as a serious political athletic figure, the writers attempted to ascribe a motive for Henry's sudden interest in topics that went beyond the batter's box. Who was putting ideas in his head? The Henry they knew cared only about hitting and sleeping. He did not fire political torpedoes. That was territory belonging to Jackie Robinson or Jim Brown, Bill Russell or that new explosive upstart Cassius Marcellus Clay. This new Henry, quoting Baldwin, channeling Malcolm X and Martin Luther King, Jr., analyzing the philosophies of both, clearly had to be the by-product of outside influence. Somebody had to be whispering in his ear.

Henry's initial approach to the disbelieving press was to forgive their past indiscretions and move forward, which revealed a larger question: Why didn't Henry turn on the press? He was famous and powerful. He was, by the mid-1960s, on a clear Hall of Fame path. He was at long last bigger than anyone else on his team, and that included Mathews. And yet he did not make the writers pay for the past transgressions of characterizing him so poorly, even cruelly. He would be angered by Furman Bisher's original profile in *The Saturday Evening Post* nearly a decade earlier, carrying the scar from that original article into his sixties. Bisher stood by his profile of Henry even decades later. Instead of excommunicating the people who had hurt him in the past, Henry in later years would collaborate on a book deal with Bisher.

One easy way to ignite Henry's fuse was to assume (as so many writers did) that he rustled himself out of bed and hit line drives. He would read the local papers and *The Sporting News* and crave that the writers would understand the work that it took to read pitchers, to learn their deliveries (Drysdale, for all his fearsome power, *always* released the ball from the same point), and what pitches they threw when the sweat began to pour (Gibson? Hard inside, but always think slider away). But when the students of the game got their due, Henry was rarely if ever listed on the attendance sheet. They said this new kid Pete Rose kept a book on how every pitcher in the game got him out. Maury Wills had his own book, a list of pitchers he stole bases against and their strengths and weaknesses. There was a story that went around that Lou Brock even *filmed* opposing pitchers. Henry was every bit a student of hitting, but he felt the writers treated him as a savant, a freak of nature who was given a gift that did not require honing.

His friends would describe him as gentle and nonconfrontational, inwardly driven but outwardly cool, and that was the reason he didn't often correct the misconceptions. In later years, when he would become a transcendent figure in his sport, beyond daily characterizations, Henry would merely give up, saying he did not feel any sentiment he projected would be accurately portrayed in the press and thus he summarily ignored the image shapers. They weren't going to give him the respect as a smart hitter. They weren't going to allow him living space other than in comparison to Mays, a comparison he would always lose on style alone. They weren't going to take him seriously as an influential social figure. They would never listen to him the way he wanted to be heard, so what was the point of explaining his positions to the writers? On this point, Henry was resigned. "It never did any good," he would say. "I would try to correct them, and they would get the correction wrong, and I'd have to correct that. So I just let people say whatever they were going to say." That left it to the growing and committed horde of Aaron protectors. "People have been treating this man like he is dumb for 35 years and it gets so tiring," recalled Allan Tanenbaum, who first met Henry in the early 1970s and would be a business associate and friend for nearly forty years. "Henry doesn't seem to mind. He stopped caring about that stuff a long time ago, but I certainly do. He does not deserve this."

Bill White, who also considers Henry a lifelong friend, believed that a little bit of Mobile always lurked inside of him. He didn't confront because the South was still talking to him. "It always bothered me when people would criticize Henry for not being more vocal. People don't understand how ingrained that hesitation about talking to whites in a certain way, or giving the impression that you're getting out of line really is for blacks from the South. When you come from other places, you can say, 'I don't give a shit.' When you're from down there, talking like that could cost you your life."

As Henry began to cultivate his new outspokenness, the baseball insiders first looked to the woman in Henry's life, Barbara. They felt it was Barbara, considered more short-tempered than Henry, who was the one pushing him to be more public on behalf of blacks.

Henry would voice displeasure regarding the state of race relations in his sport and he would be dismissed as channeling Barbara, who had put "big words" and "big ideas" into his head, but the sentiment never lost its intensity. The writer Furman Bisher would consistently parry Henry's latest stance on civil rights by essentially calling him a pawn. "Henry Aaron is a nice man," Bisher said of Henry in 2008. "But he is easily led."

BY PURE HAPPENSTANCE, it was Jackie Robinson who indirectly wound up being responsible for Henry's half century of loyalty to the Democratic party. For years, Henry had sought to pattern himself after Robinson in being a person of substance outside of the baseball diamond. And that was fine, except that Jackie Robinson was a Republican.

Almost as soon as the 1960 presidential campaign began, there was no greater irritant to John F. Kennedy than Jack Roosevelt Robinson. From the start, Robinson was unimpressed with the junior senator from Massachusetts, from his noncommittal position on civil rights to his woefully limited personal contact with black people to his lack of intimate knowledge of the black condition in general. Robinson was especially annoyed by Kennedy's early and mistaken belief that he could cultivate many of the southern politicians responsible for some of the most oppressive racial conditions in the country and still count on blacks to support him. Robinson had first met with Kennedy in 1959 and came away convinced that he could not support

Kennedy for president. Aside from Kennedy's politics, much of the reason was personal style: Robinson did not think the Kennedy brothers—John and Bobby—were particularly good listeners.

Robinson developed important relationships with two men who would cause considerable consternation to Kennedy. The first was Hubert Horatio Humphrey, Jr., the Minnesota senator, who was running for the Democratic nomination for president against John F. Kennedy.

The second was the vice president himself, Richard Milhous Nixon, who was seeking the Republican nomination and was virtually unopposed. Nixon and Robinson had met years earlier, and Robinson was taken by Nixon's impressive recall of his career at UCLA, and the two would forge a warm—if not curious, given both the cultural leanings of both men and the period of seismic change occurring in America during the growth of their association—and lasting friendship. Politically, Robinson was registered as an independent, but his politics leaned toward the Republican party of the early 1960s, which had not yet adopted the rigid platform that would define it a generation later.

ROBINSON DECIDED EARLY that either man would be better for black America than would Kennedy, and early in the political season, both Nixon and Humphrey made earnest attempts to cultivate Robinson. Robinson was a tireless correspondent, and in personal letters to both men, his voice was fiercely single-minded in the area of civil rights, but also tinged with a certain element of romance, perhaps a hope that, like he had on the baseball diamond, individuals committed to civil rights could overcome both party and societal opposition to advancements of civil rights legislation. Thus, Robinson's letters contained a certain personal fondness for Nixon. It was a position that would gain Robinson great criticism, especially from black members of the Democratic party—Adam Clayton Powell, for instance—who believed Robinson relied too heavily and too naïvely on his belief in Nixon the man, instead of following two far more telling indicators regarding the vice president: his voting record and the company he kept. It was an incongruity that exposed Robinson to the stinging charge that off of the base paths, perhaps the most daring and courageous baseball player of his time was well out of his league.

When Robinson corresponded with Humphrey, he wrote directly and boldly, both men speaking candidly of their common purpose in expanding civil rights legislation as well as changing the attitudes of the country's populace. Unlike Nixon's, Humphrey's voting record reflected his passion for civil rights. With Nixon, the letters took on a more personal approach, but Robinson regarded Humphrey as a serious man of honor and principle.

As the Wisconsin primary neared, Robinson decided he would campaign for Humphrey, with one caveat: Should Humphrey fail, he would dedicate his energies toward a Nixon victory over Kennedy.

ON FEBRUARY 3, 1960, Humphrey had been alerted by Frank Reeves, a black Democratic operative, that Robinson could be a potential ally. Among the states that held primaries, Wisconsin represented a key battleground, and in the weeks before the primary, Reeves attempted to cultivate Robinson, hoping he would use his formidable influence with black voters to gain support for the Humphrey campaign.

> *February 3, 1960*
> *MEMORANDUM TO SENATOR HUMPHREY*
> *FROM FRANK D. REEVES*
> *SUBJECT: Jackie Robinson*
> *Pursuant to general agreement, arrangements were made for me to discuss personally with Jackie Robinson whether a) he would be willing to sign a letter to be sent to a selective list of Negroes, endorsing and urging support for Senator Humphrey's candidacy, and b) he would be willing to go to Wisconsin and D.C. to support and campaign. Bill Gruver arranged a luncheon meeting for me with Robinson in New York City on 1 February, 1960.*

On March 30, 1960, Vice President Nixon's secretary, Rose Mary Woods, typed a letter to Nixon that explained Robinson's potential interest in the Nixon campaign.

To: RN
From: RMW
Fred Lowey called and wanted to talk with you. I told him you were completely tied up and he left the following message.

He would like very much to talk with you for one minute in the next couple of days in connection with the following: He had lunch yesterday with Jackie Robinson. He stressed, of course, he did not need to tell you how important Jackie was as far as the Negro vote was concerned. He feels that with the slightest persuasion Robinson could be swung around and would come on the Nixon bandwagon. To use his terms, "Robinson is more or less considered a God up here."

I asked him specifically what Robinson said and Lowey said the story is he is first of all interested in Humphrey but he feels Humphrey doesn't have a chance and his second choice would be you. Fred Lowey thinks it is very important that you get together with Robinson so that he can get to know you better. I told him that you had talked with him and that you have had correspondence with him in the past.

Ten days later, Nixon wrote that Robinson could be an asset to his presidential campaign. The letter also underscored Nixon's inherent suspicion, a characteristic that would define—and in time ultimately destroy—his political life.

April 10, 1960
To: RHF
From: RN
I think Fred Lowey has a point with regard to seeing Jackie Robinson. I would suggest the next time we are in New York that we arrange to have him drop in for a visit. Of course, we must remember that he is now employed as a columnist for the New York Post and that he will be under great pressure from his editor Wechler to take whatever nominee the Democrats select. As a matter of fact, I think a letter from me to him at this point might be in order.

To the Kennedys, friends could be more important than money. Friends, in certain cases, *were* like money, and, like any important form of currency, they existed to mitigate the effect of unexpected eventualities. That Robinson posed a powerful, unpredictable threat in what was expected to be an extremely close race was obvious, both to Kennedy and his staff, to Humphrey, and certainly to Robinson. Not so obvious was exactly what to do about him.

And it wasn't just that Robinson was a living legend; he was a legend with a platform. In 1959, Robinson agreed to write a thrice-weekly column for the *New York Post.* The column appeared on the sports page, but Robinson was given leeway to write about any subject that interested him. To the dismay of Kennedy, Robinson, by the end of 1959, wrote of politics almost exclusively.

That was when the old man—Joseph P. Kennedy, patriarch of the family, whose financial wealth was rivaled only by the wealth of his connections, former ambassador to the Court of St. James—stepped in. It was the resourceful Joe who knew whom to talk to in Wisconsin. Kennedy contacted Joe Timilty, one of his flamboyant and loyal (if not completely scrupulous) Boston associates and directed Timilty to get in touch with Duffy Lewis, the Braves traveling secretary. The connection with Lewis came, naturally, from Boston, when Lewis was (with Harry Hooper and Tris Speaker) part of Boston's Million-Dollar Outfield, winning championships with the Red Sox back in the teens, and when Joe Kennedy was what he always would be: the power behind the power. It was Joe who understood at once that the best way to neutralize the famous Jackie Robinson was to enlist the most famous black man in the state of Wisconsin, Henry Aaron. Understanding the power of advantage, Joe also asked Lewis to recruit the *second* most popular black man in the state, as well. And that was how both Henry Aaron and Billy Bruton enthusiastically agreed to campaign on behalf of John F. Kennedy for the 1960 Wisconsin primary.

For the first time, Henry was in the act, beyond the batter's box. Bruton and Henry traveled throughout the state on behalf of Kennedy. In the heavily black areas of Milwaukee, where the city's black population comprised virtually that of the entire state, Henry stood firmly for Kennedy while his hero, Robinson, went on the attack, both in his *Post* column and on the campaign trail.

When the primary ended, Kennedy had scored a decisive victory over Humphrey, beginning the end of Humphrey's campaign. Henry would always talk about his campaigning for Kennedy as one of the significant moments in his life. Two years later, with Kennedy in office, Timilty wrote to Larry O'Brien, Kennedy's top aide, about obtaining a token of appreciation that Henry would treasure.

March 3, 1962
My Dear Larry,
You will recall that during the Wisconsin Primary Campaign we needed the services of some Colored ball players to offset Jackie Robinson who appeared for Humphries [sic].

At the suggestion of the Ambassador I consulted Duffy Lewis and he obtained the services of the following players, who made personal appearances and speeches for us:
Lou Burdette
Hank Aaron
Bill Bruton
[. . .]
I would greatly appreciate it, Larry, if you would honor this request.

> *Sincerely yours,*
> *Joe*

A month later, on April 3, Timilty received the signed glossies (did they *really* think Burdette, of all people, was a "Colored ball player"?) of President Kennedy and passed them on to Duffy Lewis, but Henry would never know the backstory—that his usefulness to the campaign was not simply to help Kennedy win but to parry Robinson. Had Henry known that Robinson had chosen Humphrey, he might well have joined Robinson in supporting Humphrey against Kennedy. But he had no way of knowing he was being cultivated to neutralize the most iconic black athlete in the country's history. Henry would call his association in the 1960 campaign an "honor," and for the next half century, he would support Democratic candidates at every political level.

Although Henry had always considered Jackie Robinson his standard of courage and commitment, the perfect blend of athletic achievement and social conscience, he would not approach his activism in the often isolated, crusading Robinson manner. Following Humphrey's withdrawal from the presidential race, Robinson campaigned vigorously for Nixon against Kennedy.

Robinson seemed particularly wounded by the Nixon defeat, and even as Nixon reached his first political nadir, Robinson continued to believe in him. On Chock Full o' Nuts stationery, Robinson wrote to Nixon on November 12, 1962:

Mr. Richard Nixon
c/o Republican Headquarters
Los Angeles, California
Dear Dick:
It is difficult to write a letter such as this, but I shall do the best I can.

The only regret I have in supporting you twice is that I was unfortunate not to have been able to help more than I did. I am sorry also that most Negroes were unwilling to believe the promises you made. I personally was, and still am, convinced that you were the best candidate for the presidency in 1960 and a man we need very much in Government Service.

I am concerned because you have said that you have had your last press conference. I hope that you will reconsider, Dick, because it is the great men people attack. You are good for politics; good for America. As one who has great confidence in you and who sincerely appreciates the opportunity of having known and worked for you, I urge you to remain active. There is so much to be done and there are too few qualified people to do the job now. Your loss would be an added blow to our efforts. Do not let your critics cause you to give up your career. Each of us came into this world for a purpose. I believe that yours is service to our country.

> *Cordially,*
> *Jackie Robinson*

Robinson would always pay the heavy price of loneliness for his activism and his headfirst approach. Passion is often uncomplicated, and in complex political waters, Robinson flailed admirably and desperately, seeking a similar commitment for civil rights.

Yet in the end, before history would completely recognize Robinson's passion triumphing over his strategy, he lived as the single-minded outsider, loyal to the cause, at the cost of his allies ignoring him. Once it became clear that whatever Robinson saw in him as a man, Nixon's loyalties were with a Republican party that regarded civil rights with hostility, Robinson would eventually even break with Nixon on a political level, while maintaining a personal fondness for him.

On July 25, two days after being elected to the Hall of Fame, Robinson seemed melancholy, his fire submitting to his heart. In a sentimental moment, he wrote a letter to Walter O'Malley, an attempt at reconciliation, or at least closure.

Dear Mr. O'Malley,

Sunday night, as I had dinner with my family at the Otesago Hotel in Cooperstown, I had the opportunity of chatting with Mrs. O'Malley briefly. We talked about things I am sure she does not remember, but I really wanted to talk with her about you and I.

I couldn't help but feel sad by the fact that the next day I was entering the hall of Fame and I did not have any real ties with the game. I thought back to my days at Ebbetts Field, and kept wondering how our relationship had deteriorated. Being stubborn, and believing that it all stemmed from my relationship with Mr. Rickey, I made no attempt to find the cause. I assure you, Rae has on many occasions discussed this, and she too feels we should at least talk over our problems. Of course, there is the possibility that we are at an impasse, and nothing can be done. I feel, however, I must make this attempt to let you know how I sincerely regret we have not tried to find the cause for this breach.

I will be in Los Angeles on Friday. If you feel you have about fifteen minutes, I'll drop by. I shall call your office when I arrive.

Sincerely yours,
Jackie Robinson

After writing the letter, Robinson lived ten more years, O'Malley for another seventeen. Robinson grew as an unquestionable American icon, while O'Malley would live as one of the venerable family names in baseball. For the sake of scrubbing history, Peter O'Malley, who succeeded his father in running the Dodgers for nearly another two decades, would say that Walter never held Robinson in anything less than admiration. Of course, as Robinson grew beyond baseball to the top shelf of American legend, O'Malley criticizing him was about as smart as trading Frank Robinson for Milt Pappas. Regardless of the reason, one fact remained throughout the lives of the particulars involved: The reconciliation Robinson sought between himself and Walter O'Malley in the summer of 1962 never took place.

Henry learned a valuable lesson. Beginning in the early years of the 1960s it would be Henry who often articulated the cost of Robinson's passion, noting in interviews that Robinson was never offered a coaching, managerial, or front-office position at any level of the major-league baseball system. Nor was he asked to manage in the minor leagues or to scout. Even Branch Rickey, who had been part of two organizations, the Pirates and Cardinals, following Jackie's retirement, did not offer him a job. Where baseball was concerned, he was the loneliest immortal in history, his isolation comparable only to Babe Ruth's, who was discarded by the game as casually as a hot-dog wrapper.

INSIDE THE GAME, Henry was famous and respected and comfortable. He appeared on the television program "Home Run Derby," set out of Wrigley Field in Los Angeles, winning six straight episodes and $14,000, the most prize money during the show's run, before losing to Wally Post. When he'd arrived in Milwaukee a decade earlier, the heart and soul and imagination of the team had begun with Mathews and Spahn. Now, he was ten years older, and so, too, were the fans who had come to the ballpark for all those years. The kids who used to line Wisconsin Avenue for the parades of the 1950s had now gone to college and built families and careers, the younger ones—now that Spahn had aged and Mathews was less dominant—having grown up with Henry as their unquestioned star. Even fans like Bud Selig, who were the same age as Henry (Henry was six months older than Selig), knew the Henry Aaron routines by heart and would be as tickled by him as when they were teenyboppers looking for a prom date: the two bats he swung in the on-deck-circle dress rehearsal, no batting gloves; the front-foot stomp and drive as the pitch approached, leading easily into that signature flash of violence; the lightning spark of his bat slashing through the strike zone. They emulated him in their slow-pitch softball games, copied his moves in the backyard with their kids while playing Wiffle ball, and recalled from their lush reservoir of memories Henry's limp during his home-run trot. There was the way he stood impassively on deck, on one knee, watching the pitcher solemnly, awaiting his chance. These traits, the kids rattled off by heart. Even when he struck out, especially on a slider, Henry would pirouette, a futile corkscrew following a swing and miss, before walking, head down, toward the dugout, rarely giving the pitcher the satisfaction of that over-the-shoulder peek back at the mound. Fifty years later, Bud Selig still delighted in all of these unique stylistic traits, how Henry's bat would lash so viciously across the plate, lacing home runs into the Perini pines that didn't seem to lift more than ten feet off the ground, simple doubles in the alleys for other players. "Nobody," Selig would say, "hit more home runs that everyone else thought *might* hit the wall. With Henry, you looked up, and the ball was *gone*." Henry would lope stoically around the bases, stern as a lumberjack, only to break into smile once safely in the dugout.

The Milwaukee fans even knew how Henry held his cigarette, right arm tight to his body as he took a long drag, head always facing in the opposite direction from where he would eventually flick away the spent butt. Henry had smoked since he was a teenager shooting pool on Davis Avenue. During the 1950s, advertising campaigns often featured major-league players (*how to smoke like a big leaguer*), the perfect recruiting tool for a new generation of tobacco consumers. Sometimes, the fans with the best angle could look into the dugout and catch Henry stealing a drag before walking to the on-deck circle, extinguishing a butt on the bottom of his spikes. Like his idol DiMaggio, Henry adopted Camels as his cigarette of choice. It would always be unclear whether Henry succumbed to advertising, but

DiMaggio once appeared in a Camel ad: "Joe DiMaggio has something to say about how different cigarettes can be." Henry never admitted it to be true, but some Aaron fans distinctly remember Henry taking a drag once or twice near the on-deck circle. Take your pick of the magazines—*Sport, Sports Illustrated, The Saturday Evening Post,* and you would likely find a ballplayer selling cigarettes.

THE CAMEL MILDNESS TEST

How thorough can cigarette mildness be? Here's your answer!

In a coast-to-coast test, hundreds of men and women smoked only Camels for 30 days, averaging 1–2 packs a day. Each well-noted throat specialist examined their throats. These doctors made 2,470 careful examinations and reported not one single case of throat irritation due to smoking Camels!

VIC RASCHI—"You can't beat 'em for flavor—and they're mild!"

BOB LEMON—"Camels are great tasting, and mild!"

MEL PARNELL—"I like the taste and they get on fine with my throat. It's Camels for me!"

Seven years later, Henry got his turn, appearing in his own ad for Camels. Gracing the pages of a 1958 *Life* magazine advertisement, Henry wore a tweed jacket, a cigarette resting carefully in his left hand.

HANK AARON HIT MORE HOMERS than any other ballplayer in the majors last season. He also led both leagues in total runs batted in, won the National League's Most Valuable Player Award, and paced the Milwaukee Braves to their world championship. This real pro smokes Camel, a real cigarette. "Can't beat 'em for flavor. And Camels sure smoke mild."

The fans were protective of their hero, and he made them feel safe and good about their unexpected, glorious moment in time. The only problem was that in the 1960s, for the first time, the graphlines of Henry Aaron and those of the Milwaukee Braves trended divergently. In the beautiful 1950s, with the Braves challenging for pennants, Milwaukeeans raced through the turnstiles as if it were ten-cent beer night, and Henry was just another one of the players, an undeniably outsized talent to be sure, but without the clubhouse influence (and responsibilities) of Mathews and Spahn, Burdette and Logan and Bruton.

Within a decade, though, Henry had run right past them all. Some of the distance from his early years certainly benefited him, for he was eager to escape so much of the old life, starting with the tiresome act of having to accept the daily humiliation of being depicted as a simpleton. He had actively begun to reinvent himself, augmenting his awesome statistics with political awareness and social clout, while all the while growing more resolute in his belief that his baseball talent meant nothing if it did not translate to improving the general condition of the world around him. He was a man rounding into substantive form. Some of the changes were dramatic. He had made the conscious decision to be more outspoken on racial issues, striking up a friendship with the football player Jim Brown, then considered the most politically minded black athlete in the country. He had chosen to be more active in politics. These characteristics were easily detectable to his teammates (if not exactly understood), while others were deemed only superficial. One such change was in his dress. In the 1950s, Henry dressed like an insurance salesman—short-sleeve oxford-cloth shirt, dark, thin tie with a half Windsor knot, dark pants. Into the 1960s, as he began to make more money and grew more into himself, compared to his first years in the league, Henry looked more like a kaleidoscope: plaid and checkered suits, sunglasses, Afro, and, that great staple of the 1960s, turtlenecks with a sport coat. Both poles, those of politics and fashion, however, represented a singular truth: Henry had left one stage of his career and entered another.

And as he grew, the Braves just could not keep up. For 130 games in 1960, Milwaukee fought emerging Pittsburgh for the pennant, only to finish second, seven games back. The key sequence between the two clubs occurred in late July, with the young Pirates—led by the hard-nosed shortstop Dick Groat (who would win the league MVP that year) and featuring the passionate, determined right fielder Clemente—holding a half-game lead. Two years earlier, when the Braves won their second pennant, the Pirates had challenged but wilted at roughly the same point in the season, late July, when pitching arms die and the bats feel more like lead than lightning. And here it was, poised to happen all over again, the Braves, veterans at breaking pretenders as the summer intensified, ready to catapult the Pirates back into the land of the almost ready. On the night of July 26 in San Francisco, Sam Jones blinded the Braves lineup for six innings. He would strike out eleven, including a furious Henry, to lead off the seventh. But Milwaukee pushed home a run in the seventh, and then Henry singled and scored off Jones for payback, as well as making an eighth-inning insurance run, in a 3–1 win. The lead was still wafer-thin. Spahn and Burdette were next in the rotation, while Pittsburgh was in St. Louis to face a Cardinals team that was just beginning to show threats of being dangerous. The pressure was on the Pirates.

Then, over the next fifteen games, the Braves lost eleven times, five to the Dodgers, dropping them down to fourth place, while Pittsburgh, green to the fight, embraced the pressure and won eleven games during the same stretch. The lead was seven, and the pennant was gone. The following year, it was an inspired Cincinnati team that clubbed its way to the pennant, while Milwaukee dropped to fourth, ten games back. Nineteen sixty-two belonged to the West Coast, the renewal of the old New York rivalry to a new time zone. The Dodgers and Giants won 205 games between them, and played an epic three-game play-off that ended with Mays once again in the World Series. The Braves didn't overcome the .500 mark for good until July 25 and finished as poorly as they'd ever had since arriving in Milwaukee, fifteen and a half games out, in fifth place.

The only thing that gave 1962 special heft was that Henry's little brother Tommie made the big-league club out of spring training. For the first time in organized ball, Henry and Tommie would be teammates. Five and a half years younger, Tommie Aaron was a big kid. He stood six-one, and weighed 190 pounds, fifteen pounds more than Henry had at eighteen. He had played baseball as religiously as Henry, but also football at Central High.

The Braves had signed Tommie back in 1958, but, unlike Henry, Tommie Aaron was not a can't-miss prospect. Henry played a total of just 224 games in the minor leagues, and hit .353 in those games. Tommie followed immediately in Henry's footsteps—two seasons in Eau Claire, Class C ball, then a full season at Class B Cedar Rapids of the Three-I league in 1960, with cups of coffee in Jacksonville and Louisville. In 1961, he played 138 games in Double-A Austin of the Texas League, but the game did not seem to come easily to him. Henry believed he indirectly affected Tommie's progress, for the Aaron name produced expectations that the little brother would possess the same magic of his older, famous sibling.

For Tommie, just reaching the majors, to be on the roster, he would need to study and learn the game, find coaches interested in his success, and work at it. In the minor leagues, he was a respectable hitter—.274 his first year in Eau Claire, .299 both at Cedar Rapids and Austin—and had power. In the majors, hitting—which was the difference between staying with the club and being sent back down—would be the weakest part of Tommie's game.

Yet having Tommie in the big leagues changed the dynamic of the Braves clubhouse, and the other Braves asked themselves that old saw: How could two people who grew up in the very same circumstances, in the same house, with the same parents, be so different?

While Henry kept his distance, Tommie was the gregarious one, navigating each clique that existed in the room, soaking up the clubhouse energy, recycling it back. Henry loved baseball, but Tommie seemed to love it *and* enjoy it simultaneously. Joe Torre used to marvel at just how fast after games Henry would dress and leave the clubhouse, but Tommie was the opposite. He talked the game, chatted up the coaches and the managers and the clubhouse kids. It was part of Tommie's personality that had been evident even back in Mobile.

"He was such a good, open man," Joe Torre said. "A really good man with a really good baseball mind. Tommie was always quick with a laugh, and he made it easier for Hank."

For a time, Tommie lived with Barbara and Henry. He hadn't been on the big-league club long before he met a girl, whom he would marry. Carolyn Davenport had been a friend of Nancy Maye, wife of Braves reserve outfielder Lee Maye. Carolyn had grown up in Little Rock, but the family moved to Milwaukee when she was fifteen. Her father, Willis Davenport, was a steelworker and relocated the family after finding work at Inland Steel.

She had little interest in baseball, but she and Tommie connected quickly. "It was almost from the time we met," she recalled. "I met

Tommie at the ballpark and little did I know. I didn't know the rules, but it became normal fast. I just got used to it."

Having Tommie on the club brought Henry even closer to the city and the club, but one by one, the old cast who'd whooped it up at Ray Jackson's faded. Pafko was finished after the 1959 collapse to the Dodgers, remaining with the team as a coach. Johnny Logan lost his starting job to Roy McMillan, and he was traded to the Pirates for Gino Cimoli in June 1961. He played two more uninspired years for Pittsburgh and retired to his house on the South Side. Joe Adcock's last big year came in 1961; then the bottom fell out and he was done in Milwaukee the following year. Bruton was never again the same player defensively after the collision with Mantilla in 1957. He led the team in hits in 1960, then was sent off to Detroit that winter for Neil Chrisley and Frank Bolling, the Mobile boy against whom Henry played as a kid in the sandlots but never as a teammate, since whites and blacks were prohibited from competing in Alabama. Mantilla, who never could convince management he was good enough to be an everyday player, was gone in 1962, sent to the hapless expansion Mets, where he played for Casey Stengel. Frank Torre got hurt in 1960, played just twenty-one games, and was released, replaced in 1961 by his talented little brother Joe. There were two whippersnappers, Tony Cloninger and Joe Torre, who were destined for long, productive careers, and another, the talented Ricardo Adolfo Jacobo Carty, whom Henry would take under his wing, but many of the new faces wouldn't last. Chuck Dressen, Jackie Robinson's favorite manager, took over the club in 1960; he talked tough but lasted just two seasons. Dressen never blended with this club; he lost Spahn and Burdette almost immediately, reduced to calling the two "the Katzenjammer Kids." Birdie Tebbetts, the general manager, came down from the front office and guided the team right into fifth place. Bobby Bragan, the southerner who once preferred to be traded than to have Jackie Robinson as a teammate, took over, and the results didn't get any better.

Some of the names were still there, but they were just ghosts, closer to the Old-Timers Game than a September pennant race. Spahn stubbornly beat back time, winning twenty-three games as a forty-two-year-old in 1963, but he would be gone a year later to the

Mets and Giants and Cooperstown. Burdette won eighteen games in 1961 but would never win more than ten in a season thereafter. By 1963, he was traded to St. Louis for Gene Oliver and Bob Sadowski. Even Mathews, once projected to give Ruth a run for his money, wheezed to the finish. He would remain with Henry in Milwaukee, but he could never drive in one hundred runs or hit better than .265 after 1961. Mathews, in his time the greatest power-hitting third baseman ever, would hit thirty home runs only once more. In Milwaukee, the names were just that, names that produced a seductive whiff of sentimentality, giving off a teasing and bittersweet aroma no different from that of the old bread factory, which had long ceased production.

AND THEN THERE was Henry. As a player in his prime who could conjure up the old wistful magic and still put a hurting on Koufax, Drysdale, and the new kids who were starting to dominate the National League, there was, in Milwaukee, only Henry. And he was brilliant: .292 average, 40 homers, 126 RBI, 11 triples in 1960; 34 home runs, a .327 average, and 120 driven in the following year. Then came the two monster years that dwarfed Mays, Mantle, Maris, all of them, and put Henry on the Cooperstown track, an equal with the greats but second to nobody: .323, with 45 bombs, 128 driven in 1962, backed up by a torrid .319 average, with 44 homers, 130 RBI, and 201 hits in 1963.

Nineteen sixty-three was the *big one.* At the plate, nobody was better. He led the league in home runs, but only once, on September 10 against Cincinnati, did he hit two in a game. He led the league in runs batted in and runs scored, was second in the league in stolen bases and hits. He lost the batting title to Tommy Davis by seven points—finishing third behind Davis and Clemente—and those seven points would have given him the Triple Crown. The future Hall of Famers on the mound didn't want any part of him. Henry hit .471 against Drysdale with four homers and .318 off Marichal (though one, Bob Gibson, handled him easily, holding Henry to just two hits in fifteen at bats).

Perhaps more than any other period in his professional life, the years from 1960 to 1965 would define the enduring parameters of the

Henry Aaron story, for it was during those years when the common and convenient belief that Henry Aaron played his entire baseball career in relative obscurity was born. The press was rightfully blinded by Mays and Mantle, but the professionals knew the Aaron presence. It was after 1963 that Drysdale and Koufax nicknamed Aaron "Bad Henry," and why not? At Dodger Stadium, even though Koufax kept Henry mortal (no homers, three RBI on the year), Henry hit .406.

"The two things I remember most about being behind the plate when Henry came up was that you really couldn't pitch to him in any sort of pattern and this wonderful sound he made when he came to bat," said Tim McCarver, the Cardinals and Phillies catcher. "He would step to the plate, settle in to hit. But before he did, he would give this noise that came from the bottom of his throat.

"There were only two hitters I ever remember making that, that *sound* when they came to bat: Henry Aaron and Mike Schmidt," McCarver recalled. "It was so *regal,* the gentleman clearing his throat before going to work. Never forgot it."

The greatest Aaron protectors in the press were on the West Coast, the most prominent being Jim Murray, the legendary *Los Angeles Times* columnist. Murray believed Henry to be a better player than Willie or the rest. Henry was not exactly pleased, but he adopted the persona of the stoic construction worker building a skyscraper in the Midwest while the entire world was paying attention to Yankee Stadium to the east or to Willie Mays to the west, his peers only reminded by the enormous shadow of his cumulative achievements when he quietly passed another milestone. The other was Frank Finch, the *Los Angeles Times* writer who covered the Dodgers. Few of his paragraphs regarding Aaron were not prefaced by Finch calling Henry the game's most devastating hitter.

Though for all of Henry's determination to be that person of substance and value, to make his presence as a dominant one on the field and in the public eye, a perfect storm was taking place during these years that would permanently conspire against him and his legacy.

THE VAUNTED CHARGE that turned Spahn and Burdette, Mathews, and Aaron into superstars never again materialized. Over a span of 959 games over 1,052 regular-season days between opening day 1960 and the close of the 1965 season, the Braves never spent consecutive days in first place, and in those six years, they spent just four days *total* in first place, easily counted on one hand: one April day in 1961 (record 7–2), another April afternoon in 1963, and August 18 and 20 in 1965.

And because of that, nobody cared that Henry was making a ferocious charge toward Mount Olympus, toward Cooperstown, toward respect. As the Braves disappeared in the standings, Henry was transformed from a phenomenon to the same unassuming, workmanlike figure they remembered from the 1950s, defined by the stilted commentaries of Furman Bisher and the imperceptive beat coverage of his earlier seasons. Even when a new breed of better educated, younger reporters arrived in the clubhouse, Henry was cold. The new generation viewed race differently from their predecessors and were clearly more sympathetic, but it did not matter. By this time, Henry was no longer a kid, willing to forgive. He had built up a protective wall around his heart, his privacy, his feelings. By this time, Henry had quit trying to cultivate the press.

"Anytime you went to talk to Aaron, he wouldn't let you in. You couldn't get through. You knew that it was rough for him and you tried to let him know that, but he was just mean," said Jack O'Connell, who has covered baseball for half a century.

Aside from the periodically jarring wire headline that that quiet Henry Aaron was upset about the sport's paternalistic role with regard to blacks ("WHEN WILL BASEBALL ADMIT WE HAVE BRAINS?"—AARON) the public at large did not take real notice, either of his dramatic personal evolution or the fact that for six full seasons on top of the five he had already produced during the glory years, he was absolutely killing the baseball.

He suffered from the fact that his team had lost its relevance and from the unfortunate curse of geography, but he did not know just how right he was about money. His ambitions were easy to misread, for he did not boast as Ruth and Williams and Foxx would, nor did he roil competitively in the mold of a Robinson or Cobb. Still, he knew whom he had to beat to secure his place in the order and he also believed that, to a degree, respect was reflected in money. He had eclipsed many of his teammates on the field of play and yet could not pass them in salary. In 1960 and 1961, Henry earned $45,000, $47,500 in 1962, followed by $53,000 in 1963, $61,000 in 1964, and $63,000 in 1965, according to salary data maintained by the National League. It would not be until 1963 that he would pass Burdette in salary, and he would not pass Spahn or Mathews while each wore a Braves uniform.

Over the history of the game, there had been only a few players who could bend the system. The original, of course, was Ruth, whose first contract in 1914 called for a salary of $350 per month, but by 1921 he was earning $40,000 per year. In 1927, Ruth earned seventy thousand dollars, and by 1930, with the country in the clutches of the Great Depression, eighty thousand.

Ted Williams was another. Williams received bonuses based on the Red Sox home attendance. By 1950, Williams was earning ninety thousand dollars.

But Willie Mays set the pace. In 1960, he signed for $80,000, $85,000 in 1961, $90,000 in 1962, and $105,000 in 1963, 1964, and 1965. During the same period, Mantle earned $60,000 in 1960, followed by $70,000 in 1961, $90,000 in 1963, and $100,000 in both 1964 and 1965.

Henry did not receive substantial raises, but it was the great Clemente who was clearly the most underpaid player of his era. Clemente earned $17,500 in 1960, the year the Pirates won the World Series, and did not receive a raise. By 1965 he was earning $34,000. For his career, Clemente topped out at $63,333, which he earned in 1972, the final year of his life.

Henry understood that playing in Milwaukee may have meant free gas from Wisco, but being situated away from the marketing and intellectual capitals of the country would have a significant cost.

I don't think I've earned my due in publicity or money. I've had a few magazine stories, a few endorsements, mostly when we had a strong club in '57 and '58. A ballplayer felt it in his pocketbook when there was no National League team in New York, which is where the money is. When the Giants went to San Francisco, I never got what I should. The fans in Milwaukee have been very good to me. They never have booed me, even when I've been in some slumps and pulled some booboos on the basepaths. They've always been very courteous to me.

There's been improvement for the Negro player these last few years, but I still think a lot more can be done. Take myself—I'd like to get the same treatment that the Mantles and Marises have gotten when I do as well as them. We have Mays and Robinson and myself over here in the National League. When we do well we don't get the publicity and what goes with it like they do. Mays gets more than the rest of us, but he don't get what he should be getting.

Aaron was the first of the major black stars who did not benefit from geography, either before he reached the big leagues or after, and what other black players may have lost in financial compensation compared to their white counterparts, Henry lost both in money and, in many ways, in dignity which he would fight to regain and to protect. He came from the nation's racially charged epicenter—Alabama—where the attitudes and customs reflected those that first drove the country into the Civil War and then sheared it anew after Reconstruction.

He had sought respect, both as a man and a ballplayer. The perfect storm had conspired against him; other players better situated, with different, more marketable gifts, seemed destined always to be a step ahead of him in the public eye, even if not in the statistical columns. As the second half of the 1960s lurched forward, Henry knew what would separate him not simply from Robinson, Clemente, and Mays but also from Babe Ruth. That something was the all-time home-run record. If he corralled that, they would listen to him. They would all have no choice but to pay attention to what he had to say for the rest of his life.

CHAPTER ELEVEN

ATLANTA

THE END OF the Milwaukee Braves was ugly and litigious, grievances thrown around like third graders do in the middle of a
lunchtime food fight: the aggrieved citizens and public figures of Milwaukee versus the eager newcomers of Atlanta, lawsuits directed
toward the once-beloved Braves front office, which returned fire with
counter accusations and countersuits against the city that had once
come gallantly to its rescue. The height of the rhetoric came courtesy
of one Mr. John Doyne, an executive for Milwaukee County, who
oversaw the Braves County Stadium lease. Doyne believed God and
Commissioner of Baseball Ford Frick (in this instance, quite close to
the same person) needed to intervene on behalf of his city. "This is a
moral issue. Moral law, if you can use that term, would dictate that we
would not try to pirate someone else's club," he told United Press
International in the summer of 1964.

Now that really was a cheeky thing to say. Moving the franchise to
Atlanta contained precisely the same "moral issues" as when Milwaukee celebrated the arrival of the Braves from Boston in 1953. The
only difference this time was that instead of benefiting from the
immorality of baseball piracy, Doyne and his friends at the Milwaukee Chamber of Commerce were the ones sitting in the loser's
dugout.

The Braves, meanwhile, were quite ahead of their time, which in
the taverns along Wisconsin Avenue was no compliment. Even more
than the Dodgers and the Giants, teams more famous for their bitter
departures, the Braves had now perfected the art of playing cities
against one another for the purpose of extracting more money, better
leases, new stadiums, bigger wedges of the financial pie. In future

years, sports and business issues between municipalities would become even more important than the score on the field, and in 1964 the Braves had engineered an enduring template. After nearly a century of being a generally nondescript franchise, the Braves had now become infamous pioneers, for teams across all professional sports would, if need be, follow their model, needing nothing more than a few years of tough times before either demanding from the city a new stadium (paid for by the public, of course) or ripping the hearts out of one fan base in search of love from another.

Unlike ownership's old guard, which was convinced that television would be the ruin of its collective financial empire, any new owner entering the game needed to learn how to transition from the prewar box-office model to the radio model to television. To the misfortune of Milwaukee as a baseball town, Perini was one of the first owners who began to think about cities not as cities, but as media *markets,* best valued by the amount of revenue they could produce through electronic media.

Attendance would always be important, but over time less from actual dollars and more because of what it represented: a product with which people would want to be associated, a product advertisers would pay to support. The Milwaukee Braves radio broadcast network stretched as far as South Dakota, but the 1961 arrival of the Minnesota Twins (the old Washington Senators had run their course) began to choke the outer tributaries that once had belonged to Milwaukee. South Dakota became Twins country. Closer to Milwaukee, Cubs and White Sox games were broadcast to the city, both by grandfather rules and sheer proximity, forcing the Braves to compete with two other teams in its own city. Perini did not help matters, for he would only televise around thirty games per year, not many more than residents in the southern portions of the city and state could see from the Cubs.

ATLANTA OFFERED THE potential to own the entire region of the South. The closest baseball big-league team was the Cincinnati Reds, 450 miles away. Pro football was even more remote. Not only was it 550 miles to the closest pro city but the team happened to be those weekly Sunday football disasters, the St. Louis Cardinals. These geographic considerations represented an opportunity not to be squandered. Atlanta was the growing hub of the last region in the country not to be tapped for professional sports.

Lou Perini and the Steam Shovels packed it in in 1962, selling the team to a group of kids for $5.5 million. The head kid was an ambitious thirty-four-year-old Chicago insurance man, William Bartholomay III. The rest of the group, virtually all scions of wealthy Chicago families, wasn't much older than Bill Bartholomay, who was the youngest of the conglomerate, but it was he who was clearly in charge. And John McHale, Perini's general manager, who also joined the Bartholomay group, received a share, proof that the transition would be seamless.

At the initial press conference about the sale, November 16, 1962, Bartholomay endeared himself and his ownership group to city officials by vowing that being from Chicago, a mere eighty-five miles from Milwaukee, qualified them as "local ownership," a shrewd strategy, considering that even during the winning years, Perini's emotional and physical distance had worn thin in the city.

Thirteen years earlier, it had been Milwaukee that represented the future. Now, it was Milwaukee that was geographically challenged, flanked to the south by two teams, the White Sox and Cubs, eighty-five miles away, and now by the former Washington Senators, the American League Minnesota Twins, 375 miles to the west. The region, even though Milwaukee's population actually *increased,* had simply grown too small to support a major-league ball club.

The future was what all mortal men craved, if not the whole thing, then just a slice big enough to serve as an epitaph. In this latest version, Bartholomay thought of himself as a man of singular vision, with an ambition to open a neglected but emerging region to baseball in the same audacious manner as Walter O'Malley. Atlanta was a city with a restless business community and a political landscape undergoing a revolutionary transition, one that would either exacerbate or soothe the racial conflicts that branded the region and divided the nation.

Bartholomay believed the city represented fertile territory for the right person, someone who could see opportunity where others saw only obstacles. "I thought about history," he recalled. "The South was changing. Atlanta was the center of commerce there, with an aggressive, committed business community. I thought about how historic it would be to bring baseball to Atlanta in 1965, exactly one hundred years following the Civil War. I was very cognizant of that."

It was a good story, and maybe even parts of it were true, but little did anyone know the fix Atlanta was already in. No one admitted it, of course, but piece by piece, little by little, the forgotten scraps of details formed the entire, cynical canvas. Bartholomay may have thought about Sherman and Reconstruction and second chances a century later, but before he had even purchased the club, Perini already had his eye on moving the club to Atlanta. During the 1962 All-Star Game in Washington, McHale met with Furman Bisher, the sports editor and influential columnist (and noted Henry Aaron nemesis) of the *Atlanta Journal,* requesting a private meeting with Atlanta's mayor, Ivan Allen, Jr.

"Mr. Perini is planning to move the Braves," McHale told Bisher. "I'm certain you'll keep this in confidence at this time, but he's very interested in Atlanta and wants me to look into it. I want you to take me to see the mayor, but I want to keep my visit between us." Bisher maintained his silence for two years, and though Perini sold the team to Bartholomay and never met with Allen, events took precisely the course Perini had envisioned. Perini most likely disclosed his Atlanta plan to Bartholomay during the negotiations, and the Atlanta back channel explained why Perini did not entertain local offers to purchase the club. The secret deal with Atlanta also explained why Perini sold the club without announcing it was for sale, for perhaps a different ownership group would actually have been committed to keeping the team in Milwaukee. Moreover, the combination of forces answered the question originally posed by Doyne: The commissioner did not step in on behalf of Milwaukee because the wheels toward Atlanta were already in motion, four years before the team ever played its first game there.

The desire to move the Braves to Atlanta all along finally explained the sad case of Harry Sampson, the Milwaukee businessman who had offered to buy the Braves three months before Perini sold to Bartholomay. Instead, with an offer in hand he did not intend to entertain, Perini met with Bartholomay and another member of the ownership group, thirty-four-year-old Tom Reynolds, secretly in Toronto, and they closed the deal in just over a week.

MILWAUKEE SYNDICATE OFFER
REJECTED TWO DAYS EARLIER

MILWAUKEE, WIS. — Harold Sampson, a Milwaukee business-man, revealed after the sale of the Braves was announced November 16, that a group he had headed had tried unsuccessfully to buy the club.

"We had a firm offer on file with Lou Perini since September," Sampson said. "Our offer was kept confidential at his request. He said he did not want it generally known that the Braves were for sale. He formally declined our offer two days before he announced the sale."

Sampson said that his group was made up entirely of Milwau-keeans.

In 1964—perhaps as a last attempt to prove to the baseball cartel that economics did not make baseball untenable in Milwaukee—attendance rose by 200,000, even as the team sank to fifth place. Eugene Grobschmidt, the chairman of the governing board of County Stadium, not only accused the team of sandbagging the city but also claimed the Braves had tried to lose their remaining games to make their departure appear less egregious. In his final year with the club, even Spahn, the greatest pitcher in the history of the franchise, said that Bragan wasn't trying to win.

In Atlanta, Mayor Allen oversaw construction of an eighteen-million-dollar stadium that awaited a baseball team, soon to be named Atlanta–Fulton County Stadium. Bartholomay and the Braves foresaw arrival in Atlanta in 1965—that is, until Grobschmidt led a court battle that kept the Braves from leaving town until 1966.

The bitterness broke the link with the past. In a bygone era, young sportsmen had bought baseball teams to fulfill their own egos, to compensate for their own limited athletic abilities. Now, they were speculators, real estate prospectors whose job it was not only to build a pennant winner but to sense when a market had reached the point of diminishing returns, had outlived its usefulness. Milwaukee would be the city of firsts, the first in the modern era to provide a rebirth for a team that had languished near extinction in two-team Boston. And now it was the first in the modern era to suffer no obvious economic trauma and still somehow outlive its usefulness. As one embittered Milwaukee fan wrote of Milwaukee in *The Sporting News* when the Atlanta deal became final, "The cow had been milked."

The players did not suffer the wrath of the city. Milwaukee was loyal to Spahn, Mathews, Adcock, Logan, and, naturally, to Henry. The players would live forever as a symbol of youth and vitality, of a nostalgic time when everything seemed good, when a person's word actually meant something. In Henry's case, the ignoble actions of the front office only seemed to burnish his standing, and the last of the Milwaukee years created something of a pact between Henry and Milwaukee. He would promise the people of the city that he would never forget them, never refuse their hospitality, and, in turn, they would always consider him one of their own.

Four days before Thanksgiving, 1965, the Mary Church Terrell Club held Henry Aaron night, his first testimonial dinner. Four hundred guests crowded the Sheraton-Schroeder Hotel. Henry, wearing a dark suit, along with a skinny tie and white pocket square, was presented by Billy Bruton, who had since retired and was working in public relations for Chrysler. Henry received a silver bowl, Barbara an orchid. The crowd gave him a standing ovation, and he would later admit to being embarrassed by their warmth. It was not lost on him or the crowd that no one from Braves management was in attendance. No one from the Braves showed up, largely, because they had all since moved to Atlanta. Assistant general manager Jim Fanning sent a telegram.

For the better part of three years, while Perini had been playing cloak-and-dagger with Furman Bisher and as Bartholomay jousted with Milwaukee politicians, Henry had something else in the back of his mind: the prospect of returning to the South. For the team's black players, especially the ones who had been raised in the Deep South, the prospect of returning—the prospect of reliving indignities and humiliations—was not met with enthusiasm. Lee Maye, a young black outfielder who grew up in Tuscaloosa, began voicing his trepidation about Atlanta to Henry, who went a step further. While Bartholomay and Grobschmidt traded epithets and legal briefs, Henry initially said he would not go.

MOVE TO GEORGIA PEACHY? NOT TO AARON

The Milwaukee Braves ask the National League this afternoon for permission to move to Atlanta. There are at least two Braves players, Lee Maye and Hank Aaron, who have their fingers crossed that the league says "no," although they know that is wishful thinking.

Maye and Aaron, Negro outfielders, yesterday expressed fear of racial discrimination if the club moves to Atlanta, although both added they would go because it's their "job."

AARON AND MAYE DISTURBED BY DECISION TO GO TO ATLANTA

MILWAUKEE, WIS. — The Braves' decision to move to Atlanta was accepted with regret by two of their Negro players, outfielders Henry Aaron and Lee Maye. Both said they disliked the idea and would not move their families to the Georgia city. Both have children in integrated schools in the Milwaukee area.

Aaron even planned to take a trip to Atlanta to investigate conditions for Negroes there.

State Sen. Leroy R. Johnson, the only Negro legislator in the South, said he was writing Aaron to assure the Braves' slugger that he need have no fears about racial problems in Atlanta.

HENRY HAD NEVER considered himself as important a historical figure as Jackie Robinson, and yet by twice integrating the South—first in the Sally League and later as the first black star on the first major-league team in the South (during the apex of the civil rights movement, no less)—his road in many ways was no less lonely, and in other ways far more difficult.

He would receive credit for handling the inequities of his life with dignity, and yet he was rarely afforded the dignity of being recognized as having played a significant role in eradicating important barriers to the movement. Robinson had confronted the first, impenetrable obstacle of being allowed to compete at the major-league level; his was the first success, which made all other successes—including Henry's—possible, and Henry was never so presumptuous as to believe anything to the contrary. But after Robinson, the integration of other levels of the sport, in regions where breaking the social customs proved far more difficult (with considerably less interest), was not a story that received much coverage.

Rather, the conventional thinking concerning minor-league integration held that sooner or later, black prospects would have to play with their white teammates. Either that or the clubs would be forced to relocate their minor-league teams, moving away from the South, at considerable expense and difficulty. Thus, the breakthrough of playing baseball in the segregated South would largely be seen as an inevitablility, no real breakthrough at all.

Henry had not been recognized for his groundbreaking achievement, and now he was being told to return to the South once more. Playing in Atlanta meant confronting the South all over again, with its contradictions and its conditions. It meant being reduced once more to a person with no rights and no dignity. That had been hard enough when he was a kid, when he knew no better. But in 1966, Henry was thirty-two years old, was earning $70,000 per season, and was on a clear Hall of Fame path. He was famous and accomplished and angered that in the South all he had produced could be taken away by a teenage store clerk or an average housewife, just because they were white and he was not.

"I have lived in the South and I don't want to live there again," Henry told a reporter in 1964. "This is my home. I've lived here since I was a kid 19 years old. We can go anywhere in Milwaukee. I don't know what would happen in Atlanta."

In Milwaukee, Henry fought hard for his comfort. During one off-season, he took a job as a spokesman for the Miller Brewing Company. In another, he and Bruton formed a small real estate company, the Aaron-Bruton Investment Co. When the team struggled as Perini and Bartholomay began to distance the Braves from the city, Henry volunteered to sell season-ticket packages to fans (but even the great

Henry Aaron had little success once it became clear that Bartholomay had other plans for the franchise).

Bud Selig was eating his breakfast when he read Bob Broeg's piece in *The Sporting News* in 1964, which confirmed what he and other Milwaukeeans had refused to believe: The Braves were leaving. The Milwaukee press was quick to cover the story, albeit slower to analyze the implications. Ollie Kuechle, the sports editor and columnist of the *Journal,* had maintained that the Braves were not leaving. The mayor of Milwaukee may have been a Braves shareholder, but the king of Wisconsin, Lombardi, was one, as well, and both were in the dark. "Yes, Vince was a shareholder. He was on the Braves board," Selig recalled. "And even he couldn't save them."

Selig remembered finishing the story and thinking it was the "worst day of my life." He then began to canvass Milwaukee businessmen to mount a counterattack. If the Braves were going to be stolen, he would form a committee that would attract another team to Milwaukee, taking the first steps toward becoming the man who was synonymous with baseball in Milwaukee. From watching his team be yanked away, Selig would learn the rules of power and would vow to return big-league baseball to the city. While Doyne had once denounced "piracy," Selig was naked in his coveting of vulnerable teams. Once the Braves departed, Selig staged exhibitions for the Chicago White Sox and Cleveland Indians, with the hope of attracting them to Milwaukee.

Over thirteen years in Milwaukee, only the Dodgers outdrew the Braves on average, and that franchise played in the megalopolises of New York City and Los Angeles. As far as Bud Selig was concerned, his city had done everything right and had still ended up with a handful of sawdust. Selig was thirty-one when the Braves played their final season in Milwaukee, and he decided he would not stand on the fringes of power again. For the better part of the next half century, Bud Selig would, in his own seemingly unassuming way, become one of the game's most astute and formidable power brokers. In later years, when baseball made both men extremely wealthy, Selig recalled that Bartholomay would often joke with him, telling him that the wrenching years of the mid-1960s were the best thing that could have happened to Selig. Without his having moved the Braves to

Atlanta, Selig remembered Bartholomay telling him, Bud Selig never would have become what he would ultimately be: the most powerful man in baseball.

BARBARA AARON DID not want to believe the Braves were considering Atlanta. When the rumors first surfaced that relocation was a real possibility and that she, Henry, and the children would be moving back to the South, she felt her heart sink with profound disappointment. The house in Mequon was a handsome ranch, with a proud brick facade and a long, rambling roof that featured two cathedral peaks. The sprawling, manicured front lawn sloped sharply downward toward the street. The front of the house looked majestic in winter, a dense sheet of snow enveloping the lawn, leaving an unbroken swath of white, in contrast to the black pavement of the long driveway.

Living in Wisconsin had provided Barbara with a certain level of comfort and dignity, and she did not believe this would be true in Georgia. She was the wife of the famous Henry Aaron, and such ballplayers were always afforded special dispensation, but she also knew the codes of the South were considerably less respectful of Henry's fame. The more notorious places, the rural areas and cities such as Birmingham, which collectively seemed to revel in their reputations, even sought out prominent blacks with the intention of humiliating them, to remind them that, despite their education or accomplishment, they were still at the core niggers, permanently beneath the lowest white man of any social class.

Atlanta's historical personality was one of moderation and compromise, but the end result in the early 1960s was generally the same: Whites on top, blacks on the bottom. The family now risked having everything they'd earned in Milwaukee taken away by the denigrating ways of life in the South. Education was a primary concern for Barbara. Hankie, Gaile, Lary, and Dorinda were all enrolled in public school, and the thought of them having to leave an integrated school in Wisconsin to attend a segregated school in Atlanta particularly galled her. As a family, the Aarons had come too far to go back. Despite the fact that the Aarons were the only black family in

Mequon (and the reality that, in ostensibly tolerant Milwaukee, only Henry's outsized fame allowed them to live there), Barbara nevertheless had made friends and believed that she was part of a growing community.

She had been raised in Jacksonville, nearly as close to Atlanta as Henry had been in Mobile. She had heard the predictions about what Atlanta was going to be like, despite the apparent protections that had been promised the players and the team. During Bartholomay's and McHale's secret meetings with the Atlanta people, particularly Mayor Allen and the ubiquitous Bob Woodruff, the head of Coca-Cola and the most powerful businessman in the region, the Braves had been promised that seating in the Atlanta stadium would not be segregated. All tickets would be available to all fans. Black fans could sit in whatever seats they could afford, and Allen had promised there would be no nefarious pricing schemes that would promote de facto segregation. Allen told Bartholomay that the rest rooms, concessions, and all public facilities would be integrated.

But what if those were just words, bargaining chips necessary to get an important deal done, to keep the best player on the club from making a fuss? The Braves weren't going to refuse a multimillion-dollar move to Atlanta just because of the racial concerns the black people or players had. Had Henry's objections been a consideration, the team wouldn't have considered the South in the first place. Even if the Braves kept their promises, Barbara thought, she would have to live in the world beyond the ballpark. She'd have to take the kids to school and shop and deal with an environment she regarded with dread. What most whites did not understand, and indeed it was virtually impossible to do so, was the level of humiliation blacks in the South were forced to endure. In later years, when the confrontations of the civil rights movement would be documented in film and other media, the standard humiliations of separate drinking facilities and rest rooms would become so clichéd (and completely uncomprehensible to a new generation of black and white Americans), their mention would lose virtually all power to shock. It was not just the big humiliations that had to be borne, but the constant, daily, nagging small ones, as well. The depth of the racial prejudice, of just what whites truly believed about blacks, however, could not be underestimated. About a year before Bartholomay and Allen first began secretly negotiating the move, the relationship between Atlanta's black community and Rich's, the largest department store in the Southeast, had begun to deteriorate. For years, blacks were angered by the treatment they encountered at Rich's while spending their hard-earned money. "Not only were blacks forbidden to sit at the Rich's lunch counter," wrote Gary Pomerantz in *Where Peachtree Meets Sweet Auburn,* his groundbreaking book about the white Allens and black Dobbses, the political families who transformed modern Atlanta, "they also could not try on clothes before buying them. The Atlanta department store's rule of thumb was that white customers would not buy clothes if they knew blacks once had sampled them." When the Braves move was finalized, it was Rich's ("Atlanta born . . . Atlanta owned . . . Atlanta managed") which became one of the Braves first advertisers.

Bob Hope, an Atlanta teenager and rabid baseball fan who called the Braves for an internship a year before the team had finalized the move, knew how ingrained the white attitudes regarding black hygiene truly were. "When I was in high school, our football coach told us that the sweat of a black kid would burn you," Hope recalled. "They told us black kids wouldn't just tackle you but in the piles they would bite you and you'd get diseases. That was one of the reasons why we never played against black teams."

Whether or not whites truly believed that blacks carried diseases was secondary to the true purpose these myths served, which was to maintain the system of legal segregation.

Barbara had always been dubious about the Milwaukee club's commitment to racial equality. For the past thirteen years, when she and Henry had traveled to Bradenton for spring training, the team had offered no protections against discrimination, nor even made much effort for their basic comforts, despite the annual protestations of Henry, Billy Bruton, and Wes Covington. The lives of the wives of black players was one of the greatly underreported and underappreciated experiences, and moving back to the South meant relearning the rules, enduring the slights, large and small (the small were oftentimes the worst because they occurred so frequently). Women from Rachel Robinson to Barbara Aaron endured harsh treatment when sitting in the stands during games or when taking public transportation in the South. Some of the fan letters that protested the move echoed Barbara's personal concerns, ones that she felt had not been adequately addressed by the club.

> *Editor of The Sporting News:*
> *. . . Milwaukee . . . supported their Braves at an average of about 1,600,000 per season. The fans have lavished gifts upon the players and been good to those . . . previously . . . subject to racial discrimination.*
>
> *The fans . . . went without televised games. . . .*
>
> *In return, the new owners . . . have decided to pull up stakes and head elsewhere. . . .*
>
> > *John Wagner*
> > *Glendale, Calif.*

Bill Bartholomay would say in later years that he understood Henry's hesitancy about the region's racial climate but that he was convinced of the city leadership's commitment to break with its smothering history. Once, on a scouting trip of the area, he was immediately struck by the vast difference in racial attitudes once he arrived in Atlanta. The farther away he drove from Atlanta's center, Bartholomay found, the harsher and more unwelcoming he found the response to any level of integration. It was like entering another world, Bartholomay thought, with sharp racial divisions being only part of the difference. Even in early 1960s Georgia, remnants of the sharecropper system existed in pockets of the state's outlying areas. The complete lack of infrastructure—indoor plumbing, electricity, telephone service—underscored the level of poverty that still remained, unaffected by the postwar economic boom or advances in technology.

The contrast left him with a potentially devastating problem: The Braves were being positioned as a regional team, but outside of Atlanta, interracial competition was not a concept being met with great enthusiasm in the surrounding areas. Should the Braves be unable to penetrate the full reach of their territory, the potential advantages of the South would be immediately thwarted, and

Bartholomay was quite possibly staring disaster in the face. "There was a real hostile feel when you went to some of the outlying areas," Bartholomay recalled. "But I had to believe that while those areas might not be too accepting of an interracial team where the biggest star, alongside with Mathews, was African-American, the city itself was going to accept the team."

If Bartholomay viewed Atlanta as a prime opportunity to make his mark in baseball, many of the region's leaders saw the arrival of the Braves as key to their strategy to transform the image of the city, and by extension, the South. Geographically, Atlanta was close to perfect, and all of the reasons why it had been leveled during the Civil War were precisely the reasons why it carried such potential. Central to its value was Hartsfield Airport, named for Bill Hartsfield, the pragmatic political legend who held office for twenty-three years. Throughout the late 1950s and early 1960s, it was massive airport construction that separated Atlanta from other southern cities such as Montgomery or Memphis. The massive expansion of the airport guaranteed Atlanta would be the central hub for southern commerce. Hartsfield was so ubiquitous, a running local joke was that when a person died, before going to heaven or hell, they had to first change planes at Hartsfield.

Atlanta boasted the infrastructure, the fortuitous geography, and the population to be an economic powerhouse, but its racial undercurrent prevented it from becoming a world-class city. It had been only ten years since the state flag had been redesigned to contain a confederate flag (1956), a chilling reminder for blacks of the social order and their collective status within that structure. Atlanta had prided itself on its accommodation and moderation. But between 1960 and 1962, the Atlanta student movement staged demonstrations to integrate downtown lunch counters, not dissimilar to those protests held in Greensboro and Nashville and other southern cities, disappointing proof that the old guard—both the entrenched white political leadership and the longtime black clergymen—had moved too slowly and ineffectually for what was becoming a new, powerful movement.

During years of secret negotiation, Ivan Allen, Jr.—himself a firm segregationist less than a decade earlier—held a private optimism that by 1965 the worst was over for Atlanta. He would say often that he staked his reputation and that of the city on his commitment to undoing the rigid racial customs of Atlanta, a claim that was not exactly hyperbolic. In just the previous four years, the city had undergone tremendous turmoil. The public schools had been ordered integrated. Led by Martin Luther King, Jr., a new generation of black students impatient with the speed of progress demonstrated for the integration of downtown lunch counters, as well as other public facilities: movie theaters, auditoriums, swimming pools, and restaurants. In 1961, Allen was elected to his first term as mayor by defeating the segregationist Lester Maddox. It was an election that shifted the balance, but only uneasily. Allen defeated Maddox in a runoff by winning 98 percent of the black vote, but less than half of whites voted for him.

Allen represented the progressive political voice Atlanta required, but the power behind the change was Bob Woodruff. "The leaders of the city didn't want to go the way of Birmingham, Little Rock, and other southern cities, and all of this was a prelude to major sports," recalled Andrew Young, a former congressman and Atlanta's mayor from 1982 to 1990. "They decided that Atlanta was going to integrate from the top down. Whereas most southern cities were trying to integrate schools and come up, Atlanta made the decision—which was different from any other city—that the business community was going to lead desegregation. And so they put two black businessmen on the chamber of commerce, Herman Russell and Jesse Hill. Herman was a major contractor and Jesse Hill was VP of Atlanta Life Insurance Company. And so you had a cohesiveness with the black business community. You also had the Atlanta University Center, with Benjamin Mays and Vivian Henderson; those two were the main ones, but from that point on the business community did very little without consulting the black community."

Having professional sports in Atlanta, Allen believed, would bring the world to the city, would legitimize it. The city could not afford to be an embarrassment in front of the nation. Allen did not merely accept the Braves; he cultivated them. The fact that the Braves had chosen Atlanta was as important to the city as it was to the team. Allen wanted football next, and he began to negotiate with the NFL for an expansion team, which would become the Falcons.

"There was general agreement that one of the ways to make Atlanta a big-league city was to bring baseball and football; it was a concurrent proposal," Young recalled. "When it looked like they could get the Braves, the mayor, Ivan Allen, and Mills B. Lane, who was the president of C&S Bank, which became Nations Bank, which is now Bank of America, they almost bragged that they built a stadium with money they didn't have, on land they didn't own, for a team they didn't have yet. And if they tried to do that today, they'd all be in jail."

HENRY HAD JUST missed out on the batting title in 1965, and in the spring of 1966 he said he wanted it back. He hadn't won it since 1959, and he was suddenly being surpassed in defensive reputation by a new star, the blossoming Clemente from Pittsburgh. For years, Henry would be compared to the electric Mays, a comparison under which his playing style suffered. The same would be true of Clemente, the first Latin American superstar, but he was something more, furiously prideful, politically aware. Both Henry and Clemente possessed the political passion of Robinson, but the difference was physical. Unlike Henry, Clemente seemed to translate his fire into his physical movements. Clemente played not simply for himself but also for his people, and, like Robinson, he conveyed a message with his body. The connection of racial and ethnic pride surged through each step, each swing. Each outfield throw seemed a political statement, reminding the baseball world that he and his people had been mistreated and underestimated and he was here to address that injustice.

Clemente was a rising superstar. In addition to his consecutive batting titles, he excelled defensively. But right field was Henry's turf. In 1957, 1958, and 1959, Henry was the king of his position, both offensively and defensively. He had been awarded the Gold Glove each year, had already won an MVP, and was an all-star.

Then, like a supernova, Clemente appeared. He won his first Gold Glove in 1960, and then another, and another. By 1966, Clemente had won six straight. Henry was aware of Willie, but Willie played center. Clemente was different. He and Clemente both played right field, and the emergence of Clemente underscored both the immense level of talent in the National League and how quickly Henry could get lost as his team grew less important in the standings. Henry found himself at another disadvantage: In the television age, it was much easier to be taken by players like Clemente, a man who played with such yearning and, like Henry, smoldered at the thought of having his talent slighted.

AARON SAYS HE COULD HAVE
WON NL BATTING TITLE

LAKELAND, FLA. (UPI) — "I had a number of opportunities to win batting titles and I purposely let them pass," says Aaron. ". . . we were living and dying on home runs. So, I more or less forgot about my average and concentrated on hitting the ball hard. I believe I could have hit more than Clemente had I concentrated on it."

That Henry purposely began to eschew batting average for home runs was a telling admission. There was the moment back in 1954 when Henry sat in the hospital in Cincinnati, having snapped his ankle and ended his season. Sitting under crisp hospital sheets, surrounded by flowers and fan mail, Henry ignored the throb in his leg and the antiseptic hospital smell for a moment and allowed himself an inner smile.

"I had read so much about Musial, Williams, and Robinson," he said. "I put those guys on a pedestal. They were something special, Jackie above the rest because he was the only Negro player at the time. I really thought that they put their pants on different, rather than one leg at a time."

Then Henry let free a little secret. "Yeah, that's when I thought about eventually getting 3,000 hits. That's always been my goal."

It always had been. That is, until teammates began to notice a few changes in the way Henry went to bat. Joe Torre saw the subtleties, the way Henry would take certain pitches on the outer half of the plate, the ones he used to tattoo into the right-center gap. These were the pitches Mays used to complain about so often, the ones that Henry would wait on just that fraction of a second longer so he could find the gap and watch Mays run to the fence. Now Henry would let these pass, hoping for a pitch just a little more inside that he could jump on early, with the intention of pulling it down the line and out.

The swing Torre once marveled at was the swing that just might produce four thousand hits, and what he now witnessed was something different, something deadly but far less efficient. Henry had developed a home-run stroke, not the old swing of a prodigy, who was just so talented that the ball was going to leave the park about thirty times a year regardless, but a swing designed with one purpose in mind: to power the ball over the fence.

Musial had always been the target. More accurately, it was his National League hit record of 3,630 that Henry wanted. That was the only record he had ever craved; that was the true mark of an offensive baseball player—the number of times you came to bat and got a hit. But especially after Mantle and Maris put on a home-run show in 1961, Maris finally overtaking Ruth, the times were changing. Power was slowly growing more important to the people who ran and watched and reported on baseball—and Henry would change with them.

THE FIRST MAJOR-LEAGUE game in the 121-year history of the city—the Atlanta Braves versus the Pittsburgh Pirates—took place on April 12, 1966. The contest lasted thirteen innings, decided by a two-run homer by Willie Stargell. The Braves went on to lose four of their first five games. And then there was Henry, who hit home run number four hundred off Bo Belinsky in Philadelphia, only to follow this with a tie-breaking hit the night of April 29, when the Braves and Astros wrestled into the night, Houston tying the game at 3–3 in the top of the ninth.

Caroll Sembera, the new Houston pitcher, entered and retired Felipe Alou and Gary Geiger easily. That brought up Henry, who took two strikes and lashed a low line drive over the fence to end it. The Braves were just a couple of games out of first place.

And on June 3, at Atlanta Stadium, Henry hit another dramatic home run, this one off Bob Gibson in the bottom of the ninth. But it didn't do any good, because the Braves still lost the game, 3–2. Their record was 20–30 and the club wouldn't reach the .500 mark until September 6. Atlanta finished 85–77, and the pattern that began in Milwaukee continued. Henry was brilliant—44 homers, 127 runs batted in to lead the league—on a team that finished thirteen and a half games behind the Dodgers.

In retrospect, it was Atlanta that started him on the road to the social and political legitimacy he'd long sought. Henry preferred to remain in Milwaukee, but that was his comfort talking and, perhaps to a certain degree, his fear. Had he remained in Milwaukee, thousands of miles from the turbulence and upheaval of the South, he would have been content and praised as a solid, contributing member of a good baseball team.

To keep Hank in Milwaukee would have removed Henry from the central battleground of his life, leaving him unfulfilled. He would often say he understood his fame made it easier for him, but easy was not what Henry wanted. He wanted, like Jackie, to be counted. And there would always be that unease, that Mequon was essentially segregated, but not for him. "They don't give me a bad time, because I'm somebody special," he told *Sports Illustrated* in 1966. "But that doesn't help my brothers and sisters because anything that happens to my race, happens to me."

In Milwaukee, Henry would have been removed from the dynamics of the civil rights movement and the numerous remarkable people who would be influential in shaping his worldview. He would not have been as easily cultivated by the power brokers of the movement, the men and women who would help Henry emerge from the enormous shadow of Hank, the bigger-than-life baseball star. If Henry would lament a certain lack of relevance on a larger scale, remaining in Milwaukee would have diminished him as a person of substance even further, for Atlanta was where the Henry side of his personality would begin to be nurtured.

And it was in Atlanta where being born black collided with the promise of America, a Promethean confrontation that defined Henry's life. It was a confrontation being acted out in real time, at a place and in an era of historic significance. A year before the move, Henry met with C. Miles Smith, the president of the Atlanta NAACP, who asked Henry to reconsider his stance of refusing to play in

Atlanta. What Smith told Henry echoed Allen's gambit to Bartholomay: Atlanta had not reached its ultimate goals of true equality for all citizens, but it was charting its own path away from what many southern cities were like. Whitney Young, the director of the Urban League, reached out to Henry first in private and then in a column in the black weekly *The Chicago Defender*. Aaron, Young wrote, needed to agree to move to Atlanta to further break the will of segregationists: "Such a sacrifice is earnestly desired by Negro leaders who are hopeful that his big bat will help them hammer out an 'open city,' one in which equal opportunities are translated into reality for all."

Henry bought a handsome brick rambler that somewhat resembled the house in Mequon. It was set on two sprawling, shady acres and the address was 519 Lynhurst Drive. Almost immediately, Henry was invited to a series of informal meetings at the Braves offices, welcoming him to Atlanta. After years of being underestimated by the press and, to an extent, by the public, Henry was now in the act. Bartholomay and members of the Atlanta business community were at one meeting. At another, he met a young progressive politician named Jimmy Carter, who was running for governor against the eccentric segregationist Lester Maddox. Carter told him then and would tell him in later years, when the two men became friends, that it was not merely the arrival of the Braves that legitimized the South but the Braves specifically being led by Henry Aaron. At another meeting was a group that would not forget Henry: Martin Luther King, Sr., Martin Luther King, Jr., and Andrew Young.

"Martin was a big baseball fan," Young recalled, adding that he remembered Henry being somewhat embarrassed that he wasn't more publicly visible in the front lines of the civil rights movement. "We told him not to worry. When you talked to Henry Aaron, you knew how he felt about civil rights. We told him just to keep hitting that ball. That was his job."

In early 1966, the city held a parade to welcome the Braves. Against the backdrop of triumph, the story seems apocryphal, but Andy Young recalled the moment clearly.

"I can remember standing out at the parade. The parade came down what is now Spring Street and I was standing in front of the American hotel, which is now a Marriott Suites. It was an old hotel and I was standing behind a bunch of rednecks and I kind of moved in amongst them to see what was happening," Andy Young recalled. "Each of the major players was sitting on the back of a convertible, and when Hank came down, one guy said, 'Now, if we're gonna be a big-league city, that fella's gonna have to be able to live anywhere he wants to live in this town.' And I said, 'Oh, shit . . . *They* said that? This must *mean* something.'"

CHAPTER TWELVE

WILLIE

AS YOU ENTERED the Braves clubhouse, an oversized refrigerator loomed to the right, a frosty glass door revealing shelves of Fanta grape and orange soda distributed by the Coca-Cola Bottling Company. Next to the fridge sat the cigarette machine and a tub filled with ice and Piels beer. A side table housed assorted sundries—sunflower seeds, tobacco, bubble gum—and a jar, about ten inches high, brimming with amphetamines.

Wire-mesh dressing stalls lined the far right wall, leading to the trainer's room, the ultimate safe haven, where players got taped and massaged, and, most importantly, could hide from the press. The center of the room featured two long rectangular folding tables that stood next to the pre- and postgame spreads. The tables served as the social epicenter of the Atlanta Braves clubhouse. It was where the Dominican Rico Carty, the self-nicknamed "Big Boy" (or "Beeg Boy" if you happened to spell his moniker as he did, phonetically) preened and boasted and flexed. Felipe Alou and Felix Millan played hearts on those tables with Dusty Baker and Phil Niekro. The tables also doubled as a makeshift dais, where Joe Torre rallied support for a radical concept quickly spreading through big-league clubhouses: the creation of a strong players union to protect their interests against the owners, led by a man Torre deeply respected, Marvin Miller.

And then there was Henry, away from the tumult, at a safe distance from the rest. His locker was located along the far left wall from the clubhouse entrance, second to last from the showers. In 1968, there was no bigger, more formidable player in the Braves clubhouse than Henry Aaron, the last link to the great old days of Spahn and championships, free-flowing beer and promise. Henry could be melancholy with his role as a bridge between eras. Eddie Mathews was gone, shipped to the Houston Astros the year before. Joe Torre, eight years in the big leagues, was a perennial all-star, but it was his brother Frank who had played with the Milwaukee pennant winners. Carty could hit with anybody in the league and cut a dashing and colorful, if not annoying, figure in the clubhouse. But Carty was talent without profile, having joined Milwaukee after the glory, having never played in the postseason, having never been there when things were in full flower. Niekro was just a kid who showed immense promise, and Tony Cloninger couldn't get the pain out of his right arm after winning twenty-four games in 1965—the Braves last, lost year in Milwaukee. Henry was surrounded by good players with fine futures, professionals certainly, but he was set apart by his history and by his numbers, the great calling card for every player in major-league baseball.

As the 1968 season began, Henry was thirty-four, and enjoyed a position unique from that of anyone else playing big-league ball at that moment: He was the guy whose name invariably arose when the writers were sitting around during the interminable downtime of spring training, discussing just who might be up for the challenge, the long climb to the top of Mount Olympus, the summit, of course, being Babe Ruth and his 714 home runs. Maybe they had forgotten about Henry as Milwaukee grew irrelevant and the Braves sank from the annual pennant races, but without much warning, the gas tank on Willie Mays seemed near empty. Willie just wasn't Willie anymore. He was thirty-seven years old and 172 homers shy of Ruth, but 1967—just twenty-two homers and a career-low .263 batting average—represented an obvious distress signal. The writers and the fans (and most likely Mays himself) did the math and realized that the expected narrative of Mays passing Ruth was most likely not to be. Mays would have had to average more than forty home runs through the 1971 season (when he would be forty) even to come within breathing distance of the record. Frank Robinson was fierce and dominant and heading for Cooperstown as surely as Henry and Willie, but he was never close enough to Ruth on the home-run list ever to threaten. Killebrew? Banks? Great players, Hall of Fame–bound were each, but they had no chance. It was Henry, not yet thirty-five years old, with 482 home runs and a career batting average still over .315, who had the best shot of reaching the big guy. It was Henry, therefore, who would undergo a national reassessment. With Aaron, the calculations weren't so daunting. His back and knees were starting to give him trouble, but he was in shape. He played in Atlanta, where the ball carried, and, most important of all, he did not have to *increase* his production to reach the Babe. If he played seven more seasons, until he hit forty, in 1974, he needed to average thirty-three homers a year, one homer less than the thirty-four he had averaged over the fourteen years he had already played big-league ball. All he had to do to take a shot at Ruth was just be himself, be as consistent as he'd always been.

Even as he stood apart, the Braves were increasingly his team. Bobby Bragan and Billy Hitchcock were bounced as managers, and Bartholomay handed the reins to an Alabaman, Luman Harris, who held authority as manager but had no stature. Harris had pitched during the war years and held the distinction of losing big on a bad team, once posting a 7–21 record for the 102-loss Philadelphia A's in 1943. Henry was the best player, with the longest résumé, the greatest accomplishments, and the most respect. The veterans admired how he played so well for so long, and the kids, who not too long ago had owned his baseball card, idolized him, mesmerized by the idea that they were now not just big leaguers but shared the room with the great man himself. Respect was the proper description, for Henry did not pretend that he was anything like the younger players. He lived at a distance.

Despite their admiration for him, Henry maintained a certain curmudgeonly contempt for the new generation, by which he was now surrounded. They did not study the game as his generation had, nor did they seem to play when hurt, and to Henry Aaron, playing regardless of pain represented the ultimate mark of professionalism. After the first day of spring training, pain was a part of the game, and yet younger players seemed unaffected by sitting out a day or two until their injuries healed. And yet, this new era of modern player would earn more money than he and Spahn and Burdette and Mathews—tougher players from a tougher generation—ever saw at a similar point in their careers, either individually or, for the most part, combined.

Henry had no illusions about the power of management. He had fought every year with Bob Quinn and Birdie Tebbetts, sending back his contract every January for an extra dollar. He had been in the league thirteen seasons and still wasn't close to making $100,000.

Yet Henry could not envision baseball without the reserve clause. He believed what the owners had been telling the players and the public for a century: that free agency would destroy baseball. The league would not be able to function if players were allowed any form of free agency. Henry attended Marvin Miller's meetings. He was generally supportive of the nascent union's initiatives, but in interview settings and public statements, he would repeat various versions of the same theme: teams needed to control the players.

The center of the room was where the good players, the stars, the scrubs, and even the bug-eyed clubhouse kids commiserated. It was where a fifteen-year-old high school infielder named Stewart "Buz" Eisenberg had the greatest job in the world.

Eisenberg was a Braves batboy during the first two years the Braves were in Atlanta. While Bartholomay had been concerned how the big-league, integrated Braves would play in a region that for generations had remained strictly segregated and Jimmy Carter hoped that the arrival of the Braves would legitimize the South, Buz Eisenberg, throughout his high school years, lived out their macro concerns on a daily basis. His father, Dan Eisenberg, was a traveling salesman and had moved with his wife, Gloria, from Philadelphia to Atlanta in 1963. One of three children, Eisenberg attended North Fulton High School and later graduated from Lakeside High. He recalled that the family did not have much money and that they lived in Shallowford Downs, a brick-faced apartment complex on the northeast side of town. He was Jewish in the Deep South and remembered getting into countless fights for being called a "dirty Jew" on a daily basis, the worst of this occurring during his junior high years. Through Eisenberg's experiences, it became clear that the laws might have changed but that attitudes had not, and those attitudes were held by the very people Bartholomay needed to attract to his ballpark. These people, who were unused to interracial competition, would decide if they'd allow Henry Aaron to be their hero.

Eisenberg recalled how deeply racial attitudes defined his upbringing. As a kid in Philadelphia and, later, when the family moved to Atlanta, he did not have a black friend. He made the high school wrestling team and recalled that no one on the team wanted to pair with a talented black teammate named Jack Jones.

"There were four blacks in our high school in eleventh grade. That was the first year we integrated. The kids used to say that the black kids smelled like fish. They used to say that they ate fish because they couldn't afford meat," Eisenberg recalled.

There was the disturbing incident as a member of the junior ROTC. The instructor in charge was Sergeant Conley ("Sergeant Conley's turning green/Someone pissed in his canteen/Sound off . . . one two . . . sound off . . . say it again!") and one afternoon the sergeant hosted a first-aid seminar in the high school auditorium.

"I remember having to go to mandatory junior ROTC, back before it was ruled unconstitutional. It was totally unfair, three days a week, weapons training and things like that," Eisenberg recalled. "First aid was not integrated yet. Sergeant Conley showed us a short film and then gave us a scenario: 'You're in a truck and there's an accident. You see the victim is a black man lying in the street unconscious. So what do you do?'

"He told us, 'The first thing is you check to see if he is breathing. You find out that he isn't and you must perform mouth-to-mouth resuscitation.' And on it went. 'Look into the mouth and throat to ensure that the airway is clear. If an object is present, try to sweep it out with your fingers. Tilt the head back slightly.' Then he moved closer to the imaginary victim, approached his mouth, and instead of showing us how to give mouth-to-mouth, he yelled into it, 'GOOD-BYE, NIGGER!!!' I'll never forget that, because all the kids in the auditorium were laughing.

"For me it was different. Being with the Braves helped me out a lot with that, because in the clubhouse you talked to everyone, so when you got back to school, everything they were saying about blacks didn't make a lot of sense, because the Braves were all in the same room together."

He would remember virtually every detail of those two years with the total recall of a teenager surrounded by his heroes: how being a batboy for the Braves turned a self-described "nerdy kid" into a "hot date," both because he was associated with the hottest thing in town, the new baseball team, and because the generous tips the players bestowed upon him meant he always had more cash to take the girls out than some of his rivals at school. He remembered how the lower guys on the team, younger guys who were often closer in age to the batboys than some of their teammates, would prefer to hang out with the kids than with the established ballplayers, and how the Braves mascot, Chief Noc-A-Homa, headdress, feathers and all, always had the best weed at the ballpark, right in his tepee beyond the center-field fence. Eisenberg was particularly taken by a young pitcher named Clay Carroll, who used to go over to Shallowford Downs and swim in the pool, and how Buz and his mother, Gloria, would laugh together at just how much food Carroll could eat.

Eisenberg lived a dream. There was the time he was sitting there eating with the other clubbies when a naked Joe Torre sneaked up behind him and stood stealthily above, his penis dangling over Eisenberg's right shoulder, dangerously close to Eisenberg's right cheekbone. Upon noticing the laughter in the room and then recognizing why the team was busting up, Eisenberg kept eating, appearing not to notice Torre's dangling manhood nuzzling his cheek, before quickly striking his left hand across to his right shoulder, as if he were trying to swat a fly. Torre had by then backed away, and the room was bathed in laughter at the kid's expense, but Buz Eisenberg loved every minute of it—that just meant he was one of the guys. There was no better feeling on earth for a teenage kid who wanted to grow up to be a baseball player than to be included in the good feeling and the easy humor of the men he idolized.

He remembered Henry Aaron as a brooding figure, who always smoked and often drank a beer before and after games, at a distance from the rest. Eisenberg would recall that Henry rarely took his place in the social bazaar in the middle of the Braves clubhouse.

"Hank Aaron never even looked at me. Of all the guys, Aaron was probably the only one who I never made eye contact with, and he was the only one I really wanted to pay attention to me. I mean, here I am, fifteen and a half years old, and you're within three feet of Hank Aaron every day. He was the guy you idolized. At the end of every season, guys would tip you fifty or a hundred dollars, and Aaron stiffed me, totally. I wasn't sure if he didn't see me. But he did stiff me." The next year, as the Braves returned from spring training, Henry called out to Eisenberg and tossed him a warm-up jacket, an item that, forty-one years later, Eisenberg still owns, the jacket in beloved, precious tatters.

"I was there for eighty-one games for two seasons and Hank never, ever came over to the middle of the room. I can't say I never saw Hank Aaron smile, but I can say I never saw him belly-laugh, rap someone's ass with a towel . . . be one of the guys. I never heard what Hank Aaron's laugh sounded like, and I was aware of it because he was such a presence. I could see if he was just another guy, then maybe I never would have heard it because I wouldn't have been paying full attention. But *I was* paying full attention, because *he* was Hank Aaron.

"For any young teenage kid, being around this heroic ensemble, when they paid attention and spoke to you, it was a pretty awesome thing. Pat Jarvis, Clay Carroll, they laughed and joked and hung out with us," Eisenberg recalled. "With Aaron, it was different. With Aaron, it was worse than picking on us. He ignored us. . . . I didn't know the word at the time, but I thought it was arrogance, but later when you found out the life he was living, you sort of realized how he insulated himself from his teammates. You realize the defense mechanisms he had to set up, the walls he needed to protect himself."

IT WAS THE kids who brought Henry to life—two of them, actually, who whenever he was around acted as though they were precocious and slobbering little pups, looking up to the big man with a reverence so complete that it couldn't help but make Henry feel young and full, and, above all, appreciated. They saw him as a person of great wisdom, as somebody who wasn't just the most feared bat in the lineup but actually a person who had something important to teach. Around them, Henry let his guard down, which he had not been able to do elsewhere. He could show the dormant, mentoring side of himself that had always been present in his first fourteen years in the big leagues. With them, he could show the smile that Buz Eisenberg said he never saw.

The fact was that whether it was when he was a kid or a big leaguer, Henry never did let a lot of people in. It just wasn't his way. Though neither would ever quite understand why Henry had chosen them to be the ones to enter his private space, Johnnie B. Baker and Ralph Garr were the exceptions.

When Garr tore up the Texas League, playing for Shreveport, with his speed and they nicknamed him "Gator" and he was called up to the big club for that September 3, 1968, game with the Mets, it was Henry who was the first to greet the youngster at the door, to tell him to wait for him after the game and the two would have dinner. Garr, believing that Henry was aware of the number of black kids who were called up to the big leagues, having no guidance and only fragile confidence, always recalled the first significant words Henry ever said to him: "What got you here is what's going to keep you here. Don't let anyone take that from you. Don't you forget that." Garr came from Monroe, Louisiana, and attended Grambling University. Six hours away from graduation, in 1967, he was drafted in the third round by the Braves and immediately reported to Double-A Austin. The minor leagues, even (or perhaps especially because of the civil rights movement) during the 1960s, could be a harsh place, and Garr thrived under difficult circumstances due to baseball men, many of them white, who took an interest in his success. There were Mel Didier, who signed him out of college, and Hub Kittle, his manager in Austin, who worked with him on footwork, first on the base paths and then in the outfield. There was Cliff Courtenay in Austin. And in the background was his father, Jesse, who told him there was no turning back, not during the times Ralph wanted to return home, as most black players did at one point or another. The white man was in control, his father told him, whether he came back home or whether he played baseball. So he might as well keep on playing.

It was Henry who taught him how to be a professional. Once, during an intrasquad game during spring training in 1969, Garr made a late read on a base hit to right but tried to score from second base anyway. Henry did not just make the throw that embarrassingly wiped Garr out at the plate by a mile but also galloped into the dugout to find Garr and explain *why* the kid had been embarrassed. Getting thrown out on the base paths was not always a big deal—that is, he told Garr, unless management believed you were thrown out for not understanding the situation. White players could get away with those types of mistakes, Henry said, but blacks could not. A black player who misunderstood an in-game situation could be branded for his whole career as unintelligent, Henry told him, and Ralph Garr was not an unintelligent baseball player. During this exchange, Henry was clearly recalling his own long years of enduring the humiliating caricatures from his coaches, teammates, and the press when he was a young player. He told Garr that no matter what else they did for the rest of their lives on a baseball diamond, black players who made mental mistakes early in their careers would never be allowed to live down those first impressions, even after their careers were long over.

"He was teaching me how to play the game. He said, 'You've got the speed, but watch the game. There was no reason for you not to score.' So he threw me out and made me a better player," Garr recalled. "Because of him, what I was trying to do was make sure I didn't make it hard for the next black guy who came up. Henry led by example, so *you* led by example. I wanted to show people that we weren't monkeys."

Away from the ballpark, Henry always picked up the tab, for dinners and taxis and the small sips of hard liquor he was known to take, but each check he picked up came with a lesson about being a big-league ballplayer, whether it was about leaving the proper tip or understanding which sections of town in a given city were best avoided. And the messages were always delivered the Henry way: He would not volunteer his wisdom easily. He would wait. If Garr made a mistake in judgment, he knew Henry would say nothing until Garr felt embarrassed, beaten down enough to ask for help.

One day, Garr asked Henry why he did not chew guys out when they were not meeting his exacting standards, just to get it over with. Eddie Mathews, for example, who would return to the Braves as manager in 1972, was extremely rough and unpredictable with players. "I'll never forget it. That wasn't who Henry was. Henry wasn't going to give you the answers. He wanted you to understand the reasons why he was going to say something to you, and that could only come when you were ready to listen," Garr said. "He used to say, 'If you give a man a fish, he can eat tonight. But if you teach him to fish, he can eat for the rest of his life.'"

Henry was pleasant to the rest of his teammates, and they often sought to bathe in his aura. But Henry Aaron was no Mickey Mantle, gregarious and inclusive, the clubhouse leader of the pack when the team landed in a city, a list of friendly joints and bartenders at the ready. Few people were ever granted the golden pass to Henry's inner circle. That was why Ralph Garr and Dusty Baker were vital, for Henry had not been as close to teammates socially since Mantilla and Bruton. As much as these young men fed off of Henry, the reverse was probably just as true.

Sometimes he would surprise the others, like the time in the early summer of 1967 when Tito Francona came over from Philadelphia. The Phillies had just played two games in Pittsburgh, then flown home for a series with the Braves. The next morning, June 12, Francona was informed he'd been traded to Atlanta, thus beginning one of those strange adventures in employment germane only to baseball. Francona woke up a member of the home team, intent on beating the tar out of the Braves, but by lunchtime, with a simple change of laundry, the enemy had become the good guys.

Francona had been a big leaguer for ten years, having joined Baltimore in 1956, just two years after Henry, and was thirty-three at the time of his trade to Atlanta. A couple of days later, the club was in Houston. Francona showered and headed downstairs for dinner, and there, sitting alone in the lobby of the old Rice Hotel, was Henry, who asked Tito where he was going.

"I'm going to get a steak, I guess."

"Do you mind if I come with you?"

"We used to go out all the time. Hank liked steaks, especially in the big towns like Chicago and New York," Francona recalled. "We used to go to have lunch before a ball game and we'd flip a coin to see who would pay."

Born in 1933, a year before Henry, John Patsy Francona came from a tough-knuckles section of Pittsburgh that everyone in the neighborhood referred to as "Honky Alley." It was a neighborhood of Hungarians and Italians, with some Jews and blacks, neither group large enough to threaten the order. The real threat during the years leading up to the war was having enough food on the table. When his son, Terry, would become a successful manager with the Boston Red Sox, Tito would always tell any of his friends at the ballpark to yell out "Honky Alley!" if they wanted a foolproof method for the boys from the old neighborhood to capture his son's attention.

In New York, Tito and Henry would go to Eddie Condon's to catch some jazz and a steak. On the plane, they would play hearts. Tito never stopped being in awe of Henry's ability, but he was not one of the players (and over the years there were many) on the team who tiptoed around the superstars. "I remember when I first come up, with Baltimore, first game in the big leagues, and you know I'm nervous. I got butterflies and all, so I get to the ballpark around six a.m. We're playing the Red Sox and I'm walking along the tunnel and I see this big number nine coming toward me—it's Ted Williams. And he says, 'Hey, you're Tito Francona.' And I'm thinking, How the hell do *you* know who I am? And he tells me he was once teammates with my roommate Harry Dorish, and Harry told him to look out for me. And Ted was great, gave me advice on hitting and everything, told me not to use such a heavy bat when the weather got warm.

"Henry had so much raw talent, it was unbelievable. I remember one game I batted after him. He hit a ball bad and he was so mad that he slammed the bat down onto the dirt and snapped the bat in half. Then he looks up and the ball went out of the ballpark. Imagine being able to do that."

In terms of being cultivated by Henry, Tito Francona was one of the lucky few over the years who not only held warmth and respect for Henry but shared some intimate times with him. Yet Ralph and Dusty saw Henry in a way perhaps no one else in baseball ever did. Dusty was different from the start, for no one in Henry's inner circle ever called him Hank. Hank was the name his talent created, something the sportswriters and the ball club and the fans used. To anyone on the inside not named Dusty, he was Henry. "I never noticed it, but I guess it's true," Baker said. "But he never corrected me, either."

With those two kids, Henry was totally engaged, treating them as members of the family, and because of Henry's connection to them, Dusty and Ralph became connected to each other. Both represented the third generation of black player, post-Depression, post–World War II men who had entered the big leagues with a different set of expectations both from baseball and from life. The Negro Leagues were gone and therefore no longer the expected destination, and ambition for blacks born after the war was a less dangerous commodity. Dusty Baker grew up in Sacramento, California. For a time, he had gone to college, but in 1968, he joined the marine reserves (volunteering for six years in the reserves wasn't foolproof, but it was the best way to stay out of Vietnam). In the marines, L. CpL. Johnnie B. Baker had shown leadership qualities and was given responsibilities, yet he entered the Braves system as a nineteen-year-old kid with something of a reputation for being free-spirited, a little disdainful of authority figures, maybe one to watch. And quietly, those in the Braves front office would nudge the big man to sort of keep an eye on Dusty. But Henry was already a step ahead of the suits.

And ahead of Henry was Dusty's mother, who when Baker signed with the Braves asked Henry directly to "take care of my boy." Henry, traditionally distant and cool to the younger generation, agreed to to do.

"There were times I got called in for going certain places or being with certain people. They asked Hank to talk to me about certain things. Other times he would take it upon himself, getting me up to eat breakfast, putting the room-service card, all filled out, outside my hotel door to make sure I ate, make me go to church, invite me to go to certain meetings, NAACP meetings and things, freedom rallies back then and stuff. He promised my mom that he would take care of me as if I was his son, which he did."

And it was there, by Henry's side, that Dusty Baker saw the world. It was also where he saw the deep contradictions of race. Dusty recalled that in general the white kids and black kids and Latino kids in California were all the same. They all played together and went to the same schools. Yet when Baker considered his idea of wealth in California, the memory was always the same: whites living in exclusive neighborhoods.

In Atlanta, Baker saw just the opposite: blacks living in wealthy and upper-middle-class districts but still racially separated on a day-to-day basis. Henry's southwest Atlanta neighborhood had a white-collar sensibility, and there were civil rights meetings. It was with Henry that Dusty met Sammy Davis, Jr., and Maynard Jackson and Herman Russell, power players in local and national politics. In Chicago, Dusty dined at the home of Jesse Jackson, with Henry, of course. In Los Angeles, Henry introduced Dusty to Flip Wilson. Backstage in New York, it was Ramsey Lewis, and the start of Dusty Baker's lifelong love affair with jazz. They used to joke that even when Henry and Barbara thought they were eating alone, Dusty and Ralph were probably under the dinner table.

"He was a fun-loving guy, but a serious guy at the same time. He was a complex guy, but an everyday guy," Baker said. "He only let certain people really in. He extended himself to everybody, but he only let really certain people get in."

In Atlanta, Ralph and Dusty were part of the family. Barbara would cook for them, and they treated her as a surrogate mother, because Dusty was still a kid.

"I was there so young, nineteen years old, I was closer in age to his kids and to the batboys, so I just hung out with them all the time," Baker recalled. "I couldn't go to bars and drink with those guys, so I hung with the batboys. Lary, Hanky, Gaile, and Dorinda, who was just a little ole girl. They're all like my brothers and sisters now. We'd just hang out at Hank's house. I'd go watch their football games in high school, stuff like that. . . . Kid stuff, you know?"

Being that close, closer than all the rest, it was Dusty and Ralph who could best see the growing tension between Henry and Barbara, and it was Dusty upon whom Henry would rely. "Barbara treated me like a member of the family. She treated me like one of her own. There were people around the ballpark who said this or said that, but I'm not one of them. I was around Hank when things began to go sour between them, and it was a hard time. I have nothing bad to say about Barbara Aaron. I watched Hank deal the way Hank deals with everything—he tried to keep focused. He didn't want to put his problems off on everybody else. Those times were definitely rough on Hank."

Henry and Barbara had been together for fifteen years, since they were teenagers, were together as dreams came true and were in the public eye as America confronted itself and came steadily apart. The players' wives were often a tight sorority, enjoying the fortunes of the baseball life, but it was different for black women. They were accepted as begrudgingly at the bake sales and charity events as their husbands often were on the ball field, but sometimes it could all be too much. In a 1995 documentary, Barbara would talk about the vitriol in the stands directed at the black players, her husband among them.

Too often, she had to sit and take it. The wives always did. The baseball world, first a boys club, then an integrated boys club, was never sympathetic toward her. Barbara was not popular among those in the Braves front office; they insulted her and Henry by accusing her of being behind his evolving politics.

And then there was the infamous evening of July 30, 1966, when Barbara entered the player's parking lot at Atlanta–Fulton County Stadium before a Braves-Giants game and the attendant at the entrance gate refused to allow her in. Words were exchanged, an Atlanta policeman intervened, and Barbara drove past. The officer, L. W. Begwood, ordered her to stop. What occurred next would become a matter of debate. Barbara would say that Begwood removed his service revolver from his holster. Begwood would say that he placed his hand on his weapon but did not remove it from its holster. What was not in dispute was Barbara's arrest and the subsequent three-week suspension of three Atlanta police officers involved in the incident. The publicity was bad all around—for the Braves, who in their first season were trying to cultivate a fan base in a racially tenuous city; for Henry, who called the officers "incompetent"; and especially for Barbara, who Braves officials thought overreacted. "That woman," a Braves official said, "drove everyone crazy."

Henry would not talk much about the details of his home life, but now it was coming apart, for too many reasons to count. Henry put on a good face—the best, in fact—and Ralph loved him for it. It went back to chopping the wood. "You could never tell at the plate what was going on with Henry. We knew he had his problems, but when he came to work—professional. He might have had the worst day at home, but when he got to the ballpark—nothing. Nothing got between Henry Aaron and his business."

And in return, he was their unquestioned hero. They called him "Supe," short for "Superman." And they called him "Hammer." And they called him "44." Maybe they didn't invent the nicknames, but they used them with such affection and reverence and *frequency* that Henry was transformed into a different person, always the silent backbone of a club, but certainly now something more. He was the wise elder for this new group of kids, and they did not do anything without checking with Henry first. "You could feel it. He was that guy that you did not want thinking any less of you," Ralph Garr recalled. "In the back of your mind, he was the standard. You didn't want to do anything that Henry wouldn't do. If Henry could be on time for the team bus, *you* could be on time for the team bus. If Henry could play hurt, *you* could play hurt. We saw him do things that just made everybody want to be that much more professional. You have to understand just how much we looked up to this man, what he meant to us. Nobody wanted to be the one to disappoint Henry Aaron."

During that time, there was another youngster, too, who looked up to Henry: Clarence Edwin Gaston, who went by the nickname "Cito," a Texan from Corpus Christi who had played in the Braves minor-league system in Waycross, Georgia, and Greenville, South Carolina. During the season in spring 1967, Henry requested that Cito Gaston room with him, and, quite likely channeling his own home life with Barbara, an education ensued.

"I had the fortune to room with a guy who was my idol growing up as a kid. He taught me how to tie a tie. He taught me how to be an independent thinker coming into the big leagues," Gaston recalled. "He taught me that no matter what happened in the game to forget it. If you had a good game, leave it at the ballpark. And if you had a bad day at home, don't bring that to the ballpark. He taught me about concentration." And he told Gaston that the inverse was also true, a rule he had been practicing firsthand as his relationship with Barbara declined: If you had a bad day at the park, don't bring it home and take it out on the family.

It was the ethic that Henry wanted to impart to the kids, and sometimes he could do it with a look. If Dusty was spending too much time in the trainer's room, it was Henry who could give him *that* look and Baker would have to reassess very quickly just how hurt he truly was. Maybe he *could* play after all. And then, suddenly, Dusty would be in the lineup. If Garr looked gassed in between games of a doubleheader but saw Henry, nearly twelve years his senior, taped and ready and dressed, suddenly Garr knew he had better find that extra fuel reserve, lest he drop in Henry's esteem. Being a professional meant playing through pain, and so what if Henry's pain threshold just happened to be abnormal. Somewhere, he would always remind Dusty and Ralph and Cito (who would be with him only in 1967, although Henry would have a lifelong impact on Cito Gaston) not to forget the special burden that came with being a black player. It meant playing with pain, leading by stellar example, and being accountable, for black players were quite often the easiest ones to be gotten rid of. Make it hard on them, Henry would tell the kids. Make it hard for them to get rid of you. And it was in that context that Henry would drop his famous credo on Garr. "He used to tell me all the time, whenever something hurt and I maybe needed a break. He would always point to guys that were hurt, or maybe hurt, and maybe they could play but they didn't, and he'd say, 'Ralph, you can't help your club from the tub.' "

And then there was the question that Ralph Garr swished around in his mouth, grading its texture before offering a verdict: how to anger the cool and even Henry Aaron. The answer would have far-reaching consequences.

"Cheating," Garr said.

"You want to make the man angry? Just cheat. That'll do it. Henry wants a fair match, what you got against what he's got. I remember one time in San Francisco and Gaylord Perry was on the mound throwing them spitballs. Henry fouled one off, and instead of letting the umpire or the catcher pick it up, *he picked it up*. Then he took it, rubbed the wetness off the ball, and *rolled* it back to the pitcher's mound, looking right at him the whole time. That was Henry's way of telling Gaylord Perry, 'I'm *onto* you, son.' "

. . .

THE KIDS LISTENED, but there was one who got away. When he first arrived in Bradenton from the dusty nothingness of San Pedro de Macoris in the Dominican Republic in the spring of 1964, armed with expectations of greatness but no road map on how to attain it, it was Henry who told Joe Taylor to put Rico Carty's spring-training locker close to his. Henry wanted to teach the kid, who spoke little English—and the bit he knew was accompanied by an accent that provided an easy target for enemies—about the big leagues, wanted to make sure he succeeded. Carty was a strapping presence—six three, two hundred pounds—who swung a bat nearly as viciously as Henry. He wasn't exactly in the millionth percentile, as Henry had been, but anyone who looked at Rico Carty, from his teammates to the manager Bobby Bragan, knew that if nothing else, Carty was a major-league hitter.

There was something in the way the kid wandered around camp that spring that reminded Henry of himself ten years earlier; a black player with ability whom no one seemed to be helping. Carty was unsure of himself. Learning language was not easy and, as Henry had learned from Felix Mantilla years earlier, the southern racial customs could be jarring to Latino players unused to the Deep South.

So it came to pass that Henry *requested* that Ricardo Adolfo Jacobo Carty room with him that spring. Henry watched as the press had its way with Carty, quoting him phonetically, as it did virtually all Latin American stars, the great Clemente included. "Already he ees showing me how to talk better, how to act, what to wear," *Sport* magazine quoted Carty as saying of Henry. "He make me feel big, too. He ees even showing me about HEETING!"

Henry worked with Carty, taught him how to position himself in the outfield and how to set up pitchers at the plate. To the writers, Carty referred to Henry as "compadre." Carty told the writers that it was Henry who was making him into a good player. He had taken a promising player under his wing.

Once Carty grew comfortable in the big leagues during that summer of 1964, when he finished second in the Rookie of the Year voting (even if it was to Richie Allen, eighteen first-place votes to one) and his numbers—.330, twenty-two homers, eighty-eight runs driven in—exceeded Henry's back in 1954, well, Rico Carty started to crave the lights of the big time, and, in turn, Henry became less mentor and more nuisance. Henry was too bland. Rico wanted to be big.

Carty began calling himself "Beeg Boy," and if rookies were supposed to be seen and not heard in those days, Carty created for himself a new paradigm. He was loud in the clubhouse, full of charisma and charm and bluster, at once endearing and annoying.

He moved with a swagger. If Henry was understated in dress and public comportment, Carty had adopted an outsized personality, prone to the kind of attention seeking that ran counter to how Henry believed a big-leaguer should carry himself. Henry ran the bases, caught the ball, and swung the bat with purpose. Carty brought flair and dash to everything, from fielding to interviews. When Carty did something great at the plate, he would run out to his spot in the outfield the next inning and doff his cap to the Milwaukee crowd, waving with both hands as if he had a chance to win the Wisconsin primary. Once, after Carty tossed a ball into the County Stadium crowd after making a spectacular catch for the third out, the Texan Bragan turned to his bench coach Dixie Walker, another southerner, and said, "You know something, Dixie? I believe that fellow is capturin' their imagination."

When he struck out, he would slam the bat into the dirt half a dozen times, charismatic, maybe, but bush-league stuff to the pros— the kind of shenanigans that could get you a fastball stuck in your ear the next time up. When he thought the blue missed one, Carty would spin his head quickly backward, ready for debate, showing up the umpire but commanding the stage. When Carty began to encourage his flamboyant side, it could only mean trouble with Henry, who once explained his demeanor thusly: "I don't smile when I have a bat in my hand. That's the time for business."

In the outfield, Henry taught Carty the classic method of catching the ball: run to the spot the ball will land and wait for it. That was the way the legends did it. That was how they made it look easy. When Carty began feeling he belonged, Henry's teaching went the way of the dinosaurs, and Rico would run at full speed, hat flying, buttons popping, only to catch the ball at his waist, a basket catch, with

Broadway flair. Some of his teammates believed the showman in him *purposely* started after easy flies late, to give routine catches an added panache.

In later years, Carty's act would have been considered normal, a perfect performance for the television age, for the me show that would one day define professional sports. But in the 1960s, baseball was still a newspaper game, run by men who possessed a healthy fear of the game's ability to humble, and humility was the only way to show respect.

"I don't know if I'm talking out of school, but Rico just rubbed guys the wrong way," Tito Francona said. "But Rico was kind of a showboat and a loudmouth.

"He had loads of talent, but not many guys liked him. I remember one day we're in the clubhouse and he's got *eighty* pairs of shoes, all different styles and colors," Francona recalled. "And some of the guys are laughing, and some are just looking at him. So, I go over to Felipe Alou and I say, 'Hey, what's *with* this guy?' And Felipe looks at me and says, 'Well, what would *you* do if you had been living in the jungle your whole life?' "

There was one other thing: Henry hated the word *nigger.* Whites had used it his entire life as a way of reducing black ambitions and self-esteem. But now in the 1960s, as blacks grew more empowered and less fearful of the old guard, many young blacks called each other "niggers," if not always as a sign of camaraderie, then certainly of familiarity. Joe Torre recalled Henry tensing whenever Carty tested the limits of obnoxiousness.

Then came the famous day, June 18, 1967, when it all erupted. It was on the team plane, flying from Houston to Los Angeles, the Braves collectively smarting after being no-hit by the Astros Don Wilson. Mike de la Hoz, Henry, and Carty were sitting in the back of the plane, while Tito Francona dozed in and out of sleep, vaguely interested in their game of hearts. De la Hoz always kept a bottle of rum in his satchel and during the game got a little rowdy. Henry told de la Hoz to put the bottle away, or some words to that effect. Francona, who had been with the club for less than a week, recalled the precise moment when the gunpowder had been sparked: Carty mumbling words in Henry's direction to the menacing effect of "I wish that bottle was mine." Somewhere during the exchange, Joe Torre recalled hearing Carty refer to Henry as a "black slick."

And in a flash, Henry Aaron and Rico Carty were throwing haymakers, big punches from big men with bad intentions, Henry an overhand right that dented the overhead luggage compartment above Carty's head, Carty connecting with a shot that struck Henry's forehead, Henry returning the favor. Tito Francona, now awake, stood between the two punching teammates, along with the traveling secretary, four-foot-two inch Donald Davidson, trying to keep from getting slugged.

"Then the copilot comes rushing back and wants to know what the hell is going on," Francona recalled. "He said he thought there was an emergency, because all the weight of the plane had shifted to the back. It wasn't an emergency. It was the whole team trying to keep those two guys from killing each other."

That was it for Carty and Aaron. No more mentoring. No more cards. From that day forward, Ralph Garr recalled, "Rico was just another teammate."

"A lot of guys would brag about the fight, or keep it alive," Francona said. "But you know what Henry said about it? Henry said the thing that upset him the most was that he embarrassed himself. He used to say it was the most embarrassing moment of his life."

To THE GUYS who mattered, the ones who played the game and bled the game and, as the bars closed, wept drunkenly because their passion for baseball was far greater than their actual ability to play it, the word *superstar* was no easy term, cavalierly tossed around like a Player of the Week award. In later years, when Marvin Miller broke management's hold over the players and the baseball free market became the envy of athletes (and union members) everywhere, money was often seen as the determining factor of worth. Even the average player who signed deals with too many zeros on the check to count believed that being paid like a superstar offered instant membership to the club.

They were dead wrong, of course, and deep down in their collective heart, they knew it: There was room for only a handful on the A-list.

Superstars, the precious ones who lived in the penthouse of the Hall of Fame, were different, and with the word came a responsibility that went far beyond just talent. Being in the Hall of Fame wasn't enough, and the players themselves were the best (or worst) at parsing and policing. Nellie Fox would enter the Hall of Fame, and so would Don Sutton. But that didn't make them peers of Rogers Hornsby or Christy Mathewson.

The A-listers were different, went about their business differently, from the silent sweat of Musial, the power and bombast of Ruth, the demanding elegance of DiMaggio to the furious pride of Robinson and Clemente. They could simply do things on a baseball diamond that defied the abilities of the other 99.9 percent. But the A-listers all had one thing in common: Each went to the World Series. If they didn't play for the big prize every year like the New York stars, then at least once in their careers the best of the best turned into a pack mule, carrying the franchise and the city to the top of the sport. They were the ones whose talent placed them in the millionth percentile, the ones who by simply being on a team meant the difference between winning and losing.

The experts would always say that for this one sport, baseball, one man could never be a true difference maker. How, then, to explain why in baseball the cream of the game, virtually without exception, always played for a championship? All of the New York superstars, from Ruth, DiMaggio and Mantle of the Yankees to McGraw and Mays of the Giants to Robinson and Koufax of the Dodgers played in the World Series multiple times. Hornsby? Cobb? Wagner? Greenberg? Foxx? Killebrew? Frank Robinson? Check. Stan Musial played in the Series in 1942, 1943, 1944, and 1946, Feller in 1948 and 1954, and Walter Johnson in 1924 and 1925. Clemente went twice, won twice. Even the big-spending, no-result Red Sox went to the Series in 1946, and MVP Ted Williams was the engine. Henry Aaron played in consecutive World Series before he was twenty-five.

There were more A-listers in football (Simpson, Fouts, Sanders, Sayers, to name a few) who never played for it all than there were in baseball, so the facts trumped the folklore after all: Top-shelf base-ball greats took their teams to the heights. Past or present, sixteen teams or three divisions and a wild card, the era did not matter: Carlton, Schmidt, Jackson, Rose, Morgan, Kaline, Brett, Yastrzemski, Clemens, Henderson, Jeter, Maddux, Winfield, Pujols, and Alex Rodriguez—all of them played for a title at least once.

History wouldn't yet be finished with Ken Griffey, Jr., but for the guys who hung up the spikes for good, the great exception was Ernie Banks. Banks was the smiling ambassador of Chicago baseball, and he had toiled diligently, never once having a team rally around him in return for his years of goodwill. For Banks's first ten years in the big leagues, the Cubs never even finished .500, never better than fifth place. In 1967 and 1968, with Leo Durocher revived and running the show, the Cubs finished third, and thus it was with shock and amazement throughout baseball that during the 1969 campaign it was the Chicago Cubs who were running away toward the pennant.

THE YEAR 1969 was all about change and reaction, from a nation still reeling over the Kennedy and King assassinations to protesting (or avoiding) the war in Vietnam to a man walking on the moon. And this was time for baseball, as well. The combination of television, football, and its own slow morass had rendered baseball yesterday's game. With baseball in desperate need of a paint job, the powers gave the grand old game a makeover: an east and west division in both leagues, with a best-of-five round of play-offs between the divisions' winners for entry into the World Series, plus a lowering of the pitcher's mound to give the hitters a better chance to hit the ball, an essential act of the sport that occurred less frequently during the 1960s of Gibson, Marichal, and Koufax.

There were cosmetic nods to the future and one concrete sign of change: Those perennial punch lines, the Mets, were lurking, within striking distance of the Cubs at the all-star break.

But the rest of the year was all about the past. Banks, now in his seventeenth year, in his eighth year as a full-time first baseman, reached back into the vault to fish out one last vestige of what he once was. He would strike out more than one hundred times—a great stain on the players of that era—for the first time in his career and would hit just .253, the lowest he had ever hit up to that point. But Ernie Banks was in a pennant race. And nobody thought that the running joke—"We could put a man on the moon before the Cubs reach the World Series"—might actually end in a tie.

On August 31, after the left-hander Ken Holtzman beat Niekro 8–4 and completed a three-game sweep of the Braves at Wrigley, the Cubs held a four-and-a-half-game lead over the Mets entering the final month of the season. Twelve days before Holtzman beat Niekro, he was no-hitting the Braves at Wrigley when Henry stepped up in the seventh. The wind was blowing in, and Henry still rifled a drive to left that cut through the wind, seemed to bolt out of the park, and broke up the no-hitter and the shutout. Holtzman turned and watched it head toward Waveland Avenue. Billy Williams, the left fielder, stood against the ivy. So much for the no-hitter, Holtzman thought. At least he still had the lead.

But suddenly, the wind began chopping at Henry's ball, beating it back down to the earth and into the field of play. Williams remained leaning against the wall, and the ball, which thousands of eyewitnesses say had once been physically out of the field of play, blew back in, landing in Williams's glove. Holtzman retired the remaining hitters of the final two innings and recorded his first no-hitter.

NEIL ARMSTRONG and Buzz Aldrin, alas, could relax after all. September, and the Cubs had never come along; eight straight losses to welcome the month later, it was the Mets, who for seven seasons had never done anything but lose, who were in control of the division, staring at the play-offs. New York would win one hundred games, win the division by eight over the broken Cubs, and Ernie Banks would be gone two years later to the land of handshakes and autographs for a living, having retired without ever visiting the promised land.

Another heirloom dusting occurred during the 1969 season. Nestled amid the Braves' new pinstriped home uniforms, the trading of Joe Torre to the Cardinals for Orlando Cepeda, and the inaugural, geographically challenged National League West, where two of its six teams—Atlanta and Cincinnati—were based in the eastern time zone, was the return of another oldie: Henry Aaron and Willie Mays fighting it out for a pennant.

So much of their circling over the years had been about ability and a place in the pantheon, air most mortals would be grateful just to breathe—Willie always on top in the public imagination, the pay scale, and the proximity to immortality by way of Babe Ruth's all-time home run record, refusing to make even a little bit of room for anyone else, with Henry unfazed by Mays's poetry and stardust, convinced of his ability to chop the wood with anyone ("No way was Willie a better hitter than me, no way," he would say) while consistently diffusing the very obvious and very real rivalry that existed between the two men ("I consider us the best of friends," Henry would tell the *Wall Street Journal*).

Mays began the season with 587 home runs, Aaron 510, and the narrative that Willie Mays remained the unquestioned leader of his generation still held. The Braves, meanwhile, tore apart their new division during April, with Henry hitting .397 for the month. The Braves held on to first place, though periodically relinquishing the lead to the Giants, Dodgers, and Reds as if handing off the baton during the 4x100 relay.

Then, near Memorial Day, Henry suddenly and completely transformed the summer. On May 30, Bill Hands of the Cubs shut out the Braves 2–0 at Wrigley, the continuation of the common summer theme of the Cubs pounding Atlanta into the dirt. But the next day, after a driving rain held up the game and turned the Wrigley turf into a dishrag, Henry started matters by hitting a two-out homer off Fergie Jenkins in the first. Jenkins and Niekro would engage in a numbing stare-down that wet afternoon, until the ninth, when Niekro blinked—a Ron Santo leadoff triple and a game-winning base hit by Don Young—and the Cubs had won again.

Another day, another loss, but this time without tension: In the finale, Pat Jarvis couldn't get out of the third inning and the Cubs pounded out sixteen hits and three home runs in a 13–4 blowout.

The Braves were dropping games and the race grew so tight, four teams could soon fit in the phone booth, as if all of baseball popped in new contacts, rubbed its eyes, and for the first time saw the sharpness and burst of colors, the baseball world in true focus, all in the Technicolor form of Henry Aaron.

He had homered in four consecutive games, would hit twelve homers during June off big cats like Jenkins, old friends like Tony Cloninger (who surrendered home run number 531), and the usual assortment of unlucky no-names. By the end of June, Henry had twenty-one home runs, but it wasn't the impressiveness of his single-season total that had brought him attention, but a quick recognition among those in the sporting world that Henry, not Mays, would be yelling "Timber" when the time came to shout at Ruth.

In the span of forty-five days, after Henry had hit his twenty-ninth home run of the year, a low, serious liner off Tom Seaver, Henry had passed Mel Ott, Ted Williams, Mickey Mantle, Eddie Mathews, and Jimmie Foxx on the all-time home-run list. There were only two men left, Mays, still playing at 596 home runs, and Ruth, at 714.

The writers calculated that Henry would also reach the coveted three-thousand-hit plateau inside of a year, a milestone only Musial had reached over the past half century. Before that, you had to go back into the scrapbook forty-four years, to Eddie Collins in 1925. Henry had been abandoned when the Braves wheezed during those past summers in Milwaukee and Atlanta and the club was out of the money, but they were alive again, and so was he, rewriting the record book each day he woke up. The Braves barreled into September, unable to shake the Giants but tough enough to avoid swooning themselves, and *Sports Illustrated* first came looking for Henry, and this was just the start.

HANK BECOMES A HIT

For years, Henry Aaron performed in comparative obscurity while compiling a record that makes him one of baseball's all time hitters. Now, as Atlanta fights for a pennant, he finds he is famous at last.

And it was there, with the arrival of the austere *Sports Illustrated*, that the stage for the next act began to take shape, and this stage would be a solo one. Mays would certainly reach six hundred home runs before Henry, but implicit in the story, for the first time on a national scale, was the inevitable passing of the torch: Pursuit of Ruth belonged to Henry, not Willie Mays. It was very clear that even when he reached six hundred, Mays certainly did not have 115 more home runs left in him.

That left Henry, and even though the magazine tacitly acknowledged he would run past Mays, it did not seem to believe Ruth was in any danger. "Since he is now 35, it is doubtful that Aaron will stay around long enough to hit the 176 homers he needs to pass Ruth, but attaining his 3,000th base hit is almost a certainty, and only eight men have ever done that."

Jim Murray, the legendary *Los Angeles Times* columnist, who had loved Henry's game since the 1950s, when the rest of the world was focused on Willie, was next.

MOVE OVER, BABE . . .
AARON'S PLAYING RIGHT

Are you one who appreciates the finer things in life? . . .

If the answer to the above is "yes," you have taste. Now . . . I am going to urge you to watch the telly. . . .

What Chippendale was to furniture . . . Henry Louis Aaron is to baseball. He is an unflawed diamond, a steak in a pile of hamburger, an Old Master in a room full of abstract junk.

The Giants were in first place on September 1, half a game ahead of the Dodgers, a game ahead of a surging Cincinnati club, and three up on the Braves, but while the teams staged a raucous pennant chase, the anticipated showdown of old lions never quite came to pass. Henry had held up his end, near the leaders in the usual offensive categories. Meanwhile, for the first time in his career, it was easier to look away from than at Willie Mays. In the final heat of the pennant race, Mays was barely an everyday player. At one stretch between August and September, he had gone 63 at bats without a home run, and for the first time in his career done something he'd never envisioned: He went an entire calendar month—July—without hitting one out of the yard.

Still, the two found a way to create electricity. The Giants and

Braves met Wednesday night, September 10, Pat Jarvis against Ron Bryant. The San Francisco team arrived in Atlanta holding a game-and-a-half lead over the Braves but just half a game ahead of the Reds. It was a night of raw nerves, exposed, on both sides of the field. There was the City Too Busy to Hate being exposed as the City Too Busy for a Pennant Race, as only 10,705 showed up to the yard with their first October on the line, exposing Atlanta's indifference to baseball. Willie Mays, a dingy shell of his Broadway star, grounded into a double play in the first, perked up by nailing a runner at the plate from center, and then allowed a cheap run to score on an error during the decisive seventh inning.

Henry continued to watch Willie grow faint in his rearview mirror: a long homer off Bryant in the fourth, plus two additional runs scored in an 8–4 win. The Braves took first place the next night, when Henry hit his forty-first homer of the year while Mays wore the collar.

Five days later, when the two teams met again on September 15 in San Francisco, Atlanta this time holding a game-and-a-half lead, with fourteen to play, Willie took a few whacks at the rocking chair, driving in half of the Giant runs (including a backbreaking homer) in a 4–1 win in the opener. Marichal was the story the next night, shutting out the Braves with a four-hitter, but Mays, not quite ready to go away, went two for four and drove in the only run that mattered, and the Braves were back in second place, behind the Giants by half a game.

For the fans who remembered (or cared to remember) the old Milwaukee Braves, the scenario was too familiar: inches from the play-offs, with a dozen games left, about to blow it. Understanding the history, wondering how many different ways the trapdoor could open was not an unkind question, especially because after getting swept by the Giants, the Braves went down the coast to Chavez Ravine, to the Dodgers, Jim Bunning, and Steve Stone. Bunning, fading, couldn't get past the fifth, but the two teams jousted. And then there was Henry, who rapped a couple of hits and a run scored as the rivals slapped each other around into extra innings. Henry led off the top of the twelfth against Ray Lamb and smoked a fastball into the seats for a home run, one made even sweeter in the bottom of the inning when Henry caught the final out, and still sweeter when the team arrived in the visitors' clubhouse, took a look at the fuzzy television in the room, and saw that Larry Dierker had outdueled Henry's favorite, that cheater Gaylord Perry, up in San Francisco. Henry had put the Braves back in first.

The Dodgers would win the next night, and then the Braves wound up and delivered the knockout punch: a ten-game winning streak to ice the division title on penultimate day of the season. The scheduling gods were kind: The Dodgers and Giants beat up on each other while the Braves sliced through San Diego (110 losses) and Houston. Henry, who had finished at .300, with one hundred runs scored, forty-four homers, and ninety-seven RBI, was back in the play-offs for the first time in a decade. A year earlier, the Braves would have been packing for the off-season, having won ninety-three games but seven short of the Mets for the pennant. Now, they were in the play-offs, a young, coalescing Mets club awaiting them in the inaugural National League Championship Series.

THE PLAY-OFFS were over in an eyeblink. The Mets, racing toward destiny, finished off the Braves in three straight, but each game showed Henry in his true incandescent light.

He had never liked New York, and yet he could not escape the big town. The New York Giants beat him in 1954. Brooklyn had kept him from the World Series in 1955 and 1956. He had played in the 1957 and 1958 World Series—both times against the Yankees—and here he was once more, in the postseason in New York, playing against a team that had not existed the last time he'd played October baseball. The first game, played under the pageantry of bunting, the first big-league play-off game ever in the state of Georgia, with 50,522 aroused for baseball, was tense and muscular: Seaver against Niekro, both bound for Cooperstown, Niekro giving up two early runs in the second, the Braves nicking Seaver for three by the end of the third, both teams trading runs, getting the nerves out.

Seventh inning, one out, 4–4 game: Seaver recalled the sequence. In an earlier at bat, he threw Henry a fastball, outside corner, on which Henry was a couple of days late. In a tie ball game, nobody on,

Seaver, all of twenty-four years old but winner of a league-best twenty-five games, figured he'd get ahead with the same pitch, which Henry sent sizzling into the left-field seats for a home run, 5–4 Braves.

Even Henry was no match for destiny. The Mets knocked out Niekro the very next inning with a five spot, and the Braves went quietly the rest of the way. As if discovering the painting on the living room wall was an original Rembrandt, the New York press swarmed Henry.

In the second game, the Mets beat Ron Reed, piñata-style. It was 8–0 before the Braves batted around the order for the second time. Before the series took on a decidedly lopsided shape, there was Henry. Down 9–1 in the fifth, Henry banged a three-run homer off Jerry Koosman to offer the crowd of 50,270 a faint breath, but the final score was 11–6.

The Braves went to Shea Stadium a loss away from death. Gary Gentry took the mound for the Mets, surrounded by pennant-thirsty crazies, pumping him up, readying for the coronation.

And there, once again, was Henry, who took a Gentry fastball four hundred feet for a first-inning two-run homer. Gentry would last but two innings. Up 2–0, Pat Jarvis couldn't stop the stampede. The Braves lost leads of 2–0 and 4–3, succumbing for the final time of the year, 7–4. The hero was a twenty-two-year-old right-handed relief pitcher named Nolan Ryan, who mopped up for Gentry by giving up just three hits and striking out seven in seven innings, and it was over.

The kids on the Braves already loved Henry—there was no question about that—but what he did against the Mets elevated him to an even higher plane. Afterward, the press mobbed Henry, as if it were his team going to the World Series instead of home for the winter.

In the three games, he hit .357, homered in each one. He had five hits in fourteen at bats; none were singles. Three home runs and two doubles, and none of his hits were cheapies, either, pile-on jobs that didn't affect the final outcome. Henry had given his team the lead or given them life. And though nobody knew it at the time, he did it, essentially, with one hand.

"We were off that night after we won the division, and I was with

Henry Aaron and Clete Boyer and some of the guys, and it rained," Ralph Garr recalled. "We were in a car and it slipped into a ditch. Henry was pushing the car and cut his hand on the headlight. It wasn't two or three scratches. If you looked at his hand, you would have thought he wouldn't have played in the play-offs.

"He didn't practice, didn't say too much, and now I'm scared to death. I'm thinking, What is Henry going to tell these people, and his team has got to play the New York Mets? Me and Dusty are talking in the clubhouse when the play-offs started and Henry walks in with Dave Pursley and the team doctor. They go into in the trainer's room, and they shoot Henry in the hand with Novocain, right in between his fingers. He puts on a black glove and hit .360. . . . After that was over, it brought chills to me. You had to see that, son. You had to see it to see what Henry Aaron did to exemplify what it meant to be a baseball player."

Henry packed his bags for the year and headed to the hospital, having played through gritted teeth all season with a sore back. There would be no World Series, and he would never again play in the post-season. But in the eyes of the country, he had been reanimated, reintroduced as a superstar. He had played brilliantly during the season and was even better in the postseason. In the meantime, a process had begun—not always undertaken with great enthusiasm—the walk toward a new chapter in his life, one that would define him as one thing only. If before the 1969 season he was, in Mickey Mantle's phrase, the "greatest, most underrated player in baseball," he would leave as someone who would never go unnoticed. He had not changed, and yet he had crossed an unofficial threshold: From that day forward, he was no longer Henry Aaron. He was the man chasing Babe Ruth.

THE TABLES TURNED for good right around Thanksgiving 1971, in Mexico City. Near the beach, Willie Mays was enjoying his honeymoon with his second wife, Mae, when he was accosted by an Associated Press reporter. It was there that Mays conceded what was once the unthinkable: Henry Aaron, and not Willie Mays, would likely pass

Babe Ruth and break the all-time home-run record, sometime in either 1973 or 1974. Over the previous two seasons, the hard truth has permeated the soil that Mays had become a legend in cultivating, and others would recognize it faster than Willie. He was the one who was bigger than life, the product of his transcendent ability and the New York superhero machine. And yet during the winter after the 1971 season, for the first time in a career consistently overshadowed by star players with more charisma, playing with better media, Henry was more famous than even Willie Mays. He had 639 home runs, still seven behind Mays's total of 646, but at this juncture Henry had never been closer to Mays's career total. For the previous three seasons, with Mays in steep, heartbreaking decline, Henry had soared—44 four home runs in 1969, 38 home runs and 118 RBI in 1970, and 47 home runs, more than he'd ever hit in a year in 1971. In the opposing dugout, Mays had grown old and ordinary—as the 1972 season approached, Mays hadn't hit thirty home runs or driven in one hundred runs since 1966, hadn't scored one hundred or hit .300 since 1965. In 1971, he struck out 123 times in only 417 at bats, proof that his eyes and reflexes had weakened to the point where he could no longer make consistent contact. When Willie was Willie, say in 1962, he'd come to bat 621 times and struck out just 85 times. Numbers were meant to be massaged to political and partisan ends, but here the numbers were forcing Willie to face the larger truth that his run as *the* elite player of his time had come to a close.

There was another number Hank achieved that Willie would not, the number of which everyone in baseball was most aware: In February 1972, Henry Aaron became the highest-paid player in the history of the sport, when Bartholomay signed him to a three-year, $600,000 deal.

This, too, was Willie's territory. Willie Mays had set the standard of salaries (at least for black players) for twenty years. Now Hank was making $200,000, the first $200,000 player ever. Actually, the real number was $165,000, as $45,000 per year was deferred over a ten-year period, semimonthly, beginning immediately after his retirement or on July 1, 1973—whichever came first—but it was still more than Mays, who was earning $150,000.

AARON—600G FOR 3 YEARS—
CALLED "HIGHEST CONTRACT EVER"

ATLANTA, FEB. 29 (UPI)—Braves' superstar Hank Aaron, the man with the best chance of breaking Babe Ruth's home run record, became the highest paid player in baseball history today when he signed a contract which will reportedly pay him $600,000 over the next three years.

He was never supposed to be the guy. He didn't hit home runs in the big, bombastic way home-run hitters do. He'd led the league in home runs four times but had never hit fifty in a year, the way Ruth or Foxx or Mantle or Mays had. Even when he hit his career-best forty-seven in 1971, there was always something else a little better going on: Mays and the Giants went to the play-offs, Clemente was great again—.341 batting average, a legendary, victorious performance in the World Series—and Joe Torre hit .363 and won the MVP.

The record was never anything Henry verbalized for print, but at increasing points after 1968, he began to hone in on Ruth, doing so in his patented way: by staring at the number 714 as if through a spyglass, assessing his usual performance, subtracting for possible injuries and performance decline, but, most of all, determining that the record belonged to *him*. Periodically, he would sidle up to Wayne Minshew of the *Atlanta Journal-Constitution* and say, "Hey, Wayne, do you think I have a chance at it?"

"It was Milo Hamilton, the broadcaster, who really started doing the math and vocalizing that the record was there for him," Minshew recalled. "And sometimes that created hard feelings. I remember one time Hank and Milo were in a feud and Hank said to me, 'I can break this record if this guy would just leave me alone.' "

Along the way, on May 17, 1970, at weathered Crosley Field in Cincinnati, came hit number three thousand, a first-inning single off Wayne Simpson, the first time Henry had beaten Mays to a major milestone—Mays would reach three thousand two months later. Henry had become the first black player to record three thousand hits, the first player in baseball history to reach three thousand hits *and* hit five hundred home runs. He had always said he would retire following his three thousandth hit, but by this point his priorities had changed.

Willie would never surrender the stage easily to the man who had always played in his shadow. In Mexico City that day, Mays told the reporter that, yes, Henry would likely break Ruth's record, but he didn't stop there. Before walking away, he added halfheartedly, "Maybe I will, too."

And for years, that's how it would be. They were not friends, and if Henry'd had his way, they wouldn't have been rivals, either, because Henry truly seemed to admire Willie. The two men lived the American story with more similarities than differences. Both were black children of the Depression-era South, the defining characteristic for each. Both were unparalleled on the baseball diamond. As they aged, the similarities increased. By 1972, both men had been divorced— Barbara filed in 1970, after seventeen years of marriage, citing mental cruelty. Henry did not contest the filing, saying only that they had "grown apart." In the smoldering shadow of Robinson, neither man felt appreciated for his position on civil rights. Neither—because of his financial position and inherent conservatism with regard to power—lent enough personal clout to the elimination of the reserve clause, the rule that kept players bound to their teams for life, kept them from the money that would change the game. When Curt Flood took baseball to court, Aaron and Mays were both curiously silent. Allowing players to become free agents, Henry told the Associated Press, would be disastrous for baseball. Mays went a step further, criticizing Flood for being ungrateful to the game.

It was true that Henry Aaron was not uninterested in yapping back and forth in the papers and closed up about Mays to avoid the headaches of he-said/she-said journalism, but there was also something about Willie that wouldn't allow a real friendship with Henry. Willie wouldn't, or couldn't, ever give Henry his due as a great player, and that inability on Mays's part to acknowledge Henry as an equal was what really burned Henry.

Periodically, Mays would soften, both men apparently recognizing there was little margin for either in fostering a narrative of the two greatest black players, from the same state, no less, at each other's throats.

"I'll see how it goes," Mays said about pursuing the record along with Henry in February 1972. "But a long time ago I said Hank would pass me, and if I happened to quit within the next year or so or when he does, I'd be happy to present him with the ball that he hits out of the park."

For years, they had fought for position, but in 1954 and part of 1958 and for the whole pivotal seasons of 1959 and 1969, they fought for pennants, too, their numbers virtually identical, their legacies cemented; they were the difference between New York and London—a can't-miss either way, just depended on one's preference. Over those years, Henry had gone out of his way to praise Mays. During the Fred Haney years, when he grudgingly accepted Haney's decision to play him in center field, Henry would joke about how he would never make an all-star team because he now played the same position as Willie, a self-deprecating comment that underscored Henry's admiration for Mays and his confidence in himself. In interviews, Henry did not miss an opportunity to say Willie was the best player going, and in later years he would acknowledge Mays's contribution in easing the way for black players, first through his barnstorming team in the 1950s and later by becoming the first black team captain in baseball history. Mays was the first black player in the history of major-league baseball to be called the greatest player of all time by the mainstream, and Henry often concurred with the opinion. Around 1971, there was the story circulating around baseball about Tal Smith, then a young executive with the Houston Astros. The tale went that Smith kept two autographed baseballs at his home, side by side, one signed by Henry Aaron, the other by Willie Mays. One day, Smith's house was burglarized and the thief swiped the Aaron ball, while leaving the Mays ball in its place. Henry handled the story deftly. "All that proves," he said, "is that there's a crook in Houston who can't read."

Willie returned the favor by giving Henry back nothing. When Henry began to soar up the home-run chart, Willie was loath to give even a partial nod to Henry's ability, choosing instead to blame his own performance on his home turf, Candlestick Park, saying it was a lousy park in which to hit homers and that this was the reason for Henry's onrush. The disadvantages of Candlestick were especially obvious in comparison to that bandbox Atlanta–Fulton County Stadium, famously dubbed "the Launching Pad."

The problem wasn't that Willie was a proud and fiery competitor, but that he didn't give Henry *anything*, not even an acknowledgment that for the first twelve years of Henry's career, he played in a symmetrical park, County Stadium, whose dimensions did not favor him, while Mays played the early part of his career at the Polo Grounds, where the foul lines did not even measure three hundred feet. Mays's comment on the evening of April 27, 1971, in Atlanta, when Henry hit career blast number six hundred, ironically against San Francisco, was a prime example of this attitude. "Hank might just catch Ruth," Mays said backhandedly after the game. "He's playing in the right parks."

Willie never hit well in Milwaukee, for power or for average. From 1953 until 1965, Mays hit in County Stadium as a visiting player in his prime years and tallied a .289 average with thirty home runs in 199 games. Yet in his 2010 authorized biography of Mays, the author James S. Hirsch wrote, "Mays believes he would have hit eight hundred homers if he had not gone into the military and played in parks like Aaron's." That was what burned Henry: Willie couldn't stop slapping him in the face.

Mays did lose two years to the army, and certainly at twenty-one and twenty-two, he would have had a better-than-average opportunity to record the fifty-five home runs he would fall short of to surpass Ruth. So much of why the relationship between Mays and Aaron was perceived, often rightly, as tense, if not acrimonious, stemmed from their personalities—the self-centered Mays and the diplomatic Aaron.

After years of being asked about his own feats, Mays almost certainly must have resented at some level being asked now more about Henry. Take the end of spring training, when, during an interview session, Henry was asked about his chances to catch Ruth. "I think I can make it if I stay healthy and if I have a strong man batting behind me, so they won't pitch around me."

When the scribes asked Mays the same question, Willie's response said it all: "Well, he has to catch me first."

. . .

MAYBE MAYS DIDN'T mean to sound like a jealous rival. Maybe it was simply Willie's professional nod to the cruelty and unpredictability of the fates, for it was true that to reach the top shelf, everything had to go right: You had to play in the right park at the right time, you had to avoid missing time, and you couldn't get hurt. Ted Williams might have been the one to beat Ruth, had the Splinter not missed nearly five years to war, and played in a park, Fenway Park, where the right-field power alley was a cavernous 380 feet. Williams was generally considered the best hitter who ever lived, but he hadn't reached three thousand hits. Neither, for that matter, had Ruth or Gehrig. Maybe it wasn't jealousy, but it sounded that way. It sounded as though Willie couldn't accept the truth: Mays had the memories and the prose, but statistically, Henry had the numbers.

And that wasn't all there was. For his generation, Mays exemplified the rare combination of physical, athletic genius and a showman's gift for timing. What went less reported and, as the years passed, became an uncomfortable, common lament was just how cruel and self-absorbed Mays could be.

The veracity of one story would never be completely ascertained because Henry would refuse to discuss the details, but Reese Schonfeld never forgot it, and he believes every word of it to be true. Schonfeld would make his career in the television business, becoming a business associate of Ted Turner during the early years of the rise of cable television.

But in the summer of 1957, Schonfeld was just a kid, twenty-five years old, in Boston, excited to be sent to the Polo Grounds to interview the hottest player on the hottest team in baseball, Henry Aaron, and getting paid fifty dollars for the assignment.

"It's July 1957, I'm working for United Press/Movietone news, and I'm up at the Polo Grounds, on assignment from WBZ Boston to interview Milwaukee Braves manager, Fred Haney, left-hander Warren Spahn, and the new phenom, Hank Aaron. WBZ wanted the interviews to promote the upcoming Jimmy Fund baseball game between the Braves and the Red Sox. The Jimmy Fund had been created by the Braves when they were still the Boston Braves, and they returned to Boston every year to help raise money for the Dana-Farber Cancer Institute in the name of 'Jimmy,' a pseudonym for a twelve-year old boy who was a patient there. It was Aaron's first appearance in the game, and his potential for greatness was apparent to all. The Boston fans wanted to see him in action.

"The Braves were playing the Giants in a twi-night double-header. We arrived about five p.m., set up our camera in foul territory, just off third base. Haney emerged from the dugout, did the interview, plugged the Jimmy Fund, and then sent out Warren Spahn. Spahn told us how much he missed the fans in Boston and looked forward to seeing them shortly. All good PR. Then out came Aaron. Aaron was different. The Boston fans had never seen Aaron. WBZ had asked me to talk to him about baseball, particularly about his wrists, supposed to be 'the quickest wrists in all of baseball.'

"As we changed film for the new interview, Willie Mays came trotting in from center field, where he had been shagging flies, and knelt just on the fair side of the foul line. Dusk was falling, we had no electrician, and I had to finish the interview before the light faded entirely.

As we focused on Aaron, the cameraman measuring the distance between the lens and his subject, Mays started ragging on Aaron: 'How much they paying you, Hank? They ain't payin' you at all, Hank? Don't you know we all get paid for this? You ruin it for the rest of us, Hank! You just fall off the turnip truck?'

"Aaron is getting more and more agitated. Fred Haney trots out and explains to Aaron: 'It's the Jimmy Fund—it's charity. It's okay.' We begin the interview then to get a better shot of his wrists; we move the tripod. Now Mays lays it on thick: 'You showin' 'em how you swing? We get paid three to four hundred dollars for this. You one dumb nigger!' And he laughs. Finally we were done. Aaron shakes his head, I thank him, but half angry, half bewildered, he spits at my feet.

"When he gets back in the dugout, Haney tries to calm him down. It doesn't work. Mays has gotten into Aaron's head. Haney recognizes it and takes Hank out of the lineup. He plays not at all in the first game; in the second game he pinch-hits and walks. Willie had harassed Hank right out of the batting order. The *New York Times* cites the Mays-Aaron 'years of friendship.' I wouldn't bet on it."

If the idea that Henry Aaron, leading candidate for National League Most Valuable Player and one of the toughest, most focused clutch players in the history of the game, could be psyched out of the lineup by pregame chatter, even from Willie Mays, sounded apocryphal, it was. On July 21, 1957, just as Schonfeld recalled, the Giants and Braves did play a twi-night doubleheader at the Polo Grounds. In the first game, the Braves behind Spahn held a 4–3 lead into the bottom of the ninth, but the Giants rallied for two runs off Don McMahon and won, 5–4. Mays went one for three with a double and a run scored. Schonfeld's memory fails him in that Henry *did* play in the first game, walking as a pinch hitter in the eighth. Dick Cole pinch-ran for Henry.

Henry did not play in the nightcap, a 7–4 Braves win, but it seems apparent that his absence had nothing to do with Mays. Four days earlier, in a 6–2 win in Philadelphia, Henry went on a rampage, a perfect day: three for three with a mammoth home run off Harvey Haddix, two batted in and two walks, one intentional. In that game, he injured his ankle. He missed the next three games and wouldn't start again until July 23 in Milwaukee against the Phillies. The ankle injury, and not Mays's banter, is the more likely explanation for why Haney would scratch Henry before a doubleheader in the middle of a pennant race. It also explained why Henry, second only to Bruton as the fastest man on the Braves, would be removed for a pinch runner in a tight ball game. Clearly, he had attempted to return to the lineup too early and couldn't run.

Nevertheless, the important kernel in Schonfeld's recollections is how Mays apparently treated Henry that day, and Henry's reaction for the next fifty years—to diffuse, while not forgetting, the original offense—would be consistent with the shrewd but stern way Henry Aaron dealt with uncomfortable issues. The world did not need to know Henry's feelings toward Mays, but Henry was not fooled by his adversary. Mays committed one of the great offenses against a person as proud as Henry: He insulted him, embarrassed him in front of other people, and did not treat him with respect. Such an exchange was not the kind Henry would be likely to forget. As they say in the news business, Schonfeld stuck by his story.

"I was just a kid, and it was exciting to me to be there. It was pregame. There was nobody in the stands. I wanted to interview Warren Spahn, and I remember them playing a joke on me, because I was a rookie, too. They sent Burdette out. Luckily, I knew what Spahn looked like," he said. "You could see Hank was getting really worked up through the interview, and I thought we did a really good piece. I don't think he spit at me, but it was at my feet, like something left a bad taste in his mouth.

"Willie was calling him 'farm boy' and saying stuff like 'You're in the major leagues now.' I specifically remember Willie using the word *nigger*, but I didn't think a lot about it, because that was how a lot of blacks talked to each other. I always thought it was bench jockeying, or maybe Willie just didn't like to see the next guy coming up being just as good as he was."

BY THE EARLY months of 1972, time was breaking Henry, too. He reported to West Palm Beach in February and headed straight to the trainer's room. His ankles hurt, and so did his right knee, injured in a home-plate collision during spring training, and his back had hurt for nearly three years. And that was how in 1972 Henry would play 105 games at first base, both to ease his physical trouble and, mostly, to replace an injured Orlando Cepeda, as well as Rico Carty, who had shattered his leg.

On the good days, Henry would tell the writers during spring training that he felt like he was a kid again. "I feel like I'm eighteen again," Henry said. On the bad days, when his right knee would buckle and bite, he explained he had not elected to have off-season surgery because of his age. And there was the matter of his arthritic neck, which seemed to flare up with regularity.

The season did not start on time—the first-ever players strike made sure of that—and when it did, Henry victimized the Reds (first Don Gullett, then Jack Billingham) and then the Cardinals (Bob Gibson, then Rick Wise) during a four-day stretch in April at Atlanta–Fulton County Stadium.

Ten days later, on May 5, he returned the favor in St. Louis with a two-run shot off Gibson. The next day, May 6, 1972—also known as the forty-first birthday of Mr. Willie Howard Mays, Jr.—Henry caught Wise again, for career home run number 645. Willie, meanwhile, hadn't yet hit his first of the season. Henry was one behind Mays. Nineteen games into the season, hitting .184, with no bombs and three RBI, on May 11, the spiral was complete: The Giants traded Mays to the New York Mets for pitcher Charlie Williams (who would produce an 8.68 ERA for his new team) and fifty thousand dollars in cash.

The showman was back on Broadway, in his town, and Mays provided a nostalgia burst. May 14, in his first game as a Met (against the Giants, of course), Mays walked and scored in the first, then broke a 4–4 tie in the bottom of the fifth with a home run that stood as the game winner, 5–4 Mets. At Veterans Stadium in Philly a week later, May 21, Mays shook that year-old concrete bowl. This was a Phillies team that would win just *fifty-nine games* all season, and yet on this night they weren't pushovers, because of Steve Carlton, who would win twenty-seven games all by himself. The Phillies led 3–0 in the sixth with Carlton, on the hill when Willie led off with a double and scored on Tommy Agee's home run. On his next at bat, with one on in the eighth and the Phils up 3–2, Mays broke Carlton's heart with a two-run homer, for a 4–3 Mets win. The leader was *back*.

Willie would be respectable for the rest of the year, hitting .267, but alas, that was it for the heroics. On May 31, at Atlanta–Fulton County Stadium, Henry Aaron caught Willie Mays with home run number 648, a first-inning drive off San Diego's Fred Norman that snaked around the left-field foul pole.

WEDNESDAY NIGHT:
AARON TIES MAYS FOR 2D PLACE

It took Hank Aaron 18-plus seasons to catch Willie Mays. His next target is Babe Ruth's record.

Aaron hit his 648th home run Wednesday night. . . .

Aaron also became the second player in history to ·attain 6,000 total bases, reaching 6,001. The record of 6,134 belongs to Stan Musial. . . .

Ten days later, also at the Vet, Henry passed Mays with a little sizzle of his own: a grand slam against hulking six-foot-six-inch, 215-pound Wayne Twitchell.

Henry would never look back. He would never chase Willie Mays again as much as he would stalk the record book, passing whoever was next on the page. For the first time in his career, that next person was not Willie Mays.

Now, Henry made a marathoner's final kick toward Ruth. Atlanta hosted the All-Star Game in 1972, the first held in the Deep South, the young blazer Jim Palmer against the old pro Bob Gibson. Palmer froze Henry with a called strike three in the first and Mickey Lolich induced a lazy fly to right. But in the sixth inning, down 1–0, Henry faced his favorite spitballer, Gaylord Perry, and launched a two-run home run to deep left-center field. It was the first home-run hit in an All-Star Game in Atlanta.

The rest of the year, he followed this star turn, backing up his forty-seven-homer year with thirty-four more in 1972. That put him at 673 for 1973. The hype machine, which had generally left him alone during the 1960s, had returned for a sober, often unflattering reappraisal: to assess whether Henry was worthy of surpassing the iconic Ruth. As early as the end of the 1971 season, as Henry assaulted the record book, the combination of journalists who pointed out that Henry's consistency did not match Ruth's dominance and a segment of the public that sent him death threats returned the favor.

And it was there that Henry Aaron retrenched. He had escaped Mobile. He had realized his talent, played the game hard, and yet for all of it he was being reminded that none of it mattered, that he was again reduced, in his words, to "being just another nigger."

THERE WAS PERHAPS no better barometer that Henry was now a central figure in the national conversation than that fact that he was included in the comic strip *Peanuts*, Charles Schulz's daily masterpiece.

Schulz was the most famous cartoonist in America, and more: *Peanuts* uniquely represented the heart of the American mainstream as well as baseball's place in it. According to Schulz's biography, by

1967, the strip appeared in 745 daily newspapers across the country and in 393 Sunday papers. According to United Feature Syndicate, more than half of the nation's population made the travails of Charlie Brown part of their daily reading.

Even in the funny pages, Willie held dominion. "It's kind of fun now and then to use the names of real people in my comic strip, *Peanuts*," Schulz once told Mays biographer Charles Einstein. "And after looking over about twenty-five years' accumulation of strips, I discovered that I used the name Willie Mays more than any other individual. I suppose it's because to me, Willie Mays has always symbolized perfection."

Yet from August 8 to August 15, 1973, Schulz featured Henry, and it was a seminal moment for each. Henry was national now, and it was widely assumed that as he continued his ascension, he could pass Ruth in 1973. As such, he had taken over some of Willie's real estate.

Simultaneously, Willie had fallen once and for all. Though his team, the New York Mets, would advance to the World Series, Mays would play out the rest of the 1973 season hitting .211.

Schulz created a prescient story line, where Snoopy needed one home run to break Babe Ruth's home run record while facing a hostile public. If Henry had always been handicapped by playing in markets that were a shade below prime time, Schulz, in his ubiquitous way, had elevated Henry and the politics of the chase into the mainstream discussion, while at the same time providing a clever, biting social commentary:

Snoopy [wearing a baseball cap, reading a letter on his doghouse]: "Dear Stupid, who do you think you are? If you break the Babe's home-run record, we'll break you! We'll run you out of the country. We hate your kind!"

Charlie Brown: Is your hate mail causing you to lose any sleep?

Snoopy [now lying flat on his doghouse, a rising tidal wave of letters hovering high over him]: "Only when it falls on me."

CHAPTER THIRTEEN

RUTH

ALL WEEK LONG, Bob Hope dreamed of naked people. In the morning, he could see them, bare feet tramping blissfully across the cool, crunchy grass, bodies flapping, arms cutting feverishly in free release through the humid air. When Hope lay down to sleep, the naked people followed into his bedroom, giggling with delight as they ran him straight into ruin.

It was perfection that stood at the center of his anxieties, and so far, even as ulcers pierced his gut, he felt he was close to achieving it. He believed he had done everything right in managing the demands of Henry's pursuit of Ruth, and now, following the first week of the 1974 season, Henry stood on 714 home runs, an eleven-game home stand all but guaranteeing that Bill Bartholomay's engineering to have Henry break the record in Atlanta would pay off.

Hope had tried to provide Henry with some semblance of personal space, an oasis to ease the ordeal. Hope loved baseball so much that he was all too aware of Roger Maris—the last person to challenge Babe Ruth—and all that his team, the New York Yankees, had not done for him in 1961, when Maris would break Ruth's single-season record of sixty home runs. With history in mind, he was determined to protect Henry. Once, during the chase, word got out that the Braves had arranged for a dying boy to meet with Henry briefly before a game. "He had leukemia. He was dying and he asked can he meet Hank Aaron. Well, suddenly our phone started ringing, and with every one of these calls, every kid had one disease or another," Hope recalled. "As the pressure is growing and we're getting faster and faster toward the record, I go to an NL meeting, and the league adopted a rule that no youngsters would be allowed in the dugout before games. I told Hank we had all these requests and now we could get out of it. I told him I could get him an extra twenty minutes. And besides, I told him that all these kids, well, most of them, aren't sick. I can just tell them it's against the rules. So we go back and forth and I keep telling him, 'Hank, they aren't sick.' And Hank said, 'Yes, but some of them are.'

"So after it's all said and done, years later I'm walking through an airport or something and a man stops me and recognizes me as being part of the Braves. He tells me that his son got to meet Hank Aaron and not long after that he died on the operating table. So you can imagine how I felt."

Hope was convinced that he had successfully executed the virtually impossible balancing act of providing Henry privacy without alienating the throng of journalists, well-wishers, and dignitaries who wanted to be close to him.

Over the winter, he and his staff had updated a growing pamphlet chronicling Henry's career; the booklet had now swelled to dozens of pages, opening with the words "The Greatest Sports Story in America Is Taking Place in Atlanta." The Braves had issued daily press credentials to an average of four hundred journalists per day, forcing Hope to open the football press box at Atlanta–Fulton County Stadium for the spillover. "It was," Hope said, "like doing public relations for two teams at once: the Braves and Henry Aaron."

Bob Hope did not fear the alleged assassins who were now attracting so much attention. Since the early part of 1972, when the mathematics of Henry hitting 715 home runs grew closer to a certainty, and his was the only name to challenge Ruth's record, the threat of death increased. Carla Koplin served as Henry's personal secretary and Calvin Wardlaw, an off-duty Atlanta police officer, was assigned to Henry as a personal bodyguard. As ubiquitous as his home run total were the letters he would receive from his fellow Americans, guaranteeing his death should he continue the quest.

Hope believed that so much of the talk of murdering Henry Aaron was just that, the work of a lunatic fringe just unbalanced enough to threaten anonymously and ruin Henry's peace of mind, but not sufficiently motivated to kill. The letters Henry had received were real enough, and existed in great enough volume that Hope was not cavalier about the possibility of violence. But Hope felt that the combination of the FBI, the Atlanta police, and the two-man personal security force of Wardlaw and Lamar Harris would be sufficient to deter any maniac who may have thought his bullet could change history.

Instead, a more likely and embarrassing image continued to dominate his thinking: the sight of Henry Aaron hitting the momentous record-breaking home run, rounding first under a deafening, triumphant roar, the nation and the world's journalists chronicling every detail of the moment by typewriter, microphone, and television camera, Ivan Allen's dream of the country focusing its collective eyes on Atlanta for something other than the collision between blacks and whites at last realized. And then Hope could see the rest of the scene unfolding in his mind's eye, almost in slow motion: Henry rounding second and then, there they were, a couple of streakers running onto the field, as naked as the day they were born, zigzagging away from security, probably freaked out on LSD, upstaging Henry, embarrassing the Braves, baseball, and the city of Atlanta, his perfect night lampooned for all time.

"That's all I could think of," Hope recalled. "Can you imagine that? You have to remember that those were the days of Morganna the Kissing Bandit and kids taking off their clothes and jumping onto the field. At that moment! We would have never, ever, lived something like that down."

BOB HOPE WAS convinced that by virtue of his connection to Henry, who was challenging the home run record, he was party to something truly historic, especially in the South. The arc of his own personal life told him so, for a black person attaining such a valued place in American history in of itself represented the promise of dignity for black people that had not existed during his upbringing. Hope had grown up in the twin gulfs of class privilege and racial segregation, a classically southern motif, in an affluent section of Atlanta. His parents and grandparents routinely used the word *nigger* in their common speech, as did all of their friends. The Hope family owned a vacation home at Lake Lanier, in Forsythe County, and for years a black maid, a woman named Johnnie Lue, worked for the family.

When he was a teenager, Bob Hope was constantly frustrated by one of his responsibilities, for it cut into his free time: When the family stayed at the vacation house, he was to keep track of the time, for Forsythe County was a sundown town: No blacks were allowed within county limits after dark, and the Hope family had to shuttle Johnnie Lue out of town or risk both violation of local ordinances and their standing in the eyes of their white neighbors. "When I was sixteen, I had to watch the sun because she had to be out of the county before the sun went down," Hope recalled. "I knew it was a law, but it was a pain in the neck. It's hard to fathom that there was a time when these things were considered normal."

When he was a teenager on the football team at Northside High School in Atlanta, his coach explained to the team why Northside never played the local black high school, even though the schools were but a few miles apart.

"Clearly, growing up in the South, if you were white, you didn't have an opportunity to be around blacks. I went to high school and graduated before they had integrated sports. We had only two blacks at our school," he recalled.

"It wasn't like you had anything against them, but you hadn't affiliated with them, either. My parents and grandparents still used the N word. The white South didn't understand the black South. The black South was still a novelty. You didn't go to the same places. You heard about the colored water fountains. When I was a kid, I thought 'colored water' meant that the water was a different color, and as a kid, you wanted to drink the colored water. Then you learned the Negroes were segregated. You read the newspapers and you realized that Martin Luther King, Jr., was there. You understood what they were marching for was fair, but you didn't understand the full magnitude of what was going on."

When Hope attended Georgia State College, just ten years earlier, the law prohibited blacks and whites from competing together in the major college conference in the region, the Southeastern Conference, in either basketball or football, and now Henry was about to break a record considered unassailable, set during the tail end of the most aggressive period of segregation since Reconstruction. That the home-run record had been established at a time when blacks were not allowed to play in the major leagues carried its own degree of meaning. It was as if breaking the record would signify the hard-won fall of another barrier in the struggle for acceptance, proof of the illegitimacy of keeping blacks out of the game in the first place, proof of all that could have been possible years earlier. Henry identified with the words of Buck O'Neil, the Negro league player and manager who had never been granted the opportunity to test his skills against the great white players in the major leagues but would become the first black scout in the major leagues, discovering Ernie Banks and Lou Brock for the Chicago Cubs. "Just give us the chance," O'Neil often said, "and we'll do the rest."

PUBLICLY, HENRY ADOPTED a typically American position. He was just another in a line of kids who in this country could grow up to be anything, do anything, if they put their mind to it, he said. It was a convenient path to follow, because it made America feel good about itself and its possibilities. Henry appeared grateful and not resentful that the opportunity for blacks had been so long in coming. On March 20, 1974, an article under Henry's byline appeared in the *Montgomery Advertiser*, with Henry writing, "The Babe is a legend now. He created more excitement than any player who ever lived.

"What I find so hard to believe is that Hank Aaron, a nobody from Mobile, Alabama is the first player in 40 years to challenge that home-run record. How did it come about?"

What was clearer than the myth America liked to tell itself was how breaking the record would represent the fall of another domino in the acceptance of black athletes in professional sports, and the speed at which the old rules were being rewritten by force of time and personality. Robinson destroyed the belief that blacks weren't talented or disciplined enough to compete alongside and against whites. Ali changed the way the black athlete could express himself to the public. By challenging the all-time home-run record, Henry represented a third front: the black athlete at the top of a team sport who would break a record held by a transcendent white athlete.

By 1974, Bill Russell had been retired five years. He had won eleven NBA championships and become the first black head coach in mainstream American professional team sports, winning two championships as a player-coach. Wilt Chamberlain had statistically dominated his sport as no athlete since Ruth. Jim Brown retired as the all-time leading rusher, but in becoming the most prolific runner in his sport, Brown accumulated only numbers. He did not surpass a player who held the public imagination in a way that rivaled Ruth. In basketball, Chamberlain was every bit as dominant as Ruth in baseball, but basketball, if not exactly a fringe sport, did not define any substantial portion of America, nor did the sport's records. Who was the all-time leading scorer in NBA history before Chamberlain was a trivia question hardly even basketball fans knew the answer to.

Apart from Ruth, the sports icon with whom white America most closely identified may have been Jack Dempsey, the richest, most popular heavyweight champion of his day, and Dempsey would not fight black challengers. Joe Louis beat Jim Braddock, thereby winning the heavyweight title, but he and Jesse Owens made their initial mark nationalistically, as Americans, defeating Germans, not other Americans, for even though Louis beat the American Braddock to win the title, it would be his knockout of Max Schmeling that catapulted him into the American conscience, the symbol of American values at a time when the world faced its own larger questions of morality. Preparing to attend the first game of the Braves home stand against the Dodgers in hopes that Henry would break the record was the Georgia governor and future president, Jimmy Carter. Carter had already contributed to the anticipated celebration of Henry's victory by announcing an executive order: The state's prisoners would get right to work on a new commemorative state license plate that would read HENRY—715. Carter remembered that night in 1938 when Louis beat Schmeling and won the title, and he at once understood the deep roots of white superiority toward blacks, and by extension, this illustrated to him how Henry's surpassing Ruth would seem even more offensive to the white sense of superiority than Schmeling's losing to Louis.

Carter recalled how the whites along the dirt roads of Plains, Georgia, had rooted for Schmeling, and he could remember the roars of the black citizens down the street when Louis destroyed Schmeling in the first round. "For our community, this fight had heavy racial overtones, with almost unanimous support at our all-white school for the European over the American," Carter wrote in his book *An Hour Before Daylight*. "A delegation of our black neighbors came to ask Daddy if they could listen to the broadcast, and we put the radio in the window so the assembled crowd in the yard could hear it. The fight ended abruptly, in the first round, with Louis almost killing Schmeling. There was no sound from outside—or inside—the house. We heard a quiet 'Thank you, Mr. Earl,' and then our visitors walked silently out of the yard, crossed the road and the railroad tracks, entered the tenant houses, and closed the door. Then all hell broke loose, and their celebration lasted all night long. Daddy was tight-lipped, but all the mores of our segregated society had been honored."

Babe Ruth had held the all-time home record not for forty years, as Henry and most of America had once believed, but considerably longer. While it was true that Ruth retired in 1935 with 714 home runs, he had actually taken over the major-league lead in his eighth year in the big leagues, in 1921, when he hit his 139th homer. His record actually stood for fifty-three years. When Ruth hit his final home run in 1935, he had merely piled on his own record, as he had for fourteen years. Like Jimmy Carter, Bob Hope also felt a certain swell of civic pride that baseball history was going to be made, in Atlanta of all places, and, like Carter, he believed that even something as ephemeral as a sports team had contributed to the rehabilitation of their city. And that meant that despite the discomfort, the problems, the history, and the countless number of instances when it appeared that *change* was a dreamer's word, life in the South had actually changed dramatically. A year earlier, in 1973, Maynard Jackson, a proud descendant of one of Atlanta's most venerable black political families, the Dobbs family, was elected mayor. Carter recalled that in the years before he became president, a generation of white liberal politicians had quietly played a historic role in toppling the old order.

THE RECORD WAS going to be broken on his watch, Bob Hope thought, and on whatever night it occurred, it had to be a moment that would be remembered for all the right reasons. The first game of the home stand, Monday night, April 8, against the Los Angeles Dodgers, would be the first test of Bob Hope's expectations and preparations. Henry's father, Herbert, would throw out the first ball. Maynard Jackson and Jimmy Carter would be there. The team had arranged for Pearl Bailey, one of Henry's favorite vocalists, to sing the national anthem. The actor Sammy Davis, Jr., who had been periodically involved in trying to put together a movie deal for a biopic of Henry's life, would try to attend. Everything would be perfect. Hope believed that the night the record fell was not going to be just something that baseball fans remembered but that it would be a demarcating line in American history, another seminal moment signaling that whatever America was, it would no longer be from that day forward. That was why the naked people frightened him so much. They were the unpredictable variable. They were the one thing that could turn a seminal moment in America into a sideshow.

THE ENTIRE WINTER reminded Henry of what he wasn't able to do in 1973. On September 1, Henry stood at 706 home runs. There was nothing else to that season for the Braves, who epitomized the word *mediocre.* They had reached the .500 mark just once during those 162 games, when Henry broke a 1–1 tie in the sixth on April 12 in San Diego with career home run number 675, this one off willowy left-hander Fred Norman. The Braves won the game 3–2 and their record was 3–3, after which they would lose seven straight, and by that time, the competitive portion of the season was effectively over. The rest of the year was focused more on Henry and Calvin Wardlaw and Carla Koplin and hate mail than on winning the National League West flag.

At certain points, his stoicism would lapse, and Henry would then reveal just how sick of it all he had gotten. In the great pantheon of the game, only Ruth had hit seven hundred home runs, and during the challenge march came another drumbeat: There was only one Ruth. Baseball people, the crusty old-timers like Bob Broeg in St. Louis, made a point that Henry may have produced numbers but that Ruth was bigger than the game, the universe, life itself. Henry had played more games than Ruth, had come to bat a gazillion more times, and would have had to hit 250 homers in a season to outhomer every team in the league, as Ruth had done in 1921, and therefore Henry was not the man Ruth was. The comparisons were endless, and to Henry, they were insidious in their obvious insinuations that he was not worthy of the record.

The exact date Henry's imperturbability seemed closest to cracking was July 17, 1973. Nine days earlier, at Shea, he had single-handedly trashed the Mets—two for three, two homers—crushing the big left-hander George Stone. Stone was built like a house, six-three and 210 pounds. He and Henry had been teammates for six years in Atlanta, but now George was a Met, and Henry took him over the fence in the fourth and then again in the sixth. On the thirteenth, Bill Stoneman, the Montreal pitcher, threw Henry a mistake with two on in the fifth in Atlanta for a three-run homer and home run number 697.

On the seventeenth, against Philly, Dusty Baker, as only he and Garr could, cornered Henry in the dugout to try to pull him out of the darkness with humor. He hadn't homered in five days and had grown weary of the constant cosmic question of when he would hit number seven hundred. He was tense, annoyed, and exasperated, but he hadn't snapped. Baker saw that Henry walked around the clubhouse as if he were wearing a beauty mask, trying hard not to move a single muscle in his face. Baker angled up to Henry, holding the knob of the bat as a microphone, imitating Howard Cosell. "Hank, what do you have to do to hit seven hundred home runs?" he asked.

On this day, even Baker couldn't rescue Henry. He had not come this close to cracking since he blew up at Milo Hamilton years earlier, a confrontation so involved that Bartholomay and the front office had to broker a peace treaty. But now, Henry was having a Roger Maris moment, Ralph Garr thought. Once, in 1961, when asked one time too many if he believed he could break Ruth's single-season home-run record, Maris finally cracked, responding in a group interview session, "How the fuck should I know?"

But even on the edge, Henry did not break. He composed and steeled himself. There had been weaker, despairing moments, like the time the writers had at last left his locker after a home game and he turned to Bob Hope and pleaded softly to be left alone. "I just want to play baseball. That's it." Hope realized that Henry began to tear up; he was talking more to himself than to Hope.

At this moment, Henry looked at Baker, one of his protégés, gave a wan smile, and said before walking away, "How? Hit three more home runs. That's how."

Hours later, up 6–1 on the Mets in the sixth, Henry belted a Tug McGraw meatball into the left-center bull pen. Three days later against the Phillies, facing Wayne Lee Twitchell, another man-mountain at six-six, 220 pounds, Henry stepped in, down 5–0, with one out in the seventh, and cranked another; this one glanced off the BankAmericard sign in left-center field. The next day, the steamy Saturday afternoon of July 21, Ken Brett, with one on in the third, threw a weak fastball that Henry crunched into the seats in left, over the bull pen, and seven hundred was complete. The Braves immediately painted the seat red to commemorate the moment.

Only 16,236 fans showed up for Henry's seven hundredth, the Atlanta fan base thereby solidifying its reputation for being ambivalent to baseball. That wasn't even the worst of it, which happened to be the official baseball response to Henry's achievement. Nothing. Not a phone call or telegram congratulating him from Bowie Kuhn, the commissioner of baseball.

For two years, Henry had played it cool where baseball was concerned. He said nothing bothered him, not the pressure of the chase, not the hate mail, not the death threats that arrived by the bucketful so often on stained composition paper, the suffocating press coverage, or even the unwinnable comparisons to Ruth.

Bowie Kuhn, the commissioner, however, had insulted Henry. It would never be quite clear why Henry held Kuhn in such high esteem. The two had no previous history and it wasn't as if this commissioner was particularly fond of the players. Marvin Miller had been installed as the head of the surging Major League Baseball Players Association and he had begun to establish a new, empowering orthodoxy: The commissioner was not your friend. The commissioner was not your ally. The commissioner was not impartial. The commissioner of baseball, despite the rhetoric of using his power in the "best interests of baseball" actually used his power in the best interests of the clubs. After all, the owners hired the commissioner. If the commissioner were a nonpartisan advocate for players and owners alike, the players would have input in who actually got the job and who kept it. There was, too, the biggest of disconnects that Miller passionately imparted to the black players: No commissioner ever used his "best interest of the game" power to integrate the sport. One—Landis— actively kept blacks from playing, for it was not a coincidence that integration moved quickly after Landis's death in 1944. Nevertheless, Henry seemed to possess respect for the office of the commissioner. He was, if nothing else, a believer in the hierarchy.

If Henry had his reasons for his drive toward beating Ruth's record, people like Bowie Kuhn represented an important motivation. Kuhn was a member of the baseball establishment, first a long-time lawyer for the league before being elected commissioner in 1969. He was arrogant and uninterested in the larger tapestry of black achievement or in much beyond maintaining the power of the elite. Kuhn was an unimpressive thinker, unable to recognize the speed of change taking place in his sport and society in general. He was unprogressive, and his inability to acknowledge the reserve clause as untenable (and recognize Marvin Miller's superior intellect) cost the owners billions of dollars and years of control. His comportment was one of a man who believed himself above being held accountable to players. He was condescending and seemed totally unaware that Henry saw right through him.

The commissioner would say that he did not want to set the precedent of congratulating every player for their daily milestones—hitting for the cycle, their 100th double, 135th win, and 1,000th hit—as if he or any baseball fan had been fans when both Ruth and Aaron had reached their individual milestones. He assured Henry that he hadn't shown up for his seven hundredth because he was saving his appearance for the *big one*, when Henry broke Ruth's record. As the news cycle mushroomed, Kuhn and Henry conversed days later and the commissioner made Henry a promise: "I'll be there for seven hundred and fifteen."

Two weeks later, before the Braves played the finale of three games the perennially lost Cubs, the Reverend Jesse Jackson invited Henry to be the breakfast speaker at a gathering sponsored by Jackson's organization, Operation Push. During the late 1960s, as Jackson and Henry both gained national prominence, the two formed a budding friendship. At a south-side storefront, Henry was greeted by an overflow crowd of black Little League teams, black Boy Scout troops, and community organizers. Standing tall and athletically next to Henry, Jackson wore an olive T-shirt with green horizontal stripes and a dark collar, sporting a full Afro, a mustache, and muttonchop sideburns. Jackson was thirty-one at the time and had been a collegiate athlete. With his familiar oratory, Jackson introduced Henry:

He refused to defile his body and refused to have his mind defiled, and because he's overcome staggering odds we look to him as a success model, as one who represents the very best in our people. When we look at Hank, there's something on the outside in his presence that tells us that we can achieve, and because he's just like us, there's something on the inside that tells us that we deserve to achieve, and if he can any man can.

Henry stepped to the podium and addressed the crowd. A poster stood on the wall behind him, red bordered in gold, in the center a black silhouette of the African continent. Henry was dressed fastidiously but stylishly—a brown suit and eggshell shirt—a brown striped tie with a double Windsor knot:

I would like to read to you this morning a letter I received from Chicago and I consider this a real good letter, considering some of the letters I've gotten in the past, and it reads as follows:
Why are they making such a big fuss about you hitting 700 home runs? Please remember you have been to bat 2700 more times than Babe Ruth. If Babe Ruth came to bat 27 [*sic*] more times he would have hit 814 home runs. So Hank, what are you bragging about? Let's have the truth: you mentioned if you were white, they would give you more credit. That's ignorant. Stupid. Hank, there're three things you can't give a nigger: a black eye, a puffed lip, or a job."

In delivering the punch line, Henry gave a genuine laugh, because even gallows humor could be funny in the right crowd, and here with

Jackson, surrounded by black faces, he was protected, in a positive environment, by his people. He beamed the thousand-watt smile that had been suppressed by fog for the previous two years, the one that even Dusty Baker could not lift. Then he continued:

> And it went on to say the Cubs stink, stink, stink, and gave me a phony name and address at the end. But these are the kind of letters I receive, and when I was talking about hate mail, this is a good one compared to some of the others. So I consider this a good one. Things like this just make me push a little harder, because just as Reverend Jesse Jackson said, first of all, growing up in Mobile, Alabama being a black person, I already realized I had two strikes against me, and I certainly wasn't going to let them get the third strike against me. I figured that being a baseball player, there was only one way to go, and that was up.

A few hours later, Henry hit home run 702 at Wrigley, and then 703 and 704 the next two nights at Jarry Park in Montreal. The next one came at home, against the Cardinals, off of a weak slider from the Canadian right-hander Reggie Cleveland. He hit seven during the month of September, to finish with forty for the season, but, sitting on 713 on the final day of the season in Atlanta, in his final at bat, with the Aaron shift on against Houston pitcher Dave Roberts, he popped up weakly to second. It was over until 1974.

IT HAD ALWAYS been true that Henry found his solitude in the winter, when the baseball season had finally ended. The regular season provided no respite. At home, Henry was smothered under the crush of interview requests and public appearances. On the road, Henry had set up an elaborate plan to create a sliver of privacy: two hotels on the road, one that remained empty under the name Henry Aaron, the other—where Henry actually slept—listed under the alias A. Diefendorfer. When he was young, Henry would find the most secluded spot on Three Mile Creek and sit on the banks of the river in Toulminville, fishing and skipping rocks, usually with his friend Cornelius Giles, hidden from view. At thirty-nine, he took to the water anew, on the seventeen-foot speedboat he'd bought as a refuge, first going out into Polecat Bay and then north up the Spanish River toward Grand Bay. Henry also owned a twenty-seven-foot cabin cruiser, which he would use when he ventured south into larger bodies of water, taking down into the mouth of Mobile Bay and beyond. "It's the only place," he said of his boats in 1973, "where the phone doesn't ring."

That Henry escaped along the rivers toward the mouth of the Gulf of Mexico was somewhat incongruous, for his mother, Stella, had always discouraged him from going near the water. Even now, when he was almost forty, the owner of two boats, Henry could not swim well enough to save his own life. Yet, throughout his periods of turmoil, it was the inky waters of Mobile Bay to which he turned for catharsis. His routine was often the same: He would arrive in Mobile without warning, sneaking in a day or so early. Quite often, he would not even tell Herbert or Stella that he would be arriving, for with fame there was never any such thing as a secret. But the locals in Mobile, the ones who worked in the restaurants and the hotels, always knew when Henry was coming to town. The good ones, the ones who knew a day early, would understand, of course. But the ones who weren't connected, who found out that the great Aaron had just blown through town, unseen (*again*), began to wonder just what Henry held against Mobile, so concretely and for so long. The locals were proud of him; that was all. They couldn't exactly be blamed, either, for it was no secret that Henry's relationship with Mobile was complicated. Even when he was in his mid-seventies, there would be people in Mobile who believed Henry could never quite forgive the city for its past, for what it had done to Herbert and to so many other black men. But during the fall and winter months of 1973, Henry did not advertise his visits anywhere. One day of warning could ruin the entire purpose of the trip, which was to escape, to indulge in a moment of peace.

Safely in Toulminville, Henry would contact his brother Hebert junior, who would contact Joseph Coleman, one of Henry's old classmates, who was known as an expert with a boat, rod, and reel. Calvin Wardlaw, always armed, always watching, would be with them, as well. Sometimes, there were others, but those invitees always came at a moment's notice. On the water, Calvin enjoyed Henry best. Henry would reminisce about Mobile, point out the physical markers of his history, drift into the years that belonged to him, long before he was Hank. And it was in these moments, too precious to last, when Henry recharged, watching Joe Coleman, soft-bellied and shirtless, his torso mimicking the winding river: vertical for a moment before curving wide and growing expansive. Herbert junior looked casual in his plaid pants, the group sauntering down the river in search of croakers and bass. Croakers were the toughest ones to catch, Henry said, because once caught, their gills popped out, felt like needles.

Henry would sit in the boat, his legs dangling over the bow, like a twelve-year-old surrounded by grown-ups, the only man of the group who always wore a life preserver. He would sit on the edge of the boat, rod in his right hand, soaking in the pieces of himself that seemed so difficult to keep, immersed less in the camaraderie than in the serenity surrounding him, the chopping waters, hunched trees, and faint lavender of the wisteria, the elements upon which he would rely for regeneration.

IN DECEMBER 1973, Henry announced he had signed a five-year, one-million-dollar personal-services contract with the television manufacturer Magnavox. Henry would do commercials, make public appearances on behalf of the company, and grace virtually every Sunday paper in the country, standing next to a shiny Magnavox color TV in a full-page ad.

To the outside world, Henry stood in an enviable position; the breaking of Ruth's record would produce even greater financial opportunities. He was already the highest-paid star in the game. Things were moving quickly. Sammy Davis, Jr., flew Henry to Beverly Hills to discuss a movie project, tentatively titled *The Hank Aaron Story*.

What was not so well known at the time was that Henry was teetering on the verge of financial collapse, and he had signed the exclusivity deal with Magnavox (though he likely could have commanded more than a million) as a sure way to begin reversing his sinking

finances. When he first arrived in Atlanta, he teamed with a consortium of white businessmen for a barbecue restaurant start-up in
southwest Atlanta. The restaurant was called Hammerin' Hank's, and
the initial goal of the business plan was for the first restaurant to be
the centerpiece of a powerful local chain. The restaurant disappeared
faster than one of Henry's home-run balls into the night. Not long
thereafter, Henry connected with another business partner, who
enticed him to think big and invest in sugar futures, a risky enterprise, which sounded better than it actually was. When he looked at
the balance sheet, Henry saw he had lost twenty thousand dollars.

Then, soon after Henry signed the richest contract in baseball history, came the big fall. In the spring of 1972, Henry finalized a three-
year, $200,000 contract. He immediately teamed with two investment
bankers (men he would refuse to name) and gave them power of attorney—which is to say, complete control over his finances. His pay-
checks were signed over directly to them. The firm invested his money
for him, and it was so easy, he was told, he didn't have to lift a finger.
Over the ensuing months, Henry proceeded to hit home runs, make
the all-star team, and lose his shirt. Finally, his secretary, Carla Koplin,
suggested that he hire an auditor to check out where his money was
going and investigate the firm's legitimacy. Henry would tell the story
that when the auditors arrived, they found that the firm did not exist.
Their offices were vacated and the two men had blown town.

The swindle had damaging implications. Following the 1965 season, Henry had begun thinking about his future beyond baseball. He
had just completed his twelfth season and started to take the long
view that he naturally could not play forever. In 1966, for the first
time, he began deferring portions of his salary for when he retired, so
he would still receive income. That year, Henry's salary was $70,000
and he deferred $20,000 for future payment. The following year,
Henry received a raise to $92,500, with $42,500 to be deferred, disbursed in semimonthly cash payments following his retirement.

In 1973, Henry earned $165,000, with $50,000 to be disbursed
over a ten-year period beginning at retirement. As he grew more
involved with his real-estate and restaurant ventures, Henry needed
cash flow. On June 12, 1973, he took out a bank loan of $300,000

secured by the Braves. As part of the agreement, Henry made a handshake deal, verbally agreeing to repay the loan—$10,000 per quarter, or all of the cash flow from the project, whichever was greater. When the project went bust, Henry was on the hook for the loan, $40,000 per year.

When he totaled the damage, Henry figured he'd lost his entire life savings, well in excess of one million dollars. His lawyers told him he had been taught an expensive, cautionary lesson and that perhaps he needed to file for bankruptcy. There was only one way to assess where Henry stood during 1973 and 1974.

"I was wiped out," he said.

EVEN THE OFF-SEASON could not protect him, and during the final months of 1973, Henry's problems at least rivaled the discomfort of his fame. On November 12, 1973, a month before the Magnavox deal was announced, on November 14, 1973, Henry married Billye Williams, a former Atlanta television host, in a private ceremony at the University of the West Indies chapel in Mona, Jamaica, after nearly three years of dating. But after hearing about the Magnavox deal and his $200,000 baseball contract, Barbara wanted more money. Not long after he became the home-run king, she took him to court to get it. He was the highest-paid player in baseball, and the two would trade accusations, his that she was obstructing him from spending more time with his children, hers that now that his income had increased, so should her alimony, from $1,600 a month to $16,000.

AARON SUED FOR TENFOLD ALIMONY

ATLANTA, JUNE 3 (AP) — Hank Aaron's former wife filed a petition in Superior Court here today seeking an increase in the alimony and child support payments she currently receives from the Braves' baseball star.

Barbara Aaron said the Atlanta Braves' slugger was earning about $100,000 a year when they divorced in February 1971, but now earns "in excess" of a million dollars per year.

Years later, he would discuss these years with a fair amount of regret, saying that in some instances he had become what he had always dreaded: the rich ballplayer with no money. "I was easy, just like so many athletes today," he recalled. "It's not easy when you don't know anything about nothin' and you have all this money." He had been careful about frivolities, enjoyed being famous without the extravagances that would define the modern-day athlete. He drove a 1973 Chevrolet instead of a Porsche, wasn't the kind of player who wore a shirt once and threw it out, and yet in the months before he would break the record, he was broke.

Once the Magnavox deal was finalized, Henry began to prepare for spring training with an eye on the future. On February 5, 1974, he turned forty, and Henry had resolved that he would endeavor to make massive changes with regard to business matters. Taking better care of his finances was a given. He would be more involved. He would learn the businesses that carried his name. Women, cars, and clothes were easy, high-profile ways to lose it all, but so, too, were bad investments.

"I was angry, but I wasn't helpless. I still had my name and time to recoup," he said. "I decided to be more careful with my money."

HE DID NOT approach the challenge of breaking Ruth's record, at least privately, with self-deprecation, that "Aw, shucks, fellas" immodesty. Now that it was in sight, surpassing Ruth, being the best there ever was at hitting home runs, if not an obsession, something he craved, and now he had to wait for the entire offseason. One day in Mobile, he told Stella that he wanted the record. "He said, 'I want a record of my own,' " she recalled. To his mind, because he was so close, it was as if the record already belonged to him, and that was where his mind played such cruel tricks on him, where life teased and taunted him with its power over him and destiny, where he knew he was at his least potent. At the tail end of the 1973 season, a piece entitled "Henry Aaron's Golden Autumn" appeared in *Time* magazine. It was clear in the article that he had begun to smell the record. "I've always read Mickey Mantle, Willie Mays, Roger Maris—then Hank

Aaron. I've worked awfully hard to get my name up front," he told the interviewer. "I've waited for my time, and it's just now coming."

Still, the forces of life, Henry knew, were far more difficult to face than any hard thrower on the mound. The batter's box was the easy part. That was where Henry was king, the most powerful man on earth, in control of every facet of his life—but only at that moment. Guaranteeing that he would have another opportunity to stand in the box, to dig in and take the record in his hands and claim it for his own was another story altogether.

When his mind wandered, it brought him back most vividly to the dynamic Clemente, who had reached his three thousandth hit on the final day of the 1972 season and never lived to see the new year, killed in a tragic, unnecessary plane crash over the Caribbean. He thought about Roy Campanella, the Dodgers catcher headed for the Hall of Fame when the 1957 season ended, but after a terrible car crash on January 28, 1958, would not walk or use his hands ever again. And there was always Jackie, who had seriously thought of playing for the Giants in 1957, but then he climbed out of bed one day and life made the decision for him: He crumpled to the floor, betrayed by an arthritic knee that would never again cooperate. And maybe those nut jobs out there with their pens and their pads and stamps weren't as blustery as Bob Hope thought. Maybe he would walk down the street and one of them would see his chance, size Henry up, and take it all away with a single shot.

"I don't want to wait," Henry said when a reporter told him there was no need to worry, that he was so close to the record that it would be his within the first month of the 1974 season. "You can't wait. Look at Clemente. What would have happened to Roberto Clemente if he had waited?"

THE INVENTORY LIST for the Braves home opener looked as though it belonged to the Macy's Thanksgiving Day parade instead of to a baseball game. Bob Hope had the final figures and details for the evening: five thousand balloons, dancing girls, and two bands. For the eight previous home openers in Atlanta, an average of seventeen policemen had been assigned to work the game. But for the ninth, the April 8, 1974, home opener, the Atlanta Braves versus the Los Angeles Dodgers, that number would increase to sixty-three. Joe Shirley, the team director of security, discussed with Bartholomay the possibility of a riot when Henry hit his 715th home-run ball, so Shirley had mapped out a strategy to combat a potential free-for-all: The left-center-field bleachers had been designated ground zero, since that happened to be Henry's power alley. Shirley would dispatch six policemen, four security men, and eight extra ushers to the left-center bleachers, with the intention of keeping order should the record breaker land in the same spot as so many of his balls in the past. The grounds crew was working to beat the forecast of intermittent rain, but they were professionals, so there was no reason to worry. Nearly a full day before game time, they had completed painting a red-white-and-blue replica of the map of the United States across shallow center field: 140 feet by 80.

Hope's celebrity overtures had borne fruit. Pearl Bailey was no longer just a wish. She was on board, having agreed, per Henry's request, to sing the national anthem. Sammy Davis, Jr., had not only confirmed that he would attend but had already offered the Braves $25,000 for the home-run ball. Herbert Aaron would throw out the first pitch and both he and Stella would be part of the pregame festivities. Hope had concocted a program that would resemble the old TV show *This Is Your Life*. Herbert and Stella would stand in Alabama on the painted map, representing Mobile. Hope had contacted John Mullen, the old Braves executive who had signed Henry from the Clowns. Mullen would represent Indianapolis. Donald Davidson would stand on Boston, where the Braves were located when Henry signed in 1952. And Henry's first big-league manager, Charlie Grimm, would appear, standing in for Milwaukee. Around the chain-link outfield fence would be eight-foot-high letters that read ATLANTA SALUTES HANK AARON.

There would be no fraud, Bill Acree, the Braves clubhouse man was assured. Acree had been given the responsibility of guarding the specially marked baseballs that had been used for Braves games since Henry hit number seven hundred. It was one of the details that had been a colossal pain for the pitchers, since these were the years before memorabilia would become an industry, pitchers having gotten annoyed that a perfectly good ball was being tossed aside whenever Henry stepped to the plate. In a certain way, the pitchers felt Henry was being given an advantage, because a fresh ball was just a bit slicker, harder for a pitcher to grip. Any disadvantage to a pitcher, no matter how slight, tipped the scale in favor of a hitter of Henry's skill.

These were also the years before milestones had become marketing opportunities, moments to be captured and manipulated, and, of course, profited from. That made Bill Bartholomay the villain in the pinstriped suit, again ahead of his time for all the wrong reasons. In his first at bat in the first inning of the first game of the 1974 season in Cincinnati, April 4, Jack Billingham—who had already surrendered home runs number 528, 636, 641, and 709 to Henry—threw a sinking fastball that Henry on his first swing of the season, redirected toward the left-center gap and over the fence to tie Ruth. The businessman in Bartholomay saw potential disaster, and Bob Hope's ulcer-riddled stomach began churning anew. With eight more innings in the opener and two full games remaining in Cincinnati before the Braves went back to Atlanta to play their first home game of the season, Henry could conceivably break the record on the road, in the antiseptic bowl that was Riverfront Stadium, and rob the Braves of at least one sellout home date and possibly more. After the game, Bartholomay would tell his manager, Eddie Mathews, to sit Henry for the remaining two games, which inflamed Kuhn, who ordered Henry to play. The players had never respected Kuhn in the first place. Before the next game, Pete Rose walked to the batting cage and yelled out to Joe Morgan, "Hey, Joe, you playing today? Did you check with the commissioner?"

Given the kind of reaction Bartholomay would receive, he would have been better off fixing the World Series. The outcry would have been less. When Kuhn stepped in and ordered Henry to play in at least one of the remaining two games, which he would do, that only made matters worse, since Henry had never quite gotten over the commissioner refusing to acknowledge his seven hundredth home run. "For that," Bartholomay would recall thirty-four years later, "I got really pounded in the press, but I thought our fans deserved to see the record. I thought it was only fair to Hank, after all he went through to have the opportunity to break the record at home."

Henry's ball burned through the crisp Cincinnati air like a comet, over the heads of Billingham, Dave Concepción at short, and Pete Rose in left, before returning to earth somewhere in the seats in left center. Cornered by the press hours later, Billingham would explain his yielding a home run to Henry Aaron with a forlorn inevitability, a guy who had left his umbrella at home during a rainstorm. "I was behind three and one, so I wanted to come to him. Well, I came to him, but it didn't come like I wanted it to. It didn't sink. That was a mistake and a mistake to Henry Aaron is a home run."

The game was being televised on Channel 17, and for the people of Atlanta, Milo Hamilton was on the call.

Base hit for Lum. He gets the first base hit of the '74 season. This is the only game today. So Darrell Evans, who last year moved into superstar status—41 home runs, 104 RBIs, he led the club in spring homers with four. Jack Billingham in first inning trouble . . . walked Garr, Lum got a base hit through the left side with the runner going and pulled the shortstop over. Lum hit it perfectly through the vacated spot. . . . Darrell Evans the batter with two on as you look down the first base side and Joe Morgan is coming in to talk to Billingham . . . already on deck is the man of the hour, Henry Aaron. It's the biggest sports story in a quarter century. One away from the Babe, two to set the all-time new record . . . two balls and no strikes . . . the crowd starting to buzz. Could Henry Aaron come to bat with the bases loaded? There's nobody out, opening inning. A fly ball, left field. Pete Rose waiting . . . easy play. One out . . .

Jack Billingham was already shaken, having slept the night before on a mattress on the basement floor of his home in Delhi, Kentucky, huddled with his wife, Jolene, and his two children, John and Jennifer, as tornadoes ripped through town.

He would not fall asleep until nearly 3:00 a.m., and when he awoke, he learned that the storms that rattled his house and nerves had already killed five people.

Now the crowd warming to the introduction of Henry Aaron. Henry Aaron has three spring homers, last year hit 40. . . . Drove in 96 runs . . . had a batting average of .301. Steps in for his first at-bat of the season with two on and one down. You can actually hear a buzz in the crowd. The excitement is here, and Aaron can put on the finishing touch. Ball one . . . and the disappointment as a groan goes through the 50,000-plus crowd. They want him to be thrown something over the plate. . . . Checked his swing, missed with a curve ball. Two balls and no strikes . . . Dignitaries here from all over the country . . . some 250 writers are here from the sportswriting fraternity. . . . Stee-rike across the letters on the inside corner . . . if there's a seat empty, I can't find it. . . . Ball three! Three and one to Henry Aaron . . . We play three games here. Tomorrow is an open date. . . . We'll be home Monday night to open a big homestand with the Dodgers on Monday the eighth. Three-one pitch . . . THERE'S A DRIVE INTO LEFT FIELD. . . . THAT BALL IS GOING . . . GOING . . . AND OUT OF HERE! HENRY AARON HAS JUST TIED BABE RUTH IN THE ALL-TIME HOME-RUN PARADE. . . .

Jack Billingham was now, in his words, "salty as hell" as he stood on the mound, crouched at the waist in disgust as Henry rounded the bases, around the dirt cutouts and along the hard artificial turf. Frank Hyland, the *Atlanta Journal* beat writer, was in the press box, brimming with errata: He noted the time it took Henry to round the bases as sixteen seconds and reported that in his twenty years in the big leagues it was the first home run Henry had hit on opening day, and that the ball was the first ball in the nearly one hundred years of National League play to be made from cowhide. Horsehide was now a relic.

The game was stopped for six minutes. Vice President Ford took the microphone, and Billingham was frothing. He had not been warned that the game would be halted in the event of a home run by Henry, and now it would take little effort to fry an egg on his head. "Sure, it was irritating. It's bad enough to throw but then you gotta sit there and watch 'em give away all those trophies and listen to Bowie

Kuhn throwing a few words around," Billingham said. "Seems to me they could have picked a better time to do it, like maybe between innings."

Billingham would last five shaky innings, giving up five runs, walking four, then be bounced, with Cincinnati trailing 6–2. The Reds, with their championship pedigree and hunger, plus Pete Rose (three for five, three runs scored) and Joe Morgan (two for four, and a stolen base)—would win the game in eleven innings, 7–6, but afterward Billingham was still boiling.

"I'm happy for Aaron and all that, and don't get me wrong. I'm not badmouthing and all that, but it was embarrassing. Hell, it was frustrating enough to have to change balls every time he came up, but then to have to stand out there and go through all that. You don't know what to do."

Henry was removed in the seventh inning for the rookie, Rowland Office. In the eighth inning, a harbinger of Bob Hope's nightmare was realized. Naked people! A young boy tore off his clothes and ran naked through the aisles of the left-field upper deck to an ovation. He streaked for three minutes before being apprehended by four policemen and forced to dress. He was escorted out of the stadium, but before he was taken away, he received a louder second ovation and signed several autographs.

The specter of racial tension was never far from the chase, and for the rest of Henry's life, race would always play a determining role in his memory of that day and his inability to enjoy his accomplishments.

Before the game, Henry spoke with Jesse Jackson, who suggested that on opening day, with a chance for Henry to tie and perhaps surpass Ruth's record, the Reds should, as a courtesy, acknowledge the day, April 4, 1974, the sixth anniversary of Martin Luther King, Jr.'s assassination, with a pregame moment of silence. The Reds were angry and refused, even though the club had asked Henry before the game if there was anything the team could do for him. Cincinnati, better known for its conservatism than its progressiveness in race relations, solidified its reputation with its refusal, as did the Reds.

"It should not even have been necessary to request it," Billye

Aaron would say later about the moment of silence. She would receive ample criticism herself for her politics, and learn a bitter lesson. "After that, I figured I would just keep my mouth shut."

ON THE AFTERNOON of April 8, 1974, Henry Aaron was resting at home in southwest Atlanta, lying on his living room sofa, watching *The Edge of Night*. In his two years of isolation, locked away in hotel rooms, Henry had become familiar with and addicted to soap operas. He also followed *As the World Turns,* and was somewhat disappointed that one of his favorite diversions, *The Secret Storm,* had been taken off the air. He had outlived another one. *The Secret Storm* debuted as a fifteen-minute soap opera on February 1, 1954, on CBS, four days before Henry's twentieth birthday and a month before he stepped on the field for Milwaukee that first time in Bradenton, and was canceled three days after his fortieth birthday. At 1:00 p.m., Henry slept for a couple of hours, then drove alone to the ballpark, arriving at 4:00 p.m.

For perhaps the first time during the chase, Henry was calm, uninterrupted by reporters before the game. That was because the Braves (Eddie Mathews, in particular) had decided to violate the standing agreement between the league and the Baseball Writers' Association of America and close the clubhouse an hour before game time. Usually, the clubhouse was open to the press until thirty minutes before the game began, but Mathews, whose protection of Henry was both "fatherly and brotherly," according to Bob Hope, decided the writers had asked enough questions for the last two years. Mathews had retired six years earlier but still possessed a ferocious, erratic temper, one that left younger players on edge and gave pause to anyone not seeking immediate confrontation. Earlier, he had been set off by a reporter who asked Henry which shoe, right or left, he put on first each day. "Enough of this goddamned circus," Mathews roared. Henry thanked his old teammate and told him, "It allowed me to get some of my sanity back."

Henry stretched and walked around the clubhouse, and his teammates gave him a wide berth, no one quite willing to initiate a conversation with him. No one knew if Henry wanted to be approached or if he should be treated with total silence, like a pitcher who was throwing a no-hitter. Henry walked over to Garr, who was dressing for the game.

"Ralph," Henry said at his locker. "I'm gonna break it tonight. I'm tired. I'm going to break the record so we can get down to serious business."

"I think you are, Hank," Garr responded.

LATER IN THE afternoon, Billye arrived at the ballpark with Herbert and Stella. By the time they took the field, Henry's parents were surrounded by writers from around the globe, as important to the story as Henry. "I just feel good and happy, just to be here and see him this close to it. I saw Babe Ruth play an exhibition game once when he came through Mobile," Herbert said. While he spoke, the writers were looking for genetic clues in the father's body that would unlock the gifts of the son. Henry was known for his wrists, but it was Herbert's wide hands and long, tapered fingers that betrayed some form of athletic bloodline. With his hands, Herbert could have been a pitcher, or a pianist. Amid the crush of photographers and writers and dignitaries, it was not lost on Herbert that until his son grew into manhood, white men were an entity that required careful negotiation. Now he was shaking hands with a sitting president and future ones. Herbert was energetic that day and would spend the rest of his life in the proud position of being a celebrity dad, telling tall tales in the spirit of the moment. "I remember he hit a ball over the fence and into a boxcar. Somebody found it in New Orleans."

Henry's parents were feted as celebrities, pioneers of the American dream. They would sit next to Bill Bartholomay and Governor Carter, who was formulating a bid to rescue a wounded presidency, but amid the festivities, while Herbert offered levity, Stella was too focused on the miles she had traveled and their unique, bitter terrain—her own as much as Henry's—to be folksy.

"I'm just proud of the whole black race," she said to an interviewer. "That's what I'm really proud of."

. . .

WALTER ALSTON DID not say a word to his team about the record during the pregame meeting. The Dodgers were a stoic team, unwilling to play the role of stick figures in Henry's potential night of drama. As was the baseball custom before the first game of any series, the Dodgers went over the Atlanta scouting report with the pitching staff, and Al Downing, the night's starter, winced at what he perceived to be a whiff of the old racism that had been an insuperable ingredient of baseball soil. With regard to each of the black players in the lineup, the report echoed variations on the same theme, to pitch them in, on the hands. Invariably, someone in the meeting would say, "Garr, he doesn't like being pitched high and tight," or "Make sure you crowd Baker. That makes him uncomfortable." To Downing, the words were another insinuation that black players, even twenty-seven years after Robinson's big-league debut, were somehow less mentally and physically tough than their white counterparts, that black hitters could be intimidated in ways whites could not, that their wills, even after all this time and so much truth to the contrary, were easily broken. He asked himself, Which hitters out there *do* like to be pitched high and tight? And for the life of him, Downing couldn't come up with an answer.

Like Jack Billingham and Henry, Downing and Henry had a history. Downing had surrendered home runs number 676 and 693 to Henry. The two had met eleven years earlier, in Florida during spring training, when Downing was a rookie with the Yankees. Elston Howard, the Yankee catcher, had introduced Downing to Henry, who by that time was already a big star. Henry sized up the young pitcher quietly, shook his hand, before calling out to a reporter for a spare piece of paper and a pen. Henry scribbled quickly on the paper and handed it to Downing. "If there's anything I can ever do for you," Henry told Downing that day, "give me a call. Good luck to you."

Downing's nickname was "Ace." He had been raised in Trenton, New Jersey, by his father and two aunts after his mother was killed in a car crash when he was seven years old. From the start, he was considered a special talent: left-handed and fast. Downing's America consisted of integrated schools in New Jersey and integrated traveling baseball teams. When he was fourteen, he played on a traveling team that fielded two other blacks. When the team arrived in Frederick, Maryland, Al and his black teammates, William Crossland and Arnold Thomas, were told there were no rooms for them at the hotel and that the three boys would have to find a rooming house for blacks in a different part of town.

"One night, someone brought up the idea that we should go to the movies, not even thinking that this policy existed socially in every aspect of the city. So we get to the movies and we pay for our tickets and the usher looked at me and the other two black players and said, 'You three have to sit in the balcony and you guys can go downstairs,'" Downing recalled. "All the white guys on the team just looked at us and said, 'They go to the balcony, we'll go to the balcony.' That was a moment when I knew how special those guys were, and then we all went up to the balcony and we watched the movie."

Alston did not dwell on Henry in the pregame meeting. Steve Yeager, the brusque and unpredictable catcher, would recall years later that the scouting report on Henry contained just two words: his name. "Henry Aaron. What else did you need to say? I mean, he was Henry Aaron." Henry and Alston went back twenty years, since they were both rookies in the same season, 1954, Henry a twenty-year-old with the Braves, Alston taking over for a pennant-winning Dodgers club as a forty-two-year-old rookie manager. They were both monuments to an ancient species: baseball men who had served just one employer. As players, Alston and Aaron were polar opposites: Henry tapped for fame before he could legally drink alcohol, while Alston with career that consisted of exactly one inning and one at bat in the big leagues. The date was September 27, at Sportsman's Park, the last game of the 1936 season.

"Well, I came up to bat for the Cards in 1936 and Lon Warneke struck me out," he once said. "That's it."

Ironically, both entered the big leagues in 1954, both would retire in 1976, and both would one day be honored in Cooperstown. These days, Walt Alston resembled Charlie Grimm in Milwaukee, for somehow the Dodgers couldn't break free from second place. For the last four years, the Dodgers had been just good enough to go home, losing to Cincinnati in 1970, 1972 and 1973, and to the Giants in 1971.

Pervading the 1974 club was a combination of frustration, desperation, and old-fashioned stubbornness. Mike Marshall was the club's newest acquisition, picked up from Montreal. Marshall was an iconoclast by nature and a progressive thinker, a combination that could put one on the fast track to becoming a baseball outcast. He had been raised in Michigan and attended Michigan State, earning a Ph.D. in kinesiology. If Ted Williams was fascinated by the science of hitting, Mike Marshall was passionate about the science of pitching mechanics. He was seeking to create a new pitching orthodoxy, to develop a new method of throwing a baseball that would no longer result in the ruin of a thousand pitching arms. He wanted, essentially, to reinvent the pitching wheel. Downing had been teammates with Marshall for only three months, but he loved listening to him talk about the pitching, about torque created through the shoulder and elbow, and its heavy price. Almost immediately, a semicircle of Dodger pitchers—Al Downing, Andy Messersmith, and Tommy John—began discussing their aches, pains, and tweaks with Marshall, quite often before approaching the team medical staff, a group whose best interests for the history of baseball had always been heavily weighed toward the team and not the player. Marshall's combination of advocacy and intellect not only made him controversial when it came to Dodger management; it made him dangerous. The Dodgers would go to the World Series in 1974 and Marshall would pitch 208 innings in relief, a modern-day record. He would win the Cy Young Award, but it was apparent that as quickly as he'd arrived, his days in Los Angeles were numbered. "He was too smart for them," Downing recalled. "If you had a knot in your shoulder, you'd run it by Mike, because he knew what he was talking about and he'd give it to you straight. They didn't like that kind of competition and immediately began to create a wedge between Mike and the rest of the ball club."

The season was a week old and Marshall had not yet assessed his new team.

"I had no idea who they were, or how they competed. You can be highly talented and once the season gets going, when the pressure mounts, the talent can go the other way, and I think that was what was happening on the Dodgers," Marshall recalled. "They had the best pitching, and an outstanding offense, maybe not in terms of home runs, but certainly in the number of ways they could score runs. It was a very strong team and I was hopeful.

"In Montreal, I had been with Gene Mauch, and when we had a chance to win, he'd give me the ball and say, 'Let me know when it's over.' But there, I didn't pitch an inning in the first three games and I'm thinking, Why am I here? What I loved about Montreal was that it kept battling. What I had heard about the Dodgers was that there was lot of cross-blaming going on. My attitude had been that everyone does what they can and don't judge other people by what they can't do. We ended up becoming a very close-knit pitching staff, all mature people, not prone to getting overexcited."

Jimmy Wynn walked down the runway and into the visitors' dugout. He looked around the stadium at the placards—715 and WE WANT HANK—as he stepped into the cage for batting practice. The atmosphere, he thought, was relatively quiet nevertheless. Bill Buckner, the Dodger left fielder, sprinted toward the fence and leaped once and then twice more. He was, he later admitted, practicing scaling the fence, just in case he'd need to rob Henry of his home run. The Dodger bull pen, located behind the right-field fence, was businesslike. Downing was already in the pen, warming up.

TONY KUBEK, the Milwaukee native who had played so well for the Yankees against Henry and the Braves in the 1957 World Series, was now a broadcaster for NBC. Both he and his partner, the veteran Curt Gowdy, could feel the groundswell of the moment. "Everybody expects him to do it every time now. It's gotten that far out of proportion," Kubek said. "People won't take singles or even triples from Henry Aaron anymore. There's a lot of pressure on Henry. He's withstood it all."

The 53,775 in attendance roared when Ron Reed, the Braves hulking six-foot-six-inch, 230-pound right-hander—who, like Gene Conley, was another Braves pitcher who had played in the NBA—erased the Dodgers in the first. And they groaned when Downing, pitching carefully, walked Henry in the bottom of the second without even inducing a swing, his last two pitches very nearly in the dirt. The legendary Dodgers announcer Vin Scully, was on the call. Scully, Bronx-born, started his Dodgers broadcasting career in 1950, the same year that Henry was expelled from Central High and that the Phillies and Yankees competed in the last World Series to be played only by whites.

> Henry begins to walk up to home plate. The crowd gives him a standing ovation and the familiar number 44 steps into the batters box. Joe Ferguson, mask on, but evidently said something, and Al Downing, who also wears 44, [*who*]sat on the bench when Roger Maris broke Babe Ruth's one-year mark with 61 home runs . . . Downing doesn't want to walk Aaron. He doesn't want anyone to point the accusing fingers. He's just trying to pitch his game. Downing checking, Aaron waiting . . . and the 3–1 pitch is outside, Downing ball four, so not right now, Henry.

The night existed for one moment, its tension enveloped in only one man, who would come to bat perhaps once every thirty-five minutes, maybe get a pitch to hit or maybe not, maybe do something with that pitch or maybe not. The rest of the game—the pitches, the swings, the people—the rest was just filler: Henry raced around third and scored on a double by Dusty Baker that Buckner bobbled. When Henry crossed the plate with his 2,063rd run of his career, he broke another record, passing Mays for the all-time National League mark. But tonight, nobody cared, nor did the crowd appear particularly pained that the home team was suddenly losing as the Dodgers rallied for three runs off of Reed in the top of the third. With the possible exception of the time Maris passed Ruth back in 1961, never had the events of the baseball game seemed more secondary.

It was also clear as the night progressed that there was only one other day in the history of baseball—April 15, 1947, Jackie Robinson's debut in Brooklyn—when baseball so sharply held a mirror up to America, to its blacks and its whites and its generations and its change, reflecting what the nation was at that moment and what it was about to become. Sitting in the press box, Bob Hope could feel it, as could Jimmy Carter; Stella Aaron knew it: that the record was secondary to what it represented.

In center field, Jimmy Wynn, playing for the opposing team, had decided that he wanted Henry to hit a home run—on this night, now. Like Mike Marshall, Wynn had been focused only on assimilating with his new team and on what the Dodgers needed to do to beat Cincinnati, to finally win the division and get back to the World Series, a place Los Angeles had not been since 1966 when they were destroyed by Baltimore. At that time, Wynn was in Houston, the first star player for the old expansion Colt .45's, which by then would be known as the Astros. He had known Henry only slightly. The two had met briefly over the years, and Wynn respected Henry immensely. Wynn would recall that he did not think of Henry breaking the record until he'd reached 714, and then he began to assess Henry not in baseball terms but in historical context. He thought of his father, Joe Wynn, when Jimmy was a boy growing up in Cincinnati. Joe Wynn was a ballplayer first, playing in the industrial leagues in Ohio and Kentucky, but his generation could not dream of playing in the major leagues. Joe Wynn was the best player Jimmy had ever seen, and he had told his father he wanted to follow in his footsteps, to which the elder Wynn replied, "No, you have your own footsteps."

In between pitches, Jimmy Wynn thought about his own road to the major leagues, and the humiliations he'd endured because he wanted to be a baseball player. On numerous occasions, when the environment grew too rough, he would turn to Big Joe Wynn for comfort and sometimes to plead with his father to return home. Joe Wynn was always unsympathetic, telling him, "You're in the world now."

Jimmy Wynn would remember a game in Palatka, Florida, which probably took place in 1962 or 1963 while he was playing for the Tampa Tarpons, a farm club of the Reds. Wynn was playing third base and a pair of whites in the stands catcalled out to him, "Hey, nigger, where's your tail?"

Wynn stared straight ahead.

"Hey, nigger, I'm talking to you."

The Tarpons manager, a white man named Herschel Freeman, called time to talk to his young third baseman.

"He asked me, 'Jimmy, are you all right?' I told him I was and I told him, 'Let's play baseball.' But these two just wouldn't stop," Wynn recalled. "They're throwing the N word around and asking me where was my tail. They kept doing it, and finally, Herschel Freeman called time and went up into the stands and grabbed one of them and said, 'His name is Jimmy Wynn. If you don't want to call him that, then call him *Mr.* Wynn. If you don't want to call him that, then say nothing. And if you don't, I *will* visit you once again.'

"And the next words I heard from them were, 'Come on, Jimmy.' "

In a flash, the dense, mythic fog of the evening—of who was the greater player or who, Ruth or Aaron, had the greater impact—began to clear and there was nothing left about the night of April 8, 1974, for Jimmy Wynn, the famed "Toy Cannon," except one crystallizing thought: "It wasn't about numbers. It wasn't even really about Babe Ruth. It was about him breaking a white man's record. Everything he went through was happening because he put himself in a position to break a white man's record. You see, that record, it *belonged* to them, and in a lot of ways, to them, the ones who wrote those letters and said those things, Henry Aaron was taking it from *them* and giving it to *us*. He was giving us a little something more than what we had, something that we'd never had."

IN THE FOURTH inning, Henry received a long standing ovation for his second at bat. Darrell Evans was already on first; a throwing error by the shortstop Russell put him on. It was the top of the fourth, nobody out, and the Dodgers had already committed three errors. They would commit three more before the evening was over. Downing threw another pitch into the dirt.

Downing's next pitch would in some ways end his career as much as Henry's swing would end his. Neither man would ever be three-dimensional again. Technology—that is, television—would rob Henry of his speed, his arm, his youth, reducing him forever to a sagging forty-year-old worthy of only one moment, leaving it to his contemporaries and admirers to remind future generations of what a complete, dynamic ballplayer he once was. And Downing would no longer be the proud descendant of the denied Negro Leaguers in

general and Bill Yancey, the first black man to ever scout for the Yankees, in particular. The twenty-game season in 1971, being the first
black pitcher to start a World Series game for the Yankees—all of it
would be deleted in the public mind except for one fastball that
hugged too much of the plate, a bad pitch. For the next six years of his
life, Al Downing would spiral, referring to this period as "bitter" and
his life as "rough" because the mirror would be held up once again to
America and the divide between black and white could not be
assuaged. One day during the bad years, Downing would be in the
bull pen, a father and son ten feet above him in the stands. The father
would point at Downing and say, "There's Al Downing. He gave up
Hank Aaron's seven hundred and fifteenth home run. He's no good."
He would hear the father whisper to the son that two black men
("soul brothers" is the phrase Downing recalls hearing) conspired to
take away a white man's record. It would not be the first time nor the
last that he would be accused of purposely throwing a home run-ball
to Hank Aaron. Only after that period would Downing reclaim the
full scope of his career and his equilibrium as a man. "Let me get this
straight," Downing would say years later. "I got vilified for years for
giving up a home run to a man who hit more home runs than anyone
who ever lived? Does that make sense to anyone?"

MILO HAMILTON (*"THERE'S A NEW HOME CHAMPION OF
ALL TIME, AND IT'S HENRY AARON!"*) received more attention,
but it was the legend, Vin Scully, who offered the more poignant, tex-
tured, and lasting call of the moment:

> And swinging two bats is Henry Aaron . . . and once again a stand-
> ing ovation for Henry Aaron. He means the tying run at the plate
> now, so we'll see what Downing does. Al at the belt and he deliv-
> ers and he's low, ball one. . . . And that just adds to the pres-
> sure . . . the crowd booing. . . . Downing has to ignore the sound
> effects and stay a professional and pitch his game. One ball and no
> strikes, Aaron waiting . . . the outfield deep and straight
> away . . . fastball, high drive into deep left center field . . . Buck-
> ner goes back . . . to the fence . . . it is GONE. . . .

For twenty-five seconds, Vin Scully stayed quiet, allowing the fans to speak to America for him as Henry rounded the bases. And then he continued with the words that would make a career:

> It is over. And for the first time in a long time that poker face of Aaron shows the tremendous relief. . . . What a marvelous moment for baseball. What a marvelous moment for Atlanta and the state of Georgia. What a marvelous moment for the country and the world. A black man is getting a standing ovation in the Deep South for breaking a record of an all-time baseball idol. And it is a great moment for all of us, and particularly for Henry Aaron.

The racial divide in America was apparent even during his victorious trip around the bases. Henry rounded first and passed Steve Garvey, who attempted to give Henry a congratulatory slap of hands but missed. In the Dodger dugout, Steve Yeager, the backup catcher, watched the flight of the ball and for the next three and half decades would take little more from the evening than one number surpassing another. "It was a long time ago," he would say. "It was a historic moment, a big moment, but there are a lot of big moments in sports. But, you go on. For him to do that shows what an outstanding hitter he was, one of the best in baseball." For the black players, the home run meant so much more. The second baseman, Davey Lopes, was the first person to shake Henry's hand—the kind of shake third-base coaches give home-run hitters—then wound up with his glove hand and gave Henry a swipe on the rump. What Lopes was witnessing would resonate deeply. He is not African-American, but Cape Verdean. A small island off the westernmost point of Africa, near Senegal, Cape Verde had long been colonized by the Portuguese. In the early twentieth century, Cape Verdeans emigrated to the United States, settling largely in the old fishing and whaling towns of southern New England, places with historic names from another century, like Plymouth, New Bedford, Falmouth, Wareham, and Buzzards Bay. Lopes was raised by a single mother in Providence, Rhode Island, and his experience in America was one of being caught in between the black and the white culture, sometimes at the price of his own natural heritage. "If you told someone you were Cape

Verdean, they wouldn't even know where to begin to look," he recalled. New England does not produce many baseball players, and historically the ones talented enough to compete with players from the baseball-rich regions of California and Texas are celebrated as local heroes, inspirations. But Davey Lopes did not receive such attention and knew his darker skin to be the catalyst for his relative anonymity. In a few months after Henry's home run, Lopes and the Dodgers would play the Oakland A's in the World Series and Lopes would tell an interviewer, "I don't even think Providence knows I'm here." Like Al Downing, Lopes was proud of his special heritage as a person of color, more specifically that he was a dark-skinned second baseman wearing the uniform of the Dodgers, standing in the same position as Robinson and, after him, Jim "Junior" Gilliam. "I remember when I first came up. We'd be in spring training and Junior would tell me to come with him. I'd say, 'Where we going?' and he would just tell me to come on. We'd be in St. Petersburg and he'd point out the majestic hotels. He'd say, 'That's where the Dodgers used to stay,' and I was just in awe. Then we'd go farther into a neighborhood and he'd show me some average-looking house and say, 'And that's where *we* had to stay.' And it blew my mind, because it wasn't long ago. I thought about those things, about where we'd come as people of color, and that's why I shook Henry Aaron's hand. It felt like something I had to do."

Henry rounded second and, seemingly out of nowhere, two fans appeared and escorted him between the bases. At third, Ron Cey saw the two kids racing toward Henry and thought for a second that this was it: They might attack him.

"Well, I wasn't really sure what I was going to do when it happened. But it became clear what I was going to do when he came around, and two kids had run onto the field—I was going to stay clear of it," Cey recalled. "If he'd been running solo, I probably would have shaken his hand, but the other part of it was that this was really his moment, and you know, he should kind of walk alone."

Having grown up in socially segregated Tacoma, Washington, in the late 1950s and early 1960s, in a sense Cey was vindicated. He had always believed that sport, at its best, could be the great antidote for the American divide.

"I grew up playing sports, so I always had a relationship of playing with black kids throughout all the amateur sports: football, basketball, baseball. You know, it wasn't an issue. We grew up playing each other," Cey recalled. "I think sports, in a way, has a way of breaking down those issues. We're all trying to do something that involves a common bond. We're just making the best of it and trying to win. It [his neighborhood] was pretty segregated back then. There was a part of the town where black kids went to school. But it was a normal, everyday, middle-class place to be. There was a certain boys club downtown that was predominately black that I frequented because of my relationships with some of these players, and we didn't have any issues. This was where sports would bring you together. It's not like we all signed up on the same team to play. Somebody drafted us and we made our way to the big-league club. These were the best players. These were the players who were going to be part of our future, and when you take the field, you're all working for the same thing. If you're on a different page than that, you really shouldn't be there."

In the crowd, the two kids were racing toward Henry, and Calvin Wardlaw stood, flinching, and considered reaching for his pistol, which rested in his binocular case. A few feet away, Davey Lopes didn't even see them. "I always wondered, Where the hell did they come from?" he recalled.

Within milliseconds, it was clear the two fans had come in peace. Henry gently nudged the two kids aside as he headed toward home plate, where the home run would be official and the chase finally over. Both Britt Gaston and Cliff Courtney were students at the University of Georgia. Both would be arrested, the charge on the report alleging the two "ran onto ballfield during ballgame and interrupted ballgame." Henry would lend his name to the list of those who wanted the charges against the two kids dropped. Among those in Henry's inner circle, the running gallows joke for years would be that the smartest decision of the evening was Calvin Wardlaw's electing to leave his gun in his binocular case.

TOM HOUSE considers himself a "real low-end guy," "happy for every day" he gets to spend in the big leagues. He watched the flight of the ball and Bill Buckner climbing the fence in an attempt to put his pregame calisthenics to use. "My God, he's gonna catch it," House blurted out. The ball was beyond Buckner's reach. House threw a triumphant fist in the air. Jimmy Wynn took his glove off and began to clap.

This was the first year House had made a big-league club out of spring training without the immediate fear of being sent down. He was aware of his place in the big-league hierarchy, an environment where batting averages, strikeout totals, and earned-run averages might as well have been printed on everyone's forehead. He had noticed that during the day-to-day activities, Henry stood at a bit of a distance. In House's words, that was "because he's Hank Aaron." He said that he was "thrilled" that Henry even knew he was alive. "He was unfailingly kind. I didn't really understand the social IQ and the things he was going through, but you would never have known," House recalled. "He called me 'Tommy' and he was the same all the time—same way, same demeanor. A whole lot people were pulling for him and pulling against him, but you would never have known. I remember thinking that this guy was probably the most underrated superstar in the world. He was unbelievably civil, from the clubhouse kids to my tier of athlete all the way to the top. He was a pleasure to be around."

House had had visions not dissimilar to those of Joe Shirley, the Braves security man. "I had visions of a little old lady getting stomped by a Georgia Tech football player." But the most important baseball in the world was speeding toward him. His friend and bull-pen mate, Buzz Capra, was boxing him out to negotiate a better angle and wound up pushing House closer to the ball. House recalled what he realized at that moment: "If I don't catch it, the stitches will hit me right in the forehead."

House caught the ball and sprinted toward the infield, where Henry was being mobbed at home plate. Stella had him in a mother's embrace, a physical expression of exhalation. "He's hugging his mom and he's got a crocodile tear, and I'm thinking, Holy crap. Hank Aaron has a tear in his eye and he's hugging his mom. It's a Life Saver moment. The fact that Hank Aaron had tears in his eyes shook me more than anything," House recalled. "Then I find out a few days later from Dusty that she held him so tight to prevent anyone from shooting him. Here were a mom and a son sharing the ultimate moment in baseball, a Little League family moment in a way that nobody else would understand. But what sticks in my mind was that the tear was that he might have been happy that it was over, and the rest of the world would have killed to be in his shoes."

THE MIRROR WAS held up to America and there were the white men who did not flinch at the discomforts of the divide. They were the ones whom, back in the 1920s and 1930s, Ed Scott used to call "the good ones": whites who saw America's racial odyssey in all of its complexities and hypocrisies, and who understood its true cost and how much all of the people who called themselves Americans, and not just the blacks, had been diminished. Mike Marshall was one of those men. "He showed that it could happen. He showed all the non-sense about black people not being smart enough to be quarterbacks or as good as Babe Ruth," Marshall said. "Talent comes in all hues. That's what he did." Marshall was sitting in the dugout when Henry's ball jetted over the infield to its final destination.

"I grew up in a small town in Michigan, a farm town. It was long before the big numbers of Latinos moved in. Our farm wasn't big enough, so we didn't have crops that needed to be picked. I played in Selma and Chattanooga and Montgomery. I remember the different bathrooms and drinking fountains and places where you could sit and where you couldn't, and I remember thinking We're all the same people. How can these people be so far behind?" When Marshall suffered through difficulties in baseball, his friendship with Ronnie Woods, an outfielder Marshall met when the two were with Detroit in the mid-1960s, sustained him. The two became teammates in the big leagues in Montreal in 1972.

"Back then, even in the early 1970s, there wasn't a lot of interracial rooming. I think I was the first guy on the Expos with a black roommate, but I didn't care. His friendship made playing baseball a lot easier."

The game was stopped for eleven minutes, and Henry was too weary to be eloquent. Honesty without flourish was all he could offer.

There was no joy contained in his drained face, no desire to bask in his own afterglow. His words were not reflective or introspective or prescient, nor, upon reflecting upon this evening, would they ever be. "I just thank God," Henry said, "that it's all over with." For the next thirty-five years, Henry Aaron would not waver from this position. In San Diego, Cito Gaston heard Henry had broken the record and felt tears well up. "I was just proud. That was all I felt—pride. And years later, when I had read about how much the record hurt and how a lot of that hurt never went away, I just thought to myself, What would life be like without so much discrimination?"

THE GAME RESUMED, and Dusty Baker was amazed at how quickly the sellout crowd disappeared. "There were about fifty-five thousand people there for the record, and about ten thousand people left after it was over," Baker recalled.

In center field, Jimmy Wynn had an uncontrollable urge to speak to Henry. Players on opposing teams were discouraged from fraternizing back then, but this moment was bigger than silly rules.

"My thing was, It's over with. Now Hank can lead a comfortable life," Wynn recalled. "I kind of paused, and then told myself, The hell with it. I'm going to shake his hand. I'm going to treat this man with respect. I shook his hand and I was glad I did. You could see what the whole thing did to him. He could have said, 'I did it. I am the number-one home-run hitter of all time,' and should have been happy about it and should have enjoyed it. But you know what? He never did."

The Braves closed the clubhouse for an hour after the game and celebrated the moment as a team. There were plans for celebrations throughout the baseball world whenever Hank Aaron came to town, for the first time as the all-time leader in home runs. When the doors to the Braves clubhouse opened, Henry shook a few hands and offered a few words to the writers, the most telling to Wayne Minshew. "All he said was, 'I'm going home now,' " Minshew said. "That was it. 'I'm going home.' "

CHAPTER FOURTEEN

MORTAL

ON APRIL 8, the record-breaking home run had been Henry's only hit in three at bats. In his first three games of the season, he'd hit two home runs, and then came the swings and the misses, and, following them, the embarrassed looks, the pity, and the doubts. The night after Henry broke the record, a kid named Tommy John collared him zero for four. So did Andy Messersmith, Clay Kirby, and Randy Jones, the future winner of the Cy Young Award, who at that time couldn't get anyone out. Jones would lose twenty-two games for San Diego in 1974. Over the first sixteen at bats after hitting 715, Henry produced exactly one hit, home run number 716, off the Dodger knuckleballer Charlie Hough. His batting average was .179.

With each weak swing against a weaker opponent, Garr and Baker looked at Henry, and could see the hurt in their eyes. Nobody wanted to suggest that Supe, of all people, could no longer get around on a fastball. It was one thing to accept on an intellectual level that eventually baseball would get all of them, that even the immortals would inevitably sag and succumb as the calendar flipped forward. But it was quite another to see the Hammer getting beaten inside by a ham-and-egg fastball, needing a two-hit game, as he did April 21 in Houston, to get his average over .200. As the sun set, Henry fell deeper into himself. He was in the lineup less, playing left field now (Garr was the everyday right fielder), producing a running commentary of rejuvenation and avoidance, of willpower and resignation. "The problem is, when you've pounded baseballs for twenty years, it takes a lot of convincing to make you believe you can't do it anymore," Henry would reflect years later in his autobiography, *I Had a Hammer.* "I didn't believe it yet."

Henry did his best not to let on that he was spending more of his time in the company of doubt. "You have to understand that we looked up to him so much," Garr said. "Sure, there were pitches that he wasn't getting anymore. He was definitely missing a few, but that was what made him great to me. If you came around looking for someone to cry, you came looking for the wrong man."

THE RECORD NOW broken, the easier it became for the Atlanta front office to reach the inevitable, hard assessment that Henry Aaron could no longer play. The record belonged to him and his name could never again be mentioned without the accompanying appositive, Hank Aaron, Home Run King, but Henry was also some-thing far less regal: a forty-year-old outfielder making $200,000 a year, a player who was a full nine years older than Davey Johnson, the next-oldest position regular on the club. He was a player for whom—at least while wearing a baseball uniform—the past held far more glory than the future. The physical traits, certainly, were still apparent and they still gave Aaron watchers a nostalgic tingle: Henry resting on one knee in the on-deck circle, sometimes holding two bats to limber up, walking slowly to the plate, batting helmet in his right hand, Del Crandall–model bat dragging along behind him, leaving a caterpillar's trail. He still stepped into the batter's box as he always had, adjusting his helmet and scooping up a cupful of dirt (even in 1974, when the modern kids wore wristbands and sometimes *two* gloves, Henry did not wear even a single batting glove), as always his hitting prefaced by that deep, majestic clearing of the throat, an operatic harbinger. The routines were familiar and, in many ways, even more poignant as they yellowed.

It was his consistency that had always left his contemporaries in so much awe, how he could always hit, regardless of the circumstances, and his ability to dial it up against the best fastballs, adjust to the sharpest curves. That was what was missing right now. "With Henry Aaron, it didn't matter," Ralph Garr reflected. "He could have just come back from a funeral and you wouldn't know. You never knew what was weighing on his mind, what his mood was. You wouldn't know, because his approach was always the same to hitting. Nobody ever had that kind of concentration. If he had problems at home, you'd never know. You couldn't do anything to break him of his plan." Garr used to watch Henry's computerized mind dissect a pitcher's patterns while he sat in the dugout waiting his turn. He could be in the tunnel smoking a butt and yet he knew that he could apply the snippet of information he'd gleaned when it came his time to hit. The macho guys trying to establish themselves, guys like Kirby and Billingham, might start him out with a fastball away, a curveball in, then try to finish him with the one pitch Henry would never completely master, the slider away. Starting Henry off the plate meant that a pitcher believed he had his good stuff and could come in hard with a fastball, but only when absolutely necessary. When a pitcher started him off with a fastball in, well, that was just a show-me pitch, because unless your last named happened to be Gibson or Koufax, you didn't dare try to come inside twice on Henry in the same at bat. Gibson never gave you a chance to guess whether or not he had it on a given day, so Henry knew never to look for anything but hard and inside, and then adjust. Approaching Gibson any other way was just asking for it, for the last thing Bob Gibson would do was show weakness to a hitter, even if it meant throwing a substandard (by Gibson's measure) fastball in a dangerous location to a dangerous hitter. Against the rest of the league, Henry had the pitching sequences against him so perfectly memorized that Garr would sit back with delight and watch the guy on the mound take his inevitable pounding at the hands of the master.

The difference now was that Henry possessed the knowledge but was not producing the results, and day after day, the great man lunged where he once strode. The swagger remained intact, but now it was accompanied by fewer hits. The vaunted wrists were still plenty quick enough—until the day he walked off the field for good, nobody would easily strike out Henry Aaron—but instead of providing the gunpowder, the wrists now provided only protection, keeping him from striking out. There were times when the kids, with their hormones and muscles, would fire a fastball past Henry early in the game, thinking time had gotten the better of him. And then there he'd be, watching the fastball, sensing its movement, just as always, as some young catcher sat back, self-satisfied, waiting to watch the ball zip past the old man once more in a rush of hot air . . . only then, the wrists would spark to life, and the old baseball men, the scouts, with their Cadillacs and suspenders and their round bellies, their pens and pads and charts (in a few years, they'd be carrying radar guns, too), sitting behind the backstop would give one another that wry, wrinkly nod. *That's Henry for you. He's still got it.* And they would dig deep into their endless bags of folklore and chuckle. *You got to get up early in the morning to sneak a fastball by ole Henry Aaron. . . .* And it was right there, at that hundredth of a second in time—that unit of measure for the millionth percentiles that differentiated Mount Olympus from Cooperstown—when the universe, once so predictable, flew completely off of its axis. Once, there had been that automatic thunderclap. Now, when Henry swung, the baseball would just slide weakly off of the barrel of his bat and ricochet backward into the netting, and Henry would turn and watch the ball sail foul, poker-faced, trying to ignore the doubt. The next night, he might be beautiful again, slashing through the zone, doubles one-hopping deadly off the base of the outfield wall. And on the very next night, an average fastball might catch the bottom of his bat and trickle harmlessly toward the third-base dugout, coughing up chalk as it spun along, giving life to more whispers. And his guts would churn, because he knew better than anybody that those were the pitches that through two wars and five presidents that had routinely gotten tattooed. The wrists were no longer sparking fires, no longer doing the executioner's work. Once they'd been torpedoes, but now the legendary wrists of the great Henry Aaron were just life preservers, prolonging hopeless at bats for one more pitch.

He was still Henry Aaron. That was why Eddie Mathews batted him fourth the whole season, the same spot he had hit since the Korean War. Whatever changes Mathews might have made to the lineup, he didn't mess with one spot: When Henry played, he batted cleanup, which, whatever evidence to the contrary, made life feel normal. He fought time, even as he increasingly lost the battle. Every now and again, the old Henry would rise.

"When we would fly from Atlanta overnight to California, he normally wouldn't play the next day. We did a cross-country trip to San Francisco one time and when we got there there was a newspaper article in the *San Francisco Chronicle* about this 'Count' Montefusco, a young pitcher, maybe twenty-two years old," recalled Davey Johnson, then a Braves infielder. "He had great stuff, a nasty slider—an unhittable slider. He was complaining that he was having to pitch against the Braves. He said something like 'They're not a good team; why am I pitching against them?' And Henry read the paper and he went to [Clyde King] and said, 'I'm in the lineup.' And it was a day game after an all-night flight. I'll never forget it. We all knew what was going to happen. We'd seen it too many times. A couple of guys got on base in front of him and Henry looked for his best pitch, which was a nasty down-and-away slider. He reached out there and popped it over the left center-field wall. He came back into the dugout and said, 'I hope that kid gained more respect for us now.' Henry put him in his place. This kid was cocky. He had a really great year and felt above pitching against any club. That's what Henry said, 'We can't let this go.' And I mean to tell you, it was a wicked low-and-away slider. That was in 1974, Montefusco's first year."

Johnson could be forgiven for flashbulb memory, but the kernel of the story is nevertheless true. The game was September 18, 1974, the finale of a three-game set in San Francisco. It was true that Henry did not usually play in the opener of a West Coast series following a cross-country flight, nor did he play in this case: a day-game travel day following a night game. John Montefusco woke him, and Henry had been scheduled an off-day but put himself in the lineup. Montfusco was a rising star, twenty-four years old. He had been called up fifteen days earlier and the next year would win Rookie of the Year in the National League.

Henry led off the second, and boomed home run number 732 off Montefusco, a long, slashing drive to left center. In his next at-bat, with two on in the third, Henry singled home another run off Montefusco. Henry had put the kid down, but what didn't make sense was why Montefusco would want to upset any opponent, as the Giants would finish sixteen games behind the Braves in 1974. Pressure was like the wind, unseen by the human eye, but it could easily and obviously be detected when it descended, exerting its suffocating, downward force. The pressure Henry felt stemmed not only from his inability to catch a fastball but from *why he couldn't.* The truth was that he had indeed started the marathoner's kick to get to Ruth, gave it everything he had and soared at an age when so many of his contemporaries were washed up. Between the ages of thirty-five and thirty-nine, Mays had wilted as a baseball player. So had Frank Robinson and the rest of them. But Henry had hit 199 home runs, so suddenly, at age forty, it did not compute that the skill was no longer there. Even when he was hitting under .200, his strikeout totals were still low, and that was all the more reason for him to believe that he suffered from mechanical flaws more than from physical erosion.

In the years to come, with reflection, Henry understood the reasons were not mostly physical (other than that the nagging aches persisted a bit longer), but mental: There was, after Ruth, nothing left to chase. For five years, Ruth had been the obsession, and for the ten before that, the goal had been to prove he belonged with Mays, Mantle, and Musial, on the red carpet with the all-time greats, the ones who defined Cooperstown, instead of the other way around, and during his initial five years in the big leagues, the motivating force had been proving to himself that there was a bigger, more rewarding life beyond Mobile in which he was entitled to share. He would say he always believed he would quit the game after he had achieved three thousand hits, but the proximity to Ruth kept him going, five years after that milestone. He had wanted desperately for the chase to be over, to put an end to the pressures and the anxieties and the fears. Billye and his closest friends would spend the next three decades trying to repair the blows to his humanity that had been exacted during the chase. "There is no question he lost something he could never get back, a piece of himself," said his close friend and attorney, Allan Tanenbaum. "The chase did that."

But now that the record belonged to him, Henry realized how much the goal of vanquishing Ruth had gotten inside of him. He had weakened as a complete player since 1968, harassed by his back, his ankles, all the parts of his body that hurt. He had stolen at least fifteen bases a year for nine straight seasons, but since turning thirty-five in

1969, he hadn't stolen ten in a single season, and would not again. He did not know what would provide the inner motivation to continue playing ball.

For a time, it appeared that the pennant race would energize him. In the month before the all-star break, the Braves contended with the Reds and Dodgers, both hungry, muscular clubs. June 21, opening game of the series at Riverfront Stadium, Carl Morton against Jack Billingham: The two traded zeroes until the seventh, when Henry stroked a one-out double and later scored on a ground ball. The rest was tension, the Big Red Machine loading the bases in the bottom of the ninth, Tom House facing the murderous Johnny Bench for the game. Bench flied out to left, and the Braves took a 1–0 win. They were in second place, only five games behind Los Angeles and two ahead of Cincinnati. The Braves were making a pennant run, and it was Henry who had scored the only run of the game. Intermittently in 1974, he had spoken of retirement, but maybe there was some fun to be had after all, one last charge. Phil Niekro, the other old head on the club (even Niekro, who looked like he was seventy even when he was in his thirties, was five years younger than Henry), led the pitching staff. The kid Buzz Capra was surprising the league at 7–2, and that self-described "low-end guy, happy to be there" Tom House possessed a microscopic ERA. Where there was pitching, there was October, so even though he was no longer as dangerous, Henry somehow still found himself in the middle of big wins as the summer progressed.

A month later, the day before the all-star break, Dock Ellis beat the Braves 6–2 at Atlanta–Fulton County Stadium, and the only thing October signified to any of the long faces on the bench was uninterrupted fishing trips. The Braves had lost twenty-two of their previous thirty-three games, their record plummeted to a mediocre 50–49—a hearty fifteen games out of first—and the smiles disappeared. The loss also spelled curtains for Eddie Mathews, who, following the final out of Ellis's complete game five-hitter, was fired before he could leave the building.

Out of the race, Henry would then have to generate his own fuel, and that was precisely the problem. The ghost of Ruth had been vanquished, and even his personal life had grown normal once again. He

and Billye began to sow philanthropic seeds in Atlanta, forming charitable foundations and working with others. Gaile returned to school,
largely without incident, and during the early afternoons before night
games it was a common occurrence to see Henry, in turtleneck and
plaid pants, leaning on the fence at Marist High School, watching
Henry Aaron, Jr., play linebacker on the school football team.

Henry had even outlasted most, if not all, of his contemporaries.
Mays had gone, quietly, the last hit of his career driving in the go-
ahead run in the twelfth inning of the second game of the 1973 World
Series against Oakland, partial redemption for the moment that
would become the universal, chilling reminder for gods who can't
quit: falling down in the outfield while chasing Deron Johnson's liner
in the bottom of the ninth. Ernie Banks had retired in 1971. Mantle
and Drysdale had been gone six years, Koufax nearly ten. Robinson
and Clemente were dead, and Frank Robinson was at the end—it
was heavily rumored that he would become the first black manager in
the game at season's end. Even the roaring lion Gibson had already
announced that 1975 would be his final year. The old foes were gone,
and spiraling out of the race had cost his old comrade Eddie Mathews
his job. Henry had already achieved every important milestone in the
sport, had, in the words of Dusty Baker, broken a record every time
he climbed out of bed, and had caught every standard-bearer against
whom he had once measured himself. Stan Musial's National League
record of 3,630 hits was within striking distance, but once Ruth's
record was already under glass, rapping out singles to pass Musial
lacked the requisite emotional punch. There was nothing else for
Henry to do in the game.

THE SIGNS WERE everywhere, and had been since the beginning of
spring, when he announced that 1974 would be his final year, that the
end of Henry's career possessed the potential for trouble between
him and the Braves, the kind of trouble that could sour a legacy. One
such warning signal was that Henry was hitting less often but challenging the baseball establishment more. He was the home-run king
and, he later said, believed he had accrued the appropriate political
capital to press for rights. But there was the delicate matter of just

how the Braves felt about him as a player. His contract was up at the end of 1974 and the Braves had not initiated any discussions about renewing it. Part of the reason for this was that Henry had said during spring training he believed he would retire after the 1974 season. There were words of surprise and encouragement when Henry mentioned quitting, but no one in the Braves management really pulled on his emotional coattails to coax him to stay, and they certainly did not offer him a contract for 1975. He had become that Gibraltar of professional sports—the aging superstar too big, too accomplished, and too familiar and popular with the fans to be casually cast aside simply because his skills had eroded. History had shown that these endings were rarely resolved well. Ruth left the Yankees with an unrequited longing to manage and a sagging belly. Robinson left the Dodgers with bitterness that so heroic a journey could culminate in such cynicism, while Mays left the Giants ragged and hollow. By voluntarily retiring, Henry was following the Ted Williams model, walking away unlined, indomitable. No one in management wanted to say it, but, by retiring, Henry was solving a potentially messy problem for the Braves.

Into the season, he slogged his way through the .200s and took more days off (day games following night games, mostly and Sunday get-aways to let his body regenerate) as the club began drifting toward the future, a future that for the first time since he became the Rookie Rocket did not include him. When any chance of winning the pennant was beaten out of them during that heinous July, the end of the Aaron era became merely a matter of ripping days off of the summer calendar.

It was precisely during this time that Henry began to change his mind about the future. He had always said he would not be the ballplayer who quit only after he looked ridiculous on the field, but neither could he quite stand the idea of walking away in the grips of his mortality. Maybe he did not want to quit after all, not with a .225 batting threatening to be his final memory of wearing a big-league uniform. Maybe he would shake the tempting hand of Faust and enter into the same fatal deal that had finished other athletes, from ballplayers to boxers: He would tell himself that he would be the one who could deny time. He would say nothing, but his mind was changing about playing in 1975; he was giving himself one more chance to leave the game on top.

If the Braves were willing to reassess and allow Henry to return to the team in 1975 (and there was no evidence that they were), the series of simmering events at the end of the July appeared to end his relationship with the organization. Soon after Mathews was fired, Frank Hyland of the *Journal* asked Henry if he was interesting in managing the club. Henry retreated. "No, no, no," he replied. "I'm not interested in managing this club, or any other." Hyland went with the story and the rest of the press followed.

IT WON'T BE HANK

The job of replacing deposed Eddie Mathews as manager of the Braves is still up for grabs. . . . People are asking "could it be Tommie Aaron, Hank's brother who manages the Savannah farm club?"

It won't be Hank Aaron. Hank didn't say "no" to the suggestion. He said, "No, no, no, no, no. It won't be me. I don't know who it will be."

Then Eddie Robinson, the Braves general manager, said Henry was not a candidate for the job, and neither was Tommie, and that was when Henry began to boil. When Hyland and Wayne Minshew asked Robinson if he believed Atlanta was ready for a black manager, Robinson demurred with a terse "I'm not prepared to answer that. No comment." Two days later, Henry Aaron, batting .235, with ten home runs, flew to Pittsburgh for the All-Star Game, his twentieth consecutive one. He was voted in as a starter and shook hands with his teammates, but the game on the field was only part of the story. Baseball, commissioner Bowie Kuhn in particular, was under fire from the Pittsburgh chapter of the NAACP and the Catholic Interracial Council. The two organizations had joined forces to criticize baseball's failure to hire a black manager, with three days of protest leading up to the game. As the new home-run king, Henry smiled as a goodwill ambassador, but he was furious that neither he nor his brother had been taken seriously by Robinson as managerial material. While the NAACP protested in Pittsburgh, Robinson was making his own deal in Atlanta: Clyde King, a baseball lifer, had the job.

When the game commenced, Henry took two uninspired at bats

against his old nemesis Gaylord Perry—a weak pop to left and a grounder to first—before being replaced by César Cedeño. Some of the old faces remained—Frank Robinson, Pete Rose, and Joe Morgan—but Robinson remained the only other player in the game who, like Henry, had begun his career in the 1950s. The changes were obvious, from the soft cuts he took in the game to the new generations of stars on both sides—Rollie Fingers, Mike Schmidt, Bobby Grich—suggesting that maybe it might be time to let someone else put on the spikes.

"It's an honor," he later told Dusty Baker privately. "But I don't belong here anymore."

Almost immediately after despairing, Henry tried once more to pull himself up off the mat, giving in to will.

"The way I saw it, I had three options: hang on past my prime, do some hitting, or retire," he recalled in *I Had a Hammer.* "The option I preferred was number two."

When the game ended, Henry Aaron, white-hot, gave a nationally televised interview to Tony Kubek of NBC, where his frustration welled up into a supernova.

"I think they owe me the courtesy of asking me," Henry told Kubek, speaking of the managerial job. "I believe I deserved to be asked if I wanted it," he said. "And if they offered it to me, I would have taken it because there are no black managers."

The next day, above the news of Greece and Cypress and the Nixon impeachment and school desegregation stood Henry, above the fold, page 1A of the *Atlanta Journal-Constitution.*

RHUBARB!

Aaron Reverses Field . . .
But Braves Name King to Manage

PITTSBURGH—Clyde King . . . will be named manager of the Atlanta Braves . . . but Henry Aaron said he would have taken the job if asked. . . .

"I still prefer not to manage," Aaron replied, "but it is time he had a black manager in the major leagues." . . .

"I think Robinson should have at least had the courtesy to ask me if I was interested."

Over the next three days, Henry boiled, at the present and the past, at all that had been said and quite likely all that he had not said over the years. On Thursday, July 25, Jesse Outlar further steamed Henry with his insinuation in the *Atlanta Journal-Constitution* that Henry was nothing more than a puppet for black leaders.

PRESSURE FROM INFLUENTIAL BLACKS
LIES BEHIND AARON'S ABOUT-FACE

Henry Aaron obviously has agreed to become the Jackie Robinson of the major league dugout. He is taking the lead to change the times in baseball, even if he has to manage, something he has always vowed he did not want to do. . . .

Robinson broke the color line in baseball in 1947 with the Brooklyn Dodgers. Now influential black leaders such as Jesse Jackson apparently have persuaded Aaron that he is the man to end the managerial boycott. That's the only logical explanation of Aaron's sudden about face. . . .

The next day came the ground war—an omitted word in Jesse Outlar's column headline transformed AARON SAYS HE HAS NOT CHANGED, BUT HE'S STILL OWN MAN to AARON SAYS HE HAS CHANGED, BUT HE'S STILL OWN MAN — followed by the atom bomb: a photo accompanying Outlar's column of a cheering Billye, with the caption "Wife Billye: *Trouble?*"

That did it. He could take being called Stepin Fetchit by Furman Bisher, and a pawn by Jesse Outlar, and being left out in the cold by management, which lauded his contributions to the organization but did not seem to think enough of him to ask him if he was even interested in managing the club before announcing to the world he wasn't being considered, but putting Billye on the front page of the sports section was just the low blow required to set Henry Aaron aflame. It was also the second time Henry had seen Billye become the target. The first was months earlier, on opening day in Cincinnati, when the Reds refused his request to honor Martin Luther King, Jr., with a moment of silence. The whispers had started then, that it was Billye who was planting ideas in Henry's uncomplicated brain, that Henry had been just the nicest fellow until he married her. Now her picture was in the newspaper, adjacent to a story about him with an erroneous headline.

The cutline infuriated Henry, but it only represented a flash point. He had already been seeing red for a week. The Outlar story contained a damaging piece of fiction, one that had been voiced before and that Henry could never live down. The article suggested he did not possess the intelligence to comprehend the scope of his own struggle, whether it be the civil rights movement or the necessity for the next level of integration in his own sport, and that he needed his wife to put ideas in his head.

It all came to a head later that night, Farmer's Night at Atlanta Stadium, a quaint tradition since the Braves had first arrived in Atlanta. Each player received a carton of produce and the local farmers were celebrated in a pregame ceremony. The game with the Padres was being delayed, and while the tarp still covered the infield, Garr and Baker both told Frank Hyland to steer clear of Henry, which piqued the reporter's curiosity. Henry wanted a piece of Hyland, too, for Hyland had written that Henry had "double-talked," either to the Braves about not wanting to manage or in the NBC interview about his newfound interest. Either way, Hyland wrote, the organization could not be blamed for Henry's indecision. Henry saw Hyland and motioned for him to come to his locker. Ron Reed, the six-foot-six former basketball player, and Henry's pal Paul Casanova stood, Dusty Baker recalled, "like bouncers about to break up a bar fight." For a moment, it appeared the two were speaking civilly, and then Henry, for the first time in his career, lost it, letting Frank Hyland have it: a carton of strawberries to the face.

SPLAT! IRATE AARON SMACKS
WRITER WITH STRAWBERRIES

"Henry was pretty hot . . . he told me he had never double-talked anyone. . . . I reminded him that he had told writers one thing before the game about wanting the Braves' managing job and had said something else on television the same night.

"All of a sudden he shot out with those strawberries he was holding in his hand. . . . I don't know whether he hit me right or left-
handed—but it was flush in the face."

THE TWO WORDS the writers used almost interchangeably when
describing the opposite poles of Henry's personality were *dignity* and
bitter, the former during times when he seemed to exude uncommon
patience with the world's nuisances and injustices (which was another
way of saying that Henry often let go unpunished transgressions that
a more temperamental person would not have tolerated), the latter
when his moods and reactions to seemingly benign situations (or
worse, incidents largely of his own making) appeared to the writers
incomprehensible. In later years, Henry would admit that he was not
an easy man to understand, and throughout his public life he would
often find himself reluctant to enter public discourse, expecting little
clarity or understanding from the press, believing that any extended
attempt to explain his positions would only make matters worse. The
result would be a deepening gulf between the writers and Henry,
each growing more suspicious of the other. In Henry's view, the writers never understood him, did not take the time to understand him,
and thus he did not trust them. To the reporters who covered him,
Henry was oversensitive to slights and unaware of the power of his
own words until they produced headlines. As far as they were concerned, Henry wanted to have it both ways, to be provocative but not
to be criticized when his comments provoked.

If a modern term could be used to describe Henry during this
period of his life, *passive-aggressive* would seem the most appropriate. He enjoyed his fame, if not the constant attention, then the
recognition of his position as one of the all-time great players. He
accepted the spoils of his achievements as well earned, never falling
into the category of athletes who called attention to themselves either
by audaciousness on the field or obnoxiousness in front of the press,
and he followed in the Robinson tradition of taking a public stance
when he believed progress for blacks was being stalled.

But that did not mean that Henry was always comfortable with how the baseball hierarchy viewed his worth, which, off of the field, was not as a valuable asset. He demanded that he be taken seriously for his accomplishments, and over the years he would often be caught between conflicting positions. Breaking Ruth's record only emboldened him more. He fought with reporters during the month of July. "I've been saying the same things since 1963!" he would say. He took on Jesse Outlar in a wide-ranging interview, chastising him and anyone else who called Billye "militant."

And there was one real, unforgettable piece of evidence that Henry wasn't the Henry of yore. Ralph Garr's Henry could hit in a fog of controversies. But during July 1974, feeling assaulted by the papers, the front office, and isolated by a new generation, Henry hit just .212 for the month.

In future years, the scenario would repeat itself: Henry avoiding directness, only to bristle at what he would consider a lack of respect for his stature. What he wanted, and admitted later, was inclusion—in the case of the Mathews situation, to be afforded the courtesy of being asked if he was interested in the job, based on his credentials as a player. That was how it was supposed to work. He was baseball royalty, after all. When Mathews was hired, he didn't have to call Bartholomay and ask for the job. Bartholomay had reached out to Matthews, yet in Henry's case, no one seemed to be reaching out.

And he burned because he felt that was what happened when you were black, and if the ultimate goal of the Robinson mission was equal partnership, it was only natural that he be given consideration without having to apply, based on what he had done in the game. The number of players who had become managers was too great to count. Yogi Berra had been a Hall of Fame player and slid immediately into management, managing the Yankees when he was still playing in 1964. That same year, Stan Musial, without a day of experience in the front office, became general manager of the St. Louis Cardinals. Henry had been playing twenty years and three of his white teammates—Mathews, Red Schoendienst, and Del Crandall—were already managing in the big leagues.

What Henry discovered in a hard and embarrassing way was the curious dichotomy in baseball: It was easier for management to compensate black players for their talent than to promote them to the front office for their intellect. Compensating a player for what he could do on the field was the easy part. Understanding Henry Aaron's value to a lineup took no more acumen than picking up the sports page and perusing the daily averages. A team with Henry batting fourth every day for 162 games was a better team. But adding a black player to the front office, giving him the authority to evaluate talent, to promote and demote white players, to hire and fire white personnel, well, that was a different concept altogether. Taking such a step would not provide enough of an obvious benefit to risk upsetting the order.

And to the black players, watching Henry be treated like a beggar by upper management, despite his 725 home runs, only reinforced another long-held belief in the black baseball community: Once a black player's career was over, opportunities beyond playing did not exist.

HENRY KEPT HIS desire to continue playing largely a secret as the Braves fell behind the surging Dodgers and Reds. In the meantime, the Braves planned to send their legend off into the sunset. Even as late as September 25, a week before the season ended, the position of management was to "keep Henry around" in some undefined front-office capacity. The club had already determined to retain Clyde King as manager. The transition, at least from the management perspective, was supposed to be seamless. Henry would play his final game with the Braves, retire, and let the company take care of him. There had even been rumors that the organization had set him up with a $75,000-a-year job as a special assistant to Bartholomay.

But as the final weekend approached, Henry voiced different plans. The summer had clearly hurt him, and the desire to continue playing, he finally began to admit in his own, deliberate, cryptic way, had not yet extinguished itself. For starters, he publicly stated two embarrassing pieces of information about his organization: The first was that there was no $75,000 offer on the table; in fact, there was nothing but vagaries about what Henry's responsibilities would be when he retired; the second was that the organization had never offered him the opportunity to return to the team as a player in 1975. Henry repeated often that he did not want to "stand in the way" of the club, a passive way of reiterating that the club had not asked him back.

So when the final game of the season approached, Henry did not say good-bye to baseball. There was no pageantry. He simply said, "I've played my last game in Atlanta," which was the equivalent of taking the Braves gold watch and chucking it into the Dumpster. Henry was establishing his independence. He would play baseball in 1975, most likely in the American League as a designated hitter, maybe for the Boston Red Sox, a title contender not quite able to overcome Baltimore, or maybe he would return to Milwaukee, playing for his old pal Bud Selig and the Brewers. But he would not say good-bye to baseball, only to Atlanta.

The ripples reverberated all the way to the front office, from a chagrined Eddie Robinson, who called the announcement "a surprise," to an unaware and unenthused Bartholomay, who had been with Henry for years, since Milwaukee. Bartholomay shrugged his shoulders, offered a purple stare, and said acidly, "There's no reaction from me," then walked away. The Braves had signaled a youth movement, as Henry said often during the final two months of the season when he felt marginalized and unappreciated, and he was, it seemed, returning the favor by carving out a new path for himself, as eager to leave the Braves as the club was to look to 1975 without him. "The bottom line was that they were businessmen," Ralph Garr said. "All of Henry's people, the ones he grew up with in the game, his peers, they were all gone. The people who ran the club at that point didn't have a lot of sentimentality about him."

October 2, Atlanta, with a sparse but enthusiastic crowd of 11,081 fans on hand to say good-bye, Henry popped out, walked, and grounded out the first three at bats of the rest of his playing life with the Braves. On the fourth, in the seventh inning against a rookie named Rawlins Jackson Eastwick III, Henry launched a vicious liner over the left field fence, the ball sizzling into the bull pen. Henry trotted around the bases, head down, and ran into the dugout, the crowd begging for a curtain call, for one last look. But Henry kept going, down the stairs of the dugout, down the tunnel, and into the clubhouse, moving, he would later say, to keep from crying. He took off the uniform and would never come back.

AARON'S LAST HURRAH . . .

The Hammer Slams a Homer, And Looks to the American League

In the final swing of his 21st and final season with the Braves, Henry Aaron said farewell to Atlanta fans with a home run in the seventh inning. . . .

The Hammer said before his record 3,075 game in a Brave uniform that he would like to bow just like Ted Williams did by hitting a homer in his last time at-bat.

Henry could have been Williams, walking away with one shining last moment. He would have been even *better* than Ted, and people would have deified 1974 in a way that gave Henry his own special wing in the hero worship Hall of Fame as the guy who hit a home run not only in the *first* at bat of his final season but also in his *last.* In between, he broke Babe Ruth's all-time home run record and, just for kicks, called his home-run shot in his final at bat *before the game.* That was the kind of stuff people talked about for decades, the kind of legend that inspired the poets, the kind of outsized feats that synthesized the man and his numbers.

But after the game, Henry was not full of poetry or melancholy or reflection, content on freezing his moment. He was evasive and, in the minds of some, the Atlantans who sometimes felt as underappreciated by Henry as he did by them, sarcastic. And in his own way, he was unburdened, his mind focused on the next chapter of his life, one that did not include Atlanta. "I'm hoping that was not my last one," he said, laughing and talking with members of the Atlanta press for the final time at Atlanta–Fulton County Stadium. "I might hit my last one against Cleveland, Chicago, somebody. . . ."

Even Wayne Minshew, who felt an uncommonly close connection to Henry, was unclear about the reason for Henry's buoyancy and the lack of statesmanship on both sides. After all, he had played three thousand games with one organization.

"His mood was flippant following the homer, however, his voice teasing," Minshew wrote. "Nobody was sure how serious Aaron was. But it appears he is ready to part company with the Braves."

As had been true with the writers in Milwaukee, Henry did not have that great or lasting a relationship with any member of the Atlanta press, Minshew perhaps being the closest. But Jesse Outlar, who was not an Aaron adversary but could not be called an ally, knew he was writing for the history books. After the game, he wrote of Henry with an understanding of his weight and significance, both as a player and as a legitimizing force for baseball during his nine years in Atlanta.

AARON'S BRILLIANCE LEAVES A MEMORY

The greatest Brave obviously isn't departing on the best of terms from the only team he has ever played for.

Ironically, Ruth ended his career with the Braves, disenchanted with the Yankees. . . .

Seeing Aaron take off no. 44 for the last time was a sad scene. . . . The long summer and the longest career had ended. You see a Henry Aaron once in a lifetime, if you're lucky.

For the next month, as football season raged through the South, and Henry and Billye flew to Japan for a home-run exhibition against the Japanese home-run champion Sadaharu Oh, Bud Selig and Bill Bartholomay began private negotiations in earnest. The Red Sox were in contention to trade for Henry, but no team could compete with Milwaukee.

While Henry was in Tokyo, Davey May, still wrestling the cobwebs free from a season during which he had hit all of .226, called his home in Milwaukee from Chicago to check in on his wife, who immediately after picking up the phone informed her husband that he had been traded.

"What? Where are we going?"

"Atlanta."

"Atlanta?"

"Yes. Hank Aaron is coming here."

"Me for Hank Aaron?" he said, then hung up the phone and repeated the exchange to Wayne Minshew. "I had to call her back to make sure I heard it right."

CHAPTER FIFTEEN

ACKNOWLEDGMENT

AT VIRTUALLY EVERY major stage in Henry Aaron's professional life, a familiar pattern would develop, predictable as a 3–0 fastball: He would excel on the field and somehow become wounded off of it, slowly burning at yet another personal slight. It was only after he'd walked out the door, embarking on the next chapter in his life, that he would be rediscovered, the people he'd left behind realizing, too late, that the world without him seemed just a bit emptier. The reassessment of him, in fact, would always be the same: Henry Aaron was a treasure after all. *He carried himself with such dignity!* And the people who wanted to celebrate him anew and be close to him and tell him how much he had touched them would always wonder why he appeared to live at a certain remove, and why he did not seem particularly overjoyed by their sudden and heartfelt acknowledgment.

The answer, repeated by his handlers and friends, who were channeling the big man himself, was also almost always the same, resulting in maddening standoff: *He wasn't the one who'd changed. . . . No, he's not bitter. He is living his life. He's moved on. It's not his fault you did not realize what you had.* It happened in Mobile, when Henry grew to be one of the most famous, most accomplished people his home city had ever produced. It happened as a player (and later in retirement, during each anniversary of the record), when baseball would realize the depths of Henry's substance, that he was the difference between a gorgeous fireplace and a hearty woodstove: Other guys may have shone more elegantly, but it was Henry who was the reliable one, who burned longer and brighter, the one who always produced the most reliable heat.

So it only stood to reason that in the end, after the hugs and the kisses and the history making, leaving Atlanta would be no different from the other leave-takings. During the twenty-one-hour flight back from Japan, after the trade was announced and it was clear he was now a member of the Milwaukee Brewers American League Baseball Club—a team that did not exist until his seventeenth year in the big leagues—Henry had thought both about the significance of his return to Milwaukee and the details of his departure from the Braves franchise and, more pointedly, Atlanta. In a first interview, he gave the public a snippet of his conversation with Bud Selig.

"I'm going home," he'd told Selig, completely aware of the cutting double entendre. Yes, he was returning to the origins of his major-league career, and, no, Atlanta in the nine seasons he'd spent there had never quite felt like home. Privately, he was embittered, first that the Braves had seemed so dismissive of his potential as an organizational asset apart from his batting average, and, second, that they hadn't seemed to hesitate about siccing the newspapers on him, giving the public the impression that the club had done everything it could to keep him in Atlanta, but Henry, alas, was leaving on his own accord. In retrospect, Bill Bartholomay would view Henry's leaving Atlanta for Milwaukee as one of his great mistakes—perhaps his greatest in running the franchise, he would later say—but only after Henry was gone. At the time, in September 1974, trading Henry Aaron may very well have been a difficult choice for him, but there was another truth that Henry knew better than anyone else, Bill Bartholomay included: At no point did the Braves ever make an offer for him to stay.

If there was an exception to the rule that Henry would only be appreciated over time, at the appropriate remove, it was Milwaukee. He told the reporters that he had never wanted to leave in the first place, and though the bitterness between the Braves and the city would never be reconciled, the players only grew in stature, and Henry was now the biggest of them all. And now he was headed back.

HE HAD REJECTED the poetic imagery, the walking away unforgettably and for good with a home run, the type of Ted Williams–style departure that would have given him a swashbuckler's flourish. But

Henry did not possess the artistic instinct to walk away, not now when he could receive something just a little more concrete, more consistent with his pragmatic nature: money. His three-year, $600,000 Braves contract completed, he signed a two-year deal with the Brewers that would pay him another $240,000 per season, and that did not include his million-dollar deal with Magnavox and other rising endorsement opportunities. His finances, once crumbling and in disrepair, were rebounding.

In addition, he had gained something equally important to the cash, something that his home franchise, the Braves, had not even considered offering: a future. The Braves told Henry a job awaited him upon retirement, but when pressed, neither Bartholomay nor Eddie Robinson could specify exactly what Henry would be doing. He had wanted an opportunity that contained substance—a front-office job where he would be involved in the evaluation of players and the running of the franchise, yet the Braves would commit only to an ambiguous promise of "something in the organization." Henry did not want to be trotted out only at the appropriate time—probably for some event that required the support of the black community—to shake a few hands and smile.

When he arrived for his meeting with Brewers management, Bud Selig and his people cultivated Henry, telling him to take the long view, to think about the years after he'd hung up his spikes. Selig spoke to Henry as an equal, with respect, as a person who possessed value beyond the limits of wearing the jersey. The Selig sales pitch was the perfect approach for a man still quietly broiling from being treated like the hired help, by people to whom he had given the past twenty-one years. By their actions over the final year of his contract, the Braves had coldly reminded him—first by not considering him as a manager and later by allowing him to leave—that in the end he was just a ballplayer, and all ballplayers were replaceable.

But Bud Selig spoke to Henry about being connected to Milwaukee for life. Henry was part of the Milwaukee family and had been since he arrived in 1954. He told Henry that he was returning a family heirloom to Milwaukee, and, even better, that Henry was his friend. Selig treated Henry as royalty (in the coming years, he would even build Henry a full tennis court at the Atlanta house), and discussed with him future employment opportunities: a job with decision-making authority in the organization after he retired (general manager, farm director, perhaps). The Milwaukee people even talked about the possibility of setting Henry up in business, a local or even national beer distributorship as well, with far-flung territories and autonomy. After all, the Miller family was Milwaukee and could make things happen with a finger snap.

While Bartholomay would years later forge a substantial relationship with Henry, it was Selig who was the first owner in baseball to invest in Henry Aaron, the man. The two men had known each other since sitting on the benches at City Stadium in Green Bay, watching Lombardi's Packers, but it was the reunion in Milwaukee that began to seal their friendship. Selig, in fact, was at his most canny, his most genuine for his personal investment in Henry would pay lifelong dividends. Where his contemporaries seemed destined to underestimate Aaron, Selig immediately understood Henry's value, in the short term by providing the Brewers with the credibility the team lacked.

"He did not have as much left in the tank as I had hoped, but I always knew that bringing Henry Aaron back to this city would have an immense impact," Selig would say thirty-five years later. "We didn't win a lot of ball games, but in his own dignified manner, he legitimized us."

IN THE YEARS Milwaukee went without baseball, destiny had plans other than the family car business for Bud Selig, and the arrival of Henry represented something of a personal vindication. In the mid-1960s, after the Braves had left, he formed Teams, Inc., a loose organization of area businessmen and former Braves shareholders designed to attract a new ball club to Milwaukee. As a member of the generation that, in his words, "had their hearts ripped out" by the Braves departure, Selig had long vowed that he would avenge that bitter defeat. He would return baseball to the city, and make sure it would never leave again.

He first tried to attract a struggling franchise, the Chicago White

Sox, by having the team play exhibition games in Milwaukee during those cold four seasons the city lost big-league ball. The White Sox ultimately didn't bite, but during one season, the Milwaukee exhibitions totaled nearly a third of the White Sox attendance.

Selig had proven to baseball's curmudgeonly owners that Milwaukee still had a thirst for baseball and that Selig himself could be a persistent and capable player. It was clear another round of expansion would come soon, as cities as diverse as Montreal, San Diego, Dallas, and Seattle were all clamoring to apply for franchises. Milwaukee was an earnest but hardly exotic choice. American rust-belt cities were losing franchises, not gaining them. But Selig persisted. Before long, Bud Selig had become the face of baseball in Milwaukee and slowly began entering the cloistered world of major-league baseball.

When Selig corralled the Seattle Pilots from bankruptcy court, purchasing the club for $10.8 million in the winter of 1970, he maintained a certain historical symmetry. The Pilots had been awarded to Milwaukee at a similar point in the year—during spring training—as the Braves had been awarded to Milwaukee eighteen years earlier. In 1952, the Boston Braves had officially become the Milwaukee Braves in between innings of a spring-training game in Bradenton, and in 1970, the Seattle Pilots equipment truck had literally stopped on an Arizona highway, awaiting instructions from management on whether to drive north, back to Seattle, or northeast to Milwaukee.

Selig had done it, and in the process attempted to assuage the old hard feelings by putting the band back together. Del Crandall, the old Braves catcher, was the manager, and now Henry, forty-one years old but still Henry, would anchor the lineup. There were reunions with old friends, editorials, and luncheons, like the Play Ball Luncheon at the Marc Plaza, the one that attracted eight hundred people (the biggest turnout ever), where Henry sat sheepishly while the crowd sang "Hello, Henry" (to the tune of "Hello, Dolly!" no less). Bob Uecker, another of Henry's old teammates, was now a Milwaukee institution, a broadcaster with the club who also did funny beer commercials and told an endless stream of self-deprecating jokes.

Henry would connect to the fans (and make a little extra money) by collaborating with Uecker on "The Locker 44 Show," a pregame interview Uecker conducted with Henry before each game. "I know there are a lot of people picking us to finish fifth or sixth," Henry said when he took the microphone. "But there's not a player on this ball club who feels we're a fifth-place club." The Milwaukee people even took care of Billye, setting her up with a morning show on local television to make her feel right at home.

Still, everything was a just a little bit off. Henry was back in Milwaukee, but life is never so neat. The year 1954, when Henry was a young man on a team good enough to win the whole thing, was long gone. Going home seamlessly was nothing more than a cruel mirage, no more real than a father who stares in the face of his adult son yet still sees a boy. The nostalgia, in truth, had no value, no impact on the realities of 1975.

And there was nothing wistful about 1975. The Brewers, as a team, were awful, and they had been since arriving in Milwaukee from Seattle five years earlier as a no-name cast with little future. The Brewers were a ham-and-egg expansion team, had never finished higher than fourth place (and that year lost ninety-seven games), and had never even enjoyed a winning record. Henry was now an American Leaguer, a member of a foreign, shadowy place that played by different rules in different cities with different umpires. Worse, Henry had no love for the American League, the circuit whose collective, institutional racism fueled the black players of the National League to win nineteen out of twenty-three All-Star Games during Henry's time as a Brave.

In the AL, there was no continuity with what Henry knew. The pitching patterns were different. In the AL, they threw breaking balls in fastball counts. The umpires seemed to ignore the high strike *and* the low strike. The uniforms were purely 1970s god-awful: powder blue double-knit pullovers with yellow trim for road jerseys, not a button in sight, elastic-band belts, no buckles. The home jerseys were slightly better: white with blue pinstripes and block letters, and when Henry dressed, the strange jersey formed convexly around his paunch, meeting his waist.

Milwaukee was aflutter for his return, but Henry was no longer the eager, hungry twenty-year-old, green as a cucumber but armed with immeasurable talent, his future one of infinite visibility. He was forty-one, coming off a season of doubt and despair, the pedestrian numbers—.268, twenty homers, sixty-nine RBI—easily the least impressive of his career. He was playing for a team that was attracted to him, easily one of the greatest right fielders who ever lived, precisely because he would agree *not* to play in the outfield. The designated hitter, in existence since 1973, was the acknowledged rest home for finished ballplayers, sluggers who might still have some box-office appeal and a little pop left in their bat.

Nor was the Milwaukee of 1975 the magical place of 1954, the haven of free eggs and free gas for the players and complimentary dry cleaning, hero worship and *innocence.* Twain had it right: Youth is wasted on the young. Like the rest of the country, Milwaukee had grown up and gotten a little older, a little more scarred, a little more jaded, having lived through an unpopular war, political assassinations, civil rights, and the hard, icy blade of business cutting through the supposedly happy diversion of sports. The city now was mired in the sticky, modern big-city gumbo: integration, inflation, and unemployment. Baseball did not provide much relief. Wisconsin was particularly volatile, having weathered spirited student antiwar protests. Vietnam and school desegregation were issues that dominated all others, and Henry returned to a Milwaukee in a deep confrontation with itself. The questions of the 1960s demanded answers in the 1970s, and the time had come to vocalize what everybody knew, that racial integration was impossible while social and geographical segregation still existed.

And so much of those good old days had been nothing but a mirage anyway. Henry knew it, knew that he'd been insulated from the rough edges by his talent for hitting pennant winners for the home team. The mirage—or, more accurately, the belief in it—was a reason the current realities now seemed so harsh. Father Groppi, the activist conscience of the city, knew this better than anyone. Groppi, the heroic South Side priest who had assaulted the city's housing inequities with embarrassing protests of the city leadership— including members of his own archdiocese who preached tolerance and conciliation by day yet were members of segregated social clubs by night—found himself isolated by the 1970s, in his words, "stripped" of his parish and disillusioned by the nobility of the priesthood.

By the time Henry returned, Groppi had gone back to his old job, driving a public bus for the city for the final decade of his life. The fire for justice burned less bright. He was a weary and beaten underdog, his belief that change was possible less fervent. Nevertheless, Groppi had been more than a symbolic figure. The public protests, like the 1967 march on Kosciuszko Park, contributed to the city's first fair-housing ordinance the following year. He had joined the legendary generation of white Catholic priests who were as much a part of the civil rights movement as the better-known, historic figures they marched beside.

When Henry arrived, the nation's eyes rested upon the racial cauldron in Boston, which for years had first resisted the charge that the city's schools had been purposely segregated or denied that segregation produced an inferior education for black children—old arguments both, dating back before *Brown v. Board of Education,* yet the cornerstones of Northeast resistance. Boston had begun court-ordered busing (*forced* busing, the whites called it, lest anyone be unsure of where they stood on the issue of school integration), and in the school years of 1974 and 1975, the city erupted so violently and so completely that it would never lose its reputation as the symbol of American urban racial hostility.

Boston received the attention, and the infamy, but it was in Milwaukee where the nation's first lawsuit was filed, in 1965, challenging de facto segregation—public schools were segregated because city neighborhoods were segregated and, as such, could not be remedied without busing. It was quiet, innocuous Milwaukee that the frustrated locals, white and black, would call "the most segregated city in America." Since Milwaukee's neighborhoods were so clannish, the question of whether to bus the city's students to achieve integration was inevitable. As in Boston, Milwaukee school board officials tried every stalling tactic short of the four corners defense. When Henry and Billye moved into a condominium downtown, school desegregation was the central, roiling issue in the city, on the front page of both newspapers.

BUSING TO INTEGRATE? NOPE!

By Joel McNally of the *Journal Staff*

The popular expression is, "I am not against integration. I just don't like busing."

The NAACP Legal Defense Fund analyzed white opposition to busing differently in a study called, "It's not the distance. It's the niggers."

. . . A majority said they favored racial integration of schools, but by an even wider margin they disapproved of busing to achieve it.

. . . a closer look shows . . . busing . . . is opposed only when it would lead to racial integration.

For years, Henry had sought respect. Like Jackie Robinson, he wanted to be an important voice on significant issues. But in 1975, Bud Selig noticed a different Henry, less public, more distant, and certainly less willing to engage. Selig believed the difference, naturally, was the hangover effect of chasing Ruth. Henry veered away from the desegregation issue in Milwaukee, much to the disappointment of the local NAACP chapter, which felt Henry's voice might have made a difference. He was not hostile to the causes of integration in Milwaukee, but his kids were no longer in the public school system. The issue was not as much of a personal one. He was reticent to lend his name to the civil rights battles that had predated him. Not only did this fight seem not to be his but he did not appear to have much fight left in him at all.

ON THE FIELD, Henry had no illusions. For two seasons, sustained by nostalgia and professionalism—not to mention a healthy dose of the athlete's refusal to face his own mortality—Henry flailed at the plate. He was a tired baseball player mentally, and an increasingly limited one physically. Nevertheless, the nostalgia maintained the fantasy, and Henry played along. At each of the seemingly endless civic luncheons before spring training, Henry set his usual goals—thirty to thirty-five home runs, a .300 average—even though he'd finished 1974 with the fewest number of home runs since Eisenhower desegregated the public schools, and he hadn't sniffed .300 all season. What he didn't tell the fans was that a hitter's greatest weapon— something even more valuable than his wrists—were his eyes, and Henry could no longer see as well as he once had.

He had taken to wearing glasses, first for reading and then to drive. That meant he could not see items that were close to him nor could he see things from a distance particularly well. Most importantly, he couldn't see the ball well in batting practice. If he couldn't see a batting-practice fastball, it was only a matter of time until he would be exposed.

THE BREWERS TRAINED in Sun City, Arizona, a holdover from the days of the Seattle franchise. On the team, Henry would be surrounded mostly by kids, though they would be talented ones. The advantage in being awful all those years was drafting high. Slowly, sunshine began to peek out from behind the clouds. The second baseman, Jim Gantner, was a comer, they said. Gantner wasn't spectacular and probably wouldn't make the club in 1975, but he knew his way around the bag. And he was local, from Fond du Lac. The outfielder they drafted in the first round, back when the franchise was in Seattle, was an enigma named Gorman Thomas. Thomas looked like he should be playing third base with a can of beer by his side in the Milwaukee recreational softball leagues, but Thomas, despite his portly brawn, was oddly athletic. Even more oddly, the coaches were looking at him in center field. There was one thing in particular Thomas could do, and that was knock the hell out of the ball. The problem was, he made contact with the ball only about once a week. The catcher was the hotshot Darrell Porter, the fourth pick in the draft, who made the all-star team in his second year in the league. They were already talking about him playing for a long time.

And lastly, there was a nineteen-year-old kid shortstop from Illinois. Robin Yount was his name, and they said he had all the tools. He was a shortstop who could play anywhere and hit anything. He could even hit the ball out of the park if you weren't careful. He was another one, a top-five pick (third overall in the 1973 draft), a can't-miss. Yount was the kid whom, when he walked into the batting cage, everybody was taking notes about to see if the reports and the hype and the fanfare were true. Henry understood that.

Yount recalled being too nervous to approach Henry, calling him "Mr. Aaron," even when Henry told him to cut it out. Yount immediately realized there was no pretentiousness with Henry. In the clubhouses, the phrase for acting better than the rest was to "big-league it"—with teammates, fans, friends, everybody. But that wasn't Henry.

"He was significant. Even though I was just nineteen, I could see how important he was, and not just in baseball, either," Yount recalled. "He had already broken the record. I knew how big he was, but he didn't come off that way in person. I mean, he didn't let it get to him. We knew all he had accomplished in this game, but he acted just like anyone else."

They were just kids, but they all loved Henry. He was spent as a player, but Crandall knew the master had a way and a warmth with people. He had also accomplished more in a season than most of them had in their whole careers. So, periodically during the spring, Crandall would gather his young team in the outfield and have Henry—the man who did not enjoy public speaking—give a talk. Sometimes the conversations would be about the game—the situations, the different pitchers, what made them big leaguers different from the cats who drifted around the minor leagues. Other times, Henry would talk to them about professionalism, what it took to *stay* in the big leagues once they'd finally arrived. These were the moments that deepened his conviction that he had made the right choice in leaving Atlanta. No one in the Braves front office, by his recollection, had ever sought his counsel, despite the fact that he had hit 733 home runs and collected three thousand hits.

NOW, UNLIKE 1974, Henry could take solace in breaking the record. He could be comforted by the couple of streaks that reminded pitchers to fear him. But in Milwaukee, time also kept sending him the same overdue bill.

The first notice came in Boston, on opening day, when Henry was collared, first by the remarkable Luis Tiant (a complete-game eight-hitter) and that erratic slop-thrower, Bill Lee. Then in the home opener, against Cleveland, 48,160 saw Henry knock in his first hit and RBI as an American Leaguer, only to see his old enemy, Gaylord Perry, strike him out three times two nights later. He would avenge the insult days later in Cleveland by hitting his first home run of the season off Perry, but when the Brewers landed in Baltimore for a series with the powerhouse Orioles, Henry was hitting .095.

The second notice came April 23, after the Brewers left Baltimore and headed to New York for the first trip of the season. Henry had expected to play in Yankee Stadium, which he hadn't visited since game five of the 1958 Series, but Yankee Stadium was under renovation and the Yankees played at Shea Stadium that year. It was there, in Queens, that Henry took Crandall aside and asked his old teammate to drop him in the order. Henry Aaron could no longer bat third. He was hitting .114 at the time. In the first game against the Yankees, Henry rapped two hits, including his second homer, a floater off Pat Dobson, the Brewers only run in a 10–1 Bronx mugging.

The final notice? That came a couple of months later, when Henry Aaron, hitting all of .226, with seven home runs, was selected to play in the All-Star Game for the twenty-fourth and final time. It was all charity, and that was flattering, but charity made everything feel even worse. Henry Aaron, the charity case? He'd said he would never let that happen to him, sagging to the finish, pitied by the same eyes and ears that used to look to him for the thunder. The game was played at County Stadium, and though he received the biggest ovation, even that didn't feel as good as it should have, because Henry was voted to the team ahead of Yount, who was left off the team even though it was obvious in that half season that the teenager was the best player in uniform.

The next year, 1976, was no different, and in some ways, it was even worse. Crandall was gone, fired the season before after losing ninety-four games. Henry considered quitting, the evidence long irrefutable, but he couldn't let go.

"I knew I was better than a .234 hitter," he said. "My contract called for $240,000 and I thought I could earn it." Unlike Crandall, the new skipper, Alex Grammas, had little connection or sympathy for his forty-two-year-old designated hitter, and the season was a slog. Collectively, the Brewers finished thirty-two games out of first, having lost ninety-five games. Henry played eighty-five games, hit .229. He hit ten home runs, five of which came during a ten-day period in July.

Still, the kids sustained him, made him feel wanted, as did one veteran in particular, George Scott. Scott, the world-famous "Boomer," had been in the league for a decade, since debuting with the Red Sox in 1966. Scott was immediately popular. Scott was colorful. He often spoke in the third person and referred to home runs as "taters." He received his nickname from the majesty of his monstrous home runs and told anyone who would listen that his jewelry, particularly his necklaces, was made from the teeth of the dozens of second basemen he'd ruined.

Scott was from Greenville, Mississippi, in the deepest part of the Delta, a place of intense poverty and debilitating racial codes. At Coleman High, Scott was an accomplished basketball player, averaging more than thirty-five points per game ("Without the three-point shot," he would say a half century later. "With it, I could have averaged sixty points a game.")

The segregation was grinding. Its very existence often undermined Scott's sense of self-worth, and during his worst moments as a high school athlete, he always wondered if his best was still inferior to that of whites, simply because the two powerhouse schools were not allowed by custom and law to compete. "I always wanted to play in integrated competition. There was a good white school, Greenville High, and every year, one of us would bring home a championship. One year it would be us; the next year it would be them. But I always wanted to play them, just once, just to see who was the best."

The Red Sox had signed him as an amateur free agent in 1962, one of just a handful of black players the club had signed in its history. The Red Sox integration began in earnest with the signing of George Scott, who was signed by none other than Ed Scott, who had discovered Henry Aaron eleven years earlier. Ed Scott's firm belief in "the good ones"—the whites who treated blacks fairly—was rewarded when Milt Bolling, another Mobile native, suggested to Red Sox management that Scott would be an asset in recruiting the black players who were changing the game. The Red Sox hired Scott, who would begin a three-decade career with Boston by signing George Scott. "Had we signed him earlier," Bolling said of Ed Scott, "we might have had Hank Aaron and Ted Williams in the same outfield." Scott, like most black players, was well aware of the team's notorious reputation when it came to dealing with blacks, and his early years in the minor leagues were characterized both by his heightened sensitivity to slight and the surprising relationship he forged in Winston-Salem with Eddie Popowski, the longtime Red Sox minor-league manager. Scott did not believe he was a popular player, owing to his quick temper.

"They used to call blacks lazy all the time, and I never understood that," Scott recalled. "How can any black player be called lazy when it was so hard for us to even get to the big leagues? You couldn't *be* lazy if you wanted to make it. I was waiting for someone to use that word on me, but they never did. If anyone ever called me lazy, I'd be right there to pop him in the mouth."

Scott recalled the resistance he encountered as he moved through the Red Sox system. He was chided about his weight and his swing and his attitude, for he was part of the new breed of black player—more independent, less deferential. And each time he despaired, it was Popowski, all five feet, four inches of him, who reminded Scott of his talent and defended him to the front office, often at his own peril.

"Eddie Popowski was always there for me, and I felt the same way about him. Back in the day, when I was in the minor leagues, he told the Red Sox they'd be making a mistake by not bringing me into the organization," Scott recalled. "The Red Sox told him not to mention it again or he'd be fired. Eddie stood up for George Scott. I'll always be one of Eddie's guys."

Scott was a big player in the Red Sox magical year of 1967, hitting .303, but then struggled the next year, hitting .171 in 350 at bats. He chafed under the unsparing manager Dick Williams, who constantly attacked Scott for his weight, yet Scott believed Williams was the best manager he'd ever played for.

He had a jocular relationship with the press. He was loud and boisterous and funny. He made them laugh, and he certainly was a character, a showman by nature. But Scott also later believed his personality and physical charisma undermined him as a serious ballplayer, and in retrospect he would be wounded that his colorfulness fed into the stereotypes of the uneducated black athlete. Some of the stories of Scott's glibness bordered on the apocryphal, the by-product, he often felt, of cruel baiting by the white press to make him appear ignorant. Once, during the bloody Nigerian-Biafran war, a reporter asked Scott what he thought of Biafra, the portion of Nigeria that seceded from the country. "I don't know him," Peter Gammons once quoted Scott as saying. "But if I ever face him, I'll hit a tater off him."

He swung hard enough to generate Santa Ana winds, and during the years when it was still an embarrassment, the mark of a less accomplished hitter, Scott struck out at least one hundred times in a fourteen-year career. But he was also a perennial Gold Glove fielder as well as a devastating power hitter.

When Henry arrived, Scott was already legendary. Henry was ten years older than Scott, so the two did not travel in the same circles, but Scott and Tommie Aaron knew each other from the off-seasons Scott would spend in Mobile.

Immediately, Scott gravitated toward Henry, watching how the big man conducted his affairs. George Scott noticed how much time Henry took preparing himself to play, both offensively and defensively. Henry's work in the outfield especially impressed Scott because Henry was the designated hitter; he didn't have to work on his defense because he would not be playing the field. And yet it was Henry who set the example.

"You didn't see him dive for a lot of balls, because he didn't have to. He played the outfield the way I played first base. Watch where the hitters put the ball ninety-nine percent of the time and be at that spot," Scott said. "He knew that you weren't supposed to run after the ball; you were supposed to be where the ball was going to land. My first year with him, I had the best year of my career. Too bad I didn't play five or six more years with him, because I did everything I could to learn from his example."

SUNDAY, JULY 11, second game of a doubleheader against Texas, one of those hellish games in a baseball season: Henry twice flied out weakly to left and grounded out twice. Nobody wanted to be there, slogging through the muggy Milwaukee air, neither team going anywhere, but the Brewers had won the first four games of the five-game series and the Rangers, already salty, didn't want to get sent home like chumps, either, wearing the collar.

Texas held a 2–0 lead in the seventh before both teams decided to alternate two-spot positions: The Brewers tied it 2–2 in the bottom of the seventh; Texas went up 4–2 in the ninth, only to give up two more in the bottom of the inning. Scott fouled out to first in the bottom of the tenth. Henry, zero for four, took one pitch from Steve Foucault before belting the next one into the left-field seats for a 5–4 win. The home run was number 754, and in the clubhouse afterward, Henry took another glimpse into the way-back machine. "Only the home run I hit to win the 1957 pennant felt better than this one," he said. Only later did he admit why, because hitting home runs had become so hard that each day the great man went to the ballpark in 1976, he was never quite sure if he would ever hit another one.

Nine days later, on July 20, against Dick Drago of the Angels, Henry wafted a home run into the seats, but for the next two and a half months he would not hit another. That was it. By that time, Henry had begun collecting souvenirs. But this home run, number 755, snared by Dick Arndt, a member of the Brewers grounds crew, would never find its way to Henry. Selig would threaten his job (and later fire the kid) for not giving up the ball. Henry would plead, appealing to Arndt's sense of goodwill (then offer ten thousand dollars), but Arndt wasn't selling. Henry would never hold his final home-run ball.

FOR THE NEXT two and a half months, Henry played and sat as the drudgery and losses piled up. It all ended on a Sunday afternoon in Milwaukee, October 3, against the Tigers. Virtually nobody was there. Two years earlier, in the final game of the season, he had called his own shot. Now, in the sixth inning, down 5–1, with two out, Henry bounced a single up the middle that the Detroit shortstop, Jerry Manuel, grazed with his glove. Henry chugged to first for a run-scoring single, hit no. 3,771. Grammas sent out Gantner to replace him. Charlie Moore clapped and shook Henry's hand as he continued to the dugout.

A SINGULAR EXIT FOR KING HENRY I

By Mike Gonring of the *Journal Staff*

. . . kings deserve better. . . . Hank Aaron, the king of home runs, ended his sparkling career . . . with a .229 batting average, .232 for the two seasons. . . . Kings are supposed to go out on top. . . .

. . . After he had dressed, he smoked a cigarette and chatted with friends. . . . And then Aaron was gone, out the same door he had entered 23 seasons before. The king has ended it.

"There's something magical about going back to the place where it all began, as if it will make things begin all over again. I think the fans feel it, too. Everybody wants to turn back the clock," Henry wrote in *I Had a Hammer.* "But I discovered the same thing that Ruth, Hornsby and Mays did: you can't do it."

When he retired, nearly a century of organized baseball had been played. Only Cobb had recorded more hits. Only Cobb had scored more runs. Nobody had come to the plate more, driven in more runs, amassed more total bases, produced more extra base hits, or hit more home runs than Henry.

When the inning ended, Scott grabbed his first baseman's mitt, gave Henry a soft rap on the hip, and then jogged out to first base. It was over.

"I didn't think it bothered Hank that much and I don't think it bothered the fans that much, because everyone was so happy to have him around. I didn't see anything in his personality that said outwardly how hard it was to play when he couldn't do all the things that made him Hank Aaron," Scott recalled. "He wasn't pouting or anything, because he helped me. I knew I was playing with one of baseball's all-time greats. The way he carried himself made me a better individual, a better player. He carried himself so professionally that I never thought about him being diminished as a player. Not once. He wasn't sad. I was sad for myself that I wasn't going to get to play with this man anymore."

PART FOUR

FREE

CHAPTER SIXTEEN

DRIFT

HENRY AARON'S FIRST two decades of retirement were good years for the memories business. Many of the prewar, preintegration legends—Williams, DiMaggio, Greenberg, Feller, Spahn, Musial— were still alive and lucid, telling the stories of what would be called "the Greatest Generation." Alive, too, were their less-known, uncelebrated shadow counterparts: the ignored Negro Leaguers, whose institutional memory was now suddenly a valuable asset, both to be mined by historians and a book industry that fell in love with baseball. Baseball sought the survivors of the old Negro Leagues, too, as a sort of social penance. They would now, far too late, be called heroes by an industry once convinced their participation would undermine the standing of the sport.

The confluence of history continued with the first generation of the integrated era—Willie Mays, Frank Robinson, Joe Black, Larry Doby, and, of course, Henry—entering its golden years. The living memory of the sport went back to before World War II. Henry was still in the public eye, simultaneously present and curiously distant, a visible member of the Atlanta Braves front office—having finally been brought back by Bartholomay months after retiring—yet still uneasily removed from his contemporaries. When the public or the writers would seek out Williams or DiMaggio, it was often with wistfulness, the words on the pages of the magazines and the newspapers willfully compliant to create that special frothy brand of nostalgia: Williams's cantankerousness was no longer uncomfortable and unrefined, proof of the Splinter's classlessness. Now, a Williams broadside was reshaped into an endearing virtue—a throwback forgotten in favor of an emptier, valueless time. The longtime baseball man Joe

Klein would reminisce about the time Williams managed the Texas Rangers. It was 1972, and Ted sat in his sweltering office, watching a fuzzy black-and-white television. Klein was just a pup, a kid working in the Rangers front office, bubbling at the privilege of sitting next to the great one. On the television screen was Henry Aaron, thirty-eight years old, trotting around the bases after yet another home run, and right then, as the television replayed in slow motion Henry's home run, Williams shot out of his chair, fizzing like a bottle rocket. Just the sight of Aaron at the plate had set off in confounded admiration his cranky perfectionism.

"He was just raging," Klein recalled. "I mean, just yelling at the television: 'HOW THE HELL DOES HE DO IT? THERE'S NO SUCH THING AS A FRONT-FOOTED POWER HITTER! YOU CAN'T HIT FOR POWER OFF YOUR GODDAMNED FRONT FOOT.' That was Ted. He loved him because Hank Aaron did everything right as a hitter to Ted, except that. Ted used to say it was impossible to do what Henry did, to drive the ball out of the ballpark off the front foot. You just weren't supposed to hit that way. But Hank did it, what, seven hundred and fifty-five times?"

In retirement, Williams grew larger still in all of his fiery impatience. So, too, did DiMaggio, tailored, silvery, and elegant, a distinguished gentleman at seventy-eight years old. A PBS documentary in 1994 by the filmmaker Ken Burns unearthed another invaluable baseball artifact: the Negro Leaguer Buck O'Neil, whose love of the sport and unfailing optimism during segregation blunted the game's institutional guilt and, in turn, made O'Neil into the unlikeliest star for the rest of his life. They were celebrated as the living treasures of the game. That was the deal.

Then there was Henry. With Henry Aaron, it was all just a bit different, just a bit off, the sepia longing missing from his aura—and everybody knew why. The writers knew it, and it was the big reason someone always made the trek to Atlanta. Henry knew it, and that was what made him different from all the rest, for what he held close to his breast was a big piece of Americana, cold and irrefutable and terrible, and, unlike Williams's misanthropy, impossible to massage into wistfulness. When the writers came looking for him, they came looking for one thing—the letters, the physical pieces of paper

Henry's fellow Americans had sat down and written, one by one, threat by death threat, during the record years.

The stories would grow in psychological complexity. Stan Kasten, who worked with Henry as a kid with the Braves under Ted Turner, had heard the stories for years: that when Henry left the Braves in 1974, he took the letters with him as dutifully as he took his spikes, bats, and a few jerseys. Some people said Henry still kept the letters in the attic of his house. Other times the story went a step beyond: that in numerous instances during a calendar year, Henry would go upstairs, walled off from the world, and revisit his America, the America that robbed him of his joy, reading and rereading the threads of his country that were now fused into him like a skin graft. Some people heard the letters were in shoe boxes; others were told he kept them in an old burlap mail sack or a plastic mail tub.

The writers would come to find out if the rumors were actually true, and when he grew tired of it all, of being both reduced and defined in equal measure by the same moment, he would say, "Hate mail and home runs. You know, there's more to me than that. But nobody cares. It's the only thing people care about."

The newspapermen perked up, usually months before one of the standard milestones of his record-breaking accomplishment. April 8, 1994, for example, was a particularly big one—the twentieth anniversary of his immortality. By then, Henry was sixty years old. An unstoppable battalion of gray hairs had overtaken his dark hair, and the long parenthetical creases that bordered his mouth deepened further into his cheeks. Billye Aaron always said Henry was his mother's child, and as he aged, Henry looked even more like Stella: powerful cheekbones suppressing an arresting, wide smile, small eyes alert, surveying, flashing spontaneously at a pleasing sound. Henry wore glasses full-time now, and though he had continued to exercise, the weight he had gained began to settle at his waistline.

WAITING FIVE YEARS to be immortalized is, usually, easy-chair living. The endorsements begin to line up, almost as quickly as the various and lucrative offers to serve on this board or that charity, but from retirement in 1976 to his Hall of Fame induction in 1982, tranquillity and Henry did not spend much time together. Henry would find himself in a drift. He would always draw a paycheck from baseball, and during this period he began to make business connections that would serve him for the next three and a half decades. Yet he spoke of himself as intellectually and emotionally unsatisfied, searching for that greater purpose, in constant conflict about finding that proper balance of activism, expressing his opinion when and where it was most needed. He would often reiterate that he wanted to belong in the world of baseball, but despite his accomplishments as a player, finding his place after retirement was a challenge that proved difficult.

He would say with great frequency that he wanted baseball to be "one chapter of his life, not the entire story," and yet even as this vision crystallized, Henry was unsure exactly of what that meant in actual practice.

As the 1976 season ended, Henry had resolved to return to Atlanta. In a sense, he had it right: There's no going back. Milwaukee would never lose its emotional and personal appeal, its place in his story, but he was no longer a kid. Atlanta, for all of its seeming ambivalence toward him and baseball in general—the city would always be a notoriously poor draw, even during the years the Braves fielded a championship-caliber team—was now his home.

The real reason the promise of Milwaukee did not materialize as he had expected had less to do with nostalgia and longing and more to do with business. When he retired, promises were made, gifts exchanged, but the reality never quite matched the handshake. Bud Selig was somewhat vague about Henry's place in the organization, though without the bitter edge that poisoned Henry's final days in Atlanta.

There was talk about managing the Brewers, talk that intensified after Del Crandall was fired. In later years, both Henry and Bud Selig would say they had "discussed" the idea of Henry's becoming a manager, but the truth was that Henry was as noncommittal about managing as Selig was about making him a hard offer to take over the club. The beer-distributorship offer fell through, too, not that Miller failed to keep its word in taking care of Henry. Instead, Henry did not particularly care for the fine print attached to the deal: He could have the distributorship, but he would have to put up some of his own money: a million dollars' worth.

And the matter of what territories Henry would oversee—possibly Baltimore or Cincinnati, possibly elsewhere—was equally ambiguous. He was a big name, national news, but one was an American League city and the other had no great relationship with him. He had been burned in business during his first decade in Atlanta, and it took years for him to recover financially. He thanked Selig for his time, and the lifetime deal never took place.

At the same time, the Braves had made subtle overtures to Henry during the waning months of 1976, raising the possibility that he might return to the Braves following his retirement, overtures that took on a certain intensity following Bartholomay's sale of the club to Ted Turner.

Turner was many things—bombastic, erratic, eccentric, brilliant, visionary—but he wasn't part of the staid baseball establishment. He was not a member of the old-school club, whose members used the veneer of tradition to maintain their curmudgeonly positions of authority and, by extension, to keep the players in their place. That alone made Turner an immediate threat to the old guard. He was a businessman who could see further and wider than most anyone else in the media or baseball and he understood immediately the value of Henry Aaron. Already a millionaire at thirty-four, Turner had purchased WTCG-17 in 1974. A year later, after gaining permission from the Federal Communications Commission to broadcast nationally via satellite to a nascent cable-television viewership, Turner recognized the power and utility of sports as a programming tool. He purchased the Braves the following year and Turner had immediately thwarted baseball's rigid structure—especially its tight rules on broadcasting rights—as his cable station, renamed TBS, broadcast the Atlanta Braves in every television market in the country. And there was nothing baseball could do about it.

If one thing was clear about baseball, it was how tightly controlled the job market was. Henry himself had complained about baseball's culture of retreads, of how difficult it was to get new blood into the pipeline for managing and front-office jobs. Turner was a starting fresh, and as such, the old prejudices and baseball customs did not always exist around him. He had already hired Bill Lucas, Barbara Aaron's brother and Henry's ex–brother-in-law, to be the team's general manager.

"Bill was farm director when I promoted him to GM," Turner recalled. "And then I find out later that he was the first black person in baseball to be a general manager. Then I find out that he was the first black person in *any sport* to be a GM. When I see a person, I don't see color. I wasn't looking for points with the civil rights movement. It just didn't seem to be out of the ordinary."

Turner was bigger than life. He had no time for baseball's silly little conventions, and for Henry, that meant an opportunity. What Henry was not completely aware of was the opposition to his returning to the Braves, especially in a front-office capacity. It explained why the club had been so willing to let him go following the 1974 season. There were some men, like Dan Donahue, the Braves chief operating officer, who viewed Henry only as a hitter, not as a person who could contribute to the front office. He was a former player, and former players belonged on the field, or on their fishing boats. Superstar ex-players were even less complicated: They were given no-show jobs or jobs as spring-training instructors, an easy way to titillate the fans and keep a famous name around while the person was drawing a paycheck. In other words, Henry should have been content with the job of being Henry Aaron—leave the heavy lifting to the professionals.

But when Henry and Turner discussed Henry's return to Atlanta, it was with a real job, with an actual title and responsibilities. As Turner recalled, he asked Henry what jobs he was interested in, and Henry told him farm director because it was a position that required talent evaluation.

"When I bought the team, naturally I wanted Henry. It was the right thing to do because he was so important to the Braves," Turner recalled. "I asked him what he wanted to do and he told me he wanted to be farm director because that was a job with some teeth. I didn't worry about whether he could do the job. I didn't know very much about baseball when I came in. If I could go from nonbaseball person to owner, he could go from baseball player to the front office. After all, its not rocket science we're talking about here."

Home run no. 703. By nature, Henry did not offer entry into his inner circle. The exception was Dusty Baker (number 12), whom Henry adopted as a mentee, just as Bill Bruton had done with him years before. Davey Johnson is standing behind Baker.

With Rev. Jesse Jackson during the height of the home-run chase

By 1973, Charles Schulz's comic strip *Peanuts* was appearing in nearly a thousand newspapers nationwide. Perhaps no other individual was as adept at capturing the country's attitude. As Henry approached Ruth, Schulz inserted him into the strip during the week of Aug. 10–17, 1973, solidifying his place at the center of the national conversation.

With his second wife, Billye, and Georgia governor Jimmy Carter, on April 8, 1974, hours before he broke Babe Ruth's thirty-nine-year-old home-run record. Carter would say that Henry Aaron "did as much to legitimize the South as any of us."

Henry at the summit. Widely considered the greatest moment in the history of the game, April 8, 1974, the night Henry broke Babe Ruth's record, would hold only bittersweet moments for him. He would not talk often about that night or reflect easily. "What should have been the best time of my life was the worst, all because I was a black man. Something was taken from me I've never gotten back."

Outgoing and gregarious, Tommie Aaron (right) joined the Braves in 1962. No other teammate could bring out the lighter side in Henry like his younger brother. Tommie had been forecast as one of baseball's first African American managers in the major leagues, until leukemia ended his life in 1984.

Henry Aaron said he would never be one of those players who hung on past his prime, yet in two years with Milwaukee he hit .232, with 22 home runs and 95 RBIs. "There's something magical about going back to the place where it all began . . . Everybody wants to turn back the clock. But I discovered the same thing that Ruth, Hornsby, and Mays did: you can't do it."

Henry, in his final year in the big leagues, with Willie Mays, then a coach with the New York Mets, at an exhibition game. The two held a fierce rivalry as players, but in the next chapter of their lives Henry would escape the shadow of Mays with significant successes in the business and philanthropic worlds.

Henry and Billye in front of his plaque at the Hall of Fame. Henry Aaron and the Hall of Fame did not enjoy an easy relationship. Following his induction in 1982, he would return exactly once over the next sixteen years. Only a greater appreciation of his skills and depth by a new administration healed the wounds.

Henry had always considered himself a mama's boy, but while his features resembled those of his mother, Stella, his unpretentious approach to work was a paternal trait that would forever define the son.

Despite his accomplishments, Henry Aaron never wanted to be defined by baseball. "I want it," he said, "to be a part of my life, not the whole thing." It was his friendship with President Bill Clinton that began to elevate him from baseball great to American icon.

In June 2002, Henry flew to San Francisco to celebrate Barry Bonds's 600th home run. The two had been cordial in the past, even friendly, but the growing scrutiny over Bonds's use of performance-enhancing drugs in pursuit of the all-time home-run record forever strained the relationship.

For thirty-three years, Henry Aaron stood alone at the top of baseball's all-time home-run record. On August 7, 2007, Bonds replaced him at the top of the numerical list, but not the emotional. "Bonds may have the record," Reggie Jackson said, "but people still believe in Henry. He's the people's home-run champion."

For much of his public life, Henry had been considered distant, brooding, and embittered, but it was his bursting smile, generosity, and dry wit—a side of him suffocated by the demands of fame and his discomfort with celebrity—that his inner circle of friends recalled fondly.

Henry Aaron

With that, Henry rejoined the Braves, but it likely would not have happened without Ted Turner. Henry, Turner told him, would have a job for life with the Braves. Henry's official position was director of minor-league personnel. He would oversee the 125 players the Braves farmed out through the five clubs, from A ball to Triple-A. He would be paid fifty thousand dollars annually. Five years after Jackie Robinson's death, Henry became the first black ex–major-league player making front-office player-personnel decisions for a major-league club.

Paul Snyder worked closely with Henry during those years as director of minor-league personnel. Snyder recalled that early on he sensed a certain tension between them, now that he was Henry's peer. Henry, Snyder believed, understood that there were those within the Braves management who did not want him to have the job and thus were interested in undermining his success. Henry responded by being outwardly withdrawn—which is to say, polite but distant.

"We were sitting back in our conference room in our old stadium, at Fulton County. I was sitting straight across from him. He was being a little bit distant to me," Snyder recalled. "I assured him I didn't want his job. I had a job. I was strictly trying to help him. I was trying to make the best decisions for him and for the Braves. I had a department to run. We weren't spending a lot of money on scouting, so we had to make the most of our decisions.

"From that day forward, I felt better. Inside of that first year, he was still trying to figure out who was on his side and who wasn't. I was a minor leaguer. He didn't have to worry about me."

FOR A SHORT time, Henry seemed to embody the next stage of the Robinson mission. In addition to him, there was Bill Lucas, who was the Braves general manager. Lucas and Henry were not always on the best terms after the divorce, and Henry would admit that the relationship could be tense at times, but they maintained a mutual and professional respect. Meanwhile, Henry's sister Alfredia had married David Scott, a rising member of the Georgia House of Representatives.

Not only was Lucas an executive; he had begun to create opportunities for others to have upper-management positions. Though Bill Lucas and Henry were no longer connected by marriage, they had known each other since Bill was a freshman in college in early 1953 at Florida A&M. After that, Lucas was a Braves prospect, until, during a minor-league game, he attempted to beat out an infield hit and crashed into the first baseman. Lucas blew out his knee and his career ended.

Then, in 1979, while watching a Braves game on television, Bill Lucas suffered a severe brain aneurysm. He was admitted to Emory Hospital for five days but never regained consciousness. He was forty-three when he died.

TOMMIE AARON retired as a player in 1971. He had played parts of seven seasons in the minors and had been named Most Valuable Player at Richmond in the International League in 1967. He had worked in the organization as a player, a roving hitting instructor, and a minor-league coach. Upon taking the job, Henry pushed for Tommie to become manager of the team's top farm club, Triple-A Richmond. There was even talk that Tommie Aaron could become a big-league manager. By 1981, only three black men had managed a big league club and none of them—not Frank Robinson, nor Larry Doby, and nor Maury Wills—lasted more than three seasons.

Tommie had served as a big-league coach since 1979, first under Bobby Cox and then in 1982 under Joe Torre, another of Henry's old teammates who became a manager. It was with Torre that Tommie headed for spring training as routinely as he had for the previous twenty-five years. Only this time, following his annual physical, it became apparent something was wrong.

"He went to spring training. They did the normal blood work, and something wasn't right," Carolyn Aaron recalled. "They told him he had a certain type of anemia. That turned into the leukemia."

As much as Henry, Tommie Aaron was a member of the Braves family. Where Henry had been serious and unsure, Tommie Aaron was loose and gregarious, thought Paul Snyder.

"He played all over our system. He loved shooting craps. I remember him in that rinky-dink clubhouse in Eau Claire," Snyder said. "He loved to roll the bones. Tommie had a lot of ability. He could play six or seven positions, everything but catch. He was very genuine."

Tommie Aaron was the one person who had bridged that gap with Henry, perhaps, apart from Billye, better than any other person in Henry's life. Henry possessed a deep laugh, and a broad, engaging smile, but it was Tommie who, friends said, was able to make Henry laugh from his insides, deep from his gut. Tommie could swear and joke and loosen Henry up in public to the point where, around Tommie, Henry Aaron was a different person.

"He was just so different from Hank. Hank was so reserved," Carolyn Aaron remembered. "He was so outgoing. All the kids on our street in Mobile would come to the house and Tommie would be the one to take them to the Mardi Gras parade. He would be out raking the yard and the kids would always be there. He taught them baseball. The kids in the neighborhood talked to Tommie more than their own fathers."

Every day for over two and a half years, both at home and at Emory Hospital, it was Henry who came by with food, who called every day. Periodically, there would be hope of remission, only to have the disease return anew. On August 16, 1984, eleven days after his forty-fifth birthday, Tommie Aaron died. Henry was at the hospital that day, broken. And it was there that Carolyn watched Henry Aaron burst, his right fist slamming into the reinforced hospital window.

"It upset Hank very much. Everybody jumped when he hit that glass window," Carolyn recalled. "It was normal to grieve, normal to cry. I can't remember when I stopped crying, but when I was in public, no one knew my heart was just broken. Then, one day, you wake up and you say, 'I didn't cry today.' "

BY TEMPERAMENT, Henry was not an orator or an activist. He preferred to work through channels and to collaborate. His commitment was solid, but he did not need to be in front of the camera, at the top of the headlines. He had, in fact, discovered that very little good came from taking a personal, public stance, and his edgy relationship with the press always seemed to intensify. Behind the scenes, he lent his name and gave his time to fight teenage pregnancy, a topic most professional athletes would avoid. What made Henry's approach even bolder was his announcement that he would do a speaking tour of high schools on behalf of Planned Parenthood. On a Sunday morning, April 30, 1978, Henry arrived at Grady Memorial Hospital to lend support to a national conference on teenage sex and sexuality. After the buzz caused by his presence had subsided, Henry listened attentively to the figures: The hospital had delivered an average of six hundred babies per year between 1967 and 1977 to girls whose age ranged from twelve to sixteen. The staff told Henry that two-thirds of teen pregnancies were unwanted and that a third of all abortions in the United States were performed on teenagers. At the press conference announcing his involvement, Henry took the podium and took a prepared text from its folder.

"Something's got to be done about it," he said. "Young boys are talking about 'scoring' on dates every day. When you've gone all the way, you've scored. But I want to tell you something . . . you're not a champion in my book if you cause a young girl who doesn't want to become pregnant to become pregnant and have to drop out of school." In meeting with the Grady doctors, Henry took a modern approach toward sex education. Kids did not need to be lectured about sex, he said. "They need to know what they're doing when they do it, and accept the responsibility."

He was applauded for his principles and commitment.

But when he stepped too far out on the ledge, he was not often deft enough to avoid trouble, for he had both crafted a reputation as the mild-mannered Henry Aaron and begun to challenge conventions during a time of transition. Baseball wasn't yet prepared for this dimension of Henry. He was tired of being slapped in the face.

In 1977, a month before Henry's forty-third birthday, Fred Lieb, who had been writing about baseball since the Dead Ball Era, listed his all-time team over the past one hundred years. Lieb was white, born in the previous century, weaned on the game when it did not include blacks, and his list reflected as much: It did not contain the name of a single black player. Bill Dickey, Lou Gehrig, Eddie Collins, Honus Wagner, Pie Traynor, Ty Cobb, Tris Speaker, and Babe Ruth represented Lieb's position players. Cy Young, Christy Mathewson, Walter Johnson, Bob Feller, Lefty Grove, and Sandy Koufax were his pitchers. As far as other writers were concerned, it was Henry who seemed the clearest omission, and they questioned Lieb about this.

NO PLACE FOR AARON WITH ALL-TIME STARS. AARON NOT AN ALL-TIMER?

"I was fully aware of the racial question," Lieb told the *Chicago Tribune*. "I had to ponder for a long time about leaving off such great players as Hank Aaron, who has broken many of the records of both Ruth and Cobb; the fantastic Willie Mays and Jackie Robinson. However, I have to be true to my convictions. Having seen most of the great players, past and present, I honestly believe this is the best team one could field."

While his friends could not understand why Henry would let a dinosaur like Fred Lieb—an unimportant man from another century—get to him, Henry broiled. And some friends also wondered why the attention of a stuffed shirt like Bowie Kuhn meant so much to him. There was one problem with that elevated logic: It mattered to *him*. To Henry, this was just another injustice, another way to slight him for surpassing Ruth. Billye would attempt to soothe Henry's ire, but his anger was inspired not so much by Lieb as by an accumulation of slights.

DAYS BEFORE Willie Mays was inducted into the Hall of Fame in 1979, Henry gave an interview with Doug Grow of the *Minneapolis Star Tribune* regarding his pessimistic outlook about opportunities for blacks in baseball. Henry, perhaps thinking of Bowie Kuhn at the time, or the black players of his day who were now retired and could not get a job in the front office, was withering in his criticism of the sport.

AARON HAMMERS AT RACISM
IN MANAGEMENT AND MEDIA

Hank Aaron burns with a deep rage. It's as simple as black and white. . . .

"Look around the stadium," Aaron said. "There's not one memento of what I did. There's nothing about what I did in this stadium, but they've got a statue of Ty Cobb sliding into a base."

. . . he is baseball's only black executive. The ball is white. The game is white. . . . It is because of all the whiteness around him that Aaron discourages young blacks from considering baseball.

Then there was Kuhn, whom Henry had never forgiven for not appearing when he broke the home-run record. The wound bore deep, and it became exposed and raw at unpredictable moments. In 1980, *Baseball Magazine* named the night Henry broke Ruth's record as the most memorable moment of the decade. The magazine also named Pete Rose the player of the decade. Kuhn would be on hand at a dinner in New York to present the award, but Henry had payback for 1974 in mind. He wouldn't show up in New York. "If he couldn't spare the time for a trip to Atlanta, I don't have time to go to New York," he said.

He had said nothing that Frank Robinson had not said, nothing that Jackie Robinson had not said a decade earlier. The crime Henry had committed was not one of candor, but that he'd changed the perception of who and what he was supposed to be. He had also let his guard down. He revealed that streak in him that could not brook slights or disrespect. Wayne Minshew, the reporter who had covered Henry as a player when the team relocated to Atlanta, was now the public-relations man for the Braves. Minshew brokered an uneasy peace meeting in New York with Kuhn, at Kuhn's Rockefeller Center office.

These months were turbulent. Dick Young attacked Henry for being small in his attitude toward Kuhn and disrespecting an award in his honor. He had stepped outside of his public persona, and then came the backlash. Lewis Grizzard, the *Atlanta Journal-Constitution* columnist, struck.

WHEN DID "THE HAMMER" TURN INTO "BAD HENRY?"

. . . Did Henry Aaron get hit in the head with a foul ball? . . .

Maybe it's his wife. You know how wives can be. . . .

The writers used to write of Henry Aaron, "This man quietly goes about the job of being everybody's superstar." But oh, Henry, how you have changed.

. . . you sounded off because there was no . . . mention of . . . the anniversary of Dr. Martin Luther King's death. Suddenly, you're Hank Aaron, activist? Who put you up to that? Jesse Jackson? . . .

You could give us another great moment, Henry—a moment of silence.

It was the part of the game at which he was the least adept. He spoke the truths of his America, of what he saw, yet he was especially sensitive to the backlash. At one point, Henry told friends in frustration, "They criticize me when I don't speak, and then when I speak up, they say I'm talking too much."

CAUGHT IN THE drift, easing its force, was Billye. They had been together ten years, celebrating a decade of marriage in 1983. Henry had always been surrounded by strong women in his life, starting with Stella and his older sister, Sarah. His first wife, Barbara, had been direct, and in many ways she was placed in an impossible position. She was present for a wholly different and fundamentally difficult period, both for Henry and for America. The road for a black baseball player was a harsh one during the 1950s and much of the 1960s, a road even more difficult for a wife during those times.

If there were cliques inside the clubhouse that left the black players excluded, black women often felt isolated from the social networking that took place among the wives. Barbara, Dusty Baker thought, in a sense got the worst of the deal: She endured the crushing period when black players, regardless of their skills, would never receive their full measure of respect. By the time society had changed, she wasn't in Henry's life to enjoy the benefits.

"Any woman who had to go through what she went through, especially in the South during spring training," Baker said, "well, I don't have a bad word to say about Barbara. She took care of me like I was one of her own."

Billye did not have to make peace with the same debilitating societal forces as Barbara had, for Billye met Henry when he was Hank Aaron, His Legend and society in general had removed the barriers created by segregation, dissolving those harsh environments that had existed in the foreground of Henry's first marriage. Those old, hostile spring-training towns had been integrated for years. The fans could be vicious, but Billye's post–civil rights movement stadium environment was worlds apart from the stands in which Barbara had sat, both in Milwaukee and in the South. Both Billye and Henry were much older than most of the other families on the team, with more world experience and less necessity to assimilate. Billye attended games, but as a career woman, she wasn't there as often as the other wives. Many of the players' wives were young girls who had met their husbands early, in high school or in small minor-league towns. Many had not attended college and possessed a far different worldview than did Billye Aaron, who by the time she had met Henry had already lived through the high-pressure, high-profile civil rights years in Atlanta with her first husband, Sam Williams. While many of the wives often saw themselves as rescued from the drollery of an average life by being married to baseball players, Billye had never considered herself a "ballplayer's wife."

Billye struggled through her years in the public eye, but there was something stately about her. Her voice was lavender-soft, and she spoke with a disarming and melodic southern lilt. It was the contrast between Henry and Billye that strengthened them. Henry may have felt uncomfortable as a constant public figure, but Billye seemed the stylish natural extrovert, someone who enjoyed the perks that came with being at the very top of a world that received so much attention.

She wore elegant, expensive jewelry and furs. She was tickled by the banquets and the balls and the travel. She did not avoid the spotlight, but, rather, embraced it. And that made public life easier for Henry.

There was a part of her, she often felt, that had yearned for public attention as far back as childhood. She would refer to attaining such recognition, to actually realizing so many of her daydreams, "as a miracle."

"Maybe somewhere on the periphery of my personality I secretly wanted fame. Since I wanted to be a singer when I was young, I imagine that would mean that I wanted to be noticed. It would be hard to want to be a singer and not be noticed," she said.

Her ambitions stood in direct contrast to her realities. She had grown up Billye Suber in Palestine, Texas, the fourth of eight children—six girls and two boys. Her earliest memories were of desolation and segregation. Still, education was central to the family. Each of the eight kids attended college. Her mother left Butler High School in Tyler to marry Nathan Suber. She would always say her greatest regret was never finishing high school. Nathan Suber was a professor; he worked on the docks in Galveston part-time and was killed in an accident when Billye was twelve.

The white high school in Neches had been closer to the family's home, but Billye was bused to Clemons High School. "We got our books from the white high school and I remember that every book I got from Clemons had someone else's name in it." Billye had ambitions and wanted to go to college. Palestine, she recalled, was "too dark and isolated." For her senior year, she moved to Dallas to live with her aunt, Reba Baker, on Pennsylvania Avenue. Billye was immediately taken by the size and energy of Dallas, especially when driving down Oakland Avenue, then the black thoroughfare of the city, in her aunt's green Studebaker.

"I wanted to be a singer. My name was Billye and I wanted to be Billie Holliday. I thought she was so pretty," Billye recalled. "She had this voice and she wore a gardenia in her hair, and I just loved that. There was a theater on Hall Street, and it was for the colored people, so we didn't have to go around the corner and up the stairs into the balcony. That was our theater. Looking back where we came from," she said, "being here is almost miraculous."

In the summers as a teen, she would return to work in the fields, picking peas and cotton, laughing at her deficiencies. "I never could get the hang of it. The most I ever picked in a day was thirty-seven pounds. There were kids who could pick eighty pounds of cotton in a day.

She was adventurous. She attended San Francisco State University before receiving a fellowship opportunity in Atlanta. She felt trepidation about returning to the South. The early skirmishes of the civil rights movement had made a deep impression on her, especially the confrontation in Little Rock, as it occurred the same year, 1957, she set out for California. "It was a wonderful opportunity, but when I thought of Atlanta, all I could visualize were men hanging from trees," she recalled.

She met Samuel Williams in Atlanta, and after marrying both were active in the Atlanta civil rights movement of the early 1960s. At their house on Fair Street in Atlanta, she had dined with Martin Luther King, Jr., Ralph Abernathy, James Bevel, and the other powerful figures of the movement. They had a daughter, Ceci, and in October 1970, five days before her birthday, Samuel Williams died suddenly, due to complications following surgery.

At this time, Henry was also undergoing changes in his life, and this was the true source of their connection. When Billye met Henry on the set of WSB-TV, Henry had recently been divorced from Barbara, while Billye was in the throes of her own depression. Increasingly, during the time just prior to when she met Henry, suicide had been in her thoughts.

"I can't pinpoint how things happened in this direction except for the fact that I was very lonely. I found myself at thirty-four a widow and really thought for a short time that I wanted to die," she said. "I saw no purpose in life, no purpose in going forward. Except, when I saw my three-year-old daughter needed milk or bread, then you had to snap out of it and say, 'You have to take care of this child.' "

One of her coworkers at WSB suggested she do a series of light features on the Atlanta Braves players. The assignment, she later thought, was an attempt by the station to help her begin her reentry into the world. She had interviewed Rico Carty before Henry and immediately realized that "those two didn't want anything to do with each other." She had little, if any, interest in sports. As part of her assignment, she was given two tickets to every home game, but she had trouble finding anyone to go with her.

In 1971, when she was first scheduled to interview Henry, he did not show up for the interview, and he was late for the second. When the interview finally took place, Henry was embarrassed for Billye, due to her utter lack of baseball knowledge. He even offered to help her write her scripts for interviews with other players. Their dialogue had begun.

Billye described Henry as kind and sweet but, in their early meetings, not terribly romantic. Billye recalled one of their first dates. "He asked me to meet him at this little soul-food restaurant across the street from the stadium. He wanted to go there because it was comfortable for him and because it was close, because he had a game that night. Let's just say I was used to better. So I said to him, 'Mr. Aaron, the next time you call on me, make sure it's an off day so we could go someplace, well, a little nicer.' "

He did not write letters or send flowers spontaneously, but he was grounded, and that was important. During those years, she did not need to be swept off her feet as much as she needed comfort and stability. "He always appeared to be a family man, and that was important," she recalled. "I had heard stories about what ballplayers were like, having a woman in every port. And he could have been, but he didn't impress me as a womanizer or whatever. When he approached me, I thought he was sincere."

She carried herself with confidence and elegance. She was disarming, but that did not mean Billye Aaron was any more forgiving of the racial climate than Barbara. Her demeanor may have seemed more polished, less confrontational, but she was, friends believed, far fiercer than Henry on most racial subjects. During the home-run chase, she was particularly sensitive when it came to the pressures Henry faced and how much of it was directly attributable to his being black.

"I used to think being an athlete was the same as being an actor, but they are different. As an actor, you are playing a role. You are purposely playing someone else. As an athlete, Henry was simply expressing his talent, and the actor doesn't have to get booed, every day, in living color. I think some people can't wait for the spotlight. Either you have it or you don't. Henry does not need one iota of it."

Though Billye appeared more comfortable at public functions and was able to mingle with a natural ease, she appreciated Henry's reticence. Together, they had come to a conclusion: They would use Henry's fame for something more than wealth. For years, Henry had talked about foundation work and trying to find the proper vehicle to set his philanthropic visions in motion.

"You don't grow up in poverty and want to see other people in poverty. You know what it feels like. You know what it looks like, and you see exactly what it does to people's ambitions," she said.

WHEN IT CAME to the Hall of Fame, Henry played the waiting game on a different plane, in a reserved, exclusive strata. As they approach induction, even the best players wait and wonder about admittance. Joe DiMaggio was not inducted into the Hall of Fame on the first ballot. Others worry about securing the 75 percent of the voters needed for induction. Jackie Robinson received 78 percent. Aaron's old teammate, Eddie Mathews, corralled 79 percent.

In 1982, when it came Henry's turn, he was not worried about induction on the first ballot, but he was worried about the percentage of votes: He wanted to be the first unanimous inductee in history. In a sense, it was a cheeky thing to want, for nobody had been a unanimous choice. Ty Cobb, during the first induction in 1936, received the highest vote percentage, 98.2 percent. That was more than Ruth and Walter Johnson would get; Ruth received 95 percent, Johnson 84 percent. Mays had received 95 percent of the vote when he was inducted into the Hall of Fame in 1979.

The day arrived, January 13, 1982. Juan Marichal was on the ballot. So were Henry's old teammates Lew Burdette and Orlando Cepeda, and another Mobile legend, Billy Williams. None of them would make it this day. Four hundred and fifteen ballots were cast. Henry received 406. He missed unanimity by nine votes. The 406 votes made him second only to Mays, who had received 409. Henry's 97.8 percent of the votes was second only to Cobb's.

"I'd be lying if I said I didn't want to be unanimous, but I realize nobody has been," Henry said. "I'm happy with the number of votes I received." He would be inducted with Happy Chandler, the commissioner who succeeded Landis and integrated the game, the old Giants shortstop Travis Jackson, and Frank Robinson.

ON FRIDAY, JULY 30, Henry, Billye, Stella, and Herbert, as well as Gaile, Lary, Hank, Dorinda, and Ceci, arrived in Cooperstown and toured the Hall of Fame Museum. Stoic Henry Aaron was emotional. He slowly lowered his guard as he walked into the old museum and saw his Braves locker, which had been donated seven years earlier by Bill Bartholomay, and the symbols of his life's accomplishments. He had long been used to being famous, but that did not diminish the feeling of seeing his life on display. He had his picture taken with his parents, with Billye, and with each of the kids. He joked with Dorinda, saying that she had always wanted to go into the locker room and now was her chance. He softened at the sight of his first pro contract, which called for two hundred dollars per month, and stared at a picture of himself when he was first called to the big leagues. Embarrassed by his youthful awkwardness, or pained by the years that had passed, he asked a Cooperstown official if the photo could be replaced by one "more recent."

Induction weekend called for the lowering of swords. At the Hotel Otesaga, Henry met Bowie Kuhn for breakfast. The history between the two had been bad for years, dating back to when Kuhn failed to send Henry a telegram congratulating him on his seven hundredth home run. "Only a sick man carries grudges," Henry said. "And I'm not a sick man." After a peace meeting, they played tennis and Henry destroyed Kuhn, with a smile. The day of his induction, he awoke at 7:00 a.m. and played tennis with Frank Torre, then prepared for his speech at the Hall of Fame Library.

HAPPY CHANDLER, 84 years old, spoke first. The official transcript of his Hall of Fame speech filled three full pages. Frank Robinson's was just as long.

And then there was Henry. His speech lasted just eight minutes.

Gaile, wearing a white dress dotted by a light floral pattern, wept as she mouthed parts of Henry's speech:

> I also feel especially proud to be standing here where some years ago Jackie Robinson, Roy Campanella proved the way and made it possible for Frank and me and for other blacks, hopeful in baseball. They proved to the world that a man's ability is limited only by his lack of opportunity.
>
> The sheer majesty of this occasion and its significance overwhelms me. For truly I reflect on my life and particularly on my 23 years in baseball. I am reminded of a statement I once read, and I quote, "The way to fame is like the way to heaven. Through much tribulation." It had been for me, to quote a very popular song, the long and winding road. Nevertheless, I have been extremely blessed.
>
> I stand here today because God gave me a healthy body, a sound mind and talent. For 23 years I took the talent that God gave me and developed it to the best of my ability.
>
> Twenty-three years ago, I never dreamed of this high honor would come to me. For it was not fame I sought, but rather the best baseball player that I could possibly be.
>
> I grew up in a home where there was little in the way of material goods. But there was an abundance of love and discipline. We, therefore, had much to share. And so too is this occasion an occasion for sharing, an occasion for thanksgiving. For I did not make this journey alone.

Henry said he did not speak longer because he was on the verge of tears. If nothing else, he was generally overcome by the weekend, for he and the Hall of Fame had not enjoyed an easy relationship. Grievances rested on both sides. Henry felt the officials at Cooperstown had not treated him as they had the other greats. He believed he had donated graciously, but his items were not treated as carefully or respectfully as the donations from other great players. It started back in 1973, when the Hall of Fame published a flyer on its new exhibits. No mention was made of Henry's donations, which included the ball and bat from his three thousandth hit, and the balls for his five hundredth and six hundredth home runs. "With all the things I've done," Henry told the *New York Times,* "you'd think they could mention my name in the magazine."

And there was that eternal slight that pierced his pride the minute he walked into the building: the two statues—one of Ruth, the other of Ted Williams—that greeted each and every visitor.

Meanwhile, the collective attitude of those at Cooperstown toward Henry over the years had been that he had no tolerance for honest, simple mistakes. Henry went public with problems that could have been solved with a phone call. He read malice into the relationship, and that made him difficult.

But now he was officially a Hall of Famer. No player in the integrated era, not Mays, not Gibson, not Jackie Robinson, had received a higher percentage of votes. But Henry could not escape the nagging annoyance in his own mind that baseball had relegated him to a one-event player, and even that moment—breaking the home-run record—always came with a qualification. In a final interview in Cooperstown, Henry voiced an opinion that explained his unresolved turmoil.

> I've never been able to live down breaking Babe Ruth's home run record. They say, "If Babe had played in this park . . . if Babe had not been a pitcher all those years." But I personally had nothing to do with those things. . . .
>
> I'm a little too busy and a little too old to have any bitterness about anything. I would like to remain in baseball the rest of my life. I would like to see the Braves, my club, win a championship, and then another championship. That's the last thing I want out of baseball.

Then he flew home to Atlanta, he said, unburdened, all hard feelings dissolved by his induction, or so he claimed. His actions told a different story, and actions were the defining trait of Henry Aaron. Over the next seventeen years—when living members of the Hall of Fame were invited to welcome in the new class of inductees—Henry would return to Cooperstown exactly once.

CHAPTER SEVENTEEN

CARS

OUT OF THE wasteland of the players strike of 1994—a strike that undermined baseball's credibility and lasted 232 days—came an industry-wide gospel, one with which the sport had been unfamiliar since the dawn of the Dead Ball Era: Baseball would go into the nostalgia business. It would sell its moments, its heroes, its history, and itself. The strike served as a reminder that the resilience of the game, the fact that people *cared* so much no matter how dysfunctional its leadership, was precisely what had saved it. Gone (at least publicly) was the standard orthodoxy of tolerating the players as an unfortunate by-product of the owners' moneymaking enterprise. Refusing to recognize the wattage of the players might have watered down salaries, but it also made for lifelong enemies, and enemies got in the way of business.

The fact was, 150 years of infighting had obscured what baseball was supposed to be all about: making people feel good. A labor war had prevented baseball from making money off memories at a time when everybody else—card-show hawks, home-shopping and classic sports channels, book publishers, individual collectors—was making a killing in the memorabilia business. This was the 1990s, the information age, where promotion was not only a virtue but, in a stratified world of two hundred TV channels and the untamed Internet, an absolute necessity. The sport had already mastered warfare, its history built on grinding, century-long animosities, but now baseball had found its new religion. From now on, moments would be cherished. Players would be celebrated by the sport as the gods they were to the public. Records, milestones, championships—the history of baseball—were valuable commodities being squandered by three decades of infighting about labor.

The Yankees, of course, had always known the value of hyperbole, of feeding the hero machine. They knew it better than anyone. It was history that separated your team from the rest, history that gave baseball its special currency, made you call it the "national pastime" even though football had long dusted the national game in television ratings and popularity since before men landed on the moon. It was history that gave you pride and pedigree and protected you from the lean times, kept you from being average. It served as the reminder that you stood for something permanent, something *important,* that you weren't part of the latest popular fad, but the standard of a continuing tradition. Even the name Yankee Stadium had withstood that latest sign of the sports apocalypse—corporate naming rights for stadiums—which produced so much money that teams across all sports were willing to sell off their identity, their roots for the short-term gain. The great stadium names, the ones that gave the eye a picture of a city and a team—Comiskey, Candlestick, Tiger, Oakland, Veterans, Three Rivers—all got swallowed whole for the money. But not Yankee Stadium, even with all the money that the Yankees could have fetched by giving that piece of itself away. History was the reason the Yankees were the only team in the game never to change its home uniforms once the pinstripes and the interlocked NY became standard. It was the reason the great glories of Ruth and Gehrig, DiMaggio and Mantle, Reggie and Munson were passed down through generations of ticket buyers who wanted to identify with this New York family heirloom, fans who wanted to *belong.* Regardless of the team's current record, a trip to Yankee Stadium meant being force-fed two heaping tablespoons of the dynasty, and that made everyone feel good and close. Pregame, postgame, and in between innings, the Yankees reminded everyone in the stadium that there might be no time like the present, but yesterday, if marketed properly, was even more salable a commodity than the fleeting lilt of today's pennant race. History only increased in value. The Yankees knew that they weren't just in the business of selling hot dogs and home runs. They were in the business of selling memories.

And as it turned out, nostalgia was big business. Baseball was about the generations, father to son, son to grandfather. But for all the sugary rhetoric of how baseball linked the generations as no rival sport could, the game had no mechanism to sell its most marketable quality. The plan been for baseball to partner with the corporate world to sell its history to the public, but even before the 1994 strike exposed baseball, insiders knew it was the marketing equivalent of the *Titanic*. After the strike, the depths of the disaster became frighteningly clear.

To make it all work, baseball had to rebuild its marketing and promotions departments from within, no easy task when the talent and direction had been torpedoed by two unnatural disasters—a calamitous television deal with CBS and the mahatma of boondoggles, a failure called the Baseball Network. Both cost baseball a fortune, leaving the promotional end of the business in shambles.

And it had to undo all the old rules. Baseball didn't just play nasty with the players, but because its economy had been local for a century, it was every owner for himself. Publicity was not run from above, by the umbrella of major-league baseball. Rather, it was a mom-and-pop operation. The two leagues had been, aside from meeting in the World Series, separate entities. The American League marketed itself, as did the National. Publicity and promotions were handled at the local level, meaning the Red Sox and Yankees and Royals and Padres promoted their teams, but a coordinated national marketing for common projects—say the game itself—did not exist. Whatever national marketing did exist was left in the hands of the television-rights holders, who could choose to market selectively, or not.

It was, in short, a complete and total mess. When veteran marketing and promotions man Bill Henneberry signed on as a consultant to major-league baseball, he used an old Yiddish word, *fercockt,* and when pronouncing it, he would say it meant just what it sounded like: *fucked.*

Henneberry had started out in the business in the early 1970s, as a vice president of marketing for Hertz. One of his first accounts was the campaign that featured O. J. Simpson running through airports. He had worked for Colgate-Palmolive for eleven years before consulting for First Fidelity Bank and the NFL. His idea was a winner: team logos on credit cards. A credit card with a New York Giants helmet on it? Fans could feel connected to their teams, Henneberry argues, receiving discounts or bonus points to be accumulated like frequent flier miles on each purchase, double points if used at The Meadowlands or when purchasing tickets. Henneberry was twenty years ahead of his time. It was a moment of genius—the kind that can make a career—but Henneberry never got to expand the program to the other twenty-nine teams. The league licensed the idea to Citibank. Henneberry was out (inches from a lucrative seven-percent commission), smoldering mad that life wasn't fair (you can't copyright ideas, after all). Citibank later sold the portfolio to MBNA, which made a fortune.

When Henneberry joined baseball as a consultant, he found a sport that was "virtually leaderless." For its promotional budget, baseball produced less than four million dollars in revenue. By comparison, the promotional budget of a pro sports league tended to be nearly three times that amount. Sports advertising was all about beer and cars (*Baseball, hot dogs, apple pie, Chevrolet!*), but when Henneberry arrived, baseball's sponsors were lightweights: Scotts lawn fertilizer and Kingsford charcoal briquettes.

"We had no car, no beer. We had nothing much above one million dollars," Henneberry recalled. "We were walking into an empty room, a completely empty room. No one was running advertising that supported the theme of baseball and using baseball to build their brand. Licensing got hit like you wouldn't believe. Trading-card revenues were cut in half. And on top of that you had the CBS and Baseball Network fiascos, and then the strike. Baseball left it to whatever television network gave it the most money to market the game. It was an absolute fucking disaster."

Two accounts—Pepsi at $1.2 million and MasterCard at a contentious $1 million—accounted for more than half of the total revenues at MLB Properties. There was no money, but worse, baseball had let its most marketable quality—its history—atrophy to a fatal point.

In the years immediately following the strike, baseball got lucky, and as ballplayers always said, sometimes it was better to be lucky than good. Two strokes of good fortune hit almost simultaneously. First, the Yankees were good again, which always meant more money and more exposure for the game. As fashionable as it was to complain about the dreaded pinstripes, the facts were immutable: Good Yankee teams meant higher attendance throughout the American League, higher ratings, and increased interest. The Yankees were the rising tide that raised all boats.

On top of that came another lucky bounce: Henneberry met with representatives from MasterCard, which had an uneasy relationship with baseball. It could, then, only be described as providence that it was the credit-card company that sought out baseball and presented a golden opportunity.

The MasterCard reps unveiled a campaign they believed would work perfectly with baseball. They had even made a demo tape as part of their presentation. The video began with a young boy and his father attending a baseball game, a soft voice-over following each frame.

> Hot dog . . . $3.50
> Program . . . $1
> Pennant . . . $5
> Watching a game with your ten-year-old son . . . priceless

MasterCard called it their "Priceless" campaign and wanted baseball, the American game, to be its centerpiece. MasterCard was eager, and there was no reason to shop for a better deal—neither football nor basketball could pull as powerfully on the emotional father-son heartstrings as baseball. Baseball was already angry at Visa, which demanded exclusivity as a part of its proposal. Like the Olympic games, Visa did not want vendors to accept rival American Express cards at baseball's signature event, the World Series (" . . . and they don't take American Express" went the Visa ad campaign). MasterCard was waiting, and baseball had lucked out again, a sweetheart deal in their laps. MasterCard re-upped at $1 million, but with an ad campaign totaling $29 *million*.

HAVING RECOGNIZED ITS good fortune (instead of noticing the suspiciously increased size of its players and their subsequently ballooning offensive numbers), baseball was now hugs and kisses and Kodak moments. When Lou Gehrig played in his 2,130th consecutive game, a ceremony did not mark the occasion. A later event, which included easily the most memorable speech in baseball history, was held July 4, 1939, because everyone knew "the Iron Horse" was dying. But in the new world, there were balloons and pageantry, game stoppages and handshakes (*even from opposing players, in the middle of a game*) that night in Baltimore when Cal Ripken broke Gehrig's streak.

During the apex of the resurrection—the home-run chase of 1998—two *opposing* players, Sammy Sosa and Mark McGwire, held *joint* press conferences. When McGwire passed Roger Maris's record, Sosa sped from his position in right field to give McGwire a hug. McGwire, nodding to history, reached back and embraced the Maris family. Roger Maris had been dead for more than a dozen years, but the family was able to enjoy a moment of closure and recognition.

It was all so mushy—Sosa and McGwire even said they loved each other. Judge Landis may have rolled over in his grave, clutching his "no fraternization" rule to his breast. Bob Gibson may have looked at the sport he once dominated and thought it unrecognizable with all this lovey-dovey crap, but the cameras, the fans, and the country ate it up.

Baseball had become the king of schmaltz. But to complete the circle, the contemporaries would not be enough. The legends had to be brought back, dusted off, and restored to *their* rightful place as the game's living elders, as a link to the past, the conscience of the future.

In preliminary meetings, one man seemed unanimously perfect to be the centerpiece of the initiative, especially because 1999 marked the twenty-fifth anniversary of the all-time home-run record falling. Henry Aaron was the one the public relations and promotions departments wanted. He was, went the thought, perfect.

Yet the marketing executives in the room generally viewed the prospect of approaching Henry with a certain amount of dread, because the word had been out for years, and, unchallenged, it became fact: Hank Aaron was too bitter, too angry about baseball to be the face of any kind of promotion. The word was that he was too difficult to work with. He had already soured on baseball because of the Al Campanis affair in 1987. Besides, he probably wouldn't want to be part of it anyway.

IN THE MONTHS following Tommie Aaron's death, two major events occurred in Henry's life, one by happenstance, the other by perseverance. In 1985, Henry attended a function in New York City where he met Frank Belatti, a native New Yorker who was an emerging power player in the Atlanta business community. Belatti stood in the lobby and the receptionist, not a baseball fan of any sort, asked Belatti if he was Hank Aaron, providing Belatti a natural icebreaker when they eventually met later that night. "Henry," he said, "I've just been mistaken for you."

Bronx-born, and a lifelong baseball fan, Belatti had been chief operating officer and president of Arby's, the fast-food chain. He worked with MLB properties on the RBI/Arby's award, which had been given to each league's leader in runs batted in. The two talked about business opportunities, specifically whether Henry was interested in becoming a franchise partner with Arby's. Belatti recalled Henry demurring. The restaurant and real-estate failures of the past still carried a fresh scar, and Henry had decided he did not have the business acumen to try again.

"He told me he hadn't had much success in business," Belatti recalled. "I asked him to think about it and also I remember asking him if there were any organizations that he felt strongly about. He said the United Negro College Fund. That started the business side of things."

Henry moved with trepidation, but over time Belatti learned how important it was for Henry to have success away from the ballfield. In many ways, being a baseball player was perhaps the only area in his life where he could assume success. He had always been self-conscious about his level of formal education, and his past business ventures were not fruitful. Even inside of the baseball world, he did not feel particularly comfortable off the field, he did not feel well-regarded for his abilities in teaching, talent evaluation, or motivating players, the elements that would have made him a good executive or field manager. Thus, it became clear to Frank Belatti that Henry did not view another foray into the business community cavalierly.

Henry entered the world of fast food, obtaining his first franchise, an Arby's restaurant, in Milwaukee. He would grow his chain to sixteen before selling them to acquire a Church's chicken restaurant franchise—the competition to Kentucky Fried Chicken—in Atlanta, which would grow into a twenty-three-unit chain including Popeye's chicken, Krispy Kreme doughnuts, and Burger King.

"It was clear that success away from baseball was very important to Henry," Belatti said. "He wanted to raise money for children. I think in order for him to fill that gap in his life he needed to be, always wanted to be, more than just a former baseball player. I was very proud that Henry Aaron told me he had only done two handshake deals in his life," Belatti said. "One was with Ted Turner, the other with Frank Belatti."

Belatti felt Henry's distance, as had so many others. They came from two different worlds, Henry from the Deep South, Belatti from Arthur Avenue and 187th Street in the Bronx. Belatti recalled that the relationship warmed over time, mostly because of their conversation about ethics. Belatti impressed upon Henry that he was sympathetic to the notion of creating business opportunities for African-Americans.

Trust was something Henry did not extend easily, and in his recollections Belatti does not remember a breakthrough moment between the two men. Rather, he recalls their relationship growing from business to friendship. "Why did he trust me? Hank is a very honorable man and while he is somewhat suspicious and rightfully so, he believes in people's good nature," Belatti said. "He accepted my gesture in good faith. He realized I was only determined to make him successful."

Belatti had been a Yankees fan all his life. He remembers respecting Henry and rooting against him in the 1957 and 1958 World Series. He had worked with baseball as an adult and thus was not necessarily awed by the size and aura of professional ballplayers.

Then, on Opening Day 1986, Belatti asked Henry if he wanted to join him for a ballgame. Henry agreed and the two went to the game at Yankee Stadium.

"We got out of the car, and of course, the masses started to circle. You could hear people screaming that Hank Aaron was here," Belatti recalled. "That was when it occurred to me that this was no ordinary man. I saw how upset he got when these things happened. He just couldn't go places. People wanted things from him. They weren't there to give him respect. They wanted to get something from him. They wanted to touch him or get an autograph and he resented that. He would say to me, and he was serious, how dangerous people were, and how he did not feel safe. We realized that watching the game from our seats wasn't going to work. I sat in my seat and George Steinbrenner wound up getting Henry a seat up in a luxury box, away from everyone."

The second event that began to change Henry's outlook occurred without his knowledge. Over the course of the late 1980s and early 1990s, a chorus of people from far-flung areas of Mobile began unrelated campaigns to celebrate Henry. Kearney Windham, a diehard baseball fan and self-made sports historian, concocted the idea of a Hall of Fame for Mobile athletes. Henry would become a charter member of the Mobile Sports Hall of Fame. It was a significant start, for Henry and for Mobile, and endured a prickly relationship.

During the same period, the city of Mobile, led by a new wave of younger, diverse politicians, began a drive to improve relations with Henry. In 1977, the city named a stretch of downtown after him, the Hank Aaron Business Loop. In 1991, Mobile mayor Mike Dow was pushed by city councilor Irmadean Watson to rename Carver Park, his boyhood playground, to Hank Aaron Park. After years of frost, the city's political leadership had begun to reach out to Henry.

Where Major League baseball was concerned, however, Henry had adopted the position that given the opportunity to do the right thing, baseball would disappoint him every time. It had been that way since Bowie Kuhn chose the Yahoo Club over him. The succeeding years hadn't been much better, and the likelihood that baseball would approach him with good intentions and then do him dirt in the end became something of an expectation in his camp. His relationship with individuals inside of the game had always been solid. Ted Turner made sure he had a job for life, and Bill Bartholomay now spoke of Henry as one of his dear, dear friends. But whenever the commissioner's office got involved, whenever he had hopes that the game would finally place him in his proper context, finally give him what he believed to be his due, his first reflex was to anticipate the very worst.

For example, there was the time Henry met with Greg Murphy, the new head of MLB Properties, ostensibly baseball's marketing and promotions wing. Murphy was considered by some coworkers to be a prickly, unpopular man, but he was passionate about the necessity to cultivate Henry. Murphy told Henry that he was a baseball treasure, a true living legend. He told Henry about baseball's new initiative to revive the game's heroes with a major public campaign. The two shook hands. Months passed. Nothing happened.

Times, though, were different. After Fay Vincent's successful ownership coup, Bud Selig, who still owned the Milwaukee Brewers, was now the commissioner of baseball. There was something else about the new baseball: The sport would no longer foster the charade that the commissioner was the objective protector of the game's interest. Still, Selig at the helm meant Henry had a man in the top chair whom he absolutely trusted. Selig never missed an opportunity to elevate Henry, and the praise was genuine. It wasn't lost on the major-league executives throughout the years that the commissioner's office was supposed to give the impression of being impartial, yet Selig would routinely state publicly that Henry was the greatest player of all time. "If you noticed, he never even said 'one of the greatest,' " Henneberry said. "It was always unequivocal."

That meant that anybody at MLB who wasn't completely sold on Henry (and there were more than a few unconvinced that Henry was charismatic enough to be a leading man) now had to deal with the wrath of Bud. Mess with Henry, mess with the commissioner. Even worse for the unconvinced was the lurking notion that should things not progress to his liking, should someone at MLB treat Henry poorly, there was the probability that a phone call was being made from Atlanta to Milwaukee and that the offending parties would be swiftly punished. Selig made it a point to note that he and Henry spoke constantly, "almost daily," the commissioner would say. That kept whatever hostile elements in New York on their best behavior.

Henry also had some true believers at MLB in Henneberry, Bob Gamgort, and Kathy Francis, the lead marketing team that made the decisions on which players would become the official face of the game. The trio did not consider another legend, not Williams, not DiMaggio, not even Mays. To the group, Henry was the obvious

choice, partly because it felt the need to honor Greg Murphy's agreement with Henry, and also because there wasn't a time Henneberry
would look at the record book and not be absolutely blown away by
Henry's career numbers.

"Hank was the only choice. I think because the promise that was
made to him by Greg Murphy. I always thought there was a little bit
of guilt that they had never done right by this guy," Henneberry
recalled. "I mean, okay, he had the home-run record. Everybody
knew that, but there was the stuff only a real aficionado would know.
Thirty-seven hundred hits? First in RBI, first in home runs, first in
total bases? Third in hits? I mean, come on. What else did this guy
have to do?"

One the other hand, the whispering campaign that Henry had
turned crotchety was just prominent enough to give the marketing
people pause. There had been talk that Henry had a reputation for
being impossible to please. Baseball would accommodate him, make
good-faith attempts to placate him, to close the wounds of 1974, but
it was never enough, or so went the thought.

The first meeting was in Philadelphia in mid-1998. Henneberry,
Gamgort, and Francis met Henry and Allan Tanenbaum at the Four
Seasons in Logan Square. The meeting did not exactly get off to a
rousing start. Henneberry, like Frank Belatti, was Bronx-born, a
diehard Yankee fan, tried to break the ice with Henry and was met
with the sound of crickets.

"I walked in, and I remember him being standoffish," Henneberry
recalled. "I made a comment about him breaking my heart in '57."

More crickets.

"I was fifty years old, and I was starstruck," Henneberry said. "He
didn't give a shit about that story. He'd heard it a thousand times.
What he wanted to know was if he could trust me. I think he was reas-
sured that I wasn't a kid, that we came to him and put serious, experienced marketing guys in charge of this. Baseball had not been doing
much for him and he was a bit dubious about whether we could pull
this off. He just didn't trust baseball to do the right thing by his
image. And you know what? He was right. Baseball never before had
a plan."

Over the course of the meeting, Francis, Gamgort, and Henneberry laid out the ambitious multipronged strategy to market and promote the twenty-fifth anniversary of the record. A commemorative coffee-table book, *Home Run,* written by the respected Dick Schaap, was already in the works. Ted Williams had already agreed to put his name on the foreword. The trio told Henry the league would back a tour to a dozen parks, where, at each, Henry would throw out the first ball. There would be sponsorship and licensing opportunities, a radio and television tour. This time, they were going to do it right. He was going to be treated respectfully and regally, in the mold of DiMaggio.

And then MLB unveiled the big one to Henry and his people: The Hank Aaron Award, a new award named after Henry, honoring the best hitter in each league. He already had peripheral involvement with the Arby's RBI award, hardware given out annually to the league leader in runs driven in. Henry was, after all, the career leader in runs batted in, but his real affiliation with the award stemmed mostly from the fact that the acronym corresponded with his ownership of numerous Arby's fast-food restaurants.

The RBI award was a lesser award, a trinket few paid much attention to. The Hank Aaron Award, Henry was told at the meeting, would be different. It would be big. Henneberry's original blueprint was wide in scope. In his vision, the Hank Aaron Award would represent the player leading or near the top in each of the chief offensive categories, which made sense, because for his career, Henry had finished in the top three in each of the categories: home runs, RBIs, and hits. Henneberry also thought the award should be interactive, meaning that players and fans would be able to track the major contenders for the award during the season.

"My recommendation was a quantitative award. Most hits, HR and RBI together. We could track it throughout the year. I wanted to make a big deal out of it," Henneberry recalled. "We had the greatest living iconic player. He was first in home runs, and RBI, third in hits, first in total bases? I mean, come on. It was so obvious."

The meeting ended in success. Henneberry recalled that Henry was "ecstatic." By the end of the meeting, Henry had thawed. Where he had once been cool to the marketing group, he now told jokes, spinning yarns about the time he passed up a chance to go on *The Ed*

Sullivan Show because Lew Burdette had begged him to be in the lineup so he could snare his twentieth win of the year. Cost him two hundred fifty dollars, Henry said, and the biggest laughs came in the context of 1999, when a player's *average* annual salary was well over one million dollars. Henry delivered the line perfectly. "Two fifty was *big* money back then."

OVER THE NEXT five months came the hard part: selling Henry. The group first had to find a major sponsor that could back a major campaign, lest Henry get slighted again. Henneberry placed his target figure for the campaign between $800,000 and $1 million, but no one was biting at that figure. Over the years it would gall Henry that he was perceived as simply not charismatic enough to carry a promotion, or, worse, that he was a grumpy old man with little to offer. Henneberry accepted the talk because it was out there and the first thing a marketer does is deal with the situation instead of complain. What bothered him was how shortsighted the presumptions could be.

"Part of it was because of the perception that Hank was difficult to work with. No one knew the value of what Hank would bring to the party," he recalled. "But the big thing was this: Everything in baseball at the time was about labor and making money. MLB Properties was gutted and the baseball Network failed. No one was promoting the players that were gone. No one had touched them for fifteen years.

"We were asking for a million bucks. A few years earlier, we were selling the *whole league* for a million. No one was tying the players of yesteryear to the current game. Nobody touched anybody. It wasn't Willie, Duke, Stan, Hank, nobody. So, Hank was forgotten along with everyone else. It wasn't that he was unpopular or cast aside. *Nobody* was getting any support. It had nothing to do with Hank."

So it came to pass that the year 1999 revitalized Henry Aaron. The promotions coalesced and, in the end, baseball did not betray him as he had feared. The book, *Home Run: My Life in Pictures,* was handsome and classy, first-rate all the way. The sponsor, Country Time Lemonade, came through. The numbers were not astronomical—the $450,000 it took to get the deal done was far below Henneberry's seven-figure target—but Country Time treated Henry with the respect he believed had been nonexistent, and the executives at Country Time were delighted by his affability on the promotion trail, even if they winced each time Henry mangled the product's name.

"Hank could never say 'Country Time.' He would always say 'Country Times,' " Henneberry recalled. "It was the southern way of saying it. I told him a hundred times to say it right, and he said it wrong ninety-nine times. It drove them nuts."

Henry turned sixty-five that February and was feted with a gala event that he would never forget. The Hyatt Regency Atlanta was packed, lined with limousines, luxury cars . . . and the Secret Service. President Clinton made a surprise appearance.

That night, the Hank Aaron Award was unveiled (Manny Ramirez and Sammy Sosa would be the inaugural recipients), announced to a rousing ovation. Bill Henneberry wasn't pleased, though, for his original concept never got off the ground. Baseball stepped in and took a scalpel to the idea. Rich Levin, baseball's top public-relations man, thought Henneberry's vision encroached upon sacred turf, which was the Most Valuable Player awards, given out to each league by the Baseball Writers' Association of America, the most prestigious awards, which went back to the 1930s. The MVP was the award of Williams and Mays and Mantle. Nothing could be introduced to reduce its impact. During that time, the players union tried to compete with the BBWAA by creating the Players Choice Awards, but it didn't work. Players wanted to be associated with the hardware Hall of Famers held.

Levin was also concerned that a quantitative award based on the top offensive categories was too close to the Triple Crown, which marked the leader in batting average, home runs, and RBI.

"What we ended up with was different than what I had envisioned," Henneberry said. "I have nothing but respect for Rich Levin, but I thought it got totally screwed up. I thought we could have done more. The Triple Crown? The Triple Crown is a total anachronism. I mean, who was the last guy to win it? Yastrzemski forty years ago? The award never became as important as it should have been."

Throughout the years, Henry had met presidents. It never failed to tickle Billye that she could say without exaggeration that she and

Henry had slept at the White House more than once. They had traveled the world and dined with kings and queens and prime ministers. Usually, however, he went to them, the Home Run King as invited guest. But seeing Bill Clinton, a sitting president at the Hyatt, in town *just for him,* well, it touched a nerve in Henry Aaron that softened and humbled him.

Bill Clinton traced the roots of his relationship with Henry to March 1, 1992, when the Democratic party was slugging it out in a primary with no clear front-runner. One day it was Tom Harkin, the next day Paul Tsongas. For a time, even Jerry Brown was leading in the polls. Not that who won would matter anyway, because the winner, the pundits said, would only get demolished by the invincible sitting president, George H. W. Bush, fresh and muscular after winning the Gulf War, his approval ratings making him, if numbers were to be believed, the most popular president in history.

Still, in desperation, the phone call was made the way all important calls are made, through a maze of high-rent channels: a campaign operative called Sam Nunn, the powerful Georgia senator, who located the civil rights giant and former U.N. ambassador Andy Young, who found Henry. When he picked up the telephone, Bill Clinton, the Arkansas governor, still trying to gain a foothold in the presidential race, was on the other end, asking for Henry's help.

Clinton was holding a rally at Georgia Tech, he told Henry, and he was desperate to pump some life into his campaign. He had not yet won a single primary. Would the Home Run King allow the Clintons to use his name to raise the turnout, especially among the black voters, who, when properly motivated, could swing an election in Georgia? And one other thing, Clinton asked: Would he be willing to appear himself?

Henry told the governor he would be honored to do whatever he could to help the Clinton campaign.

On October 29, 1999, after he had won a second term, President Clinton regaled the audience at a Democratic National Committee function in Atlanta with his reminiscence of his 1993 comeback. According to the official White House transcript of the president's remarks, Clinton was consistent in his praise for Henry:

"Georgia was good to me. I remember when I ran in the Georgia primary, all the Washington experts said that Governor Clinton heads south to Georgia in deep trouble. If he doesn't get at least 40 percent in the Georgia primary, he's toast. By then, I'd already been clear dead three times. Now it's happened so often, I'm going to open a tombstone business when I leave office. (Laughter.)

"But anyway, and the people of Georgia in the primary gave me 57 percent of the vote in 1992, and sent me on my way. And I'm very grateful for that. (Applause.) And then I remember, we had a rally in a football stadium outside Atlanta, in the weekend before the election of '92. You remember that, Max [Cleland]? And we filled it. And I think Buddy Darden was there. We filled the rally. And I remember Hank Aaron was there, and there were over 25,000 people there. And we won the state by 13,000 votes. So everyone who spoke at that rally can fairly claim to have made me President of the United States, since there were twice as many people there as we won the state by. But we made it, and the rest is history."

Over the years, President Clinton would use his oratorical master-strokes to massage his message to fit the contours of his audience, but Henry always found his way into every anecdote, and in return, Henry and Billye would give the Clintons their loyalty.

"We were in a tough, tough campaign," Bill Clinton recalled. "Hank Aaron had always been a hero of mine, and at the last minute he and Sam Nunn organized a rally. It turns out that we get twenty-five thousand people to fill a football stadium, mostly, I believe, because Hank Aaron was there. We held a tremendous rally and went on to win fifty-seven percent of the vote, and later I became the first Democrat to win the state of Georgia since 1976. And no Democrat has won it since. So, when I tell everyone that Hank Aaron is a big reason I became president of the United States, it's not just hyperbole because I love the man. I say it because it's true."

At his birthday party, Henry was tearful when the president spoke, and so many emotions over the past year seemed to rush for space behind his eyes at exactly the same time. There was, always, the simple triumph of his life, but this time combined with the losses, losses he dealt with quietly and stoically. There was the photo of Henry in black suit, wearing dark sunglasses at the funeral of his father, Herbert, who had died quietly May 21, 1998. Herbert was eighty-nine years old and through his son had lived the triumph of the American story. As times changed, Herbert had been a legend in Mobile, the father of Mobile's most famous man. He had been visible around town, always known as "Mr. Herbert" or "Mr. Aaron." He had been fastidious and proud of his son. At the Episcopal Church of the Good Shepherd, Henry eulogized Herbert. "He was poor and unlearned," Henry said. "Yet he was rich and wise. You might say he had a Ph.D in common sense . . . we should all be so blessed to live a long and successful life. He did his share of bragging about me. Now, I'm bragging about him. Farewell, Dad."

A little more than two months later, on August 1, Henry held a family reunion in Atlanta. Three hundred relatives attended. Two days later, Henry's youngest brother, James, and eldest sister, Sarah, drove back to Mobile, while Henry and Billye flew to Tokyo to attend the World Children's Baseball Fair.

The next day, Sarah complained that she had trouble lifting her leg. She was admitted to the hospital, where she suffered two heart attacks. Following the second attack, Sarah slipped into a diabetic coma and never regained consciousness. She was seventy-one when she died.

Henry's brother Alfred never survived past birth. Tommie had died fourteen years earlier. Over a sixty-day span in 1998, his father and eldest sister were also gone.

The president of the United States however, had held the microphone at his birthday party, and the big man began to crack, puffy with tears. Periodically, he would talk about how fortunate he had been to be born with ability and the desire to hone his talent, but at the birthday party the words were distilled into something tangible, something real. The party would be the highlight of his life, providing him a certain energy, from which he would often draw. The emotions of the evening reinforced his desire to build a foundation that would have impact. And that wasn't all. Before President Clinton left, his presence had generated more than a million dollars for Henry's foundation.

"You never know what it means to me to have the president say those things about me," Henry recalled. "I think he was exaggerating, because he didn't need me, but it gives you a warm feeling that the president of the United States would take the time. It told me that what we were trying to do for young people was the right thing to do."

Henry sought to capitalize on his momentum by strengthening his philanthropic mission. All professional athletes touted their charitable foundations, but few of them did more than host an annual golf tournament and fly their friends around the country, tax-free. Henry felt an opportunity existed to create a model that would be truly lasting. It was, thought Frank Belatti, an opportunity for him to fuse together his two passions: separating himself from being just another ballplayer and taking an interest in the future of children, particularly children of color, who often lacked the parental guidance and educational opportunities to have a real chance in the world.

"Henry would always say, 'If you're going to influence a child, you have to do it early. Even high school is too late,' " said Allan Tanenbaum. The roots of Henry's foundation work owed its origins to an initial contribution of $100,000 from Ted Turner in connection with an Oscar-nominated documentary called *Hank Aaron: Chasing the Dream*, by an unknown film director named Mike Tollin in 1995. The foundation, now named the Chasing the Dream Foundation, was created to help 755 children—symbolically, one for each of Henry's home runs—with educational and financial support from grade school through graduation, and was aided by major fundraising coups—Bill Clinton's million-dollar birthday crash of Henry's sixty-fifth birthday, for one.

It was an ambitious project, and an expensive one that required corporate partnership. The Boys and Girls Clubs of America were in. Henry turned back to baseball, to his relationship with Bud Selig. Times had changed: the corporate and sports worlds relied heavily upon each other. The foundation needed to raise $2.5 million.

Selig was in, using his considerable muscle to further legitimize Henry's charity work. After reaching Henry's goal of sponsoring 755 kids through high school, Selig agreed in 2007 to help permanently endow the foundation with a $2.5 million gift for a new program: 44 Kids Forever, in cooperation with the Boys & Girls Clubs. In 2010, Henry took another ambitious step: a plan to fund twelve permanently endowed college scholarships, the twelve being symbolic for the number of times Henry went 4 for 4 in a game.

"Bud had a year left on his contract. The Hank Aaron Award was special to him," Tanenbaum recalled. "This wasn't a project you could execute on your own. It was more challenging. The baseball partnership recognized it's potential."

Billye had always described the motivation behind the foundation work as an opportunity to balance the scales.

"Both Henry and I had come up always being on the receiving end," she recalled. "When I look back on my life, I had someone helping me at every turn. I remember being called the teacher's pet, always into things. I remember wanting to be part of a production at school and not having the clothes. A woman named Mrs. Phillips bought me clothes. And I remember saying, 'One day, I'm going to have so many clothes.' We believed that in this position, we had a responsibility."

Henry said he knew it years before, but after the birthday party, when the president and the Secret Service and all the guests had left, his vision had crystallized: He would immerse himself in his foundation work.

PERHAPS JUST SLIGHTLY, Henry felt a certain satisfied restitution. The night did not change the hell he had endured while seeking to break the home-run record, or cure the wounds that had been so deep, but 1999 represented a breakthrough for Henry.

"I wouldn't say that the twenty-fifth was a major success for baseball, but it was a major success for Hank," Bill Henneberry said. "People said, 'We can use him,' because he can speak. He can't speak for five minutes, but he can do Q and A for an hour. He's funny, had a great sense of humor. It rebranded him. People began to find out: 'Hey, he's a wonderful guy.' He's sweet more than anything else. People didn't know that."

MasterCard hadn't backed Henry's anniversary rollout, but now it had a problem and needed help: what to do about the end of the century. The millennium was coming and baseball's biggest sponsor didn't have a plan. The year 2000 was a tailor-made marketing opportunity, and MasterCard, with $29 million invested in baseball, needed to hit a tape-measure home run. Kathy Francis went back to Bill Henneberry and asked for a concept. The result was the All-Century Team, where fans would choose the greatest lineup of the century. But there were two problems. The first was that baseball, parochially clannish to the end, could not reach a consensus on this promotional idea. The Red Sox wanted to do their own all-century team, with Red Sox players only, and Ted Williams as the centerpiece. The second problem, from a national standpoint, was finding the right person to be the face for this promotional campaign.

"The question was, Who was the most marketable? Who was still alive? Ted was sick. Musial was one hundred and five years old. So MasterCard came up with Hank, Willie Mays, and George Brett and Barry Bonds," Henneberry said. "But Brett wasn't on the All-Century Team, and nobody wanted to work with Bonds."

Henry did a commercial with the three and spent part of the year doing public appearances with Mays. The All-Century Team was a great thing for fans, debating players of different eras. It was all fun, the preferences for one player over another as harmless as choosing Kobe beef over caviar, or a Bordeaux rather than a Burgundy. But the old wounds were always close to the surface, especially when it came to competition with the two professional baseball players who always seemed to define Henry's time: Ruth and Mays.

Bill Henneberry had come a long way with Henry since their first conversation in Philadelphia. Now, when MasterCard wanted Henry to appear during the All-Century campaign, Henry would specifically request that Henneberry be the representative who traveled with him. The two crisscrossed the country.

And then, days before the public announcement of the All-Century Team, Henneberry received a phone call.

"MasterCard had done this silly online promotion, not well publicized. Only ten thousand people voted, and they told me it was Ruth, Willie, and Ted Williams. Overall, 2–3 million people voted, and Hank had gotten the second-highest number of votes, behind Ruth. MasterCard hadn't yet announced the starting lineups and didn't want to lose face for having a New York–New England-centric online vote. I'm sitting with him when I get the call. When I told Hank the news, he didn't say a word. He didn't make a sound. But you could see it in his face, that I'd hurt him. And I immediately wanted to take it back. I ruined his afternoon."

IT WAS THE corporate world that had resurrected Henry. During a period of less than three years, he had undone twenty years' worth of public perception about him. He had shown that he could be funny and engaging. His was a modest balance. In the right environment, he could take the floor. He had to open up, relax, for his true charisma to show through. During the mid- to late 1990s, he had assuaged whatever doubts existed among the sales and marketing people. He could be, in his own way, a leading man. In sporting parlance, he had made the adjustment. It was either that or the scouting report on him had been dead wrong all along.

And in so many ways, it was fitting that his revival occurred only within a particular corporate setting: He thrived behind the scenes. He still did not do many commercials, did not hawk products, did not offer his personality to every living room in America. Unlike Joe DiMaggio with Mr. Coffee or George Foreman with an electric grill, Henry would never become synonymous with a single product. He cultivated the corporate types in small gatherings, often private or semipublic. It worked better that way. Henry had always remained not only close to power but on the right side of it, and now his pragmatism was being rewarded. It was pragmatism that made him different from his idol Jackie Robinson. In Robinson's time, the issues were clear and Robinson was uncompromising: equal citizenship, nothing less. Henry took the responsibility of carrying the Robinson mantle seriously, as his politics and public statements often reflected, but his manner had always been different. Henry had always been methodical in dealing with the men in suits who controlled the money. It was not only political passion but also money that allowed projects to progress beyond the idea stage, and if Henry did not inspire in the Robinson mode, he nevertheless possessed a deft touch, to which executives tended to respond. He made the money men comfortable, and such a disposition had two consequences: The first was that he would often be exposed to the charge that he did not use his influence. The second was that making powerful men comfortable often led to financial opportunity. Now that he had been resurrected, the offers started coming in: fifty thousand for this, twenty-five grand for that. He was now part of the inner circle.

He had always loathed public speaking, but now when some corporate giant wanted him to come speak to the sales force about how to be home-run hitters in business (and in life), Henry was commanding upward of $35,000 per appearance. His foundation was growing, the backbone of his philanthropy, and lucrative invitations to serve on corporate boards followed. Ted Turner had contributed to making Henry a very rich man. Henry had served on the board of directors of TBS Broadcast Systems for a decade and a half, and he was also on the board of directors of the Braves, the Atlanta Falcons, the Atlanta Technical Institute, and Medallion Financial Corporation ("In niches there are riches," so went the company motto).

So much of it all was happening the way Bud Selig had believed it would, if baseball could just stop fighting with itself over money. Big corporate sponsorships would lift the game out of the haze of the strike. Baseball would do its part by putting a dynamic face on the game—less Bud Selig and Don Fehr, more Sammy Sosa and Mark McGwire. The game was fun now, built on an anabolic cocktail of muscles and home runs and scripted Hallmark moments, mandated directly from the commissioner's office, moments that took the rough edge off of the game and replaced sharp elbows with a "field of dreams."

The highest (players would later call it the lowest) point came during the 2003 World Series, when Roger Clemens, who said he was leaning toward retirement, left game four after the seventh inning. Clemens, pitching on the road against the Florida Marlins in a World Series game, walked off the mound to a standing ovation from *both teams.* . . . And that was the first time baseball may have overdone it with the orchestrated moments, because after the tearful, hackneyed good-bye, Clemens changed his mind. He wound up pitching for four more years.

There was the money, and the feel-good mandate, but during the great home-run chase of 1998, the summer of Sosa and McGwire, both men with different but equally powerful appeal, *USA Today* released a poll that revealed 75 percent of the country preferred that McGwire break the record, rather than Sosa. Henry appeared on an ESPN interview program soon after the poll numbers were released, and he said publicly what blacks and Latinos were saying to one another.

"It's just absolutely ridiculous that you could have that lopsided an opinion about who should break the record," he said on the air. "And I've seen other little things that happened that make me believe that McGwire was the favorite rather than Sosa. And I think the reason for that is because he's from the Dominican [Republic] and also happens to have black skin. I just don't think it's fair to him or his family or his country."

What followed was the requisite beat-down: that Henry Aaron *was* bitter after all. *And how dare he inject race into the home-run race?*

"I received hundreds of calls to do interviews," he told the *Mobile Register.* "I turned them down because I was afraid if I did it, I would be misquoted. Finally, I said yes to one, and, lo and behold, I was misunderstood."

The point was it wasn't a question of the public, or the press, misunderstanding Henry. There could be no misinterpretation of what Henry had said or what he had conveyed during the interview. Even though McGwire hit home run number sixty-two during the first week of September, the general reaction was that the record belonged to him, simply because he had surpassed the sixty-one milestone first. Three weeks still remained in the season, and for one afternoon, Sosa had tied McGwire at sixty-six, but the story line had been set: The record belonged to McGwire. Sosa would have to be content to play the stereotypical sidekick, the happy Latin.

The problem was that Henry had the temerity to talk about a real issue in this land of make-believe. He had sparked a fire with a Robinson-like resolve, and gotten smacked down for it. He had found out what was being discovered across the country: Dissent, whether it was right or wrong, was unacceptable. It got in the way of the money machine.

Henry responded to the backlash by saying nothing else on the subject. Despite the criticism, Henry held firm privately: McGwire was the chosen one because he was white, and that's the way it was in America. Publicly, however, he rushed back to the reservation, reprogrammed. "It couldn't have happened at a better time for baseball," he later said of the home runs of 1998. "Baseball had some problems because of the strike and this has helped. It's been great."

Though it had been Henry who defended Sosa, it was Sammy who eventually ran afoul of Henry. This happened a couple of years after the 1998 frenzy, when John Hancock, another big baseball sponsor, announced plans to sell its stock to the public. To commemorate the occasion, it wanted a big name to ring the bell on the floor of the New York Stock Exchange, one of the fun perks that came with being the person of the hour. It was an honor designated for visiting dignitaries, Super Bowl winners, and famous sluggers, to name a few.

Hancock, naturally, wanted McGwire, but he said no. But Sammy Sosa said yes, as did Henry. The deal was going to be simple: Two legends from their respective eras would celebrate Hancock's IPO. They would shake hands, sign autographs, and have lunch with the big shots, who then could brag to their friends. Bill Henneberry brokered the deal. Henry negotiated his usual fee, and agreed to a couple of additional events to push the numbers above a hundred grand.

But to the surprise of the Aaron people, Sosa cut his own deal: $135,000 for just the one afternoon. The day before the event, Sosa canceled, telling the firm he wouldn't be attending. Stiffing Hancock meant stiffing Henry, who was left alone to carry the event.

"So, we're going to meet and sign a hundred bats, then go to breakfast with the market makers," Henneberry recalled. "Then they get a call from Sosa's agent, who says, 'Can we do this another time?' 'What do you mean? We're going public tomorrow!' The John Hancock guy is freaked. There's all kind of shit flying around. They come back and say Sosa isn't showing. He had a signed contract. He doesn't show. I know I probably shouldn't be saying this, but people think he's this great guy. He's not."

And for the entire next day, a solo act instead of a duo, Henry was the star. He rang the bell on the exchange floor. He had them eating out of his hand. He told stories about the old days and gave that big laugh and made the executives enjoy being around him, their silvery hair turned dark and youthful for one afternoon. Everyone was taken by Henry's gentleness and humor.

"Hank had to do the whole thing, and he was delightful," Henneberry recalled. "He shook hands. He was great."

IT WAS A piece of popular fiction that Bud Selig was responsible for initiating Henry's second act. Selig's family roots were in the car business and thus it made sense to think that when Henry created the Hank Aaron Automotive Group, the umbrella for a string of car dealerships he would begin in 1999, Selig had been the inspiration.

Not only was that not the case but Selig recalled warning Henry to think twice, and then think some more, before entering the car game. "Everybody was going to blame me if it didn't work," Selig said. "So I wanted him to know exactly what he was getting into."

It was Henry's old friend Jesse Jackson who indirectly got Henry involved in cars. It turned out that, even as the millennium neared, not a single American distributorship of Bavarian Motor Works, the great BMW, was owned by an African-American. When this situation came to light, the corporate types at BMW grew skittish, at first denying the charge, while refusing to name the black-owned distributorships. This was embarrassing, even more so when Jackson began to advertise the fact. Like other status symbols, owning a BMW meant you had made it. It meant class, speed, and enough disposable income to accept no substitute. An African-American who owned a BMW represented a significant financial achievement; thus Jackson did not relent in his criticism of the company. The criticism of BMW resonated especially in Atlanta, the city that came, not always accurately, to symbolize the success of black capitalism. That meant in Atlanta, a lot of successful black people were driving BMWs, and they could afford to change allegiances, switching to, say, Mercedes-Benz. Offending such an influential constituency was not good business.

And thus it came to pass that Henry Aaron became the first black majority owner of the first BMW franchise in the country, Hank Aaron BMW, located in Union City, Georgia, just outside Atlanta. Vic

Doolan, the president of BMW, understood the importance of being on the right side of a potentially explosive issue. He reached out to Henry and his people, and from protest came progress.

As a condition of ending the pressure, which had first been exerted on luxury import car makers for years by the National Association of Minority Automobile Dealers, BMW agreed to attract black ownership of BMW franchises, starting with Henry.

That was sweet, but not as sweet as the deal Henry received. Allan Tanenbaum brokered the deal. He demanded two things, both non-negotiable: Henry would receive majority control of the dealerships and not have to put up any of his own money. After BMW, Henry acquired Jaguar, Range Rover, Honda, Hyundai, and Toyota.

Initially, not everyone was happy with the deal. The fact that Henry was receiving such a golden deal ruffled the minority professionals who had struggled and sweated in the low margins and glass ceilings of the car business. To them, it was just another example of a celebrity handout.

HANK AARON GOES TO BAT FOR BMW

But while industry insiders don't necessarily begrudge Aaron's accomplishment, some question the wisdom of appointing a high-profile franchiser with little to no automotive experience.

"Quite frankly, we were surprised," says Sheila Vaden-Williams, executive director of the National Association of Minority Automobile Dealers. "Especially since we've provided BMW with names of established dealers with an interest in the Atlanta market."

Undaunted, Henry almost immediately recognized how powerful an asset the Hank Aaron name was. He had impressed skeptics by choosing a location, Union City, that had no previous client base. He hadn't cherry-picked a ripe location, but he was determined to build a business. In the first twelve months, Hank Aaron BMW raked in $32.9 million in sales. Fans wanted to be associated with Hank Aaron, and for every new BMW he sold, he gave the buyers a Hank Aaron–signed baseball. Hank Aaron Toyota followed. As did Hank Aaron Range Rover.

Henry was vindicated, but some of his people seethed at what they considered to be more jealousy on the part of fellow professional blacks, the crab-in-a-barrel mentality that often stifled success. "There were some black folk that he knows who were calling him 'Uncle Tom' behind his back, and he wanted to prove them wrong,' " Allan Tanenbaum said. "He wasn't trying to prove anything to the white man; he wanted to prove it to other black people. I really resented that."

And it was a family affair. The kids never went into baseball, except for Lary, who became a scout with the Braves. Henry Aaron, Jr., worked at his father's dealerships. And Henry's son-in-law Victor Haydel oversaw Henry's restaurant enterprises.

"Why was I chosen?" Aaron said in an interview in the magazine *Black Enterprise.* "Just because I had been a baseball player didn't mean I didn't know how to run a business. I have 17 successful fast-food restaurants with Church's, Popeye's, and Arby's. They knew I had some experience running a franchise operation. I accepted the challenge that I could put minorities in charge and run a dealership."

When the business press came to him, it found a different Henry from the one the sporting press had been accustomed to. He was still not particularly talkative, but he seemed to regard his business successes with a heightened pride. Perhaps the reason was that because he had been so comfortable in the sports world, he now enjoyed the challenge of succeeding in business. It was this success that allowed him the opportunity to disabuse whites of the notion that blacks could not succeed in business. He found himself more engaged with sports figures who had made the transition to real business ventures (as opposed to lending their names to a product and leaving the daily operation to others). He was particularly impressed with the basketball player Magic Johnson, who had parlayed his on-court success into a financial empire of banks, movie theaters, and restaurants. Johnson did not merely own the local movie theater; he had used his clout to appeal to corporations to invest in areas heavily populated by African-Americans. Henry had done the same with his fast-food chains, but an upscale operation such as BMW would require a different approach. The result was that, as Magic Johnson had done, Henry traded off of his name to create scholarships and internships in the auto industry. Three years after entering a new business venture, BMW had (with a significant nudge from Henry) launched its first minority training program.

ON OCTOBER 10, 2002, HENRY had purchased a house at 2029 Embassy Drive in West Palm Beach, Florida—more than 3,500 square feet, nestled on the golf course of the President Country Club—for $461,250 from Anthony and Patricia Lampert. Presidents had grown upscale and exclusive, emblematic of the real estate boom sweeping the country. Just four and a half years earlier, the Lamperts had purchased the house for $97,500, but West Palm, despite an unusually high crime rate, featured enclaves of star power. Tiger Woods, Venus and Serena Williams, and Tommy Lee Jones all owned houses in the area. Henry was sixty-eight at the time and intimates knew the West Palm purchase was part of his master retirement plan. Periodically, he would drop hints that his active participation in all of his business interests was finite. In interviews, he would say that he expected to be less involved, that "he wouldn't stay in the car business forever." He remained fourth on the Braves masthead and still maintained an office at Turner Field, but even though his title grew in importance, Henry hadn't been involved in the daily operation of the Braves in years. In addition to the 755 Restaurant Corporation, he was part of various business partnerships, but in many of those he was being paid for lending his name to bring prestige to the enterprise.

His longtime assistant, Susan Bailey, who had worked with Henry since she was a teenager, was so successful at shielding him from requests (and even from people who knew him best) that she was often nicknamed "Dr. No" or "Horatius at the Bridge" by the foiled. Her stance represented Henry's increasing need for distance. And these days, Henry was saying no more than ever: no to most honorary degree offers (yes to Wisconsin's Concordia University—anything for Wisconsin; yes to George Washington University, no to Williamette College), no to speaking engagements, no to most interviews, no to commercials. You didn't see Henry pitching products as other players might. His schedule was still full, but to his inner circle, the signals were clear: He was ready to leave public life.

What was there left to prove? As he approached seventy, he had grown in stature and status. The decade had been a total success. The drift and pessimism from the 1980s were gone. The Henry Aaron of the millennium was now a regal figure. In 1997, the Mobile Stadium, which Henry could not enter as a kid and which housed the team the Mobile Bears, on which he could not play, was renamed Hank Aaron Stadium. The people in Mobile told stories about seeing Henry's dad around the ballpark, as if it were a celebrity sighting.

It was never going to be possible that Henry would be as well known for his cars as he was for his home runs, but he had nevertheless succeeded in his second act, a feat that most celebrities found increasingly elusive. He had become a wealthy man in two fields. It was during this time that even his greatest lament—that he had been rendered one-dimensional by the hate mail and the home runs and his fame—had been overcome. During the All-Century Team campaign, MasterCard ran a contest, the grand prize being dinner with Hank Aaron. The winners, a husband and wife with a couple of older children, met with Henry at the 2000 World Series.

"Hank asked what they did, and as it turned out, they owned car dealerships," Bill Henneberry recalled. "It was the perfect match. They sat down in a small conference room at Shea Stadium before one of the games and neither mentioned a word about baseball. I'll never forget the look on their faces. Their eyes were as big as saucers. They asked Hank about cars and he asked them about their dealerships. They thought they'd died and gone to heaven."

Twelve days before he left office for good, President Clinton invited Henry to the White House to honor him with the Presidential Citizens Medal for "exemplary service to the nation." A new generation of politicians—and it helped that the two most important, Jimmy Carter and Bill Clinton, were southerners—had recognized him in his fullness. The Citizens Medal, Clinton told Henry, was for his nonplaying contributions as much as for hitting home run number 715.

"In the spotlight and under pressure," Clinton said during the ceremony, "he always answered bigotry and brutality with poise and purpose." He had always burned that his interest in the world outside of baseball never seemed to translate, but apart from Muhammad Ali—who also received a medal that day—no other recipient was affiliated with sports. Henry sat next to Fred Shuttlesworth, the civil rights leader whose house was bombed by segregationists on December 25, 1956, and Dr. Charles DeLisi, the first government scientist to outline the feasibility of the Human Genome Project. Henry had become transcendent.

Eighteen months later, Henry was at the White House again, before another president, George W. Bush, to receive the Presidential Medal of Freedom, the country's highest civilian award.

The truth of it all was that Henry was never completely comfortable with the cloying demands of public life. Unassailable as he was in his position as public treasure, close friends noticed that he still never talked about 715, even though at every public appearance he signed eight-by-ten glossies of the Moment, the day he'd not mention. No one brought it up, nor did he volunteer, and that was fine, because he seemed to have softened as the years mounted.

"I don't want to say that all the wounds from what he went through were healed, but definitely it had eased some," said director Mike Tollin, who was one of the few people Henry said yes to (he allowed Tollin into his inner circle for a 1995 documentary). "I can't say for sure, but I think the way he had been so totally embraced, that times were finally different, helped a lot."

Dusty Baker would see Henry a couple of times a year, at a celebrity golf tournament or some other function, and he could sense that Henry was shifting down. One day in 2006, during his final, turbulent days managing the always tempestuous Chicago Cubs, Baker tried to explain the Aaron paradox: "The thing about Hank is that he really doesn't need any of this. There are a lot of guys who say they don't need the attention, but then you see them get mad every time someone gets mentioned ahead of them. Then all of a sudden they start giving interviews and now they're all over the place. Hank is content with what he did. He doesn't need to defend it, to compare it, nothing. He did what he did and that is enough for him."

If the private Henry sought solace as he always had, the public had one last job for him.

CHAPTER EIGHTEEN

756

WHEN A TRAIN comes speeding right at him, engines roaring, exhaust choking the easy blue sky, the instinctive man leaps blindly, hoping he will be fast enough and lucky enough to find safety. The hopeless man stands firm in the face of onrushing violence, resigned to his grisly fate. But the truly confident man, the man who knows himself, lies flat between the two rails, convinced the train will pass him by.

Beginning in 2005 and intensifying over the next two years, a locomotive of circumstances not of his own making headed directly toward Henry Aaron. And over the course of those two years, he would have to decide which of the three men he was going to be.

The amount of money was bigger than ever, and yet Bud Selig's master plan of rehabilitation through corporate synergy, orchestrated set pieces, and runaway *profits,* had, in less than a decade, collapsed. That great elixir, the home run, was now baseball's most discredited commodity. The cacophony about performance-enhancing drugs and loss of integrity was very real, even though the players, the union and the owners, all grew even richer. Alex Rodriguez earned $22.7 million in 2008, but Bud Selig was not so far behind, at $17.5 million. But because they chose money over authenticity, the heroes once credited with bringing the game back, well, they didn't look so heroic anymore.

By the time Mark McGwire had been retired a measly five years, the period most Hall of Fame–level players prepare for a lifetime of bronzed immortality, McGwire was a six-foot-five-inch, 245-pound symbol of fraud. Baseball's most carefully constructed monument, the home-run summer of 1998, was no longer a baseball heirloom, but the family disgrace, the open secret no one dare mention, in the hope it would just fade away.

No home run could ever cleanse McGwire's disastrous public appearance March 17, 2005, in front of the House Committee for Government Reform, when he was reduced to a buffed-out con man, his magical summer rendered inauthentic. The train sped toward McGwire, too, and it overwhelmed him. McGwire was unable to defend—in front of his government and his country—the outsized feats of his career that once had been celebrated. He had nothing to say, repeating the phrase that would become a punch line as well as an epitaph: "I'm not here to talk about the past." He had nothing of which to be proud, nothing at all to add. When he left room 2154 of the Rayburn Building that windy March afternoon, only the tatters of what was once his reputation remained.

Sitting next to McGwire, Rafael Palmeiro famously pointed at the committee and swore, under oath, that he'd never taken steroids. "Period," he said, only to test positive for steroids two months later. As the afternoon wore on, Sammy Sosa, McGwire's 1998 accomplice, feigned he understood not a single word of the English language, and did not answer a single question. In 2009, Sosa's name was leaked as one of dozens of names to have tested positive for an anabolic substance in 2003.

In one afternoon of stunning, devastating clarity, the years that built a renaissance not only came completely undone but proved fraudulent; a Superfund site sold as beachfront property.

The toxicity levels of what was now being called the "Steroid Era" were lethal, and it was the numbers, always the lifeblood of the sport, that contained the most cancerous cells. From the time not long after California had still been part of Mexico until 1997, the sixty-home run mark had been reached just twice, by Ruth in 1927 and by Maris in 1961. Yet between 1998 and 2001, while the profits soared, sixty had been topped *six times* and the seventy—*seventy*—home-run mark reached twice. The top six single-season home-run seasons had been recorded over a four-year period. In a four-year period, Sosa hit sixty home runs *three times* but *didn't* win a home-run title in any one of those years. Meanwhile, the cash registers *ka-chinged* melodically and the people cheered, while men like Henry Aaron, Frank Robinson, Reggie Jackson, and Mike Schmidt did a slow burn.

McGwire had hit seventy home runs in 1998, and after the last one, he said in an interview room, arms puffy and eyes shifty, that his record would *never* be broken.

But three years later, Barry Bonds hit *seventy-three* home runs.

Baseball had gotten other numbers it liked—revenues from $1.2 billion in 1994 to $6 billion in 2007 and $6.6 billion in 2008—and the public had gotten its thrills. If Bill Henneberry remembered when baseball was radioactive to advertisers and sponsors, nobody else did. But suddenly—or maybe not so suddenly—it had all gone too far, the joyride topped by one ice-cream scoop too many. McGwire-Sosa 1998 was supposed to be that ridiculous, magical year that made no earthly sense, wouldn't happen again, and gave the people who saw it that special generational unity, like DiMaggio-Williams in 1941 and Mantle-Maris two decades later. Instead, as the numbers kept increasing, one fraudulent scoop after another, the authenticity of the game seemed increasingly remote. And now, chasing Aaron, there was Bonds, already viewed suspiciously by the public for his obdurate disposition and growing head size, chased by the federal government because it believed he'd lied to a federal grand jury about taking muscle-making drugs. Bonds was so dominant and so prolific when it came to hitting the ball out of the ballpark that by 2005 he had become Henry, circa 1969: the guy for whom breaking the home run record was no longer a question of *if,* but *when.*

Historians had clung to the Black Sox—the infamous 1919 Chicago White Sox team that had thrown the World Series—as the standard of malfeasance in professional sports. They claimed that this was the cataclysmic moment when the game had been wrenched from its moorings. Steroids, they said, weren't nearly that disastrous in terms of historical importance. The contemporaries liked to point to Pete Rose, baseball's all-time leader in hits, now reduced to a cheap Las Vegas sideshow, as being worse than the rampant drug use that undermined the game.

But neither came close.

The apologists in the locker room, the front offices, and, worst of all, the press box said there was nothing in a bottle that could help you hit home runs. They demanded proof that their golden heroes would do something, *anything*, to run faster, hit harder, play more, earn more. When the information finally appeared, in the form of positive tests, grand jury investigations, sting operations, federal indictments, and empty, implausible lies, the apologists spun deftly, claiming that drugs were old news, that *everybody knew* players were using, and asking, *Couldn't we just move on?* In the face of crumbling reputations and laughable, desperate denials, the apologists turned off their brains and their intellect and their enthusiasm for the great glory of the pastime, vigorously and petulantly shaking their heads in denial.

THE PUBLIC DIDN'T want numbers anymore, not with the IRS and the federal government hunting down MVPs and Cy Young winners as though they were La Cosa Nostra. Numbers were too suspicious. Numbers just confirmed the con game. Now they wanted a hero, someone who could remind them that the currency of baseball wasn't something as unimportant as the number of times a man could hit the ball over the fence, but about the value systems and virtues that worthless feat once represented.

Reaching back into the past wasn't going to be enough. Ted Williams, the cantankerous but hearty, authentic American, was gone. So was the immigrant hero DiMaggio (though it was virtually impossible to envision the embittered, mysterious Joe leading a public debate on values). Jackie, of course, was long gone, while Willie was making more a fool of himself every day he opened his mouth about a subject he knew little about. *(I just don't think steroids help you at all. They just don't do anything.)* Mays exhibited a combination of loyalty to his godson, Barry Bonds, and a severe tone deafness to the severity of the public breach. Star power and nostalgia alone weren't going to do it this time. The word *integrity* was back in vogue, even if it was needed less as a guide and more to assuage the collective guilt. The public, as much as some of the people associated with the game, realized too late, and without enough response, that what had been lost—the belief in the difficulty that came with the game—was the very quality that gave the sport its power.

The apologists and the disbelievers and the ones who couldn't be bothered, they all tried to minimize the effects of a game without integrity. Those effects, for once, could not be measured by money, but by numbers that could not be argued: McGwire, Palmeiro, Sosa, Clemens, and Bonds, one hundred combined seasons, forty-seven all-star appearances, 2,523 home runs, 354 wins, nine MVPs, seven Cy Young Awards, two single-season home-run records, and the most famous sports record in the history of the country, all publicly disgraced during the same era by the same issue.

No other sport, at no period in the history of the republic, could ever say that. No other sport could point to half a dozen of its greatest players, and a dozen more of possible Hall of Fame caliber, all from different teams, who couldn't show their faces in public. And now the greatest record in the country was about to fall. Another tainted record. The public wanted someone who could provide a moral compass, someone who could bring them and their game back into the light.

So they turned to Henry.

There had always been a gap between Hank and Henry. Introverted and unsure in large settings, Henry thrived in tightly controlled private gatherings. There, he could relax and allow his natural suspicions to melt. He would be genuinely warm and funny and gentle, disarming his audiences with his easy laugh and quickness, like when he would take his grandson, Victor junior, to school every day. Friends would marvel at how he hated public speaking and yet shone so well in those small-group Q and A sessions, when members of the audience would file out, feeling as though they'd been talking to a familiar uncle. It was in these settings, with corporate executives, manageable groups of lucky fans, and children, where his charisma flowered.

But now, with the sport in moral crisis, the public wanted the other half of the man, not intimate-chat Henry but the great Hank Aaron, the leader of men, out in front and in public. They wanted his presence to make them feel better about a sport he hadn't played in thirty years. In the months following the 2005 congressional hearings, the number of times the public yearned to hear the voice of Henry Aaron were too numerous to count.

The old guard came out, crotchety and indignant, in defense of their time.

"Go ask Henry Aaron," Jim Bunning, the Hall of Fame pitcher turned Kentucky senator, thundered. Henry had worn out Bunning, hitting .323 against him in sixty-five at bats. In the first game of a doubleheader, May 10, 1967, in Philadelphia, Bunning gave up home run number 448 to Henry. "Go ask the family of Roger Maris," Bunning said. "Go ask all of the people who played without enhanced drugs if they would like their records compared with the current records."

On the face of it, one might have thought that Henry would have welcomed the attention, his inner desire for respect finally converging with the public's appreciation of him. For years, Henry would argue that records were always valued until they landed in his hands, the hands of a black man. He used to say the all-time home-run record was the most hallowed in all of baseball—until he broke it. Then it wasn't so important anymore. Later, he would say with no shortage of acidity that Joe DiMaggio's fifty-six-game hitting streak seemed to carry more value to the establishment than his record. Yet as Bonds approached, Henry only grew in stature. The *New York Daily News,* once the home of one of Henry's great journalistic nemeses, Dick Young, now referred to the record, *his* record, as "sacred."

After years of being dismissed as bitter and largely incurious, or disparaged and accused of being easily led by the more dominant female figures in his life, he was now an important man, the person who was being asked to be the voice of authority on the most important subject of the times. During the Steroid Era, there was no person in baseball whose word was more anticipated or carried greater moral weight than that of Henry Aaron. He had reached the position Jackie Robinson had so many years before, an athlete sought out more for his moral standing than for his past heroics.

And it was there, at the precise moment when he finally had the floor all to himself, that Henry Aaron chose not to engage. Henry's old contemporary Frank Robinson was fierce and unequivocal. "Any player found to have used steroids, well, I don't think their records should count," Robinson said. "I think they should be wiped out." It was a powerful, direct statement, emblematic of the uncompromising Robinson, who had been fourth on the all-time list for what felt like forever, with 586 home runs. "Pretty soon," Robinson said, "I'm going to be way, way, way down the list."

Robinson, Bunning, and so many of the old-timers were fierce, not just because their places in the continuum were being erased but also because for this generation of Americans, drugs were about as low as a person could go. Henry himself had been driven to action by what he saw drugs doing to black communities. He had struggled with his own brother James's drug and alcohol addictions. James was the youngest of the Aaron siblings. He had remained in Mobile and at one point was living at the Salvation Army building.

But Henry was evasive on the ethical question of steroids, about whether he believed using performance-enhancing drugs was cheating, and nobody could understand why. He refused to engage about his feelings toward specific players and their chemically enhanced accomplishments, offering vague statements about how "unfortunate" the current situation was. Henry distanced himself. Even Bud Selig had reversed field, acknowledging the degree to which his sport had been derailed. In the spring of 2006, Selig announced he would launch an investigation, headed by former senator George Mitchell, into the use of performance-enhancing drugs.

A week into the 2006 season, Henry attended a dinner in Milwaukee, where he gave an impromptu press conference, and it was here that he would begin to define his public position about Bonds.

AARON PREFERS TO FOCUS ON THE POSITIVES

"I think what the commissioner is trying to do is trying to put an end to all of this," Aaron said after a news conference at the Hyatt Regency Milwaukee. "I know people have said, 'Where is this investigation going, and what purpose?' But I think he's trying to put an end to it."

Aaron said Selig was trying to do what is right. Asked if the allegations about drug use hurt the game, Aaron sidestepped the question.

"This game has got so much to offer," he said. . . . "Yet we are focusing on one thing, and that's steroids. We need to get rid of it once and for all and, hey, let's get on with the job of playing baseball."

He frustrated certain elements of the press, which believed that Aaron was being passive-aggressive: He complained about not being taken seriously and yet shrank when the world looked to him on a serious issue. Even his supporters were often perplexed by his lack of a position, for it was incongruous with the man they knew.

"The one thing Henry *hated* was cheating. The whole thing bothered him," Ralph Garr said. "Why do you think he and Gaylord Perry never got on well? He might not have said anything, but anyone who knew Henry Aaron knew that the whole thing about drugs, that really bothered him.

"You'd have been ashamed to do stuff like that around him. He'd form his opinion from the inside. It wasn't Henry Aaron's way to tell you about your business. That's why he's not going to mention Barry. He's gonna let that train pass."

That Henry was quiet about steroids was to some degree generational. For a man of Henry's time, drugs were designed to alter the mental state of the user. Drugs made you dopey—hence the slang term *dope.* But the sophistication and purpose of designer steroids and human growth hormone—*There were drugs that could improve your eyesight?*—were outside of his sphere. Dusty Baker thought that while Henry appreciated his status as baseball royalty, he did not want this issue, so tawdry and difficult, to be the one that forced him back into the public eye. Drugs were, as they say, a dirty business. On the one hand, he was still a ballplayer, and he bought into the rhetoric that there was nothing in a bottle that could help a player once he stepped into the batter's box. The batter still had to see the ball and make contact. Yet he knew simply by looking at the numbers and the immense size of some of the players that something was amiss. "I played the game," Henry would say. "It's just not possible to hit seventy home runs." In interviews, however, such as before game four of the 2007 World Series between Boston and Colorado, he referred to performance enhancers as he would a dime bag of marijuana.

"I just don't want to get involved with conversations about dope," he said.

Yet another reason was political. His friend of a half century, Bud Selig, was under assault—from the union, from the players, from the fans and writers, and from Congress—for not being swift and decisive on the issue, and Henry was careful with his opinions. A blistering indictment of steroid use would indirectly be a criticism of his ally Selig and Selig's handling of the situation.

THE REAL POINT was, Henry thought he could not win on the Bonds issue. He would tell intimates that Bonds was a "lose-lose." If he spoke out against Bonds, then he risked the criticism that he was just a bitter old man who could not deal with his record being broken. There were people close to Henry who believed that he enjoyed being the all-time home-run leader. He had held the record for so long that it had become a part of him. It had given him the sort of legitimacy that being a transcendent player did not. And what was not to like about holding the record?

Yet, this was not a reason for Henry not to want his record broken. What Billye Aaron admired most about Henry was the comfort he seemed to have within himself. "He knows what he did," she said, "and he knows that the time would come when the record would belong to someone else. That part of it didn't bother him, as far as I'm concerned." Henry himself would repeat the same refrain: Records were made to be broken. It was a shopworn cliché, and it certainly masked whatever complex feelings he held toward Bonds, but it was true.

Henry also believed that if he said nothing, or supported Bonds in his quest to break the record, if for no other reason than to be a good ambassador to baseball, he would be tacitly condoning steroids and performance-enhancing drugs. Throughout his life, he had been proud of how he approached his profession. He didn't want to be associated with the drug culture, which had changed the game and the way the sport was viewed.

For all of his fears, there was still another section of the press that knew Henry was being placed in an impossible position. Even saying nothing about Bonds was, by definition, a statement in and of itself.

During each public appearance, he invariably would be faced with a question about Bonds. His responses were often odd, and for a press that felt Henry was in a position of leadership, this was maddening. There was, for example, the day in Milwaukee when the Brewers were dedicating a plaque for Henry's 755th home run, his last big-league home run, the record.

"Barry Bonds?" Henry said. "I don't even know how to spell his name."

To Henry's inner circle, it was a great quote, one that made everybody laugh. Henry was showing his dry sense of humor to break up a tense moment. However, the press had the opposite reaction. Flippant and evasive comments did not endear Henry to the press. And then there was the bizarre interview he gave to the Associated Press:

Q: In fact, I was just going to ask you, how closely do you follow the games?

A: Oh, I watch the Braves play every day.

Q: How many games do you go to a year?

A: I don't go to too many. I don't attend too many, but I watch on television every day.

Q: Do you have any advice for Barry Bonds?

A: For who?

Q: Barry Bonds, because he went through so much, as you did.

A: I don't have any. . . . As I said before, I don't have any advice whatsoever, no advice to anybody.

Q: Have you spoken with him?

A: No. I have not talked to anybody, really.

Q: What will you be doing when he's on the brink of tying or breaking your record?

A: I have no idea, probably playing golf somewhere.

Q: Would you reconsider your decision to stay away?

A: I will never reconsider my decision.

Q: That's pretty strong. Why is that?

A: Nothing. Just that it's the way I am. . . . I traveled for 23 years and I just get tired of traveling. I'm not going to fly to go see somebody hit a home run, no matter whether it is Barry or Babe Ruth or Lou Gehrig or whoever it may be. I'm not going anyplace. I wish him all the luck in the world.

Q: Well, if it happened in Atlanta would you go?

A: No, I won't be there.

Q: Really?

A: No.

Q: If he breaks your mark do you think it's an accomplishment on par with what you did?

A: I don't know, and as I said before, I don't want to discuss him, really. Really, I don't mean to discuss anything about it. . . . I've stayed out of this.

Behind the scenes, Henry and Bud Selig spoke numerous times each week. Henry would ask Selig for advice on how to handle the mounting questions about Bonds. Selig told Henry to speak his piece if he chose, and said the two would always be friends. It was Henry, in fact, around whom seemingly everyone in the game tiptoed. Dusty Baker found himself in the most awkward position: a commentator for ESPN during the year Bonds neared the record. Baker was trapped: For forty years, Henry had treated him like a son. But Baker had managed Bonds for ten seasons in San Francisco.

"I was caught in the middle," Baker recalled. "I'm on the air and they're asking me about steroids and Barry, but in the back of my mind I'm also thinking about Hank. So what did I do? I called Hank every week, just to make sure he was cool. He told me, 'Don't worry about me. I'm fine with it.' But I *did* worry about it, because it was Hank."

As usual, it was Selig who remained the ultimate power broker. While he remained loyal to Henry, Selig was also fielding calls from Bonds during the summer. Bonds wanted to know why Henry had not contacted him.

As Bonds approached the home-run record, members of Henry's inner circle believed he needed to take on the Bonds issue directly and candidly. There was no point, one adviser told him, to believe "this thing" could be avoided. At a meeting, Henry was inundated with ideas for how he should handle confronting the public as Bonds neared his record. One suggestion was to cultivate a friendly journalist and offer the exclusive story—Henry Aaron on Bonds and the record—to *Sports Illustrated.* It would be a cover story, of course. The people closest to him, who had known him for decades, including Bud Selig, all thought it a splendid idea: a controlled environment, with Henry on record, the kind of preemptive move public-relations experts loved. Another suggestion was to find a friendly television journalist (Tim Russert and Bob Costas were the top candidates) and have Henry do an hour-long sit-down. The freight train approached. And Henry would lie between the tracks. He said no to each strategic suggestion. And then he cut off all discussion of the matter.

The truth was, Henry was personally and permanently offended by Barry Bonds. The reasons were always sketchy, for Henry did not talk about Bonds specifically. To understand Henry, you had to know how to read body language, facial expressions, and sounds. You had to understand that Henry Aaron did not always speak with words. It was often what Henry *didn't* say that carried all the meaning. And during those two summers of 2006 and 2007, you had to be truly illiterate not to understand what he was trying to convey about both Bonds and the record.

Members of the inner circle may have sounded conflicted about the Bonds conundrum, unsure of what to say publicly (mostly out of loyalty to Henry's friend Bud Selig), but Henry shared no such uncertainty.

Bonds and Henry had done business before, back in 2002 for a Charles Schwab Super Bowl commercial, which showed Bonds taking batting practice as a mystical voice whispered in the background that Bonds needed to retire, to begin thinking about his future, in the mode of *Field of Dreams.* Finally, Bonds stopped hitting and yelled up to the press box, "Hank, will you cut it out?" The camera fixed on Aaron's surprised face and Henry delivered the commercial's punch line. "Hank? Hank who?"

It was a hilarious spot, but there was talk of a falling-out between the two men after. But what really frosted Henry was when in 2005 the Bonds people invited him to be part of what could only be termed a Barry Bonds victory tour. Bonds already had his godfather, Willie Mays, on board. Celebrations would be planned, the first when Barry hit home run number 661, passing Mays on the all-time list. The second would be after home run number 715, when Ruth was passed again, by another black man. Finally, the big fireworks would go off when Bonds hit number 756 for the all-time record.

The underlying incentive, the Bonds people told Henry, was race. Just imagine: the three greatest black players in history combining forces, finally taking history and reshaping it, turning the Bonds moment into something black America could be proud of. And there was big money to be made: exclusive appearances, limited-edition signed balls, bats, and merchandise (how many people owned memorabilia that contained the signatures of Bonds, Mays, and Aaron anyway?). The pitch ended with Henry being told his share alone might net three million dollars.

Henry spurned each overture by Bonds and his handlers to cultivate him, to make him a partner in the creation (or at least the marketing) of the beginning of a new history, the beginning of the Bonds era as home-run king, anointed by his legendary godfather, blessed by Henry. Henry made it clear to his closest advisers he would have nothing to do with Bonds. No Sunday conversation on ESPN, no traveling with Bonds to market or even aid in rehabilitating a game wounded by drugs. In a culture where everything, especially ethics, seemed to be for sale, Henry thought marketing the home-run record perhaps the crassest thing he'd ever heard. Bonds needed Henry for legitimacy, perhaps even for his own baseball salvation. But Henry Aaron needed Barry Bonds like he needed a root canal. No one would know what was exactly said during that phone conversation between the two, but there was no ambiguity about Henry's position. Confidants recalled Henry's words afterward as being "He's trying to buy me. And I resent that."

AT HIS LOS ANGELES office, Mike Tollin received a call from Rachael Vizcarra. Vizcarra was one of two women who did personal public-relations for Bonds, outside of the Giants official team sphere. She went back to Bonds's days with the Pirates and was Bonds's special envoy to Tollin, who now sat on the board of Henry's Chasing the Dream Foundation.

Tollin and Bonds had crossed paths before: A dozen years earlier, Tollin had interviewed Bonds for his documentary on Henry, *Chasing the Dream*. Given how events would ultimately unfold, it was more than a little ironic to watch the end of the film, with its interviews of stars from the mid-1990s—Frank Thomas, Ken Griffey, Jr., David Justice—and see Barry Bonds offer the last word of the documentary on Henry.

Around the same time, Tollin had been executive producer of *Arli$$*, the HBO comedy series that starred Robert Wuhl as a high-powered sports agent and featured cameos by numerous professional athletes. During the show's first two seasons, 1996 and 1997, Bonds agreed to appear, and he impressed Tollin and Wuhl (who was also an executive producer) with his professionalism and surprising serious-ness and perfectionism. What impressed Wuhl most was the time Bonds was on the set and a particular scene had not been done to anyone's satisfaction. At the time, Bonds was represented by Dennis Gilbert, and Gilbert reminded Bonds they had another appointment, a lucrative commercial for a high-powered client. They were late, he said, and would have to cut the filming short. But Bonds remained while all the necessary takes were shot and the scene was correct. Wuhl and Tollin never forgot that side of Bonds. Tollin, especially, believed it was an untapped side of Bonds that could be mined.

Now, years later, Rachael Vizcarra was calling on behalf of Barry Bonds. It was during the off-season before the 2006 season and Bonds stood at 708 career home runs. He had missed nearly the entire 2005 season due to an injury, but he came back to hit five home runs in fourteen September games. The strong finish gave the impression that Bonds would hit not only the seven homers he needed to pass Ruth in 2006 but also, the forty-eight he needed to pass Aaron to become the all-time leader.

The conversation was brief. Tollin mostly listened carefully, wait-ing for the upshot. And then, finally, he heard it: "Barry wants you to do for him what you did for Hank Aaron," Vizcarra told him.

Tollin was intrigued. As a next step in the process, he requested a meeting with Bonds. A few weeks later, the two met in Los Angeles at the apartment Bonds kept in the fashionable Wilshire Corridor. He actually kept two condominiums, one as an office, the other as a residence for when he was in town. During their talks, it seemed that Bonds was almost auditioning for the show Tollin had in mind. He told Tollin stories about growing up, about how abusive his father, Bobby Bonds, had been. He talked about the unfair treatment baseball had levied upon Bobby, and how his father's alcoholism in part could be traced to how poorly he had been treated by the game. Bonds took Tollin through the condo and Tollin found himself intrigued by Bonds's range of interests. He was interested in photography and Wall Street, movies and technology, and was in the process of a new project: a photo montage for his daughter. Yet despite the intrigue, Tollin also recognized an insulting red flag. Later that day, Bonds took Tollin to the residence portion of his condominium where his private chef was preparing lunch. Tollin was not offered any.

The discussions proceeded in earnest. Tollin wanted to know if Bonds was serious about moving forward. The project, he said, would not be hagiography: There were going to be controversial topics, such as the drug issues that swirled around him. Bonds said he was in the right frame of mind to proceed.

Tollin had been concerned about artistic integrity, and thus he demanded he have the final cut. Bonds didn't have any formal requests of his own, but wanted to know if Henry would be part of the program at some point.

After the meetings, Tollin was convinced he had sufficient cooperation from Bonds—and enough of a creative vision—to produce a compelling work. His vision was a singular one-hour documentary on Bonds. Bonds, of course, would be the star, and Tollin's challenge would be to present him in a dimension different from what Bonds believed to be the incorrect public perception of him.

Then Tollin followed up with another mantra that came from doing business in Hollywood: First you get the goods, and then you figure out where to sell them. ESPN was a natural, and the network was immediately interested—but not in a single show. Tollin recalled a conversation with Disney CEO Bob Iger at the premiere of the film *Glory Days* during which Iger told him a one-hour documentary was "leaving money on the table." The show's scope increased and Tollin agreed to film a full-season miniseries. The title Tollin wanted—*I'm Barry Bonds and You're Not*—was a nod to the seminal 1993 *Sports Illustrated* cover story. ESPN's choice—*Bonds on Bonds*—would be the title.

They made the deal, and then Tollin prepared for what he expected to be an interesting phone call—apprising Henry of the project. They had a good conversation, Tollin recalled, and Henry appreciated that Tollin showed him respect by asking him, in effect, to bless the project. But Henry was not interested. "I told him it wasn't about me taking sides. It was a chance as a filmmaker to tell a compelling story. Henry was typically gracious. Implicit in the message was that he didn't mind me doing it, but he didn't want any part of it."

BONDS WAS A polarizing figure, but also a fascinating one. John Skipper and John Walsh, two of the ESPN top executives who gave the show the green light, were enthusiastic and prepared to swat away the internal and external concerns that a reality-television show on Bonds would compromise the news operation. Walsh was particularly fascinated by Bonds, and according to intimates, he did not feel Bonds had ever been covered properly. After all, not only was Bonds bearing down on the home-run record but he was also being investigated by the federal government for perjury. Tollin and ESPN, so went the criticism, were providing a public-relations forum for a bad guy desperate to rehabilitate his image. Yet there was something of value to the show: Tollin had exclusive interviews with Barry Bonds during the season, Bonds in his own words—and nobody else had that.

That exclusivity, it turned out, would be the leverage that would ultimately destroy the show after ten episodes. Like a good-natured woman who really *believes* she can change that troubling, intriguing man she's fallen for, Tollin found out what so many people before him had discovered: There was no working with Barry Bonds.

The show debuted April 4, 2006. As the show progressed beyond the first few episodes, it was clear that Bonds believed the interviews gave him leverage over Tollin and the network. Tollin had already sensed possible trouble when, during the early blueprinting of the show, Bonds made Tollin sign a confidentiality agreement, opening him up to a multimillion-dollar lawsuit should he discuss anything that took place behind the scenes.

And then came the moment that, to Mike Tollin, said it all. Bonds had wanted Henry to be part of the project, and Tollin had an idea. If Bonds and Tollin split the cost of sponsoring a Hank Aaron scholar— roughly $25,000 apiece—Henry would most likely agree to a Chasing the Dream scholarship in the Bay Area and an appearance on the show. But Bonds just didn't get it. According to intimates, Bonds wanted nothing to do with the charity.

Later, Tollin had informed Bonds that he had a preexisting agreement with Disney to produce a $50 million film called *Wild Hogs,* a John Travolta–Martin Lawrence comedy vehicle, and he told Bonds that another producer, Fred Golding, would be taking on some of the show's duties. It was during this time that Bonds attempted in meetings to take more control over the direction of the show, which Tollin believed was in direct violation of their deal. The show was supposed to be independent, and now Bonds was trying to dictate the content during weekly planning meetings. Tollin went to ESPN, but the show was at an impasse. Bonds continued exerting control and the relationship soured. After Bonds hit his 715th home run, he insisted in dictating the content of the next week's show. "I refused and insisted on maintaining creative control," Tollin recalled. "And Barry said, 'If that's the case, I'll stop participating.' He wanted this to be his deification. I basically refused to give Bonds control. I went to John Skipper. ESPN supported my position, and we walked away."

Ultimately, the show fell flat for other reasons. Ratings were poor. Tollin believed Bonds felt betrayed over *Wild Hogs.* Yet there were a few moments he was proud of. The show captured Bonds's 715th homer, when he passed Ruth's record. After that game, Tollin went into the clubhouse to congratulate Bonds, who signed a ball for Tollin's son, Luke. The inscription was classic Bonds. "To Luke, God Bless Barry Bonds." Tollin always wondered with a certain amount of humor if the omitted comma was intentional.

And worst of all for the show, the dynamic, electric Bonds, who was expected to chase the home-run record with a fury, was hardly electric. He was a haggard old man, a sagging forty-two-year-old who, like most forty-two-year-olds still playing professional sports, accumulated numbers for a living. He could hit—occasionally. He couldn't run. He couldn't field his position.

"There's a heart beating there, but there are so many layers. I think the hardship growing up with his dad and Willie starts with mistrust," Tollin recalled. "They would tell him, 'You're better off without those people, and it's up to you to find out who those people are.'

"It was a shame. We could have made a nice show, but it became a test of wills, which wasn't what it was all about," he said. "This was his deification. So that was that. We'd rather walk away and prove to the media that we insisted on creative integrity. I saw Barry at the premiere. He was friendly. No hard feelings. It was a case of moving on. I'm not in touch with him."

THE GIANTS DESPERATELY wanted Henry to participate in the Bonds coronation. It wasn't just that a nod from Henry would give class and dignity and legitimacy to the whole sordid affair, perhaps soften the public mood that the record would always contain a steroid taint if Bonds surpassed Henry. The other reason was Henry's potential influence on Bonds himself. Perhaps having Henry involved would propel Barry into a feeling of magnanimity. Inside the Giant organization, everyone knew the real fiction surrounding Bonds was that his blood feud was a solo affair between himself and the press. That always made people who worked for the Giants laugh. The real truth was that Bonds treated Giants employees as badly as he did the writers. In some cases, certain Giants employees thought, the writers had it easier than club employees, because at least the writers could leave. They could get away from Bonds. The writers could retreat to the press box or the field or anyplace where Barry was not. They only had to deal with Bonds the player for about three hours per day. Maybe having Henry on board would give Bonds more incentive to enjoy the journey toward history. Maybe it would make Barry be nice, just for a month.

Of course, Larry Baer did not know that Bonds had already insulted Henry, and Henry Aaron wouldn't have gone to San Francisco in a million years for ten million bucks.

But Baer was persistent. Susan Bailey, upon orders from Henry and Allan Tanenbaum, was an even more ferocious gatekeeper than normal as Bonds approached the record. "Susan wouldn't even let most people finish their sentences," Tanenbaum recalled. That made one of the stories floating around—that the television network Fox had offered Henry $250,000 *per day* to travel with Bonds once Bonds came within a home run of 755—virtually impossible.

"I know that story wasn't true for two reasons," Tanenbaum said. "The first was that nobody could even get to Henry during those final three weeks. The second was that Henry had already said he had no interest in this. No amount of money was going to get him to change his mind."

Baer, though, slipped through the protective shield once, to the fury of Bailey and Tanenbaum, reaching Henry at home and asking him one final time if he would fly to San Francisco for Bonds. The Giants would cover the tab, naturally: flights, hotels, meals, transportation—everything first-class.

Henry said no.

That didn't stop Baer, who, at the league's New York offices, met with Henry and Tim Brosnan and John Brody, two members of the MLB Properties division. At that meeting, Baer told Henry he was interested in having him explain his position. Why, Baer asked, was he being so vague about his plans? Henry told Baer he did not judge Bonds but that as a seventy-three-year-old man he had no interest in following another baseball player around. He'd had his time as the record holder, he told Baer, and he wished Barry well, but he was not interested.

"Would you at least consider a taping?" Baer recalled asking, fully expecting a no. "Would you tape a congratulatory message we could show on the video board whenever he breaks the record?"

"That, I could do," Henry said.

To Henry's recollection, he had not completely committed. To Baer, Henry was on board.

Baer sprang into action. He prepared a film crew to fly to Georgia to tape Henry. He even wrote the script, telling Henry just what to say. Henry informed Baer he would do the video but that he would write the words himself . . . and he added a special caveat: Should anything "extraordinary" occur during the time between the taping and the day Bonds broke the record, he reserved the right to prohibit the Giants from airing the video. That something "extraordinary," as everyone knew, was the federal indictment for perjury that had hung over Bonds for three years.

For weeks, the video sat in a vault in the Braves offices. When Baer finally received the video—which arrived when Bonds was two home runs away from the record—he did not tell anyone he had snared the great and reticent Henry Aaron, Bonds included. The only people who knew, apart from the principals, were the scoreboard operators (who had to be sure the tape was compatible with their systems) and the commissioner's office, which had had a hand in brokering the deal.

AUGUST 7, 2007, SBC Park: fifth inning, one out. In his first two at bats, Bonds had doubled and singled against Mike Bacsik, the Washington Nationals pitcher. The day before, Bacsik had fielded the inevitable questions of what it would be like to serve up the record-breaking home run. "I dreamed about this moment since I was a kid," he said. "Except I was the one hitting the homer, not giving it up."

The record had turned into a slog, a forty-three-year-old antihero playing for nothing but himself, in joyless pursuit of a record only he wanted broken. The Giants were in last place and would stay there. If there was any suspense at all, it was about whether Bonds would be indicted before he broke the record, and, if so, whether Bud Selig would suspend Bonds immediately and save the record, an eleventh-hour clemency not so much for Henry but for the relentless assault of performance-enhancing drugs on his sport.

In the press box, the writers lived for these moments. Sitting in on history was one of the biggest reasons to be in the news business. You get only one shot to write it big, and write it well. And Bonds, with all of his bitterness and contradictions, his talent and hubris, made for great theater, if nothing else.

Dave Sheinin of the *Washington Post* was in the press box, enjoying a unique vantage point. Two years earlier, when baseball's equivalent of the Blue Wall finally crumbled in Room 2154 of the Rayburn Building during the devastating hearings on March 17, 2005, Sheinin covered Mark McGwire's disintegration and the nadir of the Steroid

Era for the front page of the *Post*, and now just one Bonds home run would provide the coup de grâce.

Now the game was tied at 4–4. Bacsik threw Bonds a fastball, which he did not miss.

"I remember the moment he hit it. I was like, 'Here we go.' And at that moment, it felt historic," Sheinin recalled. "For about as long as it took for him to circle the bases, and of course you see Hank's face on the Jumbotron, all of that felt really huge to me. There was a ten-minute window when it really felt immense. But that was it."

Bonds's ball cleared the field of play, soaring into discredited space. He was facing an imminent federal indictment, which would come less than four months later. He had determined that the moment would belong to him, that because he cherished owning the record, the record would be cherished. Weeks earlier, Bonds had sparred with the writers again about the legitimacy of his holding the record. Finally, he attempted to curb debate by declaring, "Once I break the record, it's mine."

"It's weird. It cheapened the moment but elevated the moment at the same time. It didn't feel legit. It didn't feel real. It felt fraudulent. But from a pure story standpoint, it made it richer," Sheinin said. "If it was regular old Barry Bonds with no steroids who broke Hank Aaron's record, it wouldn't have been strong. But the way it occurred made it important for society because of what it meant. It was paradoxical."

In 1998, when McGwire hit number sixty-two, every member of the Cubs infield—Mark Grace at first, Mickey Morandini at second, the shortstop José Hernandez—embraced him as he rounded the bases. Bud Selig and Stan Musial sat next to each other. The Chicago third baseman, Gary Gaetti, pounded his glove with excitement as McGwire passed. The Cubs catcher, Scott Servais, hugged McGwire and didn't seem to want to let go, even as McGwire's own team, the Cardinals, rushed to mob the hero.

Nine years later, orange-and-black streamers rained from the upper deck, and San Francisco, isolated in its joy, whooped and hollered. Bonds gave a two fisted-pump to the heavens and began his historic trot, but not a single Nationals player shook his hand as he rounded the bases. No one slapped him on the back, or even smiled. As he reached home plate, the Nationals catcher, Brian Schneider, stood away from the dish, as impassively as if play had been stopped to clear a stray beach ball from center field.

As Bonds and Willie Mays stood with their backs to the field, waving to the crowd, there came a roar within the roar. On the Jumbotron, wearing a charcoal suit and a striped tie was Henry. Those in the Nationals dugout along the first-base line, showing emotion for the first time, clapped politely.

Henry squinted and spoke his words. Bonds and Mays turned around to watch the video display.

"I would like to offer my congratulations to Barry Bonds on becoming baseball's career home-run leader. It is a great accomplishment which required skill, longevity and determination," Henry said. "Throughout the past century, the home run has held a special place in baseball, and I have been privileged to hold this record for 33 of those years. I move over now and offer my best wishes to Barry and his family on this historical achievement. My hope today, as it was on that April evening in 1974, is that the achievement of this record will inspire others to chase their own dreams." Upon completing the final sentence, Henry offered a soft little smile. Janie McCauley, a reporter for the Associated Press, put in a call to the Aaron residence in Atlanta. A woman answered the phone. "Mr. Aaron is asleep," she said, and hung up the phone.

IT TOOK SEVEN takes to complete the forty-five-second video. On the first six, Henry seemed fine, but he looked weary and tired, like he'd rather have been in West Palm or . . . Pluto . . . or . . . *anywhere* else. The words were his, but they were a scripted, clandestine, collaborative effort. E-mails circulated from Allan Tanenbaum to Henry to Mike Tollin to some staffers in the commissioner's office to Bud Selig. The message had to be subtle, yet energetic and graceful, lest Henry open himself up to the charge that, yes, he congratulated Bonds, but his heart wasn't really in it. Of course, that part was true: His heart was miles away from this compromise. But Henry had given his word to Larry Baer and the Giants, and thus he would tape a congratulatory message.

In Atlanta, Billye Aaron read each new incoming message—a

word tweak here, a change of emphasis there—a working draft for the digital age. Henry and Allan Tanenbaum proceeded to a studio in downtown Atlanta for the taping. The dark backdrop was accompanied by a montage—an Aaron home Braves jersey, a replica of the Hank Aaron Boulevard street sign.

Henry read the words carefully and dutifully, but after the sixth take, a young technician stopped him, summoning the courage to offer an artistic appraisal of the filming. Henry's delivery was fine, he said. His pacing was good. But, the young man said, this tape was being made for a celebration, for history. Was it possible, the technician asked Mr. Aaron, for him to show a little more joy? Perhaps a smile would be good.

Henry looked at the man and delivered a line that, in the face of Bonds, would forever make him the people's champion.

"Young man," Henry Aaron said. "Do you really think I have anything to smile about?"

AND SO, after thirty-three years it was over. Henry was no longer the home-run king. Bonds would hit six more that season, finish at 762, and, for his effort, never again be allowed to wear a big-league uniform.

"What was happening is that, for the first time, unlike when Babe Ruth held the all-time home-run mark, the standard-bearer and the record holder have been separated," Harry Edwards, the famed sociologist, said of the tainted Bonds surpassing Henry. "Henry Aaron, Roger Maris, these are the standard-bearers. Mark McGwire, Barry Bonds, these are record holders. For the first time ever, the standard of excellence and the record holder are totally different people.

"If you're going to maintain the integrity of the sport, the standard-bearers and the standard of excellence have to again become the same person. Right now, they're not. Henry Aaron is the standard of excellence. Because of this drug thing, baseball doesn't care about the record holder. He's just standing out there. Baseball cares about the standard of excellence, and that means people will always look to Henry Aaron."

EPILOGUE

ON OCTOBER 30, 2008, roughly thirty schoolchildren gathered at a chain-link fence in front of the Toulminville Grammar School as a rugged eighty-foot-long flatbed truck negotiated the tight, narrow maze of streets in their neighborhood of Toulminville, Alabama. The buzzing among the kids was rooted in the sheer technological undertaking of the procession, for the children did not believe what they were about to see: an entire house, sixty feet in length, twenty feet high, would be lifted off of the ground, taken in its entirety from the small tract of land where it had sat, undisturbed, for sixty-seven years, laid on the bed of the truck, and driven away. Trucks carry dirt; trucks carry cars, they confirmed to one another. But a whole house?

The moving team worked methodically, thwarted momentarily by annoying obstacles: The height of the house made it difficult for the flatbed to pass under dangerous high-tension wires. Overgrown trees hampered the crew's exit route, and no chain saw could slice through the bureaucracy: City ordinances prevented the removal of even a single tree branch without government authorization.

Police escorts awaited the convoy. An elderly woman, Mrs. Ruth, had lived next door to the house since FDR was in his third term, since the Great Depression began to slowly loosen its grip on America. Her hand covering her mouth, cheeks dampening, she stood at a slight distance from the commotion, steps removed from the construction crew and the police, from the officials from the city of Mobile and a few from the Baseball Hall of Fame and Museum, in Cooperstown, New York.

This was Henry Aaron's childhood house, 2010 Edwards Street, Mobile, the house where he had come to live when he was eight years old. That was why everyone was making such a big fuss. It was the house Herbert had built with his bare hands and lived in for the next fifty-six years, never falling to the temptation of trading up to something bigger and better, to somewhere more luxurious and exclusive, as his famous son had suggested. It was the house where Henry's mother, Estella, had lived for ten more years after her husband's death, the place where Estella Aaron and Mrs. Ruth shared a friendship that lasted a lifetime. And now they were taking the house away to the city's baseball park in central Mobile, where it would become a museum.

How the deal got done was quintessentially Henry, not the Henry Aaron who sought respect and found disappointment, but the polished and regal seventy-four-year-old who could now call presidents and CEOs directly for social visits. Bill Shanahan, the president of the Mobile BayBears, the Double-A affiliate of the Arizona Diamondbacks that played its home games at the stadium named after Hank Aaron, had an idea of how to celebrate the seventy-fifth year of Henry's life: a museum would be named after Aaron, serving as a veritable time line for the American twentieth century. Hank Aaron's childhood home more than deserved to become a civic landmark in Mobile, Shanahan reasoned. Toulminville might be a challenging locale to draw tourist traffic, so what better place for the Hank Aaron Museum than the actual house he grew up in, located at the ballpark that bore his name? The house had been boarded up for a couple of years. Its contents—photographs, furniture, clothing, and even the Presidential Medal of Freedom Henry had received from President Clinton—remained inside.

Shanahan called the Baseball Hall of Fame for help, and Cooperstown officials, finally enjoying an overdue thaw with Henry, agreed.

The consortium of builders were all southern white men, some old enough to remember the old Mobile, when people like Henry were forced by custom to defer to people like them, when Herbert Aaron was forced to give up his place in line to them. And now, in another century, a different time, these same men jumped at the chance to be close to Henry Aaron, and to honor his father's house. The bill to relocate and renovate the house would hit fifty thousand dollars. Much of the house still contained the original wood from

1942, when Herbert Aaron completed its construction. The moving expenses would be considerable, and would Henry be amenable to moving the family house in the first place? Many an honorable project wilted in the boardroom over lack of funds, but here a creative enthusiasm built up. Local architect Larry Hinkle said he'd do the entire job for free. The Hall of Fame would use its muscle. The Bay-Bears said they would maintain the museum. All Henry Aaron had to do was agree.

No one was sure how to approach Henry. The word had been out about Henry for years: He was bitter. He was angry. He was unapproachable, the guy the real fans feared most: that legend you always wanted to meet, only to have the little boy in you leveled by the jerk in him.

Mike Callahan, the general manager of the BayBears, made the call. He pitched Henry the idea. The silence was awkward.

"I really thought I'd pissed him off," Callahan recalled. "There was so much silence on the other end, I'm thinking to myself that I had this one opportunity and I blew it."

Mike Callahan realized only later that the silence on the other end was Henry holding back to keep from crying on the telephone.

THE TRUCK LURCHED before ambling slowly forward. The movers saw heaven in the form of I-65, a freeway wide enough to accommodate the flatbed. The house would travel eight miles in nine hours. The convoy passed Hank Aaron Park in Toulminville and curved around the Hank Aaron Business Loop in Mobile to reach its final destination, Hank Aaron Stadium.

Even when Henry was a boy, the house talked to him, told him in some strange way that he and his family were something special. Now the house was talking to Henry again. It had transformed honor, pride, ownership, and responsibility from airy concepts into something real, something he could hold in his hands. Henry Aaron would always be called a mama's boy, but the house was a piece of his father, an example of the unpretentious hard work he had exemplified during his adult life.

Henry was the patriarch now. Ninety-six years old, Stella Aaron died in April 2008, ten years after Herbert. She remained in Mobile until diabetes made it too difficult to keep up her house, then moved to Atlanta to live with Henry. When she was home, in Mobile, her routines were none too dissimilar from Henry's escapist tendencies when he was a boy. Henry would disappear to hook catfish on the banks of Three Mile Creek. Stella found her own spot along Mobile Bay, off of Halls Mills Road, digging up bait with a friend, trolling for redfish and white trout.

"People say over time it gets easier," Henry said one day in New York, months after Stella's death. "But it doesn't. When you lose your mother, it is always going to be hard."

Of Herbert and Stella's eight children, only three remained: Alfredia, James, and Henry. The rest were all gone, but the house still stood. In a sense, the house now mirrored what Henry had become— once intensely private, now a public institution.

THE NEXT GENERATION of Aarons remains, conflicted. The children dealt with their father's fame and its effects on them in their own ways, with varying degrees of success. Gaile Aaron speaks of her father with an intense pride, saying that he "was always a better father than a baseball player," and yet navigating her own life under his immense shadow could be complicated.

"Being introduced to someone, I was always 'Gaile, Hank Aaron's daughter,' " she said. "It was like it wasn't good enough to be just Gaile."

Lary Aaron played football in high school and then at Florida A&M. He never played big-league baseball, but he became a minor-league scout for the Milwaukee Brewers.

"There are advantages and disadvantages. When we grew up, my father told us he was really no different than anyone else," Lary Aaron said. "He just had a job that was in the limelight and people liked to see. We never thought we were better than anyone else, and he always said that he's no better than the guy who's digging a ditch."

Dorinda Aaron, Henry's youngest child from his marriage to Barbara, works for her father at the 755 Restaurant Corporation, the parent company for Henry's fast-food restaurants.

The 755 Restaurant Corporation is a reflection of Henry's closest circle. His son-in-law, Victor Haydel, oversees the operation—Popeye's, Church's Chicken, and Krispy Kreme—while Louis Tanenbaum, son of Henry's attorney Allan Tanenbaum, is also part of the management team.

Tommie Aaron, Jr., Henry Aaron's nephew, would drive to Toulminville one afternoon to visit his grandfather's house, only to see what neighbors saw in 1941: an empty square, bordered by wilted tufts of grass. Tommie junior did not know the movers had taken the house. "That," his mother Carolyn Aaron says, "was my fault. I forgot to tell him the movers had taken his grandfather's house."

The decision to dedicate the house—indeed, to give it to the world—was not a democratic one, nor was it universally popular. It was largely Henry who had maintained it, Henry who feared it being neglected and falling into disrepair if left alone in Toulminville, Henry who paid the taxes, and Henry who made the executive call to turn it over to the city of Mobile.

Herbert Aaron's granddaughter, Veleeta Aaron, passes Hank Aaron Stadium each time she drives along Interstate 65 and is vexed when she sees the house Herbert Aaron built now sitting on the grounds of a baseball stadium.

"It's sad. When you think about that house, through all the years, it was ours. It's sad just because I grew up in that house," she says. "It was something that we had to ourselves, something that was ours for our family. It was our safety place.

"I guess now, when you think about all kinds of people walking through the living room, it belongs to everybody. And that is kind of sad and kind of good. It's a part of history now."

FEBRUARY 19, 2008: Henry was in Lake Buena Vista, Florida, the spring-training home of the Braves. A group of reporters asked him about Roger Clemens, Clemens's recent testimony to the House Government Reform Committee, and the growing likelihood that Congress would seek an indictment for perjury against him. Henry responded in the same opaque manner in which he'd discussed Barry Bonds a year earlier. It was the typical, evasive boilerplate. He knew nothing about it, he said. Baseball was heading in the right direction. He didn't care about whether Clemens was inducted into the Hall of Fame. That was a decision for the baseball writers, and, he added, "I don't have a vote."

FOR THE PAST two years, when it became clear that his record would fall, a nation of baseball fans would call on him and he would confuse them. Perhaps his voice would provide cover for them, the ones who watched the bodies expand and the offensive numbers rise and yet would not make the only kind of stand—refusing to spend their disposable income on baseball—that the game's leadership would respect. Certainly, a decline in profits would have attracted the attention of Bud Selig and the baseball owners. But the fans did not do this. They spent and watched and cheered and waited for Henry to tell them that something had gone horribly wrong with the sport.

Their respect, in a sense, was the part of the hero game that Henry had long craved. For the majority of his baseball life, he had been judged based on what he wasn't. He wasn't flashy enough. He wasn't talkative enough or sufficiently articulate. He did not go on the offensive for these injustices and that made him dignified. Perhaps it was a matter of finally having what he'd always wanted and not knowing what to do with it. Or perhaps Henry's reticence was prompted by this particular issue, the drugs tied up in the runaway, unattractive commodities he did not respect, that kept him away from the calls of the nation. But that was just the problem: The leader doesn't get to choose which issue will send him into action. His only choice is whether to accept the mission.

In 2009, in Cooperstown, the day before Rickey Henderson and Jim Rice were to be inducted into the Baseball Hall of Fame, Henry Aaron erased the ambiguity. In little ways, if you paid close enough attention, he had let his feeling be known not by what he said about Barry Bonds, but by the enthusiasm he exhibited a year after Bonds broke his record, when he congratulated Ken Griffey, Jr., who in June 2008 hit his six hundredth home run. Griffey had always been considered something of a tragic figure, robbed by injuries—as well as by the widespread steroid culture around him and the prevailing belief in the baseball world that he had never used performance-enhancing drugs—of the opportunity to continue to be what he had once been: the most exciting player in the game since Mays.

If Henry was tepid in his response to Bonds when he broke the record, his message to Griffey contained no ambiguities.

"Ken Griffey Jr., congratulations on hitting your 600th home run. I got a chance to see you at the Boys and Girls Club function just recently, you and your lovely wife, and you know you've always been a favorite of mine.

"I played with your dad, I know him very well, but you know I've always said that if anybody was going to reach 700, with no pun intended to anybody, I thought you had an excellent chance. Of course we can't, we don't know how injuries played a very big part, but congratulations to reaching 600. Only a few, and you are the sixth person to do that.

"Congratulations Ken Griffey Jr., and many, many more. I'm just hoping that you'll have the greatest year you've ever had in your life. Thank you."

Now, in Cooperstown, Henry was as direct as he once had been evasive. He told a small group from the Baseball Writers' Association of America, the body that votes for Hall of Fame enshrinement, that the Steroid Era must be acknowledged in perpetuity with a scarlet letter. "If a player is elected who's known to have used steroids, then I think there ought to be an asterisk or something mentioned on the plaque that he used steroids.

"To be safe, that's the only way I see you can do it. I played the game long enough to know it is impossible for players, I don't care who it is, to hit 70-plus home runs. It just does not happen."

And with that statement, the people loved him even more. The record did not belong to him, and he did not need it. He had become the people's champion.

A MONTH AFTER Henry congratulated Ken Griffey, Jr., on his historic home run, the 2008 All-Star Game was played at Yankee Stadium. The night following the game, the television network HBO broadcast a special episode of the program *Costas Now,* hosted by veteran broadcaster Bob Costas.

"I had a good relationship with Henry going back many years and that gave me the ability to at least ask," Costas recalled. "I had been asking for a couple of years for him to appear, not with Willie, just to talk about his career. However, in such an environment in my position I would still have to be inclined to ask him about Barry Bonds. Henry was warm and respectful, but always declined. He declined everything because he saw no upside.

"First, I got Willie to agree. I told Henry, 'You'll be with Willie. The show is not about Barry Bonds, but about your respective careers, your generations.' I told him, 'You know that if that's what it's going to be about, you know I won't sabotage you.'"

Henry wore a charcoal blazer, Mays a gray suit and red paisley tie and a San Francisco Giants cap. When the two men appeared, the auditorium at the Skirball Center at New York University erupted in an extended standing ovation. Bob Gibson was the exception. Seventy-two years old and still unyielding, Gibson held out, the only person in the audience *not* to stand.

The evening was magical in its reverence for a battered game. Henry and Willie, keepers of the standard, were reinforced by the considerable supporting cast of Hall of Fame pitchers Jim Palmer and Gibson. Two kids who now borrowed the stage, Philadelphia shortstop Jimmy Rollins and Tampa Bay third baseman Evan Longoria, appeared genuinely moved.

The program began with the usual tall tales of the old romantic days—of Gibson nailing hitters and Henry and Willie nailing fastballs in return. As the evening progressed, the two men became themselves: Willie the raconteur was gregariously absorbing large chunks of space, and the night turned into yesterday afternoon, August at the Polo Grounds, the audience breathing in Willie's air, taken once more by his gifts.

And Henry sat there smiling, looking at Willie as one looks at a charmingly obnoxious cousin—equal parts humor and patience.

"Whatever tension or rivalry others have speculated, time and mutual appreciation took that away," Costas said. "Henry is a figure of tremendous dignity, Willie far more outwardly excitable and high spirited. In a way, Hank enjoyed looking at Willie. It was almost as though he was between first and second, and then we went into overtime and his hat flew off and he went into another gear."

When Henry spoke, the room went quiet and the energy changed. He was, as much as Mays, in his own element—serious and hurt, sometimes humorous and sometimes grave—and the room belonged to him. Henry spoke of serious matters, of how a piece of his life had been taken from him and how it had never come back and that no matter how many years might pass, he wouldn't speak in depth of the years from 1972 to 1974.

The show was supposed to run fifteen minutes. It lasted nearly an hour. At Willie's suggestion, the two men stood together for a final standing ovation.

"I think the difference is this," Costas said. "Henry engenders great respect, but people view Willie by excitement and fondness. They associate him with fun. With Henry Aaron, it is all about respect."

ON FEBRUARY 5, 2009, Henry Aaron turned seventy-five. The birthday party was supposed to be modest, a family-only affair, but Billye couldn't help herself and sold out the ballroom at the Atlanta Marriott Marquis. Bill Clinton was in attendance, dining at Henry's table.

"You've given us," Clinton told Henry, "far more than we'll ever give you."

Henry lived for the family; what started in Camden, under the thumb of the Tait cotton and slavery dynasty, ended with the election of Barack Obama as president, a milestone neither King nor Robinson, neither Herbert nor Stella lived to see. Henry supported Hillary Clinton in the primary. Even a month before the election, Billye Aaron was unconvinced that Obama could win, that America would do something neither she nor many Americans could envision. The country was still too racist, she said, to elect a black president.

Henry said he was "thrilled" by the Obama victory. Clinton, standing next to Henry, said the part of what Henry felt was taken from him during the Ruth chase might have been restored with the election of a black president.

"I am extremely happy with what happened in the country with having a black president," he said. "I don't think about 15, 20 years ago. I don't have time to. I think about the good time I'm having now. I've got the respect of people. That's the most important thing, trying to do everything I can and do it right."

And then Henry reverted to his usual mode of behavior, withdrawing from the fray, seeking peace while others elevated him. Ted Turner said Barry Bonds hit the most home runs in major-league history but that Henry Aaron was the home-run king. When it was his turn to speak, Tom Johnson, former chairman of CNN, took the microphone and Harry Edwards's prophecy played out in real time.

"You will always rank number one in my record book, without an asterisk," Johnson said. "Henry, you never disappointed us. Not once. Long after all of us are gone, your name, the name of Henry Aaron, will symbolize what I believe it really means to be a genuine American hero."

HENRY'S AMERICA WAS fading. In 2007, he traveled to Milwaukee to attend a dinner celebrating the fiftieth anniversary of the Milwaukee Braves only championship. Only thirteen Braves remained. Bill Bruton had died in a car crash in 1995, the accident caused by a heart attack while he was driving near his home in Delaware. Joe Adcock died in 1999. Eddie Mathews had died of a heart attack in 2001, Warren Spahn died in 2003, Lew Burdette in 2007, Billy Muffett in 2008, and the man who signed him, Ed Scott, in 2010 at age 92.

In the most complete sense, Henry Aaron had won. Winding through the city of Milwaukee is the Hank Aaron State Trail, nearly ten miles of sanctuary for bikers, runners, and skateboarders. In 2004, the city of Eau Claire erected a statue commemorating the sixty days Henry spent there. In Mobile and Atlanta, the Aaron name adorns streets and parks.

At a safe remove, when there were no more points to prove, no more misunderstandings to correct, no more slights to salve, the competitions ended and the deeds could finally speak for themselves. Henry Aaron lowered his guard and allowed the warmth of the sun of his life to bathe his face.

"Not too long ago, we went away for fifteen days on a cruise to the Panama Canal," he said. "I had been on cruises before, but never on the water for that long a time. I remember when the boat was in the Canal, in that narrow space. I looked out at the blue ocean and saw the birds swoop down into the water and then settle on the land. And then I understood how much I wanted to be like them, free. I leaned over to my wife and I told her that it was at that very moment that I finally felt like them. No one was asking me about baseball. The people that were around us weren't interested in me because I played baseball. I was free as a bird. And I told my wife. I said, 'I've never felt this free in my life.' "

ACKNOWLEDGMENTS

Over the four years it has taken to complete this project, I have accumulated serious debts to many people. Allan Tanenbaum, Henry's attorney and friend for thirty-five years, paved the way for my subsequent interviews with Henry. I am grateful for his trust, recollections, efforts, and frankness. Without him, Henry Aaron would likely not have spoken to me, and the result would have been a very different, lesser book.

Henry Aaron was never overly enthusiastic about this book, preferring to let his prodigious accomplishments speak for themselves. Nevertheless, he offered his voice on important areas that he had never before discussed publicly. Equally important, he did not impede his friends, family, and associates from speaking with me. Billye Aaron, Henry's wife, was particularly gracious. Her perspective on their remarkable journey of nearly four decades together was an invaluable one. Henry's sister-in-law, Carolyn Aaron; his niece, Veleeta Aaron; and nephew, Tommie Aaron Jr., were all generous with their time and memories.

An important figure in Henry's life, Frank Belatti, was very helpful with his recollections of meeting a Henry Aaron who in the mid-1980s was at a professional and personal crossroads and of helping him achieve a successful business career, one he is as proud of as his accomplishments on the baseball diamond. As a person who worked directly both with Henry and with Barry Bonds on television projects, Mike Tollin holds a wonderful perspective on the two men. His insights during Bonds's pursuit of Henry's record in 2007 were of unique value.

Bud Selig and I have had a contentious relationship over the past decade, but he has never wavered in his admiration of Henry Aaron. Accordingly, he was gracious with his time and remembrances of Milwaukee in the 1950s and of Henry during their fifty-plus years of friendship. I am grateful also to Jimmie Lee Solomon, Richard Levin, Patrick Courtney, Earnell Lucas, and Mike Port of the commissioner's office for their time and insights.

Research is often thankless work, but several people across various institutions were instrumental in helping with the excavation of records, court documents, census data, and other archival information vital to understanding Henry's early years. Collette King at the Mobile County Probate Court was an invaluable resource in untangling the complex web of city records during the early part of the twentieth century in segregated Mobile as well as providing me with a daily history lesson about the city. The first friendly face I encountered in Mobile, Janie Daugherty at the Mobile Public Library was kind enough to help sift through and make available the voluminous Henry Aaron file of newspaper clippings and introduce me to numerous people in Mobile who familiarized me with the city and a fair number who knew the Aaron family.

I am particularly grateful to Paulette Davis-Horton, who is a walking encyclopedia of the history of black Mobile, providing the institutional memory regarding the African-American experience in that city where little to no documentation existed.

Scotty Kirkland at the University of South Alabama's photo archives was the second friendly face I met in Mobile.

The staff at the Library of Congress Manuscript Division was diligent in helping me wade through two important collections—Branch Rickey's and Jackie Robinson's—that helped me understand Robinson's complicated relationship with organized baseball and why Henry came to admire him. The Library of Congress Periodicals Division is an invaluable source.

Constance Potter at the National Archives was helpful in providing a history of the census and in tracking down the roots of the Aaron family. The library staffs at the Atlanta History Center, the Atlanta Public Library, the Widener Library at Harvard University, the Boston Public Library, and the New York Public Library were all professional and helpful to completing this project.

My debts are endless at the National Baseball Hall of Fame and Museum, starting with Bill Francis, who did the initial heavy lifting of tracking down all things Henry Aaron and fielding my never-ending calls and e-mails. Like Bill Francis, Pat Kelly graciously accepted my frantic phone calls for photographs and was unfailingly polite and professional.

Jeff Idelson has been a great friend for many years and in addition to paving the way for me to utilize the museum's vast resources, provided me with tremendous insight into Henry's ongoing relationship with the Hall of Fame. Many thanks also go out to Tim Wiles and Claudette Burke.

There are too many people to list, but special thanks go out Dusty Baker, who has known Henry Aaron for forty years and has always been an incomparable resource about the game of baseball and the place of African-Americans. He has along the way become a great friend.

Ralph Garr and I spoke on at least a half dozen occasions and each time I learned something new about Henry and the life of that second generation of black ballplayer (the first to reach the majors without needing to play in the Negro Leagues). Of all the people interviewed for this book, Ralph understood the heart of Henry Aaron in the most unique way.

Speaking with Ed Scott, the man who discovered Henry Aaron, was one of the great pleasures of working on this book. The institutional memory of the prewar years in America fades with each passing day, and I am thankful for the opportunity to have spoken with and learned from him.

Al Downing was gracious with memories of his life in baseball and talking about a moment—the night he gave up Henry's 715th home run—about which he is beyond fatigued. I am grateful to him for being so willing to discuss his life with me.

There is no greater gentleman than Gene Conley, Henry's old teammate with the Milwaukee Braves. Gene was unfailingly polite in taking my calls to jog his memory about a young Henry Aaron, his days growing up in Oklahoma, and the early days of the Milwaukee Braves. Conversely, I realized I had worn out my welcome with the old Braves shortstop Johnny Logan, who finally fielded my calls by saying, "You again?" But I am grateful that it took a half dozen calls before he finally got fed up.

Ever since I met him in 2001, Joe Torre has been a wonderful sounding board for all topics, from race to the formation of the players' association to simply learning the game. My thanks go out to him again for his assistance and connecting me with his brother Frank, who played with Henry and was one of his closer friends on the team.

Writers in general (sports writers in particular) are very good at complaining, but I cannot thank enough two institutions for providing me with the time and resources to complete this project, especially John Skipper, John Walsh, and Rob King at ESPN. For anyone committed to journalism, there is nothing better than sitting down with John Walsh. His door was always open and I have never had a conversation with him that did not inspire me to be a better journalist, a better writer, and a better thinker while simultaneously feeling humbled by the intense sense of pride that comes with being around such a talented group as there is at ESPN.

ESPN.com executive editor Rob King was patient and supportive over the many months of 2008 and 2009 while I completed the manuscript, and like John Walsh has always been a terrific resource. Patrick Stiegman was a tremendous help both with reading sections of the manuscript and lending me a tremendous book on the Milwaukee Braves, *The Milwaukee Braves: A Baseball Eulogy*, by Bob Buege.

I am grateful for the support of my direct editors, Michael Knisley, David Kull, and especially Jena Janovy, who read portions of the manuscript's early drafts and provided helpful inspiration and suggestions.

This project originally began in May 2006 when I was a staff writer at *The Washington Post*. My former editor, Emilio Garcia-Ruiz, has always been generous with me and supported the project from the beginning.

I am thankful for the generosity of a phenomenal group of journalists at the *Post:* David Maraniss, Wil Haygood, Dave Sheinin, Mike Wise, Cindy Boren, Ed Holzinger, Meg Smith, Jonathan Krim, Jason La Canfora, and Michael Wilbon. As they say in the dugout, it was nice to hit in that lineup.

In addition, a great field of professional journalists offered insight and suggestions that were helpful to the manuscript. My thanks go to Jack O'Connell, George Vecsey, Wayne Minshew, Monte Poole, Gene Wojciechowski, Nick Cafardo, Adrian Wojnarowski, John Helyar, and the incomparable Roger Kahn.

Special thanks go out to Dan Frank at Pantheon Books, who provided the greatest gift an editor could ever offer to an author: his confidence in the project. Even at times when I wavered, he did not. His editing, guidance, and suggestions throughout the process were first-rate. Many thanks go out to his assistant, Jillian Verrillo, and her predecessors Hannah Oberman-Breindel and Fran Bigman.

My agent, Deirdre Mullane of Mullane Literary Associates, has always been the first line of defense, the staunchest advocate for any project, and still the reigning champion at putting together a saleable proposal. Many thanks also go out to Janet Pawson of Headline Media Management for her guidance and support.

For too much work and too little pay, David Kutzmann edited the manuscript from its first incarnations and, more importantly, provided an invaluable sounding board at all hours of the night, making the process a little less isolated. This is our third collaboration and, as always, it is his friendship that grows stronger with the completion of each project.

In the same vein, *Washington Post* staff writer Steve Yanda conducted several interviews and contributed research. Steve was instrumental in easing the burden of the mountains of information, and this project could not have been completed without his tremendous assistance.

There is a special group of friends upon whom I rely to such a degree that my indebtedness to them is eternal. Daily conversations with Glenn Stout rival any writing workshop in the country. Too many ideas to count have been transformed into themes and concepts that appear throughout this book. Our friendship now enters its second decade.

Often at the expense of her own writing, Lisa Davis eased the solitary exercise of writing by being a friend and confidant of the highest order. For fear of being greedy, I can only hope that the inspiration of our talks has been reciprocal.

Christopher Sauceda read the entire manuscript at each stage and as always has been a great friend during the writing process and beyond.

A special measure of thanks goes to Patricia Donohue, who also read portions of the manuscript and during the most difficult times provided the reinforcement and support that words alone can never accurately measure.

A handful of people read certain sections of the manuscript and offered valuable feedback. To Jeff Pearlman, Rachel Bachman, Geoffrey Precourt, and Buz Eisenberg, I thank you for your support.

I would also like to raise a somber glass to the late David Halberstam, who counseled me during the proposal stage of this project and offered tremendous advice and support during the early reportage of this book. My last conversation with him took place during the fall of 2006, when he urged me to "bring those tremendous Henry Aaron wrists to life." Thanks also to the late Bob Nylen, a man I knew far too little; I am lucky to have called him my friend.

Finally, there is the family who endured living with a person who for the last four years lived primarily in his head. To Veronique and Ilan Bryant, thank you. I know this is never easy.

APPENDIXES

STANDARD BATTING

Year	Age	Tm	Lg	G	PA	AB	R	H	2B	3B	HR	RBI	SI
1954	20	MLN	NL	122	509	468	58	131	27	6	13	69	2
1955	21	MLN	NL	153	665	602	105	189	37	9	27	106	3
1956	22	MLN	NL	153	660	609	106	200	34	14	26	92	2
1957	23	MLN	NL	151	675	615	118	198	27	6	44	132	1
1958	24	MLN	NL	153	664	601	109	196	34	4	30	95	4
1959	25	MLN	NL	154	693	629	116	223	46	7	39	123	8
1960	26	MLN	NL	153	664	590	102	172	20	11	40	126	16
1961	27	MLN	NL	155	671	603	115	197	39	10	34	120	21
1962	28	MLN	NL	156	667	592	127	191	28	6	45	128	15
1963	29	MLN	NL	161	714	631	121	201	29	4	44	130	31
1964	30	MLN	NL	145	634	570	103	187	30	2	24	95	22
1965	31	MLN	NL	150	639	570	109	181	40	1	32	89	24
1966	32	ATL	NL	158	688	603	117	168	23	1	44	127	21
1967	33	ATL	NL	155	669	600	113	184	37	3	39	109	17
1968	34	ATL	NL	160	676	606	84	174	33	4	29	86	28
1969	35	ATL	NL	147	639	547	100	164	30	3	44	97	9
1970	36	ATL	NL	150	598	516	103	154	26	1	38	118	9
1971	37	ATL	NL	139	573	495	95	162	22	3	47	118	1
1972	38	ATL	NL	129	544	449	75	119	10	0	34	77	4
1973	39	ATL	NL	120	465	392	84	118	12	1	40	96	1
1974	40	ATL	NL	112	382	340	47	91	16	0	20	69	1
1975	41	MIL	AL	137	543	465	45	109	16	2	12	60	0
1976	42	MIL	AL	85	308	271	22	62	8	0	10	35	0
23 Seasons				3298	13940	12364	2174	3771	624	98	755	°2297°	24•
162 Game Avg.				162	685	607	107	185	31	5	37	113	12
MIL/ATL (21 yrs)				3076	13089	11628	2107	3600	600	96	733	2202	24•
MIL (2 yrs)				222	851	736	67	171	24	2	22	95	0
NL (21 yrs)				3076	13089	11628	2107	3600	600	96	733	2202	24•
AL (2 yrs)				222	851	736	67	171	24	2	22	95	0

STANDARD BATTING

CS	BB	SO	BA	OBP	SLG	OPS	OPS+	TB	GDP	HBP	SH	SF	IBB
2	28	39	.280	.322	.447	.769	104	209	13	3	6	4	
1	49	61	.314	.366	.540	.906	141	325	20	3	7	4	5
4	37	54	.328	.365	.558	.923	151	340	21	2	5	7	6
1	57	58	.322	.378	.600	.978	166	369	13	0	0	3	15
1	59	49	.326	.386	.546	.931	153	328	21	1	0	3	16
0	51	54	.355	.401	.636	1.037	181	400	19	4	0	9	17
7	60	63	.292	.352	.566	.919	155	334	8	2	0	12	13
9	56	64	.327	.381	.594	.974	161	358	16	2	1	9	20
7	66	73	.323	.390	.618	1.008	170	366	14	3	0	6	14
5	78	94	.319	.391	.586	.977	179	370	11	0	0	5	18
4	62	46	.328	.393	.514	.907	153	293	22	0	0	2	9
4	60	81	.318	.379	.560	.938	160	319	15	1	0	8	10
3	76	96	.279	.356	.539	.895	142	325	14	1	0	8	15
6	63	97	.307	.369	.573	.943	168	344	11	0	0	6	19
5	64	62	.287	.354	.498	.852	153	302	21	1	0	5	23
10	87	47	.300	.396	.607	1.003	177	332	14	2	0	3	19
0	74	63	.298	.385	.574	.958	148	296	13	2	0	6	15
1	71	58	.327	.410	.669	1.079	194	331	9	2	0	5	21
0	92	55	.265	.390	.514	.904	147	231	17	1	0	2	15
1	68	51	.301	.402	.643	1.045	177	252	7	1	0	4	13
0	39	29	.268	.341	.491	.832	128	167	6	0	1	2	6
1	70	51	.234	.332	.355	.687	95	165	15	1	1	6	3
1	35	38	.229	.315	.369	.684	102	100	8	0	0	2	1
73	1402	1383	.305	.374	.555	.928	155	°6856°	328	32	21	121	293
4	69	68	.305	.374	.555	.928	155	337	16	2	1	6	
71	1297	1294	.310	.377	.567	.944	158	6591	305	31	20	113	289
2	105	89	.232	.326	.360	.686	98	265	23	1	1	8	4
71	1297	1294	.310	.377	.567	.944	158	6591	305	31	20	113	289
2	105	89	.232	.326	.360	.686	98	265	23	1	1	8	4

POSTSEASON BATTING

Year	Age	Tm	Lg	Series	Opp	Rsit	G	PA	AB	R	H	2B	3B
1957	23	MLN	NL	WS	NYY	W	7	29	28	5	11	0	1
1958	24	MLN	NL	WS	NYY	L	7	31	27	3	9	2	0
1969	35	ATL	NL	NLCS	NYM	L	3	14	14	3	5	2	0
3 Seasons (3 Series)							17	74	69	11	25	4	1
1 NLCS							3	14	14	3	5	2	0
2 WS							14	60	55	8	20	2	1

HENRY AARON'S AWARD HONORS AND TOP TE

ALL-STAR GAMES

1955	°	1964	°
1956	°	1965	(RF)
1957	(RF)	1966	(LF)
1958	(RF)	1967	(CF)
1959-1	(RF)	1968	(RF)
1959-2	(RF)	1969	(RF)
1960-1	(RF)	1970	(RF)
1960-2	(RF)	1971	(RF)
1961-1	°	1972	(RF)
1961-2	°	1973	(1B)
1962-1		1974	(RF)
1962-2	°	1975	°
1963	(RF)		

GOLD GLOVES

1958	NL	RF
1959	NL	RF
1960	NL	RF

POSTSEASON BATTING

SB	CS	BB	SO	BA	OBP	SLG	OPS	TB	GDP	HBP	SH	SF	IBB
0	0	1	6	.393	.414	.786	1.200	22	0	0	0	0	0
0	0	4	6	.333	.419	.407	.827	11	1	0	0	0	0
0	0	0	1	.357	.357	1.143	1.500	16	1	0	0	0	0
0	0	5	13	.362	.405	.710	1.116	49	2	0	0	0	0
0	0	0	1	.357	.357	1.143	1.500	16	1	0	0	0	0
0	0	5	12	.364	.417	.600	1.017	33	1	0	0	0	0

PPEARANCES ON SINGLE-SEASON LEADER BOARDS

MOST VALUABLE PLAYER

yr	lg	rk
1955	NL	9
1956	NL	3
1957	**NL**	**1**
1958	NL	3
1959	NL	3
1961	NL	8
1962	NL	6
1963	NL	3
1965	NL	7
1966	NL	8
1967	NL	5
1969	NL	3
1971	NL	3

BATTING AVERAGE

1955	NL	.314	5th
1956	**NL**	**.328**	**1st**
1957	NL	.322	4th
1958	NL	.326	4th
1959	**NL**	**.355**	**1st**
1961	NL	.327	5th
1962	NL	.323	5th
1963	NL	.319	3rd
1964	NL	.328	3rd
1965	NL	.318	2nd
1967	NL	.307	8th
1971	NL	.327	5th
	Career	.305	146th

ON-BASE %			
1957	NL	.378	9th
1958	NL	.386	6th
1959	NL	.401	2nd
1961	NL	.381	8th
1962	NL	.390	5th
1963	NL	.391	2nd
1964	NL	.393	3rd
1965	NL	.379	5th
1969	NL	.396	7th
1971	NL	.410	3rd
1972	NL	.390	4th
Career		.374	222nd

SLUGGING %			
1955	NL	.540	9th
1956	NL	.558	3rd
1957	NL	.600	3rd
1958	NL	.546	3rd
1959	**NL**	**.636**	**1st**
1960	NL	.566	2nd
1961	NL	.594	3rd
1962	NL	.618	2nd
1963	**NL**	**.586**	**1st**
1964	NL	.514	8th
1965	NL	.560	2nd
1966	NL	.539	6th
1967	**NL**	**.573**	**1st**
1968	NL	.498	4th
1969	NL	.607	2nd
1970	NL	.574	7th
1971	**NL**	**.669**	**1st**
1972	NL	.514	5th
1973	NL	.643	2nd°°
Career		.555	26th

ON-BASE PLUS SLUGGING					RUNS SCORED			
1955	NL	.906	9th		1955	NL	105	8th
1956	NL	.923	5th		1956	NL	106	3rd
1957	NL	.978	3rd		**1957**	**NL**	**118**	**1st**
1958	NL	.931	4th		1958	NL	109	3rd
1959	**NL**	**1.037**	**1st**		1959	NL	116	4th
1960	NL	.919	5th		1960	NL	102	5th
1961	NL	.974	3rd		1961	NL	115	3rd
1962	NL	1.008	2nd		1962	NL	127	4th
1963	**NL**	**.977**	**1st**		**1963**	**NL**	**121**	**1st**
1964	NL	.907	6th		1964	NL	103	4th
1965	NL	.938	2nd		1965	NL	109	5th
1966	NL	.895	8th		1966	NL	117	2nd
1967	NL	.943	3rd		**1967**	**NL**	**113**	**1st**
1968	NL	.852	5th		1968	NL	84	10th
1969	NL	1.003	2nd		1969	NL	100	10th
1970	NL	.958	6th		1970	NL	103	9th
1971	**NL**	**1.079**	**1st**		1971	NL	95	6th
1972	NL	.904	5th			Career	2174	4th
1973	NL	1.045	2nd°°					
	Career	.928	39th					

HITS

1955	NL	189	2nd
1956	**NL**	**200**	**1st**
1957	NL	198	2nd
1958	NL	196	3rd
1959	**NL**	**223**	**1st**
1960	NL	172	6th
1961	NL	197	3rd
1962	NL	191	6th
1963	NL	201	2nd
1964	NL	187	8th
1965	NL	181	10th
1967	NL	184	6th
1968	NL	174	10th
Career		3771	3rd

TOTAL BASES

1955	NL	325	6th
1956	**NL**	**340**	**1st**
1957	**NL**	**369**	**1st**
1958	NL	328	3rd
1959	**NL**	**400**	**1st**
1960	**NL**	**334**	**1st**
1961	**NL**	**358**	**1st**
1962	NL	366	3rd
1963	**NL**	**370**	**1st**
1965	NL	319	4th
1966	NL	325	4th
1967	**NL**	**344**	**1st**
1968	NL	302	2nd
1969	**NL**	**332**	**1st**
1971	NL	331	2nd
Career		**6856**	**1st**

DOUBLES

1955	**NL**	**37**	**1st**
1956	**NL**	**34**	**1st**
1958	NL	34	4th
1959	NL	46	2nd
1961	**NL**	**39**	**1st**
1962	NL	28	10th
1963	NL	29	10th
1965	**NL**	**40**	**1st**
1967	NL	37	2nd
1968	NL	33	6th
1969	NL	30	10th
Career		624	10th

TRIPLES

1955	NL	9	5th
1956	NL	14	2nd
1959	NL	7	8th
1960	NL	11	4th
1961	NL	10	5th
Career		98	162nd

HOME RUNS

1955	NL	27	10th
1957	**NL**	**44**	**1st**
1958	NL	30	5th
1959	NL	39	3rd
1960	NL	40	2nd
1961	NL	34	6th
1962	NL	45	2nd
1963	**NL**	**44**	**1st**
1964	NL	24	9th
1965	NL	32	6th
1966	**NL**	**44**	**1st**
1967	**NL**	**39**	**1st**
1968	NL	29	5th
1969	NL	44	2nd
1970	NL	38	5th
1971	NL	47	2nd
1972	NL	34	4th
1973	NL	40	4th
Career		755	2nd

RUNS BATTED IN

1955	NL	106	9th
1956	NL	92	9th
1957	**NL**	**132**	**1st**
1958	NL	95	6th
1959	NL	123	3rd
1960	**NL**	**126**	**1st**
1961	NL	120	4th
1962	NL	128	4th
1963	**NL**	**130**	**1st**
1964	NL	95	10th
1966	**NL**	**127**	**1st**
1967	NL	109	3rd
1968	NL	86	7th
1969	NL	97	7th
1970	NL	118	5th
1971	NL	118	3rd
Career		**2297**	**1st**

BASES ON BALLS

1960	NL	60	10th
1963	NL	78	3rd
1964	NL	62	9th
1966	NL	76	3rd
1968	NL	64	8th
1969	NL	87	7th
1972	NL	92	4th
Career		1402	25th

EXTRA BASE HITS

1955	NL	73	5th
1956	NL	74	2nd
1957	NL	77	3rd
1958	NL	68	3rd
1959	**NL**	**92**	**1st**
1960	NL	71	2nd
1961	**NL**	**83**	**1st**
1962	NL	79	3rd
1963	**NL**	77	**1st**
1965	NL	73	3rd
1966	NL	68	5th
1967	**NL**	**79**	**1st**
1968	NL	66	2nd
1969	**NL**	77	**1st**
1970	NL	65	9th
1971	NL	72	2nd
Career		**1477**	**1st**

INTENTIONAL BASES ON BALLS

1957	NL	15	2nd
1958	NL	16	3rd
1959	NL	17	2nd
1960	NL	13	3rd
1961	NL	20	3rd
1962	NL	14	3rd
1963	NL	18	2nd
1966	NL	15	4th
1967	NL	19	5th
1968	NL	23	3rd
1969	NL	19	2nd
1970	NL	15	5th
1971	**NL**	**21**	**1st**
1972	NL	15	3rd
Career		293	2nd

DOUBLE PLAYS GROUNDED INTO

1955	NL	20	2nd
1956	NL	21	3rd
1958	NL	21	2nd
1959	NL	19	4th
1961	NL	16	10th
1964	NL	22	2nd
1968	**NL**	**21**	**1st**
1972	NL	17	7th
Career		328	2nd

AB PER HR

1957	NL	14.0	3rd
1958	NL	20.0	6th
1959	NL	16.1	4th
1960	NL	14.8	3rd
1961	NL	17.7	8th
1962	NL	13.2	2nd
1963	NL	14.3	2nd
1965	NL	17.8	6th
1966	NL	13.7	2nd
1967	NL	15.4	2nd
1968	NL	20.9	7th
1969	NL	12.4	2nd
1970	NL	13.6	4th
1971	**NL**	**10.5**	**1st**
1972	**NL**	**13.2**	**1st**
1973	**NL**	**9.8**	**1st°°**
1974	NL	17.0	9th°°
	Career	16.4	37th

SALARY HISTORIES FOR HANK AARON AND WILLIE MAYS

Year	Aaron	Mays
1951	——	$7,500
1952	——	$12,500 (joined Army 5/29/52)
1953	——	Military Service
1954	$6,000	$12,500
1955	$10,000	$30,000
1956	$17,500	$50,000
1957	$22,500	$50,000
1958	$35,000	$75,000
1959	$35,000	$75,000
1960	$45,000	$80,000
1961	$45,000	$85,000
1962	$47,500	$90,000
1963	$53,000	$105,000
1964	$61,000	$105,000
1965	$63,500	$105,000
1966	$70,000	$125,000
1967	$92,500	$125,000
1968	$92,500	$125,000
1969	$92,500	$135,000
1970	$110,000	$135,000
1971	$110,000	$160,000
1972	$165,000	$160,000
1973	$165,000	$150,000
1974	$220,000	Retired
1975	$240,000	Retired
1976	$240,000	Retired

A NOTE ON SOURCES

INTERVIEWS

From the beginnings of this book, in 2006, an important question had lingered among the baseball people enthusiastic but nervous that I had undertaken the daunting task of attempting to place Henry Aaron in historical perspective. Their concern simultaneously happened to be mine as well: would Henry talk?

Numerous books have been written about Henry over the years and, except for his 1991 autobiography, all lacked a common, vital component: the true voice of Henry Aaron. He had spoken piecemeal to a handful of authors but always at a distance; the anecdotes were largely colorless or shopworn, the warmth and depth that those closest to him said were his trademark failed to permeate the page. For the first eighteen months of this project, my book would be no different.

A Murderer's Row of Henry's confidants told me they would advocate on my behalf: Dusty Baker, Joe Torre, Joe Morgan, and Bud Selig, but Henry did not respond positively to overtures, if at all.

Two weeks before Thanksgiving 2007, through two exhaustive conversations with Allan Tanenbaum, Henry's friend and attorney of nearly forty years, I found out why: the problem was Barry Bonds.

Henry had already refused to conduct any interviews largely because Bonds stood inches from his home-run record and he felt discussing Bonds created for him a no-win situation, but it was more than that. Henry had also concluded that, outside of his thoughts on Bonds, the public had no use for him. The shadow of Bonds had come to define the conflicted state of baseball, and Henry believed that Bonds defined his place in the public sphere as well, he felt. Two weeks after my last conversation with Allan Tanenbaum, I received word on December 1, 2007, that Henry would be willing to cooperate with the project, with the stipulation I would not ask him about Barry Bonds until after the record was broken. Above all, Allan Tanenbaum was the person most responsible for paving the way for interviews with Henry's closest friends and associates. Over the course of the writing of this book, he and I met in person in Atlanta and New York and spoke on dozens of occasions by telephone. More than any

545

other person, he was the reason this book had the opportunity to probe deeper into Henry Aaron the man.

Henry and I first talked on January 31, 2008, which, ironically, happened to be Jackie Robinson's birth date. We had met at length on a few other occasions—once at his home in Atlanta, once in Cooperstown, New York, at the National Baseball Hall of Fame and Museum, once at a signing event at Last Licks, the ice-cream parlor in Manhattan, and briefly during each of the 2007, 2008, and 2009 World Series—and it was clear that while Henry was cordial and unfailingly polite, he never seemed particularly enthusiastic about the existence of this project.

However, he was extremely generous. He did not ask to be paid for his involvement. No interviews in this book were made with any financial arrangement. Nor did he prohibit me from speaking to anyone close in his life. Billye Aaron, his wife, sat down with me both in person and by telephone. Henry is a regal figure to his intimates, and each member of his circle—Ted Turner, Bill Bartholomay, Frank Bellati—asked Henry to vouch for this project before speaking with me. I am eternally grateful to Henry that he did.

Thus, Henry, family members, and his closest friends comprise the primary sources for this book.

- Ed Scott, the man who discovered Henry Aaron on the Mobile sandlots, is an American treasure and one of the few remaining voices of an important, bygone time. We spoke at least a dozen times between 2006 and 2009 and his insight into life as a black man in the prewar South was an invaluable one for the early chapters of the book.
- Billy Williams, who grew up in Whistler, just outside of Mobile, was another important voice in the early chapters. There are few remaining survivors who can say they played pickup baseball at Carver Park with a young Henry Aaron, and Billy Williams's recollections of those days were important to re-creating the environment of baseball in Mobile during the war and early postwar years.
- Chuck Tanner, Johnny Logan, and Gene Conley provided great insight into Henry's first spring camp with the Braves and later his first season with the club in 1954. Baseball people have a saying that no one understands superstars on a ballclub like the nonsuperstars. All three men through their re-collections were instrumental in re-creating the early years of the Milwaukee Braves.
- Dusty Baker and Henry Aaron have known each other for more than forty years, and Dusty's graciousness with his time and recollections informed the mentoring side of Henry that he often kept well hidden from the press and the public. Dusty Baker was

also instrumental in his recollections of dates and locations of
various events that proved to be essential.

- Ralph Garr was an interesting character to interview. Though he
and Dusty Baker comprised Henry's inner circle during Henry's
years with the Atlanta Braves, Garr was not one to remember
names, dates, or places. However, few people were better in
gauging the heart of Henry, of what spurred the emotions of a
man who for a quarter century often hid what he was feeling. For
that, I am grateful.

- Frank Bellati and Bill Henneberry were excellent resources on
Henry's postcareer years. Bellati and Henry became lifelong
friends and business partners and his recollections of how Henry
began his years as a fast-food franchisee were invaluable. As
Henry began to be rediscovered by baseball in the late 1990s, it
was Bill Henneberry who was responsible for many of the
initiatives that brought Henry back into the public eye. His
recollections were important to the narrative.

The following people were also interviewed: Carolyn Aaron, Tommie Aaron,
Jr., Veleeta Aaron, David Alsobrook, Larry Baer, Bill Bartholomay, Furman
Bisher, Corey Bowdre, Della Britton-Baeza, Mike Callahan, President Jimmy
Carter, Ron Cey, President Bill Clinton, Leonard Coleman, Patrick Courtney,
Wes Covington, Janie Daugherty, Odie Davis, Al Downing, Stewart 'Buz'
Eisenberg, Vivian Davis Figures, Terry Francona, Tito Francona, Jim Frey, Ron
Gant, Cito Gaston, David Halberstam, John Helyar, Roy Hoffmann, Bob Hope,
Paulette Horton, Tom House, Jeff Idelson, Reggie Jackson, Ferguson Jenkins,
Derek Jeter, David Justice, Stan Kasten, Collette King, Joe Klein, Lee Lacy,
Bud Lea, Ron LeFlore, Richard Levin, Eric Levy, Davey Lopes, Earnell Lucas,
Felix Mantilla, David Maraniss, Mike Marshall, Tim McCarver, Fred McGriff,
Wayne Minshew, George Moore, Terence Moore, Joe Morgan, Don New-
combe, David Ortiz, Julia Payne, Jamila Phillips, Lou Piniella, Jerry Poling,
Reese Schonfeld, George Scott, Lila Sebrecht, Bud Selig, Bill Slack, Stan Slack,
Jimmie Lee Solomon, Greg Spahn, Roxanne Spillett, Paul Snyder, Brandon
Steiner, Don Sutton, Allan Tanenbaum, Mike Tollin, Frank Torre, Joe Torre,
Ted Turner, John Walsh, Tim Wiles, Ted Williams, Joy Windham, Bill White,
Kearny Windham, Jimmy Wynn, Steve Yeager, Andrew Young, and Robin
Yount.

ANONYMOUS SOURCES

For some of the more sensitive areas of the book where legal action was threatened against potential interviewees, anonymous sources were used, and I thank
them for their candor. Barry Bonds, in particular, told some intimates close to
the creation of *Bonds on Bonds,* his reality television show that appeared on

ESPN, that he would sue anyone who discussed elements of the process he deemed confidential. Through his spokespeople, Barry Bonds declined to be interviewed for this book.

BOOKS AND ARTICLES

Henry Aaron's *I Had a Hammer* (1991) is the only book in which Henry speaks in the first person about his life. Written with Lonnie Wheeler, the book is a natural first place to begin in that it laid a foundation to begin tracing Henry's life.

Clinton McCarty's memoir, *The Reins of Power: Racial Change and Challenge in a Southern City* (1999), provides an unflinching, disturbing portrait of a period in Wilcox County, Alabama, the childhood home of Henry Aaron's parents, Herbert and Estella. McCarty told me that when his book was published its candor cost him more than one African-American friend, who thought the book racist. His book offered an uncomfortable, valuable glimpse into the attitude of whites toward blacks in a place that was originally one of the strongholds of American slavery.

Leon Litwack's *Trouble in Mind: Black Southerners in the Age of Jim Crow* (1998) was an indispensable resource for understanding the depth of Jim Crow laws—not only the effects on African-Americans but its lasting effect on southern culture and, by extension, on families like the Aarons.

Pauline Davis-Horton's *The Avenue: The Place, the People, the Memories* (1991) is an essential starting point for understanding black Mobile in the twentieth century, painting a portrait of the various places on Davis Avenue a young Henry Aaron frequented as well as providing an invaluable resource for the African-American experience in Mobile.

Jerry Poling's *A Summer Up North: Henry Aaron and the Legend of Eau Claire Baseball* (2002) fills in the important period Henry spent with the Eau Claire Bears, his first step in the game of white organized baseball.

Frank Aukofer's *City with a Chance: A Case History of Civil Rights Revolution* (2007) provided color on an important period of racial change and upheaval in the city of Milwaukee and highlighted the role of Father James Groppi in the civil rights movement of the city.

Gary Pomerantz's *Where Peachtree Meets Sweet Autumn: A Saga of Race and Family* (1996) provided a thorough account of the socioeconomic and political climate of Atlanta just as the Milwaukee Braves planned to relocate to the Deep South. Pomerantz's book helped illuminate more clearly life in Atlanta and placed into greater context Henry Aaron's initial hesitancy in moving back to the South.

Eddie Mathews's memoir, *Eddie Mathews and the National Pastime* (1994), offered Mathews's unique voice in lieu of Mathews himself, who died in 2001. He was particularly close to Henry. The book, written with Bob Buege, captures the Mathews personality that spawned all three franchise locations, from Boston to Milwaukee to Atlanta.

Bob Buege's *The Milwaukee Braves: A Baseball Eulogy* (1988) filled in important gaps regarding the day-to-day triumphs and defeats of the Milwaukee Braves. Only so much color can be gleaned from poring over box scores, and Bob Buege's book helped re-create Henry's time in Milwaukee.

Bad Henry (1974), Henry Aaron's authorized collaboration with Stan Baldwin and Jerry Jenkins, was the only book that recognized Henry's relationship with the late Father Michael Sablica, an important moment in Henry's life both in reaffirming his religious beliefs as well as giving Henry's time in Milwaukee a greater dimension.

David Alsobrook's unpublished dissertation, *Alabama's Port City: Mobile During the Progressive Era, 1896–1917* (1983), is a magnificent resource for understanding the dramatic and debilitating shift from the Reconstruction Era to Jim Crow in Mobile.

Christopher Andrew Nordmann's *Free Negroes in Mobile County, Alabama* (1990) provided important context to daily life in Mobile for blacks.

NOTES

CHAPTER ONE: HERBERT

5 **My Dear Sir:** H. C. Nixon Responses to Questionnaire on Slavery, LPR91, Alabama Department of Archives and History, Montgomery, Alabama.

6 **More care must always be taken:** James A. Tait Memorandum Book, Tait Family Papers, LPR35, Alabama Department of Archives and History, Montgomery, Alabama.

10 **Blacks as a race were commented:** Clinton McCarty, *The Reins of Power: Racial Change and Challenge in a Southern City* (Tallahassee: Sentry Press, 1999), p. 113.

11 **Our name changed often:** interview with Henry Aaron.

15 **Fury Of A Texas mob:** *Mobile Daily Item,* October 22, 1902.

15 **Negro Peeper:** *Mobile Daily Item,* October 12, 1902.

16 **Bound Face To Face . . . :** *Mobile Daily Item,* October 10, 1902.

17 **Used Axe On Women: Bad Negro:** *Mobile Daily Item,* November 4, 1902.

17 **Ten More Policemen Provided:** *Mobile Daily Item,* October 16, 1902.

18 **With the disintegration of the boycott:** David Alsobrook, "Alabama's Port City: Mobile During the Progressive Era, 1896–1917." (Ph.D. diss. Auburn University, 1983), p. 145.

20 **When you own something:** interview with Henry Aaron.

23 **My grandfather believed in the work:** interview with Tommie Aaron, Jr.

23 **That was the way it was:** ibid.

24 **Absolute Segregation Of Race:** *Mobile Register,* May 28, 1943.

24 **Obviously, the black color of my skin:** *Inner City News,* June 8, 1985.

26 **I knew I was going to be a ballplayer:** Hank Aaron, with Lonnie Wheeler, *I Had a Hammer: The Hank Aaron Story* (New York: HarperCollins, 1992), p. 22.

28 **It was never one, two, three with me:** interview with Henry Aaron.

CHAPTER TWO: HENRY

30 **I did not find him to be forthcoming:** interview with Roger Kahn, April 2007.

30 My grandfather used to say all the time: interview with Tommie Aaron, Jr.

34 A lot of guys were playing a helluva baseball game: interview with Billy Williams.

34 He could hit the ball with a broken piece of wood: interview with Ed Scott.

35 I told her, if this kid was Satchel Paige: ibid.

40 I never once saw him hit cross-handed: ibid.

42 On May 23, Scott received a letter from George Sisler: This letter is from the collection of Ed Scott.

42 Major League Scouts Take Gander: *Chicago Defender,* June 7, 1952.

43 Clowns' Aaron Locks Up NAL: *Chicago Defender,* June 7, 1952.

44 The introduction might have been a pleasure: Jerry Poling, *A Summer Up North: Henry Aaron and the Legend of Eau Claire Baseball* (Madison: University of Wisconsin Press, 2002), p. 9.

45 He just would not open up to you: Interview with Wes Covington, *Eau Claire Leader-Telegram,* August 16, 1993.

46 No one can guess his IQ: Al Stump, "Hank Aaron: Public Image vs. Private Reality," *Sport,* August 1964.

47 One time I got to second base: Poling, *A Summer Up North,* p. 40.

49 It was never a romance: ibid, p. 52.

49 When you think about who Henry Aaron is: interview with Jerry Poling.

50 Jacksonville and Savannah: *The Sporting News,* April 15, 1953.

51 It was toward the country: interview with Jim Frey.

53 When you're seventeen or eighteen years old: interview with Felix Mantilla.

57 I remember one day I asked Henry: interview with Bill Slack.

58 I'll never forget that day at the depot: interview with Ed Scott.

CHAPTER THREE: STEPIN FETCHIT

59 Any amount you ask for that kid Henry Aaron: *Milwaukee Journal,* March 3, 1954.

63 Aaron Given Divided Vote By Prophets: *Milwaukee Sentinel,* March 14, 1954.

66 Aaron laid claim to a permanent roster: Mark Stewart and Mike Kennedy, *Hammering Hank: How the Media Made Henry Aaron* (Guilford, Connecticut: Lyons Press, 2006), p. 49.

67 I was playing in Sarasota: Hank Aaron, with Dick Schaap: *Home Run: My Life in Pictures* (New York: Total Sports, 1999), p. 47.

67 Red Sox Shade Braves, 3–2: *Milwaukee Journal,* March 11, 1954.

71 a little house on stilts: interview with Henry Aaron.

73 I remembered thinking: interview with Bill White.

73 Mother Gibson Serves Very Tasty Table: *Milwaukee Journal,* March 2, 1954.

74 Mrs. Gibson's was the best choice at that time: interview with Henry Aaron.

74 Behind the scenes, we made things happen: interview with Bill White.

77 "Slow Motion" Aaron Becomes: *Milwaukee Journal,* March 21, 1954.

79 He was talking about something: interview with Henry Aaron.

79 We had so many different people: interview with Chuck Tanner.

CHAPTER FOUR: MILWAUKEE

87 The whole thing is utterly fantastic: *The Sporting News,* July 18, 1951.

91 With the team we had: interview with Johnny Logan.

92 We got automobiles to drive: interview with Frank Torre.

94 The free choice of residence: Milwaukee Commission on Human Rights, *The Housing of Negroes in Milwaukee,* 1955, pamphlet 57-2402 (Milwaukee, 1955); available online at www.wisconsinhistory.org.

95 The first thing I noticed about Milwaukee: interview with Henry Aaron.

95 If it weren't for Bill Bruton: ibid.

96 There were beaches everywhere in Florida: Larry Moffi and Jonathan Kronstadt, *Crossing the Line: Black Major Leaguers, 1947–1959* (Iowa City: University of Iowa Press, 1994), p. 89.

97 My grandfather was a shortstop: interview with Greg Spahn.

99 Spahn and I: interview with Henry Aaron.

102 No way: *Milwaukee Sentinel,* March 11, 1954.

102 He knew Henry was going to have it rough: interview with Chuck Tanner.

106 Aaron Good Now: *Milwaukee Journal,* June 25, 1954.

CHAPTER FIVE: WEHMEIER

113 Aaron, who rarely shows emotion: This and subsequent quotes regarding the banquet are from *The Sporting News,* February 1, 1956.

115 I shouldn't dignify either question: *The Sporting News,* September 28, 1955.

116 Kick his ass, Joe: interview with Johnny Logan.

118 Baseball is a lot like church: interview with Roger Kahn.

118 He was more than just a manager to me: *Chicago Defender,* May 26, 1956.

119 I don't care if the guy is yellow: interview with Roger Kahn.

122 Willie's Wallop Wins Windup: *The Sporting News,* November 16, 1955.

123 It was okay to be black in the South: interview with Henry Aaron.

125 All Mays had over Henry: interview with Johnny Logan.

127 Robby Has Reds Buzzing: *Chicago Defender,* March 21, 1956.

127 Jackie, what are you doing?: interview with Roger Kahn.

128 Aaron Picked To Win: *Chicago Defender,* April 21, 1956.

129 Dodgers, Yanks Picked To Win: ibid.

130 You didn't even worry about Spahn: interview with Gene Conley.

132 Are you prepared to say that Grimm: *The Sporting News,* June 27, 1956.

146 We would have been the powerhouse: interview with Johnny Logan.

147 Burdette told me that there is no place: *New York Times,* September 12, 1956.

150 Braves Open With Cardinals: *Milwaukee Journal,* September 28, 1956.

153 What Happened To Braves?: *Milwaukee Journal,* October 1, 1956.

154 In 1956: interview with Henry Aaron.

CHAPTER SIX: JACKIE

156 An outburst by Jackie Robinson: *New York Times,* November 2, 1956.

157 Dear Jackie and Rachel: Manuscript Division, Library of Congress.

158 Dear Jackie: Manuscript Division, Library of Congress.

159 And when Jackie wants to try extra hard: *New York Times,* December 17, 1956.

159 Thank you for your letter: Manuscript Division, Library of Congress, Jackie Robinson Collection.

160 Campy is quoted as saying: Manuscript Division, Library of Congress.

161 Had something in mind: Manuscript Division, Library of Congress.

163 Some pacifist black freak: interview with Roger Kahn.

164 Southern Scribe Blames Jackie: *Los Angeles Times,* August 3, 1956.

164 If you'll forgive a personal experience: *New York Times,* December 17, 1956.

CHAPTER SEVEN: SCRIPTURE

169 Braves' Aaron Asks Pay Boost: *Chicago Tribune,* January 27, 1957.

170 I was making ten grand one year: interview with Gene Conley.

170 I think back then we all realized: interview with Henry Aaron.

171 The National League pennant has been a mirage: *Chicago Tribune,* January 19, 1957.

171 Bob Wolf always kept it to the game: interview with Chuck Tanner.

172 Jolly Cholly: interview with Gene Conley.

176 Whether I'm hitting good or not: *The Sporting News,* May 1, 1957.

176 I remember it probably better than anybody: interview with Frank Torre.

181 You have to remember: interview with Johnny Logan.

181 Ah, that was complete bullshit: ibid.

185 You *had* to drink to hang out: ibid.

185 I kept to myself: interview with Henry Aaron.

185 He went through terrible times: interview with Frank Torre.

186 He really was all business: interview with Gene Conley.

188 You had to remember that integration: interview with Henry Aaron.

189 Hank Aaron Ties Ruth Homer Mark: *Washington Post,* July 11, 1957.

189 The Wrist Hitter: *Time,* July 29, 1957.

189 I wouldn't have taken that shit: interview with Bill White.

191 We got along quite well: interview with Furman Bisher.

192 Born To Play Ball: *The Saturday Evening Post,* August 25, 1956.

197 Braves' Blazing Aaron Bids For Batting Title: *The Sporting News,* August 8, 1956.

204 I don't know if there was a way to figure it: interview with Chuck Tanner.

205 For Aaron stretched out his hand: *Time,* October 7, 1957.

CHAPTER EIGHT: BUSHVILLE

209 Fred, do you think your team will choke up: *Los Angeles Times,* October 1, 1957.

210 Before the thing even began: interview with Johnny Logan.

211 They had to beat the White Sox: interview with Greg Spahn.

211 Before the start of the 1957 World Series: ibid.

211 We weren't scared of the Yankees: interview with Gene Conley.

212 When we went in 1957: interview with Johnny Logan.

212 The Pennant Victory Ball: *Milwaukee Journal,* September 30, 1957.

213 You can't help your club from the tub: interview with Ralph Garr.

213 Aaron's Swap: Crown For Pennant: *Milwaukee Journal,* September 29, 1957.

216 Henry didn't volunteer what he thought about you: interview with Felix Mantilla.

220 Braves Welcomed At Airport: *Milwaukee Journal,* October 4, 1957.

222 "Well," the Perfesser told his pitcher: *Hank Aaron: Chasing the Dream.* Directed by Mike Tollin; produced by Mike Tollin and and Brian Robbins. Copyright 1995 TBS Productions, Inc.

224 Lary would spend three weeks: *Los Angeles Times,* December 16, 1957.

CHAPTER NINE: ALMOST

228 When you come close to winning: Eddie Mathews, *Eddie Mathews and the National Pastime* (Milwaukee: Douglas American Sports Publications, 1994), p. 150.

232 The other ballplayers were completely stunned: Mathews, *Eddie Mathews and the National Pastime,* p. 166.

232 Those guys, all they did was carry the balls to BP: interview with Gene Conley.

238 looked his friend in the eye: Henry Aaron, with Stan Baldwin and Jerry Jenkins, *Bad Henry* (Radnor, Pennsylvania: Chilton, 1974).

239 If he ever had one beer: interview with Gregory Spahn.

241 That position in center: *New York Times,* March 12, 1958.

248 Braves Frolic In Clubhouse: *New York Times,* October 7, 1958.

250 Going into the eighth: *Washington Post,* October 10, 1958.
252 You didn't want to swing it last October: *Washington Post,* March 10, 1959.
253 Braves Shade Dodgers: *Los Angeles Times,* May 6, 1959.
254 Sam Jones Guns For Hank Aaron: *Los Angeles Times,* May 21, 1959.
257 A disgracefully small crowd: *New York Times,* September 29, 1959.
258 The Coliseum was a football field: interview with Frank Torre.
260 Every team has its "ifs" and "buts": Hank Aaron, with Lonnie Wheeler, *I Had a Hammer: The Hank Aaron Story* (New York: HarperCollins, 1992), p. 143.

CHAPTER TEN: RESPECT

263 You ache with the need: Ralph Ellison, *Invisible Man* (New York: Random House, 1952), p. 4.
264 There was a reason: Frank A. Aukofer, *City with a Chance: A Case History of Civil Rights Revolution* (Milwaukee: Marquette University Press, 2007), p. 219.
265 It's nice to get attention and favors: Roger Angell, *Once More Around the Park: A Baseball Reader* (New York: Ballantine Books, 1991), p. 150.
265 You always knew he was a serious man: interview with Joe Torre.
266 Soon, a routine formed: interview with Henry Aaron.
266 My mother was so mad: interview with Ted Williams.
268 I remember it well: interview with Henry Aaron.
269 a lone black fellow who played baseball: interview with Howard Chinn.
269 Stump came away with a story: Al Stump, "Hank Aaron: Public Image vs. Private Reality," *Sport,* August 1964.
273 I know I did not make it easy: interview with Henry Aaron.
273 Things are as bad: James Baldwin, *The Fire Next Time* (New York: Dial, 1963), p. 59.
274 We've been waiting all this time: Jackie Robinson, *Baseball Has Done It.* (1964; reprint, Brooklyn, New York: IG Publishing, 2005), p. 139.
275 I was sensitive to what they would face: interview with Henry Aaron.
275 I've read some newspapermen saying: Robinson, *Baseball Has Done It,* p. 134.
276 I never knew Jackie said that: interview with Henry Aaron.
278 It never did any good: interview with Henry Aaron.
278 People have been treating this man: interview with Allan Tanenbaum.
279 It always bothered me: interview with Bill White.
279 Henry Aaron is a nice man: interview with Furman Bisher.
281 Pursuant to general agreement: Manuscript Division, Library of Congress.
282 Fred Lowey called: ibid.
282 I think Fred Lowey: ibid.

283 That was when the old man: Manuscript Division, Library of Congress.

284 My Dear Larry: ibid.

285 Dear Dick: ibid.

286 Dear Mr. O'Malley: ibid.

288 "Nobody," Selig would say, hit more home runs: interview with Bud Selig.

289 The Camel Mildness Test: *Milwaukee Journal,* April 16, 1951.

292 He was such a good, open man: interview with Joe Torre.

292 It was almost from the time we met: interview with Carolyn Aaron.

293 Dressen never blended with this club: interview with Joe Torre.

295 The two things I remember most: interview with Tim McCarver.

297 I don't think I've earned my due: Robinson, *Baseball Has Done It,* p. 140.

CHAPTER ELEVEN: ATLANTA

299 This is a moral issue: *The Sporting News,* January 16, 1965.

302 I thought about history: interview with Bill Bartholomay.

302 Mr. Perini is planning to move the Braves: *The Sporting News,* November, 7, 1962.

303 Milwaukee Syndicate Offer: *The Sporting News,* December 1, 1962.

304 The cow had been milked: *The Sporting News,* November, 7, 1962.

305 Move To Georgia Peachy? Not To Aaron: *Chicago Defender,* April 17, 1965.

305 Aaron and Maye Disturbed: Associated Press, January 16, 1965.

306 I have lived in the South: *Chicago Defender,* April 17, 1965.

311 Not only were blacks forbidden to sit: Gary Pomerantz, *Where Peachtree Meets Sweet Autumn: A Saga of Race and Family* (New York: Penguin, 1996), p. 257.

311 When I was in high school: interview with Bob Hope.

313 There was a real hostile feel: interview with Bill Bartholomay.

314 The leaders of the city didn't want: interview with Andrew Young.

316 Aaron Says He Could Have Won: *Chicago Defender,* March 2, 1964.

316 I had read so much about Musial: Associated Press, May 14, 1970.

318 Martin was a big baseball fan: interview with Andrew Young.

CHAPTER TWELVE: WILLIE

323 Eisenberg was a Braves batboy: interview with Buz Eisenberg.

327 What got you here is what's going to keep you here: interview with Ralph Garr.

329 Francona had been a big leaguer: interview with Tito Francona.

330 When his son, Terry: interview with Terry Francona.

330 In New York, Tito and Henry: interview with Tito Francona.

330 Yet Ralph and Dusty saw Henry: interview with Dusty Baker.

331 **There were times I got called in:** ibid.

333 **And then there was the infamous evening:** *New York Times,* August 9, 1966.

333 **You could never tell at the plate:** interview with Ralph Garr.

334 **I had the fortune to room with a guy:** interview with Cito Gaston.

335 **He used to tell me all the time:** interview with Ralph Garr.

336 **Already he ees showing me:** Al Stump, "Hank Aaron: Public Image vs. Private Reality," *Sport,* August 1964.

338 **I don't know if I'm talking out of school:** interview with Tito Francona.

339 **Somewhere during the exchange:** interview with Joe Torre.

343 **No way was Willie a better hitter than me:** interview with Henry Aaron.

343 **I consider us the best of friends:** *Wall Street Journal,* April 17, 1970.

344 **Hank Becomes A Hit:** *Sports Illustrated,* August 18, 1969.

345 **Move Over, Babe:** *Los Angeles Times,* October 5, 1969.

348 **We were off that night:** interview with Ralph Garr.

351 **Aaron—600G For 3 Years:** *Chicago Tribune,* March 1, 1972.

351 **It was Milo Hamilton, the broadcaster:** interview with Wayne Minshew.

353 **I'll see how it goes:** *Washington Post,* January 30, 1972.

355 **It's July 1957:** interview with Reese Schonfeld.

358 **I was just a kid, and it was exciting to me:** ibid.

359 **Wednesday Night:** *New York Times,* June 1, 1972.

361 **It's kind of fun now and then:** Charles Einstein, *Willie's Time: A Memoir* (New York: Penguin, 1989), p. 34.

CHAPTER THIRTEEN: RUTH

362 **He had leukemia:** interview with Bob Hope.

366 **Just give us the chance:** interview with Buck O'Neil.

367 **For our community:** Jimmy Carter, *An Hour Before Daylight* (New York: Simon and Schuster), 2001, p. 32.

368 **Like Jimmy Carter, Bob Hope also felt a certain swell:** interview with Jimmy Carter.

373 **He refused to defile his body:** *The Long Winter of Henry Aaron,* originally broadcast by NBC, 1973; rebroadcast by ESPN, 2006.

373 **I would like to read to you:** ibid.

375 **It's the only place:** "Hank Aaron: Going for the Record," *Ebony,* September 1973.

376 **Henry would sit in the boat:** "Chasing the Babe," *Newsweek,* August 13, 1973.

378 **Aaron Sued For Tenfold Alimony:** Associated Press, June 3, 1974.

379 **I've always read Mickey Mantle:** "Henry Aaron's Golden Autumn," *Time,* September 24, 1973.

383 **The game was being televised on Channel 17:** *Atlanta Journal-Constitution,* April 5, 1974.

385 It should not even have been necessary: interview with Billye Aaron.

387 "Ralph," Henry said at his locker: interview with Ralph Garr.

387 I just feel good and happy: *Atlanta Journal-Constitution,* April 9, 1974.

388 To Downing, the words were another: interview with Al Downing.

388 If there's anything I can ever do for you: ibid.

389 One night, someone brought up the idea: Jim "Mudcat" Grant, Tom Sabellico, and Pat O'Brien, *The Black Aces: Baseball's Only African-American Twenty-Game Winners* (Farmingdale, New York: Black Aces, 2006), p. 319.

389 Henry Aaron. What else did you need to say?: interview with Steve Yeager.

390 I had no idea who they were: interview with Mike Marshall.

391 Everybody expects him to do it every time now: *Atlanta Journal-Constitution,* April 8, 1984.

392 Henry begins to walk up to home plate: *Hank Aaron: Chasing the Dream.* Directed by Mike Tollin; produced by Mike Tollin and Brian Robbins. Copyright 1955 TBS Productions, Inc.

393 No, you have your own footsteps: interview with Jimmy Wynn.

395 There's Al Downing: interview with Al Downing.

395 And swinging two bats is Henry Aaron: *Hank Aaron: Chasing the Dream.*

396 It was a long time ago: interview with Steve Yeager.

396 If you told someone you were Cape Verdean: interview with Davey Lopes.

397 Well, I wasn't really sure what I was going to do: interview with Ron Cey.

398 I always wondered: interview with Davey Lopes.

398 Tom House considers to himself: interview with Tom House.

400 He showed that it could happen: interview with Mike Marshall.

401 I was just proud: interview with Cito Gaston.

401 There were about fifty-five thousand people: interview with Dusty Baker.

401 My thing was, It's over with: interview with Jimmy Wynn.

401 All he said was: interview with Wayne Minshew.

CHAPTER FOURTEEN: MORTAL

402 The problem is: Hank Aaron, with Lonnie Wheeler, *I Had a Hammer: The Hank Aaron Story* (New York: HarperCollins, 1992), p. 285.

403 You have to understand that we looked up to him: interview with Ralph Garr.

403 With Henry Aaron, it didn't matter: ibid.

407 There is no question he lost something: interview with Allan Tanenbaum.

411 It Won't Be Hank: *Atlanta Journal-Constitution,* July 22, 1974.

412 The way I saw it: Aaron, *I Had a Hammer,* p. 285.

412 I think they owe me the courtesy of asking me: *Atlanta Journal-Constitution,* July 22, 1974.

412 RHUBARB!: *Atlanta Journal-Constitution,* July 25, 1974.

414 like bouncers about to break up a bar fight: interview with Dusty Baker.

414 Splat!: *Atlanta Journal-Constitution,* July 26, 1974.

418 All of Henry's people: interview with Ralph Garr.

419 Aaron's Last Hurrah: *Atlanta Journal-Constitution,* October 3, 1974.

419 His mood was flippant following the homer: *Atlanta Journal-Constitution,* October 3, 1974.

420 Aaron's Brilliance Leaves a Memory: *Atlanta Journal-Constitution,* October 1, 1974.

420 While Henry was in Tokyo: interview with Wayne Minshew.

CHAPTER FIFTEEN: ACKNOWLEDGMENT

422 In retrospect, Bill Bartholomay would view Henry's leaving: interview with Bill Bartholomay.

423 But Bud Selig spoke to Henry: interview with Bud Selig.

424 He did not have as much left: ibid.

426 I know there are a lot of people picking us: *Milwaukee Journal,* April 1, 1975.

429 Busing To Integrate? Nope!: *Milwaukee Journal,* July 2, 1975.

431 He was significant: interview with Robin Yount.

432 I knew I was better than a .234 hitter: Hank Aaron, with Lonnie Wheeler, *I Had a Hammer: The Hank Aaron Story* (New York: HarperCollins, 1992), p. 285.

433 Without the three-point shot: interview with George Scott.

436 Only the home run I hit to win the 1957 pennant: *Milwaukee Journal,* July 12, 1976.

437 A Singular Exit: *Milwaukee Journal,* October 4, 1976.

437 There's something magical about going back: Aaron, *I Had a Hammer,* p. 286.

437 I didn't think it bothered Hank: interview with George Scott.

CHAPTER SIXTEEN: DRIFT

442 He was just raging: interview with Joe Klein.

443 Hate mail and home runs: interview with Henry Aaron.

446 Bill was farm director when I promoted him: interview with Ted Turner.

447 We were sitting back in our conference room: interview with Paul Snyder.

448 He went to spring training: interview with Carolyn Aaron.

450 Something's got to be done about it: *Atlanta Journal-Constitution,* May 1, 1978.

451 No Place for Aaron With All-Time Stars: Associated Press, January 3, 1977.

452 Aaron Hammers At Racism: *Minneapolis Star Tribune,* July 30, 1979.

453 When Did "The Hammer": *Atlanta Journal-Constitution,* July 20, 1977.

453 They criticize me when I don't speak: interview with Henry Aaron.

454 Any woman who had to go through: interview with Dusty Baker.

455 Maybe somewhere on the periphery of my personality: interview with Billye Aaron.

458 I'd be lying if I said I didn't want to be unanimous: *Atlanta Journal-Constitution,* July 27, 1979.

461 With all the things I've done: *New York Times,* July 30, 1982.

461 I've never been able to live down: interview with Henry Aaron.

CHAPTER SEVENTEEN: CARS

464 Henneberry had started out in the business: interview with Bill Henneberry.

465 We had no car, no beer: ibid.

471 Still, Selig at the helm meant Henry: interview with Bud Selig.

472 Hank was the only choice: interview with Bill Henneberry.

475 Levin was also concerned: interview with Rich Levin.

476 Bill Clinton traced the roots: interview with William Jefferson Clinton.

476 Clinton was holding a rally at Georgia Tech: ibid.

476 Georgia was good to me: White House transcript of President Clinton's remarks, at the Democratic National Committee dinner, October 29, 1999.

477 We were in a tough, tough campaign: interview with William Jefferson Clinton.

478 He was poor and unlearned: *Mobile Register,* May 27, 1998.

478 You never know what it means to me: interview with Henry Aaron.

480 Both Henry and I had come up: interview with Billye Aaron.

480 I wouldn't say that the twenty-fifth was a major success: interview with Bill Henneberry.

484 I received hundreds of calls to do interviews: *Mobile Register,* October 9, 1998.

485 So, we're going to meet and sign: interview with Bill Henneberry.

486 Everybody was going to blame me: interview with Bud Selig.

487 Hank Aaron Goes To Bat For BMW: *Atlanta Business Journal,* June 1, 1997.

488 There were some black folk: interview with Allan Tanenbaum.

488 Why was I chosen?: *Black Enterprise,* June 1, 2004.

491 I don't want to say that all the wounds: interview with Mike Tollin.

491 The thing about Hank is: interview with Dusty Baker.

CHAPTER EIGHTEEN: 756

497 Go ask Henry Aaron: Jim Bunning's testimony before the House Government Reform Committee, March 17, 2005.

498 Aaron Prefers To Focus On The Positives: Associated Press, June 15, 2006.

499 The one thing Henry *hated* was cheating: interview with Ralph Garr.

500 I just don't want to get involved with conversations: interview with Henry Aaron.

500 He knows what he did: interview with Billye Aaron.

501 In fact, I was just going to ask you: Associated Press, May 14, 2007.

505 The conversation was brief: interview with Mike Tollin.

506 The discussions proceeded in earnest: ibid.

508 There's a heart beating there: ibid.

509 Susan wouldn't even let most people finish: interview with Allan Tanenbaum.

510 Would you at least consider a taping?: interview with Larry Baer.

511 I remember the moment he hit it: interview with Dave Sheinin.

512 It's weird. It cheapened the moment: ibid.

513 Janie McCauley, a reporter: interview with Janie McCauley.

514 What was happening is that: interview with Henry Edwards.

BIBLIOGRAPHY

Aaron, Hank, with Lonnie Wheeler. *I Had a Hammer: The Hank Aaron Story.* New York: HarperCollins, 1992.

Aaron, Henry, with Stan Baldwin and Jerry Jenkins. *Bad Henry.* Radnor, Pennsylvania: Chilton, 1974.

Adelson, Bruce. *Brushing Back Jim Crow: The Integration of Minor-League Baseball in the American South.* Charlottesville: University of Virginia Press, 1999.

Alsobrook, David. *Alabama's Port City: Mobile During the Progressive Era, 1896–1917.* Ann Arbor: University Microfilms, 1983.

Angell, Roger. *The Summer Game.* New York: Penguin, 1972.

———. *Once More Around the Park: A Baseball Reader.* New York: Ballantine, 1991.

Aukofer, Frank A. *City with a Chance: A Case History of Civil Rights Revolution.* Milwaukee: Marquette University Press, 2007.

Baldwin, James. *The Fire Next Time.* New York: Vintage, 1963.

Biven, Shawn A. *Mobile, Alabama's People of Color: A Tricentennial History, 1702–2002.* Victoria, British Columbia: Trafford, 2004.

Bouton, Jim. *Ball Four.* New York: World Publishing Company, 1970.

Buege, Bob. *The Milwaukee Braves: A Baseball Eulogy.* Milwaukee: Douglas American Sports Publications, 1988.

Callow, Simon. *Orson Welles: The Road to Xanadu.* New York: Penguin, 1995.

Carter, Jimmy. *An Hour Before Daylight.* New York: Simon and Schuster, 2001.

———. *A Remarkable Mother.* New York: Simon and Schuster, 2008.

Cuhaj, Joe, and Tamra Carraway-Hinckle. *Baseball in Mobile: Images of Baseball.* Charleston, South Carolina: Arcadia, 2003.

Davidson, Donald, with Jesse Outlar. *Caught Short.* New York: Atheneum, 1972.

Davis-Horton. *The Avenue: The Place, the People, the Memories.* Mobile, Alabama: Horton, 1991.

Diouf, Silviane A. *Dreams of Africa in Alabama: The Slave Ship Clotilda and the Story of the Last Africans Brought to America.* New York: Oxford University Press, 2007.

Du Bois, W.E.B. *The Souls of Black Folk.* 1903. Reprint, New York: Barnes and Noble Classics, 2003.

Einstein, Charles. *Willie's Time: A Memoir.* New York: Penguin, 1989.

Ellison, Ralph. *Invisible Man.* 1947. Reprint, New York: Vintage, 1990.

Faulkner, David. *Great Time Coming: The Life of Jackie Robinson from Baseball to Birmingham.* New York: Simon and Schuster, 1995.

Flood, Curt. *The Way It Is.* New York: Trident Press, 1971.

Fussman, Cal. *After Jackie: Pride, Prejudice and Baseball's Forgotten Heroes.* New York: ESPN Books, 2007.

Gilbert, Tom. *Baseball and the Color Line.* New York: Franklin Watts, 1995.

Gibson, Bob, with Lonnie Wheeler. *Stranger to the Game: The Autobiography of Bob Gibson.* New York: Viking, 1994.

Grant, Jim "Mudcat." *The Black Aces: Baseball's Only African-American Twenty-Game Winners.* Farmingdale, New York: The Black Aces, LLC, 2006.

Halberstam, David. *The Children.* New York: Random House, 1998.

Helyar, John. *Lords of the Realm: The Real History of Baseball.* New York: Villard, 1994.

Hirshberg, Al. *Henry Aaron: Quiet Superstar.* New York: G. P. Putnam and Sons, 1969.

Kahn, Roger. *The Boys of Summer.* New York: Harper & Row, 1972.

———. *The Era: 1947–1957, When the Yankees, the Giants, and the Dodgers Ruled the World.* New York: Ticknor and Fields, 1993.

———. *Beyond the Boys of Summer: The Very Best of Roger Kahn.* New York: McGraw-Hill, 2005.

Kuhn, Bowie. *Hardball: The Education of a Commissioner.* New York: Times Books, 1987.

Leavy, Jane. *Sandy Koufax: A Lefty's Legacy.* New York: HarperCollins, 2002.

Lemann, Nicholas. *The Promised Land: The Great Black Migration and How It Changed America.* New York: Vintage, 1992.

———. *Redemption: The Last Battle of the Civil War.* New York: Farrar, Straus and Giroux, 2006.

Litwack, Leon F. *Trouble in Mind: Black Southerners in the Age of Jim Crow.* New York: Alfred A. Knopf, 1998.

Loewen, James, W. *Sundown Towns: A Hidden Dimenson of American Racism.* New York: Touchstone, 2005.

Lowery, Philip J. *Green Cathedrals: The Ultimate Celebration of Major League and Negro League Ballparks.* New York: Walker, 2006.

McCarty, Clinton. *The Reins of Power: Racial Change and Challenge in a Southern City.* Tallahassee, Florida: Sentry Press, 1999.

McKiven, Henry M., Jr. *Iron and Steel: Class, Race, and Community in Birmingham, Alabama, 1875–1920.* Chapel Hill: University of North Carolina Press, 1995.

Malcolm X, and Alex Haley. *The Autobiography of Malcolm X.* New York: Grove Press, 1964.

Maraniss, David. *Clemente: The Passion and Grace of Baseball's Last Hero.* New York: Simon and Schuster, 2006.

Mathews, Eddie. *Eddie Mathews and the National Pastime.* Milwaukee: Douglas American Sports Publications, 1994.

Mays, Willie. *My Life In and Out of Baseball.* New York: E. P. Dutton, 1966.

Miller, Marvin. *A Whole Different Ball Game: The Inside Story of Baseball's New Deal.* New York: Fireside, 1991.

Moffi, Larry, and Jonathan Kronstadt. *Crossing the Line: Black Major Leaguers, 1947–1959.* Iowa City: University of Iowa Press, 1994.

Montville, Leigh. *Ted Williams: The Biography of an American Hero.* New York: Doubleday, 2004.

Poling, Jerry. *A Summer Up North: Henry Aaron and the Legend of Eau Claire Baseball.* Madison: University of Wisconsin Press, 2002.

Polk's Mobile City Directory, 1928–1998.

Pomerantz, Gary. *Where Peachtree Meets Sweet Autumn: A Saga of Race and Family.* New York: Penguin, 1996.

Rampersad, Arnold. *Jackie Robinson: A Biography.* New York: Alfred A. Knopf, 1997.

Ribowsky, Mark. *Don't Look Back: Satchel Paige in the Shadows of Baseball.* New York: Simon and Schuster, 1994.

Roberts, Gene, and Hank Klibanoff. *The Race Beat: The Press, the Civil Rights Movement, and the Awakening of a Nation.* New York: Vintage, 2006.

Robinson, Jackie. *Baseball Has Done It.* 1964. Reprint, Brooklyn, New York: IG Publishing, 2005.

Rogers, William Warren, Robert David Ward, Leah Rawls Atkins, and Wayne Flynt. *Alabama: The History of a Deep South State.* Tuscaloosa: University of Alabama Press, 1994.

Schoor, Gene. *Lew Burdette and the Braves.* New York: G. P. Putnam and Sons, 1960.

Snyder, Brad. *A Well-Paid Slave: Curt Flood's Fight for Free Agency in Professional Sports.* New York: Viking, 2006.

Sports Illustrated. *The Hammer: The Best of Hank Aaron from the Pages of Sports Illustrated.* New York: Sports Illustrated, 2007.

Stanton, Tom. *Hank Aaron and the Home Run That Changed America.* New York: William Morrow, 2004.

Stewart, Mark, and Mike Kennedy. *Hammering Hank: How the Media Made Henry Aaron.* Guilford, Connecticut: Lyons Press, 2006.

Torre, Joe. *Chasing the Dream: My Lifelong Journey to the World Series.* New York: Bantam, 1997.

Vascellaro, Charlie. *Hank Aaron: A Biography.* Westport, Connecticut: Greenwood Press, 2005.

Zinn, Howard. *A People's History of the United States: 1492–Present.* New York: Perennial Classics, 1999.

DISSERTATION:

Nordmann, Christopher Andrew. *Free Negroes in Mobile County, Alabama.* Ph.D. diss., University of Alabama, 1990.

INDEX

Insert following page 142:

Booker T. Washington: University of South Alabama Archives
Babe Ruth: Erik Overbey Collection, University of South Alabama Archives
Davis Avenue pool hall: University of South Alabama Archives
Alabama Drydock entrance gate: Alabama Drydock and Shipbuilding Corporation Collection, University of South Alabama Archives
In Jacksonville team uniform, 1953: ICON Sportsmedia
At Lulu Mae Gibson's boarding house: Getty Images
With Bill Bruton, Jim Pendleton, Charlie White: Getty Images
With Eddie Mathews and Joe Adcock: National Baseball Hall of Fame Library, Cooperstown, N.Y.
Jackie Robinson: ICON Sportsmedia
At spring training, 1957: National Baseball Hall of Fame Library, Cooperstown, N.Y.
With Ted Williams: ICON Sportsmedia
At bat: National Baseball Hall of Fame Library, Cooperstown, N.Y.
Warren Spahn: ICON Sportsmedia
At home with Barbara and children: Getty Images
With Eddie Mathews, 1965: ICON Sportsmedia
In Atlanta: National Baseball Hall of Fame Library, Cooperstown, N.Y.
With Willie Mays and Roberto Clemente: Bettmann/Corbis
With home run 500 trophy: ICON Sportsmedia

Insert following page 446:

Home run 703: National Baseball Hall of Fame Library, Cooperstown, N.Y.
With the Rev. Jesse Jackson: National Baseball Hall of Fame Library, Cooperstown, N.Y.
Peanuts *comic strips:* © United Feature Syndicate, Inc.

With Billye and Governor Jimmy Carter: National Baseball Hall of Fame Library, Cooperstown, N.Y.

Breaking Ruth's record: National Baseball Hall of Fame Library, Cooperstown, N.Y.

With his brother, Tommie: Bettmann/Corbis

At bat: National Baseball Hall of Fame Library, Cooperstown, N.Y.

With Willie Mays: National Baseball Hall of Fame Library, Cooperstown, N.Y.

With Billye at the Hall of Fame: National Baseball Hall of Fame Library, Cooperstown, N.Y.

With his mother and father: Azalea City News Collection, University of South Alabama Archives

With President Bill Clinton: Getty Images

With Barry Bonds: ICON Sportsmedia

Bonds 756: ICON Sportsmedia

Henry Aaron: National Baseball Hall of Fame Library, Cooperstown, N.Y.

Henry Aaron: ICON Sportsmedia